The UK Economy in the Long Expansion and its Aftermath

Macroeconomic Policy Making

Series editors

Professor JAGJIT S. CHADHA *NIESR*

Professor SEAN HOLLY *University of Cambridge*

The 2007–10 financial crisis has asked some very hard questions of modern macroeconomics. The consensus that grew up during 'the Great Moderation' has proved to be an incomplete explanation of how to conduct monetary policy in the face of financial shocks. This series brings together leading macroeconomic researchers and central bank economists to analyse the tools and methods necessary to meet the challenges of the post-financial crisis world.

Published titles:

Chadha and Holly *Interest Rates, Prices and Liquidity: Lessons from the Financial Crisis*

Coffman, Leonard and Neal *Questioning Credible Commitment: Perspectives on the Rise of Financial Capitalism*

Chadha, Durré, Joyce and Sarno *Developments in Macro-Finance Yield Curve Modelling*

The UK Economy in the Long Expansion and its Aftermath

Edited by

Jagjit S. Chadha

Alec Chrystal

Joe Pearlman

Peter Smith

and

Stephen Wright

CAMBRIDGE
UNIVERSITY PRESS

CAMBRIDGE
UNIVERSITY PRESS

University Printing House, Cambridge CB2 8BS, United Kingdom

Cambridge University Press is part of the University of Cambridge.

It furthers the University's mission by disseminating knowledge in the pursuit of education, learning and research at the highest international levels of excellence.

www.cambridge.org
Information on this title: www.cambridge.org/9781107147591

First published 2016

A catalogue record for this publication is available from the British Library

Library of Congress Cataloguing in Publication data

ISBN 978-1-107-147591 Hardback

Contents

Figures

Tables

Contributors

Richard Barwell, BNP Paribas Investment Partners

Arnab Bhattacharjee, Spatial Economics & Econometrics Centre (SEEC), Heriot-Watt University

Philip Bunn, Bank of England

Jagjit S. Chadha, NIESR

Alec Chrystal, Cass Business School

Sean Holly, Fitzwilliam College, Cambridge

Paul Johnson, Institute for Fiscal Studies

Tomas Key, Bank of England

John Lewis, Bank of England

Michael McLeay, Bank of England

Alistair Milne, Loughborough University

Nicholas Oulton, Centre for Economic Performance, London School of Economics

Joe Pearlman, City University, London

Varun Paul, Bank of England

May Rostom, Bank of England

Jumana Saleheen, Bank of England

Peter Smith, University of York

Ryland Thomas, Bank of England

Martin Weale, Monetary Policy Committee, Bank of England

Tomasz Wieladek, Bank of England

Justine A. Wood, Loughborough University

Stephen Wright, Birkbeck College

Francesco Zanetti, University of Oxford

Preface

As the Series Editors of Modern Macroeconomic Policy Making, one of our purposes in this series was to encourage more work on and examination of the UK economy. The academic incentives to study macroeconomic developments in the UK have become somewhat limited, so there is only a dwindling band of those with a strong home bias to continue this important work of following the story of the First Industrial Nation. Between the conjunctural analysis of City scribblers and policy-oriented work at the Bank of England, there is room for some answers to the question of what happened to the UK economy after the end of the 1990–92 recession that left it so vulnerable to financial crisis. The conference that preceded this volume was held at Clare College, Cambridge, in September 2013, mirroring another conference held 10 years earlier in the same venue at which it was suggested that there might even be an end to monetary history. Given that we are all subject to the vagaries of fashion, in intellectual activities just as much as anything material, these new research papers allow us to set in print many of the views about the period immediately prior to the financial crisis, in the shadow of which we continue to live. We took the unusual step of having many editors, as each of Alec Chrystal, Joe Pearlman, Peter Smith and Stephen Wright acted as discussants at the conference and helped frame the set of chapters that we now hand over to posterity. We thank them, the authors and the anonymous referees of the chapters.

Cambridge 2016. JAGJIT S. CHADHA AND SEAN HOLLY

Introduction

Jagjit S. Chadha, Alec Chrystal, Joe Pearlman, Peter Smith and Stephen Wright

In the aftermath of the inflation and recessions of the 1970s and early 1980s, from the early 1990s onwards there was a major upswing in most advanced countries. In the UK it was the longest period of economic expansion on record. But it came to an abrupt end in 2007, with the freezing of the interbank markets and the collapse of Northern Rock, followed in 2008 by Bear Stearns and Lehman Brothers.

Before the crisis, many economists had begun to call this period of upswing the Great Moderation; and, echoing developments in other disciplines, such as political thought, some openly wondered whether we had found the answer to the questions that had perennially been posed by 'boom and bust'. But given the magnitude of the shocks that hit the global economy in the crisis period of 2007–08 (and since then in a number of countries) the apparent reduction in macroeconomic volatility of the earlier period now appears, with the benefit of hindsight, to have been largely illusory. We therefore argue that the period 1992–2007 can more accurately (and less ambitiously) be described as the Long Expansion – hence the title of this volume.

It is now clear that many of the problems that have occupied policymakers during the global financial crisis were being incubated during this period. And so with the twin aims of encouraging more policy-focused research on the UK, and to encourage policy debate, in the aftermath of the financial crisis and the prolonged economic recession, we commissioned 10 papers from leading UK-based researchers to look at the issues that arose during the Long Expansion and its aftermath.

The chapters in this collected volume originate in papers presented at a conference held at Clare College, Cambridge on 19–23 September, 2013.[1] The papers have been peer-reviewed and thoroughly revised since the initial versions presented at the conference. They offer a

1 The papers and previous three conferences can be viewed at: http://www.econ.cam.ac.uk/MMPM/.

comprehensive overview of the UK economy over this period in a form that we hope will offer an authoritative and enduring perspective on the British economy in the early years of the twenty-first century. We are grateful to the Bank of England, the INET Fund and the Money, Macro, Finance Research Group for support in hosting this conference. We thank Chris Harrison and Phil Good for sponsoring the modern macroeconomic policy-making series, published by Cambridge University Press. Finally, we thank Jagjit Chadha for his support in organising and thinking of this conference and book.

⋆⋆⋆

The volume opens with 'Prospects for UK growth in the aftermath of the financial crisis', by Nicholas Oulton (London School of Economics). This chapter starts by documenting the remarkable performance of the UK economy during the period 1990–2007 – the 'Long Expansion'[2] of the title of this book. By any standards – but particularly relative to what came before (and afterwards) – the productivity performance of the UK economy during this period was excellent, and looked set to continue. On the basis of pre-crisis data, using a two-sector growth model, Oulton argues that a plausible projection of the future growth rate of GDP per hour in the market sector would have been around 2½% p.a.

However, since the onset of the financial crisis and the Great Recession in the UK in spring 2008 such an optimistic projection has looked increasingly unlikely to be fulfilled. At the time when the chapter was finalised (in early 2014) both GDP and GDP per hour had fallen, and the latter was still below the level reached at the peak of the boom. The chapter shows that this fall in productivity was pervasive throughout a broad range of sectors of the UK economy. In the rest of the chapter Oulton investigates competing explanations for how this can have occurred, and then reflects on the implications for the future.

The chapter examines a wide range of hypotheses that have been proposed as an explanation of the productivity collapse: sectoral shifts; mismeasurement of banking output; overheating during the boom (with consequent overstatement of potential output); lower inputs of both physical and/or human capital input; hoarding of labour and capital; so-called "zombie firms";[3] and fiscal austerity (the impact of which Oulton concludes has been overstated). Indeed, the common feature of each of these

2 With thanks to Jagjit Chadha for this phrase to describe the period from the early 1990s to the Great Financial Crash.

3 This popular term has come to refer to firms that are just about able to meet their debt obligations to banks but are not investing.

explanations, Oulton concludes, is that none of them works: the productivity collapse remains, at the time of writing, a puzzle.

In considering future prospects the chapter considers the likely impact of the financial crisis and the 'Great Recession'. Will its impact be entirely transitory? (i.e. with productivity reverting to its previous trend). Or permanent in terms of the level of productivity? Or (in the worst case scenario) permanent both in its impact on the level and growth rate of productivity? To address this question, Oulton uses a cross-country panel dataset of 61 countries over 1950–2010 to attempt to estimate the impact of financial crises, particularly banking crises, on productivity, capital, TFP and employment. He argues that banking crises generally have a long-run impact on the level of productivity, but not necessarily on its long-run growth rate. He estimates that the permanent impact on the level of GDP per worker resulting from the crisis could be a substantial reduction of around 5½%. But, more positively, the UK can eventually be expected to return to the growth rate that would have been predicted prior to the crisis.

Oulton cautions, however, that this (relatively optimistic) prediction is conditional on the UK continuing to follow good policies in other respects, in particular not allowing the ratio of government debt to GDP to rise excessively (the final chapter of this volume, by Paul Johnson, deals with this issue in considerably more depth).

Chapter 2, 'Labor market and monetary policy reforms in the UK: a structural interpretation of the implications', by Francesco Zanetti (Oxford), examines the sources of the stability both of the growth rate of the UK, and of the macro environment more generally, during the Long Expansion. Compared to the 1970s and 1980s, GDP and inflation were less volatile, and the level of inflation decreased markedly. Zanetti identifies two possible causes: first, the labour market reforms under Mrs Thatcher, which both weakened union power and reduced the replacement ratio of unemployment benefits; and second, the use of an explicit inflation target as a nominal anchor since 1992, which culminated in a new statutory framework for price stability in the form of the Bank of England Act in 1998. He attempts to assess the impact of these changes by posing two counterfactual questions: would the introduction of these policy changes have produced a similarly favourable economic outlook if they had been accomplished in the earlier decades? And, if so, to what extent, if at all, might each of these two changes have played a role?

To assess this, using data from the earlier period 1971–91, he estimates (and for some parameters calibrates) a New Keynesian model with optimising behaviour by households and firms, where firms face a cost of adjusting nominal prices, and the labour market is characterised by search frictions and job-matching. The model also incorporates a central bank that conducts policy with a Taylor-type rule by setting the nominal interest rate in reaction to deviations of inflation from its target and output from its long-run equilibrium. Unlike the explicit inflation-targeting framework introduced in 1992, where the target of inflation is constant, during the 1970s and 1980s, monetary policy can be represented by a time-varying inflation target which changed in reaction to exogenous disturbances. In contrast, from 1992 onwards, it is assumed that the inflation target was constant, with an increased weight assigned to inflation for the monetary policy objective.

Since it is the deep preference and structural parameters, as well as the policy parameters that are estimated, the model is intended to be immune to the Lucas critique, and thus is used to draw inferences about counterfactual scenarios. These examine whether the labour market reforms and changes to the monetary policy framework would have changed the economic outlook if they had been introduced in the earlier period. Utilising these policies in the estimated model suggests that labour market reforms would have eased the transition to lower inflation for most but not all of the period, via its impact on the real wage, and hence marginal cost. But the impact is very small: the counterfactual inflation rate never reduces by more than ½%. At the same time the volatility of inflation and output growth significantly increases, so that the effects of changes in the monetary policy framework would have been mixed. A stronger reaction to inflation deviations from target would have lowered the volatility of inflation and output growth, but the introduction of a constant inflation target or a monetary policy that reacted strongly to output fluctuations would have increased volatility, so that the net effect is virtually unchanged. A potential conclusion to be drawn from these results is that the economy was simply inherently more volatile in the 1970s and at least the early 1980s, and thus that there may have been little scope for stabilisation policy to improve matters.

In the next chapter, 'Property income and the balance of payments', by Tomas Key, Varun Paul, Martin Weale and Tomasz Wieladek (Bank of England), the authors explore another puzzling feature of the Long Expansion: how the United Kingdom was able, despite a current account trade deficit and apparent net external liabilities, both to earn a positive balance of net income from abroad almost every year and to improve its net external position during the Long Expansion. The puzzle is that the current account deficit, particularly in the 10 years leading up to the financial crisis, does not square with the stability of net external assets over that period, unless there were higher systematic capital gains on the UK's assets compared with its liabilities. Indeed, between 1997 and 2012 the UK seems to have earned a total of capital gains or unidentified income worth nearly 20% of 2012 GDP despite the fact that its net asset position is shown as a debtor.

The authors carefully analyse this question by exploiting a recently constructed dataset on capital gains and asset returns. Earlier studies had suggested that the composition of UK assets as compared with liabilities is biased towards high-yielding asset classes (the composition effect). In contrast, the authors' new dataset shows that the UK, like the USA, enjoyed favourable returns on investment categories that were broadly similar for assets and liabilities. The authors note that the data do not reveal whether investors in UK foreign assets are more skilled than those investing in the UK, or whether they merely run greater risks.

This result motivates a study of the factors that may have led to this favourable position, and in particular whether the net income balance was influenced by changes in the regulatory environment. It is possible that the attractiveness of a country to foreign investors depends on the extent to which markets are regulated. In addition, the UK's capacity to borrow more cheaply than it lends might be a function of regulation. The authors study this possibility using a Bayesian Panel VAR for 13 OECD economies, which evaluates the interaction between consumption growth, inflation, the interest rate, net foreign income and the exchange rate, and allows for parameters that depend on the regulatory environment. This builds on earlier work which has shown that the way in which countries respond to shocks depends on their regulatory structure. The latter is measured using indices that represent exchange rate flexibility and financial, labour and product market deregulation. The panel approach has the usual advantage that there is more variation in the data, which makes it possible to determine the effects of regulatory changes with greater statistical significance. The Bayesian approach that is used for estimation is fairly novel in macroeconomics, and allows for the estimation of Bayesian shrinkage – the weight put on the prior covariance matrices of the time-varying parameters, which direct whether the econometrician puts more weight on the model structure or more weight on the data.

The results show that a substantial component of the improvement in the net income flow between the early 1990s and the middle of the next decade appears to have been a consequence of regulatory changes. In particular, the improvements due to financial regulation appear positive, while those due to product market regulation are negative. However, further analysis using the steady state of the VAR leads the authors to caution against accepting these results without more careful consideration. While the substantial offsetting effects from product market regulation and financial market regulation may be explained by the former having encouraged foreign investment in the UK, leading to an outflow of income, and the latter having benefited the growth of a financial sector that can earn more from foreign investments than the cost of finance, the authors note that it is more difficult to understand why labour market deregulation should lead to increased steady state income. They suggest that while the regulatory environment may have been beneficial, the upward trend of the regulatory variables may have led to an overstatement of their effects.

★★★

Given the prominence of the financial crisis at the onset of the recession that brought the Long Expansion to a dramatic close, the organisers of the conference were particularly keen to see research into the financial sector, both during the expansionary phase, and in the downturn that followed. The next three chapters all address the role of the financial sector, money and credit in the Long Expansion and the subsequent crisis, albeit with quite distinct emphases.

In Chapter 4, 'UK broad money growth in the Long Expansion 1992–2007: what can it tell us about the role of money?' Michael McLeay and Ryland Thomas (Bank of England) subdivide their investigation of the role of money into three parts. The first is a survey of the literature that covers many different approaches to the role of monetary aggregates in the economy, together with an overview of broad trends. The authors show that money and credit both grew faster than nominal GDP throughout the Long Expansion (and during the decade before) and that credit grew faster than money. The second part of the chapter reports the results of the estimation of a long-run structural vector autoregression (SVAR) model and decomposition of factors driving money, lending, GDP and inflation. The SVAR is estimated using quarterly data over a long period (1967–2012) which includes both the Long Expansion and the onset of the crisis and the Great Recession. It uses a decomposition of predictive errors into structural shocks to aggregate demand, aggregate supply and monetary policy, but with the key addition of shocks arising from the banking system. These are the cost of intermediation, the cost and availability of wholesale funding, and a variable to capture bank risk taking. They also try to identify a risk premium shock that originates in the non-bank financial sector. The estimation strategy both identifies the shocks and distinguishes between those that have permanent and temporary effects.

The impact of the standard shocks is much as would be expected. Demand shocks, for example, move output and inflation in the same direction, while supply shocks move them in opposite directions. As for the banking shocks, the cost of intermediation shock has effects on money, credit and asset prices, but no significant effect on real activity. In contrast, the wholesale funding shock has effects on credit spreads and lending, and this in turn does affect real activity. The bank risk-taking shock affects money, credit and asset prices temporarily, but has no real effect on output in the long run (by assumption).

The authors find that over their long sample, supply shocks appear to play a bigger role in driving GDP than demand shocks, in contrast to traditional macroeconomic models which have tended to put most emphasis on demand shocks. This finding may be a product of the identifying assumptions used to distinguish demand and supply shocks, but it does add support to something closer to a real business cycle approach, where technology shocks are key drivers of fluctuations, as opposed to more Keynesian approaches where aggregate demand shocks are the main source of volatility. They also provide an interesting insight into the financial crisis of 2007, which they find was preceded by credit growth originating from wholesale funding of the banking system. This result is consistent with stories about the global savings glut, the narrowing of risk premia on a wide class of assets and the 'ferocious search for yield' that helped drive the credit and housing bubble prior to the US sub prime crisis. In effect, the UK banks' 'customer funding gap' was filled by an abundance of funds channelled through the wholesale interbank market, much of which originated overseas. These flows rapidly reversed when the interbank markets froze in 2007–08 with the onset of the financial crisis.

In the third part of the chapter, the authors estimate a model of disaggregated money holdings for three specific sectors. These sectors are: other financial corporations (OFCs), proxied by insurance companies and pensions funds; private non-financial corporations (PNFCs); and households. The model is estimated for the period 1987–2008 on quarterly data. Key results are that the money growth in the OFCs sector from 2005 was linked to around 25% of the build-up in asset prices, which in turn boosted consumer spending; while the growth of money within PNFCs is sufficient to explain business investment. The authors estimate that the combined impact of these two effects added around 3% to GDP in 2005–07. In contrast, household money holding had little further informational content at this time.

The following chapter, 'An old-fashioned banking crisis: credit growth and loan losses in the UK 1997–2012' by Alistair Milne and Justine Wood (University of Loughborough), examines the origins of the financial crisis in the banking sector, focussing on the expansion of credit in the UK over the years 1997–2007 and the subsequent loan losses on UK sterling lending.

The authors provide evidence of a substantial credit expansion, especially in lending secured on property. Yet they show that this led to only relatively modest losses for UK banks on residential mortgage lending in the crisis period of 2008–13. Instead, most losses on UK bank sterling lending were associated with commercial property lending. The authors consider parallels with the two previous episodes of large-scale UK loan losses in 1973–75 and 1991–93, both of which they revisit, and draw out similarities between the most recent banking crisis and these earlier events.

The chapter also considers the role of 'shadow' banking in this boom and bust. The authors introduce a careful distinction between 'old' and 'new' shadow banking. The former takes funds from the established banking system, while 'new' shadow banking uses the modern tools of securitisation and credit risk transfer in order to create money-like substitutes for traditional bank deposits and hence disintermediate entirely from the established banks. The authors find that, in contrast to the pattern in the USA, 'new' shadow banking played only a minor role in the UK credit expansion. There was some 'old' shadow banking, with real estate investment trusts and other specialised real estate funds investing in commercial property. Securitisation of residential mortgages also helped fund what now, with hindsight, appears as an unwise extension of credit into other more risky areas of lending, notably commercial property. Otherwise, the authors conclude, this was a very old-fashioned banking crisis.

The third chapter focussing on the financial sector, 'Household debt and spending in the United Kingdom' by Philip Bunn and May Rostom (Bank of England), examines another aspect of the build-up to the crisis. It is commonly thought (rightly or wrongly) that household debt played an important role in the boom and bust of the 2007–08 financial crisis. The authors of this chapter examine this question with evidence from a panel study using household level data drawn from the ONS Living Costs and Food Survey (LCF), which covers a sample of 6,000 households on a regular basis. The data include detailed information for each household on income, spending (disaggregated by types of goods and services purchased) and debt.

The focus of this study is entirely on the influence of secured mortgage debt (which is over 80% of the total debt) on spending pattern variations across different households and over time. Mortgage debt is clearly always linked to house purchases, but there is no evidence available in this data about the role of housing net worth. There is, however, some presumption that households with high debt to income ratios will also have a high debt to wealth ratio.

The authors find evidence to show that the build-up of mortgage debt prior to the financial crisis was (unsurprisingly) linked to house price rises. However, the focus of the chapter is mainly on the extent to which high levels of secured debt affected household spending patterns. They find that higher debt households had higher consumer spending in the run-up to the 2007 crisis, and that these same households cut back spending more sharply once the crisis broke. However, while statistically significant, these effects were not substantial and provide only a small part of the explanation of consumer spending trends in general.

Three hypotheses are posed as to why high-debt households cut back more than others after the crisis: first, that high debt restricted borrowers' access to future credit; second, that high debt may have raised worries about the ability to make future interest payments; and third, households with high debts may have made larger adjustments to expectations of future income. The authors conclude that the data provide some support for the first two of these explanations, but not the third.

The implication of these results is that high levels of secured debt made consumer spending more volatile over the business cycle, as those with high debt tended to spend more during the upturn, but also cut back more during the downturn. The authors conclude that policy-makers responsible for financial and macro stability should, therefore, be concerned to ensure that debt levels do not become too high and too widespread in the household sector.

***

The period of the Long Expansion overlaps with that of the operational control of monetary policy in the UK passing to the Bank of England through the decisions of the Monetary Policy Committee (MPC). Since 1997 interest rate-setting and, more recently, non-traditional monetary policy actions in pursuit of inflation stabilisation have been carried out by this group independently of the government of the day. The Long Expansion also saw considerable stability in inflation around its target level. The next two chapters examine the activities of the MPC over this period from two quite distinct angles; while the following chapter considers the impact of global developments on UK inflation

Chapter 7, 'MPC decision-making, the Long Expansion and the crisis: integration with the global economy, heterogeneity and network dynamics', by Arnab Bhattacharjee (Heriot-Watt University) and Sean Holly (University of Cambridge), examines the conduct of monetary policy through the voting records of individual members of the MPC over the period of the Long Expansion and the financial crisis. The authors estimate a model of MPC decision-making that allows for heterogeneity and network interactions amongst members, using a panel dataset that includes both voting records and a range of macroeconomic indicators. The authors use their estimated model to show how the nature of monetary policy-making by the MPC changed over this period. They chart three distinct stages of transition: expansion from June 1997 to June 2003; the final pre-crisis stage of expansion to September 2006; and the crisis period to October 2011. Their results show an increasing influence of international developments and integration of the UK in the global economy. They also show how uncertainty and expectations of future inflation and output growth also had an increased effect on decision-making in the crisis period compared with earlier periods. This is matched in their results with better network connections and influence of external members (non-Bank of England staff) on the MPC over the crisis period.

Bhattacharjee and Holly frame their analysis in terms of a two-equation model of inflation and output growth where the monetary authorities choose the interest rate to minimise an inter-temporal loss function and that members of the MPC are assumed to follow, in their voting decisions, heterogeneous versions of the resulting interest rate rule because of factors such as differences in views of the state of the economy, varying beliefs about the size of parameters such as the effect of interest rates on inflation and the output gap, and heterogeneity in the extent of and degree of uncertainty. On top of this, interactions between the members of the MPC are allowed to include differences in the extent to which individual members influence each other.

Using the voting records of individual MPC members from 1997–2011, the authors estimate individual decision rules conditioned on a range of variables, including unemployment changes, the state of asset markets (including housing, equity and foreign exchange markets), global GDP growth, US interest rates and the standard deviation of output growth. These reaction functions are allowed to differ across the three periods identified above. The estimates are then used to generate kernel density estimates of the implied cross-sectional distributions of response coefficients in the individual decision rules. Bhattacharjee and Holly present plots of the distributions for each response for each regime. The plots for the response of monetary policy to inflation expectations across the three regimes show that MPC members were more concerned with inflation in the post-2004 period. Strikingly, increased uncertainty in output growth had a bigger impact on decision-making moving from earlier to later regimes. There is also evidence of increased heterogeneity in the output response over the regimes.

For each of the regimes in the above exercise a matrix of cross-section interaction weights is estimated separately. This spatial matrix is then used to study network dynamics. The estimates show significant asymmetries in the influence that each of the members of the MPC had on the voting behaviour of other members. Internal members of the committee (Bank of England staff) are shown to have had more influence than externals throughout; but the Governor is found not always to have been the most influential member. The network is shown to have been most well-connected during the crisis period and the external members more closely integrated into the network over that period.

Chapter 8, 'Nine votes, one view and the never-ending consensus on the MPC during the Great Stability', by Richard Barwell (Royal Bank of Scotland), is unusual amongst the chapters in this volume in that it originated as a discussant's response to the previous chapter, by Bhattacharjee and Sean Holly. The editors were unanimous in their view that the evidence presented during the discussion was sufficiently persuasive to warrant expanding into a chapter in its own right.

Barwell takes a critical approach to the question of the nature of differences in opinion amongst the members of the MPC and the outcomes of the discussions in the MPC in terms of interest rate-setting decisions. He shows that evidence of differences of view between MPC members is not reflected in differences in observed behaviour in the setting of interest rates. To assess differences in view, rather than focus on the MPC voting records or the minutes of MPC meetings, Barwell examines speeches made by members. His argument is that speeches contain the most complete public articulation of the views of members with a sufficient level of detail. The period of study is from the start of the MPC in 1997 to the author's estimate of the end of the Long Expansion from the perspective of the operation of the MPC in September 2007.

The chapter assembles evidence from speeches on a number of areas of concern for monetary policy over the period, including inflation expectations, globalisation, the operation of the labour market and structural issues in the corporate sector. These show a diversity of views on the nature and causes of developments in these areas and the likely consequences for the targets of monetary policy. Further evidence of differences in analysis by MPC members is shown in speeches referring to the behaviour of asset prices, including house prices and the exchange rate as well as financial imbalances, household debt and the behaviour of money and credit in the aggregate. These differences also include how asset price bubbles might be addressed. It is shown that whilst the behaviour of output growth and price inflation over the period appears to be rather smooth, at the time a number of shocks arrived whose interpretation and likely consequence were not agreed on by members of the MPC, as can be judged by their speeches. These differences in views are further shown to include differences in views on substantive issues such as the relative importance of the roles of data and underlying principles of economic analysis in reaching interest rate-setting decisions.

The chapter argues that, in contrast to the views expressed in speeches, in terms of actual voting, disagreement amongst the members of the MPC was modest when judged both by the relatively small number of individual dissenting votes and by the small size of the proposed changes in the interest rate which any dissenters proposed. Nearly all dissenting votes were at most 25 basis points away from the majority outcome. The question then is whether the size of this alternative setting for monetary policy would have been expected by the relevant MPC member to have had a significant effect on the economy. Barwell argues that it would be reasonable to assume that the impact of this difference was expected by them to be small, given the evidence from the Bank of England's economic models of the time, as provided to MPC members. Thus the outcome of the process of interest rate-setting is shown to have produced much greater consensus in terms of the outcome than the evidence of differences in MPC members' views might suggest would have been the case.

The chapter then asks why there was such a consensus in voting, given the range of views uncovered in the speeches. Barwell assesses the role of agreement on the central projection for the economy in the future which is part of the MPC interest rate-setting process and on the width of the fan charts which provide a measure of the degree of uncertainty surrounding the central projection. He suggests that the process that the MPC follows in agreeing on these items encourages the development of consensus. Attention is also drawn to the attitudes of MPC members to the significance of voting in dissent to the majority and the nature of consensus. Significance is also given to the nature of the economic models that the Bank supported at the time and the limited role for the modelling of financial flows that they incorporated which might have made promoting alternative views more difficult. The chapter concludes with proposals for the reform of a number of features of the operation of the MPC to encourage the presentation and discussion of alternative views by MPC members. These reforms include the publication of the views of individual MPC members and the development of a large suite of alternative economic models with different properties based on a range of views of how the economy works as well as greater resources being given to the assessment of alternative views and projections.

Inflation targeting in the UK did not take place in a vacuum. In Chapter 9, 'Emerging markets and import prices during the Long Expansion' by John Lewis and Jumana Saleheen (Bank of England), the authors start by noting the frequent claim that globalisation and the falling costs of transport and information contributed to the low-inflation experience of the developed world during the Long Expansion. Part of this was associated with the emergence of China as a major exporter of manufactured goods, due in part to its low-wage costs. Substitution of purchases towards these lower priced goods had a direct effect on inflation; but the growth of competition also put pressure on domestic producers in the developed countries to reduce costs and/or substitute new technology for high-cost labour. These forces would have been likely to exert downward pressure on inflation in importing countries, including the UK.

The authors of this chapter perform a detailed study of UK trade data, examining the impact on UK prices of import prices from specific groups of emerging economies. Emerging market exporters to the UK are collected into three main groups: China, the new members of the European Union from Eastern Europe, and other low-wage emerging economies, such as Brazil and India. All three of these groups saw a rising market share of manufactured sales to the UK, but with the growth from China outstripping the others. In non-manufactured goods trade, however, it was the other low-wage countries that saw the fastest growth of exports to the UK.

The empirical work reported in the chapter uses a database of trade in around 3,000 different products on an annual basis for the 12 years 1999–2011, where the information available includes prices and volumes of trade and the origin country. The authors test whether the growth of UK trade with these three market groups has put downward pressure on UK inflation, when other effects such as exchange rate changes are controlled for.

The authors find evidence that the growth in imports that substitutes for products from advanced economies has been associated with a reduction in import prices. They estimate that this switching to emerging-market-sourced goods reduced manufactured import price inflation by just under 0.9 percentage points per annum on average, and overall import price inflation by around 0.6 percentage points per annum. By far the biggest effect found was that coming from China in manufactured goods. There was, however, no evidence to support the hypothesis that higher inflation in emerging economies had spilled over into UK import prices.

***

Fiscal policy, and in particular fiscal retrenchment, played a crucial role in the macroeconomy as the Long Expansion ended, and rapidly became the Great Recession. In the final chapter of this volume, Chapter 10, 'UK fiscal policy before the crisis', Paul Johnson (Institute of Fiscal Studies) provides an analysis of the development of fiscal policy during the Long Expansion, including some comparisons with earlier years. Despite the apparently historically unprecedented nature of the financial crisis, he shows that there was considerable similarity between the features of the path of fiscal policy from the late 1980s and the subsequent recession and that over the period of the Long Expansion and the recession following the financial crisis. Johnson asks what lessons might be learned from the conduct of fiscal policy over these years.

A great deal of the debate over the required size and length of fiscal retrenchment in Britain following the financial crisis turns on assessment of the fiscal position immediately prior to 2008. The overall fiscal position in the UK immediately prior to the financial crisis was a significant deficit: public sector net borrowing was 2.4% of national income. Assessing how significant this was depends, in part, on measuring the cyclical position of the economy at the time. Recent estimates suggest that structural borrowing might have been as high as 3.7% of national income due to the cyclical position of the economy at the time. The chapter shows that these large deficit figures arose despite the introduction in 1997 of rules for the conduct of fiscal policy. The chapter examines first, the 'golden rule' that over the business cycle government borrowing should only be for funding public investment, and second, the sustainable investment rule that the national debt should not rise above 40% of GDP. Johnson asks whether the first was in practice open to manipulation and shows that the second was barely met immediately prior to the financial crisis. The analysis thus raises the question of whether more robust fiscal rules might be developed.

The overall fiscal position is the difference between two large numbers, so the question of sustainability is made very clear from examination of the paths of taxes and spending. Johnson shows that whilst both total tax revenue and spending show clear cyclical patterns, both also show the impact of policy choices over the period of the Long Expansion. Strikingly, spending on social security payments, which one might expect to most closely follow a cyclical pattern, followed a significantly upward path from the mid-1990s onwards despite the underlying positive growth in the economy and falling unemployment. Having shown that this increase was not due to payments related to an ageing population, Johnson suggests that these increases have not proved to be sustainable once the financial crisis arrived and output fell. On the taxation side the chapter shows that there were several discretionary changes to the overall taxation regime over recent years. As with the most recent experience with spending, significant tax cuts made in the late 1980s were subsequently undone in budgets in the early 1990s and 2000s following the failure of economic growth to be high enough to make the cost sustainable. Johnson also shows that taxation policy appears most obviously subject to a political or electoral cycle as taxes were raised in every budget following an election over the 30 years being examined. This post-election increase in taxes of an average £7.5 bn (in 2012/13 terms) has followed an average tax giveaway of £2.2 bn in the year before elections. In terms of sustainability, it is shown that revenue from North Sea oil taxation is expected to fall in the future whilst the dependence of corporation tax receipts on the financial sector appears to be less of a problem than their cyclicality. The chapter concludes with a call for future governments to introduce better fiscal rules which focus on longer term sustainability and to act with more caution and to resist calls for deviating from these rules.

★★★

Conclusion

The chapters collected here demonstrate both the complexity and interrelatedness of a modern advanced economy, such as the UK, but also how hard it is to understand key risks in real time so that policy responses can be properly calibrated. It does seem clear now that it can no longer be tenable to think about any one arm of policy as sufficient to ensure an acceptable level of economic stability. Financial (including regulatory) policy, fiscal policy and monetary policy all play a fundamental role. As Andrew Crockett once put it: 'The received wisdom is that risk increases in recessions and falls in booms. In contrast, it may be more helpful to think of risk as increasing during upswings, as financial imbalances build up, and materialising in recessions'.[4] That those

4 This point was made in a speech in 2000, 'Marrying the micro- and macro-prudential dimensions of financial stability'.

risks were allowed to build up in a period that appeared to be one of stability does represent a first-order policy error; but one that, even with the benefit of several years' hindsight, we still cannot fully understand. We hope that, if nothing else, the perspective and extended dialogue on the Long Expansion that this volume provides will mean that it will continue to be brought off the bookshelves whenever people announce the end of boom and bust.

1 Prospects for UK growth in the aftermath of the financial crisis

Nicholas Oulton

1.1 Introduction

The UK economy went into recession in 2008Q2. GDP fell in that quarter and continued falling for the next five quarters. It stopped falling in 2009Q3 and began growing again, but so slowly that in 2013Q1 its level was still 4% below the previous peak in 2008Q1 (see Table 1.1).[1] The fall in GDP per capita has obviously been even larger, since the population has continued to grow. The whole period since 2008Q1 therefore justifies the term 'slump' or even 'depression'. Few if any commentators expected a slump of this severity prior to its start. After it became apparent that the recession, though deep, was over, many expected the recovery to be equally rapid. But this didn't happen. The recovery has been slow and is still incomplete. There have been many surprising features of the five or so years since the recession began. First, despite the massive fall in output, unemployment rose comparatively modestly from 5.2% in 2008Q1 to a high of 8.4%; in September–November 2013 it was 7.1%. Second, employment and total hours worked, after falling initially, have been robust: employment and hours are both now higher than at the peak (Figures 1.1 and 1.2). The flip side of these facts is the productivity puzzle: not only has labour productivity (whether measured on an hours basis or a heads basis) stopped growing, its level has actually fallen. In 2013Q1 GDP per hour worked was still 5% below its peak level (Figure 1.4).

This is a revised and shortened version of a paper presented to the Cambridge International Macroeconomic and Finance Centre Conference on 'The Causes and Consequences of the Long UK Expansion 1992–2007', 19th–20th September 2013, Clare College, Cambridge (Oulton, 2013b). I am grateful to my discussant Tiago Cavalcanti and to other conference participants, particularly John Fender, Peter Spencer and Martin Weale, for helpful comments. I thank also Alan Castle, James Cloyne, Jonathan Haskel, Bill Martin and Peter Sinclair for useful comments and suggestions on an earlier draft. I am particularly grateful to Stephen Wright for detailed comments on the longer version and suggestions for improving and shortening it.

1 2013Q1 is the latest quarter for which national accounts data were available at the time this research was undertaken.

Table 1.1. Output, hours, jobs and productivity in the UK in and after the Great Recession (2008Q1 = 100)

Year and quarter	GDP	Hours	Jobs	Hours per job	GDP per hour	GDP per job
2008Q1	100.00	100.00	100.00	100.00	100.00	100.00
2008Q2	99.39	99.76	100.31	99.45	99.63	99.08
2008Q3	97.93	99.34	99.84	99.50	98.58	98.09
2008Q4	95.69	99.22	99.57	99.65	96.44	96.10
2009Q1	93.30	97.49	99.15	98.33	95.70	94.10
2009Q2	92.71	97.51	98.17	99.33	95.07	94.43
2009Q3	92.67	97.02	98.16	98.84	95.52	94.41
2009Q4	92.97	98.31	98.06	100.25	94.57	94.81
2010Q1	93.54	96.20	97.63	98.54	97.23	95.81
2010Q2	94.45	98.03	98.48	99.54	96.36	95.91
2010Q3	94.95	98.13	99.08	99.04	96.76	95.83
2010Q4	94.69	98.54	98.70	99.84	96.09	95.94
2011Q1	95.07	98.56	99.27	99.28	96.46	95.77
2011Q2	95.30	97.42	99.25	98.16	97.82	96.03
2011Q3	95.91	98.21	98.78	99.42	97.66	97.09
2011Q4	95.84	98.42	98.84	99.58	97.39	96.97
2012Q1	95.85	99.13	99.68	99.45	96.69	96.15
2012Q2	95.36	99.62	100.10	99.52	95.73	95.27
2012Q3	96.09	100.75	100.42	100.33	95.37	95.68
2012Q4	95.88	101.02	101.19	99.83	94.91	94.75
2013Q1	96.11	101.28	100.71	100.57	94.89	95.44

Source: GDP from *Quarterly National Accounts June 2013*; hours and jobs from *Labour Market Statistics, July 2013*. GDP is at basic prices, chained volume measure [ONS cdid: ABMM].

All this calls into question the future prospects of the UK economy, which seemed so bright during the boom. Was it all just an illusion? This is the question on which I hope this chapter will throw some light.

In 1995 I published an article with the somewhat sceptical title 'Supply side reform and UK economic growth: what happened to the miracle?' (Oulton, 1995).[2] I argued that up till the end of the 1970s the growth of the British economy had been hampered by two factors: first, our dysfunctional system of industrial relations and second a low level of investment in human capital. Despite the title, my conclusion was upbeat. The Thatcher reforms of the 1980s (reduction of union power coupled with privatisation of state-owned industries), which have been maintained and extended by subsequent governments, together with

2 Younger readers may like to note that 'miracle' was a term attached by some commentators in the 1980s to the improvement in productivity growth observed then, particularly in manufacturing.

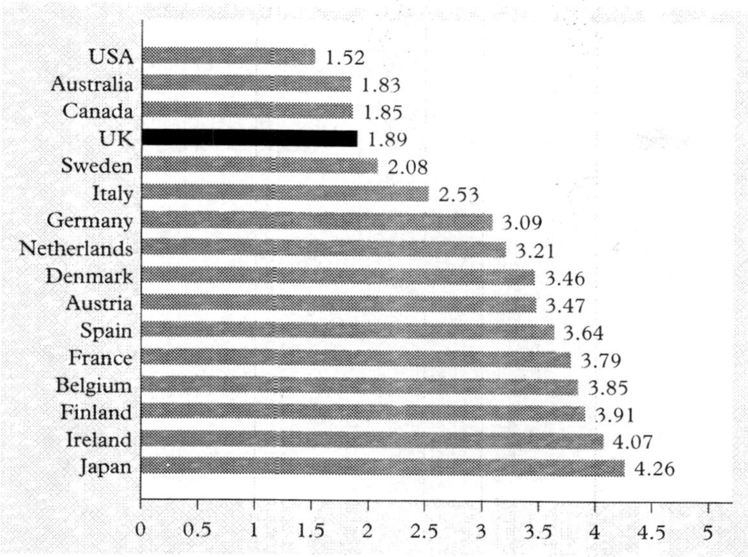

Figure 1.1. Real GDP per hour in the market sector, mean growth rate, 1970–90, % p.a.

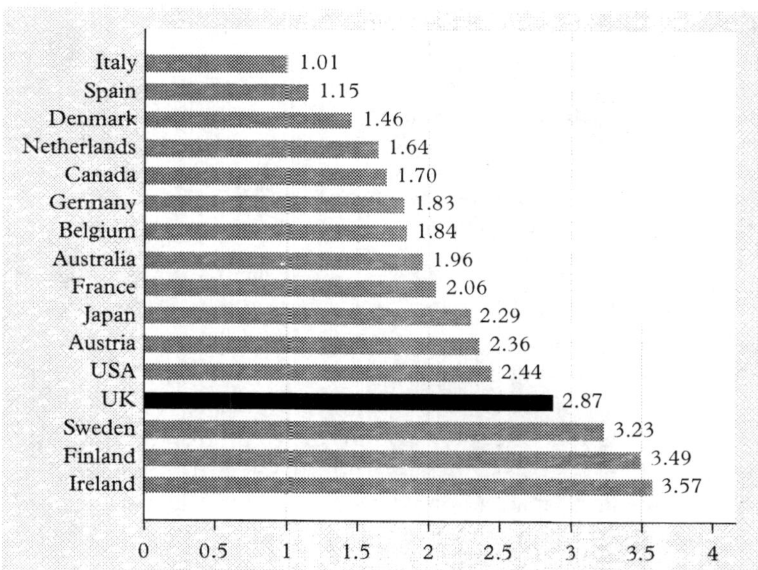

Figure 1.2. Real GDP per hour in the market sector, mean growth rate, 1990–2007, % p.a.
Source: EU KLEMS, November 2009 release (www.euklems.net).

increased investment in education, particularly higher education,[3] and improvements in primary and secondary education, had greatly improved British prospects. So I expected more rapid growth would follow. But there was an important caveat. UK performance had also been set back by poor macro policies which led to unnecessarily prolonged recessions. Optimistically, I thought these could be avoided in the future (provided we did not join the euro). At the time, mine was not a popular conclusion, at least in academic circles. A conclusion more in line with (then) received academic wisdom can be found in an article published two years after mine:

> While legal intervention has had an impact on the institutions of industrial relations, most notably in reducing the power of organised labour, this cannot be isolated from wider structural changes in labour and product markets. A review of research on economic outcomes suggests an uneven and tenuous link between institutional change and economic performance. (Brown et al., 1997)

However, since these articles were published evidence has accumulated that the UK's performance did indeed improve and growth was faster than in most comparable countries. Now the LSE Growth Commission (2013) has set its seal of approval on the view that the reforms begun under the Thatcher governments were highly effective in raising UK growth:

> Despite the current gloom, the UK has many assets that can be mobilised to its advantage, including strong rule of law, generally competitive product markets, flexible labour markets, a world-class university system and strengths in many key sectors, with cuttingedge [sic] firms in both manufacturing and services. These and other assets helped to reverse the UK's relative economic decline over the century before 1980. Over the course of the following three decades, they supported faster growth per capita than in the UK's main comparator countries – France, Germany and the US.[4]

Perhaps the clearest way to see this is to look at the growth of GDP per hour worked in the market sector (thus avoiding incompatibilities in the way public sector output is measured in different countries). In Figures 1.1 and 1.2 I compare 16 countries over two periods, 1970–90 and 1990–2007, using the EU KLEMS database (O'Mahony and Timmer, 2009). In the first period GDP per hour grew at 1.89% p.a. in the UK, the fourth slowest in this group of countries, behind France, Germany, Italy and Japan amongst others, though slightly ahead of the

3 The proportion of people aged 25–34 in Britain who have a university degree is approaching 50% and is the 6th highest in the OECD. This proportion is now higher in the UK than in the USA, while the proportion aged 25–64 with a degree is close behind the US one (OECD, 2013).

4 See too Van Reenen (2013), who also credits the reforms begun in the Thatcher era.

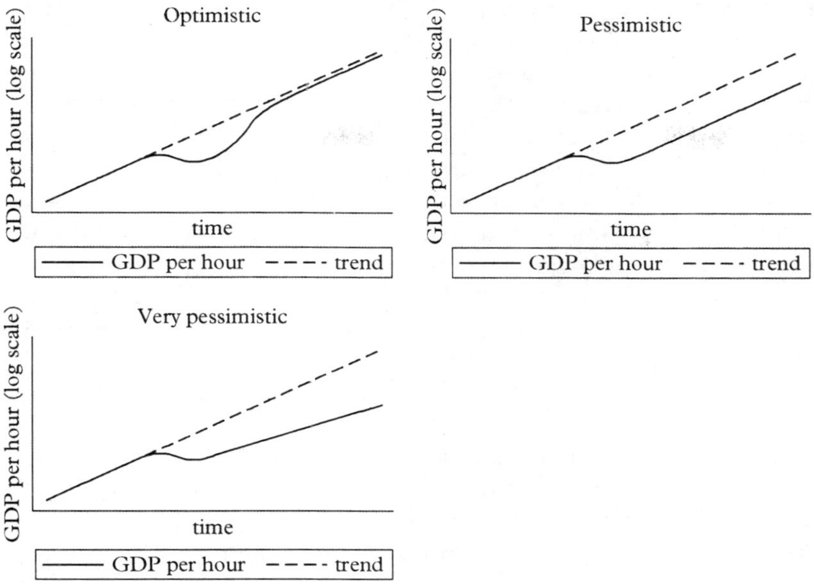

Figure 1.3. Hypothetical paths for GDP per hour during recession and recovery

USA. In the second period it grew at 2.87% p.a., ahead of all the above countries and behind only Ireland, Finland and Sweden.

But all this optimistic evidence has been called into question by the worldwide financial crisis which has led (most commentators would argue) to the worst recession in the UK since the 1930s.[5] Figure 1.3 sets out in schematic form three possible scenarios for the future after a crisis-induced recession, labelled 'optimistic', 'pessimistic' and 'very pessimistic'. Here the dashed lines represent trend (potential) GDP per hour, based on pre-crisis conditions. Under the 'optimistic' scenario the economy recovers, the original trend growth rate prevails again (possibly after a lengthy period) and furthermore the *level* of GDP per hour eventually returns to the value it would have achieved if the crisis had somehow been avoided. In other words, the economy eventually returns to the track (the dashed line) it would have been predicted to be

5 This may be unfair to the 1930s, which saw a private house-building boom and imaginative infrastructure projects like electrification and the National Grid. The main reason the 1930s have such a bad image is the high rate of unemployment.

on in the absence of the crisis. Of course, even under this scenario the crisis has not been costless, since there has been a permanent loss of output relative to potential during the recession and recovery. But after a bit this is just a bygone. Under the 'pessimistic' scenario, the economy eventually regains its trend growth rate but it never gets back on the original track: GDP per hour is always below what it would have been without the crisis. (It has become something of a commonplace to say that the recovery from a financial crisis tends to be long and slow. But this statement might describe either the pessimistic or the optimistic scenario, because it does not distinguish clearly between levels and growth rate effects.) Finally, under the 'very pessimistic' scenario, not only does the economy never get back on the original track but it falls progressively further and further below it. In other words the trend growth rate has fallen as a result of the crisis.

Which of these scenarios is closer to the truth for the UK? My argument in this chapter is that the pessimistic scenario is the most likely: the UK will eventually regain its previous trend growth rate, but will have suffered a permanent loss in GDP. The main reason for this conclusion is that it is what we would expect as a result of a banking crisis (on the basis of econometric evidence presented below). This argument is not advanced with 100% confidence and clearly much depends on external conditions over which we in the UK have no control. And it also depends on a continuation of reasonably good policies, particularly with regard to government debt, as discussed later.

1.1.1 Plan of the chapter

I start in Section 1.2 by setting out a framework for estimating long-run growth, based on a neo-classical two-sector model. I argue that two sectors are necessary to take proper account of the impact of information and communication technology (ICT), which is of continuing importance in my view. I use this model to develop a projection for the long-run growth rate of labour productivity (output per hour) in the UK market sector. This projection takes no account of the financial crisis and is calibrated entirely on pre-crisis data. It shows if you like what might have happened (on reasonable assumptions) had the recession somehow been avoided: it corresponds to the dashed lines in Figure 1.3. Next, in Section 1.3 I look at what has actually happened to the British economy since the boom came to an end in early 2008. As we all know there has been not just a decline in the productivity growth rate but an actual fall in the level of productivity from its peak, which has yet to be regained. I consider various hypotheses that have been advanced to explain the productivity puzzle, including GDP mismeasurement, declining human and physical capital intensity, labour and capital hoarding, zombie firms and austerity. In Section 1.4 I look at international evidence on the effects of banking crises on output per worker, capital per worker, total factor productivity (TFP) and output per capita, via a panel data study of 61 countries over 1950–2010. This enables one to quantify the permanent loss of GDP that is due to the crisis. However, this model does not enable one to distinguish between the pessimistic and the very pessimistic scenarios (since the pessimistic scenario is the maintained hypothesis). I therefore turn in Section 1.5 to consider two case studies: the USA in the aftermath of the Great Depression of the 1930s and Japan after the bubble burst in 1990 when it entered on its so-called 'lost decade(s)'. As we shall see the USA supports the case for the 'pessimistic' scenario, while Japan supports the case for the 'very pessimistic' one. Section 1.6 concludes.

1.2 A pre-crisis projection of UK productivity growth[6]

In this section I first make the general case for explicit consideration of ICT in making projections of future growth. Then I discuss the basic neo-classical (Solow) growth model and why it is deficient when ICT is important. I next set out a two-sector model in which the second sector produces ICT investment goods. Technical progress is assumed to be more rapid in the ICT sector. Finally I calibrate this model using pre-crisis data only.

1.2.1 The importance of ICT

The approach adopted here recognises the central importance of ICT in the modern world. After the growth rate of US labour productivity started to rise in the latter half of the 1990s, a number of highly influential growth accounting studies were published. These included Oliner and Sichel (2000, 2002), Jorgenson and Stiroh (2000a,b), Stiroh (2002), Jorgenson et al. (2004, 2005, 2007) and Oliner et al. (2007). These studies all attributed a high proportion of the productivity resurgence to ICT, and found that most of the improvement was due to the *use* of ICT equipment by other industries (capital deepening) rather than to the *production* of ICT equipment by the ICT industries themselves. See also Oulton (2002), Oulton and Srinivasan (2005) and

6 This section draws heavily on Oulton (2010) and (2012) where more detailed justification for some of the methods and assumptions can be found.

Marrano et al. (2009) for the UK, and for the G7 Schreyer (2000); a US–UK comparison is Basu et al. (2004) and an EU–US comparison is van Ark et al. (2008).

By their nature academic studies are always somewhat out of date, at least when they come to be published. So some more recent data is worth noting. Those who think that the ICT boom of the late 1990s was all irrational exuberance, a product of dotcom fever and Y2K hysteria, might like to note that in the USA the net stock of computers was 111% higher in 2007 than it had been in 2000, while the net stocks of software and communications equipment were 54% and 62% higher respectively (source: Bureau of Economic Analysis, Fixed Asset Tables, Table 1.2, available at www.bea.gov; accessed 11/02/2014).

1.2.2 The textbook one-sector model

I start with the textbook one-sector (Solow) model, expanded to include human capital. Consideration of this model will motivate the move to a two-sector model. Here we assume just one sector whose output can be used for either consumption or investment. For simplicity and for consistency with the two-sector model below, I assume that the production function is Cobb–Douglas with constant returns. The equations of the model are:

$$Y = C + I = BK^{\gamma}[hH]^{1-\gamma}, \quad 0<\gamma<1 \tag{1.1}$$

and

$$\dot{K} = I - \delta K \tag{1.2}$$

where Y is output, C is consumption, I is investment, B is the level of TFP, K is capital, H is hours worked, h is the average level of skill (human capital) per worker, and δ is the geometric rate of decay (depreciation) of capital. Output per hour (y) is

$$y = \frac{Y}{H} = Bh^{1-\gamma}k^{\gamma} \tag{1.3}$$

putting $k = K/H$. TFP is assumed to grow at the exogenous rate μ, hours worked (H) at the exogenous rate n, and human capital (skill) at the exogenous rate g_h.

As is well known, under standard assumptions this model possesses a steady state in which output per hour grows at a constant rate given by:

$$\hat{y}^* = \frac{\mu}{1-\gamma} + g_h \tag{1.4}$$

where a hat (^) denotes a growth rate and a star (*) denotes the steady state. In the basic Solow model there is only one engine of growth, the exogenous growth of TFP (μ). Here there is also a second engine, the growth of human capital (g_h). Physical capital plays an important role, but in the long run all capital deepening (growth of k) is induced by growth of TFP or growth of skill.[7]

In this model, forecasting the long-run growth rate of hourly labour productivity (y) is fairly straightforward: it requires just a forecast of TFP growth (μ), an estimate of the parameter γ which corresponds to the capital (profit) share and an estimate of the growth rate of skill (h). Assuming that inputs are paid their marginal products, TFP growth can be measured by

$$\mu = \hat{B} = \frac{\dot{Y}}{Y} - v_K\left(\frac{\dot{K}}{K}\right) - v_L\left(\frac{\dot{H}}{H}\right) - v_L\hat{h} \tag{1.5}$$

where $v_K(v_L)$ is the income share of capital (labour) and $v_K + v_L = 1$. (In terms of the model, $v_K = \gamma,\ v_L = 1 - \gamma$). A forecast of TFP growth can be based on its own history, which empirically could be measured using a discrete-time Törnqvist index. A forecast of the growth of skill could also be based on its own past history.[8]

Where does ICT appear in the solution for the equilibrium growth rate, Eq. (1.4)? If we applied the model to an economy with some ICT production, then the fact that TFP growth has been (and will probably continue to be) higher in ICT than in non-ICT industries will influence the past and projected future aggregate TFP growth rate. But suppose instead we are considering a small, open economy with no ICT production at all (not an unrealistic assumption). Then the one-sector model predicts zero impact from the ICT revolution. But surely the ability to import ICT capital at ever-declining prices must be beneficial to growth? As we are about to see, this is exactly what the two-sector model predicts.

7 The derivation assumes a Cobb–Douglas production function, but this is only for comparability with what follows. Essentially the same results could be derived from any neo-classical production function with purely labour-augmenting technical progress.

8 The growth of skill can be measured by the difference between a quality-adjusted index of the growth of hours and the unadjusted growth of hours. In the quality-adjusted index each type of labour is weighted by its wage. So quality is rising if the composition of the labour force is shifting towards more highly paid forms of work. For UK measures of skill growth, see Bell et al. (2005); similar measures appear in the EU KLEMS database. The ONS also now produces a similar measure (Franklin and Mistry 2013).

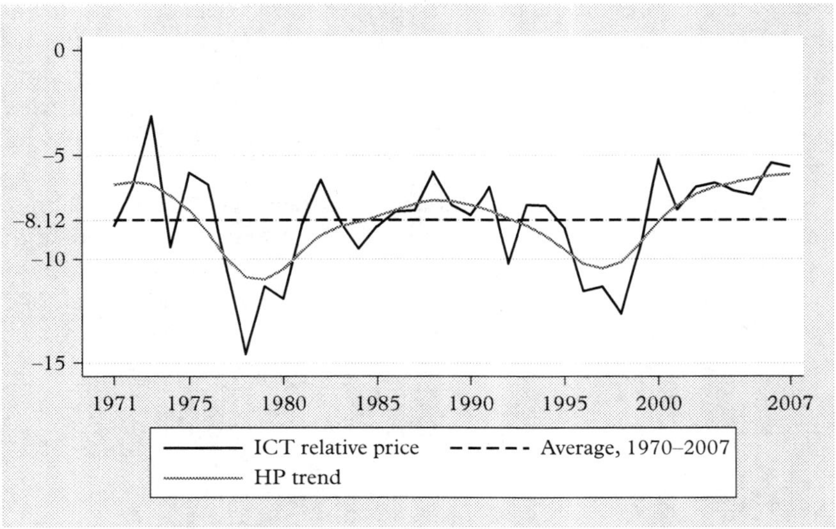

Figure 1.4. Rate of decline of relative price of ICT in the USA, % p.a. *Source:* U.S. NIPAs, Table 5.5.4; ICT price relative to price of non-farm business sector output.

1.2.3 *A two-sector model*[9]

The one-sector model assumes in effect that there are no persistent changes in the relative prices of the myriad goods which make up a real economy. It thus fails to capture the most striking feature of recent economic history in the industrialised economies, namely the dramatic and persistent falls in the relative price of ICT investment goods. For example, in the USA between 1970 and 2007 the relative price of computers in terms of the price of output in the non-farm business sector was falling at an average rate of 20.32% p.a.; the relative price of the broader category of 'information processing equipment and software' was falling at 8.12% p.a. (source: U.S. National Income and Product Accounts (NIPA); see Figure 1.4). This rate of decline, sustained over four

9 The present model draws on Oulton (2007) and (2012). A model similar in structure to the present one but with a quite different interpretation is in Barro and Sala-i-Martin (1995), Chapter 5. The two-sector model with faster technical progress in investment goods was revived by Whelan (2001) and applied by Martin (2001) to study the US economy and by Cette et al. (2005) to compare France and the USA. It was also employed by Bakhshi and Larsen (2005) to analyse the impact of macroeconomic shocks in the UK context. Oliner and Sichel (2002) employ the steady state of a five-sector model for some of their projections of the US economy. The main difference between the earlier work and the present application is the extension of the two-sector model to an open economy.

decades and more, is unprecedented. So I now consider a two-sector model in which the relative price of the good produced by the second sector is changing.

I assume that the output of the first sector can be used either for consumption (C) or for investment (I_C); the output of the second sector, which we can think of as the sector producing ICT goods, can only be used for investment (I_{ICT}). For brevity, I refer to the sector producing consumption and non-ICT investment goods as just the consumption sector. The production function for this sector is given by

$$Y_C = B_C (K_C^C)^\alpha (K_{ICT}^C)^\beta (hH_C)^{1-\alpha-\beta}, \quad 0<\alpha,\beta<1,\ \alpha+\beta<1 \tag{1.6}$$

where K_C^C, K_{ICT}^C are capital services of non-ICT and ICT capital respectively that are used by the consumption sector (here the superscript represents the industry), and H_C is hours worked in that sector. In per hour terms,

$$y_C = \frac{Y_C}{H_C} = B_C h^{1-\alpha-\beta} (k_C^C)^\alpha (k_{ICT}^C)^\beta \tag{1.7}$$

Here $k_C^C = \frac{K_C^C}{H_c}$ and $k_{ICT}^C = \frac{K_{ICT}^C}{H_c}$, the capital intensities in the consumption sector. I assume as before that skill is growing exogenously at rate g_h and that TFP in the consumption good sector (B_C) is growing at rate μ_C.

For the ICT-producing sector, I make a crucial, simplifying assumption: the production function is the same as in the consumption sector, except for TFP. As a result, in equilibrium the capital intensities will be the same in both sectors and equal to the whole-economy input endowments. The production function for the ICT sector is:

$$y_{ICT} = \frac{Y_{ICT}}{H_{ICT}} = B_{ICT} h^{1-\alpha-\beta} (k_C^{ICT})^\alpha (k_{ICT}^{ICT})^\beta \tag{1.8}$$

Here $k_C^{ICT} = \frac{K_C^{ICT}}{H_{ICT}}$ and $k_{ICT}^{ICT} = \frac{K_{ICT}^{ICT}}{H_{ICT}}$, the capital intensities. The growth rate of TFP in the ICT sector, $\mu_{ICT} = \hat{B}_{ICT}$, is assumed exogenous. I also assume that $\mu_C < \mu_{ICT}$.

The model is completed by equations stating that input supplies must equal demands, by two accumulation equations for the two types of capital, and two balance equations stating that the supply (domestic output plus imports) of each industry's output must equal demand (home plus foreign). It is also useful to define the price of ICT goods relative to that of consumption goods, p: $p = P_{ICT}/P_C$ where P_{ICT},P_C are the nominal prices of the ICT and consumer goods respectively.

Oulton (2012) shows that the model possesses a steady state (defined as a state where the real interest rate and the proportion of aggregate hours allocated to each sector are constant) with the following properties. The growth rate of consumption per hour worked ($c = C/H$) is constant in the steady state:

$$\hat{c}^{\star} = \frac{(1-\beta)\mu_C + \beta\mu_{ICT}}{(1-\alpha-\beta)} + g_h \tag{1.9}$$

It can also be shown that

$$\hat{p} = \mu_C - \mu_{ICT} < 0 \tag{1.10}$$

since by assumption $\mu_C < \mu_{ICT}$. So the steady state growth rate can also be written as:

$$\hat{c}^{\star} = \frac{\mu_C - \beta\hat{p}}{(1-\alpha-\beta)} + g_h \tag{1.11}$$

This second form of the solution is useful in empirical work.

To complete the solution of the model, the steady state growth rates of output per hour in the two sectors are:

$$\begin{aligned} \hat{y}_C^{\star} &= \hat{c}^{\star} \\ y_{ICT}^{\star} &= \hat{c}^{\star} - (\mu_C - \mu_{ICT}) = \hat{c}^{\star} - \hat{p} > \hat{y}_C^{\star} \end{aligned} \tag{1.12}$$

We see that in steady state output and productivity of the consumption good grow less rapidly than does output and productivity of the ICT good. It can also be shown: (1) the stock of ICT capital grows faster than the stock of non-ICT capital; and (2) the ratios of investment to GDP, the capital–output ratios and the savings ratio, all in value (current price) terms, are constant in the steady state.

Intuitively, where there were two engines of growth in the one-sector model, TFP and skills growth, there is now a third: TFP growth in the ICT sector, which is faster than in the consumption sector. This third engine drives up the growth rate of consumption permanently.

A Divisia index of the steady state growth rate of real GDP per hour (y) can now be derived as:

$$\hat{y}^{\star} = \frac{\mu_C - \left[\beta + (1-\alpha-\beta)w_{ICT}^{\star}\right]\hat{p}}{(1-\alpha-\beta)} + g_h \tag{1.13}$$

where $w_{ICT}^{\star} = pY_{ICT}^{\star}/(Y_C^{\star} + pY_{ICT}^{\star})$ is the steady state output share of the ICT sector. The growth rate of GDP per hour is obviously positively related to the two TFP growth rates. It is also positively related to (a) the parameter β, which can be interpreted as the income share of ICT capital and (b) the share of ICT output in GDP ($w^{\star}_{ICT}$). It is easy to see that real GDP grows more rapidly than real consumption in the steady state if the ICT output share is positive (i.e. if $w^{\star}_{ICT} > 0$). Note that the solution to the two-sector model, Eq. (1.13), reduces to that of the one-sector model, Eq. (1.4), if $\hat{p} = 0$, i.e. if TFP growth is the same in both sectors (and noting that in this case $\alpha + \beta = \gamma$).

The solution just given applies just as much to an open as to a closed economy. It shows how misleading the one-sector model can be. For that model predicts that the long-run growth rate of a small economy which is completely specialised in the non-ICT good is determined entirely by TFP growth in that sector (and the labour share and the growth of skill). So such an economy apparently derives no benefit at all from the ICT revolution. But we now see that it does benefit in the form of improving terms of trade and the two-sector model allows us to quantify this effect. If the ICT output share is zero ($w^{\star}_{ICT} = 0$), then the boost to growth coming from the fact that technical progress is faster in ICT is $-\beta\hat{p}/(1 - \alpha - \beta) > 0$.

1.2.4 *Implementing the two-sector model empirically*

The empirical counterpart of the theoretical Eq. (1.13), describing the steady state growth of GDP per hour, can be written as follows:

$$\Delta \ln \overline{y} = \frac{\Delta \ln \overline{B}_C - [\overline{v}_{K_{ICT}} + \overline{v}_L \overline{w}_{ICT}] \Delta \ln \overline{p}}{\overline{v}_L} + \overline{g}_h \qquad (1.14)$$

where bars over variables indicate projected values; $\overline{v}_{K_{ICT}}$ is the projected income share of ICT capital, $\overline{v}_L$ is the projected income share of labour, $\overline{w}_{ICT}$ is the projected output share of the ICT sector and $\overline{g}_h$ is the projected growth rate of skill. Values for these parameters are required for medium/long-run projections of GDP growth.

Annual data for the UK for the income and output shares of ICT, the labour share, the growth of skill and overall TFP growth[10] can be found in the EU KLEMS database for the years 1970–2007.[11] The growth rate of the relative price of ICT is taken from the US NIPA. Most researchers who study the impact of ICT consider the US price indices to be more reliable than their counterparts in other countries

10 Given an estimate of overall TFP growth, say $\Delta \ln \overline{B}$, we can apply Domar aggregation to obtain $\Delta \ln \overline{B}_C = \Delta \ln \overline{B} + \overline{w}_{ICT} \Delta \ln \overline{p}$.

11 In EU KLEMS the income share of an ICT asset is measured by standard growth accounting techniques. It is the rental price (user cost) of the asset times the stock divided by nominal GDP in the market sector; the rental price is the Hall–Jorgenson measure. The output share of ICT is nominal value added in ICT-producing industries divided by nominal GDP in the market sector.

Table 1.2. Projected growth rates of GDP per hour for the UK market sector derived from one-sector and two-sector models (parameter values calibrated on pre-crisis data)

Description	Parameter: *Theory*	Parameter: *Measurement*	Method	Value
TFP growth rate (whole economy)	μ	$\Delta\ln\overline{B}$	Mean, 1990–2007	0.0114
TFP growth rate (consumption sector)	μ_C	$\Delta\ln\overline{B}_C$	Mean, 1990–2007	0.0087
ICT income share	β	$\overline{v}_{K_{ICT}}$	HP trend (level)	0.0641
ICT output share	$w^{\star}_{ICT}$	$\overline{w}_{ICT}$	HP trend (level)	0.0183
Labour share	$1-\alpha-\beta$	$\overline{v}_L$	Mean, 1990–2007	0.7301
Rate of decline of ICT price	$\mu_C-\mu_{ICT}$	$\Delta\ln\overline{p}$	HP trend (growth rate)	−0.0590
Growth rate of skill	g_h	$\overline{g}_h$	Mean, 1990–2007	0.0057
Projected growth rates of GDP per hour				
One-sector model		$\Delta\ln\overline{y}$	Equation (1.4)	0.0213
Two-sector model		$\Delta\ln\overline{y}$	Equation (1.14)	0.0261

Source: Parameter values derived from pre-crisis UK data in EU KLEMS (November 2009 release, available at www.euklems.net). Rate of decline of relative price of ICT ($\Delta\ln\overline{p}$) from pre-crisis data from U.S. NIPA (www.bea.gov). Projected growth rates derived using Eqs. (1.4) and (1.14). See text for details.

(Schreyer (2002), Oulton (2002); Oulton and Srinivasan (2005)).[12] I follow suit here and measure the relative price of ICT as the US price of ICT equipment (computers, software and communications equipment) relative to the price of gross value added in the non-farm business sector (the latter being close to the EU KLEMS market sector).

All these series (in log levels for TFP and the ICT relative price, in levels for the shares) were passed through a Hodrick–Prescott filter. I have used two methods to pick parameter values, depending on the nature of the time series. In the case of series which appear stationary like the labour share I use the mean over 1990–2007. In other cases I use the value of the HP trend of that variable (or its growth rate) in 2007. The parameter values I adopted are in Table 1.2. The value for $\Delta\ln\overline{p}$, the projected rate of decline of the ICT relative price, is quite a conservative one. It is (numerically) smaller than its mean value over 1990–2007 (–8.12%) since the HP trend picks up an apparent

12 In the UK the Office for National Statistics now employs a similar methodology to that of the US Bureau of Economic Analysis to measure the price of computers, but this new methodology has only been applied to recent years of the computer price series. So the UK series moves in a similar way to the US one in recent, but not in earlier, years.

deceleration after 2000 (Figure 1.4). Plugging the parameter values in the table into Eq. (1.14), the growth rate of the UK's GDP per hour in the market sector is projected to be 0.0261 or 2.61% p.a. The extra boost to growth coming from the falling price of ICT is estimated as

$$\frac{-\bar{v}_{K_{ICT}}\Delta\ln\bar{p}}{\bar{v}_L}=0.0052 \tag{1.15}$$

or 0.52% p.a., i.e. about a fifth of future growth is projected to come from the falling price of ICT. The projected growth rate is slower than the rate actually achieved over 1990–2007, 2.87% (see Figure 1.2) mainly because of the assumption that ICT prices will fall more slowly in future. If to the contrary they continue to fall at the average rate actually observed over 1990–2007 (8.12% p.a.) then the projected growth rate would rise to 2.79% p.a. with the ICT contribution rising to 0.71% p.a.

It is also worth noting that the projected growth rate generated by the one-sector model is much lower. The mean TFP growth rate in the UK market sector was 1.14% p.a. over 1990–2007. Applying Eq. (1.4) generates a projected growth rate of only 2.13%. This is much slower than the actual rate experienced over 1990–2007 (2.87% p.a.); see also Oulton (2010), Annex B. Recall that all these calculations are based on pre-crisis data.

ICT has been an important source of growth for the UK since the UK has been an early adopter of the new technologies. Out of 19 leading economies the ICT income share was higher in the UK than in 15 of the others, being surpassed only by the US and Swedish shares (Oulton 2012, Table 1.3). Cette and Lopez (2008) found that across countries the ICT income share varies positively with the extent of higher education and negatively with product and labour market rigidities. It is likely therefore that the high UK share reflects our advantages on these dimensions.

1.3 Labour productivity during and after the Great Recession: puzzles and explanations

This section reviews the course of labour productivity in the UK in and after the Great Recession. I consider first some puzzling facts and then turn to possible explanations.

1.3.1 Puzzles

GDP started falling in 2008Q2 and continued falling in the subsequent six quarters up to and including 2009Q3. It began rising again in

2009Q4 (Table 1.1). 2009Q3 therefore marks the trough of the present cycle while 2009Q4 marks the end of the recession in a technical sense and the start of the recovery (Source: *Quarterly National Accounts, June 2013*). Relative to its peak in 2008Q1 to the trough of the recession, labour productivity (GDP per hour) fell by 4.5% (Table 1.4). Comparing the latest period, 2013Q1, with the previous peak, labour productivity was lower still, by 5.1%. And relative to the pre-crisis HP trend, labour productivity in 2013Q1 was 16% lower. So relative to the peak labour productivity fell in the recession and has since stagnated. This is the productivity puzzle.

Labour productivity on a 'heads' basis, GDP per job, looks even worse than on an hours basis, at least up till the last three quarters (Table 1.1). This is because hours fell more than did jobs, an interesting example of the UK's labour market flexibility. Weekly hours per job were declining prior to the recession. But they fell below their previous trend during the recession, though they are now back to their pre-recession level (Table 1.1).

The UK experience is in sharp contrast to that of the USA. There, output per hour in the non-farm business sector fell initially as the recession began but then recovered strongly. In 2009Q1 it surpassed its previous peak level of 2007Q4. Though growth slowed in 2012, by 2013Q4 productivity was 10% higher than the previous peak. On average it grew by 1.9% p.a. between 2007 and 2011. By comparison, productivity grew at 2.6% over 2000–07 and 2.2% over 1990–2001.[13] So there has been a slowdown but no crisis in US labour productivity, despite the fact that during the recession GDP fell by about the same proportion in the USA as in the UK. The UK productivity performance post-recession also seems to have been worse than in most EU countries (Hughes and Saleheen, 2012).

1.3.2 Aggregate and sectoral analysis

Further insight into the productivity puzzle comes from breaking down the economy firstly into broad aggregates and secondly more finely by sector (see Table 1.3).

1.3.2.1 The influence of hard-to-measure or otherwise problematic sectors Initially I check whether the overall picture is changed by looking at broad sectors such as the market economy, i.e. GDP excluding

13 Source: US Bureau of Labor Statistics, www.bls.gov.lpc/prodybar.htm, accessed 11/02/2014.

Table 1.3. Sectoral breakdown of the UK economy in 2007

Sector		Share of GDP, %	Share of total hours, %	Relative productivity, ratio
A	***Agriculture, forestry & fishing***	0.6	1.6	0.39
B	***Mining & quarrying inc. oil & gas***	2.5	0.3	10.65
C	Manufacturing	11.1	10.9	1.01
D	Electricity, gas, steam, etc	1.3	0.4	2.93
E	Water supply, sewerage, etc	1.1	0.5	2.19
F	Construction	7.7	8.4	0.91
G	Wholesale & retail trade	11.5	15.0	0.76
H	Transport & storage	4.8	5.3	0.91
I	Accommodation & food services	2.9	5.4	0.54
J	Information & communication	6.0	4.3	1.34
K	***Financial & insurance activities***	8.3	4.1	2.07
L	***Real estate***	8.7	1.4	6.37
M	Professional, scientific & tech. activities	7.3	7.5	0.96
N	Administrative & support activities	4.5	7.5	0.59
O, P, Q	***Government services***	18.4	22.7	0.81
R	Arts, entertainment & recreation	1.5	2.2	0.67
S–U	Other services & household activities	1.8	2.4	0.72
	Total	100.0	100.0	1.00

Note: Classification is in accordance with SIC 2007. Relative productivity is GDP share divided by hours share. Sectors in *Bold Italic* are those described in the text as 'problematic' for various reasons. Output of Real estate includes the imputed rent of owner-occupiers. Government services include Public Administration and defence, Education, and Health and social services. Relative productivity is GDP share divided by hours share, i.e. value added per hour in the sector in question divided by value added per hour in the whole economy.
Source: Office for National Statistics.

government services (Public administration and defence, Education, and Health and social services, sectors O, P and Q), which was 74.1% of GDP in 2010. Next I also exclude sectors which are problematic in various ways. There are some sectors where labour productivity was declining prior to the recession and other sectors whose performance cannot be taken at face value (see below). Some of these problematic sectors are natural resource-dependent, such as Agriculture (A) and oil and gas (B); in others there may be measurement issues, e.g. Financial and insurance activities (K).[14] It is often suggested that banking output was overstated in the boom (more on this below). I also exclude the

14 See Burgess (2011) and Oulton (2013) for discussion of the problems in measuring the output of financial services.

Table 1.4. Estimates of labour productivity (GVA per hour) for broad sectors: ratio of GDP per hour in (a) the trough of the recession (2009Q3) and (b) the latest period (2013Q1) to GDP per hour in the previous peak (2008Q1 = 100.0)

	Whole economy	**Market sector (GDP exc. O, P and Q)**	**Market sector, exc. problematic sectors (A, B and K)**	**Whole economy, holding labour shares at 2007 values**
Ratios	(1)	(2)	(3)	(4)
Trough (2009Q3) to peak (2008Q1)	95.52	95.31	94.54	95.89
Latest period (2013Q1) to peak (2008Q1)	94.89	94.93	96.23	94.19

Source: Office for National Statistics. Column (1) from Table 1.1; columns (2)–(4) from data underlying the *Productivity Bulletin, June–July 2013*. See text for further explanation.

imputed rent of owner-occupiers from Real estate (L) since there are no hours worked associated with this form of output. The resulting aggregate (MEX) was 61.6% of GDP in 2010. Market services (MS) is the market economy with the production sector and utilities (A–F) excluded, 51.9% of GDP in 2010. I calculate real gross value added (GVA) in these broad aggregates using the ONS methodology (annually chain-linked Laspeyres indices).

Productivity performance is shown in Table 1.4. Column 1 shows the official figures for labour productivity, GDP (at basic prices) per hour. Column 3 shows the market economy (ME) and column 4 shows the MEX aggregate. There is very little difference between the performance of these aggregates, though MEX has perhaps done a shade better since the trough.

Figure 1.5 shows the course of quarterly labour productivity (GDP per hour worked) in these aggregates from 1997Q1 up till the latest date available at the time of writing, 2013Q1. These and the following figures have a common format. What actually happened (according to the most recent information) is shown as a solid line, with a dashed line showing the trend estimated over the pre-recession period. The trend is calculated by the Hodrick–Prescott (HP) filter (with parameter set to 1600 since these are quarterly data) over the pre-crisis period 1997Q1–2008Q1 and extrapolated beyond then to the end of the period (2013Q1). The vertical axis is on a log scale so that growth rates can be read off from the slopes of the lines. The figures also show the Great Recession (the period of falling GDP, 2008Q2–2009Q3) marked

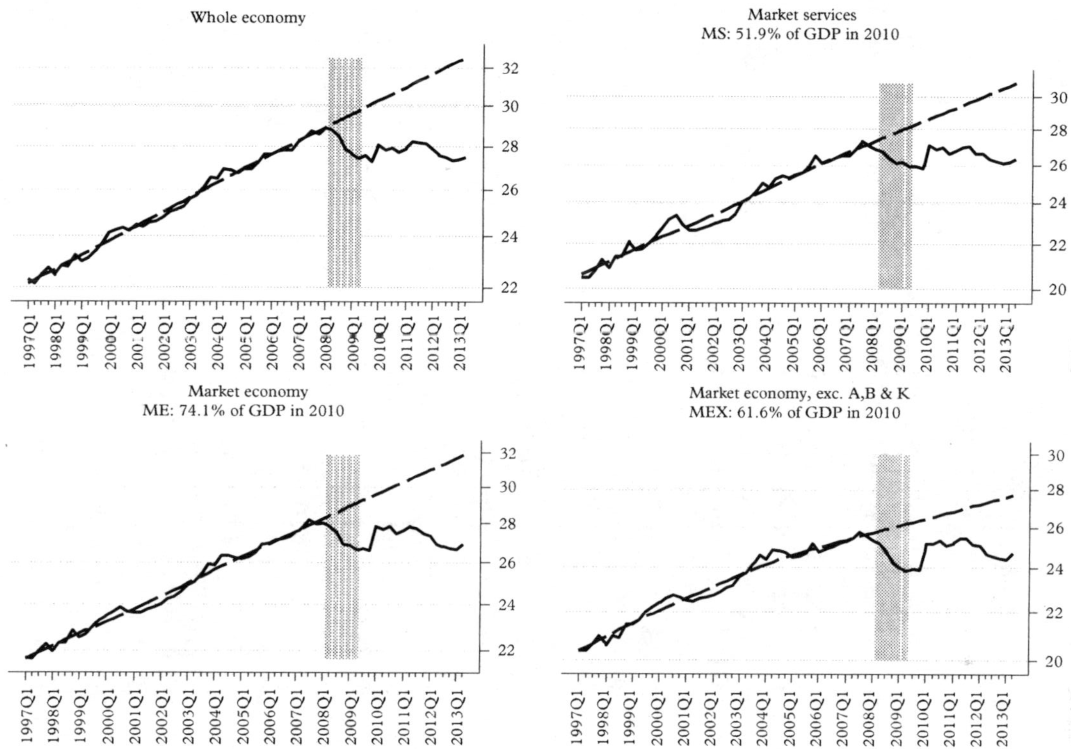

Figure 1.5. Real GVA per hour – whole economy (log scale, 2010 £)
Note: Seasonally adjusted. Grey bar (red bar in web version) marks Great Recession (2008Q2–2009Q3). Dashed lines are Hodrick–Prescott trends estimated over 1997Q1–2008Q1.
Source: Office for National Statistics, *Labour Productivity Bulletin*, September 2013

by a grey bar (red bar in web version). Figure 1.5 confirms the evidence of Table 1.4: excluding sectors which may be problematic for various reasons does not resolve the productivity puzzle. Productivity fell in each of these aggregates and has yet to regain its previous peak.

1.3.2.2 Reallocation of labour to sectors where productivity is lower Has the aggregate productivity performance been materially affected by resources shifting from high productivity sectors to low productivity ones? Table 1.3 shows a breakdown into 17 sectors. This table shows the share of each sector's value added in aggregate value added (GDP) in the last year of the boom, 2007. Also shown are the 2007 shares of each sector in aggregate hours worked. If we divide the share in GDP by the share in aggregate hours we get the relative labour productivity of each sector (value added per hour in each sector divided by aggregate value added (GDP) per hour); this is shown in the last column. The level of labour productivity varies widely across the 17 sectors, from a low of 0.39 in 'Agriculture, forestry & fishing' to a high of 10.65 in 'Mining and quarrying including oil and gas'. So, hypothetically, holding the productivity growth rate in each sector at its observed value but reallocating labour towards (say) a sector with a low productivity *level* could lower aggregate productivity by a significant amount.

We can see whether this actually happened by calculating what GDP per hour would have been if productivity had risen in each sector at the rate actually observed but the allocation of labour across the sectors was the same as in 2007, i.e. the 2007 labour shares continued unchanged at their Table 1.3 values. The result is in column (4) of Table 1.4: holding labour shares constant makes virtually no difference (a conclusion already reached by Martin (2011)).

Despite this negative result, a shift away from high productivity to low productivity activities *within* (rather than between) sectors might have further explanatory power. Suppose that in the recession shoppers shift from high-margin to low-margin stores. The high-margin stores offer a better shopping experience or better service, but their prices for comparable products are higher (think of buying bananas in Harrods Food Hall compared to in your local Tesco). This shift would show up as a fall in output and productivity in the official statistics. The same effect could arise if there is a shift towards cheaper, own-brand products within a given store.[15]

15 Philip Clarke, Tesco chief executive, argues that such a shift has indeed taken place since the recession began ('Lessons from the supermarket for austerity Britain', *Financial Times*, 19 October 2012).

1.3.2.3 The productivity puzzle at the sectoral level Figure 1.6 shows the course of labour productivity in each of the 17 sectors of Table 1.3.[16] More recent data has substantially changed the picture formed on the basis of earlier evidence. Patterns which were discernible in data released in mid-2012 are now not so apparent (Oulton and Sebastiá-Barriel, 2013). The general conclusion from looking at these figures is that the productivity puzzle is very widespread. Most sectors now fall into the 'very pessimistic' category, including Manufacturing (C), Wholesale and retail trade (G) and Finance and insurance activities (K). Previously government services (O, P, Q) looked to have performed quite well, but now they seem just as subject to the productivity puzzle as other sectors. Information and communication (J) now also appears to be in the 'very pessimistic' category. There are some maverick sectors. Productivity growth in Construction (F) is very erratic, but the trend was declining prior to the recession. The more recent data puts this sector right on its falling trend. In the utilities too (D and E) trend productivity was declining prior to the recession and actual performance has worsened since. Presumably regulation (e.g. the cost of meeting higher environmental standards) has played a role here. Other sectors on a declining trend before the recession were Agriculture (A), and Oil and gas (B). The latter has done particularly poorly since then. Presumably geology is the main explanation. Finally, Real estate (L) is a particular puzzle. Before the recession productivity was declining, but after the recession it rises sharply, and this despite the fact that we have stripped out the imputed rent of owner-occupiers.

1.3.3 *Mis-measurement of GDP due to mis-measurement of banking output*

It is frequently argued that the output of the banking industry was overstated during the boom. Bankers were selling financial products of low or no social value ('toxic rubbish') to ignorant or greedy clients. So if banking output were measured correctly it would be seen to have grown more slowly than the official figures suggest. Consequently, since banking is a large industry in the UK, the growth of real GDP must have been overstated too. If this argument is correct, it would

16 These data can be found (with considerable difficulty) on the ONS website at http://www.ons.gov.uk/ons/about-ons/what-we-do/publication-scheme/published-ad-hoc-data/economy/index.html. I have used the spreadsheet dated June–July 2013. Note that total hours worked are derived from the Labour Force Survey (LFS), as is self-employment, and hours worked in each sector are scaled so that they add up to the LFS total.

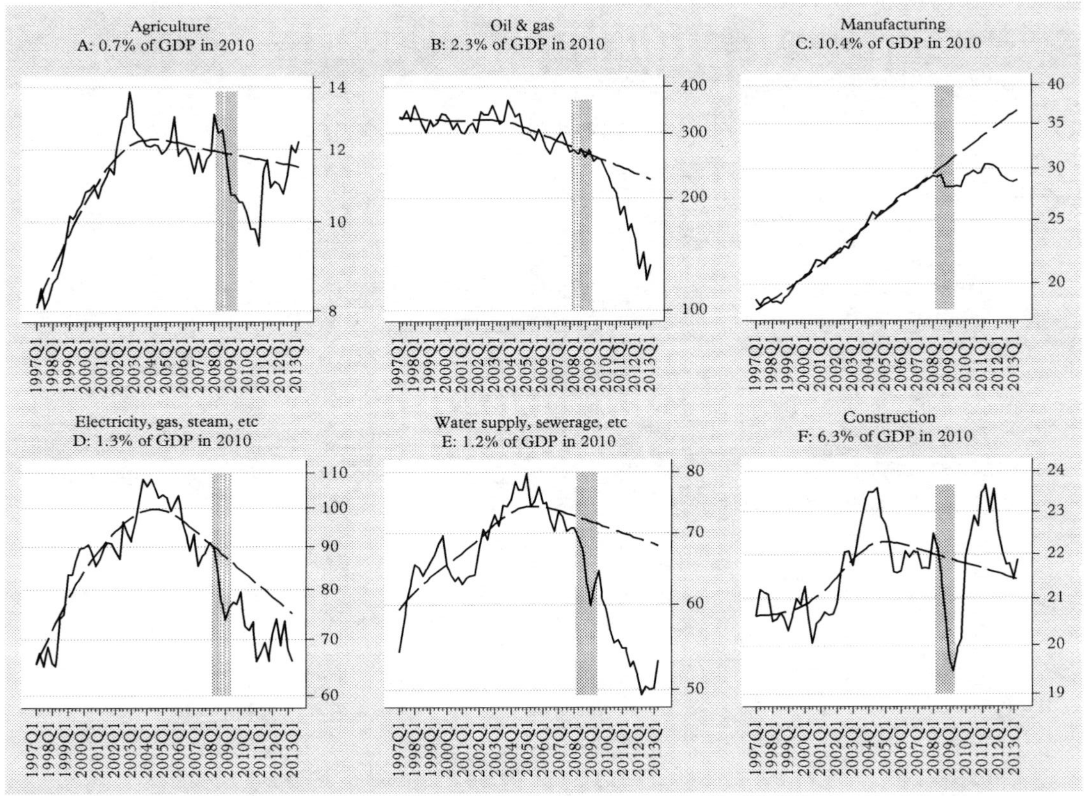

Figure 1.6. Real GVA per hour – sectors (log scale, 2010 £)
Note: Seasonally adjusted. Grey bar (red bar in web version) marks Great Recession (2008Q2–2009Q3). Dashed lines are Hodrick-Prescott trends estimated over 1997Q1–2008Q1.
Source: Office for National Statistics, *Labour Productivity Bulletin*, September 2013.

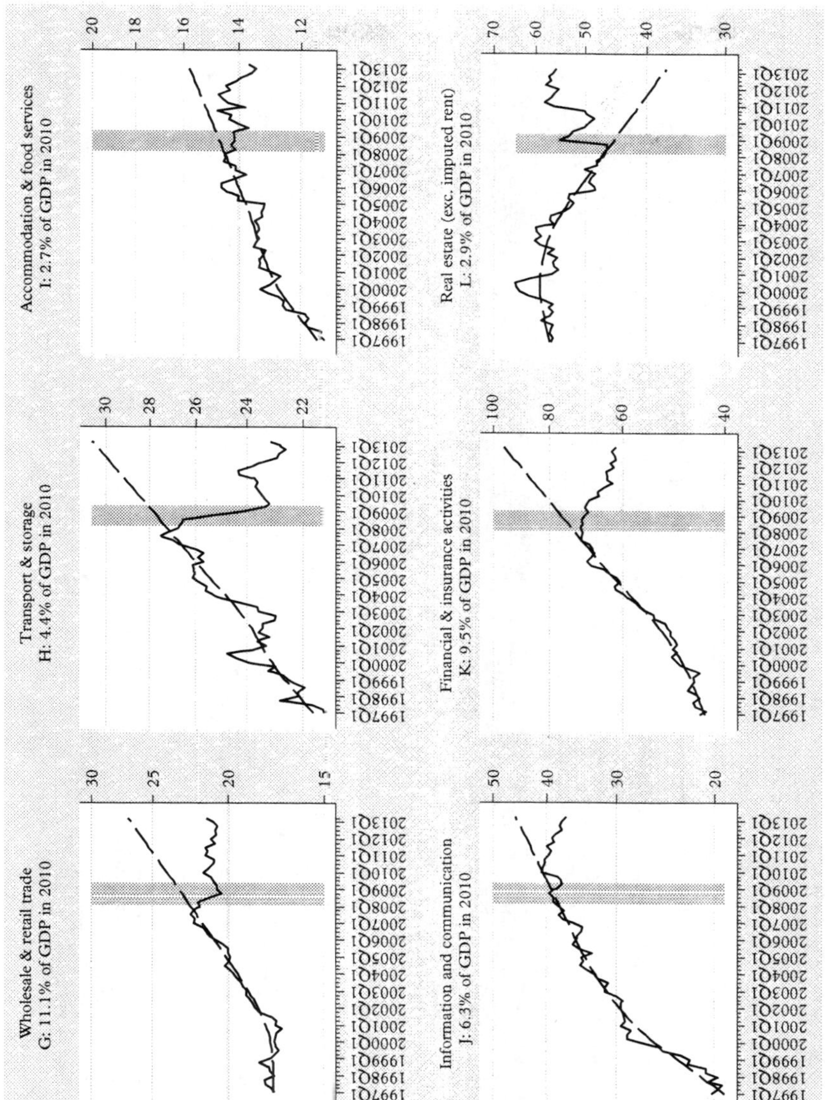

Figure 1.6. *(Continued)*

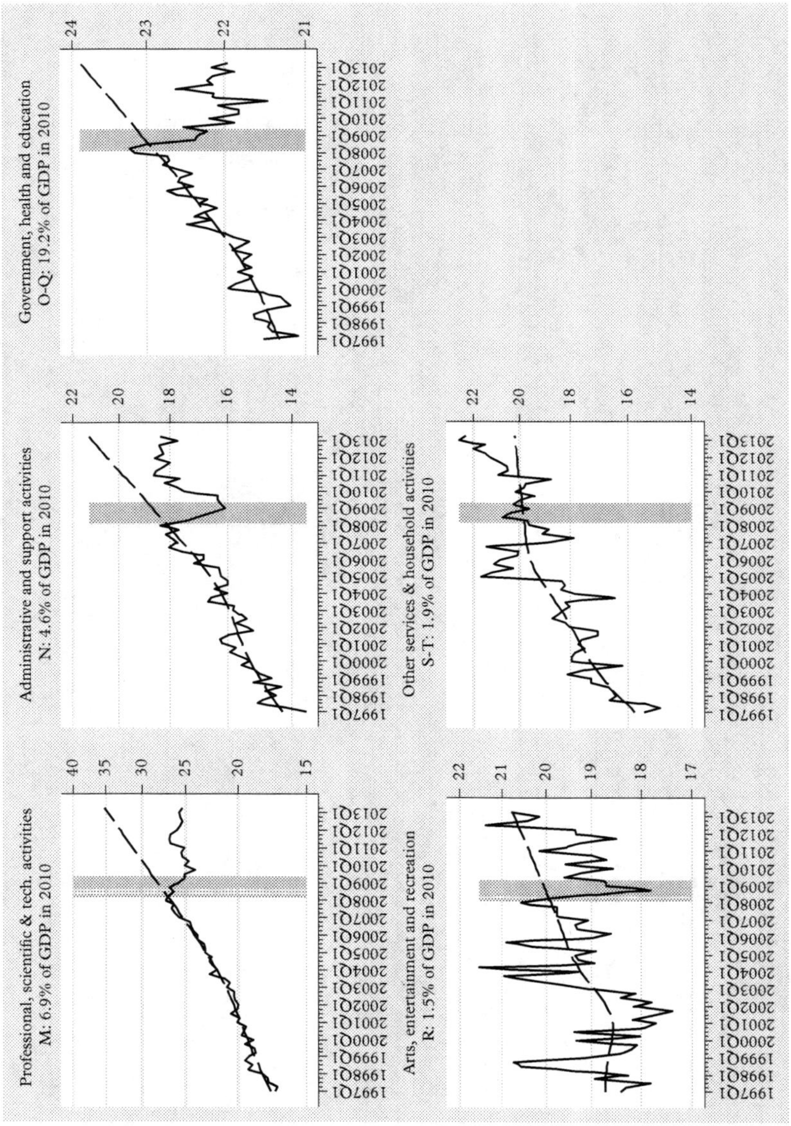

Figure 1.6. (*Continued*)

have serious consequences, not just for our view of the recent past but also for our view of the likely future. For if British growth in the run-up to the crisis was slower than we originally thought, then our view of the likely future path of GDP should be correspondingly more pessimistic, even when the economy has fully recovered from the Great Recession. Equally, if GDP in the boom was overstated, but is more accurately measured now, then some of the sting from the productivity puzzle will have been removed.

Elsewhere I have argued that this argument is wrong (Oulton, 2013a). Even if the premise is correct ('Banking output has been overstated'), the conclusion ('GDP growth has been overstated') does not follow. The error in the argument derives from a failure to understand how the ONS actually constructs its estimates of real GDP. Closer to the truth would be the assertion: 'if banking output has been overstated, then the output of some other industry or industries must have been understated'. Briefly, the reason why the argument is wrong is that the Office for National Statistics measures the real growth of GDP primarily from the expenditure side (GDP(E)). And from the expenditure side most of the problematic part of banking output drops out, since this part is intermediate consumption rather than final expenditure. For example, any financial product sold to a domestic business is intermediate consumption and the services generated by selling mortgages to owner-occupiers are also intermediate (they show up as a cost of producing the implicit rent of owner-occupiers).

The ONS also measures the growth of real GDP from the output side (GDP(O)). But the output side estimate is 'reconciled' with the expenditure side one by adjusting the growth rate of some industries (including banking) till the two estimates are equal (within narrow limits). I calculated that any overstatement of GDP growth due to errors in measuring final expenditure on banking services is not likely to have exceeded 0.1% p.a. over 2000–07.

1.3.4 Overheating in the boom?

Suppose that in the boom the economy was operating at a progressively higher level of demand pressure. In other words, productivity was growing faster than its true trend rate. Then the fall in productivity experienced after the boom ended would exaggerate the true decline or even conceivably eliminate it altogether. Figure 1.7 gathers together four indicators of demand pressure. From the expenditure side there is the growth of the GDP deflator (at basic prices) and the ratio of net exports

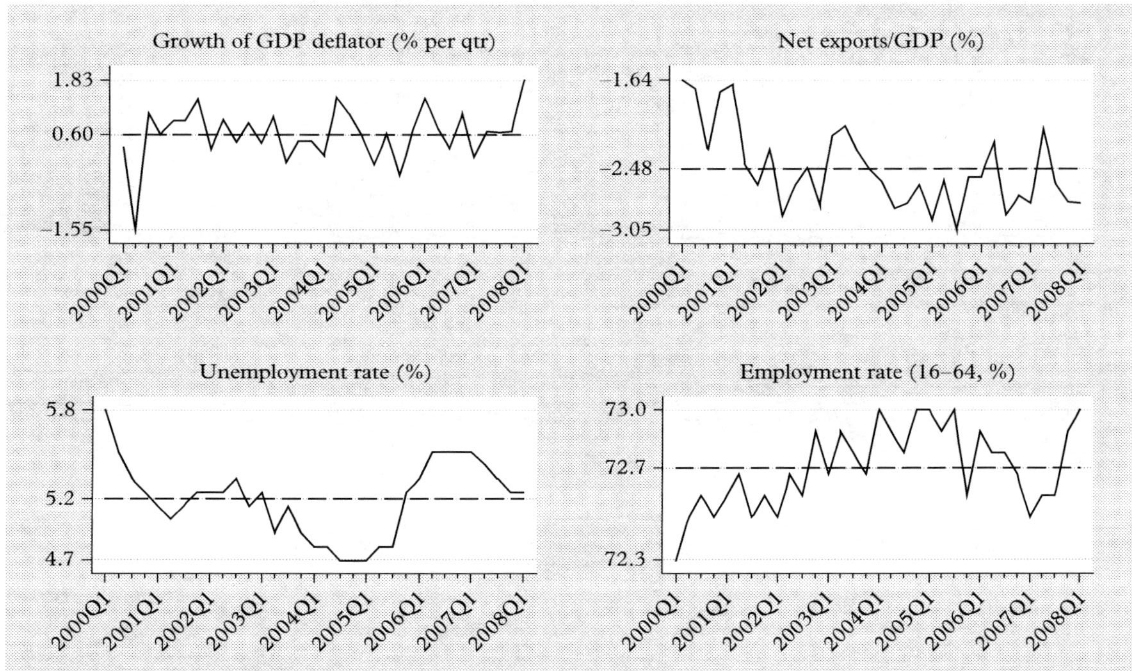

Figure 1.7. Indicators of overheating during the boom
Note: Dashed lines show mean levels over 2000Q1–2008Q1
Source: Office for National Statistics, Quarterly National Accounts and Labor Force Statistics

to GDP (in current prices). From the labour market side there is the unemployment rate and the employment rate of those aged 16–64.[17]

None of these indicators show any sign of trending upwards over the period 2000Q1–2008Q1. True, the unemployment rate fell, and the employment rate rose, over 2000–02, but after that they stabilised. The net export ratio also fell between 2000 and 2002, but it too stabilised. Given that inflation was low and showed no sign of accelerating over this period (which was, after all, part of the 'Great Moderation'), there is no evidence of excessive pressure of demand, still less of growing pressure.

1.3.5 *Lower physical capital input?*

One possible explanation for lower labour productivity is a decline in capital services per unit of labour ('capital shallowing'), due to lower investment since the Great Recession began. The UK labour market is now exceptionally flexible. In the face of a massive demand shock, real wages have fallen by about 4% (Table 1.6) while the cost of capital has risen. This has led firms to reduce the quantity of capital per hour worked. Consequently, output per hour, i.e. productivity, has fallen (Pessoa and Van Reenen, 2013). This is a seductive story but is it true? Business investment has of course fallen massively since the Great Recession began. But a fall in investment does not necessarily imply a fall in the capital stock, still less a fall in capital per hour worked.

The ONS has recently published estimates of TFP which go up to 2012 (Field and Franklin, 2014). They find that capital deepening in the whole economy was positive in each of the years 2008–11, though it was negative in 2012. But the level in 2012 was still 3% higher than in 2007. So there has been capital deepening during and after the recession, not capital shallowing. Estimates for the market sector by Goodridge et al. (2013) also show no capital shallowing up to 2009 (their latest year).

Because of the importance of this issue, and because the ONS has massively revised its investment series, I have made some estimates of my own, employing both the old and the new series. I use business investment, which is arguably more appropriate for productivity analysis, with a range of assumptions about depreciation. I use the Perpetual Inventory Method (PIM) and the standard capital accumulation equation:

$$K_t = (1 - d)K_{t-1} + I_t$$

17 Sources: GDP deflator at basic prices [ABML/ABMM] and net exports (exports minus imports) as a proportion of GDP at market prices [IKBJ/YBHA] from *Quarterly National Accounts June 2013*; unemployment rate [MGSX] and employment rate [LF24] from *Labour Force Statistics, July 2013*.

Here K is capital, I is gross investment and d is the depreciation rate. My measure of capital deepening is the growth of capital per hour worked in the market sector.

A quarterly ONS series on real investment in the business sector (chained volume measure; ONS code NPEL) is available from 1987 up till the present. A perpetual inventory calculation requires an initial capital stock, which in this case is lacking. So to start with I assume an initial stock of zero at the beginning of 1987: this is the first round. This already produces estimates of the stock in later years which are not too bad (given the other assumptions): at an 8% annual depreciation rate any initial stock has decayed to only about 12% of its 1987 level by the end of the period 25 years later. But we can do better. I take the capital–investment ratio at the end of the period as estimated by the first round and assume that it applies at the beginning of the period too. This generates a better estimate of the initial stock. The process can be repeated. After the third round the growth rates of capital do not change much. My estimates from the third round appear in Table 1.5. Looking first at the left-hand panel, my preferred results use an annual depreciation rate of 8% (2.063% quarterly, the first column) but I also show results for 6% and 10% annual rates (columns 2 and 3).

It turns out that the growth rates of capital are not very sensitive to the assumed depreciation rate in the period of the Great Recession and its aftermath (2008Q2 onwards, though the peak for capital per hour was in 2007Q4). The growth rate of capital has been positive in every quarter from 2008Q1 to 2012Q4 though only half as fast as in the boom period.

Hours initially fell, but have been generally rising since 2010Q2. As a result, there have been quarters when capital deepening was negative, particularly from 2011Q3 to 2102Q3. Nonetheless, the broad trend is upward: assuming an 8% annual depreciation rate, capital per hour had in 2010Q3 increased by 9% relative to the pre-recession peak (see Table 1.5). Since then capital per hour has been declining. But the level in 2012Q4 was still 7% above the pre-recession peak in 2007Q4.

These estimates use what I call the 'old series' for business investment. In July the ONS released what I call the 'new series', which it claims to be an improvement mainly due to more disaggregated deflation of nominal investment in different assets. The new series differs in many respects from the old and some of these differences seem highly implausible (and unexplained): the new series is much more volatile and has a much flatter HP trend over the run-up to the recession. So it would not be surprising if the new series were eventually revised. However that may be, the right-hand panel of Table 1.5, derived from

Table 1.5. Estimates of capital per hour in the UK market sector in and after the Great Recession: ratio of current level to previous peak in 2007Q4 (2007Q4 = 100.00)

	Based on old (pre-July 2013) series for NPEL			**Based on new (July 2013) series for NPEL**		
	Quarterly depreciation rate			**Quarterly depreciation rate**		
Year and quarter	0.02063	0.01535	0.025996	0.02063	0.01535	0.025996
2007Q4	100.00	100.00	100.00	100.00	100.00	100.00
2008Q1	98.63	98.62	98.63	98.86	98.81	98.91
2008Q2	101.23	101.21	101.23	101.58	101.50	101.65
2008Q3	102.19	102.20	102.18	102.37	102.34	102.39
2008Q4	104.30	104.34	104.25	104.12	104.19	104.04
2009Q1	107.05	107.15	106.93	106.42	106.63	106.19
2009Q2	108.01	108.21	107.79	107.61	107.87	107.32
2009Q3	108.56	108.88	108.22	108.01	108.42	107.58
2009Q4	108.64	109.09	108.18	108.10	108.63	107.55
2010Q1	109.69	110.23	109.13	109.16	109.77	108.52
2010Q2	108.57	109.22	107.91	107.94	108.68	107.18
2010Q3	108.17	108.91	107.41	107.45	108.30	106.58
2010Q4	107.59	108.43	106.74	106.70	107.67	105.71
2011Q1	108.19	109.15	107.23	107.03	108.16	105.89
2011Q2	109.35	110.40	108.29	108.10	109.34	106.86
2011Q3	108.85	109.98	107.73	107.45	108.78	106.13
2011Q4	108.78	109.97	107.60	107.14	108.57	105.72
2012Q1	108.67	109.93	107.43	107.06	108.57	105.58
2012Q2	108.44	109.76	107.16	106.51	108.10	104.95
2012Q3	107.55	108.91	106.22	105.40	107.07	103.77
2012Q4	107.74	109.18	106.36	105.06	106.87	103.30
2013Q1	...	...	...	104.46	106.42	102.58

Notes: Capital stock estimated by the Perpetual Inventory Method applied to quarterly Business investment (CVM; ONS cdid: NPEL), 1987Q1–2012Q4 (old series) or 1987Q1–2013Q1 (new series). The initial capital stock is estimated by an iterative method: see text for details. Market sector hours are from an ONS spreadsheet underlying the *Productivity Bulletin*. The quarterly depreciation rates of 0.02063, 0.01535 and 0.025996 correspond to annual rates of respectively 8%, 6% and 10%.

the new series, shows a very similar picture to the left-hand one: there is no evidence of capital shallowing.

These calculations show that, far from falling, capital per hour has been rising since the recession began. On my preferred depreciation measure (8% p.a.), in 2012Q4 it was 7% above the pre-recession peak of 2007Q4, using the old series, and 4% higher using the new series.[18]

18 I therefore disagree with the conclusion of Pessoa and Van Reenen (2013) that capital shallowing has occurred: see Oulton (2013) for more detail.

Table 1.6. Real average weekly earnings, 2008Q1 = 100.0

	Private sector	Public sector	Whole economy
2008Q1	100.0	100.0	100.0
2008Q2	99.2	101.1	99.6
2008Q3	98.4	100.9	99.0
2008Q4	96.8	99.7	97.4
2009Q1	92.8	99.7	94.3
2009Q2	96.4	100.8	97.3
2009Q3	94.5	100.5	95.8
2009Q4	94.8	101.1	96.3
2010Q1	94.4	100.9	95.7
2010Q2	94.6	102.2	96.3
2010Q3	94.5	101.6	96.0
2010Q4	94.8	102.1	96.4
2011Q1	95.8	103.1	97.4
2011Q2	95.7	102.9	97.4
2011Q3	95.4	102.6	96.8
2011Q4	95.9	102.8	97.3
2012Q1	95.1	102.5	96.8
2012Q2	96.3	103.0	97.5
2012Q3	96.4	103.9	97.8
2012Q4	95.6	103.1	97.0
2013Q1	93.4	101.9	95.6

Note: Average weekly earnings (seasonally adjusted monthly data, converted to quarterly) deflated by GDP deflator.
Sources: Average weekly earnings from *Labour Market Statistics, July 2013*; GDP deflator from *Quarterly National Accounts, June 2013* (at basic prices, calculated as ABML/ABMM).

These calculations employ the concept of investment laid down in the current System of National Accounts under which some types of intangible investment, such as software, are included, but others, such as R&D, are excluded. Goodridge et al. (2013) argue that intangible investment is part of the explanation of the productivity puzzle. Intangible investment, particularly expenditure on R&D, has held up well during and after the recession. So if R&D is included in GDP as a form of investment (as it will be when the new System of National Accounts is implemented), GDP will be seen to have fallen by less than on the current official estimate; they estimate that GDP in the market sector would have been 1.6% higher in 2012.[19]

19 They also argue that intangible investment, particularly in R&D, generates positive externalities. Intangible investment slowed down in the early 2000s and this could have led to a slowing of TFP growth after the boom. These two effects together could account, they argue, for about a third of the 16% percentage point fall in labour productivity relative to trend in 2012.

1.3.6 *Lower human capital (skill)?*

Falling labour productivity might be explained by falling labour quality. Unfortunately for this explanation, labour quality has increased steadily since 2007. It was 5% higher at the end of 2012 than in 2007. This is not very surprising, since in a downturn less skilled workers are more likely to lose their jobs. So, far from helping to explain it, this deepens the productivity puzzle (Franklin and Mistry, 2013).

1.3.7 *Labour/capital hoarding?*

That output per hour should fall during a recession is not surprising. This is in fact the normal experience. One common explanation is labour hoarding: firms tend to hang on to labour during a downturn to avoid firing costs and subsequent hiring costs during the subsequent upturn. An alternative explanation is that some labour has an overhead character; for example the security guards looking after a building (as long as the building continues in use and is not sold, abandoned or demolished). What is puzzling in the British case is that six years after the onset of the recession labour productivity is still below its previous peak and well below its previous trend. Certainly output too is below its previous trend, but why have firms not adjusted to this by reducing labour input (either hours or jobs)? If potential labour productivity has been growing at something like the pre-crisis rate, it is hard to understand why firms should want to hang on to labour. In fact, jobs in the market sector have been increasing since 2010Q1. And evidence from business surveys (reviewed by Dale (2011)) suggests that there is little spare capacity.

The case for labour hoarding has been forcefully argued by Martin and Rowthorn (2012). Their argument mainly rests on the importance of overhead labour. They also point out that both human and physical capital per worker have increased during the recession (see above), so on these grounds we would expect labour productivity to have risen, not fallen. They also argue that the alternative damage hypothesis is inherently implausible: why should disruption in the banking sector lead to loss of knowledge of how to produce output in the rest of the economy? (I return to this issue below.)

The cost of making a worker redundant in the UK is quite substantial: about £12,000, or slightly less than half the average annual wage according to the CBI (cited in Faccini and Hackworth (2010)). So this could easily explain why firms are reluctant to fire workers at the beginning of a recession, especially if they expect to have to rehire the same or similar workers in about a year's time. But six years after the recession began this explanation looks increasingly thin. According to Faccini and Hackworth (2010) again, employment protection legislation (EPL) has not changed much since the mid-1980s on the OECD's measure, though it may now possibly be enforced more rigorously. They also find two other factors which go the other way. First, the flexibility of real wages has increased since 1993 (partly due to the decline in unionisation), which has helped to maintain employment in the downturn. Between 2008Q1 and 2013Q1 real producer wages fell by 4.4%; in the private sector they fell by 6.6% (Table 1.6). Second, the costs of hiring may have increased since the average skill level of the workforce is now higher than in previous recessions; this would make firms more reluctant to fire workers in the downturn.

Given the length of the productivity downturn the labour hoarding hypothesis must rely on firms retaining labour because of its overhead character. However (to use the earlier example), a building, say a shop, may require a security guard, but at some point it is cheaper to sack the guard and close the shop down rather than keep it in operation in anticipation of an upturn in sales.

Capital rather than labour hoarding, i.e. lower capital utilisation, may be a more plausible mechanism. Consider a firm which runs a chain of shops. Though previously in profit, the firm is running at a loss after the recession hits. So it closes one or more of its stores, which raises footfall in its surviving stores and restores the firm to profit. If real wages fall it might be worthwhile for the firm to increase employment in its surviving stores, since competition may be more intense in the new environment, i.e. *effective* (utilised) capital per unit of labour could fall.

What about the stores which are standing empty? At some point the firm will want to sell these if sales do not revive. But selling them right away might be difficult if all retail firms are facing the same difficulties. And transferring them to other uses may be costly and time-consuming in a country like Britain, where planning permission would be required. Demolishing the stores is unlikely to be a more profitable (or legal) option than just leaving them standing empty.

This story of falling *effective* capital per unit of labour is compatible with rising *actual* capital per unit of labour. So a typical PIM calculation would still give the correct answer (since the boarded-up shops still exist), but does not take into account the fall in utilisation. The story is potentially applicable outside retailing, e.g. to manufacturing: the mothballing of plants or production lines could lead to a similar result. In summary, in this story labour is fully utilised, but capital is not. Capital is not fully utilised because it takes time to dispose of or to convert to some new use.

1.3.8 *Crippled banks and zombie firms?*

There is considerable anecdotal evidence of apparently sound firms being denied credit on reasonable terms after the banking crisis began. Banks were trying to repair their balance sheets and this was at the expense of their business customers (as well as of potential home owners). The opposite accusation is also often made: banks have exercised forbearance, i.e. they have rolled over loans to insolvent businesses, or forgiven interest payments, because they were unwilling to recognise the losses on their balance sheets. Certainly the number of insolvencies has been surprisingly low given the depth of the recession.

The denial of credit to sound firms presumably affects small and medium-sized enterprises (SMEs) more than large ones, since the latter have access to stock market finance, which is available now at very low interest rates; in any case the corporate sector as a whole is in financial surplus and holds very large cash balances. Denial of credit has to show up somewhere. It may be part of the reason why business investment has fallen. If so, we have already taken it into account in the discussion of capital input above. It might show up in other ways. One possibility is that firms economise on working capital, and this could lead to lower productivity; for example a manufacturing firm might hold fewer spare parts and this would lead to more down time and so to lower labour productivity. But inventory–sales ratios do not seem to have fallen since the recession began. Another way that firms could economise on finance is by employing fewer people. But here the evidence goes the other way. It is SMEs who have been less willing to shed labour than larger firms, who are presumably less affected by credit constraints.

The zombie firms story bring an element of *déjà vu* to those of us who remember the controversies surrounding the 1980–81 recession. Then it was often claimed that the apparent productivity improvement in manufacturing was due to a 'batting average' effect: the elimination of the lowest productivity firms through bankruptcy (for cricket fans, this is like not allowing the tail-enders to bat, which raises the average but not the total score). The zombie firms claim is the batting average argument in reverse: now it is supposedly the least productive firms who survive through forbearance by the banks, so dragging down the average productivity level. But when the economy is still in a slump, loss-making firms are not necessarily the same as low-productivity firms. In principle this question could be settled through microdata analysis.[20]

20 Microdata analysis eventually settled the issues around the 1980–81 recession. A large part of the productivity improvement was due to productivity growth in surviving firms (Oulton, 2000; Disney et al., 2003).

At the time of writing, this analysis has yet to be done. For the moment I am sceptical that zombies can account for a large part of the productivity puzzle.

1.3.9 *Austerity*

The picture painted by numerous bloggers and commentators is that the UK has been passing through a period of unparalleled austerity ('the cuts'). If this picture is correct, then austerity by depressing aggregate demand must be a candidate explanation for the productivity puzzle. There is considerable debate on the size of the fiscal multiplier, with many asserting that it is particularly large when (as now) the economy is at or close to the zero lower bound (ZLB). In Oulton (2013b) I argued that on neither theoretical nor empirical grounds is the evidence on the effectiveness of fiscal policy quite as clear cut as many claim. But whatever we conclude on these issues, before we can estimate the impact of austerity on GDP we need to know how large the cuts have been. Prior to examining this, let us first note that whatever may have been the case for fiscal policy, monetary and financial policy have been extremely supportive. First, UK banks were supported by a huge bail-out and two of the largest (RBS and Lloyds-HBOS) were effectively nationalised. Second, Bank Rate was cut. It was 5.75% in November 2007. By April 2008 it had been cut in three steps to 5%, a level maintained till October 2008. From then on it was rapidly reduced till it reached 0.5% in March 2009, where it has remained up till now (February 2014). Third, the exchange rate fell abruptly. The sterling exchange rate index (ERI) stood at a peak of 104.6 in 2007Q1. The low point was reached in 2009Q1 at 77.8, a fall of 26%. It has risen a little since then, but still stood at 80.5 in 2013Q1, a fall of 23% from the peak. Though not explicitly the result of policy (no currency manipulation here!), the depreciation was certainly allowed by and a result of our monetary framework. Fourth, once Bank Rate reached virtually the ZLB the policy of quantitative easing was wheeled out, under which the Bank of England has acquired 29% of the stock of gilts with the possibility of more to come if the MPC were to so decide. Fifth, there have been various programmes to encourage bank lending to business, such as the Funding for Lending Scheme.

1.3.9.1 Public sector employment and expenditure One measure of austerity is jobs in the public sector. Between March 2008, when the boom ended, and December 2012 the number of public sector workers fell by 288,000 or by 4.8%. Taking account of transfers into and out of the public sector (i.e. reclassifications) increases the fall to 6.5%.[21] By itself this represents a fall of 1.3% in total employment. But over the same period total employment actually rose by 0.7%, i.e. gains in the private sector more than compensated for losses in the public sector.

However, because of changes in the degree of outsourcing of activities in the public sector, the number of jobs may not be a very good measure of the government's impact on the economy. So it is better to look at government spending on goods and services, both current and capital. Columns 1–3 of Table 1.7 show real government (central plus local) expenditure on goods and services, capital, current and total, using the official (ONS) concepts.[22] Real government current spending has been higher in every quarter since the recession began than it was at the peak (2008Q1). Real government investment has followed an erratic course since the recession began. It mainly rose in the last two years of the Labour government and has mainly been lower after the coalition came to power in spring 2010. But its average level has been about the same as in 2008Q1. Investment is much smaller than current spending. So total expenditure has unambiguously risen since the peak: in 2013Q1 total government expenditure was 6% higher than in 2008Q1. In other words, far from austerity, we have had a fiscal stimulus.

We can measure the contribution of government expenditure to growth as the government share (in nominal terms) times the growth rate of real expenditure. The government's contribution since the recession has on average been positive, at 0.09 percentage points per quarter.

It might be objected that the official measures of real government spending are misleading, since they incorporate many disputable assumptions about how to measure productivity in the public sector. So I have calculated two alternative, 'Keynesian' measures. The idea here is to forget about the social value of government expenditure (the education of children, the care of the sick etc.) and just consider it as an engine for pumping effective demand into the economy. In the first Keynesian measure nominal government expenditure is deflated by the GDP deflator (column 4). Done in this way, government expenditure is higher than at the peak up till 2011Q1, before falling back.

21 Source: Office for National Statistics, a spreadsheet available online as emp02 mar2013_tcm77-301480.xls. Employees in Lloyds-HBOS and Royal Bank of Scotland were transferred from the private to the public sector in October 2008. 196,000 employees in Further Education Corporations and Sixth Form Colleges Corporations were transferred from the public to the private sector between March and June 2012.

22 Total real government expenditure on goods and services is not published by the ONS. I have calculated it as an annually chained Laspeyres index of current and capital spending. In accordance with the official methodology for calculating chain-linked GDP, the weights for 2011 to the present are those of 2010.

Table 1.7. Real government expenditure on goods and services: official versus Keynesian measures (2008Q1 = 100.00)

	Official			**Keynesian**	
	CVM	**CVM**	**CVM**	**Deflated by GDP deflator**	**Deflated by wage index (AWE)**
	(1)	**(2)**	**(3)**	**(4)**	**(5)**
Year and quarter	**Current**	**Capital**	**Total**	**Total**	**Total**
2008Q1	100.00	100.00	100.00	100.00	100.00
2008Q2	100.41	99.08	100.29	99.62	100.62
2008Q3	101.27	98.72	101.02	100.15	101.14
2008Q4	102.49	100.67	102.31	101.98	104.19
2009Q1	101.57	111.50	102.55	103.90	108.79
2009Q2	101.29	103.63	101.54	101.66	103.43
2009Q3	101.97	116.02	103.41	104.23	107.99
2009Q4	102.29	120.73	104.14	103.32	106.78
2010Q1	101.99	115.73	103.42	102.80	107.34
2010Q2	102.49	108.50	103.24	101.85	105.86
2010Q3	102.37	112.87	103.55	101.21	105.48
2010Q4	102.29	110.36	103.24	101.47	105.53
2011Q1	102.23	110.39	103.19	102.48	106.17
2011Q2	102.39	95.67	101.99	97.18	100.73
2011Q3	101.94	100.56	102.10	97.47	101.97
2011Q4	102.38	95.73	102.01	97.99	102.05
2012Q1	105.15	107.55	105.73	101.93	106.62
2012Q2	104.19	109.10	105.01	96.68	100.17
2012Q3	105.08	99.13	104.89	97.73	101.09
2012Q4	105.90	101.52	105.87	98.26	102.90
2013Q1	106.01	95.45	105.35	97.87	103.71

Source: Government current spending (central and local government), nominal and real, and GDP deflator (at market prices, YBHA/ABMI) from *Quarterly National Accounts, June 2013*. Government investment, nominal and real, from corrected figures in *Business investment, Q1–2013 results* (Office for National Statistics, 2013b). The 'total official' measure is my own calculation and is a chained-linked Laspeyres index of the official current and capital expenditure series. Average weekly earnings index from Office for National Statistics (2013a).

In 2013Q1 it was 2% lower than at the peak. From 2008Q2 to 2013Q1 its average level was 100.5. For the second Keynesian measure I take a leaf from the master's book and measure volumes in wage units, i.e. by deflating nominal values by a wage index, as recommended by Keynes in the *General Theory* (Keynes, 1936[1961], p. 41). Using the Average Weekly Earnings index as the deflator, the results of this alternative calculation appear in column 5. Again we find that there was a fiscal stimulus: real spending is now nearly 4% higher than at the peak of the boom. On this measure the stimulus was highest in 2009Q1. Though declining since then, it has remained positive.

1.3.9.2 Budget deficits In the boom period from 2000Q1 to 2008Q1, net lending by the government (central and local) averaged −1.69% of GDP, i.e. there was a budget deficit. In the period since then net lending by the government has averaged −8.01% (Table 1.8 and Figure 1.8). In other words since the crisis began there has been a huge blow-out in the budget deficit. The latter, though falling, is still considerably larger than in France, a country where unemployment (11.1% in December 2013) is much higher and which has supposedly been pursuing Keynesian anti-austerity policies. The deficit is currently larger than in some countries, such as Greece, which the financial markets regard as basket cases.

Of course the present UK government has not exactly chosen to run a deficit as large as this. Its size is largely a function of the automatic stabilisers kicking in as GDP fell. But clearly with the exception of a rise in VAT the coalition government has done little to counteract the automatic stabilisers, and also, as we have seen, has not yet substantially cut real spending on goods and services. The continuing large deficits have meant that the debt–GDP ratio has risen at (to me at least) an alarming rate. Public Sector Net Debt, one measure employed by the Office for Budget Responsibility (OBR), was 75.1% of GDP in March 2013. Between 1987 and 2007 it had hovered around 40% of GDP (Office for Budget Responsibility, 2013). The OBR projects that on current 'austerity' policies the net debt ratio will peak at 85.6% in 2016–17. This projection assumes that government keeps to its spending plans and that the Bank of England succeeds in keeping inflation at the 2% target for the CPI.

In summary, reports of savage cuts seem greatly exaggerated. Fiscal policy has reinforced monetary policy and has been mildly expansionary. Consequently, it is unlikely that 'austerity' can explain much if any of the productivity puzzle. Of course, it is always possible to argue that

Table 1.8. Mean net lending by sector as % of GDP

	2000Q1–2008Q1	**2008Q2–2013Q1**
Government	−1.69	−8.01
Corporations	2.17	5.29
Households	−2.50	0.61
Rest of world	2.02	2.00

Source: ONS, *Quarterly National Accounts, June 2013*. GDP is at market prices. Government is central and local government combined.

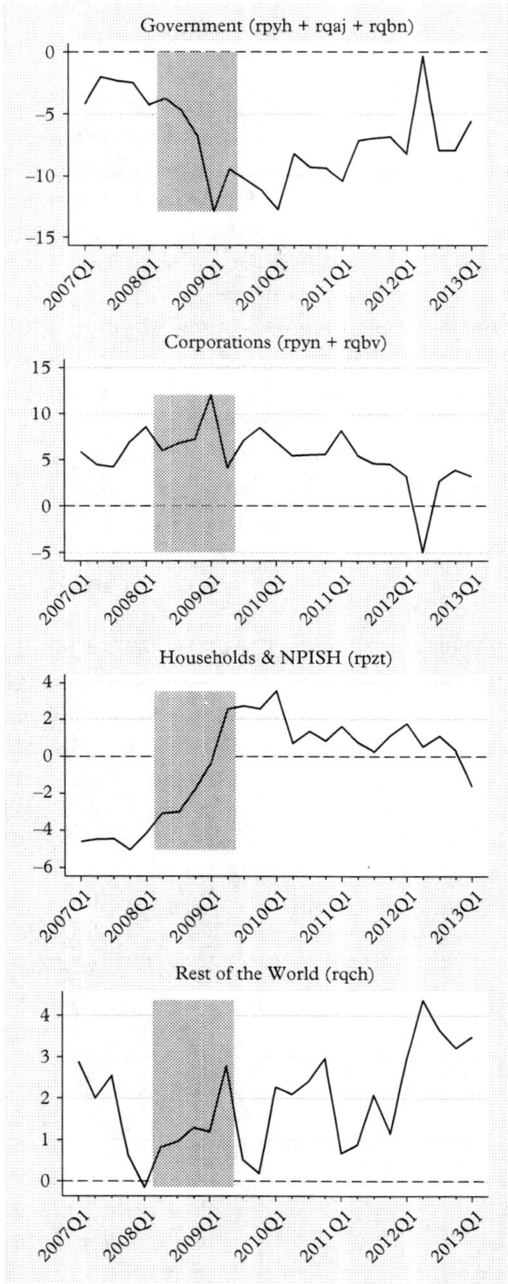

Figure 1.8. Net lending by sector, % of GDP at current market prices
Note: Seasonally adjusted. Black bar (red bar in web version) marks Great Recession (2008Q2–2009Q2).
Source: ONS, Quarterly National Accounts, June 2013 (ONS ccids in brackets).

government expenditure should have been even higher given the depth of the recession. But any proposal for a more expansionary fiscal policy than the present one should explain what the effect will be on the debt–GDP ratio and what the economic consequences will be of any significant increase in that ratio, which is anyway expected to rise substantially on current policies.[23]

1.4 The long-run effects of banking crises: evidence from cross-country panel data

All the candidate explanations for the productivity puzzle discussed in the previous two sections arguably relate to the short-term effects of the financial crisis and the slump which followed it. Even the 'crippled banks and zombie firms' hypothesis, which relies directly on a malfunctioning banking system, suggests only short-term effects: when the banking system is restored to health these effects will disappear. So I turn now to possible long-term effects. I start by reviewing evidence and theory on the long-term effects of financial (particularly banking) crises. Then I summarise the findings of a recent cross-country panel analysis covering 61 countries over 1950–2010 (Oulton and Sebastiá-Barriel, 2013).

1.4.1 Previous empirical findings on financial crises

Reinhart and Rogoff (2010) find that, based on data for 44 countries spanning about 200 years, GDP growth rates fall as the gross central government debt–GDP ratio rises (they assign the debt–GDP ratios to four buckets: below 30%, 30–60%, 60–90% and above 90%). The growth effects are similar in advanced and emerging economies.[24] Reinhart and Rogoff (2012) argue that the negative association between debt–GDP ratios and growth cannot be entirely due to cyclical effects (recessions causing high debt) since low growth is highly persistent in highly indebted countries (so high debt is causing low growth). The very pessimistic case of Figure 1.3 finds some support in Broadberry and Crafts (1992), who argue that the Great Depression cast a long shadow over the British economy, since it led to productivity-reducing policies such as protection and cartelisation of industries.

A number of other studies, e.g. Cerra and Saxena (2008), Furceri and Mouragane (2012), Barrell et al. (2010), Papell and Prodan (2011)

23 For further discussion of fiscal policy and the UK's debt ratio, including the fascinating 'expansionary contraction' of 1945–46, see Oulton (2013b).

24 My interpretation takes into account the critique of the published results by Herndon et al. (2013) and the subsequent response by Reinhart and Rogoff (2013).

and IMF (2009, Chapter 4), also find that the recovery from financial crises is very slow. For example, Papell and Prodan (2011) argue that 'The preponderance of evidence for episodes comparable with the current US slump is that, while potential GDP is eventually restored, the slumps last an average of nine years'. Like Barrell et al. (2010), they argue that advanced countries are different from developing ones: the latter can and do suffer permanent damage from severe financial crises. The claim that advanced countries are relatively immune to the effects of financial crises is based on the evidence for the period since the Second World War. However, based on a study of nearly 200 recession episodes in 14 advanced countries between 1870 and 2008, Jordà et al. (2012) find that more credit-intensive booms tend to be followed by deeper recessions and slower recoveries.

1.4.2 Long-run effects of financial crises: theory

Why might we expect long-run effects from financial crises? A number of factors might reduce the long-run level of potential GDP, and of potential GDP per hour, even when recovery from the recession is complete (in the sense that GDP is growing at its long-run rate and unemployment is at a level consistent with a constant rate of inflation).

Reinhart and Rogoff (2011) argue that financial crises have a tendency to raise the stock of government debt relative to GDP, either because of the cost of recapitalising failed banks or because government expenditure is not cut in proportion to reduced tax revenues. High levels of debt require high levels of taxation to service the debt and this may lead to efficiency losses; also, high debt interest payments may crowd out socially productive public expenditure if there is resistance to higher taxes (Barro, 1979).

In the recent boom, real interest rates were very low, reflecting a mispricing of risk. When the recovery is complete and official rates return to normal levels, the rates at which firms can borrow are likely to be higher due to an additional risk premium. So they will want to hold a lower level of capital in relation to output. Suppose that the real interest rate (the required return on capital) rises from (say) 7% to 9%. The depreciation rate averaged over all types of capital can be taken to be 8%. Then the cost of capital rises from (7 + 8 =) 15% to (9 + 8 =) 17%, i.e. by 13.3%. The elasticity of capital with respect to its cost is −0.4 according to Barnes et al. (2008). And the elasticity of output with respect to capital is about 1/3 (the profit share). So the effect of the rise in the real interest rate on the long-run level of GDP is (13.3 × −0.4 × 1/3) = −1.8%. This calculation suggests that the effect is not negligible.

Higher unemployment during the recession reduces the human capital of the unemployed, by preventing them from gaining the experience that would raise their productivity. Of course, this effect eventually disappears when the affected workers leave the labour force (through emigration, retirement or death) and are replaced by workers who enter the labour market after the Great Recession is over. But even if not permanent, this effect could clearly be long-lasting, since youth unemployment has risen particularly sharply in many countries. Suppose that an additional 3.5% of the labour force becomes unemployed as a result of the Great Recession, that this higher rate of unemployment lasts for a period of 5 years, and that each additional unemployed person is unemployed for one year. This is equivalent to (5 × 3.5 =) 16.5% of the labour force losing one year's experience. If the rate of return to experience is (say) 7% p.a. (which is consistent with estimates of the return to schooling), then the effect on GDP is a reduction of (16.5 × 0.07 × 2/3 =) 0.8%.

There could be a long-run effect on the level of TFP. According to this argument the amount of innovation taking place in the economy is temporarily reduced by the recession. Innovation is implemented through or accompanied by investment in intangibles (e.g. R&D, in-firm training or expenditure of management time on corporate restructuring) or it could take the form of new entrants into an industry bringing new products, new technology or new business methods. All this is (arguably) what lies behind TFP growth as conventionally measured (Corrado et al. (2009); Marrano et al. (2009)). Now since innovation is a cumulative process and since the supply of workers and entrepreneurs capable of innovating is inelastic, a reduction in innovation in one period cannot easily be made up in a subsequent one: in other words, less innovation today means that the future *level* of TFP is permanently lower. For illustration, suppose that prior to a crisis, assumed to last one year, the economy is capable of generating a stream of innovations a, b, c, … from the current year t onwards. As a result of the crisis the first innovation a is now delayed to year $t + 1$; the subsequent innovations b, c, … are now also delayed one year to years $t + 2$, $t + 3$, … Though all innovations are eventually introduced, the level of TFP will clearly be lower in every year after the crisis is over than it would have been in the absence of the crisis. A reduction in the TFP level will also lead to a secondary effect, a reduction in the desired level of capital, again reducing labour productivity.

These are of course just illustrative calculations. What we need is a theoretical framework which would allow us to assess the size of any such effects empirically.

1.4.3 A theoretical framework

It is important to adopt a theoretical specification which allows financial crises to have both short-run and long-run effects and for the latter to be on both the level and the growth rate of productivity. It will then be an empirical issue how large or small these effects are. A fairly general framework for productivity growth can be written as follows:

$$\begin{aligned} q_{it} - q_{it-1} &= \lambda(q^{\star}_{it} - q_{it-1}) + \beta(q_{it-1} - q_{it-2}) + (1 - \lambda - \beta)(q_{it-2} - q_{it-3}) \\ &\quad + \gamma crisis_{it} + \varepsilon_{it}, \quad 0 < \lambda < 1,\ 0 < \beta < 1,\ \lambda + \beta \leq 1,\ \gamma < 0 \end{aligned} \tag{1.16}$$

Here q_{it} is the log of the level of (labour) productivity in the *i*th country, $q^{\star}_{it}$ is the log of the long-run productivity level in that country (long-run is indicated by a star (⋆)), $crisis_{it}$ is a one-zero dummy indicating the presence or absence of a financial crisis and ε_{it} is a mean-zero error term. The first term on the right-hand side, $\lambda(q^{\star}_{it} - q_{it-1})$, is a simple partial adjustment mechanism whereby a fraction λ of the gap between actual and long-run productivity is removed each period, presumably through investment in the broad sense. The second and third terms, $\beta(q_{it-1} - q_{it-2})$ and $(1 - \lambda - \beta)(q_{it-2} - q_{it-3})$, reflect persistence in productivity growth: aggregate demand takes a while to recover from a recession, so factor utilisation is lowered, which reduces productivity growth till recovery begins; also investment is depressed for a while. The third term, $\gamma crisis_{it}$, is the short-run effect of a financial crisis on productivity growth. It may reflect a temporary disruption to credit which further reduces investment. We expect that $\gamma < 0$. Note that for the equation to make sense in the long run, the sum of the coefficients on the first three terms on the right-hand side must equal 1 and the specification imposes this restriction.

A simple model of the long-run productivity growth rate is:

$$q^{\star}_{it} - q^{\star}_{it-1} = \alpha_i + a_t + \theta crisis_{it} + \xi_{it} \tag{1.17}$$

Here α_i is a country-specific fixed effect and α_t is a time effect common across countries. The long-run effect of financial crises on productivity levels is measured by the parameter θ, which is expected to be negative. The long-run growth rate is *temporarily* influenced by a financial crisis only while the latter is ongoing. Once a crisis is over, it ceases to influence the long-run growth rate (since then $crisis_{it} = 0$). But even when the crisis is over, the long-run productivity *levels* $q^{\star}_{it+1}, q^{\star}_{it+2}, \ldots$ will be lower than they would otherwise have been. A more complex model would allow the long-run growth rate also to be *permanently* affected by a crisis. But this seems to be asking too much of the data.

In summary, in the specification suggested here, a financial crisis may have a temporary effect on the productivity growth rate (measured by γ in Eq. (1.16)) and hence a temporary effect on the productivity level. A financial crisis may also have a permanent effect on the productivity level (measured by θ in Eq. (1.17)). But there is no permanent effect on the productivity growth rate. The latter is assumed to be dependent on other factors, such as the worldwide development of science and technology and the country's own institutions, all of which are assumed independent of financial crises.

To obtain an estimating equation, substitute Eq. (1.17) into Eq. (1.16), lag Eq. (1.16) once and subtract the result from Eq. (1.16). Then after some manipulation we get:

$$\begin{aligned}\Delta q_{it} =& \lambda a_i + \lambda a_t + (\lambda\theta + \gamma) crisis_{it} - \gamma crisis_{it-1} \\ &+ [1 + \beta - \lambda]\Delta q_{it-1} + [1 - \lambda - 2\beta]\Delta q_{it-2} - [1 - \lambda - \beta]\Delta q_{it-3} \\ &+ \Delta\varepsilon_{it} + \lambda\xi_{it}\end{aligned} \tag{1.18}$$

In econometric form this can be written as

$$\begin{aligned}\Delta q_{it} =& \phi_{i0} + \sum_{u=0}^{T-1} \phi_{1u} D_{t-u} + \phi_2 crisis_{it} + \phi_3 crisis_{it-1} + \phi_4 \Delta q_{it-1} \\ &+ \phi_5 \Delta q_{it-2} + \phi_6 \Delta q_{it-3} + \eta_{it}\end{aligned} \tag{1.19}$$

The relationship between the underlying parameters and the coefficients (the ϕs) is:

$$\begin{aligned}\beta &= (\phi_4 - \phi_5)/3 = (\phi_4 + \phi_6)/2 \\ \lambda &= 1 + \beta - \phi_4 \\ \gamma &= -\phi_3 \\ \theta &= (\phi_2 - \gamma)/\lambda\end{aligned} \tag{1.20}$$

The first line of Eq. (1.20) shows that the specification imposes a restriction on the coefficients on lagged productivity growth:

$$\phi_4 + 2\phi_5 + 3\phi_6 = 0 \tag{1.21}$$

If this restriction is not imposed then there will be two possible estimates of the underlying parameter θ. From Eq. (1.20), these two estimates are

$$\begin{aligned}\theta_1 &= \frac{3(\phi_2 + \phi_3)}{3 - 2\phi_4 - \phi_5} \\ \theta_2 &= \frac{2(\phi_2 + \phi_3)}{2 - \phi_4 + \phi_6}\end{aligned} \tag{1.22}$$

The main interest in what follows attaches to the size of the long-run effect of financial crises, i.e. the absolute size of θ.

1.4.4 *Productivity and financial crises: data*

We use the data on financial crises gathered and analysed by Reinhart and Rogoff (2009). The actual data are taken from spreadsheets accompanying their book, which are publicly available at http://www.reinhartandrogoff.com/data/. The productivity data derive from The Conference Board's Total Economy Database (TED) for 2011 which is also publicly available online at http://www.conference-board.org/data/economydatabase.[25]

1.4.4.1 The Reinhart–Rogoff database of financial crises Reinhart and Rogoff (2009), hereafter R–R, have gathered data for six types of crisis (see their Chapter 1): (1) Currency; (2) Inflation; (3) Stock market; (4) External debt; (5) Domestic debt; (6) Banking. Each crisis is measured by a dummy variable, equal to 1 when a country is judged to be in this type of crisis and 0 otherwise. Their data cover 63 countries over the period 1800–2010. I use just the data from 1950 onwards, i.e. the potential number of observations is $61 \times 63 = 3843$.

Here I report results just for banking crises which R–R define as follows: '(1) bank runs that lead to the closure, merging or takeover by the public sector of one or more financial institutions and (2) if there are no runs, the closure, merging, takeover or large-scale government assistance of an important financial institution (or group of institutions) that marks the start of a string of similar outcomes for other financial institutions'. This is because some of the other R–R crises might be considered *consequences* of banking crises, e.g. a stock market crash. Or they might be thought of as *responses* (whether market-induced or policy-induced). For example, the sharp fall in sterling which accompanied the Great Recession and the UK banking crisis was a market response (though unlike many currency crises in developing or emerging countries it was against the background of an inflation-targeting rather than an exchange rate-targeting monetary regime). So for the UK the fall in sterling was not a crisis but part of the adjustment process. Banking crises on the other hand are very hard to predict: models designed to do so have a poor fit even in sample (Corder and Weale, 2011).

For each of the six types of crisis the percentage of total years for which countries were in crisis has increased between the first and second halves of the whole 61-year span 1950–2010. The increase in

25 For further details on data, sources and methods, see Oulton and Sebastiá-Barriel (2013).

frequency is particularly sharp for banking crises: over 1950–79 only 0.9% of country-years was spent in a banking crisis, but this rose to 19.8% over 1980–2010 (Oulton and Sebastiá-Barriel, 2013, Table 1.3). The major events were the Latin American debt crises of the 1980s, the Asian financial crisis of 1997–98 and the current global financial crisis.

1.4.4.2 Output and productivity The 2011 version of The Conference Board's Total Economy Database (TED) contains national accounts data for 128 countries covering the period 1950–2010, though with missing values for some countries. Labour productivity is available for most countries over the whole 61-year period in heads form, but for a much smaller number of countries in hours form. Hours are better than heads, but we do not want to confine the analysis to the richer countries with better statistics. So we use GDP per person engaged (GDP per worker). We construct a measure of capital per worker by applying the PIM to a total investment series from the national accounts data underlying the Penn World Table; we assumed an 8% depreciation rate. Then we constructed the growth of TFP as the growth of GDP per worker minus the share-weighted growth of capital per worker; capital's share was taken to be 1/3. Finally, population is available also from the TED and we used this to construct GDP per capita.

After merging the R–R data with the TED, we lose about half the countries included in the latter. There are now 61 countries for which we have both labour productivity and crises data for at least some of the 61 years (in fact an average of about 53 years per country, with the missing years being mostly in the 1950s and 1960s). The 61 countries cover the whole planet, not just the OECD; 23 countries are classified as developed and 38 as developing.[26]

1.4.5 The effect of crises: regression results

Sub-section 1.4.3 set out a framework within which the average short- and long-run effects of crises across our sample can be estimated. We now seek to test this model using the dataset just described. We ran the regression specified in Eq. (1.19) with successively the growth of GDP per worker, the growth of capital per worker, the growth of TFP, and the growth of GDP per capita as the dependent variable. The right-hand side variables were the banking crisis dummy, the banking crisis

26 The data used to generate the results reported below can be found in Stata and Excel format at http://www.bankofengland.co.uk/publications/Pages/workingpapers/2013/wp470.aspx.

dummy lagged, two lags of the dependent variable, country fixed effects and year dummies. Full details of the results are in Oulton and Sebastiá-Barriel (2013). Here we report results just for the parameter of most interest, θ, which measures the effect of a banking crisis on the long-run level of the dependent variable. These results come from estimating Eq. (1.19) by the Arellano–Bond (difference) method; OLS estimates are similar.

The first column of Table 1.9 reports the results for the full sample (all countries and all years). Let us consider first the effect on GDP per worker. The solution for θ says that a banking crisis has a long-run, permanent impact on the *level* of productivity: it reduces it by about 1.1% for each year that the crisis lasts. In other words a crisis lasting five years would reduce the level of GDP per worker by (5 × 1.1% =) 5.5%, permanently. Of course, the estimated effects are for an 'average' crisis as experienced by these 61 countries over the period 1955–2010. The estimate of θ is significant at the 1% level.

The remaining columns of Table 1.9 report various sensitivity tests:

Column (2): exclude the Great Recession (2008–10).
Column (3): exclude countries affected by the Asian financial crisis of 1997–98. (Korea, Malaysia, Sri Lanka, Taiwan, Thailand, Indonesia, India, Philippines and China).
Column (4): exclude countries affected by the Latin American debt crisis of the 1980s (Argentina, Bolivia, Brazil, Chile, Columbia, Costa Rica, Ecuador, Mexico, Peru, Uruguay and Venezuela).
Column (5): developed countries only (23 countries).
Column (6): developing countries only (34 countries).
Column (7): early years only (all countries, 1950–79).
Column (8): later years only (all countries, 1980–2010).

Still sticking with GDP per worker (the top panel of Table 1.9), the size of θ varies in an interesting way across these sub-samples, though with two exceptions it is always large numerically and negative. Excluding the Great Recession reduces θ numerically from −1.096 to −1.005, or by 4%, surprisingly little; this may be partly due to the fact that our observation period ends in 2010. Excluding the Latin America countries roughly halves the size of θ numerically; θ now also fails to be significant.[27] This may be another way of saying that these countries managed their crises of the 1980s comparatively poorly. If the regression is run on developed

27 This is a Latin American effect since excluding each Latin American country in turn one by one has little effect on the size and significance of θ.

Table 1.9. Long-run percentage effects on levels of GDP per worker, capital per worker, TFP and GDP per capita of one year spent in a Reinhart–Rogoff banking crisis (estimates of θ derived from Eq. (1.19), estimated by Arellano–Bond (difference) method; standard errors in parentheses)

Variable affected by crisis	(1) All countries and years	(2) Exc. Great Recession	(3) Exc. Asia	(4) Exc. Latin America	(5) Developed countries only	(6) Developing countries only	(7) 1950–79	(8) 1980–2010
GDP per worker								
$100 \times \theta$	−1.096***	−1.005***	−1.112***	−0.550	0.362	−1.258***	0.831	−1.231***
(s.e.)	(0.356)	(0.380)	(0.417)	(0.382)	(0.278)	(0.467)	(1.954)	(0.382)
Capital per worker								
$100 \times \theta$	−1.137***	−1.419***	−0.997**	−0.755*	−0.0423	−1.677***	−0.832	−1.229***
(s.e.)	(0.411)	(0.462)	(0.405)	(0.392)	(0.379)	(0.397)	(1.122)	(0.418)
TFP								
$100 \times \theta$	−0.813**	−0.718**	−0.807**	−0.373	0.394	−0.864**	1.019	−0.854**
(s.e.)	(0.340)	(0.341)	(0.379)	(0.329)	(0.288)	(0.437)	(1.916)	(0.358)
GDP per capita								
$100 \times \theta$	−1.794***	−1.574***	−1.849***	−1.444***	−0.789**	−1.773***	0.390	−1.875***
(s.e.)	(0.372)	(0.386)	(0.406)	(0.396)	(0.386)	(0.495)	(2.170)	(0.410)

Note: *** $p < 0.01$, ** $p < 0.05$, * $p < 0.1$. Standard error for θ estimated by Stata's *nlcom* procedure. Fixed effects, year dummies and constant included in all regressions. In the full sample ('All countries and years') the number of countries is 61, the period is 1950–2010 (61 years) and the total number of observations is 3277; 23 countries are classified as developed and 38 as developing. For full details of estimation results, data sources and methods, see Oulton and Sebastiá-Barriel (2013). The data can be found at: https://ideas.repec.org/p/boe/boeewp/0470.html.

countries only then θ is positive and insignificant (column 5). An optimistic interpretation is that developed countries possess institutions able to deploy policies capable of neutralising the effect of banking crises. A more pessimistic interpretation is that these countries have up till now suffered only mild and isolated crises, e.g. the UK's secondary banking crisis of the 1970s. Or if the crisis was quite severe, as Sweden's was in 1991–94, it was against a benign international background. So for the developed countries past experience will not necessarily be a reliable guide to the effects of the present crisis, especially when we consider that the developed countries in our sample include Greece, Ireland, Portugal and Spain. That suggests we should place more weight on the full sample results. Finally, θ is positive and insignificant when the regression is run just over the first half of the observation period, 1950–79 (column 7). As we have already seen, banking crises were much less frequent then.

What are the channels through which banking crises damage productivity? In the present framework there are two: by reducing capital per worker or TFP. The results for capital per worker appear in the second panel of Table 1.9 and can be seen to be very similar to the results for GDP per worker, both overall for the whole sample and for the various sub-samples. But now θ is significant (at the 10% level) even when Latin America is excluded. (However, θ is not significant when only developed countries are included.) So a reduction in the long-run level of the capital stock per worker seems to be a consequence of a banking crisis and helps to explain the earlier finding of a long-run reduction in labour productivity. But this does not necessarily rule out a channel running from TFP, since a long-run reduction in TFP would also induce a long-run reduction in capital per worker. And these estimates of the fall in capital per worker are too small by themselves to account for the fall in GDP per worker: if we weight the capital effect by capital's share (say one third), then the capital channel can explain only about a third of the hit to GDP per worker. Looking down to the next panel of Table 1.9, we see that a banking crisis does indeed reduce the level of TFP. In the full sample, it reduces it by 0.81% for each year of crisis. Again, the effect is not significant for developed countries.

1.4.5.1 Effects on GDP per capita via labour force participation A possible criticism of our results is that the effects on labour productivity that we find may reflect differences across countries in labour market institutions.[28] In some countries the response of employment to a shock to output may be smaller than in others. Adjustment may be smaller *either*

28 We owe this point to Chris Pissarides.

because of labour market rigidities, which make it hard to fire people, *or* because of real wage flexibility, which reduces the incentive to do so. One way to look at this is to consider the effect of a financial crisis on GDP per capita rather than on GDP per worker. The relationship between the two is: GDP per capita = GDP per worker times the employment ratio (workers as a proportion of the population). So in countries where employment is cut when output falls there will be a fall in the employment ratio.

There is another reason why the employment ratio may fall. If a banking crisis reduces TFP and there is also an induced fall in capital per worker, then the demand for labour shifts to the left. Unless labour supply is completely inelastic there will be a fall in employment relative to population.

We can test for this by running our regression Eq. (1.19) with the dependent variable redefined as GDP per capita instead of GDP per worker. We find that the long-run effect of a banking crisis on GDP per capita is substantially larger than the effect on GDP per worker and more significant: see the lowest panel of Table 1.9. One year of a banking crisis reduces the long-run level of GDP per capita by 1.79%. The effect is highly significant at the 1% level, even when Latin America is excluded. When only developed countries are included in the regression, the long-run effect is lower, though still large – a reduction of –0.79% – and this is significant at the 5% level. In other words, part of the effect of a banking crisis comes in the form of a long-run fall in the employment ratio (whether due to higher unemployment or inactivity rates).[29]

1.4.6 *Conclusions on crises*

The results suggest that banking crises as defined by Reinhart and Rogoff have on average a substantial and statistically significant effect on the long-run level of labour productivity. The long-run level of labour productivity is reduced by about 1.1% for each year that the crisis lasts.[30] There is also a substantial and statistically significant effect on the long-run level of GDP per capita, a reduction of 1.79% for each year of crisis. That is, the long-run employment ratio also falls. This effect is statistically significant overall and also for just the developed countries.

29 IMF (2009) also finds long-lasting effects on the employment ratio following a financial crisis as do Furceri and Mourougane (2012).

30 No such significant long-run effects were found for the five other types of financial crisis distinguished by Reinhart and Rogoff if these latter were not accompanied by a banking crisis (Oulton and Sebastiá-Barriel, 2013).

Two qualifications should be noted. First, the crisis variable is a one-zero dummy. We have no measure of the severity of crises, other than the circular one of observing their consequences. Second, it is part of the maintained hypothesis that crises do not affect the long-run productivity growth rate. I attempt to address this second qualification in the next section.

1.5 Two case studies: the USA and Japan

I now consider two case studies: the USA after the Great Depression of the 1930s and Japan after the bubble burst in 1990. As we shall see, the US case provides evidence that growth can eventually resume at its previous trend rate, albeit after a massive hit to the level of GDP. This is consistent with the maintained hypothesis of the previous section. The Japanese case to the contrary seems to support the view that the long-run growth rate can be permanently affected by a financial crisis.

1.5.1 The USA after the Great Depression of the 1930s

The Great Depression started in the USA in 1929. The peak-to-trough decline in GDP was about 27%, and real output did not surpass its 1929 level till 1937 (Crafts and Fearon, 2010). Perron (1989) studied the question of whether US GDP has a unit root, i.e. whether it is trend stationary or difference stationary. He found that it was trend stationary: after a one-off shock like the Great Depression is properly taken into account, the US growth rate reverts to its long-run trend. This means that the Great Depression (which was also accompanied by a banking crisis) reduced the long-run *level* of US GNP, but left the long-run *growth rate* unchanged. In fact, though this was not the focus of his study, it is possible to deduce from his results that the hit to the GDP level was about 17%: see Perron (1989) Table VII and his parameter θ in particular. Ben-David et al. (2003) report similar results.

This result leads to a paradoxical conclusion. Suppose that in 1937 you had been asked to project the long-run future growth of the US economy. Naturally you would look at past GDP. But as it turned out you would have made a much better forecast if you had only looked at data up to 1929 and ignored everything that had happened afterwards. This would have been a brave thing to do in 1937, and no doubt you would have been regarded as a very foolish person by sensible people.

Why didn't the Great Depression cast an even longer shadow? One reason may be that the policy changes which it induced were not too bad for long-run growth. True, the USA slid into protectionism (the Smoot–Hawley tariff introduced under the Hoover administration), but in a large economy this had a less deleterious effect than similar policies did in smaller European countries. Some of the Roosevelt administration's more damaging policies, such as price-fixing and cartelisation of industry, were rolled back by the courts. The administration also passed legislation making it easier for unions to organise and get recognised. But US industry never conceded control over working practices on the shop floor to the unions to the extent that UK industry did, and some union gains in this area were rolled back after 1945 (Ulman, 1968, p. 333, citing earlier work by Slichter, Healy and Livernash). By contrast, in the UK protection and cartelisation in the 1930s were followed by nationalisation of key industries in the 1940s; together with increased union power, all this arguably hampered UK growth (Broadberry and Crafts, 1992). Finally it is interesting to note that the US debt–GDP ratio was quite low on the eve of the Great Depression. While it more than doubled during the 1930s, this was from a low base. The total gross central government debt–GDP ratio was 16.3% in 1929 and still only 43.9% in 1939.[31] Part of the reason why the debt did not rise by more was that (as is well known) Keynesian fiscal policies were not actually employed by Roosevelt.[32]

1.5.2 *Japan after the bubble burst in 1990*

It is often said that Japan has suffered 20 years of stagnation since the bubble burst in 1990. And Japan is often pointed to as an example of the dire consequences of a financial and banking crisis. So my contention that in the long run the UK growth rate will be unaffected by our own banking crisis might seem questionable in the light of the Japanese case.

However, while Japan is certainly a cautionary tale, the Japanese performance has not in fact been quite as bad as it is often made out to be. Using annual data, the bursting of the bubble did not lead to an actual fall in GDP: in other words, any fall in output was swiftly made up within the year. It is true that GDP fell in 1998 and 1999, but this was hardly a direct result of the bubble bursting; it is usually associated with a temporary fiscal tightening and contagion from the Asian financial crisis. Apart from that episode post-bubble GDP grew steadily, if slowly, right up till the global financial crisis hit in 2008 (Figure 1.9). However, the growth rate of GDP has been much lower after the bubble than

31 Source for debt ratios: a spreadsheet named 20_data.xls, available from Carmen Reinhart's website (http://www.carmenreinhart.com/data/browse-by-country/countries/united-states), accessed 23/08/2013.

32 See Crafts and Fearon (2010) for an overview of the US experience, also the more detailed articles in this special issue of the *Oxford Review of Economic Policy*, especially Hannah and Temin (2010).

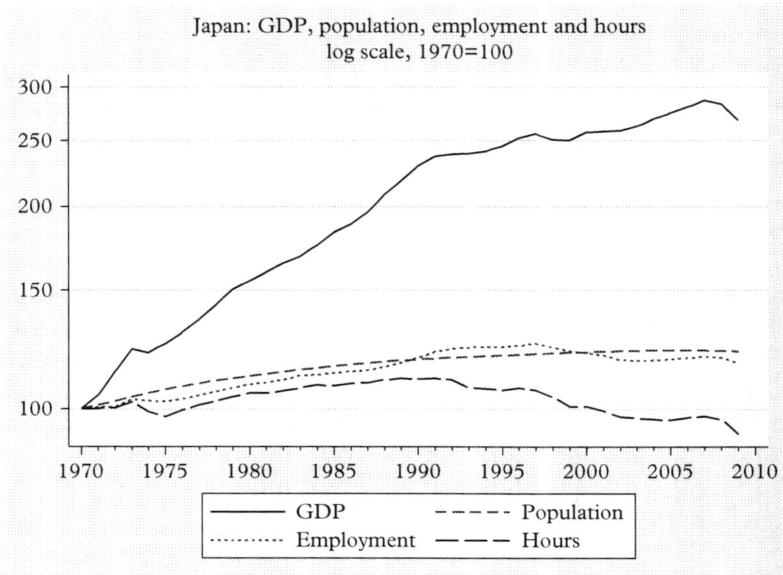

Figure 1.9. Japan: GDP, population, employment and hours
Source: The Conference Board, Total Economy Database (http://www.conference-board.org/data/economydatabase)

Table 1.10. Japan: average annual growth rates before and after the bubble, % p.a.

	1970–90	1990–2007
GDP	4.14	1.33
Population	0.84	0.18
Employment	0.87	0.02
Hours	0.51	−0.74
GDP per head	3.30	1.15
GDP per worker	3.27	1.30
GDP per hour	3.64	2.06

Source: The Conference Board, Total Economy Database, 2011 release. (http://www.conference-board.org/data/economydatabase).

before (Table 1.10): between 1970 and 1990, GDP grew at 4.14% p.a., but between 1990 and 2007 at only 1.33% p.a.

A closer look shows that this is partly due to a slower growth of employment, which in turn is due to a slower growth of population (coupled with ageing). But the really striking change is the fall in hours and in hours per worker (Figure 1.9). In 1990, the average Japanese worker worked 2031 hours per year; by 2007 this had fallen to 1785 hours, a decline of 12%. Out of 34 countries in The Conference Board's Total Economy Database for which hours data are available, Japan came 7th in 1990 in the length of the working year. By 2007 its rank had fallen to 19th (Table 1.11). The consequence is that the

Table 1.11. Hours worked per worker per year (number) and growth rate of GDP per hour (% p.a.): 34 countries

	Hours worked per worker			**Growth rate of GDP per hour**		
Country	*1990*	*2007*	*% change*	*1959–73*	*1973–90*	*1990–2007*
Argentina	1850	1841	−0.5	3.42	−0.73	2.80
Austria	1832	1678	−8.4	6.02	2.45	2.11
Belgium	1652	1560	−5.6	5.84	2.57	1.65
Brazil	1879	1841	−2.0	3.39	1.37	1.27
Canada	1788	1735	−3.0	2.10	1.05	1.42
Chile	1984	2168	9.3	2.53	0.41	2.17
Colombia	1969	1956	−0.7	2.88	1.33	1.27
Denmark	1525	1547	1.4	3.74	2.31	1.53
Finland	1769	1706	−3.6	5.15	2.95	2.72
France	1705	1556	−8.7	5.42	3.07	1.75
Germany	1572	1430	−9.0	5.25	2.98	1.95
Greece	2233	2115	−5.3	7.96	2.00	2.30
Hungary	1945	1985	2.1	...	1.73	3.06
Iceland	1839	1808	−1.7	4.27	2.44	1.90
Ireland	2179	1869	−14.2	5.04	4.01	3.68
Italy	1867	1816	−2.7	7.22	2.40	0.92
Japan	***2031***	***1785***	***−12.1***	***8.11***	***3.21***	***2.06***
Mexico	2121	2177	2.6	3.47	−0.47	0.80
Netherlands	1508	1389	−7.9	5.47	2.29	1.65
New Zealand	1759	1704	−3.1	2.06	−0.14	1.17
Norway	1502	1419	−5.5	4.61	3.06	2.18
Peru	1930	1926	−0.2	3.85	−2.67	2.96
Poland	1750	2078	18.7	...	−3.76	3.16
Portugal	1839	1942	5.6	7.15	1.77	1.26
Romania	1638	1878	14.7	...	−9.56	2.99
Singapore	2318	2307	−0.5	6.36	3.26	2.52
Spain	1742	1636	−6.1	6.60	4.04	1.14
Sweden	1561	1618	3.7	4.36	0.97	2.29
Switzerland	1700	1643	−3.4	3.51	1.12	1.05
Taiwan	2364	2166	−8.4	6.49	6.04	4.48
Turkey	2057	1918	−6.8	4.64	3.80	3.86
UK	1783	1673	−6.2	3.48	2.20	2.87
USA	1724	1709	−0.9	2.49	1.25	1.83
Venezuela	1889	1931	2.2	1.08	−1.79	0.73
Mean	*1847*	*1809*	*−1.9*	*4.64*	*1.38*	*2.10*

Source: The Conference Board, Total Economy Database, 2011 release. (http://www.conference-board.org/data/economydatabase).

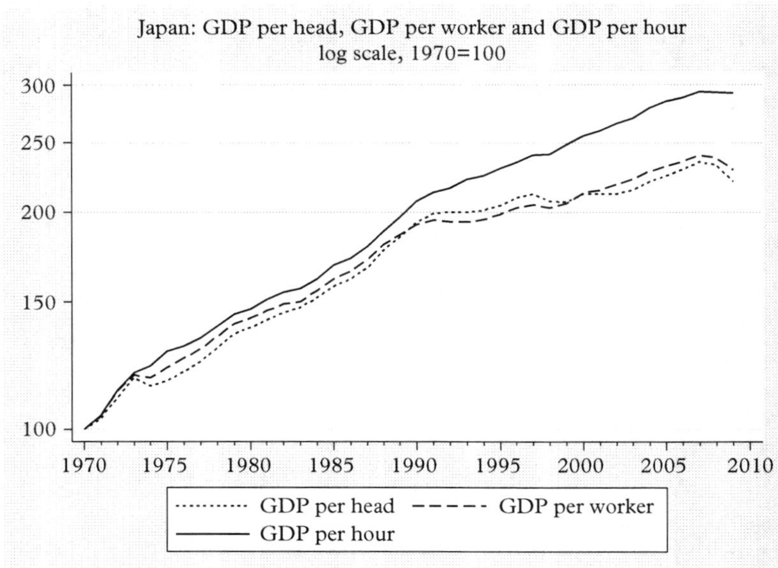

Figure 1.10. Japan: GDP per head, GDP per worker and GDP per hour
Source: The Conference Board, Total Economy Database (http://www.conference-board.org/data/economydatabase)

growth rate of GDP per hour worked was still a respectable 2.06% p.a. post-bubble (and a bit faster in the market sector, see Figure 1.2), even though down from 3.64% pre-bubble. By contrast, GDP per worker grew at only 1.30% p.a. (see Table 1.10 and Figure 1.10).[33]

The fall in hours worked in Japan was certainly large. But hours worked were falling in most of these 34 countries over the same period: see Table 1.11. Whatever the reasons for the steady decline in hours worked in the Japanese case, it is difficult to associate it directly with the bursting of the bubble. It looks more like a belated adjustment to the rich country norm.

33 Curiously, neither Krugman (1998) nor Koo (2008) mentions the fall in hours worked. Nor has either anything to say about productivity, though Krugman does mention the possibility that TFP growth has fallen. By contrast, Hayashi and Prescott (2002) do discuss the fall in hours worked and cite a law of 1988 mandating a gradual cut in the workweek from 44 to 40 hours. They also dispute the credit crunch or 'zombie banks' explanation for the productivity slowdown: 'There is no evidence of profitable investment opportunities not being exploited due to lack of access to capital markets. The problem then and today is a low productivity growth rate'. But Hayashi and Prescott offer no explanation for the fall in the TFP growth rate. Nor do they discuss fiscal policy and the possible role of rising debt in reducing the efficiency of the Japanese economy.

How does Japan's growth of GDP per hour compare with that of other countries? Table 1.11 gives the answer for the periods 1959–73, 1973–90 and 1990–2007. In 1959–73 Japan was growing much faster than the average of these countries (8.11% p.a. versus 4.64% p.a.), in 1973–90 its growth was again more rapid, at 3.21% p.a. compared to 1.38% p.a., but in 1990–2007 its performance was average: 2.06% p.a. versus 2.10% p.a. In the last period labour productivity in Japan was still growing more rapidly than in other large, rich countries like Canada, France, Italy and the USA, though not so rapidly as in the UK. So we might interpret Japan's slowing productivity growth not as a consequence of its financial crisis, but as a result of its exhausting the opportunities for catch-up.[34]

This is probably too optimistic an interpretation. Data on the growth of Japanese TFP (value added basis) are available from the EU KLEMS database, November 2009 release, for 1973–2006 (http://www.euklems.net/euk09ii.shtml). They show that for the whole economy TFP grew at 1.46% p.a. over 1973–90, but at only 0.05% p.a. for the post-bubble period 1990–2006. The corresponding figures for manufacturing are 3.65% p.a. and 0.63% p.a. So there has been a huge slowdown in TFP growth. The sense that the Japanese economy has been malfunctioning is strengthened by looking at the real rate of return to capital in the market sector. Figure 1.11, also derived from the EU KLEMS database, shows this to have fallen steadily since 1990. As Koo (2008) has amply documented, the Japanese government has applied an endless series of fiscal stimuli since the bubble burst. The deleveraging undertaken by the corporate and household sectors after asset prices collapsed has been offset by huge government budget deficits. This was good in a way, since it probably prevented a large rise in unemployment. It is widely believed, however, that much of the stimulus has gone into construction projects of dubious social value ('bridges to nowhere'). And the upshot is that Japan now has one of the highest debt–GDP ratios in the world. The gross general government debt–GDP ratio rose from 68.0% in 1990 to 225.9% in 2010.[35] This may be

34 By 1990 Japan's GDP per capita had reached 81% of the US level (source: The Conference Board Total Economy Database, 2011 release).

35 Source: Reinhart–Rogoff data available at Carmen Reinhart's website (http://www.carmenreinhart.com/data/browse-by-country/countries/japan/).; accessed 19 August 2013. The net ratio was a lot lower (about 110%), but net ratios can be problematic. For example, the net ratio is much lower than the gross one in the USA, one reason being that the former excludes federal government debt held by the social security fund. But the net rate also excludes the liabilities of the social security fund, which are of course enormous. There was presumably a reason why the framers of the Maastricht Treaty set the maximum acceptable debt–GDP ratio at 60% in gross not net terms.

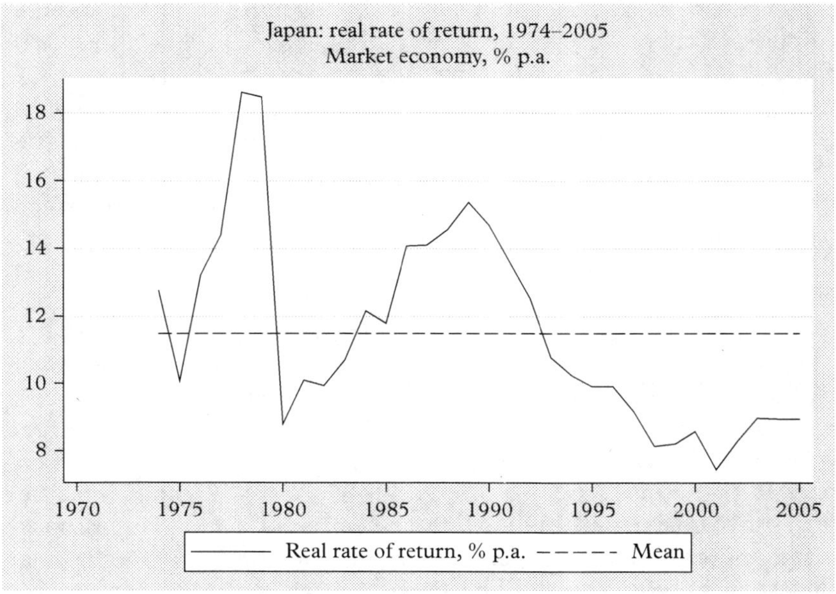

Figure 1.11. Japan: real rate of return, 1974–2005 market economy, % p.a.
Source: Oulton and Rincon (2012), based on EU KLEMS database (November 2009 release, www.euklems.net).

sustainable, in the sense that the government is not about to go bust and will continue to meet its debt obligations, partly through financial repression and (perhaps) higher inflation.[36] But the high and rising debt–GDP ratio may not have been costless: it may have induced inefficiencies in capital markets which have lowered the rate of return to capital and introduced frictions into the normal process of creative destruction. Arguably, TFP growth has slowed as a result.

In summary, though the Japanese experience is not as bad as it is often portrayed, it does provide some evidence for financial crises reducing the growth rate of productivity over a lengthy period, in this case 17 years (after which of course Japanese growth has plunged still further in the wake of the worldwide financial crisis). But it may be that the way the Japanese government dealt with the crisis, by large fiscal stimuli leading to a high and still growing debt–GDP ratio, has also played a role in

36 Hansen and Imrohoroglu (2013) argue that Japanese fiscal policy is unsustainable on its present trajectory, since it would require average tax rates of the order of 40–60% in the near future (2020 onwards).

reducing long-run growth. This may in fact be an illustration of the point made by Crafts (2013), that the *long-run* effects of financial crises depend very much on how policy responds, and these responses may either promote or hinder growth (see also Broadberry and Crafts, 1992).

1.6 Conclusions

Before the financial crisis British growth prospects looked bright. Labour productivity was growing faster in the UK than in our major competitors and British performance on other dimensions, such as inflation, employment and unemployment, was good. I have presented a projection of UK labour productivity growth (output per hour), based on a two-sector model and calibrated entirely on pre-crisis data. This projection is for the market sector (i.e. excluding government and government-financed activities like health and education). The projected figure is 2.61% p.a. About a fifth of future growth is projected to derive from the falling prices of ICT equipment from which the UK can continue to gain as a freely trading nation. The projected growth rate is a little slower than the rate actually achieved over the period 1990–2007, 2.87% p.a., mainly because I am projecting that the ICT price will fall more slowly in the future.

The crisis has called all this into question. Not only has growth stopped, but the level of labour productivity has actually fallen and is still (at the end of 2013) below the level achieved during the boom. In other words, six years after the recession began the recovery is still incomplete, an unprecedented situation for Britain. I have examined nine hypotheses put forward to explain the productivity puzzle. These were:

- Reallocation of labour to sectors with lower productivity
- Excessive influence of hard-to-measure sectors
- Mis-measurement of GDP due to mis-measurement of banking output
- Overheating in the boom
- Lower physical capital input
- Lower human capital input
- Labour/capital hoarding
- Crippled banks and zombie firms
- Austerity

The first four hypotheses are essentially measurement issues. I found that none of them holds water. The reallocation effects are negligible and eliminating the hard-to-measure sectors leaves the puzzle intact. Banking output may have been mismeasured, but this does not mean that GDP was mismeasured. There is little evidence that demand was pressing on supply during the boom, still less that there was increasing pressure on supply. Likewise both physical and human capital per hour worked have *increased*, not decreased, since the recession began in 2008Q1. Similarly, it is hard to blame austerity for reducing labour productivity, since contrary to the common perception government expenditure on goods and services has increased, not fallen, since 2008Q1. Also the government budget has been in substantial deficit, thus allowing the automatic stabilisers to play a role. All this has been accompanied by highly supportive monetary policy (with Bank Rate almost at the ZLB plus QE) and a steep fall in the exchange rate.

That leaves labour or capital hoarding and financial frictions, the latter either in the form of reduced funding to business or excessive forbearance to zombie firms. The strongest argument against labour hoarding is that it is implausible that it should continue for six years after the recession began, and also be accompanied by rising employment and hours worked since mid-2010. Rather than labour it may be capital that is being hoarded, so that the *effective* amount of capital per unit of labour has fallen, motivated by the fall in real wages. But this explanation is speculative, since we have no adequate measure of capital utilisation.

Turning to financial frictions, certainly bank lending to business has been reduced and this may well be part of the explanation of why business investment has fallen. But this has already been taken into account in the discussion of capital input. Keeping zombie firms alive on a financial drip may have reduced productivity, but the size of this effect has yet to be quantified. In any case, in a slump loss-making firms are not necessarily low-productivity firms. At the moment we lack the micro evidence to assess the strength of this hypothesis.

Arguably, all the hypotheses just summarised relate to short-term effects. So when the economy does eventually recover, what will be the long-term effect of the financial crisis? Theory suggests that banking crises can have long-lasting effects. One plausible mechanism is through a temporary interruption in TFP growth (or more broadly, innovation) which cannot be made up later. A cross-country panel analysis suggests that banking crises do indeed have long-lasting effects: they cause a fall in the long-run *level* of labour productivity, while leaving its long-run *growth rate* unaffected. They also lead to a long-run fall in the levels of capital per worker, TFP and employment. This finding corresponds to the 'pessimistic' scenario of Figure 1.3. For each year of a banking crisis as defined by Reinhart and Rogoff (2009), the long-run levels of GDP per worker, capital per worker, TFP and GDP per head are reduced by respectively 1.10%, 1.14%%, 0.81% and 1.79%. For a crisis lasting (say) five years, the reduction in levels is five times the one-year effect. These are the average effects across all countries.

In the panel analysis it was just assumed that the long-run growth rate was unaffected by banking crises, since testing this hypothesis seemed to be asking too much of the data. So instead I took a case study approach and looked at the experience of the USA after the Great Depression of the 1930s and of Japan after the bubble burst in 1990. In the US case the long-run growth rate does not seem to have been affected, even though the long-run GDP level took a huge hit (a 17% reduction). In the Japanese case, there was certainly a big fall in the growth rate of GDP after 1990 and up to 2007. But much of this was due to a fall in hours worked per worker. The growth rate of output per hour remained good by international standards. Nevertheless, output per hour grew much less rapidly after 1990 than before, as did TFP. So there is certainly a case to be made that the bursting of the bubble reduced the long-run growth rate in Japan.

So why the difference between the Japanese and US cases? One possibility is the response of the Japanese government to the crisis: tight monetary policy accompanied by very lax fiscal policy. The former led to declining prices (negative inflation) over the 1990–2007 period. The latter led to a steeply rising government debt–GDP ratio, which has now reached over 225%. I argued (tentatively) that the distorting effects of high debt may have led to the sharp decline in Japanese TFP growth since 1990.

The following hypothesis should therefore be considered as a topic for further research. Expansionary fiscal policy in the aftermath of a banking crisis may succeed in raising output and employment, but if it leads to excessive debt levels it will reduce long-term growth. So there may be a trade-off between output and employment today and growth tomorrow. Applying this argument to the UK, whether or not the UK will revert to its projected long-term growth rate of GDP per hour (2.61% p.a. in the market sector) will depend on the government debt–GDP ratio not rising excessively. Even so, the cross-country evidence suggests that, assuming the banking crisis lasted five years and that the UK is an 'average' country, the UK will suffer a permanent hit to the level of GDP per worker of about 5½% and an even larger hit to the level of GDP per capita of about 9%.

References

van Ark, B., O'Mahony M. and Timmer M.P. (2008). "The productivity gap between Europe and the United States", *Journal of Economic Perspectives*, 22(1), 25–44.

Bakhshi, H. and Larsen, J. (2005). "ICT-specific technological progress in the United Kingdom", *Journal of Macroeconomics*, 27(4), 648–669.

Barnes, S., Price, S. and Sebastiá-Barriel, M. (2008). "The elasticity of substitution: evidence from a UK firm-level data set", Bank of England Working Paper No. 348.

Barrell, R., Davis, P., Karim, D. and Liadze, I. (2010). "The effects of banking crises on productive potential output in OECD countries", National Institute of Economic and Social Research Discussion Paper 358.

Barro, R. (1979). "On the determination of the public debt", *Journal of Political Economy*, 87(5), 940–971.

Barro, R.J. and Sala-i-Martin, X. (1995). *Economic Growth*. New York: McGraw-Hill, Inc.

Basu, S., Fernald, J., Oulton, N. and Srinivasan, S. (2004). "The case of the missing productivity growth: or, does information technology explain why productivity accelerated in the United States but not in the United Kingdom?". In *NBER Macroeconomics Annual 2003* (edited by Mark Gertler and Kenneth Rogoff), Cambridge, MA: The MIT Press. Reprinted in *The Economics of Productivity* (The International Library of Critical Writings in Economics 236), edited by Dale W. Jorgenson, 2009. Cheltenham, UK: Edward Elgar. [Discussion paper version: http://papers.nber.org/papers/w10010].

Bell, V., Burriel-Llombart, P. and Jones, J. (2005). "A quality-adjusted labour input series for the United Kingdom (1975–2002)", Bank of England Working Paper No. 280; available at http://www.bankofengland.co.uk/publications/workingpapers/wp280.pdf.

Ben-David, D., Lumsdaine, R.L. and Papell, D.H. (2003). "Unit roots, postwar slowdowns and long run growth: evidence from two structural breaks", *Empirical Economics*, 28(2), 303–319.

Broadberry, S.N. and Crafts N.F.R. (1992). "Britain's productivity gap in the 1930s: some neglected factors", *Journal of Economic History*, 52, 531–558.

Brown, W., Deakin, S., and Ryan, P. (1997). "The effects of British industrial relations legislation 1979–97", *National Institute Economic Review*, 161, 69–83.

Burgess, S. (2011), "Measuring financial sector output and its contribution to GDP", *Bank of England Quarterly Bulletin*, 2011 Q3, 234–246.

Cerra, V. and Saxena, S.C. (2008). "Growth dynamics: the myth of economic recovery", *American Economic Review*, 98, 439–457.

Cette, G. and Lopez, J. (2008). "What explains the ICT diffusion gap between the major advanced countries? An empirical analysis", *International Productivity Monitor*, 17 (Fall), 28–39.

Cette, G., Mairesse, J. and Kocoglu, Y. (2005). "ICT and potential output growth", *Economics Letters*, 87(2), 231–234.

Corder, M. and Weale, M. (2011). "Banking crises and recessions: what can leading indicators tell us?" Bank of England, External MPC Unit, Discussion Paper No. 33.

Corrado, C., Hulten, C. and Sichel, D. (2009). "Intangible capital and U.S. economic growth", *Review of Income and Wealth*, 55(3), 661–685.

Crafts, N. (2013). "Long term growth in Europe: what difference does the crisis make?" *National Institute Economic Review*, 224, R14–R28.

Crafts, N. and Fearon, P. (2010). "Lessons from the 1930s Great Depression", *Oxford Review of Economic Policy*, 26(3), 285–317.

Dale, S. (2011), "Productivity and monetary policy", speech to the South Tyneside Manufacturing Forum. http://www.bankofengland.co.uk/publications/Documents/speeches/2011/speech519.pdf.

Disney, R.F., Haskel, J. and Heden, Y. (2003). "Restructuring and productivity growth in UK manufacturing", *Economic Journal*, 113(489), 666–694.

Faccini, R. and Hackworth, C. (2010). "Changes in output, employment and wages during recessions in the United Kingdom", *Bank of England Quarterly*, 2010 Q1, 43–50.

Field, S. and Franklin, M. (2014). "Multi-factor productivity, indicative estimates to 2012". http://www.ons.gov.uk/ons/rel/icp/multi-factor-productivity--experimental-/indicative-estimates-to-2012/art-indicative-estimates-to-2012.html.

Franklin, M. and Mistry, P. (2013). "Quality-adjusted labour input: estimates to 2011 and first estimates to 2012". http://www.ons.gov.uk/ons/rel/icp/quality-adjusted-labour-input--experimental-/estimates-to-2011-and-first-estimates-for-2012/art-estimates-to-2011-and-first-estimates-to-2012.html.

Furceri, D and Mouragane A (2009). "The effect of financial crises on potential output: new empirical evidence from OECD countries", OECD Economics Department Working Papers No. 699.

Furceri, D. and Mourougane, A. (2012). "The effect of financial crises on potential output: new empirical evidence from OECD countries", *Journal of Macroeconomics*, 34, 822–832.

Goodridge, P., Haskel, J. and Wallis, G. (2013). "Can intangible investment explain the UK productivity puzzle?" *National Institute Economic Review*, 224, R48–R58.

Hannah, L. and Temin, P. (2010). "Long term supply implications of the Great Depression", *Oxford Review of Economic Policy*, 26(3), 561–580.

Hansen, G. and Imrohoroglu, S. (2013). "Fiscal reform and government debt in Japan: a neo-classical perspective". NBER Working Paper No. 19431.

Hayashi, F. and Prescott, E.C. (2002). "The 1990s in Japan: a lost decade", *Review of Economic Dynamics*, 5, 206–235.

Herndon, T., Ash, M. and Pollin, R. (2013). "Does high public debt consistently stifle economic growth? A critique of Reinhart and Rogoff", Political Economy Research Institute, University of Massachusetts Amherst, Working Paper No. 322. http://www.peri.umass.edu/fileadmin/pdf/working_papers/working_papers_301-350/WP322.pdf.

Hughes, A. and Saleheen, J. (2012). "UK labour productivity since the onset of the crisis — an international and historical perspective", *Bank of England Quarterly Bulletin*, 2012 Q2, 138–146.

International Monetary Fund (2009). "What is the damage? Medium term output dynamics after financial crises", *World Economic Outlook*, October, chapter 4, pp. 121–151.

Jordà, O., Schularick, M. and Taylor, A.M. (2012). "When credit bites back: leverage, business cycles, and crises", Federal Reserve Bank of San

Francisco Working Paper No. 2011–27. http://www.frbsf.org/publications/economics/papers/2011/wp11-27bk.pdf.

Jorgenson, D.W. and Stiroh, K.J. (2000a), "U.S. economic growth at the industry level", *American Economic Review, Papers and Proceedings*, 90, 161–168.

Jorgenson, D.W. and Stiroh, K.J. (2000b), "Raising the speed limit: U.S. economic growth in the information age", *Brookings Papers on Economic Activity*, (1), 125–211.

Jorgenson, D.W., Ho, M.S. and Stiroh, K.J. (2004), "Will the U.S. productivity resurgence continue?", *Federal Reserve Bank of New York, Current Issues in Economics and Finance*, 10(3), 1–7.

Jorgenson, D.W., Ho, M.S. and Stiroh, K.J. (2005), 'Growth in U.S. industries and investments in information technology and higher education'. In Corrado, C., Haltiwanger, J. and Hulten, C.R. (eds), *Measuring Capital in the New Economy*. Chicago: University of Chicago Press.

Jorgenson, D.W., Ho, M.S. and Stiroh, K.J. (2007), "A retrospective look at the U.S. productivity growth resurgence", Federal Reserve Bank of New York, Staff Reports No. 277; available at http://www.newyorkfed.org/research/staff_reports/sr277.html.

Keynes, J.M. (1936[1961]). *The General Theory of Employment, Interest and Money*. London: Macmillan & Co Ltd.

Koo, R.C. (2008). *The Holy Grail of Macroeconomics: Lessons from Japan's Great Recession*. Singapore: John Wiley and Son (Asia) Pte. Ltd.

Krugman, P.R. (1998). "It's baaack: Japan's slump and the return of the liquidity trap", *Brookings Papers on Economic Activity*, 2, 137–205.

LSE Growth Commission (2013). "Investing for Prosperity: Skills, Infrastructure and Innovation" (P. Aghion, T. Besley, J. Brown, F. Caselli, R. Lambert, R. Lomax, C. Pissarides, N. Stern and J. Van Reenen). Centre for Economic Performance, London School of Economics and Political Science. (http://www.lse.ac.uk/researchAndExpertise/units/growthCommission/documents/pdf/LSEGC-Report.pdf).

Marrano, M.G., Haskel, J. and Wallis, G. (2009). "What happened to the knowledge economy? ICT, intangible investment, and Britain's productivity record revisited", *Review of Income and Wealth*, 55(3), 686–716.

Martin, B. (2001). "American potential", UBS Asset Management, mimeo.

Martin, B. (2011). "*Is the British economy supply constrained: a critique of productivity pessimism*". Centre for Business Research, University of Cambridge.

Martin, B. and Rowthorn, R. (2012). "*Is the British economy supply constrained II? A renewed critique of productivity pessimism*". Centre for Business Research, University of Cambridge.

OECD (2013). *Education at a glance* 2013. Paris. http://www.keepeek.com/Digital-Asset-Management/oecd/education/education-at-a-glance-2013_eag-2013-en.

Office for Budget Responsibility (2013). *Fiscal Sustainability Report*. http://budgetresponsibility.independent.gov.uk/fiscal-sustainability-report-july-2013/.

Office for National Statistics (2013a). *Labour Market Statistics*. http://www.ons.gov.uk/ons/dcp171778_315111.pdf.

Office for National Statistics (2013b). *Business investment, Q1 2013 results*. http://www.ons.gov.uk/ons/dcp171778_316065.pdf.

Oliner, S.D. and Sichel, D.E. (2000), "The resurgence of growth in the late 1990s: is information technology the story?", *Journal of Economic Perspectives*, 14(4), 3–22.

Oliner, S.D. and Sichel, D.E. (2002), "Information technology and productivity: where are we now and where are we going?", *Federal Reserve Bank of Atlanta Review*, 87(3), 15–44.

Oliner, S.D., Sichel, D.E. and Stiroh, K.J. (2007), "Explaining a productive decade", *Brookings Papers on Economic Activity*, (1), 81–152.

O'Mahony, M. and Timmer, M.P. (2009). "Output, input and productivity measures at the industry level: the EU KLEMS database", *The Economic Journal*.

Oulton, N. (1995). "Supply side reform and UK economic growth: what happened to the miracle?" *National Institute Economic Review*, 154, 53–70.

Oulton, N. (2000). "A tale of two cycles: closure, downsizing and productivity growth in UK manufacturing, 1973–89", *National Institute Economic Review*, 173, 66–80.

Oulton, N. (2002). "ICT and productivity growth in the UK". *Oxford Review of Economic Policy*, 18(3), 363–379. Reprinted in The Economics of Productivity (The International Library of Critical Writings in Economics 236), edited by Dale W. Jorgenson, 2009. Cheltenham, UK: Edward Elgar.

Oulton, N. (2007). "Investment-specific technological change and growth accounting", *Journal of Monetary Economics*, 54(4), 1290–1299.

Oulton, N. (2010). "Long term implications of the ICT revolution: applying the lessons of growth accounting and growth theory". Centre for Economic Performance, Discussion Paper No. 1027. http://cep.lse.ac.uk/pubs/download/dp1027.pdf.

Oulton, N. (2012). "Long term implications of the ICT revolution: applying the lessons of growth accounting and growth theory". *Economic Modelling*, 29, 1722–1736.

Oulton, N. (2013a). "Has the growth of real GDP in the UK been overstated because of mis-measurement of banking output?" *National Institute Economic Review*, May, 224, R59–R65.

Oulton, N. (2013b). "Medium and long run prospects for UK growth in the aftermath of the financial crisis". Centre for Economic Performance, Occasional Paper No. 37, October 2013, and Centre for Macroeconomics Discussion Paper No. CFMDP2013-7, December 2013. http://cep.lse.ac.uk/pubs/download/occasional/op037.pdf; http://www.centreformacroeconomics.ac.uk/pdf/CFMDP2013-7-non-technical-summary.pdf.

Oulton, N. and Rincon-Aznar, A. (2012). "Rates of return and alternative measures of capital input: 14 countries and 10 branches, 1971–2005". In *Industrial Productivity in Europe: Growth and Crisis*, edited by Mathilde Mas and Robert Stehrer, Edward Elgar. Discussion paper version: http://cep.lse.ac.uk/pubs/download/dp0957.pdf.

Oulton, N. and Sebastiá-Barriel, M. (2013). "Long and short-term effects of the financial crisis on labour productivity, capital and output". Bank of England Working Paper No. 470 and Centre for Economic Performance,

Discussion Paper No. 1185. http://www.bankofengland.co.uk/publications/Documents/workingpapers/wp470.pdf; http://cep.lse.ac.uk/pubs/download/dp1185.pdf.

Oulton, N. and Srinivasan, S. (2005), "Productivity growth in UK industries, 1970-2000: structural change and the role of ICT", Bank of England Working Paper No. 259.

Papell, D. and Prodan, R. (2011). "The statistical behaviour of GDP after financial crises and severe recessions", paper prepared for the Federal Reserve Bank of Boston conference on "Long-Term Effects of the Great Recession".

Perron, P. (1989). "The great crash, the oil price shock and the unit root hypothesis", *Econometrica*, 57(6), 1361–1401.

Pessoa, J.P. and Van Reenen, J. (2013). "The UK productivity and jobs puzzle: does the answer lie in labour market flexibility?". Centre for Economic Performance Special Paper No. 31.

Reinhart, C.M. and Rogoff, K.S. (2009). *This Time is Different: Eight Centuries of Financial Folly*. Princeton: Princeton University Press.

Reinhart, C.M. and Rogoff, K.S. (2010). "Growth in a time of debt", *American Economic Review*, 100(2), 573–578.

Reinhart, C.M. and Rogoff, K.S. (2011). "From financial crisis to debt crisis", *American Economic Review*, 101, 1676–1706.

Reinhart, C.M., Reinhart, V.R. and Rogoff, K.S. (2012). "Public debt overhangs: advanced-economy episodes since 1800", *Journal of Economic Perspectives*, 26(3), 69–86.

Reinhart, C.M. and Rogoff, K.S. (5, 2013). Errata: "Growth in a time of debt". http://www.carmenreinhart.com/user_uploads/data/36_data.pdf.

Schreyer, P. (2002), 'Computer price indices and international growth and productivity comparisons', *Review of Income and Wealth*, 48, 33–57.

Stiroh, K.J. (2002), "Information technology and the U.S. productivity revival: what do the industry data say?", *American Economic Review*, 92, 1559–1576.

UK Debt Management Office. (2013). Quarterly Review April–June 2013. www.dmo.gov.uk.

Ulman, L. (1968). "Collective bargaining and industrial efficiency". Chapter VIII of R E Caves and associates, *Britain's Economic Prospects*. Washington: The Brookings Institution.

Van Reenen, J. (2013). "Productivity under the 1997–2010 Labour government", *Oxford Review of Economic Policy*, 29(1), 113–141.

Whelan, K. (2001). "A two-sector approach to modeling U.S. NIPA data", *Journal of Money, Credit and Banking*, 35, 627–656.

2 Labour market and monetary policy reforms in the UK: a structural interpretation of the implications

Francesco Zanetti
University of Oxford

2.1 Introduction

Two key changes can arguably be said to have characterised the economic landscape in recent UK history: first, labour market reforms enforced by the Thatcher government in the late 1980s and, second, the introduction of an explicit inflation target in 1992, which entrusted the monetary authority with the mandate of stabilising inflation around a numerical target. Subsequently, the UK economy experienced a step change in macroeconomic performance. Figure 2.1 shows the growth rate of real Gross Domestic Product (GDP) and the growth rate of the GDP deflator, an inflation indicator, in the UK from 1970 to the present: it suggests that both real output growth and inflation have been more stable than they were in the 1970s and the 1980s. Moreover, the level of inflation has decreased remarkably since the early 1990s. Would the introduction of these policy changes have produced a different economic outlook if they had been accomplished in the earlier decades? And, if so, to what extent, if at all, might each of these two changes have played a role?

To answer these questions, this chapter uses a model that details the functioning of the UK economy during the 1970s and 1980s which is able to incorporate the policy reforms described. It then uses the model to draw inferences about how these policy changes might have altered the economic outlook had they been introduced in the early 1970s.

I am very grateful for insightful discussions with John Fender and the extremely useful comments and suggestions of Richard Barwell, Arnab Bhattacharjee, Jagjit Chadha, Gulcin Ozkan, Joe Pearlman, Peter Sinclair, Martin Weale and seminar participants at the conference on 'The Causes and Consequences of the Long UK Expansion: 1992 to 2007' at the University of Cambridge. Correspondence: Francesco Zanetti, University of Oxford, Department of Economics, Manor Road, Oxford, OX1 3UQ, United Kingdom. Email: francesco.zanetti@economics.ox.ac.uk.

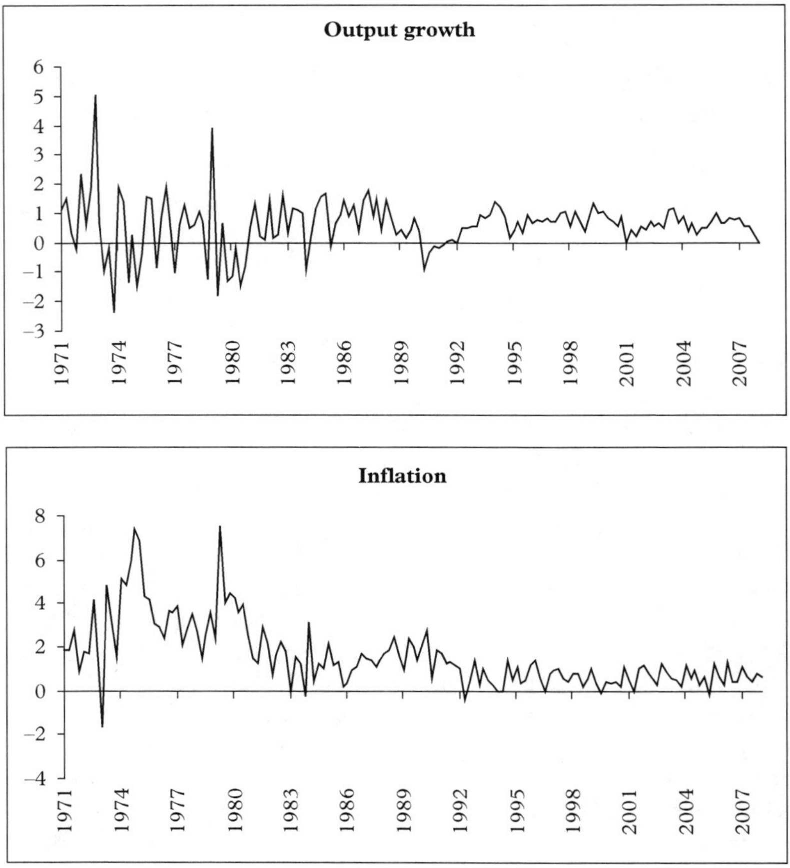

Figure 2.1. Real output growth and inflation in the UK
Notes: Output growth is measured by the growth rate of the real GDP (upper figure) and inflation is measured by the growth rate of GDP deflator (lower figure).

The analysis is conducted using a microfounded New Keynesian model where firms face a cost to adjusting nominal prices and the labour market is characterised by search frictions. The theoretical framework also incorporates a monetary authority that conducts monetary policy by setting the nominal interest rate in reaction to deviations of inflation from its target and output from its long-run equilibrium. Unlike the explicit inflation-targeting framework introduced in 1992, where the target of inflation is constant, during the 1970s and 1980s, the monetary authority could be perceived as having an implicit time-varying inflation target, where the target was allowed to change in reaction to exogenous disturbances. Although the monetary authority never explicitly announced an inflation target before 1992, to the extent that 'inflation is always and everywhere a monetary phenomenon', as suggested by Friedman (1968), changes in actual inflation should not have taken place without changes in at least the monetary authority's implicit inflation target. Hence, this modelling strategy seems an appropriate representation of the conduct of monetary policy before the introduction of an explicit and constant inflation target in 1992. The outcome is a setting similar to those of Blanchard and Galì (2010), Zanetti (2011) and Ireland (2007), which offers a detailed description of the optimising behaviour of households, firms and the monetary authority, and their interactions in the determination of macroeconomic outcomes. The model is then taken to the data and estimated on the UK 1971–91 period to provide a detailed characterisation of the UK economy prior to these policy changes. The econometric estimation separates out the policy parameters, such as those representing monetary policy and the structure of the labour market, which may vary due to changes in policy, from those which represent the household's preference and firm's technology, which ought to be policy-invariant. Hence, the model is immune to Lucas's (1976) critique and can be used to draw inferences about how the introduction of these policy changes may alter the economic outlook. For this reason, counterfactual scenarios, described below, are used to determine to what extent either labour market reforms or changes in the monetary policy framework, or both, could explain the changed economic outlook.

The counterfactual scenarios presented in this chapter aim to establish whether the labour market reforms designed to reduce the unions' power and the replacement ratio of unemployment benefits, and the changes to the monetary policy framework, such as the constant inflation target and the consequent increased weight assigned to inflation as an objective of monetary policy, would have changed the economic outlook if they had been introduced in the earlier decades. The exercise therefore consists of imposing these policy changes on the estimated model for the period 1971–91 to establish to what extent, if at all, each of them would have altered the economic outlook. The findings of this exercise suggest that labour market reforms are unlikely to have produced a considerably different economic outlook. Although a decrease in either unemployment benefits or the power of unions generates a lower level of inflation, the volatility of inflation and output growth significantly increases. The effects of changes in the monetary policy framework are mixed. The degree of reaction to deviations of inflation from the target is important for explaining the lower variance of inflation, output growth and the reduced inflation level. On the other hand, the introduction of a constant inflation target, or a monetary policy that responds more forcefully to output fluctuations, actually increases the volatility of inflation and output growth.

The remainder of the chapter is organised as follows: Section 2.2 relates this chapter to the literature, Section 2.3 provides an overview of the economic context, Section 2.4 sets up the model, Section 2.5 derives the equilibrium and the model's solution, Section 2.6 presents the results and Section 2.7 concludes.

2.2 Related literature

This chapter relates closely to two branches of the literature. First, a number of works have investigated the causes of the reduced macroeconomic volatility in the UK from the early 1990s onward, the period often referred to as an era of 'Great Moderation'. Benati (2008) uses econometric techniques to find that smaller shocks might have caused the muted economic outlook. Canova et al. (2007) use a time-varying VAR to show that changes in the transmission of demand shocks and the reduced volatility of supply and monetary policy shocks account for the improved macroeconomic stability. On the other hand, Batini and Nelson (2009) document that the change in view of policymakers about the importance of monetary policy that culminated with the introduction of inflation targeting, is likely responsible for the post-1990 UK macroeconomic stability. Bianchi et al. (2009) use a FAVAR model to show that the slope of the yield curve is related to a lower and stable inflation in the UK. Unlike these works, this chapter is the first to investigate the importance of labour market reforms and the introduction of a constant inflation target using an estimated, dynamic, stochastic, general equilibrium model. It therefore provides an empirically grounded assessment of the effect of these reforms and enables the model to quantify the structural shocks, which are used to derive the counterfactual scenarios. A closely related study is Blanchard and Galì (2007), which investigates the effect of oil shocks on the US economy. Like this chapter, they find that changes in the labour market, by decreasing real wage rigidities, and a more credible monetary policy, which reacted more aggressively to inflation, played a role in the more muted effect of oil shocks and therefore the different economic outlook in the post-1980 period compared to the 1970s. However, both their approach and focus are different. In Blanchard and Galì (2007) the labour market rigidities are not microfounded, since they assume that wages are exogenously prevented from adjusting, whereas here they are derived from first principles. While they interpret the degree of wage rigidities as a measure of changes in the labour market, this chapter investigates the effect of two well-defined labour market reforms. Moreover, they calibrate the model's parameters, while here the estimation uses the data to determine the parameters' values. Furthermore, the analysis here also focuses on the introduction of a constant inflation target, which is uncovered in Blanchard and Galì (2007).

Second, this chapter also contributes to the estimation of structural models for the UK economy, which is an understudied area of research, as emphasised by DiCecio and Nelson (2007). Unlike DiCecio and Nelson (2007), who estimate the model using a vector autoregression to match the responses of variables to a monetary policy shock, this chapter uses maximum likelihood estimation to fully exploit the ability of the structural model to match the data. In addition, this chapter also incorporates labour market frictions, which, as advocated by Nickell (1997), are an important feature of the UK labour market, and therefore provide a more accurate description of the economy. This chapter also relates to recent works by Kamber and Millard (2008) and Harrison and Oomen (2010), who estimate an array of New Keynesian models to investigate the monetary transmission mechanism in the UK. Finally, the chapter is also related to Faccini et al. (2013), who estimate a general equilibrium model with labour market frictions on UK data. While these works focus on the period from the 1980s onward, this chapter is the first study to provide a detailed description of the economy during the 1970s and 1980s. Moreover, the focus here is broader, as it uses the model to perform normative analysis to determine the relevance of labour market reforms and the introduction of inflation targeting.

2.3 The economic context

To place the analysis in context, before proceeding with the analysis it is worth describing the economic situation and the actual policy changes that took place. In the late 1970s UK economic performance had been subdued: Bean and Crafts (1996, Table 6.1) document that the UK had the lowest growth rate of GDP per capita among a sample of 12 OECD countries and that output dropped more sharply during the 1980s recession than in other developed counties. The top panel of Figure 2.1 shows that output growth was low during the 1970s, and that the second half of the 1980s was characterised by a high level of growth. Interestingly, the strong economic performance of the UK economy coincided with far-reaching labour market and monetary policy reforms.

In the late 1980s the Thatcher government introduced a series of labour market reforms aimed at reducing the distortions in the labour market considered responsible for the poor performance of the UK economy. In particular, as pointed out by Minford (1983), the unemployment benefit system and the power of the unions were regarded as particularly damaging. Consequently, legislation such as the Trade Union Act of 1984 and the Employment Act of 1988 led, as documented by Blanchflower and Freeman (1993), to a steady decline in union density and to a reduction of the replacement ratio of unemployment benefits. In particular, Gregory (1998) documents that union membership declined from 11.7 million in 1979 to 7.2 million in 1996 and union density of employment also declined from 50 per cent in 1979 to 31.3 per cent in 1996. Moreover, Millward, Stevens et al. (1992) reports that the decline of the unions' role was concentrated in the late 1980s.

In the late 1980s the UK government started to reconsider the monetary policy framework. Following Britain's departure from the Exchange Rate Mechanism in September 1992, the Chancellor of the Exchequer, Norman Lamont, established an explicit numerical target for the rate of inflation and gave the legal mandate to the monetary authority to maintain inflation around the target in the medium term. The 1998 Bank of England Act made the Bank independent to set interest rates. The Bank of England became accountable to parliament and started to implement the annual explicit target for the rate of inflation set by the Government. The bottom panel of Figure 2.1 shows that inflation became remarkably low and stable from the early 1990s.

2.4 The economic environment

The theoretical model resembles those used by Blanchard and Galì (2010) and Zanetti (2009, 2011), which combine a standard New Keynesian model with labour market search. In addition, monetary policy accounts for a time-varying inflation target as in Ireland (2007). The model economy consists of a representative household, a representative finished-goods-producing firm, a continuum of intermediate-goods-producing firms, indexed by $i \in [0, 1]$, and a monetary authority.

The labour market is similar to that in Blanchard and Galì (2010), which is based on the Diamond–Mortensen–Pissarides model of search and matching. This framework relies on the assumption that the processes of job search and recruitment are costly for both the firm and the worker. Job creation takes place when a firm and a searching worker meet and agree to form a match at a negotiated wage, which depends on the parties' bargaining power. The match continues until the parties exogenously terminate the relationship. When this occurs, job destruction takes place and the worker moves from employment to unemployment, and the firm can either withdraw from the market or hire a new worker.

The goods market is comprised of a representative finished-goods-producing firm, and a continuum of intermediate-goods-producing firms indexed by $i \in [0, 1]$.[1] During each period $t = 0, 1, 2, \ldots$, each intermediate-goods-producing firm hires workers and produces a distinct, perishable good. During each period $t = 0, 1, 2, \ldots$, the finished-goods-producing firm purchases intermediate goods from the intermediate-goods-producing firms and sells them at an established price on the market. Each intermediate-goods-producing firm sets the price as a markup over its marginal cost, and it faces a cost to adjusting its nominal price, as in Rotemberg (1982). This cost to price adjustment allows the monetary authority to influence the behavior of real variables in the short-run.

The monetary authority is modelled with a modified Taylor (1993) rule as in Clarida et al. (1998): it adjusts the nominal interest rate in response to deviations of output from its steady state and inflation from its target. Similarly to Ireland (2007), monetary policy also allows the inflation target to adjust in response to exogenous shocks.

The next section describes the agents' tastes, technologies, the policy rule and the structure of the goods and labour market in detail.

2.4.1 *The representative household*

During each period $t = 0, 1, 2, \ldots$, the representative household maximises the expected utility function

$$E_0 \sum_{t=0}^{\infty} \beta^t a_t (\ln C_t), \tag{2.1}$$

where the variable C_t is consumption, β is the discount factor $0 < \beta < 1$, and a_t is the aggregate preference shock that follows the autoregressive process

$$\ln(a_t) = \rho_a \ln(a_{t-1}) + \varepsilon_{at}, \tag{2.2}$$

1 Note that the model abstracts from issues of heterogeneity and distribution among economic agents, since it is based on the representative agent framework.

where $\rho_a < 1$. The zero-mean, serially uncorrelated innovation ε_{at} is normally distributed with standard deviation σ_a. The representative household enters period t with bonds B_{t-1}. At the beginning of the period, the household receives a lump-sum nominal transfer T_t from the central bank and nominal profits D_t from the intermediate-goods-producing firms. The household supplies N_t units of labour at the wage rate W_t to each intermediate-goods-producing firm $i \in [0,1]$ and receives unemployment benefits b_t during period t. Then, the household's bonds mature, providing B_{t-1} additional units of currency. The household uses part of this additional currency to purchase B_t new bonds at nominal cost B_t/R_t, where R_t represents the gross nominal interest rate between t and $t+1$. The household uses its income for consumption, C_t, and carries B_t bonds into period $t+1$, subject to the budget constraint

$$C_t + B_t/P_tR_t = [B_{t-1} + W_tN_t + D_t + T_t + (1 - N_t)b_t]/P_t, \tag{2.3}$$

where N_t lies between 0 and 1 for all $t = 0, 1, 2, \ldots$. Thus the household chooses $\{C_t, B_t\}_{t=0}^{\infty}$ to maximise its utility (Eq. (2.1)) subject to the budget constraint (Eq. (2.3)) for all $t = 0, 1, 2, \ldots$. Letting $\pi_t = P_t/P_{t-1}$ denote the gross inflation rate, and Λ_t the non-negative Lagrange multiplier on the budget constraint (Eq. (2.3)), the first-order conditions for this problem are

$$\Lambda_t = a_t/C_t, \tag{2.4}$$

and

$$\Lambda_t = \beta R_t E_t(\Lambda_{t+1}/\pi_{t+1}). \tag{2.5}$$

According to Eq. (2.4), the Lagrange multiplier must equal the household's marginal utility of consumption. Equation (2.5), once Eq. (2.4) is substituted in, is the representative household's Euler equation that describes the consumption decision.

2.4.2 The labour market

During each period $t = 0, 1, 2, \ldots$, the flow into employment results from the number of workers who survive from the exogenous separation and the number of new hires, H_t. Hence, total employment evolves according to

$$N_t(i) = (1 - \delta)N_{t-1}(i) + H_t(i), \tag{2.6}$$

where $N_t(i)$ and $H_t(i)$ represent the number of workers employed and hired by firm i in period t, and δ is the exogenous separation rate and $0<\delta<1$. For all $t=0,1,2,\ldots$, the fraction of aggregate employment and hires supplied by the representative household must satisfy $N_t=\int_0^1 N_t(i)di$, and $H_t=\int_0^1 H_t(i)di$ respectively. It is convenient to introduce the variable x_t, labour market tightness:

$$x_t=H_t/U_t, \tag{2.7}$$

and assume, as in Blanchard and Galì (2010), full participation in the labour market such that

$$U_t=1-(1-\delta)N_{t-1} \tag{2.8}$$

is the beginning of the period of unemployment. Finally, it is useful to define

$$u_t=1-N_t \tag{2.9}$$

the fraction of the population left without a job after recruitment. Since all new hires are from the part of unemployed workers, $0<x_t<1$. Hence, x_t also represents the probability that an unemployed worker finds a job.

Let $\mathcal{W}_t^N$, and $\mathcal{W}_t^U$, denote the marginal value of the expected income of an employed, and unemployed worker respectively. The employed worker earns a wage, suffers disutility from work and might lose her job with probability δ. Hence, the marginal value of a new match is:

$$\mathcal{W}_t^N=\frac{W_t}{P_t}+\beta E_t\frac{\Lambda_{t+1}}{\Lambda_t}\{[1-\delta(1-x_{t+1})]\mathcal{W}_{t+1}^N+\delta(1-x_{t+1})\mathcal{W}_{t+1}^U\}. \tag{2.10}$$

This equation states that the marginal value of a job for a worker is given by the real wage and the expected-discounted net gain from being either employed or unemployed.

The unemployed worker expects to move into employment with probability x_t. Hence, the marginal value of unemployment is:

$$\mathcal{W}_t^U=\frac{b_t}{P_t}+\beta E_t\frac{\Lambda_{t+1}}{\Lambda_t}\left[x_{t+1}\mathcal{W}_{t+1}^N+(1-x_{t+1})\mathcal{W}_{t+1}^U\right]. \tag{2.11}$$

This equation states that the marginal value of unemployment is made up of unemployment benefits together with the expected-discounted capital gain from being either employed or unemployed. Similarly to Zanetti (2011), unemployment benefits are set as a proportion, ρ_b, of the established wage, such that $b_t=\rho_b w_t$, where ρ_b represents the replacement ratio.

The structure of the model guarantees that a realised job match yields some pure economic surplus. The share of this surplus between the worker and the firm is determined by the wage level, in addition to compensating each side for its costs from forming the match. As in Pissarides (2000), the wage is set according to the Nash bargaining solution. The worker and the firm split the surplus of their matches with the absolute share η, and $0<\eta<1$. The difference between Eqs. (2.10) and (2.11) determines the worker's surplus. The firm's surplus is simply given by the foregone cost of hiring, G_t, which, as in Blanchard and Galì (2010), is an increasing function of aggregate technology, z_t, and labour market tightness:

$$G_t = z_t B x_t^{\alpha}, \tag{2.12}$$

where $\alpha \geq 0$, and $B \geq 0$.[2] The aggregate technology, z_t, follows the autoregressive process

$$\ln(z_t) = \rho_z \ln(z_{t-1}) + \varepsilon_{zt}, \tag{2.13}$$

where $\rho_z < 1$. The zero-mean, serially uncorrelated innovation ε_{zt} is normally distributed with standard deviation σ_z. Hence, the total surplus from a match is the sum of the worker's and the firm's surpluses, given by $\mathcal{W}_t^N - \mathcal{W}_t^U + G_t$. Nash bargaining sets the worker's surplus as a fraction η of the total surplus, $\mathcal{W}_t^N - \mathcal{W}_t^U = \eta(\mathcal{W}_t^N - \mathcal{W}_t^U + G_t)$, and therefore the wage bargaining rule for a match is:

$$\eta G_t = (1-\eta)(\mathcal{W}_t^N - \mathcal{W}_t^U).$$

Substituting Eqs. (2.10) and (2.11) in this last equation produces the agreed wage:

$$W_t = b_t/P_t + [\eta/(1-\eta)]\{G_t - \beta(1-\delta)E_t(\Lambda_{t+1}/\Lambda_t)[(1-x_{t+1})G_{t+1}]\}, \tag{2.14}$$

where η is the bargaining power of the worker. Equation (2.14) shows that the wage equals the unemployment benefits together with current hiring costs, and the expected savings in terms of the future hiring costs if the match continues.[3] The influence of these last two terms on the wage depends on the relative power of the worker in the wage bargain.

2.4.3 The goods market

As described above, the production sector is comprised of a representative finished-goods-producing firm and a continuum of intermediate-goods-producing firms, indexed by $i \in [0, 1]$, characterised by staggered price-setting as in Rotemberg (1982).

2 Note that the cost and benefit of posting a job are the same in equilibrium.
3 Note that the wage of newly hired workers is applied to existing workers.

2.4.3.1 The representative finished-goods-producing firm During each period $t=0,1,2,\ldots$, the representative finished-goods-producing firm uses $Y_t(i)$ units of each intermediate good $i\in[0,1]$, purchased at nominal price $P_t(i)$, to produce Y_t units of the finished product at constant returns to scale technology

$$\left[\int_0^1 Y_t(i)^{\frac{\theta_t-1}{\theta_t}} di\right]^{\frac{\theta_t}{\theta_t-1}} \geq Y_t,$$

where θ_t is the time-varying elasticity of substitution among intermediate goods, as first introduced by Smets and Wouters (2007), Steinsson (2003) and Ireland (2004, 2007). This parameter follows the autoregressive process

$$\ln(\theta_t)=(1-\rho_\theta)\ln(\theta)+\rho_\theta \ln(\theta_{t-1})+\varepsilon_{\theta^t}, \tag{2.15}$$

where $\rho_\theta<1$. The zero-mean, serially uncorrelated innovation ε_{θ^t} is normally distributed with standard deviation σ_θ.

Hence, the finished-goods-producing firm chooses $Y_t(i)$ for all $i\in[0,1]$ to maximise its profits

$$P_t\left[\int_0^1 Y_t(i)^{\frac{\theta_t-1}{\theta_t}} di\right]^{\frac{\theta_t}{\theta_t-1}} - \int_0^1 P_t(i)Y_t(i)di,$$

for all $t=0,1,2,\ldots$ The first-order conditions for this problem are

$$Y_t(i)=[P_t(i)/P_t]^{-\theta_t}Y_t \tag{2.16}$$

for all $i\in[0,1]$ and $t=0,1,2,\ldots$ The aggregate shocks θ_t can be interpreted as intermediate-goods-producing firm markup over marginal cost.

Competition drives the finished-goods-producing firm's profit to zero at equilibrium. This zero profit condition implies that

$$P_t=\left[\int_0^1 P_t(i)^{1-\theta_t} di\right]^{\frac{1}{1-\theta_t}}$$

for all $t=0,1,2,\ldots$

2.4.3.2 The representative intermediate-goods-producing firm During each period $t=0,1,2,\ldots$, the representative intermediate-goods-producing firm hires $N_t(i)$ units of labour from the representative household in order to produce $Y_t(i)$ units of intermediate good i according to the constant returns to scale technology

$$Y_t(i) = z_t N_t(i). \tag{2.17}$$

Since the intermediate goods are not perfect substitutes in the production of the final goods, the intermediate-goods-producing firm faces an imperfectly competitive market. During each period $t = 0, 1, 2, \ldots$ it sets the nominal price $P_t(i)$ for its output, subject to satisfying the representative finished-goods-producing firm's demand. The intermediate-goods-producing firm faces a quadratic cost to adjusting nominal prices, measured in terms of the finished goods and given by

$$\frac{\phi_p}{2}\left[\frac{P_t(i)}{\pi P_{t-1}(i)} - 1\right]^2 Y_t,$$

where $\phi_p > 0$ is the degree of adjustment cost and π is the steady state gross inflation rate. This relationship, as stressed in Rotemberg (1982), accounts for the negative effects of price changes on customer–firm relationships. These negative effects increase in magnitude with the size of the price change and with the overall scale of economic activity, Y_t.

The problem for the firm is to choose $\{P_t(i),\ N_t(i),\ H_t(i)\}_{t=0}^{\infty}$ to maximise its total market value given by

$$E_0 \sum_{t=0}^{\infty} (\beta^t \Lambda_t / P_t) D_t(i), \tag{2.18}$$

where the variable $D_t(i)$ is profits, subject to the constraints imposed by Eqs. (2.6)–(2.8), (2.12) and (2.17). In Eq. (2.18), $\beta^t \Lambda_t / P_t$ measures the marginal utility value to the representative household of an additional dollar in profits received during period t and

$$D_t(i) = P_t(i) Y_t(i) - N_t(i) W_t - H_t(i) G_t - \frac{\phi_p}{2}\left[\frac{P_t(i)}{\pi P_{t-1}(i)} - 1\right]^2 Y_t \tag{2.19}$$

for all $t = 0, 1, 2, \ldots$ Thus the firm chooses $\{N_t(i), P_t(i)\}_{t=0}^{\infty}$ to maximise the profit (Eq. (2.19)) subject to the demand function (Eq. (2.16)), the production technology (Eq. (2.17)), and law of employment accumulation (Eq. (2.6)). Solving Eq. (2.6) for $H_t(i)$ and substituting the outcome, together with Eq. (2.16), into Eq. (2.19), and letting Ξ_t denote the non-negative Lagrange multiplier on Eq. (2.17), permits us to write the first-order conditions for this problem as

$$\frac{W_t}{P_t} = \frac{\Xi_t}{\Lambda_t} z_t - \frac{G_t}{P_t} + \beta(1-\delta)\frac{\Lambda_{t+1}}{\Lambda_t}\frac{G_{t+1}}{P_t}, \tag{2.20}$$

and

$$\phi_p\left[\frac{P_t(i)}{\pi P_{t-1}(i)}-1\right]\frac{P_t}{\pi P_{t-1}(i)}=(1-\theta_t)\left[\frac{P_t(i)}{P_t}\right]^{-\theta_t}+\theta_t\frac{\Xi_t}{\Lambda_t}\left[\frac{P_t(i)}{P_t}\right]^{-(1+\theta)}$$
$$+\beta\phi_p E_t\left\{\frac{\Lambda_{t+1}}{\Lambda_t}\left[\frac{P_{t+1}(i)}{\pi P_t(i)}-1\right]\frac{P_{t+1}(i)P_t}{\pi P_t^2(i)}\frac{Y_{t+1}}{Y_t}\right\}. \tag{2.21}$$

Equation (2.20) is the firm's labour supply condition, which equates the real wage with the marginal product of labour minus the hiring costs to pay in period t, plus the expected saving on the hiring costs forgone in period $t+1$, if the job is not dismissed. Equation (2.21) is the New Keynesian Phillips curve in its non-linearised form and it states that the firm sets prices as a markup over marginal cost, accounting for price adjustment costs. As Ravenna and Walsh (2008) and Chadha and Sun (2008) point out, the presence of labour market search frictions enables the New Keynesian Phillips curve to track inflation fluctuations more precisely.

2.4.4 *The monetary authority*

During each period $t=0,1,2,\ldots$, the monetary authority conducts monetary policy using a modified Taylor (1993) rule,

$$\ln(R_t/R)=\rho_y\ln(Y_t/Y)+\rho_\pi\ln(\pi_t/\pi_t^\star)+\ln(v_t), \tag{2.22}$$

where R and Y are the steady state values of the nominal interest rate and output, and $\pi_t^\star$ is the monetary authority time-varying inflation target for the period t. According to Eq. (2.22), the monetary authority adjusts the nominal interest rate in response to movements in output from its steady state and inflation from the target. As pointed out in Clarida et al. (1998) and Nelson (2003), this modelling strategy for the central bank consistently describes the conduct of monetary policy in the UK since the early 1970s. The monetary policy shock v_t follows the autoregressive process

$$\ln(v_t)=\rho_v\ln(v_{t-1})+\varepsilon_{vt}, \tag{2.23}$$

where $\rho_v<1$. The zero-mean, serially uncorrelated policy shock ε_{vt} is normally distributed, with a standard deviation σ_v. Similarly to Ireland (2007), the time-varying inflation target $\pi_t^\star$ evolves according to

$$\ln(\pi_t^\star)=\ln(\pi^\star)+\delta_a\varepsilon_{at}-\delta_\theta\varepsilon_{\theta t}-\delta_z\varepsilon_{zt}+\sigma_\pi\varepsilon_{\pi t}, \tag{2.24}$$

such that it may vary exogenously, when $\sigma_\pi > 0$, and may adjust to preference, cost-push and technology shocks, when $[\delta_a, \delta_\theta, \delta_z] > 0$. Note that, as in Ireland (2007), since negative realisation of $\varepsilon_{\theta t}$ and ε_{zt} and positive realisation of ε_{at} increase prices, positive values for δ_θ, δ_z and δ_a generate more persistent movements in the inflation target. The presumption here, as detailed at the outset, is that changes in inflation should not have happened without changes in at least the implicit inflation target, and that the implicit inflation target reacts to shocks similarly to the underlying inflation.

2.5 Equilibrium and solution

In a symmetric, dynamic, equilibrium, all intermediate-goods-producing firms make identical decisions, so that $Y_t(i) = Y_t$, $N_t(i) = N_t$, $H_t(i) = H_t$, $D_t(i) = D_t$ and $P_t(i) = P_t$, for all $i \in [0, 1]$ and $t = 0, 1, 2,$. In addition, the market clearing conditions $T_t = M_t - M_{t-1}$ and $B_t = B_{t-1} = 0$ must hold for all $t = 0, 1, 2, \ldots$ These conditions, together with the firm's profit conditions (Eq. (2.19)) and the household's budget constraint (Eq. (2.3)), produce the aggregate resource constraint

$$Y_t = C_t + (\phi_p/2)(\pi_t/\pi - 1)^2 Y_t + G_t H_t, \tag{2.25}$$

where the term $G_t H_t$ expresses the resources spent in hiring. Substituting the Lagrange multiplier, Λ_t, from Eq. (2.4) into Eqs. (2.5), (2.14) and (2.20)–(2.21), and deriving the labour market equilibrium condition by combining the agreed wage (Eq. (2.14)) with the labour demand (Eq. (2.20)), the model describes the behavior of 14 endogenous variables $\{b_t, C_t, G_t, H_t, \Lambda_t, \Xi_t, N_t, \pi_t, \pi_t^\star, R_t, U_t, W_t, x_t, Y_t\}$ and four exogenous shocks $\{a_t, \theta_t, v_t, z_t\}$. The equilibrium is then described by the representative household's first-order conditions (Eqs. (2.4) and (2.5)), the law of employment (Eq. (2.6)), the definition of labour market tightness (Eq. (2.7)), the definition of unemployment accumulation (Eq. (2.8)), the definition of cost per hire (Eq. (2.12)), the agreed wage (Eq. (2.14)), the production function (Eq. (2.17)), the labour market equilibrium condition (Eq. (2.20)), the New Keynesian Phillips curve (Eq. (2.21)), the monetary authority policy rule (Eq. (2.22)), the time-varying inflation target (Eq. (2.24)), the aggregate resource constraint (Eq. (2.25)), the definition of unemployment benefits and the specification of the exogenous shocks as in Eqs. (2.2), (2.13), (2.15) and (2.23).

The equilibrium conditions do not have an analytical solution. Instead, the model's dynamics are characterised by log-linearising them around the steady state. The log-linearised equilibrium conditions are

$$\hat{\Lambda}_t = \hat{a}_t - \hat{C}_t,$$

$$\hat{\Lambda}_t = \hat{R}_t + E_t\hat{\Lambda}_{t+1} - \hat{\pi}_t,$$

$$\hat{N}_t = (1-\delta)\hat{N}_{t-1} + \delta\hat{H}_t,$$

$$\hat{x}_t = \hat{H}_t - \hat{U}_t,$$

$$\hat{U}_t = -(1-\delta)\ (N/U)\hat{N}_{t-1},$$

$$\hat{G}_t = \psi\hat{z}_t + \alpha\hat{x}_t,$$

$$\begin{aligned}\hat{W}_t = {} & (b/W)b_t + [\eta/(1-\eta)](G/b)\hat{G}_t + (1-\delta)\beta(x/b)[\eta/(1-\eta)]E\hat{x}_{t+1} \\ & - (\beta/b)(1-\delta)(1-x)[\eta/(1-\eta)](\hat{G}_{t+1} + \hat{\Lambda}_{t+1} - \hat{\Lambda}_t),\end{aligned}$$

$$\hat{Y}_t = \hat{z}_t + \hat{N}_t,$$

$$\begin{aligned}\hat{b}_t = {} & (\Xi z/\Lambda b)(\hat{\Xi}_t - \hat{\Lambda}_t + \hat{z}_t) - \{1 + [\eta/(1-\eta)]\}(G/b)\hat{G}_t \\ & + \beta(1-\delta)\{1 + (1-x)[\eta/(1-\eta)]\}(G/b)(\hat{\Lambda}_{t+1} + \hat{G}_t - \hat{\Lambda}_t) \\ & - \beta(1-\delta)(xG/b)[\eta/(1-\eta)]E\hat{x}_{t+1},\end{aligned}$$

$$\hat{\pi}_t = \beta E_t\hat{\pi}_{t+1} + (\theta\ \Xi/\phi\Lambda)(\hat{\Xi}_t - \hat{\Lambda}_t + \hat{\theta}_t) - (\theta/\phi)\hat{\theta}_t,$$

$$\hat{R}_t = \rho_y\hat{y}_t + \rho_\pi(\hat{\pi}_t - \hat{\pi}_t^{\star}) + v_t,$$

$$\hat{\pi}_t^{\star} = \delta_a\varepsilon_{at} - \delta_\theta\varepsilon_{\theta t} - \delta_z\varepsilon_{zt} + \sigma_\pi\varepsilon_{\pi t},$$

$$\hat{Y}_t = (C/Y)\hat{C}_t + (GH/Y)(\hat{G}_t + \hat{H}_t),$$

$$\hat{a}_t = \rho_a\hat{a}_{t-1} + \varepsilon_{at},$$

$$\hat{\theta}_t = \rho_\theta\hat{\theta}_{t-1} + \varepsilon_{\theta t},$$

$$\hat{v}_t = \rho_a\hat{v}_{t-1} + \varepsilon_{vt},$$

and

$$\hat{z}_t = \rho_z\hat{z}_{t-1} + \varepsilon_{zt},$$

where a hat on a variable denotes the logarithmic deviation from its steady state and a variable without the time index represents its value at the steady state. The solution to this system is derived using Klein (2000), which is a modification of Blanchard and Kahn (1980), and takes the form of a state space representation. This latter can be conveniently used to compute the likelihood function in the estimation procedure.

2.6 Estimation and findings

The econometric estimation uses UK quarterly data for output growth, consumption growth, the nominal interest rate, inflation and the growth rate of wages for the sample period 1971:1 through 1991:4. Output growth is defined as the quarterly growth rate of gross domestic product at basic prices; consumption growth is defined as the quarterly growth rate of final consumption expenditure; the nominal interest rate is defined as quarterly averages of daily readings on the three-month UK Treasury Bill rate; inflation is defined as the quarterly growth rate of the GDP deflator; and wages growth is defined as the quarterly growth rate of the Average Earnings Index. All the data are taken from the Office for National Statistics dataset, with the exception of the series of the three-month UK Treasury Bill rate, which is from the Statistical Interactive Database. The data are demeaned prior to the estimation.

As in other similar studies, such as Ireland (2004), a first attempt to estimate the model produced implausible values for the discount factor. Thus the real interest rate is set to 4 per cent annually, a number commonly used in the literature, which pins down the quarterly discount factor β to 0.99. Consistent with UK data, the steady state value of the job finding rate, x, and unemployment rate, u, are set equal to 0.4 and 0.3 respectively. This yields a value for the separation rate, $\delta = ux/((1-u)(1-x))$, equal to 0.29, which is in line with the UK estimate by Jolivet et al. (2006). Also the parameter B, which determines the steady state proportion of hiring costs of total output, is difficult to identify and is calibrated. Since there is no precise empirical evidence on this parameter, following Blanchard and Galí (2010) it is set approximately to 0.0438 so that hiring costs represent 1 per cent of total output, which seems a reasonable upper bound. Of special interest is the bargaining power parameter, η, which represents the fraction of the total surplus attributed to the worker. The estimation was unable to identify this parameter and therefore it is set equal to 0.5, as estimated by Petrongolo and Pissarides (2001), so that the household and the firm have the same bargaining power. Consequently, in order to satisfy the Hosios (1990) condition, which guarantees that allocations of the economy are Pareto optimal, the parameter of the elasticity of hiring costs with respect to labour market tightness, α, is set equal to one.[4] Another parameter that the estimation procedure was unable to identify is the replacement ratio, ρ_b, that represents the ratio of unemployment benefits to the past wage, which is set equal to 40 per cent, as estimated

4 A similar calibration strategy is used in Blanchard and Gali (2010) and Zanetti (2008).

by Bean (1994) and Nickell (1997). The steady state value of the elasticity of substitution between intermediate goods, θ, is set equal to six so that the equilibrium markup is equal to 20 per cent, as suggested in Britton et al. (2000). The gross steady state value of inflation, π, is set equal to 1.02, matching the average inflation rate in the data. Finally, Eqs. (2.14) and (2.20) pin down the parameter χ which is set equal to 0.9985.

Table 2.1 displays the maximum likelihood estimates of the model's parameters together with their standard errors. The estimate of the degree of nominal price rigidities, ϕ_p, is equal to 24.3425. As shown in Ireland (2000), given that θ is equal to six, it implies that approximately 20 per cent of the firms adjust their price each period, a value in line with Britton et al. (2000). It is worth noticing that, given the sizable standard error of this parameter, considerable uncertainty remains about the degree of nominal price rigidities in the economy.

The parameter estimates of Eqs. (2.22) and (2.24) characterise the conduct of monetary policy. The estimate of the reaction coefficient to the fluctuations of output from its steady state, ρ_y, is 0.1229, and the estimate of the reaction coefficient to the fluctuations of inflation from the inflation target, ρ_π, is 1.1019. These estimates suggest that the monetary authority responded weakly to inflation and output. This is in line with the estimates in Nelson (2003) and the documentation in Batini and Nelson (2009). The estimates of Eq. (2.24), which describes the inflation target, point out that preference, cost-push and technology

Table 2.1. Maximum likelihood estimation and standard errors

Parameters	Estimates	Standard errors
ϕ_p	24.3425	29.3824
ρ_π	1.1019	0.0557
ρ_y	0.1229	0.0922
δ_a	0.2375	0.2779
δ_θ	0.1428	0.1824
δ_z	0.2612	0.8819
ρ_a	0.9938	0.0003
ρ_θ	0.8557	0.0148
ρ_v	0.4280	0.1954
ρ_z	0.6506	0.0307
σ_a	0.2920	0.5819
σ_θ	1.1144	0.6935
σ_π	0.1420	0.5678
σ_v	0.0008	0.0047
σ_z	0.6763	0.0723

shocks are all important components to determine the implicit inflation target. In fact, the estimates of δ_a, δ_θ and δ_z are equal to 0.2375, 0.1428 and 0.2612 respectively. Interestingly, the monetary authority leaves the target to react more aggressively to technology shocks while giving less weight to preference and cost-push shocks.

The estimates of the exogenous disturbances show that preference shocks are highly persistent, with ρ_a equal to 0.9938, while cost-push and technology shocks are less so, with ρ_θ and ρ_z equal to 0.8557 and 0.6506 respectively. The estimates of the volatility of the exogenous disturbances show that cost-push and technology shocks are highly volatile, with σ_θ and σ_z equal to 1.1144 and 0.6763 respectively, while shocks to the monetary policy rule, inflation target and households' preferences are of lower magnitude, with σ_v, σ_π and σ_a equal to 0.0008, 0.1420 and 0.2920 respectively. Clearly, these values suggest that cost-push and technology shocks are important components of economic fluctuations.

To investigate how the variables of the model react to each shock, Figures 2.2 and 2.3 plot the impulse responses of selected variables to one standard deviation of each of the exogenous shocks. The first column in Figure 2.2 shows that after a one standard deviation technology shock, output and unemployment both rise, while inflation falls. The fall in inflation allows for an easing in monetary policy such that the nominal interest rate falls. Finally, the one-period immediate increase in unemployment leads to a fall in labour market tightness, which then increases due to the subsequent fall in unemployment. The second column in Figure 2.2 shows that a one standard deviation cost-push shock causes a fall in inflation and the nominal interest rate, and a rise in output. The increase in output triggers a fall in unemployment that generates a rise in labour market tightness. Given the opposite reaction of output and inflation in the case of technology and cost-push shocks, these disturbances behave as supply-side shocks, as mentioned in the outset. The third column in Figure 2.2 shows that a one standard deviation monetary policy shock translates into an increase in the nominal interest rate and into a fall in output. The fall in output generates an increase in unemployment and a consequent fall in the number of hires. Opposite shifts in the number of hires and unemployment generate a fall in labour market tightness. Since the monetary policy disturbance is serially uncorrelated, the reaction of each variable dies off over a period of one year. The first column in Figure 2.3 shows that after a one standard deviation preference shock both output and inflation rise, leading the nominal interest rate, due to the modified Taylor rule, to increase. Unemployment falls, and therefore labour market tightness rises due to

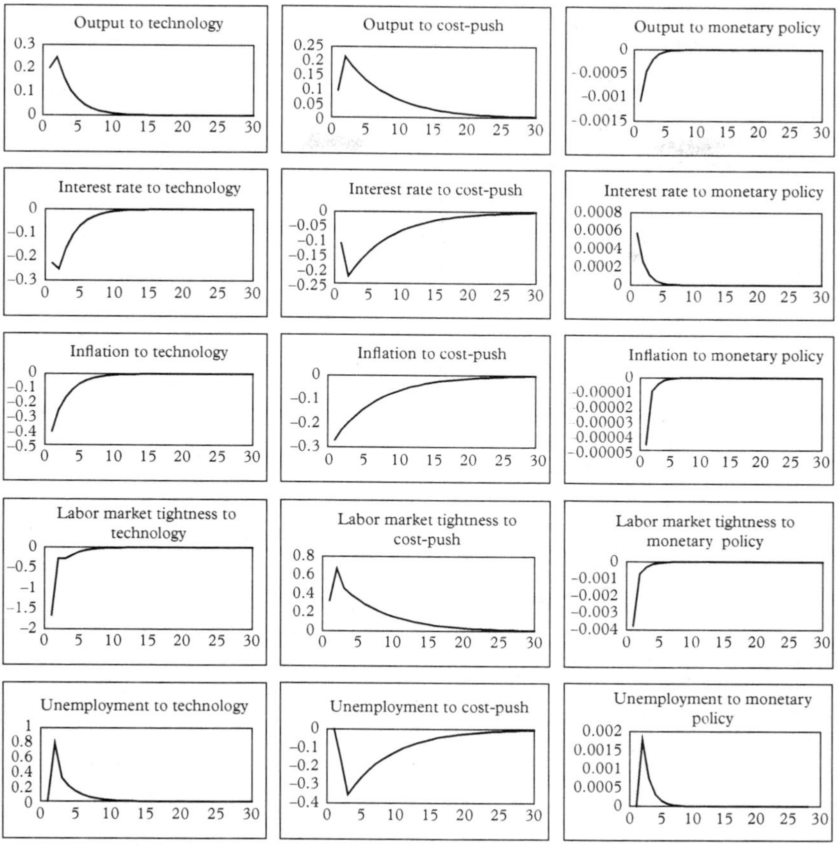

Figure 2.2. Impulse responses to technology, cost-push and monetary policy shocks

Notes: Each panel shows the percentage-point response of selected models' variables to a one standard deviation shock. The horizontal axis measures the time, expressed in quarters.

the lower response of vacancies. Finally, the second column in Figure 2.3 shows that a one standard deviation inflation target shock decreases the nominal interest rate and raises inflation, whose combined movements generate a decrease in the real interest rate and therefore a rise in output. Unemployment falls and so labour market tightness increases.

Looking across all these impulse responses also provides some insights into how the presence of labour market search and the introduction of a time-varying inflation target affect the transmission

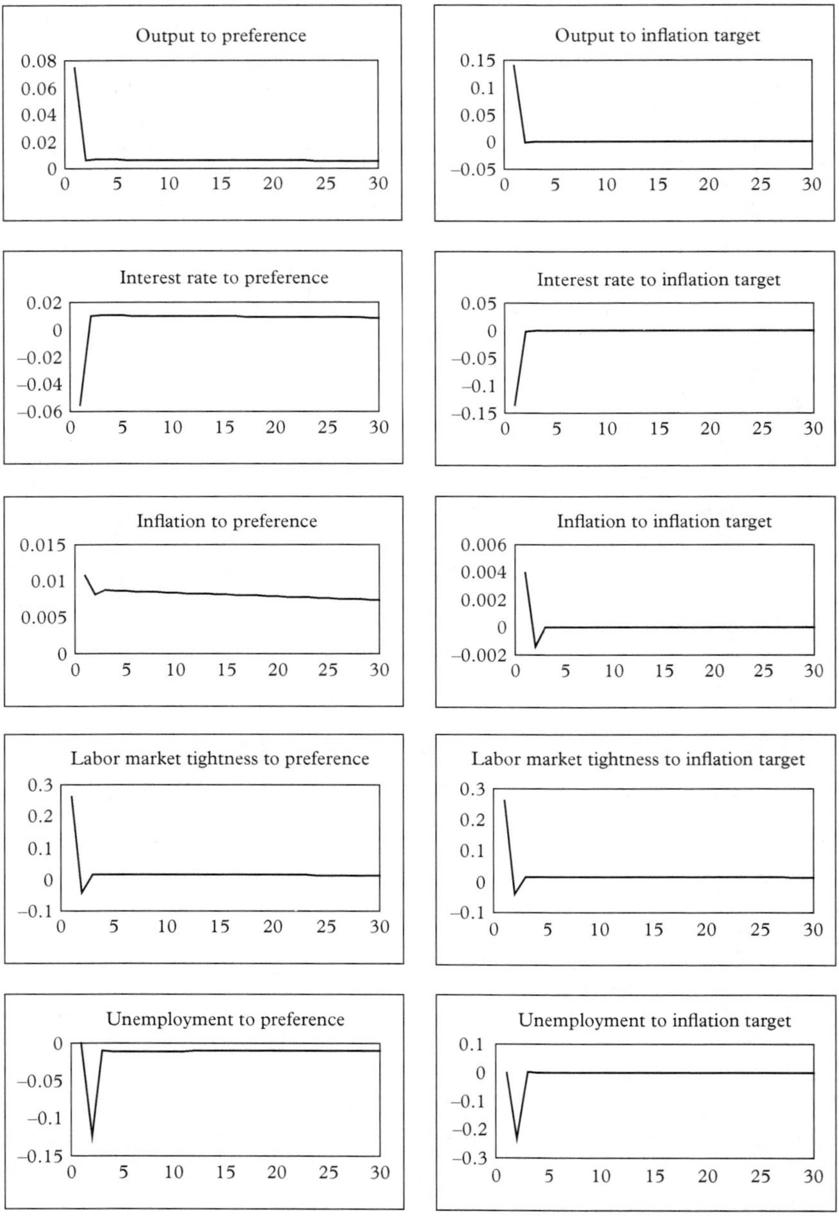

Figure 2.3. Impulse responses to preference and inflation target shocks
Notes: Each panel shows the percentage-point response of selected models' variables to a one standard deviation shock. The horizontal axis measures the time, expressed in quarters.

mechanism of a standard New Keynesian framework. For all shocks, the coexistence of these two features leaves the baseline transmission mechanism of a New Keynesian setting qualitatively unaffected: all the variables respond to shocks similarly to a standard New Keynesian model without labour market search and a time-varying inflation target, as in Woodford (2003). This corroborates the findings in Christoffel et al. (2006) and Ireland (2007), who show that each of these two features on its own leaves the qualitative response of the underlying New Keynesian model unchanged. Nonetheless, as detailed below, the joint presence of labour market search and the time-varying inflation target affects the model's quantitative response to disturbances.

To understand the extent to which the movements of each variable are explained by the shocks, Table 2.2 reports the asymptotic forecast error variance decompositions for the estimated model. The results show that cost-push shocks explain low-frequency movements in output and the nominal interest rate, while technology shocks play an important role in driving long-run fluctuations in inflation, labour market tightness and unemployment. On the other hand, preference and inflation target shocks explain a small fraction of aggregate fluctuations.

To detail how the exogenous shocks have evolved during the estimation period, Figure 2.4 plots the estimate of each shock using the Kalman smoothing algorithms from the state space representation of the estimated model. These estimates point out that monetary policy shocks, in the form of exogenous shocks to either the inflation target or the policy rule, were of smaller magnitude compared to technology or cost-push shocks, suggesting that, in line with the findings of the forecast error variance decomposition, the latter had a more relevant role in affecting aggregate fluctuations. These stochastic shocks, once fed into the state space representation of the model, generate time series for all the model's variables. This therefore allows the derivation of the unobserved time-varying inflation target, which is plotted in Figure 2.5

Table 2.2. Asymptotic forecast error variance decomposition

	Technology	**Cost-push**	**Monetary policy**	**Preference**	**Inflation target**
Output	41.17	50.69	0	2.59	5.54
Interest rate	40.84	51.51	0	3.03	4.63
Inflation	50.19	48.66	0	1.15	0
Labour market tightness	63.92	28.67	0	2.02	5.39
Unemployment	58.61	35.67	0	1.82	3.90

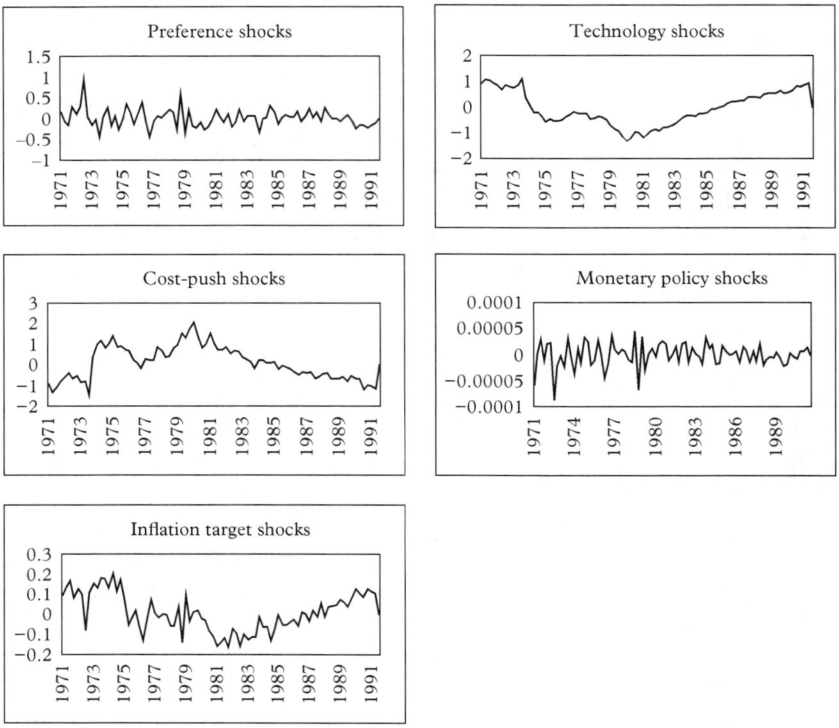

Figure 2.4. Smoothed estimates of preference, technology, cost-push, monetary policy and inflation target shocks
Notes: Each panel shows estimates of the exogenous shocks using the Kalman smoothing algorithm from the state space representation of the estimated model.

against the observed inflation. The figure shows that during the 1970s the monetary authority translated adverse technology shocks into higher inflation, by allowing the implicit inflation target to grow. In the early 1980s, it had taken advantage of the positive supply shocks to reduce inflation and it subsequently allowed the implicit inflation target to grow throughout the 1990s. This is in line with the narrative evidence in Batini and Nelson (2009).

As detailed at the outset, since this model is immune to Lucas' (1976) critique, counterfactual scenarios can disclose whether the introduction of labour market reforms or a monetary policy framework based on a constant inflation target might have altered the economic outlook if they had been introduced in the earlier decades. The exercise consists in superimposing these policy changes on the model, assuming

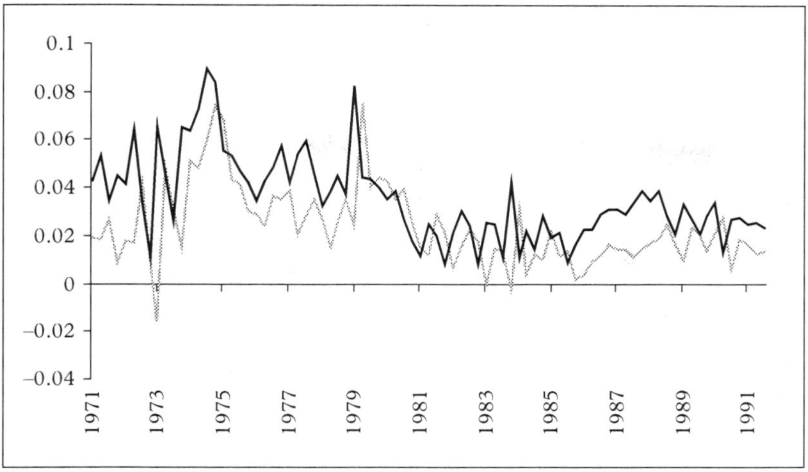

Figure 2.5. Estimate of the time-varying inflation target and inflation
Notes: Unobserved time-varying inflation target (black line) and observed inflation (grey line).

that all the other parameters and stochastic shocks remained unchanged, to generate time series for the alternative scenarios. To this end, Figures 2.6 and 2.7 compare the historical series of inflation and output growth against the series that would have been generated under counterfactual scenarios. Figure 2.6(a) shows the counterfactual case of a reduction of 10 per cent in the replacement ratio of unemployment benefits, ρ_b, such that it equals 0.36 instead of its estimated value. This policy change would have had a sizable effect on the level of inflation, which would have been on average lower compared to its realised counterpart: 2.1 per cent instead of 2.3 per cent. However, inflation volatility would have increased somewhat (0.0292 instead of 0.0273). Interestingly, output growth would have displayed a substantially unchanged level, but a slightly higher variance (0.0140 instead of 0.0138). Figure 2.6(b) shows the observed series against those generated under the counterfactual scenarios of a 10 per cent reduction in the household's bargaining power, η, such that it equals 0.45 instead of 0.5. The level of inflation would have been materially lower, 1.6 per cent instead of 2.3 per cent, while the variance of inflation would have doubled, 0.0560 instead of 0.0273. Similarly, both the level and variance of output growth would have remained substantially unchanged compared to their realised counterparts. This suggests that the implementation of these labour market reforms would have contributed to the reduction of the level of inflation, but would have been unable to

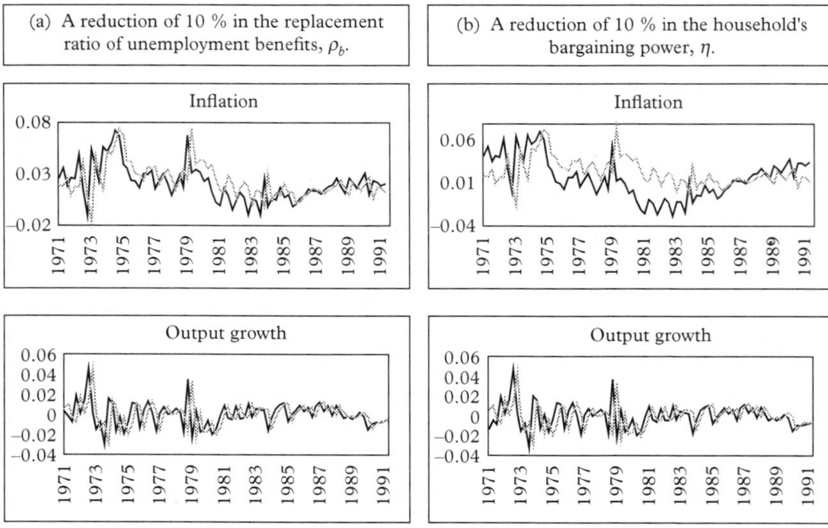

Figure 2.6. Labour market reforms counterfactual scenarios
Notes: Counterfactual experiments. Each panel shows the actual series (grey line) and the model estimates (black line) of how the actual series would have behaved under some alternative scenarios.

generate a lowering of inflation and output growth volatility. This echoes the results in Zanetti (2009, 2011) who finds that a decrease in labour market regulation, in the form of either lower workers' bargaining power or unemployment benefits, increases the volatility of inflation.

Figures 2.7(a)–(c) show counterfactual cases for changes in the monetary policy framework. Figure 2.7(a) shows time series generated by assuming that the monetary authority undertakes a constant inflation target instead of allowing the target to vary in reaction to shocks, by imposing the parameters δ_a, δ_θ, δ_z and σ_π equal to zero. Under this scenario the level of inflation would have lowered to 1.4 per cent instead of 2.3 per cent, while the variance of inflation would have approximately tripled to 0.0652 instead of 0.0273. By keeping a constant inflation target the monetary authority would have offset adverse technology shocks with more pronounced change in the nominal interest rate, which would have produced higher variance of inflation. Instead, output growth would have remained at the same level, but with higher volatility, 0.0327 instead of 0.0138. Figure 2.7(b) shows how the path would have changed for a 5 per cent increase in the monetary authority response to the deviation of inflation from its target, such that

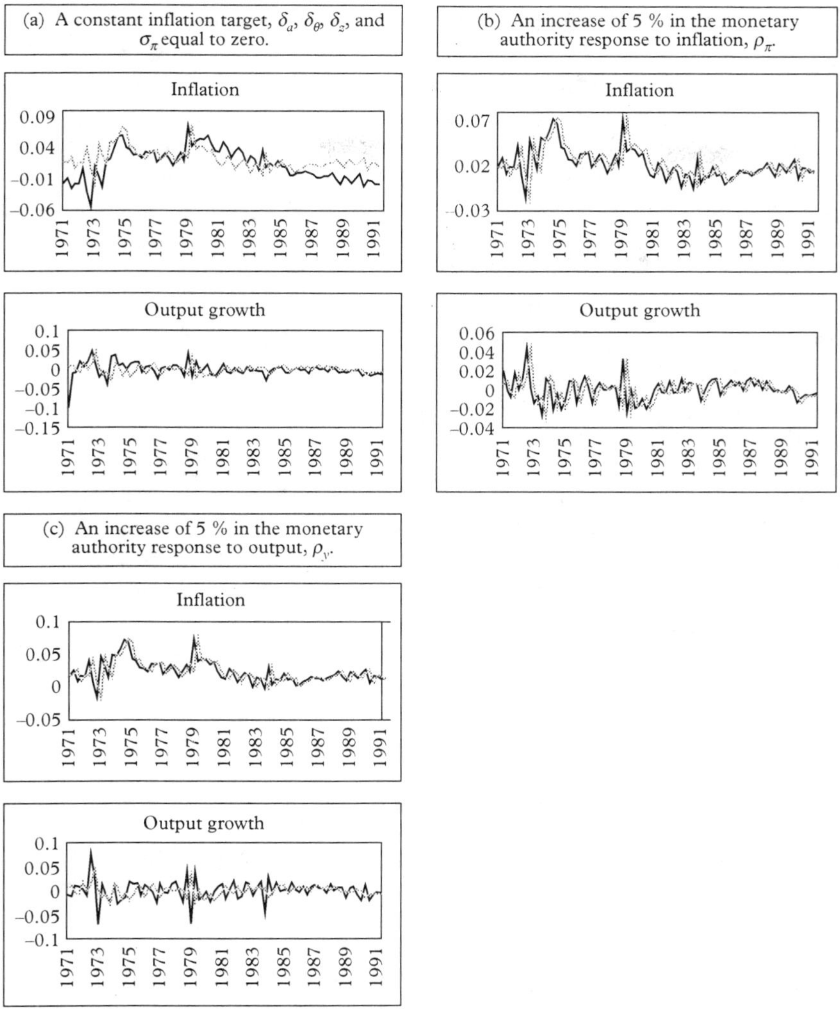

Figure 2.7. Monetary policy reforms counterfactual scenarios
Notes: Counterfactual experiments. Each panel shows the actual series (grey line) and the model estimates (black line) of how the actual series would have behaved under some alternative scenarios.

ρ_π equals 1.1571. Differently from the case that superimposes a constant inflation target, if the monetary authority had increased the degree of reaction to the deviation of inflation from its time-varying target both the level and variance of inflation would have been lower, at 2.2 per cent instead of 2.3 per cent and 0.0260 instead of 0.0273 respectively, while output growth would have remained substantially unchanged. Finally, Figure 2.7(c) displays the counterfactual case where the monetary authority would have increased by 5 per cent its reaction to deviations of output from its steady state, such that ρ_y equals 0.1291. Under this scenario, inflation would have been substantially unchanged from its historical counterpart, while output growth would have displayed higher volatility, with its variance equal to 0.0418 instead of 0.0138. This analysis suggests that the degree to which the monetary authority reacted to inflation deviations from the inflation target would have contributed to a decrease in the variance of inflation and output growth and also to a lower level of inflation. On the other hand, the introduction of a constant inflation target or a monetary policy that would have reacted strongly to output would have been unlikely to produce a different economic outlook. These findings are in line with numerous related studies on other economies. For instance, Clarida et al. (2000), Boivin and Giannoni (2006), Lubik and Schorfheide (2004) and Castelnuovo (2007) find that by responding more strongly to inflation, monetary policy has stabilised the US economy more effectively in the post-1980 period. Gambetti and Pappa (2008), using sign restrictions on a VAR, find that the introduction of inflation targeting is unable to explain the reduced volatility of inflation in several economies.

2.7 Conclusion

This chapter has developed a general equilibrium model that details the functioning of the UK economy during the 1970s and 1980s to investigate to what extent labour market reforms enforced by the Thatcher government in the later 1980s, in the form of reduction of unemployment benefits and union power, and the introduction of a constant inflation target in 1992, might have changed the economic outlook if they had been introduced in the early 1970s. The econometric estimation of the model has permitted us to separate out the policy parameters, such as those representing monetary policy and the structure of the labour market, which may vary due to changes in policy, from those which represent the household's preference and firm's technology that ought to be policy-invariant. Hence, the model positively answers Lucas' (1976) critique and can be used to draw inferences about how these policy changes might have altered the economic outlook. The exercise shows that the decreases in unemployment benefits and union power are unlikely to have produced a different macroeconomic performance. The results on monetary policy reform are mixed. A stronger reaction to inflation deviations from target would have lowered the volatility of inflation and output growth. By contrast, the introduction of a constant inflation target or a monetary policy that had reacted strongly to output fluctuations are unlikely to have changed the economic outlook.

But while the results do support the importance of the way in which the monetary authority reacts to inflation, it should also be noted that the model abstracts from some relevant attributes of the economy. For instance, it ignores the oil sector, which, as Blanchard and Galì (2007) and Nakov and Pescatori (2010) point out, may alter the propagation of exogenous disturbances and therefore interact with the policy changes to reduce macroeconomic volatility. Similarly, the model also sets aside important developments of the period, such as improved inventory management, as emphasised in McConnell and Perez-Quiros (2000), or the development of financial innovations, as pointed out by Dynan et al. (2006), whose presence may also have a non-trivial effect on the way in which the economy reacts to policy changes and how these interact with aggregate disturbances. Furthermore, although the model developed here allows aggregate productivity, cost-push shocks and nominal disturbances to have effects on the economy, in practice a variety of other aggregate shocks may play a role. To establish to what extent the results hold for refinements of the theoretical framework remains an outstanding task for future research.

References

Batini, N. and Nelson, E. (2009). 'The U.K.'s rocky road to stability', *Global Economic Studies*. Nova Science Publishers.

Benati, L. (2008). 'The Great Moderation: in the United Kingdom', *Journal of Money Credit and Banking*, 40, 121–148.

Bean, C. R. (1994). 'European unemployment: a survey', *Journal of Economic Literature*, 32, 573–619.

Bean, C. R. and Crafts, N. (1996). 'British economic growth since 1945: relative economic decline ... and renaissance?,' CEPR Discussion Papers 1092, C.E.P.R. Discussion Papers.

Bianchi, F., Mumtaz, H. and Surico, P. (2009). 'The UK great stability: a view from the term structure of interest rates', *Journal of Monetary Economics*, 56, 856–871.

Blanchflower, D.G. and Freeman, R.B. (1993). 'Did the Thatcher reforms change British labor market performance?' Conference paper. CEP/NIESR.

Blanchard, O. J. and Kahn, C. (1980). 'The solution of linear difference models under rational expectations', *Econometrica*, 48, 1305–1311.

Blanchard, O. J. and Galì, J. (2010). 'Labor markets and monetary policy: a new Keynesian model with unemployment', *American Economic Journal: Macroeconomics*, 2, 1–30.

(2007). The macroeconomic effects of oil price shocks: why are the 2000s so different from the 1970s? NBER Chapters. In: *International Dimensions of Monetary Policy*. National Bureau of Economic Research, Inc., pp. 373–421.

Boivin, J. and Giannoni, M. (2006). 'Has monetary policy become more effective?', *The Review of Economics and Statistics*, 88, 445–462.

Britton, E., Larsen, J. D. and Small, I. (2000). 'Imperfect competition and the dynamics of mark-ups', *Bank of England Working Paper No. 110.*

Canova, F., Gambetti, L. and Pappa, E. (2007). 'The structural dynamics of output growth and inflation: some international evidence', *The Economic Journal*, 117, C167–C191.

Castelnuovo, E. (2007). 'Assessing different drivers of the Great Moderation in the U.S', *University of Padua Working Paper Series.*

Chadha J. and Sun Q. (2008). Labour market search and monetary policy—a theoretical consideration. In: P. Arestis and J. McCombie (Eds). *Unemployment: Past and Present*. Palgrave Macmillan.

Christoffel, K., Kuester, K. and Linzert, T. (2006). 'Identifying the role of labor markets for monetary policy in an estimated DSGE model', *European Central Bank Working Paper No. 635.*

Clarida, R., Galì, J. and Gertler, M. (1998). 'Monetary policy rules in practice: some international evidence', *European Economic Review*, 42, 1033–1067.

(2000). 'Monetary policy rules and macroeconomic stability: evidence and some theory', *Quarterly Journal of Economics*, CXV, 147–180.

DiCecio R. and Nelson, E. (2007). 'An estimated DSGE model for the United Kingdom', *Federal Reserve Bank of St. Louis Review*, 89, 215–231.

Dynan K., Elmendorf D. W. and Sichel, D. E. (2006). 'Can financial innovation help to explain the reduced volatility of economic activity?', *Journal of Monetary Economics*, 53, 123–150.

Faccini, R., Millard, S. and Zanetti, F. (2013). 'Wage rigidities in an estimated dynamic, stochastic, general equilibrium model of the UK labour market,' *Manchester School, University of Manchester*, 1, 66–99, 09.

Friedman, M. (1968). Inflation: causes and consequences. In: *Dollars and Deficits: Living with America's Economic Problems*. Englewood Cliffs: Prentice-Hall.

Gambetti, L. and Pappa, E. (2008). 'To target inflation or not to target: a conditional answer', *Universitat Autònoma de Barcelona Working Paper*.

Gregory, M. (1998). 'Reforming the labour market: an assessment of the UK policies of the Thatcher era', *Australian Economic Review*, 31, 329–344.

Harrison, R. and Oomen, O. (2010). 'Evaluating and estimating a DSGE model for United Kingdom', *Bank of England Working Paper 380.*

Hosios, A. (1990). 'On the efficiency of matching and related models of search and unemployment', *Review of Economic Studies*, 57, 279–298.

Ireland, P. N. (2000). 'Interest rates, inflation, and Federal Reserve policy since 1980', *Journal of Money, Credit, and Banking*, 32, 417–434.

(2004). 'Technology shocks in the New Keynesian model', *Review of Economics and Statistics*, 86, 923–936.

(2007). 'Changes in the Federal Reserve's inflation target: causes and consequences', *Journal of Money, Credit, and Banking*, 39, 1851–1882.

Jolivet, G., Postel-Vinay, F. and Robin, J. M. (2006). 'The empirical content of the job search model: labor mobility and wage distributions in Europe and the US', *European Economic Review*, 50, 877–907.

Kamber, G. and Millard, S. (2008). *Understanding the Monetary Transmission Mechanism in the United Kingdom: The Role of Nominal and Real Rigidities*. Bank of England: Mimeo.

Klein, P. (2000). 'Using the generalized Schur form to solve a multivariate linear rational expectations model', *Journal of Economic Dynamics and Control*, 24, 1405–1423.

Lubik, T. and Schorfheide, F. (2004). 'Testing for indeterminacy: an application to US monetary policy', *American Economic Review*, 94, 190–217.

Lucas, R. E., Jr. (1976). 'Econometric policy evaluation: a critique', *Carnegie-Rochester Conference Series on Public Policy*, 1, 19–46.

McConnell, M. and Perez-Quiros G. (2000). 'Output fluctuations in the United States: What has changed since the early 1980's?', *American Economic Review*, 90, 1464–1476.

Millward, N., Stevens, M., Smart, D. and Hawes, W.R. (1992). *Workplace Industrial Relations in Transition: The ED/ESRC/PSI/ACAS Surveys*. Aldershot: Dartmouth Publishing.

Minford, P. (1983). *Unemployment—Cause and Cure*. Oxford: Martin Robertson.

Nakov A. and Pescatori A. (2010). 'Oil and the Great Moderation', *Economic Journal*, 120, 131–156.

Nelson, E. (2003). UK monetary policy 1972–97: a guide using Taylor rules. In: Mizen, P. (Ed.). *Central Banking, Monetary Theory and Practice: Essays in Honour of Charles Goodhart, Volume One*. Cheltenham, UK: Edward Elgar, pp. 195–216.

Nickell, S. (1997). 'Unemployment and labor market rigidities: Europe versus North America', *The Journal of Economic Perspectives*, 11, 55–74.

Petrongolo, B. and Pissarides, C. (2001). 'Looking into the black box: a survey of the matching function', *Journal of Economic Literature*, 38, 390–431.

Pissarides, C. (2000). *Equilibrium Unemployment Theory*. MIT Press.

Ravenna, F. and Walsh, C. (2008). 'Vacancies, unemployment and the Phillips curve', *European Economic Review*, 52, 1494–1521.

Rotemberg, J. (1982). 'Monopolistic price adjustment and aggregate output', *The Review of Economic Studies*, 49, 517–531.

Smets, F. and Wouters, R. (2007). 'Shocks and frictions in US business cycles: a Bayesian DSGE approach', *American Economic Review*, 97, 586–606.

Steinsson, J. (2003). 'Optimal monetary policy in an economy with inflation persistence', *Journal of Monetary Economics*, 50, 1425–1456.

Taylor, J. (1993). 'Discretion versus policy rules in practice', *Carnegie-Rochester Conference Series on Public Policy*, 39, 195–214.

Woodford, M. (2003). *Interest and Prices: Foundations of a Theory of Monetary Policy*. Princeton University Press.

Zanetti, F. (2008). 'Labor and investment frictions in a real business cycle model', *Journal of Economic Dynamics and Control, Elsevier*, 32(10), 3294–3314.

(2009). 'Effects of product and labor market regulation on macroeconomic outcomes', *Journal of Macroeconomics*, 31, 320–332.

(2011). 'Labor market institutions and aggregate fluctuations in a search and matching model', *European Economic Review*, 55, 644–658.

3 Property income and the balance of payments

Tomas Key, Varun Paul, Martin Weale and Tomasz Wieladek

3.1 Introduction

Concerns about the UK's balance of payments position have a long history. For most of the period of the Bretton Woods system there was a sense that the balance of payments constrained the ability of the economy to grow (Houthakker and Magee, 1969). The end of the fixed exchange rate system in 1972 raised the hope that the balance of payments might become self-equilibrating. Certainly balance of payments crises, of the type that the UK had faced in the 1950s and 1960s and in some respects similar to the more recent problems of countries in the euro Area, have affected the UK since sterling started to float.[1]

Nevertheless, in the years leading up to the global financial crisis the UK sustained a balance of payments deficit of the order of 2% of GDP; doubts about the sustainability of this might have been thought to have been a factor behind the sharp fall of sterling in 2007/08. The depreciation did not, however, have the impact on the trade balance which was hoped for. Since the crisis the balance of payments deficit has increased. An important factor behind the worsening of the balance of payments deficit has been a decline in net income from abroad. In 2012 this was lower, by about 2% of GDP, than it had been in 2007.

In this chapter we explore the phenomenon whereby the UK was able, despite a trade deficit and apparent net external liabilities, both to earn a positive balance of net income from abroad and to improve its net external position. We then use a VAR framework to quantify the shocks which might account for both the relatively favourable level of net income before the crisis and the sharp decline in the five years following the crisis.

The views expressed here are those of the authors and not those of the Monetary Policy Committee or the Bank of England.

1 In 1976 concerns about the UK's inflation prospects did lead to a sharp fall in sterling. Monetary policy was tightened sharply to support sterling and in that sense the situation was not very different from what might have been expected with fixed exchange rates.

A VAR framework offers a means of exploring these issues. It is often suggested that the attractiveness of a country to foreign investors depends on the extent to which markets are regulated. It may also be the case that the UK's net income from abroad, and in particular, any capacity to borrow more cheaply than it lends, might be a function of regulation. But, if this is the case, these influences need to be reflected in the VAR. And furthermore, estimation needs to take account of the possibility that they have non-linear effects, affecting the way in which the economy responds to different disturbances. It is possible, for example, that financial deregulation made it easier for the country to earn high returns from a low asset base, because it attracted skilled financiers to the City of London.

We develop a panel framework which allows us to explore these issues. The panel approach has the advantage over working only with the UK that there is more variation in the data and thus that it is possible to determine the effects of regulatory changes more satisfactorily. This builds on earlier work which has shown that the way in which countries respond to shocks depends on their regulatory structures. For example Assenmacher-Wesche and Gerlach (2010) estimate panel VARs for two groups of countries and find that responses to shocks depend on the flexibility of financial markets. Calza et al. (2013) come to similar conclusions when looking at mortgage markets.

In Section 3.2 we describe the evolution of the UK's net asset position, its current balance and its net receipts of income from abroad. We present estimates of how rates of return on the UK's assets differ from those on its liabilities. Section 3.3 presents our econometric analysis of the relationship between regulation and net income from abroad. Section 3.4 concludes.

3.2 Property income and the balance of payments puzzle

The puzzle posed by the UK's external position in the ten years before the crisis can be easily set out. Figure 3.1 shows two variables. The first is net external assets as a proportion of GDP. The second is a hypothetical value which net assets, as a proportion of GDP, would have taken if the asset position had built up simply by adding the current account balance to the net balance of the previous year. Obviously movements in net assets arise from capital gains and losses as well as from current account surpluses or deficits. The downward slope of the cumulated current account position shown in Figure 3.1 reflects a steady annual current account deficit. The net asset position, however, appears to be stationary. The implication is that there have been systematic capital gains.

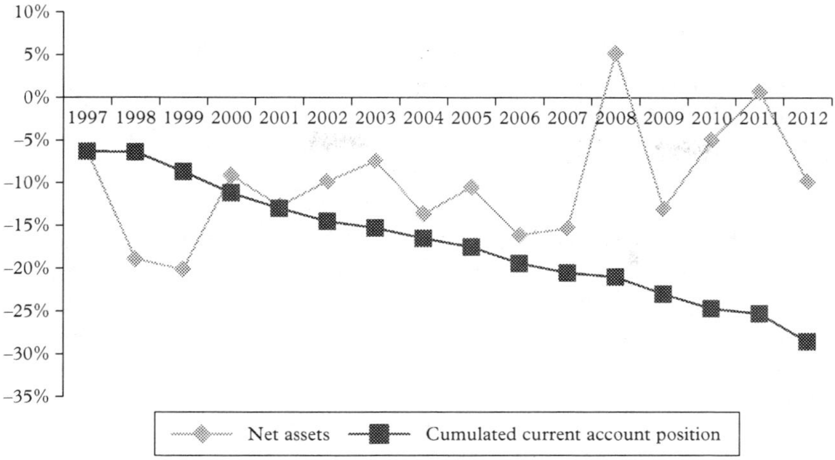

Figure 3.1. Net assets, net income and the UK current account (% of GDP)

Accounting conventions define the boundary between capital gains and property income, and reflect a general sense that capital gains are one-off while income is more likely to be stable. The pattern, which has persisted over 15 years might, however, lead to the view that positive capital gains can be expected and that these might therefore be seen as unobserved property income. Since 1997 the UK seems to have earned capital gains or unidentified income worth nearly 20% of 2012 GDP despite the fact that its net asset position is shown as a debtor.

3.2.1 *Rates of return and capital gains*

Gourinchas et al. (2010) provide a detailed international comparison of the rates of return earned by different countries on their foreign investments. They work with the four categories of foreign assets identified in the balance of payments statistics: foreign direct investment, equity and debt portfolio investment and other assets and liabilities. The latter include the network of assets and liabilities generated by cross-border banking, which has become such an important feature of the UK's economy. To the extent that different countries can choose a mix of assets different from their mix of liabilities, it is possible to influence the return on net assets, in much the same way as a bank aims to borrow cheaply and lend out or invest what it borrows at a higher rate of return. But the figures produced by Gourinchas et al. suggest that the USA earns higher returns than it pays on each category of foreign assets. So, even without any mismatch between the composition of its assets and its liabilities, it would enjoy an income account which was particularly favourable given its asset position. They describe this as 'exorbitant privilege', the term adopted by M. Giscard d'Estaing in the 1960s to describe the USA's ability to run a current account deficit.[2]

But Pratten (1996) and Nickell (2006) have argued that official external asset figures are subject to a distortion arising from the fact that foreign investment is valued at book values rather than market values. The consequences of retained profits are reflected, because, for foreign-owned firms, all profits are treated as remitted to the owner, with retained profits then being counted back as capital flows. But changes in the notional market value of foreign direct investment are not transmitted to the official statistics.

Pratten estimated the extent of the misvaluation of the UK's foreign direct investment position, by comparing the book values of the relevant investments with the stock market valuations of the relevant companies. For a UK business with direct investment abroad, he assumed that the overall market value of the company, as measured by its stock market value, was split in proportion to the ratio of the average of domestic to foreign profits over a three-year period. After making subjective adjustments for biases he thought present in his calculations, he suggested that, in 1991, UK foreign investment abroad was worth about 75% more than its book value, while foreign direct investment in the UK was worth about 50% more than its book value.

Colleagues of ours at the Bank of England have produced updated series for UK investment abroad and foreign investment in Britain, on the assumption that investment values move in line with the stock markets of the countries where they have taken place (updating the work described by Elliott and Wong Min (2004)). Adjustments for the effects of exchange rate changes are also made. The book and market value foreign direct investment data are shown in Figure 3.2, while the overall impact on net foreign assets can be deduced from Figure 3.3.

These figures show the country as a significant net creditor because (1) Britain has, even on ONS figures, a positive balance in foreign direct investment, and (2) Britain's overseas assets are upvalued by more than foreign investment in Britain. Plainly, it becomes easier to understand why Britain should run a net surplus on the income account

2 M. d'Estaing arguably meant something rather different – that since the reserve currency was the US dollar in the Bretton Woods system, the USA did not face problems financing its deficit, while other countries with similar deficits would have faced financing problems.

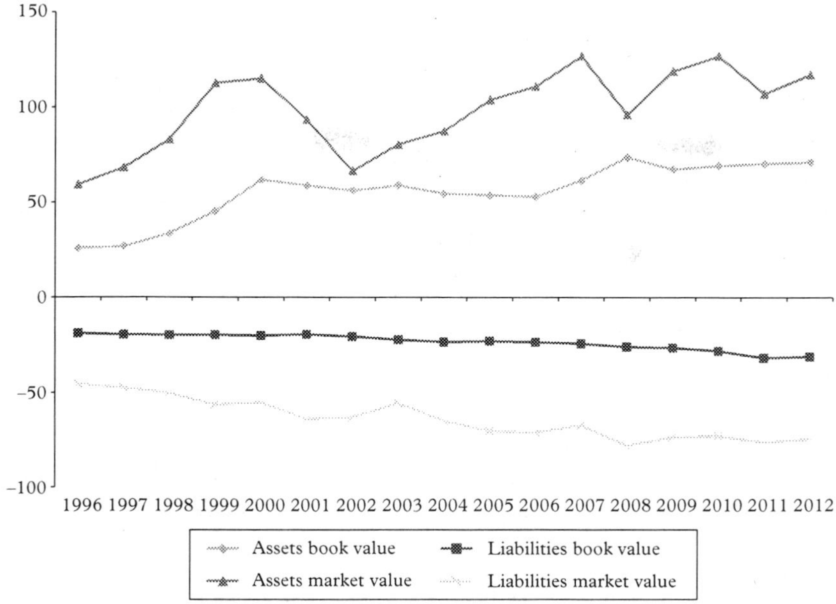

Figure 3.2. Foreign direct investment: assets and liabilities at book and market values (% of GDP)

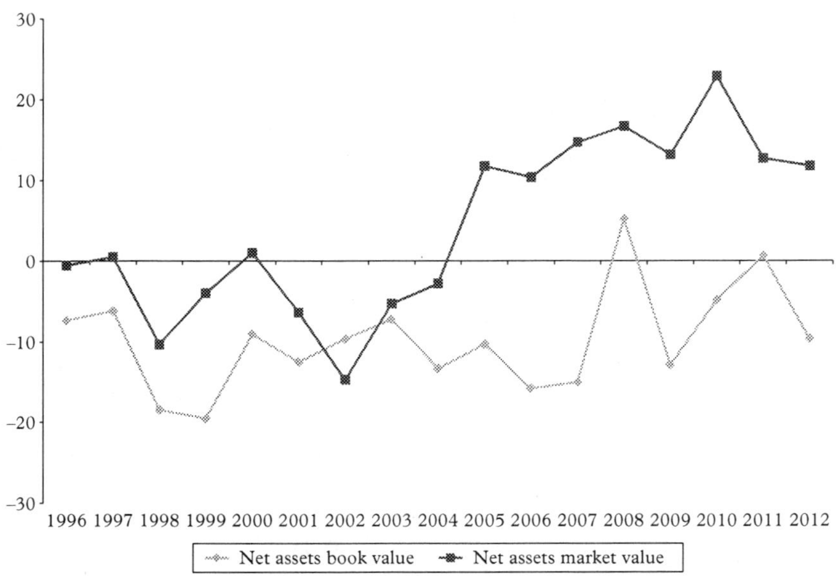

Figure 3.3. Net foreign assets with foreign investment at book and market values (% of GDP)

if it is actually a net creditor. But that does not, on its own, account for the fact that the net external balance seems to have improved even while Britain was running an external deficit. The true surplus on the property income account needs to be larger than the deficit on the balance of trade and on transfer income.

We proceed to examining the real rates of return on Britain's assets and liabilities, with the returns on foreign direct investment calculated using the series adjusted to market values. We also show, however, estimates computed from the published book values, so that the effects of the adjustment to market values are clear.

3.3 The rate of return on Britain's external assets and liabilities

Table 3.1 shows implied real rates of return for the period from 1997Q1 to 2007Q4, while Table 3.2 shows the analogous figures for the period from 2008Q1 to 2013Q3. But, making the distinction suggested by Gourinchas et al. (2010), Habib (2010) suggests that none of the other advanced economies, including the UK, enjoy the return effect and that only the USA can enjoy exorbitant privilege. However, UK data have been substantially revised since Habib (2010) completed his study. Tables 3.1 and 3.2 show the returns on the different types of asset, both for the period from 1997–2007 and for 2008–11. The returns are

Table 3.1. Rates of return on UK external assets and liabilities, 1997–2007 (% annualised)

	UK assets		**UK liabilities**			
	Ex gains	**Inc gains**	**Ex gains**	**Inc gains**	**Share of total assets**	**Share of total liabilities**
FDI	5.4	8.5	3.7	5.3	25.9	17.4
Equity	2.6	6.6	2.9	9.0	10.8	14.0
Debt	4.8	6.0	4.9	4.0	14.2	12.7
All long-term investment	4.6	7.3	3.7	5.6	50.8	44.1
Other	3.0	6.9	3.4	6.9	49.2	55.9
All	3.7	7.0	3.5	6.3	100	100
Memo FDI book value	*10.0*	*7.9*	*7.5*	*3.8*		
Memo all with FDI book value	*4.2*	*7.0*	*3.9*	*6.3*		
Excess return on assets		0.7				
Excess return with FDI book value		*0.6*				

Table 3.2. Returns on UK external assets and liabilities: 2008Q1–2013Q3 (% annualised)

	UK assets		UK liabilities			
	Ex gains	**Inc gains**	**Ex gains**	**Inc gains**	**Share of total assets**	**Share of total liabilities**
FDI	4.6	1.3	3.0	1.0	16.3	10.6
Equity	2.6	6.5	3.2	1.4	6.6	8.0
Debt	2.8	6.8	2.9	3.8	12.3	15.0
All long-term investment	3.6	4.0	3.0	2.2	35.2	33.5
Other	0.8	4.0	1.0	3.8	64.8	66.5
All	1.8	4.0	1.7	3.4	100	100
Memo FDI book value	*7.7*	*7.2*	*4.4*	*5.3*		
Memo all with FDI book value	*1.9*	*4.9*	*1.7*	*3.8*		
Excess returns on assets		0.6				
Excess return with FDI book value		*1.1*				

calculated both from reported income alone and after taking account of capital gains. The latter are calculated from the residuals needed to reconcile the published figures for transactions in assets with the balance sheet data provided by ONS. Thus they include measurement errors and discrepancies. These may be particularly marked for 'other' assets. These data suggest that returns including gains seem to be mostly higher on UK assets than on UK liabilities, although this was not true of equity in the period 1997–2007, and the returns on 'other' assets and liabilities were equal then. Total returns, including those earned from the fact that, relative to UK liabilities, the composition of UK assets is biased towards high-yielding forms of investment (the composition effect) on UK assets exceeded those on liabilities by 0.7% per annum in the period from 1997–2007 and by 0.6% from 2008 onwards. The very high capital gains associated with other assets and liabilities between 2008 and 2011 are, as noted above, derived by comparing reported assets transactions with reported balances, and there is more than a small risk that they may be artefacts resulting from misrecording.

Looked at overall, the information available on the UK's external assets and liabilities suggests, in contrast to the findings of Habib (2010), that the excess return comes from a return effect rather than a composition effect. Between 1997 and 2007 our calculations show that differences in the composition of external assets and liabilities are not the cause of the excess return, whilst between 2008Q1 we find that this composition effect is actually negative (–0.5%).

This suggests that the UK, like the USA, enjoys favourable returns on its investments rather than biasing its investments towards the broad categories which offer the highest measured returns. Capital gains, on top of flows of investment income, have offered a second means by which the UK's external position has financed itself. But, as we noted earlier, it is not possible to say whether this is the consequence of the skill of the UK's investing community or it is simply because they run greater risks with the UK's overseas investments than do the foreigners who invest in the UK.

The sterling depreciation of 2007 is an interesting case study, however. Just as the financial crisis weakened equity markets around the world, the UK's specialisation in financial services resulted in a disproportionately large fall in UK equities. Meanwhile, while UK investors suffered a reduction in the return on their foreign investments, the depreciation raised the sterling value of those foreign assets by up to 25%, providing a substantial revaluation of the UK's net external asset position.

3.4 Econometric analysis: regulation and income flows

These observations raise the question of whether one can say rather more about the factors which have contributed to the UK's favourable balance of payments position over the last 20 years. We examine, in particular, whether changes in the regulatory environment in the UK have influenced the net income balance. We do this by estimating a Bayesian Panel VAR for advanced economies. In this VAR we study the interaction between real consumption growth, inflation, the short rate of interest, net income from abroad and the real exchange rate.[3] Thus our model, although not structural, represents the interactions between the key monetary and real forces of each domestic economy with the net income variable. The model is estimated on data for 13 OECD countries. We estimate allowing for the possibility that changes in regulatory structure affect the parameters by which the endogenous variables influence each other.

3.4.1 Regulatory variables

We explore whether the VAR coefficients vary with the degree of exchange rate flexibility, financial, labour and product market deregulation. We describe each index in turn. Figure 3.4 shows the financial

3 CPI and real exchange rate data were taken from the OECD Main Economic Indicators and the BIS effective exchange rate database, respectively. The remaining variables were taken from the OECD Economic Outlook database.

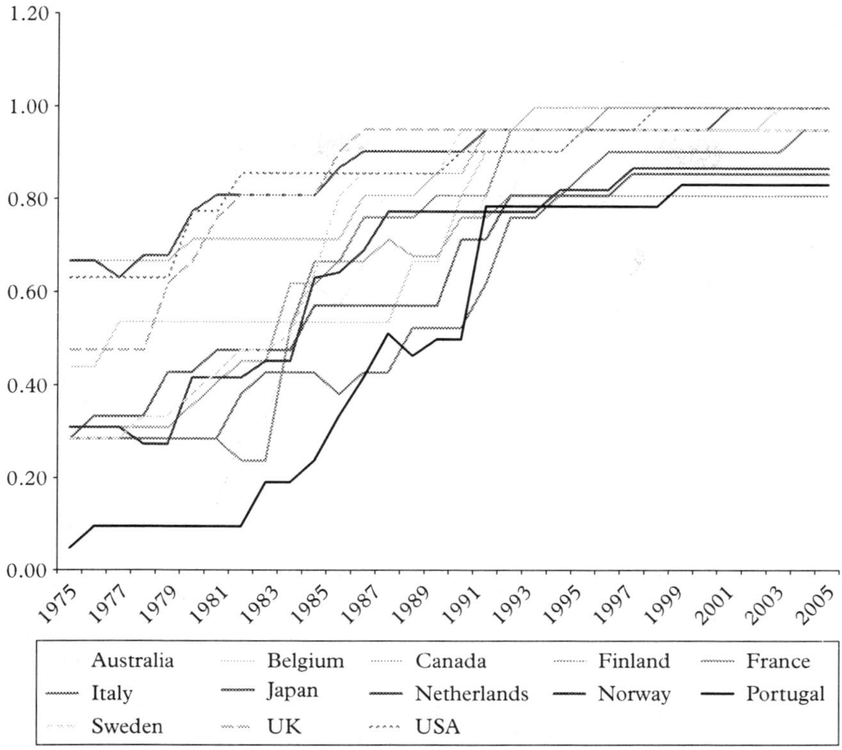

Figure 3.4. Index of financial liberalisation
Source: Abiad et al. (2010). Higher values indicate greater liberalisation.

liberalisation index for each of countries in our study. This is taken from Abiad et al. (2010) and has seven different components of the dataset. These are credit controls, interest rate controls, entry barriers, state ownership in the banking sector, prudential regulation, securities market policy and capital account restrictions. Each component can take the values {0, 1, 2, 3}, with higher values meaning fewer restrictions. We sum all components to come up with the aggregate financial liberalisation index we use in our empirical exercise. This index is normalised to 1.

As a proxy for product market regulation (Figure 3.5) we use the ETCR index constructed by Conway et al. (2006). This captures the level of regulation in seven non-manufacturing sectors: airlines, telecommunication, electricity, gas, post, rail and road freight. These sectors represent a substantial proportion of economic activity and the area in which domestic economic regulation is most concentrated and has a major impact due to limited import competition. The index

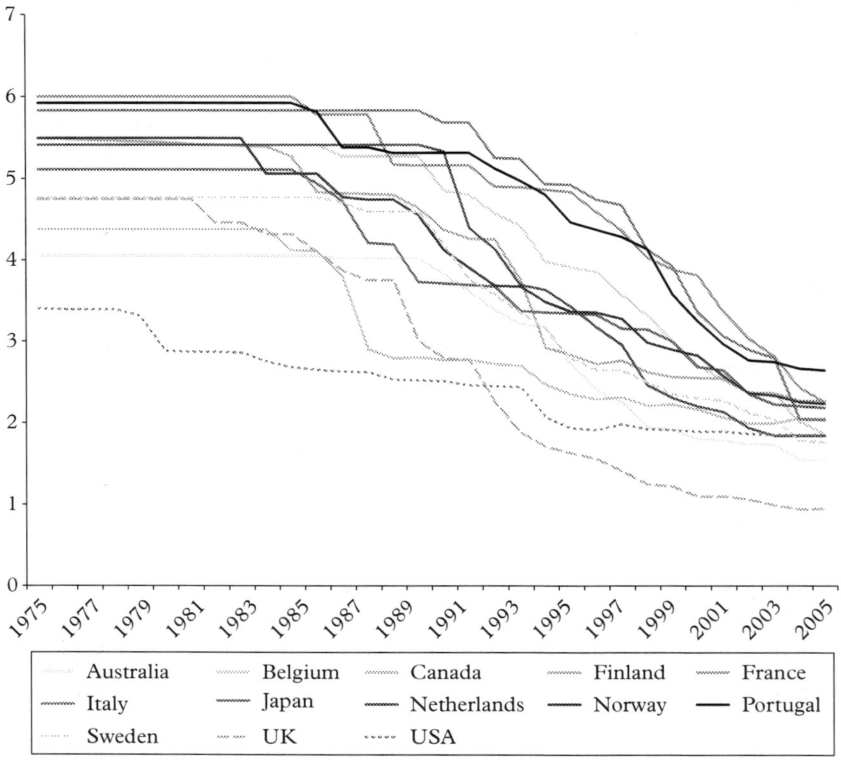

Figure 3.5. Index of product market liberalisation
Source: Conway et al. (2006). Lower values indicate greater liberalisation.

takes into account characteristics of the markets, such as the presence of barriers to entry, public ownership, vertical integration, monopolies and the presence of legally imposed price controls, which typically distort competition in these sectors.

The index of labour market liberalisation (Figure 3.6) broadly reflects minimum wage regulation, hiring and firing practices, the share of the labour force whose wages are set by centralised collective bargaining, unemployment benefits and the use of conscription to obtain military personnel.

The indicator of exchange rate regime flexibility (Figure 3.7) is taken from Ilzetzki et al. (2008). Finally, our VAR model consists of five endogenous variables: Quarterly real consumption growth, CPI inflation, the short-term interest rate, the current account to GDP ratio and the real effective exchange rate.

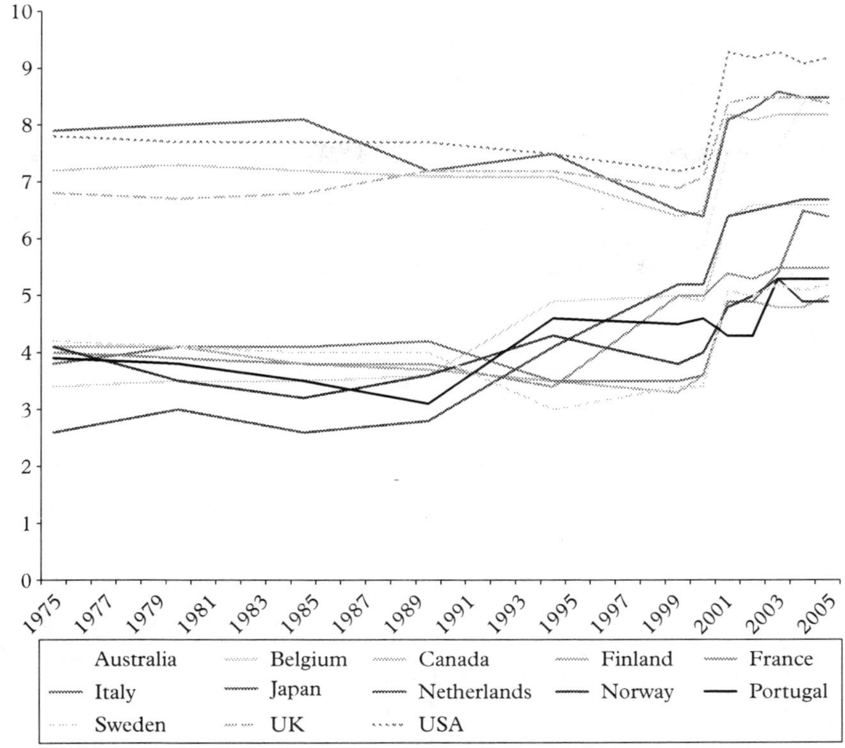

Figure 3.6. Index of labour market liberalisation
Source: Fraser Institute. Higher values mean greater liberalisation.

3.4.2 *The varying-coefficient Bayesian Panel VAR model*

We are interested in examining how changes in the structure of the macro-economy affect the economic structure in OECD countries so as to be able to infer from this how the UK may have been affected. Previous work relied on either time-series information within individual countries or cross-sectional differences across countries to answer questions of this type. Some recent work has used the 'interacted panel VAR' approach (IPVAR) to exploring the role of changes in regulatory structures (Abbritti and Weber, 2010; Towbin and Weber, 2013). But this approach assumes that all of the heterogeneity in coefficients is explained by the differences in regulatory frameworks. There is no room for other variation in the coefficients either between countries or over time.

If this assumption is violated, the estimates will be subject to dynamic heterogeneity bias (Pesaran and Smith, 1995). Sa et al. (2014) use the

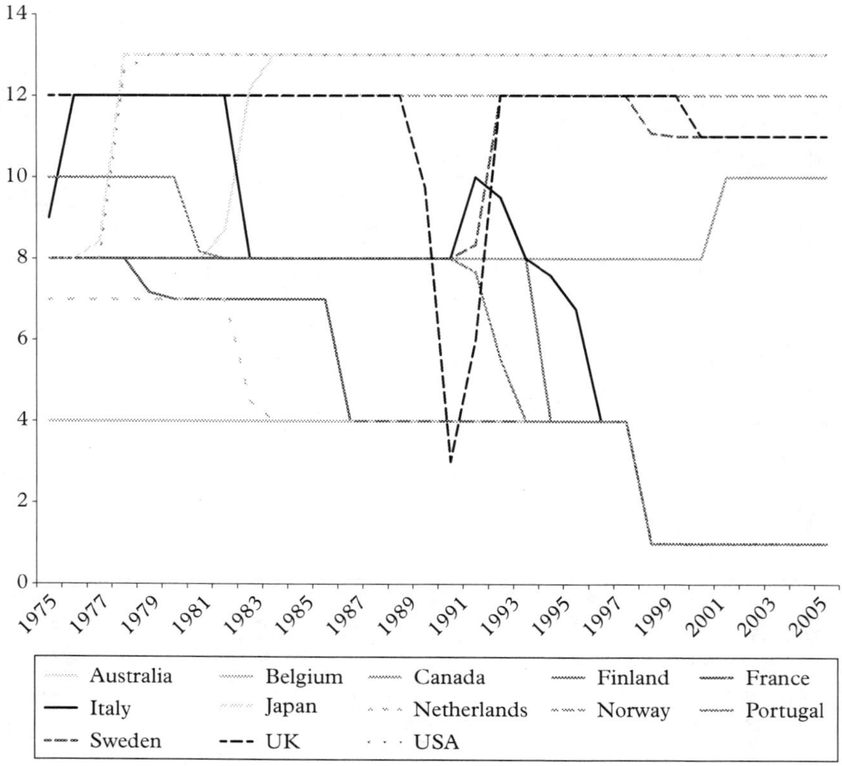

Figure 3.7. Index of exchange rate flexibility
Source: Ilzetzki et al. (2008). Higher values indicate greater flexibility.

mean group estimator to address this potential problem, but since that approach requires estimation country-by-country, degrees of freedom considerations typically constrain the number of structural characteristics that can be analysed to two. Wieladek (2015) proposes a Bayesian shrinkage approach to estimating panel VAR models where the coefficients are functions of other exogenous variables. Since his approach allows for both dynamic heterogeneity and multiple structural characteristics, this is the econometric approach that we choose to follow. It delivers a random effects estimator; the structure resulting from Bayesian shrinkage permits random variation both across countries and over time.

Here we follow the approach outlined in Wieladek (2015) and model the individual VAR coefficients as functions of the exchange rate regime and the financial, product and labour market deregulation in each country within a panel data structure.

We estimate the following panel VAR[4] model:

$$\boldsymbol{Y}_{c,t} = \boldsymbol{X}_{c,t}\boldsymbol{B}_{c,\tau} + \boldsymbol{k}_{c,\tau} + \boldsymbol{e}_{c,t} \qquad e_{(c,t)} \sim N(0, A'_{c,\tau}\boldsymbol{\Sigma}_c\boldsymbol{A}_{c,\tau}) \tag{3.1}$$

$$\boldsymbol{B}_{c,\tau} = \boldsymbol{B}_0 + \boldsymbol{D}_{c,\tau}\delta_{\boldsymbol{B}} + \boldsymbol{u}_{\boldsymbol{B}c,\tau} \qquad \boldsymbol{u}_{\boldsymbol{B}c,\tau} \sim \boldsymbol{N}(0, \Lambda_{\boldsymbol{B}c}) \tag{3.2}$$

$$\boldsymbol{k}_{c,\tau} = \boldsymbol{k}_0 + \boldsymbol{D}_{c,\tau}\delta_{\boldsymbol{k}} + \boldsymbol{u}_{\boldsymbol{k}c,\tau} \qquad \boldsymbol{u}_{\boldsymbol{k}c,\tau} \sim \boldsymbol{N}(0, \Lambda_{\boldsymbol{k}c}) \tag{3.3}$$

$$\boldsymbol{A}_{c,\tau} = \boldsymbol{A}_0 + \boldsymbol{D}_{c,\tau}\delta_{A} + \boldsymbol{u}_{Ac,\tau} \qquad \boldsymbol{u}_{Ac,\tau} \sim \boldsymbol{N}(0, \Lambda_{Ac}) \tag{3.4}$$

where $\boldsymbol{Y}_{c,t}$ is a matrix with N endogenous variables in the columns at time t, in country c, with the total number of countries C. $\boldsymbol{X}_{c,t}$ contains the lags of the variables in $\boldsymbol{Y}_{c,t}$ and for country $\boldsymbol{c}$ at time t. $\boldsymbol{B}_{c,\tau}$ is the array of associated coefficients for country $\boldsymbol{c}$ at time $\boldsymbol{\tau}$ and $\boldsymbol{k}_{c,\tau}$ the array of terms which are independent of the endogenous variables of the model. We assume that the corresponding matrix of VAR residuals $\boldsymbol{e}_{c,t}$ is distributed with zero mean and a covariance matrix that is the product of the lower triangular matrix $\boldsymbol{A}_{c,\tau}$ and a diagonal matrix of structural shocks $\boldsymbol{\Sigma}_c$, which is assumed to be normally distributed. $\boldsymbol{B}_{c,\tau}$, $\boldsymbol{k}_{c,\tau}$ and $\boldsymbol{A}_{c,\tau}$ are modelled as linear functions of exogenous variables $\boldsymbol{D}_{c,\tau}$ with the associated coefficients $\boldsymbol{\delta_B}$ and $\boldsymbol{\delta_A}$, respectively. It is important to note that we allow the variables in $\boldsymbol{D}_{c,\tau}$ to vary at a lower frequency, since most economic liberalisation indicators are at annual, as opposed to quarterly, frequency. Our model therefore naturally deals with such mixed frequency issues. In that case, $\boldsymbol{D}_{c,\tau} = \frac{\sum_{l=1}^{Z} \boldsymbol{D}_{c,t-l}}{Z}$, where $Z = 4$. Our labour market indicator is only available every five years up until 2000. We therefore set $Z = 20$, meaning that most of the other annual indicators are five-year averages for the corresponding annual indicators. In other words, if the sample period starts in 1976, then $\boldsymbol{D}_{c,1}$ is the average for 1976–81. $\boldsymbol{B}_{c,\tau}$, $\boldsymbol{k}_{c,\tau}$ and $\boldsymbol{A}_{c,\tau}$ would then be the corresponding array of coefficients for that period. A second advantage of this approach is that five-year averages of these indicators are less likely to be endogenous with respect to the business cycle and monetary policy specifically, and hence more likely to satisfy the assumptions of the model.

Previous work has adopted three different ways of estimating panel VAR models with the structure as set out in Eqs. (3.1)–(3.3). Abbritti and Weber (2010) and Towbin and Weber (2013) assume that $\boldsymbol{u}_{\boldsymbol{B}c,\tau} = 0$ and $\boldsymbol{u}_{Ac,\tau} = 0$, which means that the vector of exogenous coefficients can explain all of the country-specific variation in $\boldsymbol{B}_{c,\tau}$, $\boldsymbol{k}_{c,\tau}$ and $\boldsymbol{A}_{c,\tau}$.

4 The description of most the components of our proposed model closely follows the presentation of Jarocinski (2010) and Wieladek (2014). See their work for more details on the remaining parts of the model.

In that case Eqs. (3.2)–(3.4) can be substituted back into Eq. (3.1) and the model can be easily estimated via OLS equation by equation. But if this assumption is violated, as it is likely to be in practice, estimating the model with country fixed effects will lead to dynamic heterogeneity bias (Pesaran and Smith, 1995).

Sa et al. (2014) use the mean group estimator to address this problem. But to the extent that this approach requires estimation country-by-country, modelling variation in coefficients as a set of more than two exogenous variables is typically not feasible, even in moderately sized VARs, due to degree of freedom considerations. Wieladek (2015) proposes Bayesian shrinkage[5] for estimating this type of model by extending the hierarchical linear model approach presented in Jarocinski (2010). This is similar to the Litterman (1986) prior assumption popular in economic forecasting, but rather than shrinking towards a random walk, coefficients are shrunk towards a set of explanatory variables. Given that this approach allows for both multiple interaction terms and dynamic heterogeneity, this is the approach we choose to follow. The model is estimated by repeatedly drawing from the posteriors of the Gibbs sampling chain 150,000 times, discarding the first 50,000 draws as burn-in and retaining one in a hundred of the remaining draws for inference.

3.4.3 Identification

Previous work has identified monetary policy shocks in Bayesian VAR models in two different ways. One strand of work imposes exclusion (zero) restrictions on the matrix of contemporaneous relationships, $\boldsymbol{A}_{c,t}$, typically in a lower triangular fashion.[6] Consumption growth and CPI inflation are ordered before the interest rate, which means that the main identification assumption is that real activity and prices react with a lag to monetary shocks. In larger VAR systems, it is less clear how to order

5 Bayesian econometricians typically impose priors on the underlying econometric model to make estimation feasible when degrees of freedom are limited. Shrinkage then refers to both the process and the degree to which the model priors are superimposed on the data. In our example, our prior belief is that the coefficients in Eq. (3.1) evolve according to Eqs. (3.2)–(3.4), with the corresponding variance matrices, Λ_{Bc}, Λ_{kc}, Λ_{Ac} determining the weight that is put on these priors. Smaller variance matrices imply that the econometrician wants to put more weight on the model structure and less weight on the data. In other words, smaller variance matrices imply greater shrinkage towards the priors. But setting these variance matrices pre-estimation is to a certain extent arbitrary. This is why, as discussed in the main text, the degree of shrinkage is treated as a parameter that is estimated in our approach.

6 See Sims (1980) for a first application and Christiano et al. (1999) for a survey on this approach.

the remaining variables. An advantage of this approach is that both the number, as well as the ordering, of restrictions imply that the VAR system is globally identified, meaning that parameters obtained with these restrictions are globally unique within the likelihood function (Rubio-Ramirez et al., 2010). We therefore identify the monetary policy shock via a lower triangular decomposition of $\boldsymbol{A}_{c,t}$, with the short-term interest rate ordered after consumption and prices, but before the current account and the real exchange rate. Given that the interest rate is ordered after consumption and prices, our identification scheme encompasses the standard assumption that real activity only reacts to monetary policy with a lag. The second implicit assumption in this identification scheme is that the monetary policy authority reacts only with a lag to the real exchange rate and to movements in income from abroad.

3.5 Results: the income balance of the UK

This model makes it possible to address two questions of interest. First of all, what contribution has each of the shocks made to the net income balance? And secondly, how far have changes in the regulatory structure in the UK affected the net income balance? Since we now focus on the UK, we drop the country subscript. We also simplify the exposition by setting out the algebra on the assumption that there is only one lag rather than the four actually present in our model. We have also represented the time-varying components of the coefficients by subscripts showing the period to which they relate, notwithstanding that they change only every five years.

Based on Eqs. (3.1)–(3.4), it is possible to write the endogenous variables, $\boldsymbol{Y}_{c,t}$, as:

$$\boldsymbol{Y}_t = \prod_{j=1}^{t} \boldsymbol{B}_j \boldsymbol{Y}_0 + \sum_{j=1}^{t-1} \prod_{\tau=j}^{t-1} \boldsymbol{B}_{\tau+1} \boldsymbol{k}_j + \boldsymbol{k}_t + \sum_{j=1}^{t-1} \prod_{\tau=j}^{t-1} \boldsymbol{B}_{\tau+1} \boldsymbol{A}_j \boldsymbol{u}_j + \boldsymbol{A}_t \boldsymbol{u}_t \qquad (3.5)$$

This standard historical decomposition allows us to calculate the structural shocks, $\boldsymbol{u}_t$ iteratively. We can then explain the path of each of the macroeconomic variables in terms of the movements in the constant terms, $\boldsymbol{k}_t$ and the structural shocks $\boldsymbol{u}_t$. All of these shocks are taken from our identification scheme, meaning that we can decompose each series into the contributions from real exchange rate (RFX), balance of payments income account (BoP), output, inflation and monetary policy shocks. The shocks do not, on their own, add to the data because there are additional components generated by the initial position and the constant terms. The latter, of course, themselves depend on the regulatory regime.

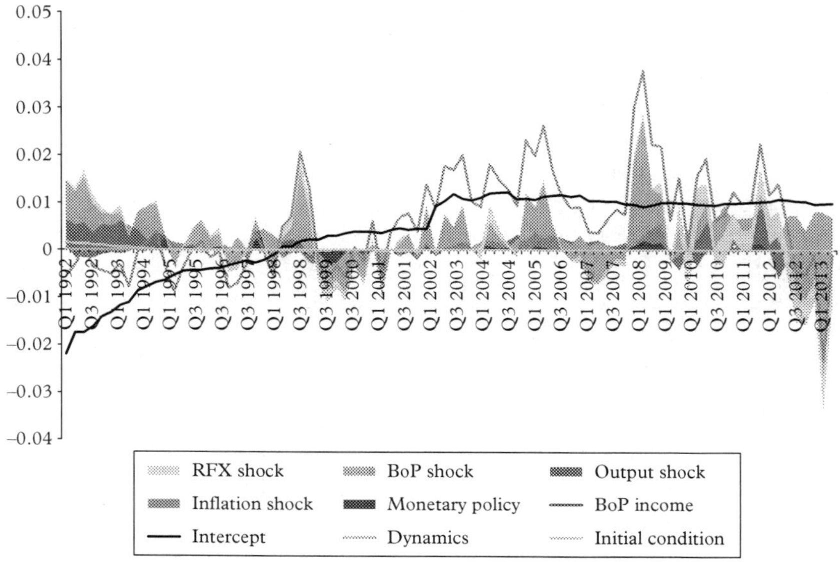

Figure 3.8. The contributions of shocks to the UK's net receipts of income from abroad

This suggests, perhaps not very surprisingly, that for most of the period short-term fluctuations were driven directly by shocks to the income account. In the period since the economic crisis, however, real exchange rate shocks have also played a role. But the model also shows, in the black line, the effects of the movements in the intercept which are a consequence of regulatory changes. If the model had only an invariant constant term, it would have settled down at a steady state by 1992 (in much the same way as the transient arising from the initial conditions in 1976 has died out by 1992). But because both the intercept terms and the other coefficients vary over time, the second and third terms of Eq. (3.13) are prone to movement. This suggests that a substantial component of the improvement in the net income flow between the early 1990s and the middle of the next decade is a consequence of regulatory movements.

Is this plausible? Looking at the results in more detail suggests that, while underlying changes over time have probably been important, it is not clear that the effects of time variation are in fact due to regulatory changes. The reasons for this can be seen by considering the long run of the model. The steady state of the system is, with the subscript T representing the parameter values associated with the regulatory regime

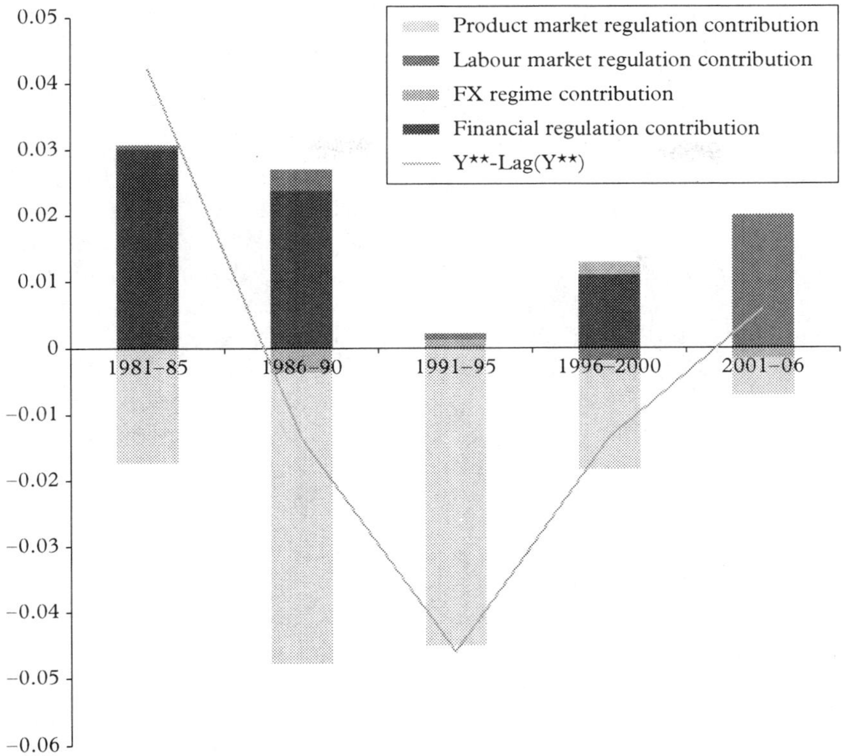

Figure 3.9. Changes in the steady state arising from changes in regulation

of quinquennium T and with the country subscript dropped for simplicity, given from Eq. (3.1), since, in the steady state $\mathbf{Y}_T = \mathbf{X}_T$, as

$$\boldsymbol{Y}_{\boldsymbol{T}}^{**} = (\boldsymbol{I} - \boldsymbol{B}_{\boldsymbol{T}})^{-1}\boldsymbol{k}_{\boldsymbol{T}}$$

If we write $\boldsymbol{B}_{\boldsymbol{T}} = \boldsymbol{B}_{\boldsymbol{T}-1} + \Delta\boldsymbol{B}_{\boldsymbol{T}}$ and $\boldsymbol{k}_{\boldsymbol{T}} = \boldsymbol{k}_{\boldsymbol{T}-1} + \Delta\boldsymbol{k}_{\boldsymbol{T}}$ we can then make use of a linear approximation to write

$$\boldsymbol{Y}_{\boldsymbol{T}}^{**} - \boldsymbol{Y}_{\boldsymbol{T}-1}^{**} \cong (\boldsymbol{I} - \boldsymbol{B}_{\boldsymbol{T}-1})^{-1}\Delta\boldsymbol{B}_{\boldsymbol{T}}(\boldsymbol{I} - \boldsymbol{B}_{\boldsymbol{T}-1})^{-1}\boldsymbol{k}_{\boldsymbol{T}-1} + (\boldsymbol{I} - \boldsymbol{B}_{\boldsymbol{T}-1})^{-1}\Delta\boldsymbol{k}_{\boldsymbol{T}} \tag{3.6}$$

Equation (3.6) is linear in the contributions made by changes to each type of regulation from one quinquennium to the next. We show the individual components in Figure 3.9.

These point to very large, but generally offsetting, effects from product market regulation and financial market regulation. Now it is plausible that deregulation of product markets has encouraged foreign investment in Britain and, as a result, led to an outflow of income to the rest of the world. Deregulation of financial markets might well have encouraged the development of the modern City institutions, and fostered their ability to earn more from the rest of the world than they pay for their financing, as Section 3.3 suggested. It is rather harder to see why a reduction in labour market regulation should have led to a marked upward movement in steady state income, except on the grounds that it led to an increase in supply which exceeded the associated increase in demand, and thus encouraged the accumulation of foreign assets. But the more general point is that the effects shown are large relative to the absolute value of net income from abroad shown in Figure 3.8, and indeed relative to the underlying gross inflows and outflows of income. So, while changes in the regulatory environment have probably been a favourable influence on the underlying external income account, there are probably some effects of time which have been correlated with the regulatory variables we have identified and which may also have played a role.

3.6 Conclusion

During the period of long expansion, Britain's balance of payments position was supported by net receipts of income from abroad, despite the fact that the published balance sheet shows the country to be a net debtor. To some extent this position can be reconciled by valuing foreign direct investment at market value rather than book value. But even then, a continuing external deficit would have been expected to lead to a deterioration of the net asset position. This was largely avoided because, asset by asset, Britain seemed to earn more on its foreign investments than it paid out on investments by foreigners in Britain.

It might be expected that changes in the regulatory environment would influence the attractiveness of Britain to foreign investors, and also the ability of City institutions to earn interest and dividend income from the rest of the world. A VAR analysis suggests that this is indeed the case. The long-run movements attributed to changes in the regulatory environment are, however, very substantial, and it is probable that the work we have done has identified only some of the key factors influencing net income flows, thereby overstating the impact of these changes.

References

Abiad, A., Detragiache, E. and Tressel, T. (2010). 'A new database of financial reform', IMF working paper 08/266.

Abbritti, M., Weber, S. (2010). 'Labour market institutions and the business cycle: unemployment rigidities vs. real wage rigidities', working paper series 1183. European Central Bank.

Assenmacher-Wesche K., Gerlach S. (2010). Financial structure and the impact of monetary policy on property prices. Swiss National Bank. http://www.stefangerlach.com/Asset%20prices%20(21%20Apr%202010).pdf.

Calza, A., Monacelli, T. and Stracca, L. (2013). 'Housing finance and monetary policy', *Journal of the European Economic Association*, 11, 101–122.

Christiano, L., Eichenbaum, M. and Evans, C. (1999). 'Monetary policy shocks: what have we learned and to what end?' *Handbook of Monetary Economics*.

Conway, P., de Rosa D., Nicoletti G. and Steiner, F. (2006). 'Product market regulation and productivity convergence', *OECD Economic Studies*, 2, 39–76.

Elliott, J. and Wong Min, E. (2004), 'The external balance sheet of the United Kingdom: recent developments', *Bank of England Quarterly Bulletin*, Winter.

Gourinchas, P.-O., Rey, H. and Govillot, N. (2010). Exorbitant Privilege and Exorbitant Duty. http://www.imes.boj.or.jp/english/publication/edps/2010/abst/10-E-20.html.

Habib M.M. (2010). 'Excess returns on net foreign assets – the exorbitant privilege from a global perspective', working paper 1158. European Central Bank.

Houthakker, H. and Magee, S. (1969). 'Income and price elasticities in world trade', *Review of Economics and Statistics*, 51(2), 111–125.

Ilzetzki, E., Reinhart, C. and Rogoff, K. (2008). 'Exchange Rate Arrangements into the 21st Century: Will the Anchor Currency Hold?' University of Maryland. http://www.carmenreinhart.com/user_uploads/ERA-Country%20chronologies.pdf.

Jarocinski, M. (2010). 'Responses to monetary policy shocks in the East and the West of Europe', *Journal of Applied Econometrics*, 25(5), 838–68.

Litterman, R. (1986). 'Forecasting with Bayesian vector autoregressions-five years of experience', *Journal of Business and Economic Statistics*, 4, 25–38.

Nickell. S. (2006). The UK Current Account Deficit and All That. Nuffield College, Oxford. http://www.nuffield.ox.ac.uk/users/nickell/papers/TheUKCurrentAccountDeficitandAllThat.pdf.

Pesaran, M.H. and Smith, R. (1995), 'Estimating long-run relationships from dynamic heterogeneous panels', *Journal of Econometrics*, 68(1), 79–113.

Pratten, C. (1996), The Valuation of Outward and Inward Direct Investment. Report for the CSO. Department of Applied Economics. ISBN 0-906251-11-7.

Rubio-Ramirez, J., Waggoner, D.F. and Zha, T. (2010), 'Structural vector autoregressions: theory of identification and algorithms for inference', *Review of Economic Studies*, 77(2), 665–96.

Sa, F., Towbin, P. and Wieladek, T. (2014), 'Low interest rates and housing booms: the role of capital inflows, monetary policy and financial innovation', *Journal of the European Economic Association*.

Sims, C. (1980). 'Macroeconomics and Reality', *Econometrica*, 48, 1–48.

Towbin, P. and Weber, S. (2013), 'Limits of floating exchange rates: the role of foreign currency debt and import structure', *Journal of Development Economics*.

Wieladek, T. (2015), 'Varying coefficient Bayesian panel VARs', *Bank of England Staff Working Paper*.

4 UK broad money growth in the Long Expansion 1992–2007: what can it tell us about the role of money?

Michael McLeay and Ryland Thomas

4.1 Introduction – the behaviour of money during the long expansion: what are the puzzles?

The recent financial crisis has re-focused attention on the role of money and credit in the real economy. The recession associated was a sharp contraction of credit, suggesting that credit supply factors have important macroeconomic effects (see e.g. Bell and Young (2010) and Barnett and Thomas (2013)). The monetary policy response to the crisis involved various unconventional measures that led to an expansion of central bank balance sheets and, at least in the case of quantitative easing in the UK, was aimed at increasing the stock of broad money in the economy (Bridges and Thomas (2012), Butt et al. (2012)). So understanding the movements in money and credit is very much back on the macroeconomic agenda.

Prior to the crisis much of macroeconomic analysis was typically interested in explaining movements in macroeconomic variables in terms of only a small number of aggregate level shocks, such as aggregate supply, aggregate demand and monetary policy shocks. Movements in money were largely on the periphery of macroeconomic analysis, and many economists doubted the relevance or information content in money holdings given the poor experience with targeting monetary aggregates in the 1980s. Movements in credit were not ignored over this period, but they were typically treated within the umbrella of aggregate demand shocks. Furthermore, little attention was paid to the potential for credit to have allocative effects that boosted the supply potential of the economy. As discussed by Chadha et al. (2013), models with a banking system suggest that it is important to look at money and credit when the banking system is a source of shocks.

The views expressed in this chapter are those of the authors, and not necessarily those of the Bank of England. This chapter was finalised on 28 February 2014.

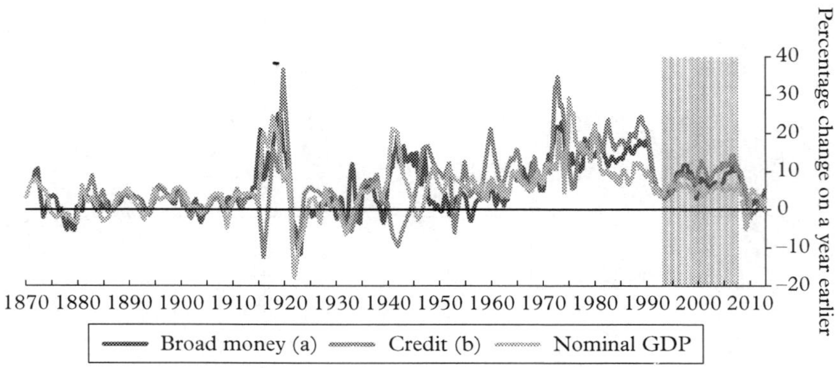

Figure 4.1. Money, credit and nominal spending – a long-run perspective
Sources: Capie and Webber (1985) and Bank of England, see Hills et al. (2010). Shaded area represents the long expansion 1993–2007Q3. (a) M3 1945–63, M4 1963–98, M4 excluding intermediate 'other financial corporations' (IOFCs) 1998–2012. (b) M4 Lending 1963–1998, M4 Lending excluding intermediate 'other financial corporations' (IOFCs) 1998–2012. Data are adjusted to exclude the impact of securitisations and loan transfers.

This chapter goes back to the long period of expansion from the mid-1990s leading up to the financial crisis in 2007 to examine what movements in money and credit were telling us about the UK economy. Figure 4.1 shows that from a long historical perspective the period does look like a relatively more stable nominal environment given the large swings in money, credit and nominal spending in previous decades. And yet there were many features of money and credit growth that were pointing towards the impending financial crisis. In particular, during the Long Expansion between 1993 and 2007 there are several noteworthy features and puzzles in the behaviour of money and credit:

(i) Credit grew faster than money

In the 1980s the expansion of money largely matched that of credit in flow terms, but this was not the case during the Long Expansion. Figure 4.2 shows the changes in UK banks' balance sheets over three six-year periods from 1993. Until around 1998, money grew broadly in line with credit, as it had in the 1980s. But over the next six years, credit started to grow faster than money, and it did so at an increasing rate leading up to the crisis. For the aggregate banking sector, that

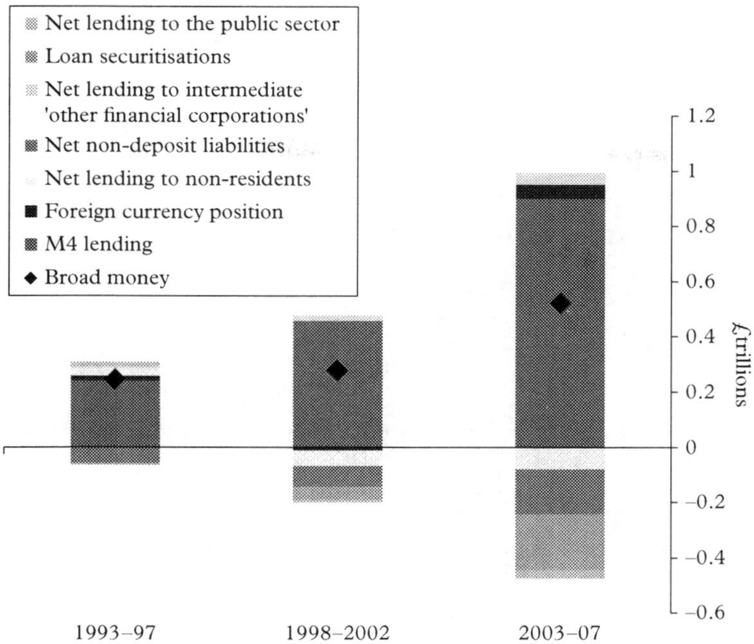

Figure 4.2. Sterling counterparts to broad money over the Long Expansion

created a 'customer funding gap' of loans not financed by customer deposits – broad money. The other bars in the figure show how banks filled that gap.

Banks' net foreign currency positions were little changed over the long expansion, so the expansion of credit must have led, in aggregate, to other changes in the *sterling* components of banks' balance sheets. In the 1998–2002 period, credit creation in excess of money was partly matched by an increase in banks' net non-deposit liabilities, possibly representing their increased use of wholesale funding markets. That change was even more evident over the final six years before the crisis. There was also a trend towards greater securitisation of loans over the period. When those securitised loans were sold on to non-banks it would have reduced the deposits of the non-bank private sector, further increasing the wedge between credit and broad money. Finally, between 1998 and 2007 there was also a fall in the net lending position of banks to non-residents, suggesting that some of the customer funding gap was filled with increased deposits from overseas.

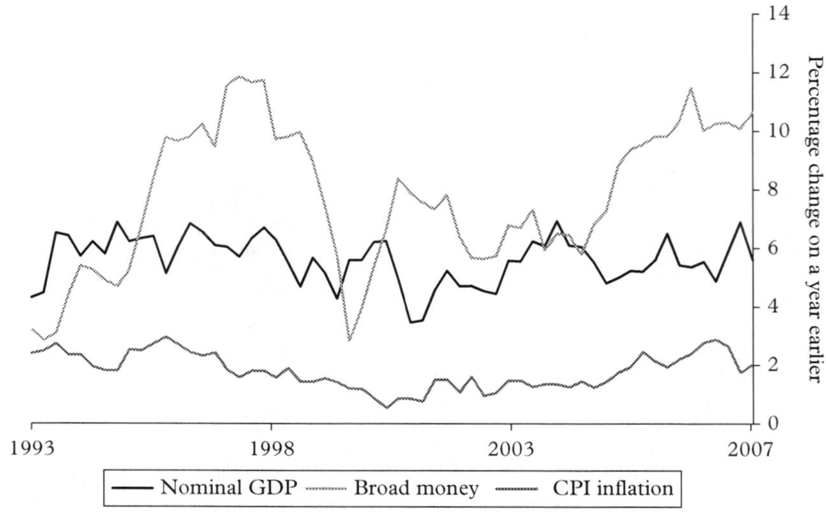

Figure 4.3. Inflation, broad money growth and nominal GDP growth

(ii) The expansion of money did not lead to a large pick-up in inflation

Despite double-digit money growth, inflation was low and stable over the Long Expansion, with consumer price index (CPI) inflation never rising above 3%, shown in Figure 4.3. For much of the 15 years prior to the crisis, broad money growth grew strongly. This was particularly conspicuous in the years immediately prior to the crisis, but over the entire period, annual money growth was rarely lower than 6%. Such high average growth rates would usually be associated with upward inflationary pressure. One explanation could be that there were offsetting shocks bearing down on inflation at the same time. Alternatively, something inherent in the shocks which boosted money may have prevented them from becoming inflationary, for example if they simultaneously boosted the supply potential of the economy.

(iii) All measures of money grow faster than nominal spending over this period

Figure 4.4 show that all measures of money – narrow (notes and coin), broad and weighted Divisia indices – grew strongly over the period. And as shown in Figure 4.3, this growth was generally stronger than that of nominal spending: in other words, money's velocity of circulation fell over the period, under any measure of the money stock. That broad money velocity declined suggested that, at least temporarily, the use of money as a store of value did not decrease over the period. But what

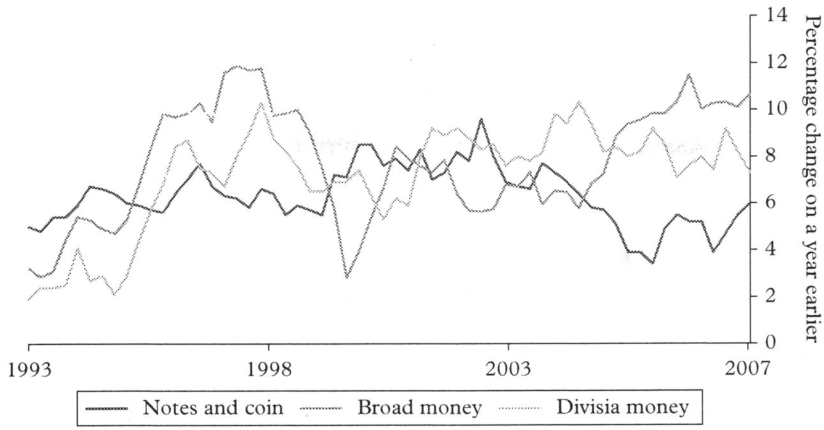

Figure 4.4. Measures of money growth

drove this fall in velocity? Was it a continuation of the trend in financial liberalisation seen in the 1980s or did it represent other shocks?

(iv) Corporates were responsible for much of the pick-up in money growth

Breaking down aggregate broad money growth into the contributions of different sectors shows that much of the strength in money was driven by the non-intermediate 'other financial corporations' (NIOFCs) sector and to a lesser extent by private non-financial companies (PNFCs). The money holdings of households grew at a reasonable rate, and relatively steadily, over the entire period. By contrast, the NIOFCs sector, containing financial companies such as pension funds and asset managers, was both more volatile and grew more strongly. Berry et al. (2007) posited that it was possible that the increase in the money holdings of this sector were mostly matched by an increase in its money demand, driven by the positive wealth effects of strong growth in asset prices. But that depends on what drove asset prices in the first place. The expansion of money in the NIOFC sector may have led to increased asset prices as an equilibrium response (Figure 4.5).

To investigate these issues and puzzles the rest of the chapter is structured as follows. The first section reviews the literature on the role of money and credit in the transmission mechanism. We discuss various theories, both conventional and unconventional, that suggest that the money-creating sector is a source of macroeconomic fluctuations and that the money created by those shocks plays an important role in the transmission of economic shocks. Section 4.2 then discusses how a

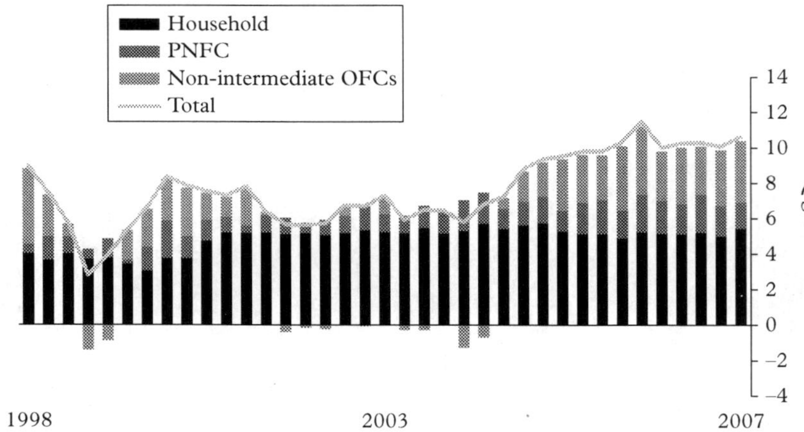

Figure 4.5. Contributions to broad money growth by sector

structural VAR analysis can be used to distinguish the role of these shocks from the standard aggregate shocks that are typically looked at in macroeconometric analysis. Section 4.3 then carries out a historical decomposition of the data to quantify the role of different shocks, including those emanating from the money-creating sector over the Long Expansion period. Section 4.4 then goes on to look at the sectoral data on money and credit to elucidate the role of money holdings in propagating different shocks. Section 4.5 concludes.

4.2 Recent literature on the role of money in the transmission mechanism

4.2.1 Conventional and unconventional theories of money

Assessing the impact of money and credit on demand and inflation is difficult using the conventional models that were typically used for the analysis of macroeconomic fluctuations in the lead-up to the financial crisis. Indeed, there were two conventional frameworks that were used to analyse inflationary pressures in the economy, each with polarised assumptions about the role of money.

4.2.1.1 Standard New Keynesian framework At one end of the spectrum many economists were happy to use the standard New Keynesian model that emphasises the dynamic link between various interest rates (including possibly loan rates if we crudely introduce spreads) and 'real' spending decisions. Real spending then has an impact on inflation via the real marginal cost gap and, in simpler variants, the output gap. In this world there is little role for the quantities of money and credit other than as incidental output variables. A cash in advance constraint can be incorporated, but is little more than an add-on. Nominal spending is also relegated to this category and 'drops out' as a recursive accounting identity from prices and output.

4.2.1.2 The quantity theory + money multiplier approach Given that the standard New Keynesian model often had little to say about money and credit, economists often turned to the Quantity Theory of money for insight. The appeal of this theory is that it is explicitly one about nominal spending determination and its link with the money supply. The price level is then determined when nominal demand is set against real supply in the economy. The problem with the theory is that it is an identity, and causality has to be imposed *a priori*. There is no real theory of what M is and how it is determined, except as possibly some simple multiple of base money (the 'money multiplier') which is prevalent in many textbook descriptions. It is also a static theory of nominal spending. In particular it makes no predictions about how the velocity of circulation 'V' moves in response to a shock to money. Typically velocity is treated as pinned down by transactions technology and other structural developments in the financial sector with full proportionality assumed between money and nominal spending. It is very much a black box that says little about which components of demand are affected by an increase in the money supply.

The problem with both theories is that they do not offer a clear way of integrating the money supply process with the consumption and investment spending decisions of households and firms. The ultimate answer is to think harder about how a monetary economy actually differs from the more abstract frameworks we typically use. And this ultimately means thinking about the frictions that money overcomes – if you like, what determines the 'demand for money'?

This has been recognised as a tough challenge for dynamic optimising models, as inevitably (if these problems are taken seriously) it means dispensing with the Walrasian auctioneer assumption and dealing with sequence economies, decentralised markets and heterogeneous agents. It also means generating a role for banks and financial intermediation, given that most of the money used today represents the liabilities of the private banking system.

Progress on this in the academic literature has proceeded along various lines and in various directions over the years. But it is fair to say that a consensus has not emerged in how to integrate money and credit into a standard macroeconomic model, particularly in a way that can

Table 4.1(a). Alternative literature on money

- Older literature
  - Aftermath of the general theory, loanable funds and the finance constraint, Ohlin (1937), Robertson (1940), Tsiang (1956, 1980), Clower (1967)
  - Asset imperfect substitutability e.g. Tobin (1969), Brunner and Meltzer (1987)
  - Buffer-stock money (Laidler 1984)
- Extensions of NK/RBC paradigms
  - Limited participation with cash in advance constraints (Fuerst 1992, Christiano and Eichenbaum (1992))
- Alternative academic literature
  - New monetary economics (Kiyotaki and Moore (2002), Williamson and Wright (2010))
  - Market monetarists (Christensen (2011))
  - Loans create deposits (Benes and Kumhof (2012))
  - Post-Keynesian endogenous money (Moore (1988), Howells(1995))
  - Circuitist theory (Rochon and Rossi (2003))
  - UK broad monetarism (Congdon (1992))
  - Flow of funds modelling (Godley and Lavoie (2006))

straightforwardly be taken to the data. That of course does not mean there are not key insights from this literature that we can try to use to investigate the data. Rather than attempt a long literature survey of the various ideas and approaches, we list some of the key alternative frameworks for analysing money and credit in Table 4.1(a), and we simply draw out some of the key strands and ideas from this literature that are either missing or implicit in the conventional frameworks used pre-crisis.

What are some of the key themes from the literature?

- Pretty much all of these theories would suggest that the existence of various frictions means that trade is carried out in decentralised markets rather than a Walrasian auction. That means transactions are necessarily carried out in a sequential or non-synchronous manner by heterogeneous agents. And to overcome the problems of a double coincidence of wants and trust money is required to some degree in all transactions, in both goods and asset markets. Sometimes money needs to be held 'in advance' for transactions when it is the explicit medium of exchange, but sometimes it is only needed 'in arrears' when used mainly as a means of final settlement, e.g. for transactions made using credit cards and trade credit. It also means that an injection of money in one market or sector will inevitably spill over into another market, and that means attempting to track the distribution of money holdings over a time. In many optimising models this is hard to do and some modelling device is needed to unwind any redistributive effects to avoid having to deal with degenerate distributions.

- Many theories stress that it is important to think of the demand for money in terms of a circulating flow among agents. It is not sufficient to think of the demand for money just as simply a stock demand at any one moment. The stock concept only applies to idle money held in the banking system as a store of value ('hoarding'). A (stationary) monetary equilibrium (in a closed economy) is when a given stock of money is circulating at a sufficient rate or velocity to make investment and saving plans consistent at the natural rate of interest.

- Underlying the circular flow is the idea that in normal times money will always be 'accepted' in exchange for either goods or financial assets. And it will be held in the short-run as a 'temporary abode of purchasing power' between transactions, despite the fact that it bears little or no interest. This 'acceptance' of money in exchange does not necessarily mean that agents want to 'hold' the money in equilibrium. In this sense there can be a divergence between actual and equilibrium money holdings – a monetary 'overhang' – that can persist over time and have a dynamic impact on goods and asset markets. In other words, money is pinned down by supply factors in the short run and may only be made consistent with demand in the longer term.
- Base money (consisting of currency and reserves) is the ultimate means of settlement in the economy. But in practice this settlement is largely carried out by banks via their reserve accounts with the central bank. Bank money or deposits are by and large the chief medium of exchange in the economy, and are typically the means of settlement for many credit transactions. So the focus should be on the determination of the broad money supply and bank behaviour. Banks' reserves and holdings of currency are demand-determined and only important in the sense that banks need an inventory to maintain convertibility of their deposits into the ultimate means of settlement.
- When interest rates are the policy instrument, the supply of broad money is endogenous and created by the banking system in response to the demand for credit and its willingness to supply that credit. When banks make loans they automatically create deposits. In particular, it is important not to think of banks as 'taking in money and lending it out', as a conventional financial intermediary is described. Nor should banks be thought of as receiving 'injections of reserves' and then lending out a multiple of them along the lines of the money multiplier that appears in many textbooks. In normal times the whole process operates in reverse. Banks first meet the demand for credit. This automatically creates its own deposit funding given agents' willingness to accept money in exchange for the initial set of transactions (i.e. the deposits created are initially retained in the banking system).

That can then generate a monetary overhang that spills over into asset and goods markets. Banks may well demand more reserves or hold more notes and coin in their tills as a precaution to maintain convertibility given the higher stock of deposits. But reserves are largely incidental if the central bank allows the banking system to hold what it likes. It is the deposits created and the possibility of a broad money overhang that matters for analysing demand and inflation.

4.2.2 A simple monetarist framework for analysing money

Given the current state of flux in monetary economics and the lack of an accepted method of incorporating money and credit into a model, an empirical analysis of the role of money necessarily implies an eclectic approach, but drawing where it can on the various strands of literature outlined above. This section provides an overview of the simple analytical framework we use in this chapter for investigating the role of money in the Long Expansion period. Our framework is, to all intents and purposes, explicitly monetarist in its nature. It emphasises the role of financial yields, asset prices and nominal spending in bridging a discrepancy, possibly incipient, between the supply of money and the demand for money. But it recognises explicitly that money will respond endogenously to different shocks. We outline the different factors affecting money supply and demand and consider the mechanisms through which the literature suggests that money supply and demand are made equal. We then use this framework to investigate to what extent the money-creating sector could be a source of shocks and the role that money plays in propagating shocks more generally.

As noted earlier, the *supply* of broad money in a financially developed economy such as the UK is pinned down by the behaviour of the banking system (including the central bank) and the various transactions it carries out with the non-bank private sector. The most important of these transactions historically has been the provision of credit by the banking sector to the non-bank private sector. When a bank or building society makes a loan to a household or company, it automatically creates a deposit – either for the borrower or for the recipient of the borrowers' expenditure if the loan is spent immediately (as in the case of purchasing a house, spending on a credit card or drawing on an overdraft facility). More generally, any transaction between the banking sector and the non-bank private sector will involve the creation or destruction of banking sector deposits and will thus affect the supply of broad money. For example, paying out dividends will create money when a bank credits shareholders' accounts with a deposit. And issuance of bank long-term debt or equity will destroy money as asset managers purchase the instruments using their deposits.

So the supply of money at any point in time will depend on:

(i) The determinants of the demand for credit, such as consumption and investment spending, and the value of housing transactions.
(ii) The willingness of banks to supply credit and the relative cost to household and companies of borrowing from banks relative to the cost of borrowing from capital markets.
(iii) The cost of issuing bank debt and equity or attracting funding from overseas relative to the cost of deposits

The *demand* for broad money can be understood in terms of its two uses in the economy: first, it is used as a means of carrying out and settling transactions – its 'medium of exchange' role; second, it is also held as a financial asset in household and company portfolios – its 'store of value' role. So the demand for money is likely to depend on:

(i) the value of transactions in the economy – nominal spending on goods and services and the value of asset transactions.
(ii) the overall value of asset portfolios – households and companies would be expected, other things equal, to hold a certain share of their portfolio in money;
(iii) the relative rate of return on money – the yield on deposits compared to other assets will determine the share of the portfolio that households and companies choose to hold in money. These alternative assets include longer-term financial assets, such as gilts and equities, but also potentially real assets such as consumer durables. The responsiveness of the demand for money to the relative rate of return on money will depend on the substitutability between money and other assets. Money might be a highly imperfect substitute for other assets because of various frictions, costs and degrees of market segmentation, as discussed for example in Goodfriend (2004) and Andrés et al. (2004).

Given these determinants of money supply and demand we need to consider two issues.

First, how do the supply and demand for money respond to different shocks. Do they both respond equivalently so that typically money demand and supply move simultaneously and there is no disequilibrium or overhang to unwind? In that case money will just be a corroborative indicator of the shocks hitting the economy. Or do they move differently, so that the determinants of money supply and demand must move over some time horizon to make them consistent? The answer is likely to depend on the shock hitting the economy.

Second, if certain economic shocks do lead to a persistent discrepancy between the supply and demand for money, what, if anything, needs to adjust to make them consistent in the longer term. In other words, what role does money play in the propagation of shocks and can this information be used to inform the future behaviour of other variables? Will nominal spending need to respond or will other variables move so that money and credit simply shift relative to income and only velocity changes? That too will depend on the type of shock hitting the economy.

Crudely speaking we might think of classifying shocks into those that originate outside the banking system, such as shocks to aggregate demand, aggregate supply and monetary policy, and those that occur as a result of a shift in the behaviour of the money-creating sector itself, such as factors affecting the willingness of the banking system to supply credit or the degree of competition among banks for both loans and deposits. And a key question we want to ask is whether shocks that originate in the money-creating sector affect the economy in a different way to standard shocks to aggregate demand and supply. We consider both sets of shocks in turn, using some simple stylised models that originate from the literature we discussed earlier.

4.2.3 Money and standard macroeconomic shocks

Typically shocks originating outside the banking system will affect the supply and demand for money by changing the nominal spending plans and demand for credit by companies and households. To see how this works we can look at a simple example of money supply and nominal spending determination in a loanable funds model. We use this in preference to an IS-LM framework as it makes the dynamic role of money and credit clearer.

Figure 4.6 shows a standard investment-savings or 'loanable funds' diagram where planned investment (saving) is negatively (positively) related to the interest rate. In this economy we assume money is required to buy both goods and assets. To introduce monetary frictions in a meaningful way an arbitrary timing friction is imposed on the goods market which says that the money income received in a given period cannot be spent or is not 'disposable' until the next period. This is to introduce some non-synchronicity between payments and receipts of income and to allow for a finite velocity of circulation. Because this

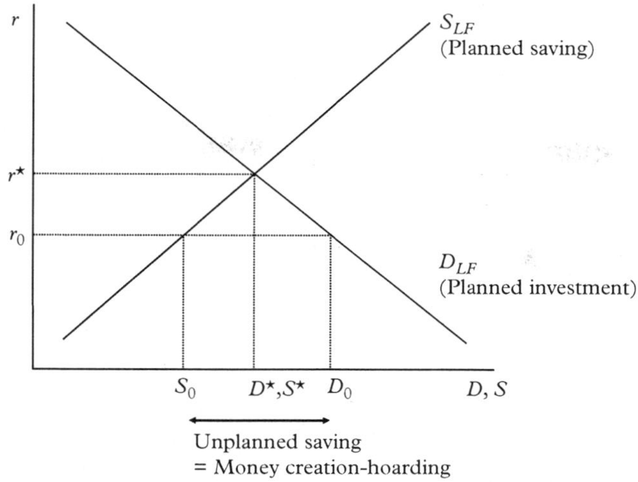

Figure 4.6. Money creation and its link with nominal saving and investment plans

is a monetary economy the saving and investment flows represent supplies and demands for loanable funds or 'credit', i.e. an exchange of money today in return for a payment of money in the future. In particular, the schedules here represent *nominal* flows of money between savings and investors and the rate of interest is the nominal rate prevailing in the money market.[1]

Figure 4.6 initially shows an economy in 'monetary equilibrium' at the natural rate of interest r^*. In this equilibrium a given stock of money is circulating between firms and households sufficient to finance a level of nominal spending consistent with full employment. This is equivalent to saying that investment and saving plans are consistent with a fixed stock of money.

Let's now consider what happens in response to a monetary policy shock when interest rates are reduced below the natural rate (or equivalently there is a shift in planned investment or consumption spending that raises the natural rate and the central bank holds interest rates unchanged). Other things being equal this implies a gap between planned investment and savings ($D_0 - S_0$) because nominal investment and consumption plans are both higher. That also implies in a closed economy that nominal spending plans exceed the income earned in

1 So expectations of inflation are taken as given when drawing the saving and investment schedules.

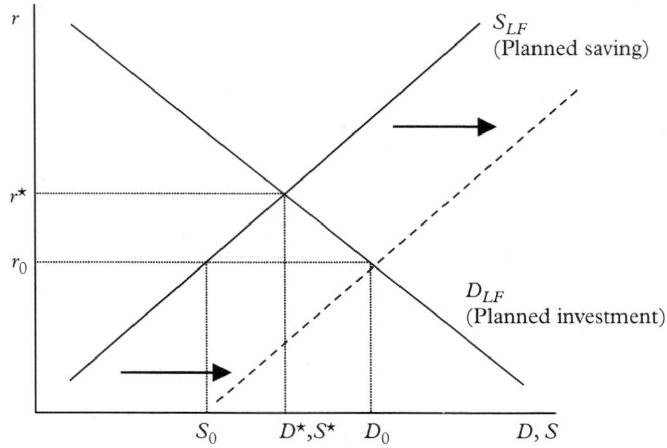

Figure 4.7. Restoration of equilibrium

(and money carried over from) the previous period (see Tsiang (1980)). So how can the central bank hold interest rates at this level and allow nominal spending in the economy to increase, i.e. what stops rates from rising back to the natural rate in this shock? The answer can only be through money creation by the banking system that plugs the planned investment-savings gap (net of any increase in hoarding or the asset demand for money). Firms wanting to invest at the lower rate of interest will have to borrow from banks.

The deposits created by such lending are initially 'accepted' by the recipients of the spending and this acceptance automatically 'funds' the new lending in the short term. The acceptance of the newly created deposits can be thought of as representing unplanned saving or 'unanticipated income' (or even as 'convenience lending', e.g. Moore (1988)). This bridges the planned investment-savings gap. The higher broad money stock calls for banks to hold higher central bank reserves and cash holdings to ensure convertibility of these deposits into base money should they be called upon. But the central bank supplies these on demand at the lower level of rates, so these are purely demand-determined increases in reserves that flow from the higher level of deposits. The causation is not vice versa as discussed earlier.

This initial increase in nominal spending and the money supply is not a new equilibrium position. If the same investment-saving plans were to persist into the next period a further increase in the money supply would be required to maintain the same *level* of nominal spending and the velocity of circulation would be continuously declining.

Equilibrium can only come about once agents in the aggregate are happy to pass around a higher stock of money, i.e. when money is circulating at the same rate as previously (and crudely money demand is equal to money supply). And for this to happen planned nominal savings need once again to equal planned investment. Ultimately, in equilibrium households need to want to buy extra corporate securities and bonds rather than hold their savings in idle deposits, and firms need to want to issue those bonds and equities to finance the higher level of investment rather than increasing their borrowing from banks. This is the only way in which higher nominal spending can be financed using a stationary (but circulating) stock of money. In a simple Keynesian multiplier model, for example, this comes about via the multiplier process, where agents spend a proportion of their unanticipated income (the marginal propensity to consume is less than 1) on other goods and services and this generates successive rounds of nominal income expansion until saving expands sufficiently so that planned savings once again equals planned investment.

So in this simple model broad money is endogenous and reflective of the initial higher level of nominal spending, but it would also be predictive about the future rounds of spending in the multiplier process. The initial expansion of broad money in response to demand initially represents higher unplanned saving and so would predict future rounds of spending and income expansion until planned savings expand sufficiently. In a more general setting there would be a variety of channels through which nominal spending would expand in response to this monetary disequilibrium, including expectations and other financial market prices which we have abstracted from here. The key point is that even though money is endogenous, standard shocks to aggregate demand, policy and supply can lead to monetary disequilibria that could be predictive of additional rounds of spending.

4.2.4 Money and shocks to the banking sector

In addition to standard macroeconomic shocks there could also be shocks originating from a shift in the behaviour of the money-creating sector itself – the banking sector. Such shocks can be split into two broad categories: those changing the size of the wedge between loan and deposit rates[2] and those mainly affecting the wedge between *both rates* and the risk-free rate, for a given loan–deposit spread.

2 This is the type of spread which features in Curdia and Woodford (2010) and Goodfriend and McCallum (2007) among others.

Examples of the first kind of shock are increases in the competitiveness of the banking sector (such as occurred in the UK in the 1980s) or improvements in intermediation technology. These would simultaneously increase the supply of money (through increased credit creation at lower loan rates) and the demand for money (due to a higher return on deposits). Another type of shock in this category would be a change in bank risk-taking that would lower loan rates for given deposit rates. That would lead initially to supply moving for a given demand for money.

The second type of shock would instead move *both rates in the same direction*. It could be any shock that lowered the cost to banks of funding themselves from wholesale markets, increasing their supply of credit and reducing the rate paid on their substitute source of funding, deposits. Faced with this shock the money supply and its demand would move in opposite directions.

The different types of shocks affecting the banking sector can be motivated using a simple partial equilibrium model of a profit-maximising bank, in the spirit of Monti–Klein.[3]

$$\Pi = L(i_L - w - c) - D(i_D + c) - F(i_F + \rho) - LK \tag{4.1}$$

$$L = l(i_L), l'() < 0 \tag{4.2}$$

$$D = d(i_D), d'() > 0 \tag{4.3}$$

$$w = x + \varepsilon, \varepsilon \sim N(0, \sigma^2) \tag{4.4}$$

$$L = D + F \tag{4.5}$$

$$K = k(Var(\Pi/L)), k'() > 0 \tag{4.6}$$

Equation (4.1) gives the bank's profit condition. The first term, $L(i_L - w - c)$, is the revenue the bank makes from granting L loans, paying interest rate i_L, before deductions for loan write-offs w, and the marginal operating cost of intermediation c. The rest of the terms represent the bank's cost of funding the loans. That cost is split between D deposits on which the bank pays interest i_D and a cost of intermediation[4] and F units of wholesale funding on which it pays the risk-free rate i_F and a risk premium ρ over that rate. The bank's balance sheet constraint Eq. (4.5) requires that it fund its loans through either the deposit or wholesale market. Finally, the bank is assumed to pay an

3 See Freixas and Rochet (1997) for an exposition of the Monti–Klein model.

4 For simplicity, this is assumed to be the same as the cost of intermediating loans, with no economies of scope.

extra cost of capital K to cover for unexpected losses on the loans it makes. Equation (4.6) describes how this cost depends positively on the variance of the bank's profits per loan. It could be thought of as representing the risk aversion of the bank's wholesale investors, or as a Value-at-Risk constraint imposed by regulators.

Equations (4.2) and (4.3) show that the bank's credit (and money) demand schedules are assumed to depend negatively (positively) on the interest rates paid. The write-off rate is made up of a deterministic component x and a shock around that component: $\varepsilon \sim N(0, \sigma^2)$ – Eq. (4.4). As the rest of the model is deterministic, this is also the variance of the bank's profits per loan: $Var(\Pi/L) = \sigma^2$. Substituting Eqs. (4.2)–(4.6) into Eq. (4.1) gives the bank's profit maximisation problem. The bank sets its loan and deposit rates to maximise its expected profit, given by Eq. (4.7). The bank satisfies all demand at its optimal interest rates, so there is no role for Stiglitz–Weiss type quantity rationing.

$$\max_{i_L, i_D} E(\Pi) = l(i_L)(i_L - x - c) - d(i_D)(i_D + c) - (l(i_L) - d(i_D))(i_F + \rho) - l(i_L)k(\sigma^2) \tag{4.7}$$

Assuming an interior solution, solving Eq. (4.7) gives the first-order conditions for the bank's optimal choices of interest rates (and so credit supply and equilibrium money demand):

$$-\frac{(i_D + c - i_F - \rho)}{i_D} = \frac{d(i_D)/i_D}{d'(i_D)} \equiv \frac{1}{\eta_D} \tag{4.8}$$

$$\frac{(i_L - c - i_F - \rho - x - k(\sigma^2))}{i_L} = -\frac{l(i_L)/i_L}{l'(i_L)} \equiv -\frac{1}{\eta_L} \tag{4.9}$$

In the limiting case of perfect competition in the loan and deposit markets the right-hand side of both equations will be equal to 0. So the rate paid on deposits will be equal to the risk-free rate less the cost of intermediation, plus the risk premium paid on the substitute source of funding: $i_D = i_F + \rho - c$. The risk premium increases the marginal cost of wholesale funding, causing banks to bid up the price of deposit funding until the two sources equate. The marginal cost of intermediation has the opposite effect, as it increases the cost of raising deposits relative to wholesale funding, pushing down on the rates actually paid on deposits.

The rate charged on lending under perfect competition is given by: $i_L = i_F + \rho + c + x + k(\sigma^2)$. The first two terms are identical to those on the deposit rate, representing the marginal cost of wholesale funding. But the marginal cost of intermediation pushes *up* on the loan rate, because the real resources expended on intermediation reduce the actual return earned by the bank. The final two terms represent the expected loss per loan x that the bank faces due to write-offs, as well as a charge from investors or regulators for the risk around that expectation: $k(\sigma^2)$. A higher mean or variance of write-off costs on a loan increases the rate charged on the loan.

This framework suggests there are three types of shock that can arise in the monetary sector which are likely to have different effects on the economy:

(i) Shocks to competition and technology that lower the cost of intermediation

Relative to perfect competition, more market power for the bank will push down on its (equilibrium) elasticities of demand η_D and η_L.[5] This would allow the bank to make positive profits by paying a lower rate on deposits and charging a higher rate on loans. With some inelasticity, the bank could do this without losing all of its demand. And in equilibrium it would always choose to trade off some of that demand against the gain it would make on the higher price.

A positive shock to competition in the banking sector could come about in two ways. New entrants or more aggressive competition could drive up the (own-rate) demand elasticity of loans and deposits faced by an individual bank. The bank would lose a larger proportion of its loans and deposits from charging a mark-up/mark-down over the marginal cost of wholesale funding, so would reduce the rate charged on its loans and increase that on deposits, towards that marginal cost. Another possibility would be an improvement in intermediation technology reducing the marginal cost of intermediation. This would close the gap between the rate paid and received on deposits, at least some of which the bank would optimally pass on to its customers.

Although to the bank the two shocks to the cost of intermediation are different (the first would reduce profitability and the second increase it), to the private sector both would be identical, pushing down on loan rates and up on deposit rates. That would simultaneously increase both the supply of money (lower loan rates would stimulate credit demand, boosting the supply of money through higher credit creation) and the demand for money, due to the higher return on deposits relative to

5 Unless there is perfect, or Dixit–Stigitz CES competition, these elasticities will depend on the interest rate chosen, so are note exogenous variables to the bank.

other assets. No movement in nominal spending would therefore be required to make them consistent. There would be a permanent shift in money holdings relative to nominal spending in the economy or – equivalently – a fall in the 'velocity of circulation' of broad money.

(ii) Shocks to the cost of providing wholesale funds to the banking system

In contrast, a shock decreasing the perceived riskiness of the banking sector, or to investors' willingness to take on risk, would reduce the risk premium paid by bank on its uninsured wholesale debt, reducing banks' marginal cost of wholesale funding. As with a positive competition shock, banks would pass at least some of this on to borrowers by lowering the lending rate. In addition, to the extent that this shock might reflect the introduction of new unregulated sources of wholesale funding, such as securitisation, it might also allow banks to work around existing regulatory capital constraints on lending and increase the supply of loans directly.

So overall this shock would have the same effect as a positive competition shock, increasing credit supply, equilibrium credit creation and so the money supply. But the effect on money demand would differ. Faced with a cheaper substitute source of funding, banks would face less pressure to pay high deposit rates, lowering these until the marginal cost was equal to that on wholesale funding. Lower rates on bank deposits relative to other assets would reduce the private sector's demand for money. What happens to the money supply over time depends on the liability management of UK banks and the extent to which banks actually use the cheaper wholesale funding at the expense of deposit financing. For example, banks may be more willing to issue some unsecured debt to an overseas resident who, following the shock, is now happy to take the risk of holding that debt and running down a safer but lower-yielding sterling deposit with that bank (or another UK resident bank). To the extent that supply and demand move to a different degree in the short run, e.g. if banks cut deposit rates but are slow to carry out active liability management, then this could create a monetary disequilibrium, requiring additional adjustment from one or more of the determinants of money supply or demand.

In the long run this shock is likely to lead to a larger expansion of credit than of money, given that much of the cheaper wholesale funding could be in the form of overseas deposits or non-deposit liabilities, such as unsecured debt or mortgage-backed securities. In other words this shock is likely to lead to a funding gap.

Table 4.1(b). Summary of differences between different banking sector shocks

	Loan rates	**Credit**	**Deposit rates**	**Money demand (M*)**	**M – M***
Cost of intermediation	↓	↑	↑	↑	0
Wholesale funding costs	↓	↑	↓	↓	↑?
Bank risk taking	↓	↑	0	0	↑

(iii) Shocks to the risk-taking behaviour by the bank itself

A shift in the perception of risk and the expected write-off rate by the bank would tend to lower the spread of loan rates relative to the safe rate. That might be due to a perceived improvement by banks in their ability to evaluate and monitor risk or increased expectations about the growth of the economy. So this shock would affect the overall cost of intermediation, but largely through the loan spread component. It should have little impact on the deposit spread component of the cost of intermediation. That should lead to an expansion of both money and credit. But again it may well lead to a positive money disequilibrium to the extent that the money created by extra credit will not initially be consistent with the long-run demand for money given unchanged deposit rates.

Table 4.1(b) summarises the differences between the different banking sector shocks. All three shocks would predict a cut in loan rates and a rise in credit provision, but they imply different responses for money, deposit rates and the gap between money supply and long-run money demand (M – M*). We use these predictions to help us identify the shocks empirically in Section 4.2.

4.2.5 *Money as a propagation mechanism – how do monetary disequilibria unwind?*

In previous sections we have shown in various stylised settings that different shocks can, in principle, lead to at least incipient discrepancies between the supply and demand for money. But how in general will any significant monetary overhang get unwound? This issue has resurfaced recently in the blogosphere,[6] where many commentators have

6 See for example
http://www.bloomberg.com/news/2013-08-23/an-economist-confused-about-banking.html
http://krugman.blogs.nytimes.com/2013/08/24/commercial-banks-as-creators-of-money/?_r=0
http://www.interfluidity.com/v2/4522.html

been discussing Tobin's famous 1969 article 'Commercial banks as creators of money'. In general, different schools of thought emphasise different adjustment mechanisms to a discrepancy between the supply of money and the demand for money, as discussed in Howells (1995).

Some would argue there cannot be a discrepancy and therefore nothing needs to change, or at least the private sector will unwind the discrepancy with little inducement. This was the essential point made by Tobin. For example, Eggertsson and Woodford (2003) argue that even if there is imperfect asset substitutability between money and other assets, there are Modigliani–Miller type arguments to suggest that a central bank purchase of riskier assets that boosts the money stock (in terms of either reserves or deposits) should not require a change in asset prices or consumption. The private sector will simply attempt to undo the effects of the central bank's purchase of risky assets – the demand for risky assets by the private sector falls by exactly the same amount as supply. This is because such a trade simply transfers risk from the private to the public sector and the private sector hedges against the increased riskiness of future taxes and transfers by holding safer assets. Such arguments are similar to those made by Fama (1980) and Wallace (1981) about the irrelevance of open market operations.

Post-Keynesians and circuitists would argue the irrelevance from a different angle. Any incipient disequilibrium between money supply and demand is quickly removed by repayment or extension of bank credit – 'the reflux principle' – with little need for a change in asset prices or spending.

A monetarist would argue that these irrelevance propositions are all special cases and that once one allows for (collectively) market segmentation, preferred habitats, costs of adjusting portfolios, heterogeneity among different agents and the transactions motive for holding bank deposits, there could in principle be significant effects on asset prices and nominal spending as different agents rebalance their portfolios. As a result, once the money circulates it does not necessarily pass into the hands of agents who want to repay debt, even if this would be Pareto optimal from the Walrasian auctioneer's point of view. The process of unwinding a disequilibrium could be much more protracted for two reasons.

First, adjustment in the determinants of the demand for money at the individual level may take time. According to the buffer-stock theory of money demand (see Laidler (1984)), the demand for money by households and companies is a target level of money balances that they wish to hold on average over a given period. But at a particular moment in time they will often accept holding more or less than that amount, as a (possibly very temporary) means of bridging the gap between payments and receipts. Over time they will attempt to return to their target level following a change in their money holdings. As noted earlier, this suggests that, in the short run, the aggregate stock of money is largely determined by supply factors and is only made consistent with the underlying demand for money over a longer horizon. But this time horizon may differ hugely between different sectors in the economy. For example, financial institutions are likely to want to eliminate any discrepancy between actual and desired money holdings relatively quickly; whilst households and non-financial companies may take longer due to inattention and portfolio adjustment costs.

Second, a further key distinction is the difference between the individual agent's or sector's attempt to reduce its money holdings and the adjustment of the economy in the aggregate. Individuals can only reduce their surplus liquidity by passing that liquidity on to someone else. So there is a whole sequence of adjustments that may need to be made by diverse individual agents/sectors in the economy before equilibrium in the economy as a whole is reached. This is the genesis of 'hot potato' effects, where money gets passed on among agents until ultimately the transactions underlying the transfers of deposits lead to sufficient changes in asset prices, nominal spending and other yields so that the demand for money is made equal to supply.

As noted earlier, the difficulties of incorporating this type of heterogeneity and associated hot potato effects into macro models with a banking system means investigating these issues has to be, for the time being at least, based on a purely empirical approach.

4.2.6 An empirical approach for addressing the propagation role of money

A significant body of research work has gone into estimating systems of equations that explore the linkages between money and credit aggregates on the one hand, and asset prices and spending on the other (Thomas (1997a,b), Brigden and Mizen (2004), Chrystal and Mizen (2005a,b), Dhar et al. (2000), De Santis et al. (2008), Papademos and Stark (2010)). Although the approach is largely empirical, these estimated systems do capture some of the linkages discussed earlier and some theoretical restrictions can be placed on them. In particular, efforts to develop systems based around estimated equations for the long-run demand for money – the '$M - M^*$' approach – are the most directly related to the buffer stock monetarist idea. This approach attempts to map out empirically how the restoration of monetary equilibrium, at either an aggregate or sectoral level, occurs following an increase in money holdings (Figure 4.7).

These buffer-stock or M–M⋆ models have several core properties:

(i) Money demand is estimated as a function of activity, value of assets ('wealth') and rates of return as noted earlier.
(ii) *Money is modelled jointly with asset prices and activity* in a VAR framework. So money can in principle have feedback effects on asset prices and activity as well as vice versa.
(iii) *Theory is used to pin down the long run.* A cointegrated VAR approach is used, as advocated by Pesaran and Shin (2002). The idea is that theory pins down the form of certain long-run (cointegrating) relationships, the most important of which is the money demand relationship. But the dynamics of each variable around those long-run relationships are then freely estimated.
(iv) Additional identifying restrictions are then required to produce impulse responses to different 'shocks'.

The typical approach in this type of model is relatively straightforward. First, a long-run demand for money equation – M⋆ – is estimated. This equation attempts to capture the transactions and asset demands for money either for aggregate money or for a particular sector.

$$M^{\star} = f(\text{nominal demand, deposit rate, other rates of return, wealth})$$

From this one can construct 'monetary overhangs', the gap between the actual stock of money and equilibrium money holdings – 'M – M⋆'.

Second, a cointegrated VAR or vector error correction mechanism (VECM) can then be estimated. In this system, nominal spending, rates of return and money itself are a (lagged) function $g(L)$ of M – M⋆ and other disequilibria terms (such as the output gap).

$$\text{Nominal demand, rates of return, wealth, money} = g(L)(\text{M} - \text{M}^{\star}, \text{ other disequilibria})$$

In this approach, it is therefore possible to investigate which variables, including money itself, are affected by the money disequilibria generated by particular shocks. For example, if M – M⋆ negatively affects the aggregate money stock and nothing else, this would give more weight to the Kaldor–Tobin view that surplus money is easily extinguished via repayment of bank debt.[7] In contrast, if M–M⋆ is found to affect asset prices and nominal spending, that would give more weight

7 See for example Kaldor and Trevithick (1981).

to the monetarist hypothesis. The key feature of these systems is that the estimated money equilibrium condition must hold in the long run through some mechanism. The system then identifies how equilibrium has typically been restored over the particular period examined.

The linkages tend to be clearer at an individual sectoral level (Thomas (1997a,b), Brigden and Mizen (2004)). So, for example, the expansion of the money stock resulting from QE occurs as a result of medium-long maturity gilt purchases. So one might focus on the pension fund (ICPF) sector, given that it is likely to end up holding most of the newly created deposits. And you would expect that the immediate effect of them attempting to rebalance their portfolios would to be bid up the prices/lower yields on other assets in their portfolio. This is fine if the money circulates like a hot potato within the ICPF sector (they all attempt to buy shares off each other). But you then face the issue mentioned earlier of analysing how the economy reaches an equilibrium in aggregate if money spills over into the other sectors (e.g. ICPFs may buy new issues of shares from PNFCs). Ideally you would like to estimate these systems at a sectoral level and integrate them into a complete flow of funds model to link up the various sectors and determine the distribution of money balances at any one time. This is by no means a simple, straightforward task, although the Godley and Lavoie (2006) flow of funds work represents one attempt.

The aggregate and sectoral models we use in this chapter are now addressed in more detail.

4.3 A model for investigating the role of the monetary sector as a source of shocks

4.3.1 An aggregate cointegrated SVAR model

To quantify the role of different shocks we use an aggregate Structural Vector Autogression model or SVAR. This approach involves decomposing the movements in a set of variables into the contribution of a number of structural shocks where each shock is identified using theoretical restrictions. The advantage of an aggregate model is that we can obtain a general equilibrium response of all the variables in the system to a particular shock. The model we use here is an extension of the model used by Dhar et al. (2000) and Bridges and Thomas (2012) to include a role for both credit aggregates and prices. It includes a set of key variables of interest for analysing the role of credit and money in the economy and explicitly builds in a long-run money demand relationship alongside other equilibrium relationships. So, as discussed in the previous section, our VAR allows for cointegration and is sometimes known as a Strucutral Vector Equilibrium Correction Mechanism or SVECM following the approach of King et al. (1991) and Mellander et al. (1992).

The model is estimated on quarterly data over a long sample of around 50 years, 1964Q1–2012Q4. That allows us to look back at various periods of financial expansion and contraction that occurred in the UK in the post-war period, with which we can compare the period of the Long Expansion. A long sample covering various economic cycles helps identify long-run cointegrating relationships in the data especially given the end of the sample period is dominated by the trough following the financial crisis. Attempting to identify cointegrating relationships on shorter samples containing this period is often difficult. The cost is that we are estimating over a number of policy regimes and there may be periods of structural change both in terms of the trend behaviour of the economy and in terms of the cyclical relationships between variables.

4.3.2 Data choices

To disentangle the role of standard aggregate shocks from shocks emanating from the money-creating sector we estimate a system that includes the standard macroeconomic variables used to identify these shocks, namely inflation, real GDP and short-term interest rates. We augment these with measures of money, credit and the rate of return on loans and deposits, plus a number of financial market variables, such as long-term bond yields, equity prices and the real exchange rate. That allows us to investigate the role of money and credit and their effect on various asset markets. In all we use 10 series. The data we use are as follows.

(i) For inflation (π) we use a seasonally adjusted measure of quarterly CPI inflation extended back to the 1960s using the ONS's long-run measure of consumer prices (see O'Donaghue et al. (2004)).
(ii) For real GDP (y) we use the headline measure of real GDP at market prices.
(iii) For the short-term interest rate (is) we use Bank Rate.
(iv) For the long-term interest rate (il) we use a zero-coupon UK 10-year government bond yield.
(v) For our measure of broad money (m4x) we use the break-adjusted stock of M4 excluding the deposits of intermediate OFCs as shown in the introduction. The GDP deflator is used to deflate the series to create real broad money balances.

(vi) For the growth of credit quantities (m4lx) we use the real break-adjusted[8] stock of M4 lending (bank and building society lending) to households, PNFCs and non-intermediate OFCs. This measure is also adjusted for the impact of securitisations, so any securitised loans are retained within the stock. This 'headline' measure of M4 lending is often referred to as M4Lx(ex). The GDP deflator is used to deflate the series.

(vii) For the own rate on M4 (id) we use a weighted average of the effective interest rates on currency (zero), sight deposits, time deposits and other savings instruments such as ISAs. Each weight is based on the share of each instrument in the stock of M4. The inclusion of currency and non-interest-bearing deposits in the calculation of the average allows us to pick up the falling share of these components in overall deposits, which pushes up the own rate over time.

(viii) To proxy the rate of interest on borrowing (ib) we use investment-grade UK corporate bond yields covering all companies, including financial companies. Our use of corporate bond spreads reflects the fact that we have a relatively continuous series we can take back to the 1960s. The yields we used are measures from Bank of America which go back to 1997. Prior to this we use yields from Global Financial Data back to 1966. Corporate bond yields have been found to be a useful summary measure of credit conditions in US studies (e.g. Gilchrist et al. (2009) and Gilchrist and Zakrasjek (2012)). And the inclusion of financial company spreads means that we should pick up movements in bank funding costs which would feed into the borrowing rates faced by households. A preferable alternative would be to have used actual bank borrowing rates faced by companies and households. But these were less readily available before the mid-1990s.

(ix) For real equity prices (pk) we use the FTSE-all share index deflated by the GDP deflator.

(x) The real exchange rate (e) is the narrow UK real effective exchange rate index from the BIS based on consumer prices.

From these series we can construct a number of auxiliary series such as the deposit rate spread (*id–is*), credit spreads (*ib–il* given the maturity of corporate bonds is similar to that of 10-year gilt yields), the cost

8 The break-adjustment method corrects for any breaks in the stock series arising from changes in the reporting population, classification changes, revaluation effects and write offs. The break-adjusted stock takes the latest estimate of the unadjusted stock of lending and projects this backwards using transactions data on the flow of lending. See http://www.bankofengland.co.uk/statistics/Pages/iadb/notesiadb/Changes_flows_growth_rates.aspx for more details.

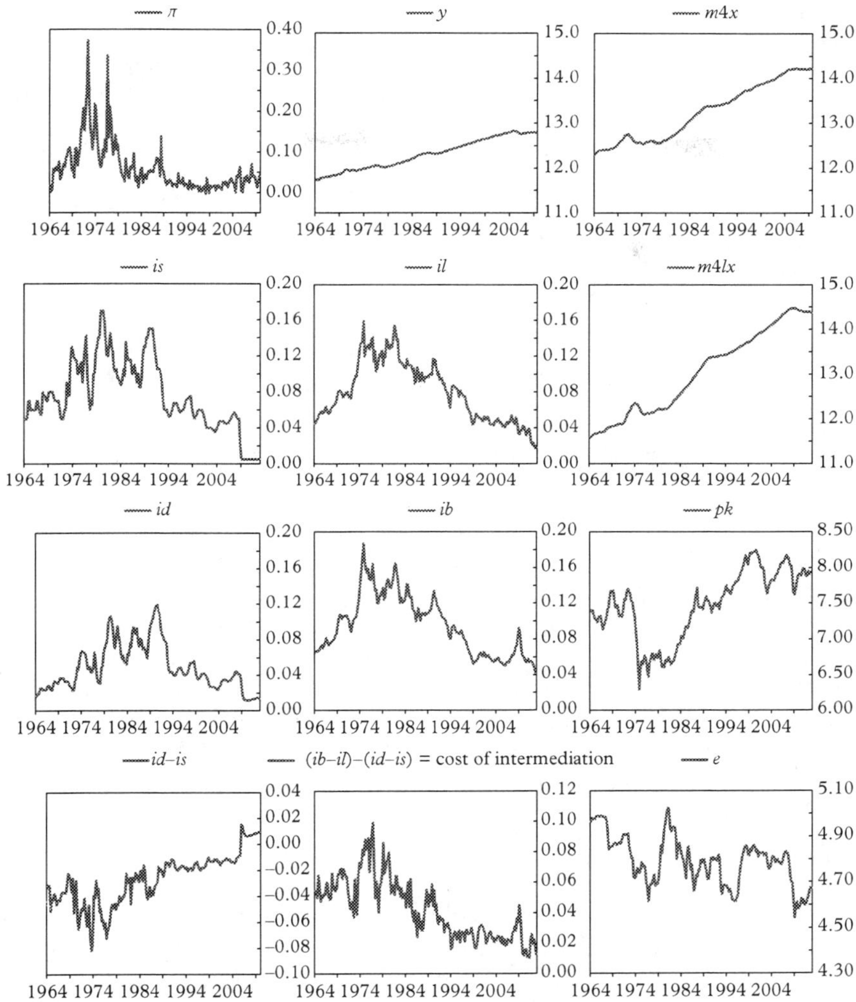

Figure 4.8. Data series used in the SVAR

of intermediation (*ib–il*)–(*id–is*), and velocity (*y–m*4). The data series are charted in levels (for interest rates and inflation) and logged levels (for other variables) in Figure 4.8.

4.3.3 *Stationarity of the data and cointegration*

As a first step we look at the data in log levels (except for inflation and the interest rate variables which are just levels of the relevant interest

Table 4.2. ADF stationary tests

Series	*t*-stat	*P*-value	Lag based on Akaike Information Criterion
Inflation (annual)	−3.23 (−1.67)	0.02 (0.4466)	1 (4)
Real GDP	−1.3729	0.5949	0
Bank rate	−1.5088	0.5273	0
Long-term government bond yields	−0.7967	0.8175	1
Deposit rate	−2.2773	0.1804	1
Corporate bond yield	−1.4671	0.5483	1
Real M4x	−0.2984	0.9215	2
Real M4Lx	−0.7638	0.8265	2
Real equity prices	−1.4447	0.5595	1
Real exchange rate	−2.7930	0.0611	1

rate/inflation rate) and test the stationarity of our series using standard Augmented Dickey–Fuller statistics. This is summarised in Table 4.2. All the series appear to be integrated of order one in the levels of the data but can be made stationary by first differencing. That includes the inflation rate and interest rate series that are often treated as stationary variables in shorter sample periods. In particular, quarterly inflation can appear stationary on standard ADF tests given its volatility, but annual CPI inflation is non-stationary over the whole sample period. As discussed in more detail in Appendix 1 the non-stationarity of the series means that the underlying trends in all these series are stochastic trends with a potential drift component with a sign that depends on the series.

The next step is to look for cointegration among the variables. That will determine how many common stochastic trends there are driving our 10 variables. For example, if we find six long-run relationships between the variables that means there will be four common stochastic trends driving our 10 series (see Appendix 1 for details).

In Table 4.2 we apply the procedure of Johansen (1988) to determine the degree of cointegration in our system. The degree of cointegration appears very sensitive to lag length of the VAR. The Schwarz and Akaike information criterion suggest a short lag length of two and on that assumption the Johansen test indicates there are three cointegrating vectors. But longer lag lengths, required to make the errors serially uncorrelated and closer to normality, suggest six or possibly seven vectors. In part, that probably reflects the fact that inflation and interest rates are close to being stationary series.

We start off the analysis assuming there are four cointegrating vectors based on the earlier results of Dhar et al. (2000) and Bridges and Thomas (2012) using a subset of the variables here. Those four cointegrating relationships should still be valid in a larger system. They estimated a long-run money demand function; a term structure relationship; a real interest rate or Fisher relationship; and an asset price relationship linking equity prices to GDP. This implies the following long-run relationships (where constant terms reflecting the equilibrium means are defined as k_1 to k_4):

$$m4x - p = 0.5^{\star}y + pk + 8^{\star}(id - is) + k_1$$

$$is = il + k_2$$

$$is = \pi + k_3$$

$$pk = y + k_4$$

In summary, there is a long-run demand for real money balances that depends on the spread between deposit rates and long rates and also on output and asset prices (as a proxy for wealth). The short-long rate spread and the real interest rate are stationary around their sample means, as is the asset price to GDP ratio, suggesting equity prices are proportional to dividends for a given profit share. So these vectors deliver appealing long-run economic relationships that we can justify on the basis of theory.

Table 4.3 suggests that choosing four cointegrating vectors and imposing the restrictions consistent with the relationships above is rejected. That suggests there may indeed be more cointegrating relationships when credit quantities and prices are added. We first attempted to identify an additional cointegrating vector based on a credit demand relationship where credit is dependent on yields, GDP and asset prices, but we failed to find an acceptable relationship that could not be rejected by the data. That suggests there may be a stochastic trend in credit supply that works independently of spreads and output reflecting shifts in non-price factors (e.g. terms and conditions) and other quantitative restrictions (e.g. loan to value ratios). We then experimented with testing for cointegration between the corporate bond rate and long-term bond yield, i.e. that credit or borrowing spreads are stationary.

$$ib = il + k_3$$

That produced a set of vectors that could not be rejected at the 1% level (Table 4.4), but could be rejected at the 5% level of significance. Inspection of the vectors themselves suggests that the real interest rate

Table 4.3. Johansen cointegration trace test statistics

H0:rank<=	Trace test [Prob] : two lags	Trace test [Prob]: four lags	Trace test [Prob] : six lags
0	333.86 [0.000] **	320.73 [0.000] **	335.96 [0.000] **
1	236.93 [0.000] **	241.65 [0.000] **	257.60 [0.000] **
2	163.58 [0.028] *	181.48 [0.002] **	194.02 [0.000] **
3	117.57 [0.139]	138.30 [0.006] **	136.80 [0.008] **
4	84.278 [0.237]	102.55 [0.014] *	99.428 [0.026] *
5	61.047 [0.205]	71.538 [0.034] *	69.663 [0.050] *
6	40.355 [0.212]	47.546 [0.052]	45.517 [0.080]
7	21.540 [0.335]	26.697 [0.112]	26.029 [0.131]
8	9.5994 [0.319]	9.8662 [0.297]	9.6977 [0.310]
9	1.4373 [0.231]	1.6356 [0.201]	2.7204 [0.099]

Note: A '**' represents rejection of the null hypothesis at the 1% level, and a '*' a rejection at the 5% level

Table 4.4. Summary of restrictions on β

	β_1	β_2	β_3	β_4	β_5
	0.00	0.00	−1.00	0.00	0.00
y	−0.50	0.00	0.00	−1.00	0.00
is	7.93	0.00	0.00	0.00	0.00
il	0.00	−1.00	0.00	0.00	1.00
id	−7.93	1.00	1.00	0.00	0.00
m4x	1.00	0.00	0.00	0.00	0.00
m4lx	0.00	0.00	0.00	0.00	0.00
pk	−1.00	0.00	0.00	1.00	0.00
ib	0.00	0.00	0.00	0.00	−1.00
e	0.00	0.00	0.00	0.00	0.00

LR test of restrictions: $\chi^2(24) = 42.004$ [0.0129]*

and corporate bond spread vectors are the ones most likely to be leading to a rejection of the restrictions. In particular, the corporate bond spread shows some evidence of a mean shift at the start of the crisis, but until we observe the behaviour of spreads over the next few years it is probably too early to confirm that through statistical tests. So given: (a) the theoretical appeal of these cointegrating relationships; (b) that they proved acceptable in a smaller system; and (c) that they cannot be ruled out at the 1% level in this larger system, we use these as the basis for our cointegrated SVAR.

So our VECM model is given by.

$$\Delta x_t = d + B\Delta x_{t-1} + \Pi x_{t-1} + e_t$$

where Π can be written as $\Pi = \alpha\beta'$, where β is our 5×5 matrix of five cointegrating vectors, and α is an 5×5 matrix of response coefficients to those disequilibria. Given a lag length of two in the levels of the variables the effective sample period is from 1964Q3 to 2012Q4.

Once estimated we are then going to invert the VAR to obtain the moving average representation of the model, which describes the evolution of the variables in terms of current and past shocks.

$$x_t = x_0 + \mu_t + C(1)\sum_{i=0}^{t-1} e_{t-i} + C^\star(\mathrm{L})e_t$$

Unlike the standard non-cointegrated VAR, $C(1)=F$ is a reduced rank matrix (rank $= n - r = 5$), which Engle and Granger (1987) and Engle and Yoo (1991) show can be written as the product of two matrices $C(1) = \gamma\theta'\gamma{\cdot}\gamma$ and θ are $n \times n - r$ (or equivalently $n \times k$) matrices related (non-uniquely) to the parameters of the cointegrating vectors α and β through the relationships $\beta'\gamma = 0$ and $\theta'\alpha = 0$. The model can then be written as a trend-cycle decomposition of x_t:

$$x_t = x_0 + \mu t + \gamma\,\tau_t + C^\star(\mathrm{L})e_t$$

where there are $n - r$ common stochastic trends (CSTs) given by:

$$\tau_t = \theta' \sum_{i=0}^{t-1} e_{t-i}$$

So in general, when there are r cointegrating relationships among the n variables in x_t, the MA representation is defined in terms of $k = n - r$ common stochastic trends (made up of cumulated permanent shocks) and r temporary shocks. But the reduced-form errors e_t that make up the common trends and temporary shocks cannot be given a structural interpretation without additional restrictions.

4.3.4 *Identification of structural shocks*

The challenge here is to identify both the five permanent shocks or stochastic trends driving the system and the five temporary shocks that merely have a cyclical effect on each of the variables. The technicalities of identification are discussed in more detail in Appendix 1. Here we concentrate on outlining the economics of our identification procedure, based on the models we discussed in Section 4.1.

As discussed earlier, we want to distinguish between the standard aggregate shocks that are typically analysed in macroeconomics from those shocks originating in the monetary sector. But we need to allocate these across both the permanent and temporary shocks. We deal with the standard macroeconomic shocks first:

For the standard macroeconomic shocks – aggregate supply, aggregate demand and monetary policy shocks – we can think of splitting each type into permanent and temporary shocks. For example, we might think of aggregate supply shocks being split into those that permanently affect the level of output, such as TFP shocks, and those that are typically viewed to have a transitory effect, such as cost-push or mark-up shocks. Similarly, for monetary policy we might think of the permanent component as the inflation target or nominal anchor that pins down inflation expectations in the economy, whereas temporary shocks to policy represent the deviation from some rule designed to hit that inflation target. Finally, for aggregate demand shocks we can think of shocks that (in a small open economy) will shift the equilibrium exchange rate (which we showed earlier was non-stationary) such as shocks to world demand or preferences for UK exports, as opposed to shock to domestic demand, which would not affect the structural trade balance and should only have a temporary effect on output and other real variables. That gives us six shocks we can try to identify, shown in Table 4.5.

Earlier we identified three shocks that might arise in the money-creating sector. These are listed in Table 4.6. Two of these shocks are likely to be candidates for permanent shocks. The cost of intermediation has trended downwards largely on account of the rising deposit rate spread, so one of the stochastic trends is likely to reflect this shock. The gap between the stock of lending and money has also been non-stationary given the cointegration evidence, so the shock to the cost and

Table 4.5. Standard macroeconomic shocks

Type of shock	Permanent shocks	Temporary shocks
Aggregate supply	Technology/TFP	Cost-push/mark-up
Aggregate demand	World demand/preferences	Domestic demand/confidence
Monetary policy	Core inflation	Deviations from rule

Table 4.6. Shocks arising in the monetary sector

Type of shock	Permanent and temporary
Cost of intermediation	Permanent effect
Cost and availability of wholesale funding	Permanent effect
Bank risk-taking	Temporary effect

availability of funding is likely to be a permanent shock that leads to a long-run shift in the customer funding gap of banks. As we noted earlier the shock to bank risk-taking should mainly affect the spread of loans over risk-free rates, which we noted was stationary. This would suggest it mainly has a cyclical effect, so we treat this as a temporary shock.

The remaining shock we try to identify as a shock to risk premia that originates in the non-bank financial sector. So it affects financial markets such as bond, equity and FX markets, but does not initially lead to an expansion of money and credit.

Given these theoretical priors about the permanency of the candidate shocks we set about trying to identify these shocks through a set of restrictions. We decompose the reduced-form residuals of the VECM into a linear combination of structural shocks as shown below:

$$e_t = \Gamma_0 \eta_t \quad \text{and}$$

$$C(L) = \Gamma(L)\Gamma_0^{-1} \quad C(1) = \Gamma(1)\Gamma_0^{-1} \quad \Omega = \Gamma_0^{-1} \sum \Gamma_0$$

We need enough restrictions on the shocks to identify the mapping matrix Γ_0. This is a 10 × 10 matrix, so we need 100 restrictions to identify this matrix. We already have placed 25 restrictions on this matrix by uniquely identifying five cointegrating vectors. In the presence of cointegrating relationships, KPSW (1991) and Warne (1991) show that Γ_0 can be partitioned into two matrices=$[H\ J]$ so that $\Gamma(1)\Gamma_0^{-1} = [F\ 0]$, which just says that five of our shocks will have no long-run effect on the variables in our system. Importantly the cointegrating vectors have placed some restrictions on the long-run impact matrix. For example, our permanent shocks will affect short and long rates by the same amount in the long run, given that they are cointegrated in a one for one relationship. We can also get $n^\star(n+1)/2$ restrictions from assuming the structural shocks are mutually uncorrelated so that Ω is a diagonal matrix. That provides 55 restrictions. That means we need 20 additional restrictions: 10 on the permanent shocks and 10 on the temporary shocks. These can come from imposing restrictions on either the timing, sign or long-run impact of each shock, as discussed in the Appendix 1.

For the permanent shocks it seems natural to use long-run identifying restrictions in the spirit of Blanchard and Quah (1989) and King et al. (1991). The long-run restrictions applied are as follows:

(i) Only the core/target inflation shock is allowed to affect inflation in the long run. So only monetary policy determines the inflation rate in the long run. This implies four zero restrictions on the long-run impact of the other shocks.

(ii) The aggregate demand shock does not have a permanent effect on output, even though it has a permanent effect on the real exchange rate. This assumes that potential supply is invariant to the real exchange rate and would imply, for instance, that there is little long-run real wage resistance by workers (see Layard et al. (1991) for a discussion). It also assumes there are no hysteresis effects from demand shocks. So this is a somewhat controversial restriction, especially as we allow the core/target inflation shock to affect output in the long run.

(iii) Aggregate supply and demand shocks are assumed to be neutral for finance. They do not have an impact on the cost of intermediation or the ratio of M4 lending to GDP in the economy. That implies that the aggregate demand shock has no impact on the stock of real lending in the economy, given that it has no impact on GDP. That delivers five restrictions.

(iv) Finally, the funding cost shock is also assumed not to affect the cost of intermediation in the long run as it should push down on both loan and deposit rates relative to safe rates. But unlike the aggregate demand and supply shocks it is allowed to permanently affect the ratio of lending to GDP in the economy.

For the temporary shocks we can either use timing or sign restrictions on the shocks. Sign restrictions have the advantage of avoiding arbitrary timing assumptions. But, as found in Canova and de Nicoló (2002) and Barnett and Thomas (2013), they can produce implausibly large contemporaneous effects of demand and monetary policy shocks on GDP and inflation. Here we apply standard timing restrictions. We then gauge the plausibility of the restrictions by assessing whether the sign and size of the responses look plausible given what theory would suggest. The short-run restrictions applied are as follows:

(i) We assume prices are sticky in response to demand and financial shocks so that only mark-up or cost-push shocks such as VAT have an immediate impact on prices. That provides four restrictions.

(ii) Only aggregate demand and mark-up shocks can have an immediate effect on output (i.e. within the quarter). That provides three restrictions. Financial market, banking sector and monetary policy shocks only affect output with a lag.

(iii) Monetary policy shocks have an immediate effect on Bank Rate. But the financial and banking sector shocks are assumed to just affect risk premia and credit spreads in the short-run and not affect risk-free rates immediately. This is based on a Taylor-rule assumption that monetary policy only responds immediately to output and inflation and these shocks only affect inflation and output with a lag.

(iv) The financial market risk premium shock is assumed to have no immediate effect on money, as it originates outside the money creating sector.

Our identifying restrictions on both the permanent and temporary shocks are summarised below.

$$\begin{array}{cc}\textbf{Permanent shocks}: & \textbf{Temporary shocks}: \\ \textbf{Long-run restrictions} & \textbf{Impact restrictions}\end{array}$$

$$\begin{bmatrix}\pi \\ y \\ is \\ il \\ id-is \\ ib-id \\ m4x \\ m4lx \\ pk \\ e\end{bmatrix} = \begin{bmatrix}0&0&0&0&\star \\ \star&0&0&0&\star \\ \star&\star&0&0&\star \\ \star&\star&\star&\star&\star \\ \star&\star&\star&\star&\star \\ \star&\star&\star&\star&\star \\ \star&\star&\star&0&\star \\ \star&\star&\star&\star&\star \\ \star&\star&\star&\star&\star \\ \star&\star&\star&\star&\star\end{bmatrix}\begin{bmatrix}\eta_{AD} \\ \eta_{Pol} \\ \eta_{brisk} \\ \eta_{Prem} \\ \eta_{mu}\end{bmatrix} \qquad \begin{bmatrix}\pi \\ y \\ is \\ il \\ id-is \\ ib-id \\ m4x \\ m4lx \\ pk \\ e\end{bmatrix} = \begin{bmatrix}0&0&0&0&\star \\ \star&0&0&0&\star \\ \star&\star&0&0&\star \\ \star&\star&\star&\star&\star \\ \star&\star&\star&\star&\star \\ \star&\star&\star&\star&\star \\ \star&\star&\star&0&\star \\ \star&\star&\star&\star&\star \\ \star&\star&\star&\star&\star \\ \star&\star&\star&\star&\star\end{bmatrix}\begin{bmatrix}\eta_{AD} \\ \eta_{Pol} \\ \eta_{brisk} \\ \eta_{Prem} \\ \eta_{mu}\end{bmatrix}$$

Permanent shocks	**Temporary shocks**
η_{TFP} = neutral aggregate supply shock	η_{AD} = aggregate demand shock
η_{for} = overseas demand/preference shock	η_{Pol} = monetary policy shock
η_{nom} = core/target inflation shock	η_{brisk} = Bank risk-taking shock
η_{coi} = cost of intermediation shock	η_{prem} = Risk premia shock
η_{fun} = wholesale funding shock	η_{mu} = Mark – up/cost – push

4.3.5 *Validating the shocks*

We can examine whether our identifying restrictions produce sensible responses by carrying out impulse response analysis and a forecast error-variance decomposition. A full set of impulse response charts and forecast error-variance tables can be found in the Appendices 2 and 3. First we consider the standard macroeconomic shocks.

Both the permanent and temporary aggregate supply shocks produce responses that suggest that output and inflation move in opposite directions in the short run, despite the absence of explicit sign restrictions. In the long run a positive TFP shock produces a depreciation of the real exchange rate, suggesting that higher exports are needed to offset the higher import spending resulting from the permanent expansion of output. Monetary policy also appears on average to have tried to offset the inflationary implications of a permanent TFP shock, but appears to accommodate mark-up shocks and minimise the output implications. The response of output under the temporary mark-up shock is relatively small. Both shocks account for over half the variance of inflation up to a two-year horizon.

The aggregate demand shocks we identify produce responses of output and inflation that move in the same direction in the short run, which is in line with theoretical priors. They also produce a stabilising policy response. The rise in output and inflation following the overseas demand shock is rather short-lived and insignificant, suggesting that the crowding out effect of policy and the real exchange rate happens relatively rapidly. The main effect of the shock is on the real exchange rate. The temporary aggregate demand shock has a more persistent effect on output and explains around 30% of the variance of output at very short horizons.

The monetary policy shocks that we identify also have sensible effects. A negative core inflation shock raises real (*ex post*) interest rates and leads to a fall in output and a depreciation of the real exchange rate, following an initial appreciation. The temporary policy shock also appears sensibly signed on output and inflation at the one- to two-year horizons. So we have no 'price puzzle' effects despite the use of timing restrictions. But the output response is very small and insignificant compared to the impact on inflation, which appears to mainly operate through the exchange rate and import prices. The temporary policy shock also appears to have a perverse effect on long rates via the term/risk premia. That could reflect higher uncertainty about monetary policy goals following any deviation from the 'average policy rule' used by policy-makers over the sample period.

The banking sector shocks produce some interesting differences and are compared in Figures 4.9–4.11 (again see the Appendix 2 for a full set of responses and standard error bands).

The cost of intermediation shock although it leads to a permanent impact on both money and credit, has only a very small impact on output in either the short or long run. A fall in the cost of intermediation also leads to a fall in equity prices, suggesting that it leads to a switch between equity and bank debt for a given level of activity. Overall, this shock accounts for about 36% of the movements in money at long horizons and around 36% of the movements in credit.

The wholesale funding shock appears to have a more significant effect on the economy. A fall in wholesale funding costs lowers credit spreads

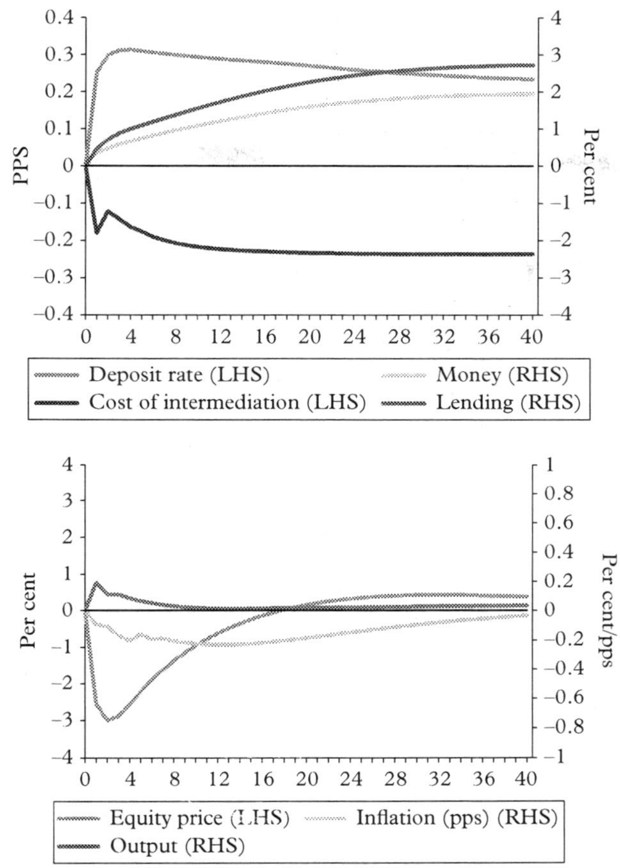

Figure 4.9. Impulse responses to a cost of intermediation shock

and boosts lending. That in turn leads to a rise in output that is significant and permanent (see Appendix 2 for standard error bands). There is also a significant fall in inflation. That in part may be driven by the initial appreciation of the exchange rate, but it also suggests that this shock has a permanent effect on potential supply, perhaps reflecting that the higher lending finds its way into riskier, more productive sectors. Money expands following this shock but by significantly less than lending. Unlike the cost of intermediation shock the expansion of money and credit is associated with a persistent pick-up in equity prices, in this case perhaps suggestive of some of the hot potato effects discussed earlier. Deposit rates fall by a similar amount to loan rates, as

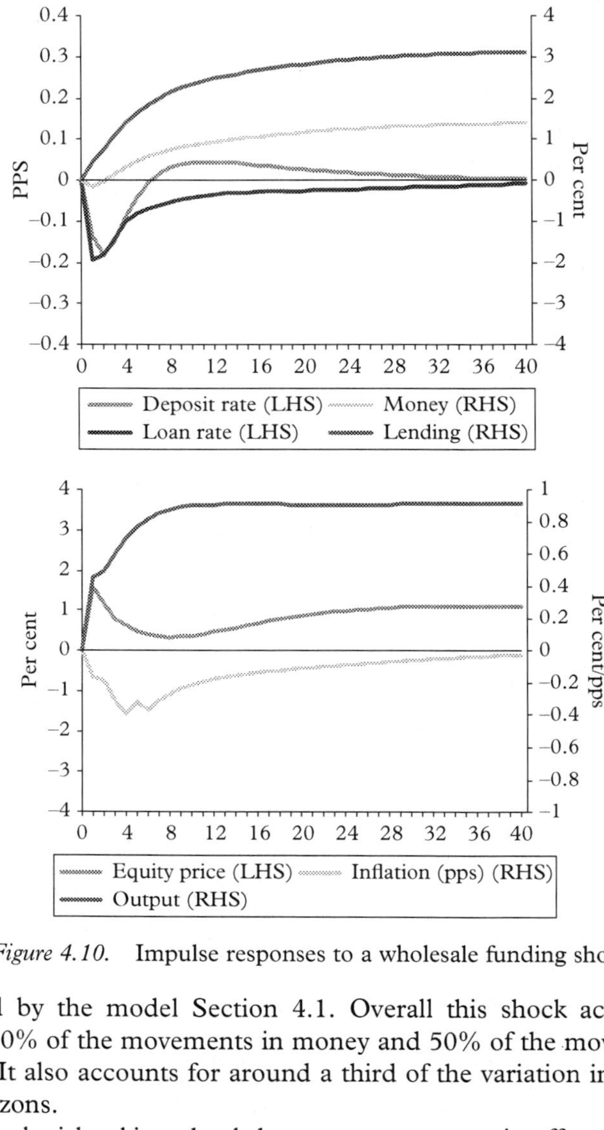

Figure 4.10. Impulse responses to a wholesale funding shock

predicted by the model Section 4.1. Overall this shock accounts for around 20% of the movements in money and 50% of the movements in lending. It also accounts for around a third of the variation in output at long horizons.

The bank risk-taking shock has a more symmetric effect on money and credit than the wholesale funding cost shock. It also leads to a significant fall only in loan rates rather than deposit rates, as suggested by the model in Section 4.1. Although this shock only has a temporary effect it accounts for around 10–20% of the movements in money and credit at the two- to three-year horizon. A positive shock to bank risk-taking that boosts money and credit also increases output, like the

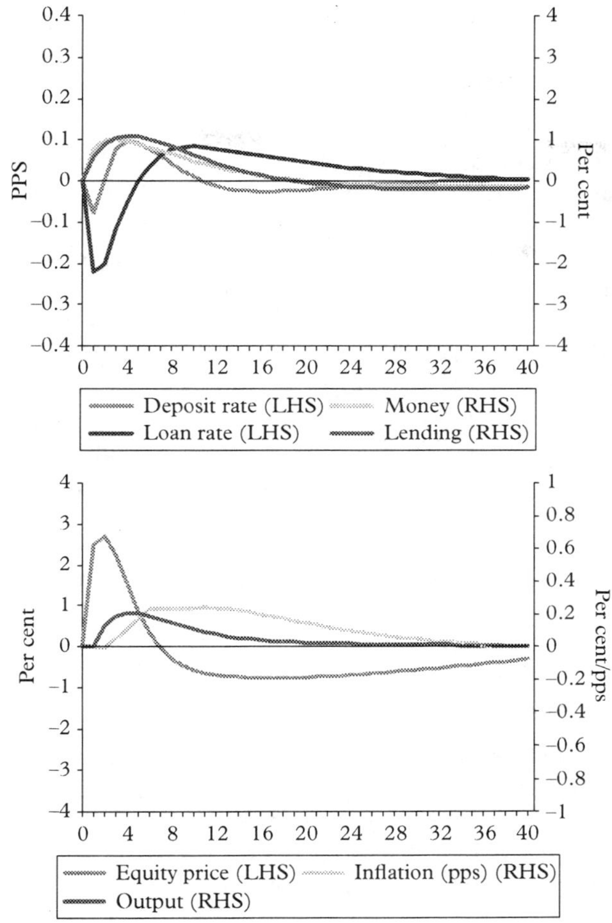

Figure 4.11. Impulse responses to a bank risk-taking shock

wholesale funding shock. By definition this shock is assumed not to have a permanent effect on output and potential supply, so inflation also rises in response to this shock. Asset prices also appear to respond positively to this shock, again suggesting that the money created by credit expansion finds its way into financing asset transactions.

Overall it suggests that our identifying restrictions on the banking sector shocks have led to meaningfully different shock responses that accord with our priors about how money and credit should behave and produce contrasting impacts on inflation and output that may help us explain the various features of the Long Expansion period.

4.4 Analysing the Long Expansion period – to what extent was the monetary sector the source of shocks driving the economy?

In this section we use historical decomposition analysis to analyse the importance of different shocks over the Long Expansion period and to see what light it sheds on the puzzles we outlined in the introduction. The advantage of having a long sample back to the 1960s is that we can also compare the Long Expansion period with other periods, including the subsequent financial crisis. A historical decomposition involves running a sequence of dynamic forecasts starting at a particular point in time. The first forecast is a base projection that takes the value of each variable at the start of the decomposition (reflecting the impact of shocks that have occurred before the start point) and maps out how each variable would return to its trend path in the absence of further shocks. Given this base projection, the path of each structural shock is then sequentially fed into to the SVAR until the resulting forecast is equivalent to the observed data. The marginal impact of each shock is then recorded to produce the historical decomposition.

4.4.1 What explain the movements in money and credit over the Long Expansion period?

Figures 4.12 and 4.13 show historical decompositions of real M4x and M4Lx growth over the entire historical period. We divide the period up into the Great Inflation period from 1967 to 1979, the Thatcher era from 1979 to the early 1990s, the Long Expansion period from the mid-1990s to mid-2007 and then finally the financial crisis to the end of 2013.

The contributions of the banking sector shocks we identify appear to tell a conventional story about the period before the Long Expansion. All three shocks contribute negatively to money and credit growth in the late 1960s prior to the introduction of Competition and Credit Control (CCC) in late 1971 reflecting the various controls put in place following the 1967 devaluation. After the introduction of CCC and during the Barber boom that followed these shocks then account for much of the expansion of money and credit growth before the introduction of the Corset in late 1973, although high inflation and weak activity contributed to the sharp slowdown in real money and credit growth. During the 1980s money and credit expanded relative to nominal GDP and all three shocks contributed to this. So financial liberalisation involved not only increased competition and a reduced cost of

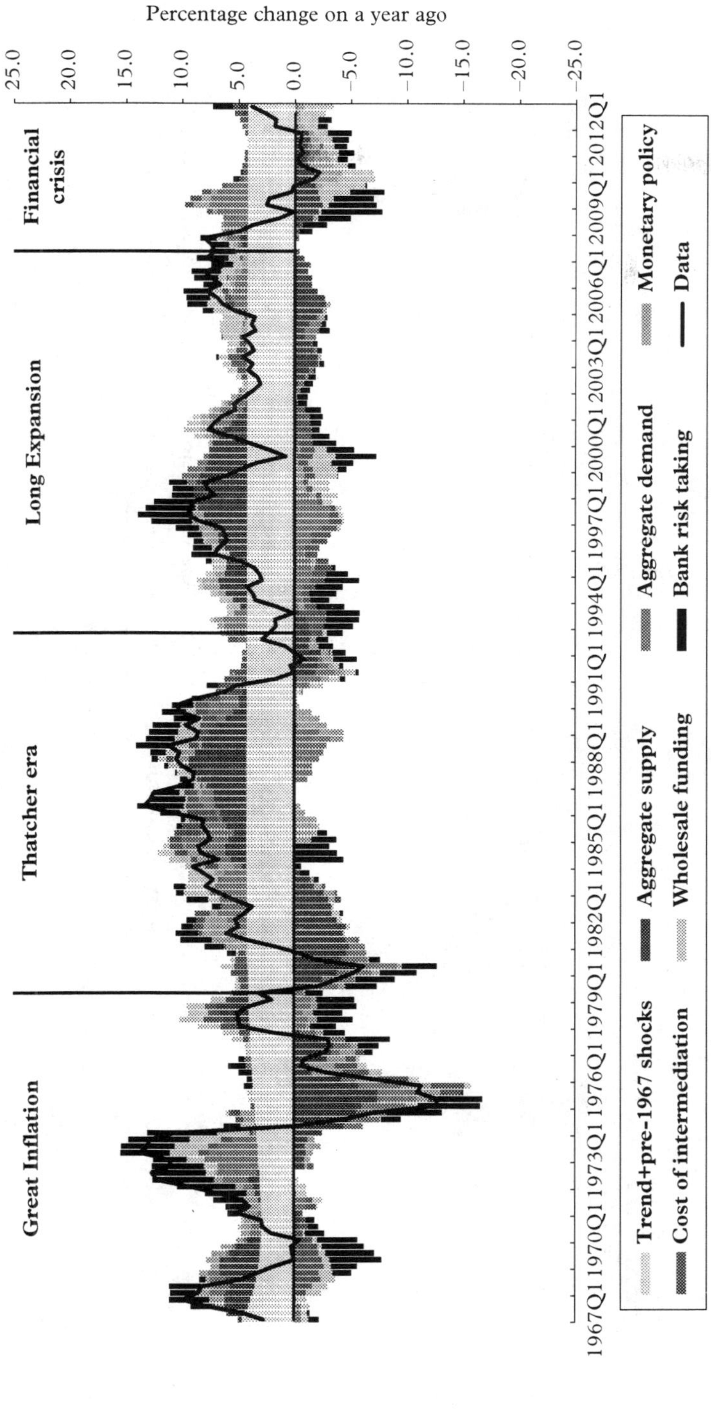

Figure 4.12. Historical decomposition of real M4x growth

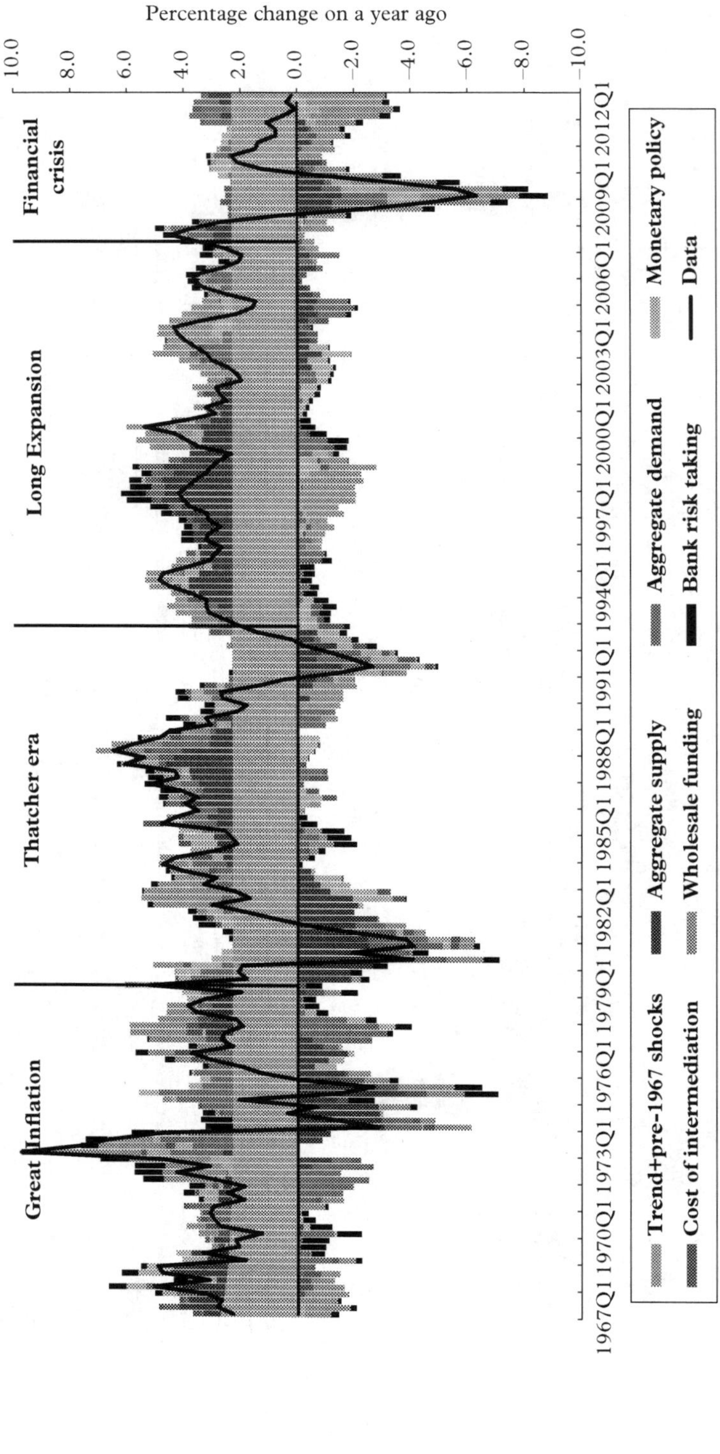

Figure 4.13. Historical decomposition of real lending growth

intermediation, but also an expansion of wholesale funding and extra risk-taking by banks, at least until the early 1990s recession, following which these shocks went into reverse and credit and money growth remained subdued until the mid-1990s. So the historical contributions suggest that the banking sector shocks we identify look plausible when seen in the context of the past 50 years of UK economic history.

During the Long Expansion period the wholesale funding shock appears to be the most important driver explaining the pick-up in credit growth ahead of the start of the financial crisis. That mainly reflects the expansion of securitisation and overseas deposit liabilities that we noted in the introduction. But interestingly the wholesale funding shock appears most prevalent in the period leading up to around 2005/06. The contributions to money growth from this shock are also positive, but of smaller size, consistent with the impulse responses shown earlier. So this shock can account for much of the wedge between lending growth and money growth over this period.

From 2005 to the start of the financial crisis in mid-2007 the bank risk-taking shock appears to be more important and reflects the fact that the wedge between credit and money growth started narrowing. So excessive risk-taking by the banking system may only have occurred late in the Long Expansion period. Prior to that it seems to have reflected the international search for yield by wholesale investors and the ability of UK banks to tap into that finance. While there is some evidence of increased competition pushing down on yields and the cost of intermediation it looks to be a smaller contribution than from the other two shocks.

During the financial crisis the wholesale funding and bank risk-taking shocks can account for almost all the collapse in lending over this period, reflecting the closure of wholesale funding markets and balance sheet retrenchment of the banking system.

4.4.2 *The impact of shocks on GDP and inflation*

Figures 4.14 and 4.15 show a historical decomposition of annual GDP growth and CPI inflation.

Standard aggregate demand and supply shocks account for a significant proportion of the movements in output over the past. As we noted earlier, the distinction between aggregate demand and supply shocks rests heavily on the assumption that demand shocks have no permanent effect on output, but the demand shock contributions do show some correlation with noteworthy fiscal episodes, such as the fiscal contraction in the early 1980s and expansion later in the decade. The banking

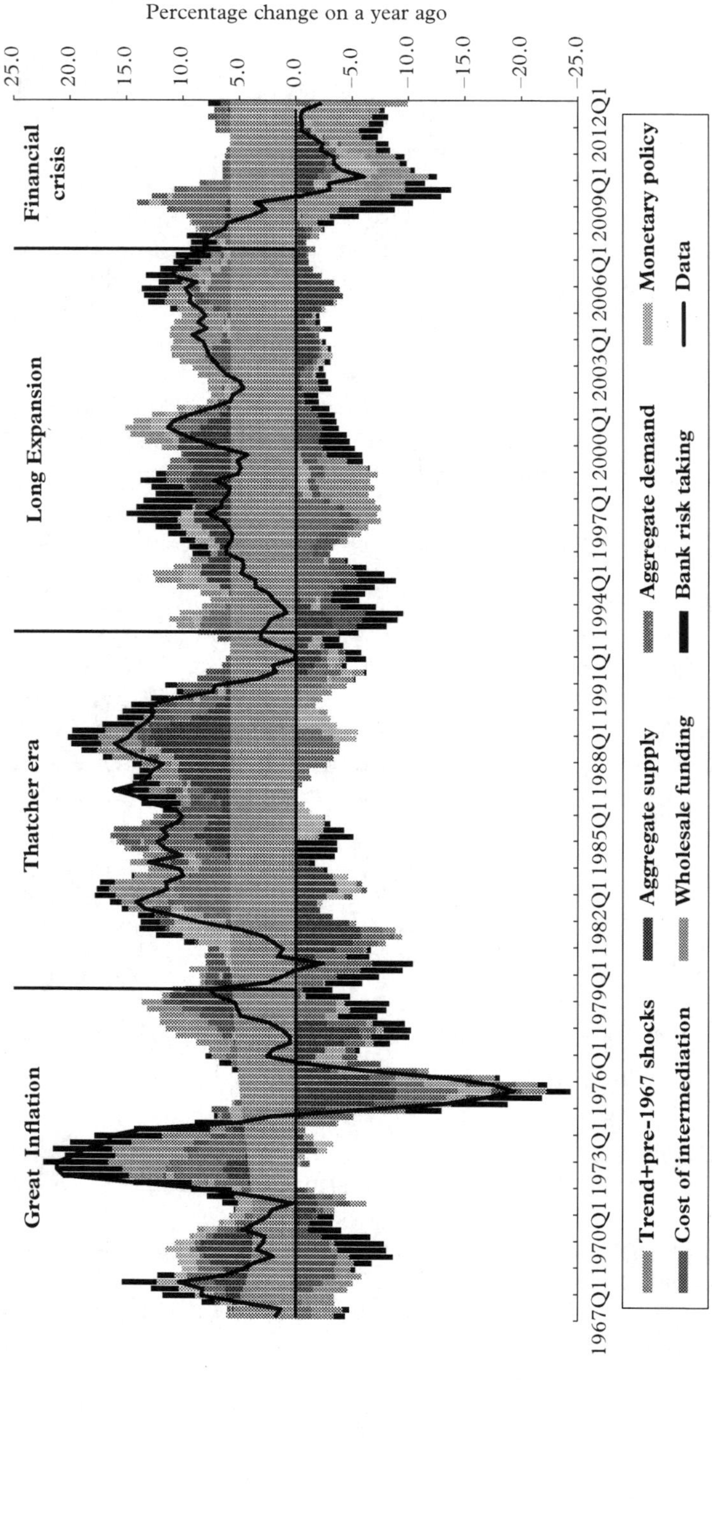

Figure 4.14. Historical decomposition of GDP growth

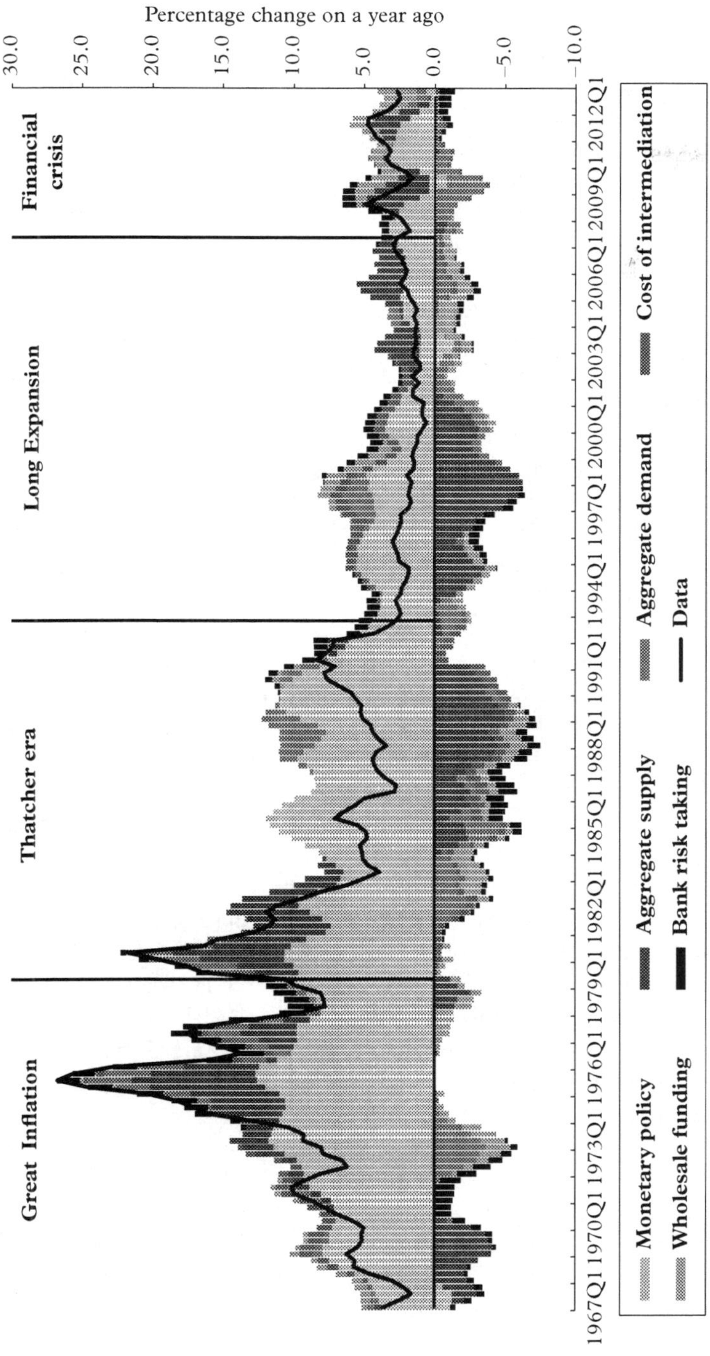

Figure 4.15. Historical decomposition of CPI inflation

sector shocks have also been important. In particular, during the early 1970s and 1980s the expansion of money and credit associated with the wholesale funding and bank risk-taking shocks looks to have had a powerful effect on output.

During the early part of the Long Expansion period aggregate supply shocks seem to have been the most important drivers of growth, perhaps reflecting the fall in the relative price of ICT capital goods over this period. Aggregate demand shocks played less of a role, though that may just reflect the fact that we have restricted the aggregate demand shock to have no effect on output in the long run. But from around 2000 onwards the wholesale and, to a lesser extent, bank risk-taking shocks were the most important drivers of growth. They explain why output growth was above its historic trend over this period. So these shocks, while they increase the ratio of credit and money relative to GDP, also worked to raise output itself. The importance of these shocks carried through into the financial crisis. The large negative shocks to wholesale funding and bank risk-taking can explain around half of the fall in GDP in 2009; the rest is explained by negative aggregate demand shocks and supply shocks. That probably reflects the collapse in world trade – the effect of a global credit shock – and higher energy prices. They can also explain almost all of the slowdown in GDP growth in 2011 and 2012. That probably reflects the impact of the euro area on bank funding costs.

In terms of inflation, the permanent and temporary monetary policy shocks naturally dominate the explanation of the large swings in inflation during the 1970s and 1980s. But from the mid-1990s onwards the other shocks become relatively more important. Importantly, over the Long Expansion period *the wholesale funding shock was important in keeping inflation down* over this period, despite it pushing up strongly on output growth. That reflects the possibility that this shock has a beneficial impact on potential supply as noted earlier, perhaps because credit was directed to more productive risk-taking industries. That may seem surprising given that a lot of credit was being channelled into commercial and residential property over this period. But the downward pressure on inflation occurs mainly in the 2003–07 period, when non-commercial and real estate (non-CRE) lending also picked up strongly. So this shock acted as a beneficial supply shock that offset the upward pressure from oil prices and other aggregate supply and cost-push shocks over this period. This can also explain why inflation has remained stubbornly high over the financial crisis. The collapse in credit associated with the negative wholesale funding shock is estimated to have significantly pushed up on inflation over this period, suggesting that weak credit growth has had a detrimental impact on potential supply.

So overall it appears that shocks emanating from the money-creating sector were important drivers of both output and inflation in this period and appear to have had beneficial effects on the supply side.

4.5 The role of money as a propagation mechanism

Although aggregate models are useful, because they allow us to look at the complete macroeconomic response to structural shocks, they are less useful for looking at the role of money as a propagation mechanism. The cointegrated VAR we estimated in Section 4.3 did contain a money disequilibrium term, and this, together with lags of money growth, did feed significantly into a number of the reduced-form VAR equations. But the linkages between money, asset prices and spending have tended to be clearer at the sectoral level in the UK data (see Congdon and Ward (1993), Fisher and Vega (1993), Thomas (1997a,b), Thomas (1997b), Brigden and Mizen (2004), Chrystal and Mizen (2005a,b)). In particular, in structural econometric models of sectoral money holdings, where money is estimated jointly with other sectoral variables, money appears to have some incremental information about future movements in asset prices and spending that are not detectable in aggregate models. As noted earlier, there were notable differences in the sectoral movements of money in the Long Expansion period. In particular, much of the pick-up in money growth in the early to mid-2000s leading up to the crisis was due to corporate sector money holdings, both financial and non-financial. So in this section we look at what these movements in sectoral money holdings may have been able to tell us about asset prices and spending over this period. Unlike the previous section we abstract from the underlying shocks that drove these money holdings, but rather investigate how the money, once created, may have flowed through the rest of the economy.

The key challenge with sectoral models is that they need to be augmented with assumptions that allow us to link the sectors together to produce an aggregate picture of how the wider economy is affected. The identification method is also different from that used in the aggregate CVAR model of the previous section. The models start off as small cointegrated VARs estimated at the sectoral level, where, say, personal sector money holdings are jointly estimated with consumption. These systems are additionally conditioned on certain aggregate variables that are treated as exogenous to the sector for estimation purposes, such as household income and GDP. Some structural restrictions are then placed on the short-term contemporaneous relationships between the variables. Unlike the structural VAR approach adopted in the aggregate model, it is more difficult to identify independent 'shocks' at the sectoral level using theoretical restrictions. Instead, the models are identified by placing restrictions on the short-run interactions between the variables or on how the long-run cointegrating relationships enter particular equations. In this sense, the aim is to identify structural 'equations' that have some plausible theoretical interpretation, rather than to identify specific 'shocks'. In the econometric literature these models are known as structural econometric models or 'SECMs'.

We use three sectoral models, one for the household sector, one for the PNFC (private non-financial company sector) and one for the financial company sector. The key properties of each model are briefly articulated in turn.[9] We then discuss how the three models can be combined to investigate the role of sectoral money holdings in the build-up to the crisis.

4.5.1 *The financial company sector model*

The financial company sector model consists of a four-equation VAR of financial company real sterling money holdings, real sterling asset values, the real deposit rate and a composite yield that weights together the dividend yield of the FTSE All-Share (plus a constant 3% as a proxy for real dividend growth) and the ten-year real zero coupon government bond yield. The weights reflect the shares of gilts and equities in financial companies' portfolios.

The appropriate definition of the financial company sector is a difficult one. Our preferred measure would be to include the range of institutions that would typically hold the assets purchased by the APF. This would include insurance companies and pension funds, asset managers and other fund managers. In the UK monetary statistics, these institutions are termed non-intermediate OFCs or (NIOFCs).[10] Unfortunately, the data for this sector are only available back to 1998 and are confined to their money holdings. Longer runs of data on both money and total asset holdings are available back further for the narrower insurance company and pension fund (ICPF) sector. We therefore use VAR estimates based on the ICPF sector as a proxy for the broader NIOFC sector.

9 More details on the econometric approach and identification procedure can be found in Thomas (1997a,b) and Brigden and Mizen (2004).

10 This classification excludes financial companies that either intermediate between banks, such as the London Clearing House (LCH), or are bank holding companies or subsidiaries. For a more detailed discussion of the UK's monetary aggregates, see Burgess and Janssen (2007).

The model, estimated over the period 1987Q1–2008Q3, suggests that there is one long-run relationship in the data. This is identified as a money demand relationship of the form:

$$m = w + \theta^{\star}(rd - rg)/100$$

where m is the log of money holdings, w is the log of 'wealth' or total financial assets, rd is the own rate on money (the deposit rate) in percentage points and rg is the weighted rate of return on non-monetary assets (gilts and equities) in percentage points. θ is the semi-elasticity of money holdings with respect to a change in the opportunity cost of holding money.

The dynamics of the VAR system suggest that asset values and yields both respond to an increase in money holdings in the financial company sector. In particular, the gap between actual and equilibrium money holdings has a significant positive effect on asset prices and a negative effect on yields. But the feedback of this gap onto money itself is not significant (see Table 4.7 for details). It may seem odd that excess money does not feed back into actual money holdings, but in fact it is supportive of a monetarist transmission mechanism. It suggests that when money holdings increase in the financial company sector, asset managers do not repay bank debt or purchase many assets directly from overseas residents. Rather, they purchase assets from each other in a financial merry-go-round. In this way, financial companies respond to monetary disequilibria by buying assets from one another, causing money to circulate like a 'hot potato' within the sector. The results suggest that this process would continue until asset prices are bid up sufficiently and financial yields fall sufficiently to make financial companies willing to hold additional money, restoring equilibrium.

The long-run impact on asset prices depends on the size of the percentage increase in money and on the semi-elasticity of money with respect to non-monetary yields. To see this we can 'invert' the long-run money demand function (legitimately, given that causality appears to go from money to asset prices) to give:

$$\%\text{ change in } w \approx \%\text{ change in } m + \theta^{\star}\text{pp change in } rg$$

where deposit rates are held constant. If we assume that yields are inversely related in the long run to their price with a coefficient of γ we get:

$$\text{pp change in } rg = -\gamma^{\star}\ \%\text{ change in } w$$

$$\%\text{ change in } w \approx (\%\text{ change in } m)/(1 + \theta\gamma)$$

This suggests that in general the change in financial asset prices will be less than proportionate to the change in NIOFCs' money holdings if θ

Table 4.7. ICPF (insurance company and pension funds) system of equations

Variables:

rm4icpf=log of real M4 holdings of ICPFs
rwicpf=log of real total sterling asset values of ICPFs
rdicpf=real rate of return on deposits
ryield=real rate of return on ICPFs domestic assets proxied by a portfolio share-weighted average of: (a) the real return on ten-year gilts; and (b) the FTSE All-Share dividend yield+the average growth rate of private sector output over the sample period (3% pa).

Cointegration and weak exogeneity test: four lags; sample 1988(1) to 2008(3)

Long-run money demand cointegrating vector (β), standard errors in brackets

rm4icpf	1.0000
rwicpf	−1.0000
rdicpf	−0.10403
ryield	0.10403 (0.041642)

Loading vector (α), standard errors in brackets

rm4icpf	0.00000
rwicpf	0.10431 (0.034)
rdicpf	0.00000
ryield	−0.45922 (0.172)

LR test of weak exogeneity restrictions: $\chi^2(4)=4.9826$ [0.2891]

$\beta_1=1;\beta_2=-1;\beta_3=-\beta_4;\ \alpha_1=0;\alpha_3=0$

System estimated by FIML over sample: 1988(1) to 2008(3)

Δrwicpf =	+ **0**.06692***Δrm4icpf**(− **1**)	+ **0**.06692***Δrm4icpf**(− **2**)	
(*SE*)	(0.03003)	(-----)	
	+ **0**.0882***ECMicpf**(− **1**)	+ 0.0163*Δrdicpf(− 2)	+ 0.2633
	(0.02946)	(0.007181)	(0.0854)

Standard error of the equation=0.0457

Δryield=	−**0**.2344***Δrm4icpf**	−0.0975*Δrdicpf(−2)	−**0**.3892***ECMicpf**(−**1**)	−1.1449
(SE)	(0.235)	(0.0358)	(0.1463)	(0.424)

Standard error of the equation=0.226

ECMicpf = rm4icpf–rwicpf–0.104*(rdicpf-ryield)

is non-zero.[11] As a result, money holdings will rise as a share of total financial assets. This reflects the fact that money demand is made consistent with a higher supply in part by a wealth or scale effect (the '1' in

11 Throughout we make the simplifying arithmetic assumption that the change in asset values is approximately equal to the overall change in the asset prices of the securities held in NIOFCs' portfolios.

'$1 + \theta\gamma$') and in part by a substitution effect (given by the '$\theta\gamma$' component). In the extreme case where θ is infinite, money is a perfect substitute for other assets, and higher money holdings can be accommodated with little or no change in financial yields and prices. When θ is zero, money and other assets are perfect complements and will increase proportionately together. In our estimated system, θ is estimated to be around 10 and γ is around 0.04 in the long run. This implies that a 10% increase in NIOFCs' money will lead to around a 7% increase in asset prices and a 0.4 percentage point fall in yields.

4.5.2 *The private non-financial corporation (PNFC) sector*

The PNFC sector model uses a three-equation system of PNFC money holdings, borrowing and investment based on Brigden and Mizen (2004). Money is required for investment spending and investment itself depends on output, the cost of capital and capacity utilisation. But, like the financial company and household sectors, there is two-way feedback between money and investment. In particular, the gap between actual money holdings and equilibrium money demand has a positive effect on investment as highlighted in Table 4.8. This introduces some direct effects of money holdings on investment. This gives a structural interpretation to the leading indicator property of PNFC money holdings found in other studies (see e.g. Astley and Haldane (1995)).

4.5.3 *The household sector*

The household sector model used is a simple two-equation system of household M4 and consumption spending based on Thomas (1997a). As discussed in that paper, for estimation purposes, income, financial and housing wealth and rates of return are treated as weakly exogenous. In this system, personal sector money holdings depend on consumption according to the transactions demand for money, and both consumption and long-run money demand depend on total net financial and housing wealth (asset values). But there is also a direct effect of money holdings on consumption spending, suggesting some form of liquidity effect on consumption. These terms are highlighted in bold in Table 4.7.

4.5.4 *Linking the sectoral models together*

The three sectoral systems outlined above need to be connected by various linking equations between asset prices, household wealth and the cost of capital. In particular, assumptions are required about how real

Table 4.8. Household sector model equations

Variables:

rm4hh=log of real M4 holdings of households
rwhh=log of real household total financial and tangible wealth
c=log of real consumption
y=log of real household disposable income
rdhh=own rate on household deposits
rb=Bank Rate
pc=log of consumption deflator

System estimated by FIML over sample: 1977(4) to 2008(4)

Δrm4hh =	+ 0.7947*Δrm4hh(− 1)	− 0.04283*ECMrm4hh(− 1)	+ 0.00837	+ 0.1174*Δrwhh
(SE)	(0.152)	(0.0166)	(0.00258)	(0.0377)
	+ 0.06627*Δrwhh(− 1)	+ 0.1568*Δy	+ 0.1568*Δ*y*(− 1)	+ 0.002506*(Δrdhh-Δrb)
	(0.0413)	(0.072)	(0.072)	(0.0019)
	+ 0.002219*(Δrdhh(− 1)	− Δrb(− 1))	− 1.259*ΔΔpc	− 0.8127*Δc
	(0.00172)		(0.248)	(0.314)

Standard error of the equation=0.00987802

Δlc =	+ **0**.6778*Δ**rm4hh**	+ **0**.3145*Δ**rm4hh**(− 1)	− 0.2814*ECMc(− 1)	+ 0.2963	+ 0.05385*Δrwhh
(SE)	(0.138)	(0.126)	(0.0446)	(0.0474)	(0.0279)
	+ 0.04429*Δrwhh(− 1)	+ 0.1421*Δ*y*	+ 0.07056*Δ*y*(− 1)	− 0.003302*Δrb	
	(0.0279)	(0.0655)	(0.0634)	(0.000902)	
	+ 0.003119*Δrdhh(− 1)				
	(0.00115)				

Standard error of the equation=0.00835391

ECMrm4hh = rm4hh − 0.55*c − 0.45*rwhh − 0.075*(rdhh-rb)

ECMc = c − 0.6*y − 0.25*rwhh + 0.00975*rdhh − 2.2854*Δpc

GDP responds for a given increase in real consumption and investment and how that in turn affects inflation. We make the following assumptions in our preferred baseline specification:

(i) The real cost of capital is assumed to fall according to the impact of higher equity and bond prices on the dividend and corporate bond yield. Household equity and bond wealth are assumed to move in line with the value of financial company assets. We assume that house prices and housing wealth are unchanged.
(ii) To produce an impact on GDP we combine the consumption and investment impacts according to their expenditure shares, but also assume that imports increase in proportion to GDP. Dwellings investment is assumed to rise in proportion to business investment. Exports are held fixed, as we assume that the exchange rate is unchanged in our baseline case. Note that consumption depends on income, so there will be feedback or multiplier effects of higher GDP back on to household spending. Similarly, investment depends on capacity utilisation which we model as a function of GDP growth and the level of output detrended by a linear time trend. So there are also investment accelerator effects embodied in the system. This means the system response of consumption and investment will be stronger than the partial effects of higher money holdings shown in the previous section.
(iii) We close the model with a simple Phillips curve equation linking the output gap to inflation, which we base on the specification of the Bank of England quarterly model (see Harrison et al. (2005)).
(iv) We also assume that nominal deposit rates and Bank Rate are unchanged. So there are no monetary policy feedbacks incorporated in these simulations. We also implicitly assume that inflation expectations are unchanged, given that they are not explicitly identified in the sectoral models. So *ex ante* real policy and deposit and loan rates are implicitly fixed in these simulations (Table 4.9).

4.5.5 Quantifying the propagation role of money in driving asset prices and GDP during the run-up to the financial crisis

To try to calibrate the role of money as a propagator of shocks we take the bolted together sectoral models and feed the increase in corporate money holdings observed between 2003 and 2007 into the equations for asset prices, yields and investment spending, which contain terms in monetary overhangs and current and lagged money growth. So in essence we are ignoring how the extra money balances were created, but then asking ourselves how that increase in the supply of money

Table 4.9. PNFC sector model equations (with lending variables and terms removed)

Variables:

rm4pnfc=log of real M4 holdings of PNFCs
ibus=log of real business investment
y=log of real output
profits=log of real PNFC profits
rdpnfc=own rate on PNFC deposits
rl=effective PNFC loan rate
rb=Bank Rate
pgdp=log of GDP deflator
rcc=log of real user cost of capital
util=CBI capacity utilisation
D85=dummy variable for 1985 Q1

System estimated by FIML over sample: 1978(3) to 2008(3)

Δibus =	−0.1172*ECMpnfci(−1)	+**0**.0721***ECMpnfcm**(−**1**)	
(*SE*)	(0.0226)	(0.025)	
	−0.02279*ΔΔrl	+0.02252*ΔΔrb	
	(0.00585)	(0.00544)	
	+0.1169*ΔD85	+0.03665*util(−1)	−0.4706
	(0.0198)	(0.00828)	(0.114)

Standard error of the equation=0.0227437

Δrm4pnfc =	−0.06761* ECMpnfcm(−1)	+0.0264* (Δrdpnfc − Δrb)	+0.0170*(Δrdpnfc(−1) − Δrb(−1))
(*SE*)	(0.0179)	(0.00775)	(0.00803)
	+0.03414*Δprof	−1*Δpgdp	
	(0.0152)	(-----)	
	+0.02628*ΔD85	+0.05605	
	(0.0173)	(0.0111)	

Standard error of the equation=0.0241983

ECMpnfci = ibus − y + 0.5 ∗ rcc + 0.082 ∗ (rl-rb)

ECMpnfcm = m4pnfc − 0.5 ∗ ibus − 0.5 ∗ y − 0.068 ∗ (rdpnfc-rb) might have passed through to the rest of the economy. So it is a partial 'helicopter drop' experiment designed to isolate the role of money holdings on particular expenditure components and allowing those to feed through to the economy with the typical multiplier and accelerator effects on GDP. As noted earlier, we assume no monetary policy or other stabilising response to these partial simulations. So they should be viewed as an upper bound on how much money might be contributing to the propagation of shocks over this period.

We look at the 2003–07 period in particular as the money created over this period is dominated by banking sector shocks and is the period during which there was a particular build-up in corporate sector money holdings. This arguably makes the partial simulation exercise discussed above more relevant/appealing as these are shocks that directly affect the supply of money and may be more likely to lead to monetary overhangs than other aggregate shocks. Figures 4.16 and 4.17 show the impact on asset prices, investment and real GDP compared with the actual increases for both variables over the 2003–07 period split into the partial contributions from PNFC money and NIOFC money holdings.

- The build-up of NIOFC money holdings was mainly concentrated in 2005 onwards and the sectoral models suggest the build-up of money on this scale might have been enough to raise equity prices by around 25%, which is just under a third of the actual increase in equity prices of around 85%. This is sufficient to boost consumption by 1.8% and

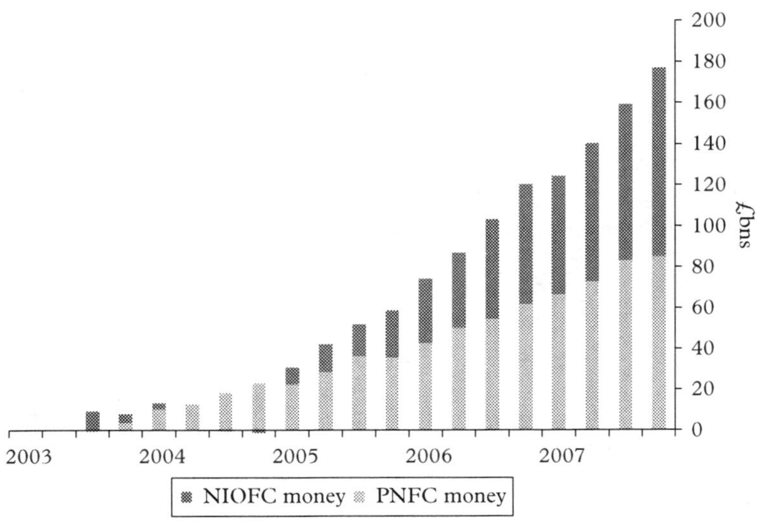

Figure 4.16. The build-up in corporate money 2003–07

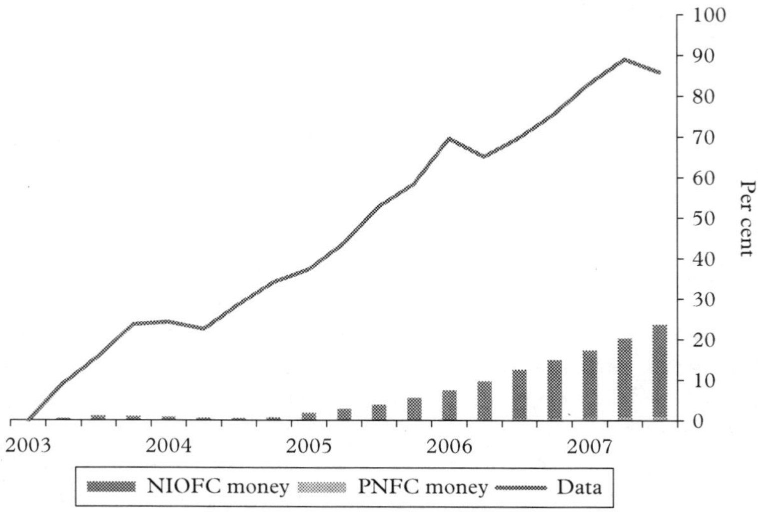

Figure 4.17. The impact on equity prices

GDP by just over 1% by 2007Q3 and would have doubled over the following year had the financial crisis not occurred.

- The £60bn increase in PNFC money holdings is sufficient to explain the entire increase in real business investment over this period. This is sufficient to have raised the level of GDP by around 2% by the start of the financial crisis.
- Collectively the increase in money holdings over this period may have been sufficient to raise the level of GDP by 3% through liquidity effects and the impact of monetary disequilibria on investment and equity prices. That is around a fifth of the actual increase and half of the increase of GDP relative to its historic trend. That suggests that money may have been a significant propagator of the banking sector shocks that occurred over this period (Figures 4.18 and 4.19).

4.6 Conclusions

This chapter has examined the behaviour of credit and money in the lead up to the financial crisis of 2007. We use the information from both money and credit and their rates of return to help identify different types of banking sector shocks over the past. We also use the information in sectoral money holdings to identify the role of money in the propagation of shocks. Our results suggest several qualitative and quantitative conclusions.

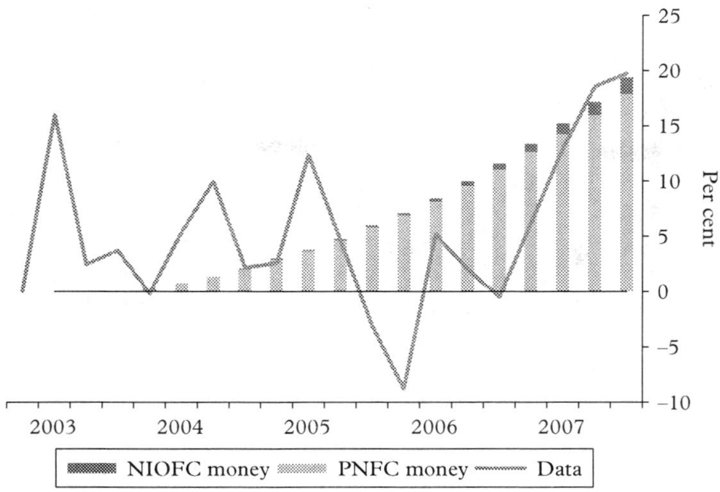

Figure 4.18. The impact on business investment

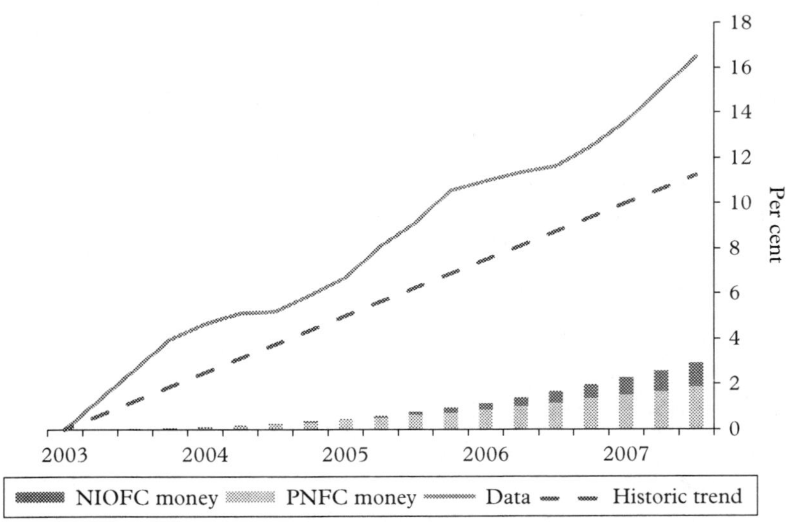

Figure 4.19. The impact on GDP

A key driver of credit growth over this period appears to be a shift in the willingness of wholesale investors to provide funds to the UK banking system, which we attribute to increased risk-taking by wholesale investors. This can explain the more rapid expansion of credit relative to money growth over this period. That shock boosted asset prices and demand, but also appears to have had a beneficial effect on the supply side of the economy, which partly explains the lack of an inflationary response. There is also evidence of increased risk-taking by banks in the immediate lead up to the crisis. This did provide some impulse to GDP and inflation, but was cut short by the financial crisis where the willingness to both supply wholesale funds and take risks collapsed.

A partial analysis of sectoral money holdings suggests that money may well have played a significant part in the transmission of banking sector shocks to GDP in the lead up to the financial crisis. The circulation of increased money in the financial sector can potentially explain around a third of the increase in equity prices and 20% of the GDP increase over the four-year period.

Overall our results suggest that it is important to look at *both* money and credit and their rates of return in order to understand what happened in the lead up to the financial crisis and what occurred in its aftermath. A joint analysis helps distinguish between different types of banking sector shocks and allows a better understanding of their propagation. This will be important in monitoring the recovery of the UK economy going forward and assessing the appropriate response of policy.

Appendix 1: Long-run restrictions methodology

In this section, we describe the general approach to modelling the time series in the cointegrated SVAR discussed in Section 4.3. In particular, we describe what we mean by the terms 'permanent' and 'temporary' shock and the terms 'trend' and 'cycle'. We also explain how we 'identify' them, i.e. give them an economic interpretation.

(a) Trends and cycles The cointegrated SVAR approach involves modelling our time series as the sum of two components, a trend and a cycle:

$$x_t = x_0 + \mathrm{F}\tau_t + \Phi(\mathrm{L})\, v_t \tag{A.1}$$

where

x_t = a vector of the n time series of interest at time t.

$\mathrm{F}\tau_t$ = the non-stationary or permanent components of x_t, with τ_t = the trends and F = loading matrix (i.e. how each trend affects each of the variables in the long run).

$\Phi(\mathrm{L})\, v_t$ = the stationary or temporary components of x_t, with v_t a vector of white noise disturbances, which generate dynamic or 'cyclical' effects through the distributed lag matrix $\Phi(\mathrm{L})$, where L is the lag operator ($\mathrm{L}^n\, v_t = v_{t-n}$). So $\Phi(\mathrm{L})v_t$ is a stationary distributed lag of current and past disturbances $= \Phi_0 \, v_t + \Phi_1 L v_t + \Phi_2 L^2 v_t \ldots$ or equivalently $= \Phi_0 \, v_t + \Phi_1 \, v_{t-1} + \ldots$

(b) Stochastic trends and permanent shocks In addition to the usual deterministic growth or 'drift' term, we allow the trends to have a stochastic or random component, made up of a sequence of small random disturbances. Since these disturbances have a permanent effect on each of the variables, they are termed the 'permanent shocks'.

$$\tau_t = \mu + \tau_{t-1} + \eta_{1t} \tag{A.2a}$$

or

$$\tau_t = \mu_t + \sum_{j=0}^{t} \eta_{1t-j} \tag{A.2b}$$

where μ represents deterministic growth and η_{1t} are the permanent shocks. So our stochastic trends are simply a vector of random walks with drift. And the stochastic part of the trend is simply the sum of the current and past permanent shocks to hit the economy.

Since our trends are stochastic, there is no reason to restrict the permanent shocks driving these trends from having cyclical effects (i.e. dynamic effects that differ from the long-run effects). So the vector v_t contains both permanent and temporary shocks:

$$v_t = [\eta_{1t} \; \eta_{2t}]'$$

where η_{2t} are purely temporary shocks, which do not have a long-run impact on x_t and so do not form part of the stochastic trends.

So in general, our trend-cycle model for x_t can be written in terms of the permanent and temporary shocks as:

$$x_t = x_0 + \mu_t + F \sum_{i=0}^{t-1} \eta_{1t-i} + \Phi(L) \begin{bmatrix} \eta_{1t} \\ \eta_{2t} \end{bmatrix} \tag{A.3}$$

where F is a $n \times k$ matrix, where k is the number of permanent shocks driving the system. Such a representation is often called a moving-average ('MA') representation, as it describes movements in x_t as a weighted moving average of current and past shocks.

(c) Alternative ways of modelling the trends There are of course other ways of modelling the non-stationary components of our series. One obvious alternative is to model them as simple linear deterministic trends. In this case, the shocks in the model affect only the cyclical movements of each variable and are independent of the systematic forces driving the trends.

Another way of modelling the trends is as a sequence of one-off deterministic regime shifts:

$$\tau_t = \mu + \mu^{\star} D_t + \tau_{t-1} \tag{A.4a}$$

$$\tau_t = \mu_t + \mu^{\star} \sum_{i=0}^{t} D_{t-i} \tag{A.4b}$$

where D is a vector of impact dummy variables and $\sum_{i=0}^{t} D_{t-i}$ a vector of one-zero step-dummies.

In this case, the non-stationarity of x_t is the result of a number of large relatively infrequent 'regime' shifts, rather than a sequence of successive small random changes. This may be important for some of the trends we wish to identify. For example, the underlying nominal anchor or permanent component of inflation may be best modelled as a series of known shifts in the policy regime, rather than as a sequence of small incremental changes. A similar argument may be used for modelling the trend in financial liberalisation.

(d) Estimating a common trends model The estimation of a model such as (A.1) proceeds by recognising that it is the inverse representation of a VAR model:

$$A(L)x_t = d + e_t \tag{A.5}$$

where $A(\mathrm{L}) = A_0 + A_1\mathrm{L} + A_2\mathrm{L}^2 \ldots$ and the structural shocks that we ultimately recover, through the use of economic identifying restrictions, are simply a transformation of the VAR residuals e_t. For the moment, we leave the identification issue aside and proceed as if the VAR residuals, e_t, are equivalent to the economic shocks we wish to recover, denoted earlier as η_t. This is to focus attention on determining the number of permanent and temporary shocks driving the system. This has an important bearing on how we invert the VAR representation to yield an MA representation.

The number of permanent shocks depends upon the cointegrating properties of the data. Loosely speaking, two or more non-stationary variables are said to cointegrate if a linear combination of them is found to be stationary. In other words, the non-stationary or trend components of the variables tend to move together over time in some proportion, and the linear combination of the variables can be thought of as defining a long-run equilibrium relationship. This in turn implies that the non-stationary components of these variables are driven by a 'common' stochastic trend (or trends). The implication is that there are fewer stochastic trends or permanent shocks than there are endogenous variables. And the number of columns in the matrix

$$F = k < n.$$

To see the duality between cointegration and the existence of common stochastic trends, we rewrite the VAR above in vector error-correction (VECM) form, where the long-run relationships between the levels of the variables in x_t are isolated in the matrix Π:

$$B(\mathrm{L})\Delta x_t = d + \Pi x_{t-1} + e_t \tag{A.6}$$

If none of the variables cointegrate, then $\Pi = 0$, and we are left with a standard VAR in the first differences of the variables

$$B(\mathrm{L})\Delta x_t = d + e_t \tag{A.7}$$

This, in most cases, can be easily inverted to yield the MA representation:

$$\Delta x_t = \mu + C(\mathrm{L})e_t \text{ where } C(\mathrm{L}) = B(\mathrm{L})^{-1} \tag{A.8}$$

and rewriting in terms of trends and cycles

$$x_t = x_0 + \mu_t + C(1)\sum_{i=0}^{t-1} e_{t-i} + C^{\star}(\mathrm{L})e_t \tag{A.9}$$

where $C^{\star}(\mathrm{L}) = (1-\mathrm{L})^{-1}[C(\mathrm{L}) - C(1)]$ and $C(1)$is the long-run impact matrix equivalent to F above. In this case, the matrix F is an $n \times n$ matrix, and there are $k = n$ stochastic trends driving x_t.

If the variables are cointegrated with r cointegrating vectors or long-run relationships in the data, then rank (Π) = r and Π can be written as $\Pi = \alpha\beta'$, where β is an $n \times r$ matrix of r cointegrating vectors, and α is an $n \times r$ matrix of factor loadings. Inverting the VAR is more difficult in this case. We can still write the model as

$$x_t = x_0 + \mu_t + C(1)\sum_{i=0}^{t-1} e_{t-i} + C^{\star}(\mathrm{L})e_t \tag{A.10}$$

But this time, $C(1) = F$ is a reduced rank matrix (rank = $n - r$), which Engle and Granger (1987) and Engle and Yoo (1991) show can be written as the product of two matrices $C(1) = \gamma\theta'\gamma$ and θ are $n \times n - r$ (or equivalently $n \times k$) matrices related (non-uniquely) to the parameters of the cointegrating vectors α and β through the relationships $\beta'\gamma = 0$ and $\theta'\alpha = 0$. In this case, the trend cycle decomposition of x_t should be written:

$$x_t = x_0 + \mu t + \gamma\tau_t + C^{\star}(\mathrm{L})e_t \tag{A.11}$$

where there are $n - r$ common stochastic trends (CSTs) given by:

$$\tau_t = \theta' \sum_{i=0}^{t-1} e_{t-i} \tag{A.12}$$

So in general, when there are r cointegrating relationships among the n variables in x_t, the MA representation is defined in terms of $k = n - r$ common stochastic trends or permanent shocks and r temporary shocks.

Example: King, Plosser, Stock and Watson (KPSW) model (1991)

To see the duality between cointegration and common trends, consider the example in KPSW (1991).

x_t consists of consumption, investment and output:

$$x_t = [con_t \; inv_t \; gdp_t]'$$

KPSW suspect that consumption, investment and GDP are ultimately all driven by a single common stochastic trend – productivity. The 'great ratios' (ie $con_t - gdp_t$ and $inv_t - gdp_t$) are stationary, so that there are two cointegrating relationships between consumption and output and investment and output.

$$\beta' x_t = \begin{bmatrix} 1 & 0 & -1 \\ 0 & 1 & -1 \end{bmatrix} \begin{bmatrix} con_t \\ inv_t \\ gdp_t \end{bmatrix} \tag{A.13}$$

Given that there is one common stochastic trend, γ is a $(n \times (n - r))$ matrix, i.e. a (3×1) matrix:

$$\gamma = \begin{bmatrix} 1 \\ 1 \\ 1 \end{bmatrix} \tag{A.14}$$

And the trend-cycle decomposition is then given by:

$$\begin{bmatrix} con_t \\ inv_t \\ gdp_t \end{bmatrix} = \begin{bmatrix} con_0 \\ inv_0 \\ gdp_0 \end{bmatrix} + \begin{bmatrix} 1 \\ 1 \\ 1 \end{bmatrix} \tau_t + c^{\star}(L) \begin{bmatrix} \Delta\tau_t \\ e_{2t} \\ e_{3t} \end{bmatrix} \tag{A.15}$$

(e) The identification issue The identification issue refers to how we recover the structural shocks from the VAR residuals, which we put to one side in the above. It has a natural corollary with the identification of simultaneous equations models, except that we are putting

restrictions on the MA rather than the VAR representation of the data. In the previous section, it was assumed that the residuals of the VAR and the structural shocks were the same. But the VAR is a reduced-form representation. Every variable is modelled on the lags of itself and the lags of other variables. So there are no contemporaneous relationships among the variables: A_0 in (A.5) and B_0 in (A.6) are simply the identity matrix. This implies two things for the reduced-form MA representation of x_t:

(i) only one shock affects each of the variables contemporaneously (C_0 is an identity matrix, so that e_{1t} only affects x_{1t} contemporaneously, e_{2t} only affects x_{2t} and so on…); and
(ii) the shocks are likely to be correlated, since any contemporaneous interaction among the variables will be captured in the variance-covariance matrix of the VAR residuals Σ.

In general, (i) and (ii) are not properties we would want our structural shocks to satisfy. Ideally, we would want our structural shocks to be mutually uncorrelated, since we want them to represent distinct and independent economic processes. We also want them to satisfy certain theoretical criteria. So, for example, we might like to restrict some of the long-run properties of the shocks, leaving the contemporaneous effects to be determined by the data, rather than *vice versa*.

So as a first stage, we define a structural model as one that allows each shock to have a contemporaneous effect on each of the variables in x_t. This involves pre-multiplying the reduced-form VAR or VECM representation by a matrix, $A_0 = \Gamma_0^{-1}$ as in KPSW (1991), which in MA form for both cointegrated and non-cointegrated systems yields:

$$\Delta x_t = \Gamma(\mathrm{L})\eta_t = \Gamma(1)\eta_t + \Gamma^{\star}(\mathrm{L})\eta_t \qquad \text{(A.16)}$$

where the variance-covariance matrix of the structural shocks is denoted Ω, and the relationship between the reduced-form and structural parameters is given by:

$$\begin{gathered} \mathrm{e}_t = \Gamma_0 \eta_t \quad \text{and} \\ C(L) = \Gamma(L)\Gamma_0^{-1} \quad C(1) = \Gamma(1)\ \Gamma_0^{-1} \quad \Omega = \Gamma_0^{-1}\Sigma\Gamma_0 \end{gathered} \qquad \text{(A.17)}$$

Note that this is merely a transformation of the reduced-form model. It places no testable restrictions on the data. In the simultaneous equations literature, if Γ_0 is appropriately defined, the model would be said to be 'just' or 'exactly' identified. So the key to identifying both the permanent and temporary shocks is to identify the matrix $\Gamma_{0,}$ since this is the link between the structural and reduced-form parameters.

We can see from the relationships above that we can identify the elements of Γ_0 in several ways:

(i) We can place contemporaneous or sign restrictions on the shock. For example, we could prevent a shock from having a particular effect on a variable because of known or assumed timing lags. This would imply restricting certain elements of Γ_0 to be zero. Or we could exploit theory and look at the set of different Γ_0 matrices that satisfy certain sign restrictions (e.g. only select matrices where the identified demand shocks move inflation and GDP in the same direction, and the identified supply shocks move them in opposite directions); one could then take the median or use some other criterion to pick the appropriate central case for impulse response and historical decomposition analysis.

(ii) We can place restrictions on the dynamic effects of the shocks. For example, we may wish to impose some cross-equation restrictions implied by the rational expectations hypothesis, though in general these are over-identifying (i.e. they do place testable restrictions on the data). Given that the reduced-form $C(L)$ parameters are known, this would mean restricting the elements of $\Gamma(L)$ so that the structural MA parameters $\Gamma(L)=C(L)\Gamma_0$ take a particular form.

(iii) We can place restrictions on the long-run impact of the shocks. This is often preferable to placing contemporaneous or dynamic restrictions on the shocks, as economic theory often has more to say about the long run. This would mean choosing Γ_0 so that $\Gamma(1)$ takes a particular form. Note that any cointegrating relationships will play an important part in this, since the matrix of long-run multipliers is of reduced rank and can be split into $\Gamma(1) = [F\ 0]$ satisfying $\beta'\Phi = 0$ (see KPSW (1991) and Wickens (1996)).

(iv) Finally, we can place restrictions such that the variance–covariance matrix of the structural shocks takes a particular form. As argued earlier, we would want our structural shocks to be orthogonal to one another, and so we might want to place the restrictions that

$$\Gamma_0^{-1}\Sigma\Gamma_0 = \Omega = \mathrm{I}.$$

In this chapter, we use a combination of restrictions (iii) and (iv) to identify the permanent shocks, and (i) and (iv) to identify the temporary shocks. In the presence of cointegrating relationships, KPSW (1991) and Warne (1991) show that Γ_0 can be partitioned into two matrices$=[H\ J]$, which allows us to break down the identification of Γ_0 into several stages:

(i) Cointegrating restrictions that determine the rank of H and J, and place some restrictions on the pattern of H. These impose $(n-r) \times r$ restrictions on Γ_0.

(ii) Identifying the permanent shocks. This involves orthogonality restrictions on the permanent shocks, as well as long-run restrictions. This provides $(n-r)^2$ restrictions (see Mellander et al. (1992)).
(iii) Orthogonality between the permanent and temporary shocks. This imposes $r(n-r)$ restrictions.

In all, we impose n^2 restrictions on Γ_0, which is the minimum we need to identify exactly its n^2 elements. Following KPSW (1991), we also place some testable over-identifying restrictions on the cointegrating vectors at stage (i). This is to ensure that our cointegrating vectors represent, as far as possible, sensible long-run equilibrium relationships. This is useful in tying down some of the long-run multipliers.

Appendix 2: Impulse responses

For each shock the response shown is the impact of a one standard error shock introduced in 1964Q1. Error bands represent one standard deviation away from the mean.

Impulse responses:
TFP shock

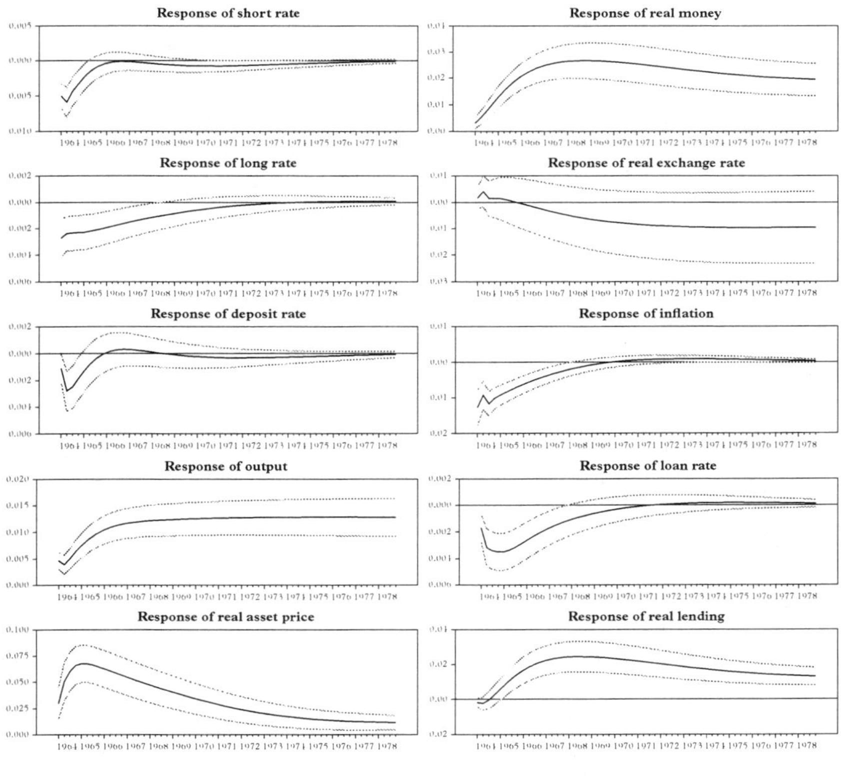

**Impulse responses:
overseas demand shock**

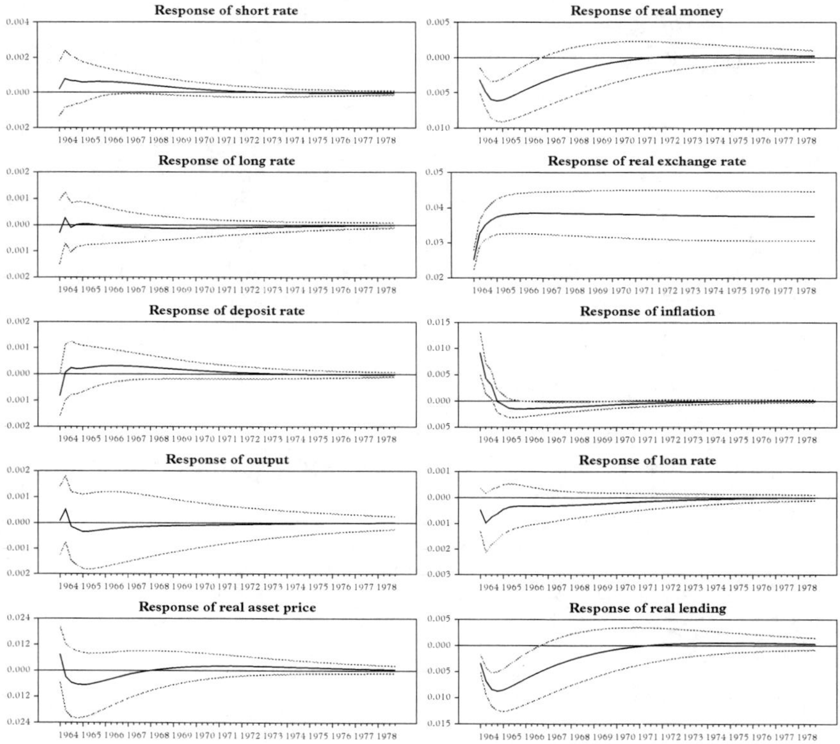

Impulse responses:
core inflation shock

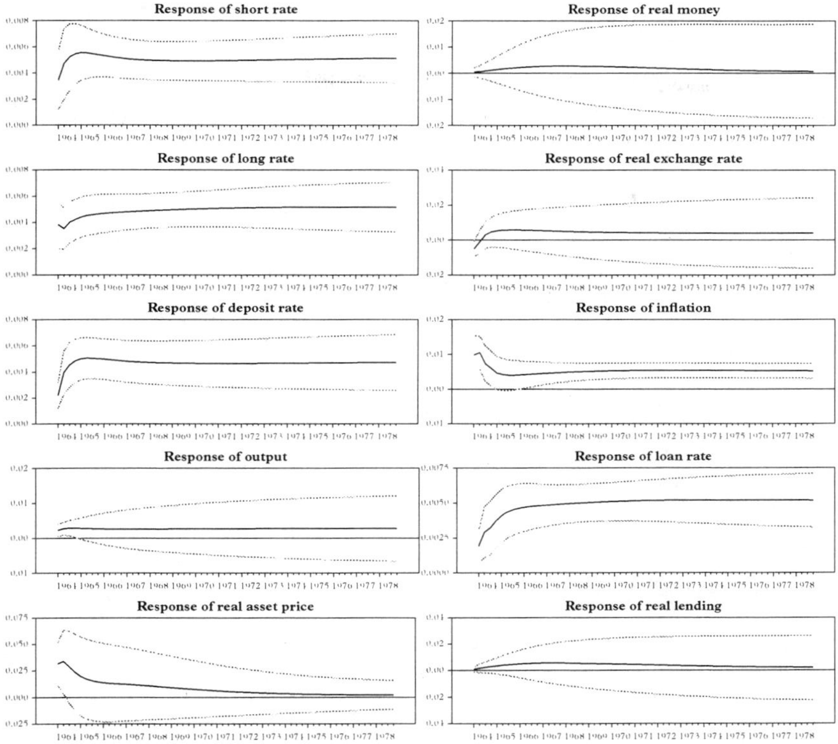

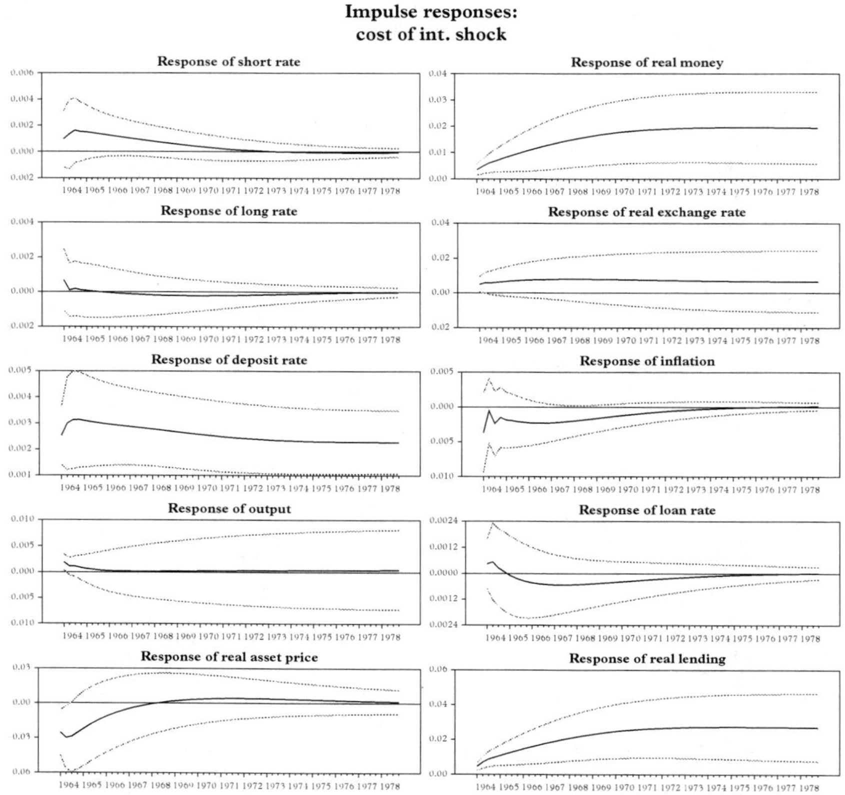
Impulse responses:
cost of int. shock
Response of short rate
Response of real money
Response of long rate
Response of real exchange rate
Response of deposit rate
Response of inflation
Response of output
Response of loan rate
Response of real asset price
Response of real lending
1964 1965 1966 1967 1968 1969 1970 1971 1972 1973 1974 1975 1976 1977 1978

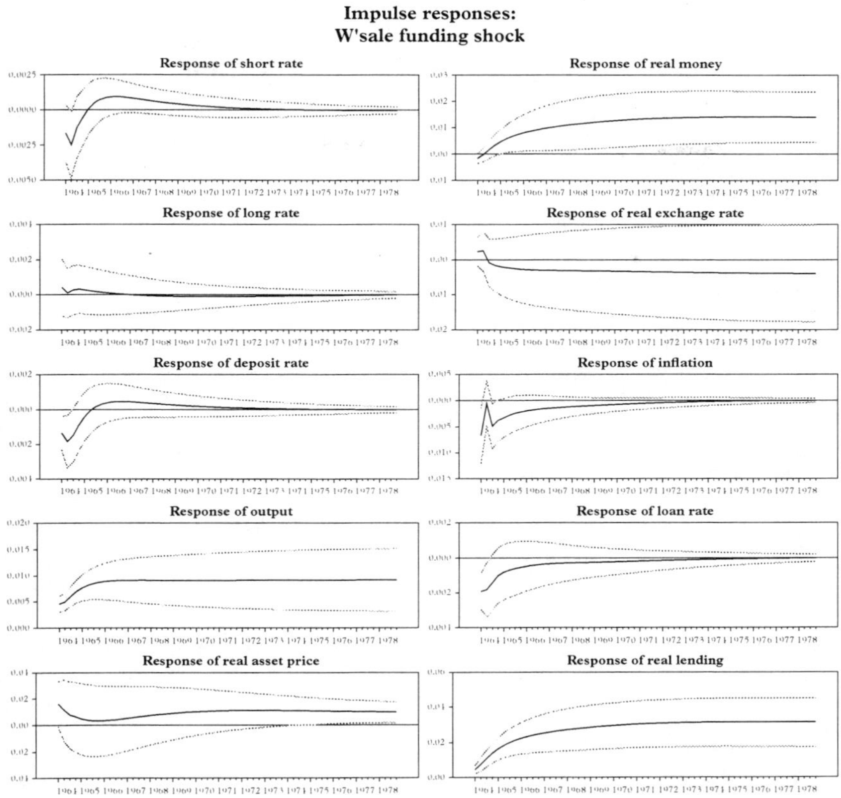
Impulse responses:
W'sale funding shock
Response of short rate
Response of real money
Response of long rate
Response of real exchange rate
Response of deposit rate
Response of inflation
Response of output
Response of loan rate
Response of real asset price
Response of real lending

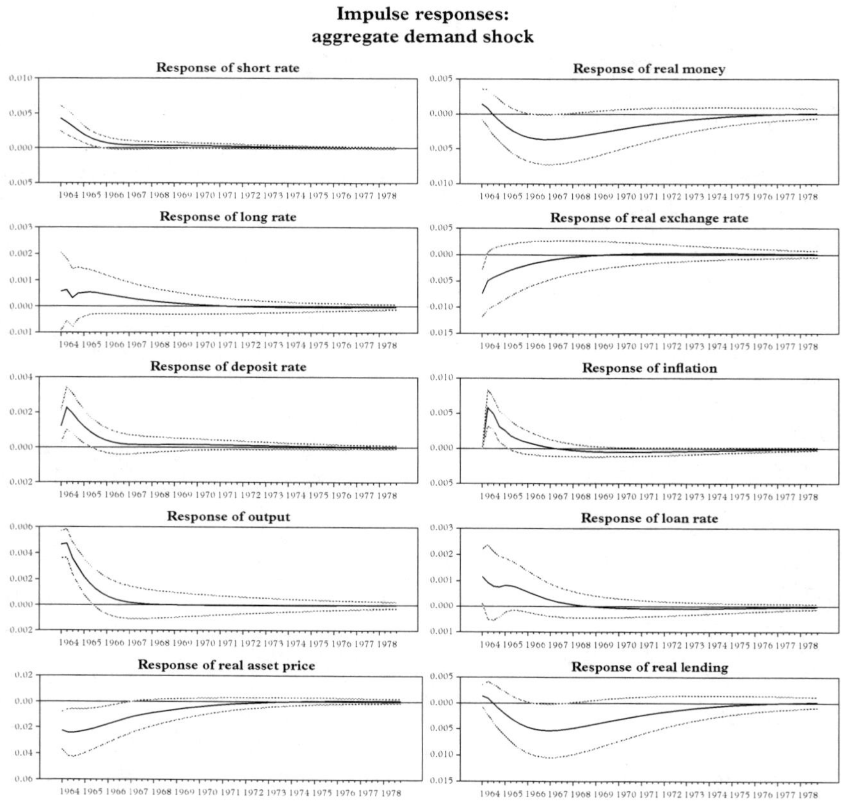
Impulse responses:
aggregate demand shock
Response of short rate
Response of real money
Response of long rate
Response of real exchange rate
Response of deposit rate
Response of inflation
Response of output
Response of loan rate
Response of real asset price
Response of real lending
1964 1965 1966 1967 1968 1969 1970 1971 1972 1973 1974 1975 1976 1977 1978

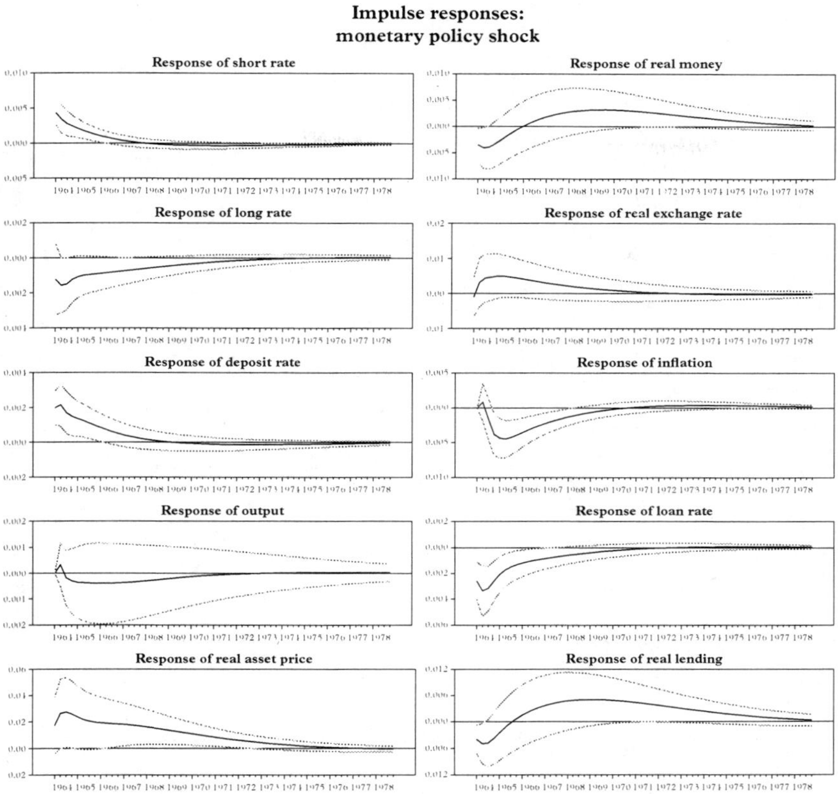
Impulse responses:
monetary policy shock
Response of short rate
Response of real money
Response of long rate
Response of real exchange rate
Response of deposit rate
Response of inflation
Response of output
Response of loan rate
Response of real asset price
Response of real lending

Impulse responses:
bank risk shock

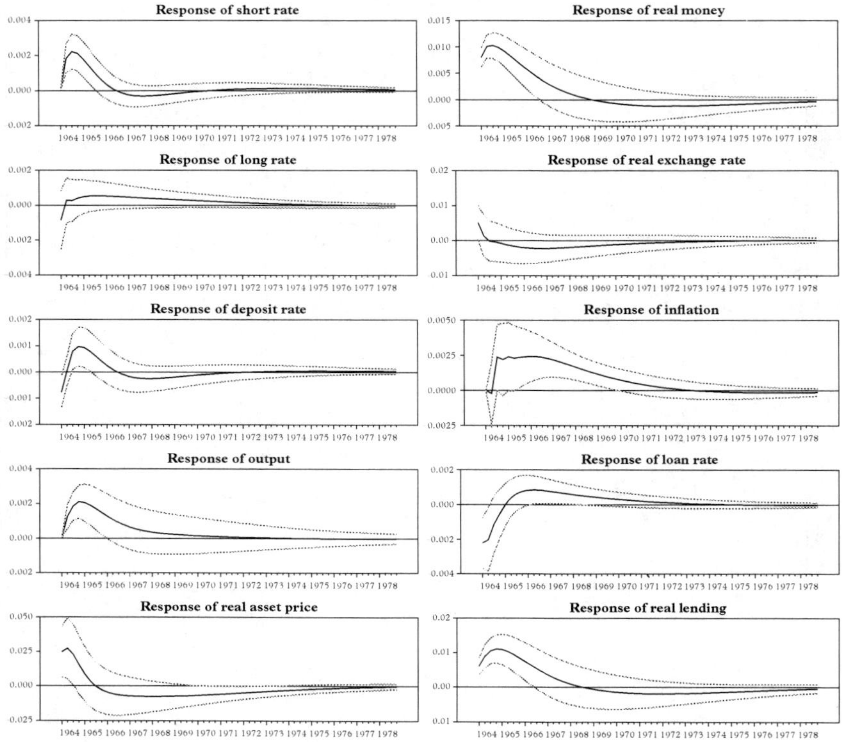

**Impulse responses:
risk premium shock**

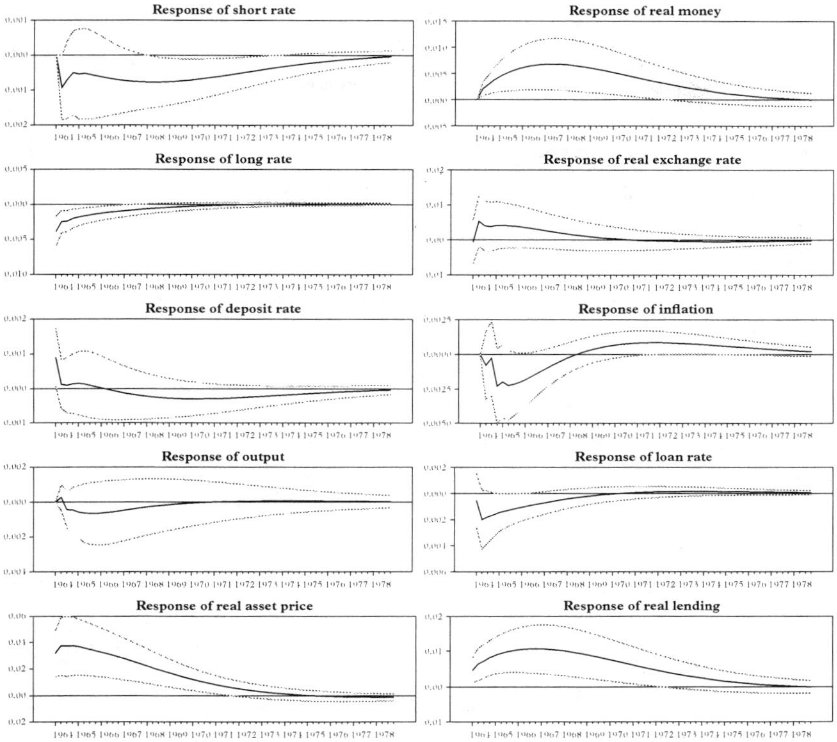

Impulse responses:
cost push shock

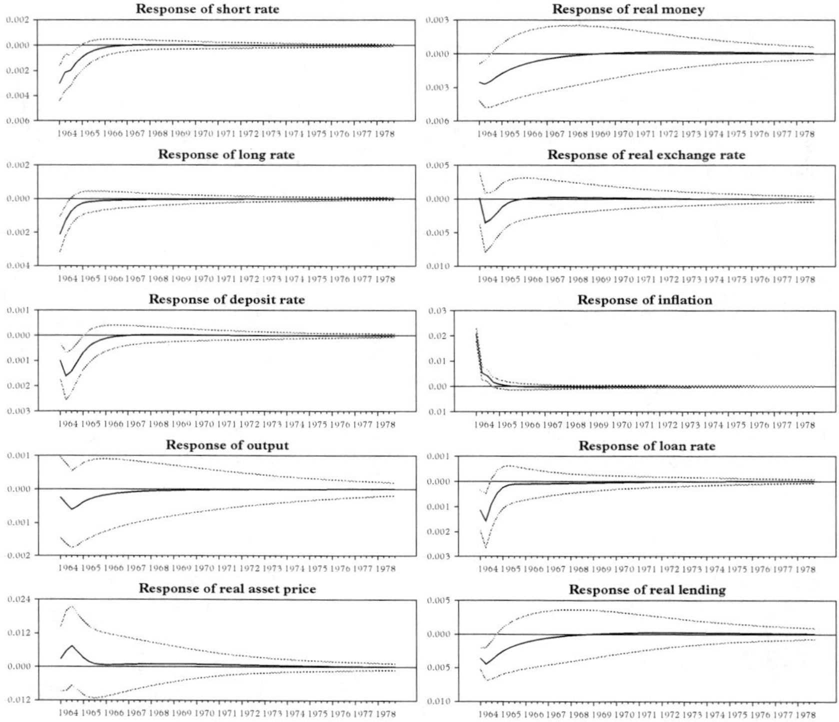

Appendix 3: Forecast error variance decompositions

	Permanent shocks					Temporary shocks				
Horizon (qtrs)	η_{TFP}	η_{for}	η_{nom}	η_{coi}	η_{fun}	η_{AD}	η_{pol}	η_{brisk}	η_{prem}	η_{mu}
Inflation										
1	0.193	0.101	0.115	0.016	0.053	0.000	0.000	0.000	0.000	0.521
4	0.336	0.074	0.218	0.013	0.045	0.030	0.002	0.002	0.001	0.278
8	0.428	0.042	0.202	0.017	0.053	0.041	0.041	0.015	0.011	0.152
12	0.431	0.038	0.199	0.025	0.051	0.034	0.062	0.025	0.016	0.119
20	0.390	0.036	0.247	0.038	0.049	0.028	0.064	0.035	0.015	0.098
100	0.191	0.019	0.619	0.023	0.025	0.014	0.032	0.019	0.011	0.047
	0.119	0.012	0.763	0.015	0.016	0.009	0.020	0.012	0.007	0.029
GDP										
1	0.299	0.000	0.071	0.050	0.283	0.296	0.000	0.000	0.000	0.001
4	0.300	0.001	0.083	0.019	0.376	0.189	0.001	0.027	0.001	0.003
8	0.420	0.001	0.059	0.008	0.410	0.076	0.001	0.023	0.002	0.001
12	0.491	0.001	0.046	0.004	0.398	0.042	0.001	0.014	0.002	0.001
20	0.555	0.000	0.037	0.002	0.375	0.021	0.001	0.008	0.001	0.000
100	0.626	0.00	0.030	0.001	0.338	0.003	0.000	0.001	0.000	0.000
200	0.632	0.000	0.030	0.001	0.335	0.002	0.000	0.001	0.000	0.000
Bank rate										
1	0.290	0.000	0.137	0.011	0.031	0.210	0.215	0.000	0.000	0.106
4	0.275	0.005	0.279	0.023	0.033	0.149	0.133	0.005	0.039	0.060
8	0.202	0.006	0.425	0.031	0.025	0.115	0.109	0.006	0.039	0.043
12	0.162	0.007	0.515	0.033	0.025	0.094	0.091	0.007	0.031	0.034
20	0.122	0.007	0.619	0.031	0.022	0.071	0.068	0.011	0.024	0.025
100	0.039	0.002	0.882	0.009	0.007	0.021	0.020	0.006	0.007	0.007
200	0.021	0.001	0.938	0.005	0.003	0.011	0.011	0.003	0.004	0.004
10 year gilt yield										
1	0.165	0.002	0.324	0.010	0.004	0.007	0.033	0.338	0.016	0.100
4	0.179	0.001	0.455	0.004	0.003	0.008	0.057	0.234	0.008	0.052
8	0.171	0.001	0.569	0.002	0.002	0.008	0.045	0.164	0.009	0.028
12	0.153	0.001	0.640	0.002	0.001	0.008	0.039	0.128	0.009	0.020
20	0.117	0.000	0.736	0.001	0.001	0.005	0.030	0.088	0.008	0.013
100	0.026	0.000	0.941	0.001	0.000	0.001	0.007	0.019	0.002	0.003
200	0.013	0.000	0.970	0.000	0.000	0.001	0.003	0.010	0.001	0.001
Deposit spread										
1	0.375	0.025	0.039	0.060	0.002	0.229	0.134	0.020	0.014	0.102
4	0.363	0.023	0.036	0.119	0.008	0.169	0.107	0.035	0.084	0.058
8	0.314	0.023	0.037	0.197	0.017	0.148	0.094	0.044	0.079	0.047
12	0.277	0.022	0.035	0.273	0.022	0.130	0.081	0.051	0.068	0.041
20	0.226	0.019	0.030	0.402	0.020	0.102	0.064	0.054	0.052	0.031
100	0.067	0.005	0.028	0.808	0.006	0.028	0.018	0.018	0.014	0.008
200	0.035	0.003	0.030	0.883	0.003	0.015	0.010	0.010	0.007	0.004
Cost intermediation										
1	0.012	0.004	0.003	0.144	0.011	0.000	0.690	0.067	0.069	0.001
4	0.024	0.018	0.026	0.174	0.002	0.023	0.569	0.083	0.077	0.004
8	0.108	0.016	0.022	0.257	0.008	0.014	0.447	0.077	0.049	0.004
12	0.148	0.016	0.017	0.317	0.013	0.011	0.366	0.066	0.043	0.008

(*continued*)

Appendix 3. (*cont.*)

	Permanent shocks					**Temporary shocks**				
Horizon (qtrs)	η_{TFP}	η_{for}	η_{nom}	η_{coi}	η_{fun}	η_{AD}	η_{pol}	η_{brisk}	η_{prem}	η_{mu}
20	0.142	0.017	0.013	0.416	0.017	0.008	0.289	0.051	0.044	0.002
100	0.075	0.010	0.024	0.679	0.010	0.005	0.144	0.029	0.024	0.001
200	0.048	0.006	0.027	0.782	0.006	0.003	0.092	0.019	0.015	0.001
Money										
1	0.080	0.083	0.002	0.104	0.022	0.018	0.102	0.535	0.000	0.053
4	0.219	0.116	0.003	0.126	0.018	0.004	0.060	0.398	0.029	0.026
8	0.423	0.078	0.005	0.138	0.058	0.009	0.023	0.209	0.045	0.011
12	0.529	0.048	0.007	0.147	0.078	0.013	0.011	0.114	0.048	0.005
20	0.586	0.023	0.007	0.173	0.096	0.011	0.009	0.049	0.044	0.002
100	0.463	0.004	0.003	0.331	0.175	0.002	0.003	0.008	0.011	0.000
200	0.432	0.002	0.002	0.361	0.191	0.001	0.002	0.004	0.005	0.000
Lending										
1	0.023	0.079	0.003	0.149	0.139	0.013	0.106	0.252	0.146	0.090
4	0.010	0.134	0.011	0.161	0255	0.003	0.050	0.224	0.116	0.037
8	0.091	0.086	0.017	0.165	0.357	0.009	0.016	0.140	0.104	0.014
12	0.180	0.053	0.018	0.171	0.377	0.014	0.010	0.080	0.090	0.007
20	0.250	0.025	0.016	0.200	0.379	0.013	0.010	0.035	0.069	0.003
100	0.145	0.004	0.006	0.341	0.478	0.003	0.004	0.005	0.014	0.000
200	0117	0.002	0.004	0.362	0.502	0.001	0.002	0.003	0.007	0.000
Real equity price										
1	0.168	0.011	0.187	0.123	0.049	0.097	0.056	0.117	0.191	0.001
4	0.372	0.005	0.115	0.099	0.016	0.073	0.078	0.069	0.169	0.004
8	0.488	0.005	0.078	0.073	0.009	0.067	0.070	0.037	0.170	0.002
12	0.532	0.004	0.066	0.057	0.008	0.061	0.069	0.029	0.172	0.002
20	0.568	0.003	0.058	0.043	0.009	0.052	0.071	0.026	0.168	0.001
100	0.590	0.003	0.051	0.035	0.060	0.040	0.062	0.024	0.135	0.001
200	0.597	0.003	0.048	0.030	0.100	0.034	0.053	0.020	0.115	0.001
Real exchange rate										
1	0.004	0.817	0.033	0.032	0.007	0.071	0.001	0.035	0.000	0.000
4	0.005	0.894	0.012	0.028	0.003	0.023	0.011	0.006	0.012	0.005
8	0.002	0.905	0.017	0.029	0.003	0.013	0.013	0.003	0.011	0.003
12	0.002	0.909	0.018	0.032	0.004	0.009	0.012	0.003	0.010	0.002
20	0.007	0.912	0.017	0.035	0.005	0.005	0.008	0.003	0.007	0.001
100	0.044	0.900	0.012	0.030	0.008	0.001	0.002	0.001	0.001	0.000
200	0.049	0.900	0.011	0.029	0.009	0.000	0.001	0.000	0.001	0.000

References

Andrés, J, López-Salido, D J, Nelson, E (2004). Tobin's imperfect substitution in optimising general equilibrium. *Journal of Money, Credit and Banking*, 36 (5), 665–90.

Astley M, Haldane, A (1995). Money as an indicator. *Bank of England Working Paper No. 35.*

Barnett, A, Thomas, R (2013). Has weak lending and activity in the United Kingdom been driven by credit supply shocks? *Bank of England Working Papers 482.*

Bell, V, Young, G (2010). Understanding the weakness of bank lending. *Bank of England Quarterly Bulletin*, 50(4), 311–20.

Benes, J, Kumhof, M (2012). 'The Chicago plan revisited', *IMF Working Paper*, 12/202.

Berry, S, Harrison, R, Thomas, R, de Weymarn, I (2007). Interpreting movements in broad money. *Bank of England Quarterly Bulletin*, 47(3), 376–88.

Blanchard, O, Quah, D (1989). The dynamic effects of aggregate demand and supply disturbances. *The American Economic Review*, 79(4), 655–73.

Bridges J, Thomas, R (2012). 'The impact of QE on the UK economy – some supportive monetarist arithmetic', *Bank of England Working Paper*, No 442.

Brigden, A, Mizen, P (2004). Money, credit and investment in the UK industrial and commercial companies sector. *The Manchester School*, 72, 72–79.

Brunner, K, Meltzer A (1987). 'Money and the economy: issues in monetary analysis', presented at the 1987 Raffaele Mattioli Lectures, Carnegie Mellon University, Pittsburgh.

Burgess, S, Janssen, N (2007). Proposals to modify the measurement of broad money in the United Kingdom: a user consultation. *Bank of England Quarterly Bulletin*, 47(3), 402–14.

Butt, N, Domit, S, McLeay, M, Thomas, R (2012). What can the money data tell us about the impact of QE?, Bank of England Quarterly Bulletin 2012 *Q4.*

Canova, F, De Nicoló, G (2002). Monetary disturbances matter for business fluctuations in the G-7. *Journal of Monetary Economics*, 49(6), 1131–59.

Capie, F, Webber, A (1985). '*A monetary history of the United Kingdom, 1870–1982*', vol. 1, Routledge.

Chadha J, Corrado L, Holly, S (2013). 'A note on money and the conduct of monetary policy', *Cambridge Working Papers in Economics 1329*, Faculty of Economics, University of Cambridge, Cambridge.

Christensen, L (2011). 'Market monetarism: the second monetarist counter-revolution', Mimeo.

Christiano, L, Eichenbaum, M (1992). Liquidity effects and the monetary transmission mechanism. *American Economic Review*, 82(2), 346–53.

Chrystal, K A, Mizen P (2005a). Other financial corporations: Cinderella or ugly sister of empirical monetary economics? *International Journal of Finance & Economics*, 10(1), 63–80.

Chrystal, K A, Mizen, P (2005b). A dynamic model of money, credit, and consumption: a joint model for the UK household sector. *Journal of Money, Credit and Banking*, 37(1), 119–43.

Clower, R (1967). A reconsideration of the microfoundations of monetary theory. *Western Economic Journal*, 6(1), 1–8.

Congdon, T (1992). '*Reflections on monetarism*', Clarendon Press, Oxford.

(2005). 'Money and asset prices in boom and bust', Institute of Economic Affairs, *Hobart Paper No. 152*, London.

Congdon, T, Ward, S (1993). 'The personal sector's demand for M4 balances', *Lombard Street Research Econometrics Research Note*, May.

Curdia, V, Woodford, M (2010). The central-bank balance sheet as an instrument of monetary policy. *Journal of Monetary Economics*, 58(1), 54–79.

De Santis, R, Favero, C, Roffia, B (2008). 'Euro area money demand and international portfolio allocation', *ECB Working Paper Series No. 926*

Dhar, S, Pain, D, Thomas, R (2000). 'A small structural empirical model of the UK monetary transmission mechanism', *Bank of England Working Paper No. 113.*

Eggertsson, G, Woodford, M (2003). The zero bound on interest rates and optimal monetary policy. *Brookings Papers on Economic Activity*, 34(1), 139–235.

Engle, R F, Granger, W J (1987), Co-integration and error correction: representation, estimation, and testing. In Harvey, A (ed), '*Time series, volume* 1', p. 65.

Engle, R F, Yoo, B S (1991), Forecasting and testing in co-integrated systems. In Engle, R F, Granger, C W (eds), '*Long-run economic relationships: readings in cointegration.*'

Fama, E (1980). Banking in the theory of finance. *Journal of Monetary Economics*, 6(1), 39–57.

Fisher, P G, Vega, J L (1993). 'An empirical analysis of M4 in the United Kingdom', *Bank of England Working Paper No. 21.*

Freixas, X, Rochet, J (1997). '*The microeconomics of banking*', MIT Press, Cambridge.

Fuerst, T (1992). Liquidity, loanable funds, and real activity. *Journal of Monetary Economics*, 29(1), 3–24.

Gale, D (1982). '*Money: in equilibrium*', Cambridge University Press.

Gilchrist, S, Zakrajsek, E (2012). Credit spreads and business cycle fluctuations. *American Economic Review*, 102(4), 1692–1720.

Gilchrist, S, Yankov, V, Zakrajsek, E (2009), Credit market shocks and economic fluctuations: evidence from corporate bond and stock markets. *Journal of Monetary Economics*, 56(4), 471–493.

Godley, W, Lavoie, M (2006). '*Monetary economics an integrated approach to credit, money, income, production and wealth*', Palgrave-Macmillan, London.

Goodfriend, M (2004). Narrow money, broad money, and the transmission of monetary policy. In Faust, J, Orphanides, A, Reifschneider, D (eds), '*Models of monetary policy*', Board of Governors of the Federal Reserve System, DC, 2005, pp. 277–303.

Goodfriend, M, McCallum, B (2007). Banking and interest rates in monetary policy analysis: a quantitative exploration. *Journal of Monetary Economics*, 54(5), 1480–1507.

Harrison, R, Nikolov, K, Quinn, M, Ramsay, G, Scott, A, Thomas, R (2005). *The Bank of England Quarterly Model*, Bank of England, London.

Hills, S, Thomas, R, Dimsdale, N (2010). The UK recession in context – what do three centuries of data tell us? *Bank of England Quarterly Bulletin*, 50(4), 277–91.

Howells, P (1995). The demand for endogenous money. *Journal of Post Keynesian Economics*, 18(1), 89–106.

Johansen, S (1988). Statistical analysis of cointegrating vectors. *Journal of Economics, Dynamics and Control*, 231–54.

Kaldor, N, Trevithick, J (1981). A Keynesian perspective on money. *Lloyds Bank Review*, 1–19.

Khan, A, Thomas, J (2010). 'Inflation and interest rates with endogenous market segmentation', Ohio State University, *Working Paper*.

King, R G, Plosser, C I, Stock, J H, Watson, M W (1991). Stochastic trends and economic fluctuations. *American Economic Review*, 819–40.

Kiyotaki, N, Moore, J (2002). Evil is the root of all money. *The American Economic Review*, 92(2), Papers and Proceedings of the 114th Annual Meeting of the American Economic Association, pp. 62–66.

Laidler, D (1984). The buffer stock notion in monetary economics. *The Economic Journal*, 94, Supplement: Conference Papers, 17–34.

Layard, R, Nickell, S, Jackman, R (1991), *Unemployment: macroeconomic performance and the labour market*, Oxford University Press.

Mellander, E, Vredin, A, Warne, A (1992). Stochastic trends and economic fluctuations in a small open economy. *Journal of Applied Econometrics*, 7(4), 369–94.

Moore, B (1988). '*Horizontalists and verticalists: the macroeconomics of credit money*', Cambridge University Press, Cambridge.

O'Donoghue J, Goulding L, Allen G (2004). 'Consumer Price Inflation since 1750', *ONS Economic Trends 604*, March.

Ohlin, B (March 1937). Some notes on the Stockholm theory of savings and investment I. *The Economic Journal*, 47(185), 53–69.

Papademos, L D, Stark, J (eds) (2010), '*Enhancing monetary analysis*', ECB, Frankfurt.

Pesaran, M H, Shin, Y (2002). Long-run structural modelling. *Econometric Reviews*, 2.

Robertson, D (1940). Mr Keynes and the rate of interest. '*Essays in Monetary Theory*', Taples Press, London

Rochon, L, Rossi, S (2003). '*Modern theories of money*', Edward Elgar, London.

Thomas, R (1997a). 'The demand for M4: a sectoral analysis, Part 1 – the personal sector', *Bank of England Working Paper No. 61*.

(1997b), 'The demand for M4: a sectoral analysis, Part 2 – the corporate sector', *Bank of England Working Paper No. 62*.

Tobin, J (1969). A general equilibrium approach to monetary theory. *Journal of Money, Credit and Banking*, 1(1), 15–29.

Tsiang, SC (1956). Liquidity preference and loanable funds theories, multiplier and velocity analysis: a synthesis. *American Economic Review*, XLVI(4), 539–64.

(1980). Keynes's 'finance' demand for liquidity, Robertson's loanable funds theory, and Friedman's monetarism. *The Quarterly Journal of Economics*, 94 (3), 467–91

Wallace, N (1981). A Modigliani-Miller theorem for open market operations. *American Economic Review*, 71, 267–74.

Warne, A (1991). 'A common trends model: identification, estimation and asymptotics', *Mimeo*, Stockholm School of Economics, Sweden.

Wickens, M R (1996). Interpreting cointegrating vectors and common stochastic trends. *Journal of Econometrics*, 255–71.

Williamson, S, Wright, R (2010). New monetarist economics: models, In Friedman, B, Woodford, M (eds), *Handbook of Monetary Economics*, 3(2), pp. 25–96.

5 An old fashioned banking crisis: credit growth and loan losses in the UK 1997–2012

Alistair Milne and Justine A. Wood

The goal of this chapter is to investigate the role played by new forms of banking and by financial innovation in supporting the expansion of UK domestic credit during the years 1997–2007 and in the subsequent credit losses of 2007–12. Our conclusion, surprisingly, is that the most important mechanism operating was much the same as during earlier similar episodes in the UK, the secondary banking crisis of 1973–75 and the property-related banking losses of 1991–93. In all three cases, unsustainable lending secured on property was the main culprit; sometimes, but not always, this was intermediated via 'shadow' banks outside of the regular banking sector, but this was a characteristic of the 1973–75 credit expansion just as much as during the final years of the long expansion. Credit derivatives and other financial innovations, and maturity mismatch conducted by non-bank intermediaries, both of which contributed to a rapid growth of so called 'shadow banking' in the USA and to subsequent losses on US structured credit securities in recent years, played only a relatively minor role in the UK credit expansion and loan losses of 1997–2012.

This is not to say that shadow banking played no role at all in the UK, but this was an 'old' form of shadow banking, different from the 'new' shadow banking that was so prominent in the credit losses and liquidity problems of the US financial system in 2007–08. The 'new' shadow banking is characterised by substantial maturity mismatch and funding through 'deposit-like' liabilities (short-term money-like assets, notably shares in money market mutual funds, regarded as entirely safe but without deposit guarantees or the liquidity support provided by direct access to the central bank lender of last resort facility). The 'old' shadow banking consists of non-bank credit providers that rely to an important extent on borrowing from established banks, and where they

We thank Charles Nolan and Stephen Wright for detailed comments.

borrow in money markets do so on an uncollateralised basis (so their liabilities are recognised as relatively risky short-term investments, not entirely safe substitutes for bank deposits).

We show that, in contrast to the situation in the USA in the run-up to the crisis of 2007–08, almost all the domestic (i.e. sterling lending) in the UK was extended directly or indirectly by established UK regulated banks and most of the associated risks were retained on their balance sheets. In comparison to the USA, shadow banks played a lesser and more conventional role in the form of specialised financial intermediaries, such as REITs and other property investment companies, which borrowed from the established banking sector to finance investment in commercial property; 'new' shadow banks did not significantly compete with the established banks for short-term deposit and wholesale sterling funding.

The chapter is organised as follows. Section 5.1 reviews the existing literature on shadow banking and its role in the build-up of systemic risk before the recent global financial crisis. Section 5.2 then uses available Bank of England data to examine both the build-up of credit and subsequent UK sterling banking losses during the years 1997–2013 and the role of shadow banking in their finance. Section 5.3 provides a brief comparison with earlier episodes of property-related banking losses in the UK in 1973–74 and 1991–93. Section 5.4 concludes.

5.1 Shadow banking and the global financial crisis

A substantial recent literature has addressed the role of shadow banking during the global financial crisis of 2007–08, focussing largely on US experience. There are two reasons for this focus on the USA: in the years preceding the crisis a large US dollar 'shadow banking' system emerged that played a key role in financing the subprime mortgage lending in the USA. The literature, though, has largely ignored 'shadow banking' in other currencies, primarily for the reason that data on the structured credit securities and other instruments are much more readily available for the USA than for other countries. This section reviews this literature, emphasising the contrast between the way shadow banking has recently operated in the USA ('new' shadow banking) with the way in which it has operated in other countries and at other times ('old' shadow banking).

Although most work on shadow banking refers to US experience, there has more recently been a shift in interest to various forms of shadow banking across the world. Beginning in 2011, the Financial Stability Board has published an annual monitor of shadow banking activities, the latest of which covers 20 jurisdictions together with the euro area (Financial Stability Board, 2013). The Financial Stability

Board has also, in August 2013, proposed a global approach to the regulation of shadow banking.

5.1.1 *'New' versus 'old' shadow banking*

The Financial Stability Board defines shadow banking as 'credit intermediation involving entities and activities outside the regular banking system'.[1] This broad definition includes, for example, specialised or offshore banks subject to lighter regulation and scrutiny than established banks, as well as non-bank intermediaries. Within this broad definition, it is useful to contrast two characterisations of shadow banking, which we label respectively as the 'new' and 'old'. The new characterisation dominates much of the current research literature (Adrian and Shin, 2009; Pozsar et al., 2010; G.B. Gorton and Metrick, 2010a; Singh, 2010; Pozsar and Singh, 2011), but we will argue that the experience of the UK which we examine is better characterised as 'old' shadow banking.[2]

Four key features of this 'new' US dollar shadow banking (or rather shadow banking system) are: first and most importantly that it engaged in extensive maturity transformation using liabilities (shares in money market mutual funds) that investors regarded as extremely safe and therefore as close substitutes for bank deposits; second that it provided intermediation from ultimate savers (households and companies) right through to ultimate borrowers (a wide range including sub prime mortgage borrowers and other lending secured on property) entirely outside of the established banking system; third that it operated without the liquidity support provided by access to the lender of last resort facility from the central bank and is thus subject to runs; and fourth and finally that it made extensive use of innovative instruments such as credit derivatives, structured credit securities and various forms of collateralised short-term funding, both on and off balance sheet, in order to transform illiquid loans into apparently safe and liquid short-term liabilities.

While the recent literature has focused almost exclusively on this 'new' shadow banking and its role in the build-up of both credit and liquidity risk in the USA over the years 2002–07, a different and older form of shadow banking has appeared in many other jurisdictions and on previous occasions, making little or no use of the technologies of securitisation, repo and credit derivatives and not perceived as creating

1 Financial Stability Board (2013)

2 Our distinction between 'old' and 'new' is reflected in the past usage of the term 'shadow banking'. It seems to have been first used to describe what we call 'new' shadow banking by (McCulley, 2007), but had previously been used to refer to what we call 'old' shadow banking, for example by (Bradshaw, 2004).

liabilities that are a close substitute for bank deposits. In this 'old' form of shadow banking, smaller institutions, operating offshore or under looser regulatory oversight than established banks, provide an important share of domestic credit; but this shadow bank lending is funded by some combination of direct lending from established banks and short-term *unsecured* money market borrowing, i.e. its short-term liabilities are explicitly recognised as being risky. Frequently these shadow banks satisfy the substantial demand for lending in property booms, providing secured lending on residential and commercial property. Examples of losses arising from this 'old' form of shadow banking include the UK in 1973–75 and 2008–12 and Thailand in 1997–98.[3] Other examples go back at least as far as the failure of US trust companies during the panic of 1907.[4]

To sum up: the 'new' US dollar shadow banking that emerged during the years 2002–07 used structured credit securities as repo collateral for raising short-term money market finance, especially from money market mutual funds that captured deposits away from traditional banks. This in turn allowed credit to be extended directly to borrowers without direct intermediation by banks. The literature on this 'new' shadow banking emphasises the demand for money-like assets, i.e. liquid, risk-free interest-bearing assets that can be exchanged without requiring costly assessment of their value. But other forms of shadow banking ('old' shadow banking) have emerged at other times and in other jurisdictions, engaging in conventional lending, and funded either directly by banks or with liabilities that were recognised as being riskier than bank deposits.

Figure 5.1 illustrates the possible links between regular banks, shadow banks and financial market participants. The figure is complicated, a reflection of the great variety both in the ways in which shadow banks can be funded and in assets they hold. As we have described, the 'new' shadow banking that emerged in US dollar markets in the years 2002–07 was characterised by (a) the holding of securities, especially short-term paper and structured credit securities; and (b) using these securities to obtain collateralised money market funding either from money market mutual funds or from long-only institutional investors. These links are thus illustrated in the figure by the linkages contained with the dotted circle: the 'new' shadow banking nexus.

This configuration can be contrasted with the case of the UK during the period 2003–09 – as illustrated by the dashed lines in Figure 5.1

3 The UK examples are documented later in this chapter. For Thailand see Leightner and Lovell (1998), Alba et al. (1999) and Charumilind, Kali, and Wiwattanakantang (2006).

4 See Moen and Tallman (1992) and Frydman, Hilt, and Zhou (2012).

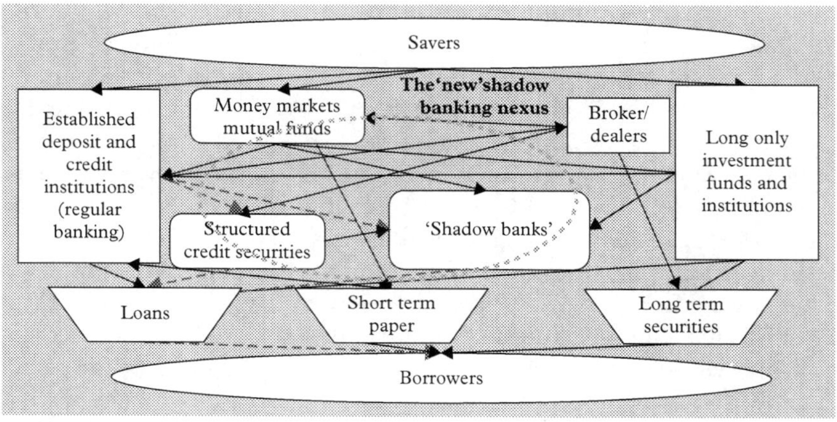

Figure 5.1. The variety of 'shadow banking' linkages

and documented in our Section 5.3 below. In the UK in these years sterling shadow banking was primarily funded directly by traditional deposit and credit institutions, *not* from money markets; and these UK shadow banks made relatively little use of structured credit instruments; rather, they mostly provided credit directly to borrowers.

Some further interpretation of this figure can be offered:

- The shape labelled 'shadow' banks represents the very wide range of different institutions, operating outside of the regular banking system, that have been a source of systemic vulnerability in previous financial crises. Examples (there are many) include (a) the secondary banking crisis in the UK of 1973–74; (b) centralised mortgage lenders that were most exposed to losses on UK mortgage lending during the downturn of 1992–93; (c) the Thai finance houses that were the first casualties of the Asian financial crisis of 1997–98; (d) the 'structured investment vehicles' (SIVs) that collapsed at the onset of the global financial crisis in 2007 and triggered substantial losses for German and other banks; and (e) the private commercial real estate funds that have been a prominent source of recent UK bank credit losses following the crisis of 2007–08.
- A further dimension, not fully captured in the figure, is the role of money market (short-term) lending, both secured and unsecured. Money market intermediation is a major source of short-term funding to commercial banks, leveraged credit funds and specialised lenders, and also to broker/dealers and (via direct investment in short-term paper) private non-financial companies. Maturity mismatch using

short-term money-market instruments has contributed to many episodes of financial instability, including those in Scandinavia, Japan and the UK in the early 1990s; the Asian crisis of 1997–98 (where Thai and South Korean institutions especially borrowed on a large scale in foreign currency in money markets, assuming that their currency peg meant that they were not exposed to exchange rate risk); and in the USA in 2007–08.[5]

- The shape labelled 'structured credit securities' represents the novel instruments (mostly issued in US dollars) that played a central role in the global financial crisis of 2007–08.[6] The most important of these were residential mortgage-backed securities (RMBS), commercial mortgage-backed securities (CMBS), credit card and other loan structures (usually referred to as ABS), syndicated loan structures (CLOs), structures built on credit derivatives (synthetic CDOs) and finally re-securitisations of credit structures (often referred to as ABS-CDOs). A key vulnerability of 2007–08 was that the tranched instruments (in order of seniority: senior, mezzanine, junior and equity tranches) issued by these credit structures were held to a large extent in trading books by banks, broker dealers and leveraged credit funds, and funded in money markets.[7] Long-only investment funds and institutions made only very limited investments in these new dollar-denominated credit instruments.[8]

While the 'shadow banking' linkages illustrated in Figure 5.1 have often been a source of financial instability, financial crises have often occurred without them. Over the years commercial banks have proved quite capable of getting into deep trouble, often needing government intervention to ensure their survival, without recourse to either novel financial instruments or off-balance sheet intermediation. Before the recent problems of UK banks such as HBOS or RBS, other examples include the Latin American debt crisis, the US Savings and Loans losses of the 1980s and many banking failures in emerging markets

5 Contrary to widespread perceptions, the UK bank Northern Rock made only limited use of money market borrowing: its main sources of wholesale funding were through the issue of mortgage backed securities and covered bonds (see Milne and Wood (2008)). The reason that it got into liquidity problems was that it adopted a practice of lending first, using unsecured money market borrowing as a temporary source of funds, before later transferring repackaging loans into mortgage-backed securities. When the markets for securitisation froze in 2007 it had no alternative source of funding available to it.

6 See Milne (2009a) Table 3.2 for an analysis of the various components of this $13 tn market.

7 Milne (2009b) Chapter 6 describes these trading book strategies, in particular the 'negative basis trade' and their role in the crisis of 2007–08.

8 See Milne (2009b) for further analysis and discussion.

since the early 1970s. Such direct exposure has also been a feature of euro area banking problems, with for example the recent large-scale losses on property lending amongst both Irish and Spanish banks and the exposure of many banks to periphery euro-area sovereign debt. These cases of financial instability have been associated with unsustainable credit expansion and with excessive maturity mismatch using short-term wholesale money market funding, but undertaken *directly* by banks or other established deposit institutions, rather than through leveraged credit funds or specialised investors.

It should also be acknowledged that most episodes of financial instability, whether involving shadow banks or not, have been associated with excessive extension of credit secured on residential and commercial property and often, but not always, with unsustainable external borrowing.[9] In a few other cases (Latin American exposures in the 1980s or recent crises in the periphery of the euro area) banking problems have resulted from exposures to sovereign lending or sovereign debt. Occasionally, in some emerging markets with poor standards of governance, serious banking problems have been associated with large-scale misuses of funds or other banking fraud.

5.1.2 Shadow banking in the USA and offshore US dollar markets

In order to highlight the differences between 'new' and 'old' shadow banking, this subsection and the one following contrast the operation in recent years of shadow banking in US dollar markets with the shadow banking that developed in Europe and the UK.

According to Gorton (2010), the ability to diversify their loan portfolios, and hence back bank deposits with comparatively safe if illiquid assets, made banks historically the natural suppliers of deposit money; but the new technologies of securitisation, secured lending (repo) and the hedging of associated default risk using credit derivatives allowed non-bank intermediaries to displace traditional banks in the supply of seemingly riskless short-term liabilities backed by illiquid long-term lending.

The most important of these liabilities was the sale or repurchase agreement (or repo), a form of secured borrowing. By agreeing to sell an asset and then subsequently repurchase at a slightly higher price, a borrower pays the equivalent of an interest rate; but risk is limited by the practice of requiring 'haircuts', i.e. the extent to which the actual market value of the asset (for example $100) exceeds the agreed

9 Some references from an extensive literature include Goodhart and Delargy (1998); Kaminsky and Reinhart (1999); Davis and Zhu (2004); Reinhart and Rogoff (2009).

repurchase price (for example $95).[10] Another important form of secured borrowing used to finance securitised loans was 'asset-backed commercial paper' or ABCP, a short-term tradable paper secured on structured credit securities.[11]

Adrian and Shin (2009) highlight the use of repo by US broker-dealers (investment banks) for the leveraged purchase of structured credit and other financial assets. Adrian and Shin (2010a,b) document a strong *positive* relationship between changes in US broker-dealer leverage (largely through repo) and changes in balance sheet size.

The rapid growth in the issue of mortgage-backed securities and other structured credit assets, financed using these various forms of short-term borrowing, came to a sudden halt in mid-2007. A major reason was the lack of transparency regarding underlying asset quality: investors were acquiring shadow banking exposures with little regard to which assets were safe and which had more underlying risk; asymmetric information became an inherent problem.[12]

As depositors panicked, the highly liquid market shrank drastically and liquidity vanished. Gorton and Metrick (2010b, 2012) interpret the crisis of 2007–09 as a banking panic centred on the repo market and triggered by a loss of confidence in structured credit securities. This created a feedback effect in which stronger balance sheets feed greater demand for the asset, which in turn raises the asset's price and leads to stronger balance sheets; while weakening balance sheets trigger the reverse mechanism, a mechanism that had been analysed even before the crisis by Brunnermeier and Pedersen (2008).

To illustrate this mechanism, (Gorton and Metrick, 2009) document the dramatic rise in haircuts across asset classes. Before the financial crisis, haircuts were close to zero for many asset classes, and only a little higher at around 5 per cent when used on subprime mortgage-backed securities and related assets as collateral. From July 2007 onwards the haircuts on subprime mortgage-backed and related securities rose rapidly, eventually climbing to 100 per cent; i.e. these assets were no longer acceptable as collateral in repo. Haircuts on non-subprime-related asset classes also rose sharply, to a maximum of 20 per cent.

A related mechanism that again contributed to the panic was that of rehypothecation, i.e. the practice of reusing collateral that had been obtained in return from extending repo finance in order to raise funds.

10 In this case the haircut of $5 ($100–$95) protects the repo lender from loss in the event of default, because even if the value of the asset should fall by $5 they can still sell the asset and get back the money owed ($95).

11 For description and discussion see Pozsar et al. (2010).

12 For elaboration see for example Ashcraft and Schuermann (2008) and Gorton (2009).

In this way collateral could be passed on in a chain from one institution to another. Singh and Aitken (2009) show how the amount of rehypothecation has declined substantially since Lehman Brothers' bankruptcy due to the fear of losing collateral if the broker dealer becomes insolvent. Also, as documented by researchers at the Bank for International Settlements, much of the financing of US dollar-structured credit securities was offshore, booked by institutions in Europe and elsewhere, and triggering a worldwide dollar shortage when the crisis broke (McGuire and Von Peter, 2009; He and McCauley, 2010).

What was the magnitude of US dollar shadow banking? The answer depends on what exactly is included as shadow banking. The volume of low-risk mortgage-backed securities issued by the US government-sponsored agencies Fannie Mae and Freddie Mac meant that assets held outside of the US banking system surpassed those held by commercial banks as early as the mid-1990s.[13] However, this is not the 'shadow banking' that proved so unstable during the global crisis, because most of these agency securities were held by long-term investors without maturity mismatch.

An alternative measure is to look at total repo borrowing. Gorton (2010b) estimates the US repo market to have been $12tn in 2007, just before the crisis, compared with the total assets in the US banking system of $10tn. Hördahl and King (2008) claim that the former top US investment banks funded roughly half of their assets using repo markets, with additional exposure due to off-balance sheet financing of their customers. The collateral often consisted of securitised loans and other structured credit instruments. Gorton and Metrick (2012) estimate that net repo financing provided to broker dealers fell by $1.3tn from the second quarter of 2007 to the first quarter of 2009. The flight of capital was driven by money market funds, foreign financial institutions and domestic and offshore hedge funds, as well as other unregulated cash pools.

Other researchers reach even higher estimates of the size of US shadow banking. Only bi-party, not tri-party, agreements are captured by the Federal Reserve data (tri-party is when repo assets are held with a third party institution – a common arrangement in the USA, but not in Europe). Therefore, allowing for tri-party repo, even larger estimates of the magnitude of shadow banking can be obtained. Pozsar et al. (2010) estimate the US shadow banking sector to be $20tn in March of 2008, falling to $16tn in 2010. Pozsar and Singh (2011) estimate that the size was $25tn in the USA at the end of 2007 and $18tn at the end of 2010.

13 For a detailed discussion see Pozsar et al. (2010).

All these repo-based estimates, however, substantially overstate the total amount of shadow banking, because only a share of repo finance is used to support bank-like credit intermediation. A better approach is to identify more directly the type of intermediation supported by different groups of institutions, an approach adopted by the Financial Stability Board and described in the next subsection. This approach suggests that US shadow banking (excluding the GSEs) was only around $3tn at end 2012.

5.1.3 *Shadow banking in the euro area and the UK*

Having described US dollar shadow banking, we now review available statistical information on shadow banking in euro and sterling markets in the years before and after the global financial crisis. Our main conclusion is that, while there is considerable uncertainty about the amount of shadow banking intermediation, the overall amount of credit intermediation by shadow banks independent of the established banking system remains relatively small in other currencies than the US dollar. This is consistent with the fact that euro and sterling securitisation took place on a much smaller scale than in US dollars and these securities were to a much larger extent retained on bank balance sheets, for example to be used as collateral for borrowing from the Bank of England and the ECB.[14]

The most comprehensive measures of shadow banking activities are those being developed by the Financial Stability Board, in their 'Global Shadow Banking Monitor' which aims to reveal detailed trends in shadow banking activity on a global and jurisdiction by jurisdiction basis. The most recent of these (Financial Stability Board, 2013) includes relatively aggregated data for 20 jurisdictions and also the euro area. Total intermediation by 'other financial intermediaries' grew from $66tn in 2011 to $71tn in 2013. This represents about 24 per cent of total financial sector assets, half of banking system assets and 117 per cent of the GDP of the countries covered, a little below the 125 per cent of GDP in 2007.

This measure is, however, far in excess of the actual level of shadow banking activity, since it includes intermediation by *all* 'other financial intermediaries' and much of this intermediation is not shadow banking at all. It includes a number of intermediaries, such as hedge funds, equity mutual funds, private equity funds, broker-dealers and others that do not intermediate credit or engage in maturity mismatch and are therefore not shadow banks. The intention of the FSB is that this statistical framework should eventually be refined to identify separately shadow banks, i.e. those 'other financial intermediaries' engaged in

14 For comparison of European and US securitisation before the crisis see Milne (2009a).

credit intermediation and exposed to bank-like risks from leverage and maturity mismatch, but to date their statistics do not provide this level of disaggregation.

A further concern with the FSB measures, especially when looking at their reported figures for individual jurisdictions, is that they do not distinguish offshore intermediation between non-domestic investors and borrowers from onshore intermediation. This boosts the magnitude of other financial intermediation relative to GDP in jurisdictions with substantial offshore activity, such as the UK, Hong Kong and some parts of the euro area.[15]

Financial Stability Board (2013) provides some supplementary breakdown of 'other financial intermediation' for 25 jurisdictions (the coverage of the euro area is incomplete). This reveals (see especially Exhibit 4.2) that at end 2012, structured finance vehicles – which are central to the 'new' shadow banking documented by Gorton and Metrick (2010b) and others – amounted globally to around $5tn (of which 35 per cent were booked in the USA and 13 per cent in the UK, but many outside the USA were in fact holding US dollar assets); finance companies (in our terminology 'old' shadow banks) were also around $5tn; money market mutual funds were about $4tn; and real estate investment trusts less than $1tn.

An alternative attempt to estimate the magnitude of shadow banking in the euro area and the UK can be found in Bouveret (2011) (see Table 5.1). Bouveret estimates the size of the European shadow banking sector to be around $13tn at the end of 2010 compared to $15.8tn in the USA. The sector has declined by 20 per cent since the beginning of 2008 in the USA, but did not decline in Europe, in part because the ECB took mortgage-backed securities and other forms of structured credit instrument as collateral for its liquidity provision in the euro zone.

A more detailed examination of Bouveret's numbers, shown in Table 5.1, suggests that there are problems with the interpretation of these estimates, especially for Europe. First, there is considerable double counting, arising from the inclusion of both shadow banking liabilities (money market mutual funds, repo) and shadow banking assets (structured credit securities) in the total estimate of aggregate shadow banking. Second, like researchers examining the size of US shadow banking, Bouveret does not distinguish between the use of repo to finance holdings of structured credit instruments from their use to finance other positions, including taking both long and short positions in government and

15 A related concern applies to FSB figures for the Netherlands, where around two-thirds of 'other financial institutions' are some 14,000 'Special Financial Institutions' used by foreign owned multinationals to facilitate intergroup transactions and raise external funding. See Financial Stability Board (2013), footnote 30.

Table 5.1. Bouveret (2011) estimates of US and European shadow banking (2010Q4, US$bn)

Component	U.S.	Europe
Total outstanding open market paper	1057	563
Total repo liabilities	1213	8086
Net securities loaned	733	–
Total shares outstanding of money market mutual funds	2755	1550
Total for maturity transformation	**5758**	**10199**
Total liabilities of ABS issuers (non-GSE structured credit)	2333	2860
Total GSE liabilities	6561	–
Pool securities	1166	–
Total for credit transformation	**10060**	**2860**
Total for the shadow banking sector	**15818**	**13060**
Commercial bank liabilities	12828	59640*
Traditional banks liabilities(a measure of deposits)	7791	28675
In % of banks' liabilities	**123%**	**22%**
In % of traditional banks' liabilities	**200%**	**46%**

Notes on sources of data: MMFs info is taken from the industry (European Fund and Asset Management Association, EFAMA), central banks or commercial providers (Lipper). In 2010Q4 MMFs were measured as £1182bn (EFAMA), or £1132bn (ECB), or £1120bn (Lipper). Commercial paper info is taken from the ECB and the STEP (Short Term European Paper) programme. In 2010Q4 CP was £411.3bn. Contrary to the US CP market, the European CP market did not experience a downturn during 2008Q4, and instead stabilised in early 2009. ABS info is taken from AFME (Association for Financial Markets in Europe). In 2010Q4 ABS balances were £2090bn. September 2010, around £500bn of ABS were held on repo at the ECB according to AFME (2011), accounting for 24 per cent of total collateral posted. Repo data is taken from the International Capital Market Association (ICMA). December 2010, value of repo contracts outstanding was £5908bn. While the European repo market declined during the crisis (by roughly 30 per cent between 2008Q2 and 2008Q4), it has since increased. The US repo market declined by more than 50 per cent from 2008Q2 to 2010Q4.

corporate bonds. Bouveret adds repo and reverse repo and divides by two to obtain an average figure;[16] but a brief examination of the figures for repo finance in bank accounting statements suggests that this could exaggerate the amount of net repo funding available to finance holdings of structured credit instruments by ten or more times.[17]

Third, Bouveret does not take account of the very different institutional features of money market mutual funds in the USA and Europe.

16 Reverse repo is simply the other side of a repo contract, so repo is used for collateralised borrowing of money by offering a security as collateral, while reverse repo is used to lend money while in return holding a security as collateral.

17 We also note the inconsistency between the Bouveret measure of US repo markets, which is an order of magnitude lower than that provided by other researchers. This may be due to his aggregation method.

Many MMFs in Europe, especially in France, are in fact bank sponsored and used for financing their parent bank (in France for example the 'Livre A' funds are created largely to take advantage of tax concessions) and do not represent disintermediation. Fourth, the Bouveret figures on 'ABS' (mortgage and other asset-backed securities) do not distinguish the large amount of ABS created in Europe simply for the purpose of obtaining liquidity from the ECB and the Bank of England.

Another comparison of repo activities, this time between the USA and the UK, is presented by Hördahl and King (2008). Since 2002, repo markets had doubled in size; $10tn in both the US and euro repo markets, and $500bn in the UK repo market at the end of 2007. As liquidity dried up, repos became increasingly concentrated in the shortest maturities and only against the highest-quality collateral. The Bank of England gathers data from roughly 60 banks and broker-dealers for the UK repo market. Total repos and reverse repos reached a peak of £662bn or around 50 per cent of UK GDP in mid-2007 (this includes both sterling and, more importantly, foreign currency repo). Approximately four to six banks dominated the market, with banks accounting for three quarters of transactions while securities houses, building societies, fund managers and insurance companies account for the remainder. Strikingly, in mid-2007, while the repo market in the USA was under stress the euro area and UK markets operated under much calmer conditions.

To conclude: there are considerable statistical uncertainties about the magnitude of shadow banking in the USA, the euro area and the UK. The more detailed breakdowns from the Financial Stability Board suggest that the core activities associated with shadow banking, in which bank-like risks of maturity mismatch and leverage have often arisen – both the structured credit vehicles characteristic of what we call 'new' shadow banking and the finance companies and real estate investment trusts associated with what we describe as 'old' shadow banking – are together only $11tn across 20 major jurisdictions, including the USA, the UK, Germany, France and Italy. The repo-based estimates that have been so widely quoted by economics researchers as suggesting that shadow banking has grown worldwide to as much as $30tn or more (approaching 50 per cent of global GDP) are therefore a substantial overstatement of the overall magnitude of shadow banking.

Moreover, it remains unclear whether anything like the 'new' shadow banking that emerged in the USA has financed domestic credit to any significant degree in the euro area or the UK. We now turn to examine the case of the UK in much greater detail, showing that what happened in this case was 'old' rather than 'new' shadow banking based on bank lending and unsecured money market funding of non-bank specialised lenders, especially in the commercial property sector.

5.2 Shadow banking and the UK credit expansion

This section documents, using available data, the UK credit expansion of 1997–2008 and the role played by 'shadow banking', wholesale funding and securitisation to support the expansion of UK credit. It also compares this episode with the earlier property-related credit losses of 1973–74 and 1991–93.

5.2.1 UK credit expansion prior to the crisis

All the data presented here are for sterling money and credit of UK monetary and financial institutions.[18] Foreign currency lending and deposit takes place in the UK on a large scale, but this is not part of the UK credit expansion since it is overwhelmingly offshore banking in which both borrowers and depositors are non-residents.

Figure 5.2 shows the evolution of UK broad money (M4), as a percentage of GDP from 1982 to 2013. The substantial difference between the two upper lines in this figure highlights a challenge in understanding

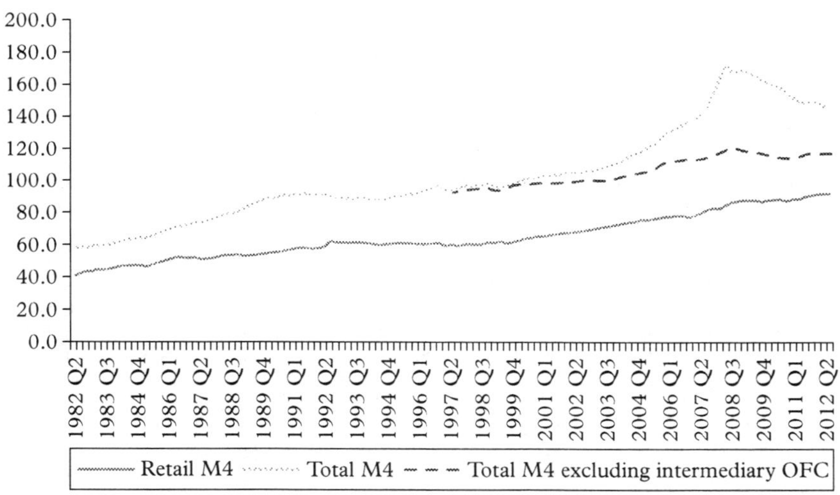

Figure 5.2. UK broad money (% of GDP, 1982–2013)

18 The data in Figures 5.2–5.7 are mostly taken from the Bank of England Statistical interactive database (http://www.bankofengland.co.uk/boeapps/iadb/). An online appendix details our use of this data.

the data on the UK credit expansion of 2002–07: there was a dramatic growth in both bank lending to and funding from what the Bank of England statistics describe as the 'Intermediate OFC (Other Financial Corporations)' sector.[19] As described by the Bank of England these Intermediate OFCs consist of 'non-bank credit grantors (including securitisation vehicles); mortgage and housing credit corporations; bank holding companies; other activities auxiliary to financial intermediation; and other financial intermediaries, to the extent that these deposits are held with MFIs in the same group of financial companies (i.e. 'intra-group' deposits)'.[20] For the purpose of analysing monetary conditions, for example in their Inflation Report, the Bank of England prefers to monitor M4 excluding deposits from these entities, on the ground that this narrow measure of money has a closer relation to nominal spending and is therefore economically more meaningful.

As Figure 5.2 indicates, much of the notable growth in intermediate OFC deposits occurred *post*-crisis, their ratio to GDP increasing from 19 per cent of GDP in 2008Q2 to 50 per cent of GDP in 2010Q1, before falling back to 29 per cent of GDP in 2013Q2.[21] There is also a notable growth in intermediate OFC deposits in the period running up to the crisis, rising from around 2½ per cent of GDP in 2003 to 19 per cent of GDP in 2008. In the late 1990s the ratio was close to zero. Over the same period, lending to intermediate OFCs grew even more rapidly (see the discussion of Figure 5.3 below).

19 Even larger levels of broad money result, including deposits from other OFCs, such as life insurance and pension funds, central counterparties or securities brokers; these are excluded entirely from Figure 5.2.

20 For more detailed discussion see Janssen (2009). According to the Bank of England Statistical Interactive Database, Table C further analysis of deposits and lending, the breakdown of intermediate OFI lending in Dec 2012 was as follows: loans to 'activities auxiliary to financial intermediation' (apparently fund management) £121bn, 'intra-group lending' £150bn, lending to securitisation special-purpose vehicles £19bn, loans to bank holding companies £29bn, loans to non-bank credit grantors £13bn and loans to mortgage and housing credit corporations £55bn, a total of £387bn. The corresponding sterling deposits and repos were: from securitisation special-purpose vehicles £212bn, intragroup deposits £110bn, from bank holding companies £18bn, from mortgage and housing credit corporations £14bn, from non-bank credit grantors £2bn and finally from fund management companies £60bn.

21 This is largely accounted for by a substantial increase in deposits from securitisation special-purpose vehicles/mortgage and housing credit corporations from March 2008 until December 2010 (during this period these two series are not reported separately, although it is clear for later figures that most of these deposits are from special-purpose vehicles). The Bank of England database provides no further detail, but the most obvious interpretation is that this large increase from March 2008 resulted from the Bank of England lending large sums to securitisation vehicles via 'repo' of residential mortgage-backed securities, with these funds in turn being deposited with sponsoring banks. These numbers may also be affected by changes in the reporting base or a changed accounting treatment of SPVs when they required support from their sponsoring banks.

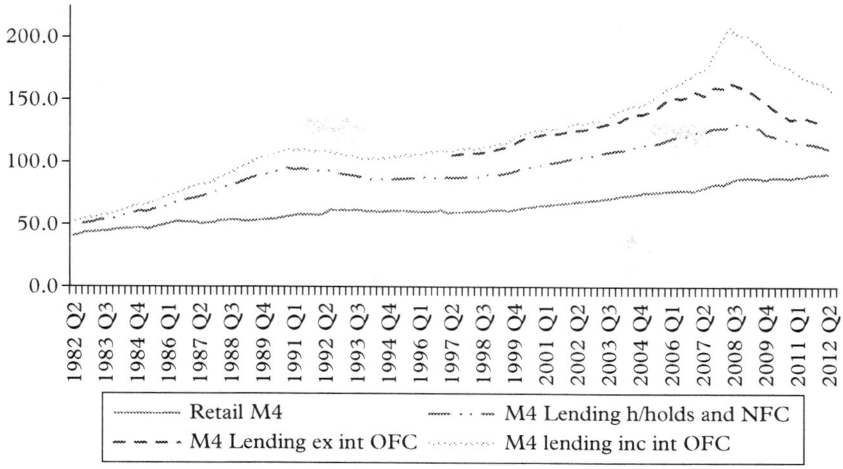

Figure 5.3. M4 lending and retail funding (% of GDP, 1982–2013)

Figure 5.2 indicates that during the run-up to the crisis wholesale funding of UK monetary institutions, *excluding* deposits from intermediate OFCs, grew at a similar rate to retail deposits in M4 (the two lower lines in the figure). However, since lending was growing more rapidly than deposits (documented in Figures 5.3 and 5.4), other further sources of funding must have been used to support lending growth.

The relatively rapid growth of M4 lending to the non-financial private sector, relative to the stock of retail deposits, is shown in Figure 5.3.[22] This uses three measures of sterling lending available from the Bank of England statistics. The first and lowest in most years is lending on balance sheet (sometimes called M4L). The second (sometimes called M4Lex) is described on the Bank of England website as 'M4 lending excluding the impact of securitisation', a rather confusing description, since this measure, rather than excluding securitisation, actually adds back securitised lending which is not reported on balance sheet. This chart also reports the broadest measure of M4 lending, including that to intermediate OFCs. Since intermediate OFCs includes lending to securitisation vehicles and to housing and mortgage credit and housing

22 Apart from lending to intermediate OFCs this graph excludes all M4 lending to other financial corporations, described by the Bank of England as follows: 'Other financial corporations (Items 15–17) are private financial corporations (other than monetary financial institutions) engaged primarily in provision of financial services. Examples include financial intermediation, insurance companies and pension funds and activities auxiliary to financial intermediation (e.g. fund management)'. (http://www.bankofengland.co.uk/statistics/pages/iadb/notesiadb/industrial.aspx)

institutions, this additional measure is the most comprehensive measure of lending; however, it also includes a lot of lending which is redeposited with the monetary financial institution sector. In addition, Figure 5.3 reports two narrower members of M4 lending, excluding intermediate OFCs and to households and non-financial companies (NFCs).

Figure 5.3 reveals a fairly stable relationship between on-balance sheet sterling lending to households and non-financial companies and retail deposits, with total 'conventional' lending of this kind exceeding retail deposits by around 40 per cent of GDP from the early 1990s to the late 2000s. In contrast, other forms of lending to other (non-bank) financial institutions grew rapidly throughout this period (and as indicated by Figure 5.2 accompanied by substantial growth in bank deposits from non-bank financial institutions).

There is, though, evidence of lending outstripping deposits in Figure 5.4, constructed using Bank of England statistics for household lending and deposit-taking. As indicated in this figure, household lending grew much faster than household deposits from the late 1990s to 2008, all of which can be accounted for by an increase in the ratio of mortgage lending to GDP from 52 per cent of GDP in mid-1999 to 86 per cent of GDP in the first half of 2009. Over the same period the gap between household deposits and total household lending grew from 7 per cent of GDP to 23 per cent of GDP. It has since fallen back to around the 1997 level as UK households have rebuilt their balance sheets.

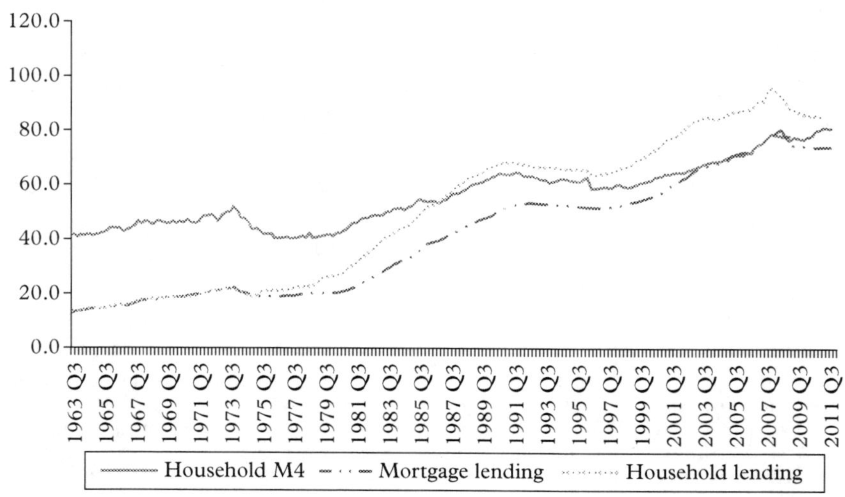

Figure 5.4. Household lending and deposits (% of GDP, 1963–2013)

M4 lending only includes lending to the non-financial corporate sector monetary financial intermediaries. A recent Bank of England analysis by Benford and Burrows (2013a) provides a fuller picture of one major corporate lending market, that for commercial real estate (CRE). They report that £247bn of the outstanding debt secured on CRE at end 2010 was bank lending, with about two-thirds of this lending provided by UK-owned banks and the rest by foreign owned banks. This amounts to about two-thirds of all UK resident bank lending to non-financial corporations.

Compiling data from a variety of sources, they report that total debt secured on commercial real estate rose rapidly in the year preceding the crisis, growing from around £110bn at end 2002 to around £300bn at end 2008 (Benford and Burrows (2013a), p. 55, Chart A) . This represented an increase from 11 per cent of nominal GDP in 2002 to 23 per cent of GDP in 2008, and accounts for close to one-third of the increase in the ratio of M4 lending to GDP over the same time period shown in Figure 5.2.

The CRE lending documented by Benford and Burrows (2013a) can be roughly matched to the industrial and sectoral allocation of M4 lending to the non-financial corporate sector in the Bank of England statistical database. Table 5.2 uses this data to present a breakdown of total M4 lending into various property related and other components as a percentage of GDP.

Much of this lending is captured by the database series RPQTBUT 'Sterling lending to firms involved in undertaking the buying, selling and renting of real estate' (column (2) of Table 5.2), a component of lending to the non-financial corporate sector. This lending to GDP grows from 2½ per cent of GDP in 1986 to over 7 per cent in 1991, the peak of the Thatcher–Lawson credit boom. After declining to 4 per cent of GDP in 1997 it then rises strongly again, reaching a peak of 19 per cent of GDP in 2009. Subsequently it has fallen back to 12 per cent of GDP in 2012.

A further part of property-related lending is recorded by the Bank of England as part of lending of Other Financial Corporations (OFC) as series RPQTBVN 'Sterling lending to mortgage and housing corporations' (column (3) of Table 5.2). Until December 2010 this series also includes lending to special-purpose securitisation vehicles. This lending series rises from 1 per cent of GDP in 1997 to 6½ per cent of GDP in mid-2007 (and rises further to 12 per cent of GDP in 2009; we believe this is because many banks were forced to lend money to fund their own securitisation vehicles).

The sum of these two property-related lending series rose from 5 per cent of GDP in 1997 to around 25 per cent of GDP at the beginning of

Table 5.2. Property-related lending components of M4 (% of GDP)

	Construction companies	Real estate agents and funds	Mortgage and housing corporations	Residential mortgage lending	Total property-related lending	Non-property-related M4 lending
	(1)	(2)	(3)	(4)	(5) = (1) + (2) + (3) + (4)	(6)
1997	0.9	4.3	1.3	51.9	58.4	29.3
1998	0.9	4.7	1.3	51.8	58.7	29.4
1999	0.9	5.1	1.9	53.1	61.1	29.6
2000	1.2	6.3	1.7	55.9	65.2	31.7
2001	1.4	7.6	1.9	58.2	69.1	32.1
2002	1.5	8.7	2.5	62.2	74.8	31.7
2003	1.4	9.4	3.2	65.9	79.9	29.4
2004	1.5	10.4	4.7	69.3	86.0	27.9
2005	1.6	11.7	5.0	71.8	90.0	29.2
2006	1.6	13.1	6.1	75.7	96.5	29.9
2007	2.0	14.8	6.4	78.6	101.8	30.3
2008	2.4	18.6	12.6	83.3	116.9	20.9
2009	2.0	18.8	6.3	85.7	112.8	25.9
2010	1.7	16.6	5.3	75.1	98.7	22.6
2011	1.6	13.4	4.3	74.1	93.4	23.4
2012	1.5	12.1	3.7	74.0	91.3	22.5

Source: Bank of England Interactive Statistical Database and authors' calculations. There is a break in the series for mortgage and housing corporations in 2010 when lending to securitisation vehicles is excluded.

the crisis. Over the same period residential mortgage lending rose from 52 per cent to 85 per cent of UK GDP. Taken together with a much smaller rise in lending to property construction companies (column (1) of Table 5.2) from about 1 per cent to 2 per cent of GDP, property-related lending accounts for all of the increase in sterling M4 lending relative to GDP during the credit expansion of 1997–2007. Non-property-related lending (column (6) of Table 5.2) actually fell slightly over the same period. This was an old-fashioned property lending boom.

Figure 5.5 shows the impact of this property-lending boom on the composition of total M4 lending (including securitised loans, excluding lending to intermediate OFCs but adding back lending to mortgage and housing credit corporations) to the personal, non-personal household and corporate sectors. This share of mortgages in total lending actually falls slightly during the years 1997–2008, due to the even more rapid growth of lending secured on commercial real estate. The share of personal

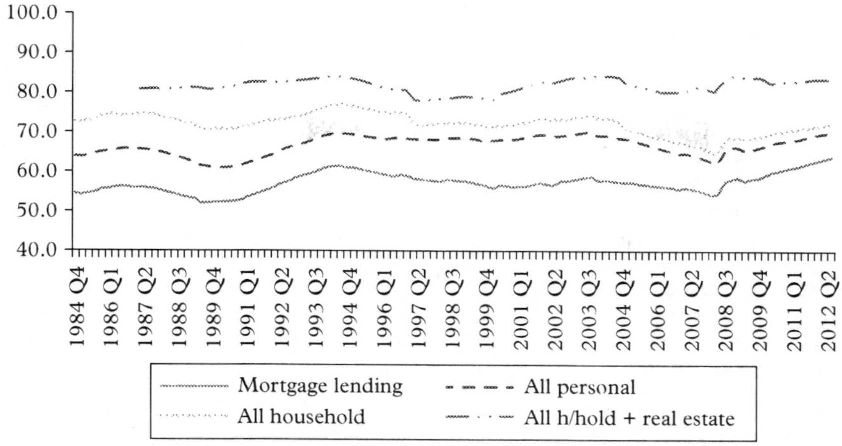

Figure 5.5. Composition of M4 lending ex int OFC (% of total, 1984–2013)

non-mortgage lending and lending to the rest of the household sector (this includes lending to unincorporated businesses) declines.

The share of M4 lending going to real estate and construction companies of all types, including the listed and unlisted CRE funds analysed by Benford and Burrows (2013a), is represented by the gap between the dotted lines and upper dash lines of Figure 5.5. While this lending expanded extremely rapidly over the period 1997–2008, over the same period other forms of lending to non-financial companies fell from over 20 to less than 15 per cent of total M4 lending (although the total amount of this other lending did not change much as a share of GDP).

While the credit boom of 1997–2008 was dominated by lending on residential and commercial property, the risk exposures that resulted from this lending varied considerably from one category of loan to another, and also, depending on the quality of their loan books, from one lender to another. Table 5.3 shows five-year cumulative loan write-offs for major categories of lending, again taken from Bank of England statistics.

Table 5.3 reveals that a total of £71.8bn of UK lending has been written off since the second quarter of 2008, representing 2 per cent of the average stock of loans over the period 2008Q2–2013Q2. Of these, the major contributions have been from credit card lending (£17.5bn, 24 per cent of the total), other unsecured personal lending (£15.1bn, 21 per cent of the total) and lending on commercial real estate (although not shown in this table, these write-offs amounted to approximately

Table 5.3. Cumulative five-year write-offs

All monetary institutions UK sterling lending		2003Q3–2008Q2 £bn	Share	Annual rate	2008Q3–2013Q2 £bn	Share	Annual rate
Non-financial corporations	(1)	6.5	18%	0.4%	30.3	42%	1.3%
Other financial corporations	(2)	0.3	1%	0.4%	2.2	3%	2.5%
Residential mortgages	(3)	0.5	1%	0.0%	3.4	5%	0.1%
Credit card lending	(4)	12.1	33%	3.7%	17.5	24%	5.0%
Other unsecured personal	(5)	15.7	43%		15.1	21%	
All lending to individuals	(6)	28.3	78%	0.6%	35.9	50%	0.6%
Unincorporated businesses	(7)	0.9	2%	0.4%	1.4	2%	0.6%
Non-residents	(8)	0.5	1%	0.1%	2.0	3%	0.5%
Total	(9)	36.5	100%	0.2%	71.8	100%	0.4%

Source: Bank of England Interactive Statistical Database and authors' calculations.

£20bn, or 28 per cent of the total).[23] These three forms of lending together account for very close to three-quarters of all of these UK sterling loan write-offs.

Despite the very large increase in the ratio of residential mortgage lending to GDP, write-offs on residential mortgage loans to individuals accounted were only £3.4bn; 5 per cent of the total write-offs and less than ½ per cent of the 2008 stock of residential mortgages. Similarly low write-off rates were recorded for lending to other financial corporations and to non-residents. Finally, about £10bn of write-offs, 14 per cent of the total, are against non-financial corporations not involved in commercial real estate.

Although credit card lending and unsecured personal lending both made a substantial contribution to total write-offs on sterling lending, the *increase* in UK sterling loan write-offs in this period (compared to the previous five years) is mostly from lending to non-financial corporations (and most of this was on commercial real estate lending). Comparing the first and fourth columns of Table 5.3, this category of write-offs accounts for £24bn of a total £35bn increase in write-offs between 2003–08 and 2008–13. Write-offs on credit cards rose by only just over £5bn and on mortgages by just under £3bn, while write-offs on other unsecured personal lending actually fell from £15.7bn to £15.0bn.

23 The breakout of write-offs for CRE lending is not available in the Bank of England database, and hence not distinguished in this table, but it is reported by Benford and Burrows (2013a).

Table 5.4. Comparison of sterling credit write-offs with other losses

	£bn
UK sterling credit write-offs (from Table 5.3)	71.8
Royal Bank of Scotland: 2008 write down of goodwill and other intangible assets	32.6
Losses on London investment banking operations (UK and International Banks, January 2007–March 2009)	150
HSBC credit provisions for North American operations 2006–10	28.8

Sources: Table 5.3 plus RBS (2009); FSA (2010), HSBC 10-K reports to the SEC, and authors' calculations.

The high level of write-offs on credit cards and other unsecured personal lending reflects the fact that these categories of loans are always risky, regardless of the state of the wider macroeconomy. This is not such a problem to banks, because the high levels of write-offs are anticipated and therefore interest rates on these forms of lending are set at sufficiently high levels to cover anticipated losses. The large increase in write-offs on loans to commercial real estate was a much bigger problem for UK banks because it was not anticipated, and therefore interest rates on this secured (and therefore supposedly safe) lending were far too low to absorb the losses.

These write-offs of domestic sterling exposures were not the only source of losses to UK owned banks and to other banks operating in the UK. Other major losses arose from (a) trading losses, including especially losses on investments in US dollar structured credit securities; (b) losses on lending outside of the UK, principally those of HSBC on its North American subsidiary HFC; and (c) the large write-down of the Royal Bank of Scotland share of the acquisition of ABN-AMRO bank. Table 5.4 compares some measures of these further losses with those shown in Table 5.3.[24]

Note that these losses on London investment banking are to a large extent accounted for by the activities of North American, Swiss, German and other international investment banks in London. The UK banks with substantial investment banking operations (HSBC, Barclays and Royal Bank of Scotland) account for a relatively small proportion of these losses (the FSA report from which this figure is taken does not distinguish the losses of these three UK-owned investment banking subsidiaries from those of others). On the other hand the table excludes the losses of

24 Note that Table 5.4 arguably overstates investment banking trading losses, because it does not allow for recovery in market values since March 2009, and may not capture all UK bank loan losses, since some further write-offs could possibly take place after 2013 (though with a recovering economy there could equally well be write-backs).

investment banking subsidiaries of these three banks outside of the UK. What Table 5.3 does show is that these UK sterling credit write-offs in Table 5.1 account for a major share of the losses of UK banking sector.

The sterling credit exposure and experience of loan losses by banks and building societies in the UK, in the build-up to and materialisation of the financial crisis of 2007–09, were similar in many ways to those experienced in the earlier major credit loss episodes in the UK of 1973–75 and 1991–93. As in the earlier crises there was a rapid growth of property-related lending, through both residential mortgage lending and lending secured on commercial real estate.

One difference from 1991–93 is that this most recent growth in mortgage lending was followed by relatively modest write-offs of mortgage loans. The most obvious explanation for this is that in 1990–91 short-term interest rates were maintained at very high levels in an effort to keep sterling within the European exchange rate mechanism. In the most recent period, in sharp contrast, short-term interest rates were reduced sharply. This, however, did not prevent substantial write-offs on unsecured personal lending and on commercial property lending.

To what extent was this related to shadow banking? Figures 5.6 and 5.7 report some indicators of UK shadow banking activity. The most salient feature of these charts is the substantial growth in issue of residential mortgage-backed securities (RMBS) in Figure 5.6, from less than 2 per cent of GDP in 1999 to nearly 27 per cent of GDP at the start of the crisis in 2007, i.e. an increase of 25 per cent of GDP, matching the increase in residential mortgage lending (Figure 5.4) over the same period from 52 per cent to 77 per cent of GDP.[25]

Regrettably there are no statistics on the holding of these sterling residential mortgage-backed securities: some tranches will have been placed in conduits used by the issuing banks to raise funding; other tranches will have been sold to long-term investors; yet other tranches will have been purchased as trading assets by other banks or by hedge funds. Still, regardless of who was purchasing the securitisations, most risk will have been retained by the issuing banks. This is because even before the crisis only low-risk mezzanine and senior tranches of RMBS could be readily sold.[26]

The AFME statistics used for Figure 5.6 also provide a breakdown of different types of securitisation in the UK (but without distinguishing

25 Bank of England data for securitisation in Figure 5.6 is available only back to 2010Q1, but this matches fairly well with the other series reported in Figure 5.6, AFME data for sterling securitisation that goes back to 1999.

26 Milne (2009) Chapters 4–6 discusses the role of securitisation in the global financial crisis in detail. There was no equivalent in sterling markets of the 'ABS-CDOs' used to resecuritise unsold junior tranches of US$ RMBS.

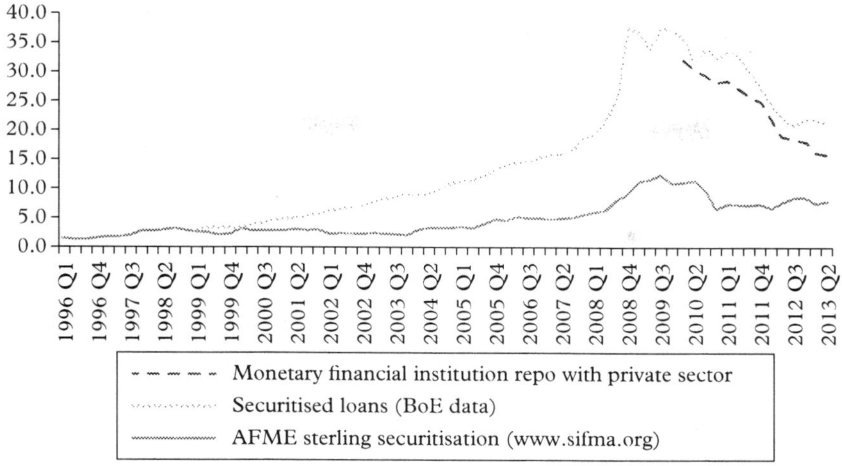

Figure 5.6. Securitisation and repo (% of GDP, 1996–2013)

sterling from foreign currency). These figures indicate that total outstanding securitisation in the UK in 2007Q2 was equivalent to 49 per cent of GDP (about one-fifth higher than the sterling securitisation shown in Figure 5.6), with securitised residential mortgage-backed securities amounting to 31 per cent of GDP, securitised commercial mortgage-backed securities 8 per cent of GDP and all other securitisations (credit cards, business loans and 'collateralised debt obligations or CDOs') adding up to 10 per cent of GDP, i.e. residential mortgage-backed securitisation was much more important than any other form of securitisation in the UK. Finally, Figure 5.6 shows sterling repo financing by monetary financial institutions. This is much smaller than securitisation, but the series are not really comparable.[27]

Figure 5.7 shows two indicators of property-related lending (other than residential mortgages provided to individuals), both taken from Table 5.2 above. These are Bank of England data on loans to real estate agents and funds (a component of lending to non-financial corporations) and lending to housing and mortgage credit corporations (a component of lending to intermediate other financial corporations). The definitions of these two series are both rather broad. Included in 'housing and

27 There will be other repo by financial institutions which are not classified as monetary financial institutions. The ICMA/University of Reading for June 2007 indicates that total sterling repo in 2007Q2 amounted to £280bn, about four and a half times the level shown in Figure 5.6. At the same time, as discussed in Section 5.2, much of this repo will be used for financing trading positions, not for holding structured credit securities such as RMBS.

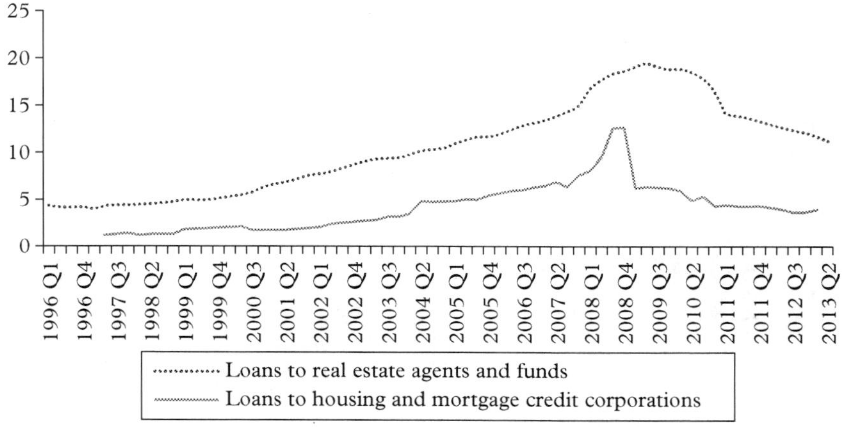

Figure 5.7. Other sterling property-related lending (% of GDP, 1996–2013)

mortgage credit corporations', before 2010, are special purpose vehicles used for the issue of RMBS and the conduits used for holding and financing RMBS. With the onset of the crisis, from 2007Q2 onwards, as these off-balance-sheet vehicles were unable to obtain short-term funding in the markets, banks were forced to lend to the vehicles they sponsored, increasing lending to Housing and Mortgage Corporations shown in Figure 5.6 substantially from 5 per cent to 13 per cent of GDP. This need to lend then declined as the Bank of England provided substantial repo finance secured against RMBS and CMBS.

As described by Benford and Burrows (2013), a large part of UK bank lending secured on commercial property was to property companies (with much of the rest to wealthy individuals). This property company lending is included in the second series in Figure 5.7 – loans to real estate agents and funds. The large expansion of commercial real estate lending is a major reason for the increase in this category of lending from around 5 per cent of GDP in the late 1990s to nearly 15 per cent of GDP in 2007.

Two main conclusions can be drawn from Figures 5.6 and 5.7. While Bank of England statistics are not particularly informative about financial activities outside the banking sector, there is little evidence to be found of 'new' shadow banking in sterling markets of the form that developed in the USA in the years preceding the global crisis. The securitisation of mortgages and other sterling lending was conducted by established banks, not by competing shadow banks, and used as a tool to secure further funding to continue the credit expansion. While banks were using off-balance-sheet vehicles to raise short-term funding using securitised loans as collateral, the amount of 'emergency' lending to these vehicles suggested by Figure 5.7 was only about 5 per cent of GDP, indicating that the size of these off-balance-sheet vehicles was much less than total sterling securitisation.

The second conclusion is that the main exposure that led to the large increase in sterling loan write-offs (shown in Table 5.3) was a substantial increase in rather conventional lending to property companies. Some form of 'shadow' banking may have played a secondary role in this boom and subsequent bust, but this was through REITs and other leveraged investment funds investing in commercial property (see Benford and Burrows (2013) for more detailed discussion of the activities of these other investors in commercial property).

5.3 Comparison with the UK banking losses of 1973–74 and 1991–93

This section briefly compares the most recent episode of bank credit losses in the UK with the earlier episodes of 1973–74 and 1991–93.

The 1973–74 shadow banking crisis has been documented in some detail by Reid (1982). While sterling foreign exchange controls continued to be applied until 1979, a gradual deregulation of domestic UK banking occurred from the late 1950s until the early 1970s. The relaxation of strict controls of lending for the purchase of consumer durables ('hire purchase') led to the creation of a number of finance groups seeking to provide loans to consumers and smaller businesses, but they had no banking license and their legal status as banks was unclear. As recognised in a famous judgement (United Dominions Trust Ltd v. Kirkwood BT – QB 1966) by Lord Denning, Master of the Rolls, these finance houses had a claim, under UK common law, to be regarded as banks simply by virtue of having practised a lending business with rights to reclaim debts, and having been accepted as such by the investors and financial intermediaries that funded them.

This somewhat unsatisfactory situation was addressed by Section 123 of the 1967 Companies Act, allowing the Board of Trade to issue certificates for organisations to engage in banking, alongside the already established banks: *either* those recognised under Schedule VIII of the 1948 Companies act or subsequently under Section 127 of the 1967 Companies Act (these were the most prestigious banks and included all the major high street clearing banks as well as the discount houses and merchant banks in the City of London) *or* a number of other banks authorised by the Bank of England for participation in the London markets and largely engaged in foreign exchange business.

A large number of institutions took up the opportunity to obtain Section 123 banking certification, engaging in a wide range of credit provision, especially property finance lending to housebuilders and to commercial real estate developers, not just consumer lending. By the autumn of 1973, just before the secondary crisis broke, there were 133 banks certificated by the Board of Trade and a further 323 banks recognised or licensed by the Bank of England (the so called 'listed banks' because they were listed as contributors to the Bank's banking statistics). Amongst these listed banks Reid (1982, p. 52) identifies some 34 banks that were engaged in similar business activities (property and consumer finance) to the new certificated banks, and can thus also be regarded as part of the secondary banking sector.

There was no clear responsibility for regulatory oversight. The Bank of England was primarily concerned with maintaining contacts with the clearing banks and discount houses with which it conducted its own market business. The City banks were regarded as self-policing because they engaged only in wholesale business. This freedom was reinforced, in 1971, by the introduction of the new monetary regime of 'Competition and Credit Control'. The direct controls on lending of the larger banks that had been a major instrument of monetary policy for two or more decades were scrapped; the clearing and other banks were encouraged to compete fiercely for business; and the primary monetary instrument became Bank of England control over short-term interest rates.

The final say on the setting of interest rates remained, however, that of HM Treasury and its political masters. This political constraint on the raising of interest rates, combined with the expansionary fiscal stance of the new Conservative Chancellor Anthony Barber ('the dash for growth') laid the foundations for a rapid boom in property prices, for which the newly liberalised banking system was only too ready to provide the necessary credit. Reckless expansion was encouraged by extremely lax controls over lending risks amongst both established and secondary banks.

Reid (1982, pp. 61–63) records that between October 1971 and December 1973 total sterling (listed) bank advances to domestic residents rose 148 per cent (from 14 per cent to 27 per cent of nominal GDP, modest proportions by the standards of later years, but a rapid rise nonetheless). These figures contain relatively little lending secured on residential property, because at that time banks were still not allowed to compete with building societies in the provision of long-term residential mortgages.

This figure also understates the total creation of credit, because the 'unlisted' Section 123 banks appear in these statistics as borrowers rather than as lenders (the property and financial sector accounted for some £6.7bn of total bank lending in December 1973). Many of these unlisted Section 123 banks were able to extend much greater credit than they obtained from the listed banks by borrowing on the rapidly expanding London wholesale money markets. Between October 1971 and December 1973 total money market deposits (unsecured interbank lending and sterling wholesale certificates of deposit) rose from 8 per cent to 18 per cent of GDP, with much of this money lent by Section 123 banks. While there are no comprehensive figures, the situation of various individual institutions documented by Reid (1982) suggests that many of the secondary banks – which took very little in the way of retail deposits – often raised half or more of their funding from wholesale markets.

While the property boom itself slowed in mid-1973, the crisis itself was not triggered until December of that year, when (in the context of a gloomy economic environment with deteriorating industrial relations in the UK and the current threat of substantial oil price increases by OPEC) liquidity problems emerged at Cedar Holdings, one of the most prominent of the secondary banks. In an emergency overnight meeting on 19–20 December, the Bank of England persuaded major shareholders and Barclays Bank to provide £72m of funding to refinance the wholesale money market borrowing of Cedar. But the announcement of this rescue only triggered rumours of problems at other secondary banks. By Friday 21 December the major clearing banks and the Bank of England agreed and announced the 'lifeboat operation' through which the major clearing banks would 'recycle' funds to replace wholesale deposit withdrawals from the secondary banking sector.

Eventually, by mid-1975, the lifeboat loaned out some £1.2bn (around two-fifths of the equity capital of the clearing banks that backed the lifeboat) to 25 secondary banks (with £500m provided to United Dominions Trust, the largest of the secondary banks that had listed status). This lending, while gradually wound down after its 1975 peak, remained on the books of the clearing banks for several years. Of the 25 beneficiaries of the lifeboat, most disappeared, either through liquidation or through absorption into larger financial groups, and the remainder substantially contracted. Other secondary banks, strong enough to avoid the need to take lifeboat funds, similarly either exited from banking or were absorbed into larger financial groups.

It is not possible, even from the detailed research of Reid (1982), to compare the total property-related losses that emerged following the 1971–73 property boom with the commercial property losses experienced in the period 2009–13. Much of the loss was at secondary banks outside the compass of Bank of England banking statistics. If anything, the scale of problems in the property sector seem to have been more severe than in 2003–07 (see Reid (1982) Chapter 8 for discussion of property loan difficulties), but the rapid inflation of 1974–75, following the OPEC oil price shock, transferred resources from bank depositors to bank creditors, easing the burden of repayment and limiting loan losses.

The 1991–93 UK banking problems remain relatively poorly documented compared to either 1973–75 or 2007–13. There are no comprehensive reviews of this crisis, of comparable detail to that provided by Reid (1982) for the secondary banking failures of 1973–75. Still information about the problems of these years can be obtained from subsequent Bank of England research (Jackson (1996); Logan (2000); Hoggarth and Soussa (2001)).

The banking sector problems of 1991–93, like the earlier episodes of 1973–75 and 2007–12, were driven by a property lending cycle in which smaller 'shadow' banks participated. In 1991 there were 116 small banks in the UK, a large proportion of which engaging in lending secured on residential and commercial property lending; of these, by 1993 25 had failed. But these shadow banks (in our terminology 'old' shadow banks because while much less closely regulated than the established banks they were not competing for deposit-like liabilities) accounted for a very much smaller share of total credit provision than the secondary banks in 1973. Logan (2000) reports that the total assets of the 92 small banks for which he was able to assemble data amounted to only £15bn (2.6 per cent of 1991 GDP) compared to the total assets of Barclays, the largest UK banking group at the time, which had total assets of £138bn (23.2 per cent of GDP).

As documented by Vander Weyer (2000), Barclays was by some margin the most important lender in commercial property markets (for example, Barclays was the principal creditor in the bankruptcy of Olympia and York, the property developers who built the Canary Wharf tower). Active participants in UK commercial property market lending also included a number of foreign banks. Shadow banks played a relatively small role in the property lending problems of 1991–93.

Chart 1 of Pain (2003) reports the stock of loan loss provisions (as a percentage of total lending) of the largest UK banks over the years 1982–2000. The biggest source of losses was unconnected with the UK economy and property cycle: from the early 1980s it came from Latin American and other overseas exposures of Lloyds, Midland and Standard Chartered (resulting in cumulated loan loss provisions of 9 per cent, 7 per cent and 6 per cent of loan assets respectively). Barclays did not have the same substantial losses on international exposure in the 1980s, but in 1991–93 it accumulated loan loss provisions of close to 4 per cent of its total lending, much of this arising from its UK commercial property exposures. The accumulated provisions of other UK banks were around half those of Barclays. The overall level of loan loss provisions in UK domestic banking was broadly similar, as a proportion of total lending, in 1991–93 to the level of loss provisions reported in Table 5.3 for the period 2008–12.

While Barclays was hit especially hard, the magnitude of the commercial property lending boom appears to have been slightly smaller in the early 1990s than in the 2000s (Figure 5.5). Total non-household real estate-related lending increased from around 2 per cent of GDP in 1986 to 8 per cent of GDP in 1991; this compares with a rise of this lending category in the later commercial property boom from around 7 per cent of GDP in 1997 to 15 per cent of GDP in 2007.

While the problems in commercial property appear slightly smaller in 1991–93 than in 2007–12, this is not true of residential mortgage lending, Chart 2 of Pain (2003) reports the ratio of the stock of loan loss provisions to loans of the four largest UK mortgage banks. These rose to nearly 1.75 per cent of lending (Alliance and Leicester) and around 0.8 per cent of lending for the other three mortgage banks (Halifax, Abbey National and Northern Rock). Thus residential mortgage loan losses were much more severe in 1991–93 than in the most recent mortgage market downturn of 2007–12, most obviously because of the policy of maintaining high levels of interest rates in 1990–92 to maintain the UK's fixed exchange rate in the European ERM.

5.4 Summary and conclusions

This chapter has examined the expansion of credit prior to the financial crisis of 2007–09 and the subsequent loan losses in UK sterling lending. A central question we have addressed is the role of new forms of intermediation ('shadow banking') and new credit instruments. We have reviewed the literature on shadow banking (Section 5.1); examined magnitude, financing and subsequent losses on the credit expansion of UK banks and the role played in this episode by shadow banks (Section 5.2) and provided a brief comparison with the earlier episodes of property related credit losses in UK domestic lending in 1973–75 and 1991–93 (Section 5.3).

We draw a distinction between 'old' shadow banking, taking funds from the established banking system, and 'new' shadow banking, using the modern tools of securitisation and credit risk transfer in order to create money-like substitutes for traditional bank deposits and hence disintermediate entirely from the established banks. We argue (Section 5.1) that while 'new' shadow banking of this kind played an important role in the USA, bypassing commercial bank intermediation, it did not operate in this way in the markets for euro and sterling lending. The only element of the 'new' shadow banking, of the kind described by Gorton and Metrick (2010b), relevant to UK domestic (sterling) lending was the extensive use of securitisation, especially of residential mortgages, in the years preceding the crisis, but these securitisations were all conducted by established UK banks, not by competing shadow banks.

Bank of England statistics reveal that residential mortgage lending led to relatively modest losses for UK banks in the period 2008–13. Losses on sterling exposures emerged instead, primarily from lending secured on commercial property and unsecured personal lending, with most of the increase in losses associated with commercial property. This was a property boom (as documented by Benford and Burrows (2013b), commercial property lending increased to about two-thirds of total UK bank lending to the non-bank corporate sector (by UK-owned and foreign banks)), followed by substantial loan losses.

A form of 'old' shadow banking played some role in this boom and bust, with real estate investment trusts and other specialised real estate funds investing in commercial property. In this respect the most recent episode of loan losses has some parallel to the UK lending losses of 1973–75, discussed in our Section 5.3, in which smaller 'secondary banks', drawing funding from larger established banks, invested substantial funds secured in commercial property. There are also parallels with the UK in 1991–93 (the end of the Thatcher–Lawson boom), where again much of the lending was secured on property, with banks relying on market-based valuation of the underlying collateral.

This does not mean that 'new' shadow banking played no role in the recent UK credit expansion or had no impact on UK banks. Royal Bank of Scotland, Barclays and HSBC were also active investors in offshore US dollar shadow banking, with substantial holdings and large subsequent trading losses on US dollar RMBS, CDOs and other structured credit instruments. Securitisation of residential mortgages also helped fund what now appears as an unwise extension of credit into other more risky areas of lending, notably commercial property. The loss of confidence and resulting collapse in the marketability of residential mortgage-backed securities during the crisis then had a further immediate impact, starving UK banks of liquidity, most notably in the failure of Northern Rock in September 2007. Apart, though, from this novelty – the widespread use of securitisation to fund loan expansion – this was a very old-fashioned banking crisis.

References

Adrian, Tobias and Shin, Hyun Song. (2010a). The changing nature of financial intermediation and the financial crisis of 2007–09. *FRB of New York Staff Report*, (439).

(2010b). The changing nature of financial intermediation and the financial crisis of 2007–09. Staff Reports. New York. http://www.newyorkfed.org/research/staff_reports/sr439.html.

(2009). The shadow banking system: implications for financial regulation. *SSRN Electronic Journal*, doi:10.2139/ssrn.1441324. http://papers.ssrn.com/abstract=1441324.

Alba, Pedro, Leonardo Hernandez and Daniela Klingebiel. (1999). *Financial Liberalization and the Capital Account: Thailand, 1988–97*. The World Bank, Washington, DC.

Ashcraft, Adam B and Til Schuermann. (2008). Understanding the securitization of subprime mortgage credit. Staff Report, Federal Reserve Bank of New York.

Benford, James and Oliver Burrows. (2013). Commercial property and financial stability. *Bank of England Quarterly Bulletin* (1): 48–58. http://www.bankofengland.co.uk/publications/Documents/quarterlybulletin/2013/qb130105.pdf.

Bouveret, Antoine. (2011). An assessment of the shadow banking sector in Europe (July 6). Available at SSRN:http://ssrn.com/abstract=2027007.

Bradshaw, Keith. 2004. Informal lenders in China pose risks to banking system. *New York Times*. http://www.nytimes.com/2004/11/09/business/worldbusiness/09yuan.html?pagewanted=print&position=&_r=0.

Brunnermeier, M.K. and L.H. Pedersen. 2008. Market liquidity and funding liquidity. *Review of Financial Studies* 22(6): 2201–2238.

Charumilind, Chutatong, Raja Kali and Yupana Wiwattanakantang. (2006). Connected lending: Thailand before the financial crisis*. *The Journal of Business* 79(1): 181–218.

Davis, E Philip and Haibin Zhu. (2004). Bank lending and commercial property cycles: some cross-country evidence. 150. Working Paper. BIS working paper.

Financial Stability Board. (2013). Global Shadow Banking Monitoring Report 2013. http://www.financialstabilityboard.org/publications/r_131114.htm.

Frydman, Carola, Eric Hilt and Lily Y Zhou. (2012). *Economic Effects of Runs on Early'Shadow Banks': Trust Companies and the Impact of the Panic of 1907*. National Bureau of Economic Research, Harvard, MA.

FSA. (2010). The Prudential Regime for Trading Activities. 10/4. Discussion Paper. http://www.fsa.gov.uk/pubs/discussion/dp10_04.pdf.

Goodhart, Charles and P.J.R. Delargy. (1998). Financial Crises: Plus Ça Change, plus C'est La Même Chose. *International Finance* 1(2): 261–287.

Gorton, Gary. (2009). The subprime panic*. *European Financial Management* 15(1): 10–46.

Gorton, Gary B and Andrew Metrick. (2009). Haircuts. 15273. Working Paper. National Bureau of Economic Research, Harvard, MA.

Gorton, Gary B. (2010). *Slapped by the Invisible Hand: The Panic of 2007*. Oxford University Press, UK. http://books.google.com/books?id=8mExI4boLqIC&pgis=1.

Gorton, Gary B. and Andrew Metrick. (2010a). Regulating the shadow banking system. *SSRN Electronic Journal*, doi:10.2139/ssrn.1676947. http://papers.ssrn.com/abstract=1676947.

Gorton, Gary B. and Andrew Metrick. (2010b). Regulating the shadow banking system. *Brookings Papers on Economic Activity* (2): 261–297, doi:10.1353/eca.2010.0016. http://muse.jhu.edu/content/crossref/journals/brookings_papers_on_economic_activity/v2010/2010.2.gorton.html.

Gorton, Gary and Andrew Metrick. (2012). Securitized banking and the run on repo. *Journal of Financial Economics* 104: 425–451, doi:10.1016/j.jfineco.2011.03.016. http://linkinghub.elsevier.com/retrieve/pii/S0304405X1100081X.

He, Dong and Robert N. McCauley. (2010). Offshore markets for the domestic currency: monetary and financial stability issues. 02/2010. *SSRN Electronic Journal*. Working Paper, doi:10.2139/ssrn.1699740. http://papers.ssrn.com/abstract=1699740.

Hördahl, Peter and Michael King. (2008). Developments in repo markets during the financial turmoil. *BIS Quarterly Review*, 37–53.

Hoggarth, Glenn and Farouk Soussa. (2001). Crisis management, lender of last resort and the changing nature of the banking industry. *Financial Stability and Central Banks*. London: Routledge for CCBS and the Bank of England.

Jackson, Patricia. (1996). Deposit protection and bank failures in the United Kingdom. *Bank of England Financial Stability Review* (1): 38–43.

Janssen, Norbert. (2009). Measures of M4 and M4 lending excluding intermediate other financial corporations. *Bank of England Monetary & Financial Statistics*: 1–4. http://www.bankofengland.co.uk/statistics/Documents/ms/articles/art1may09.pdf.

Kaminsky, Graciela L and Reinhart Carmen M. (1999). The twin crises: the causes of banking and balance-of-payments problems. *The American Economic Review* 89 (3): 473–500, doi:10.2307/117029. http://www.jstor.org/stable/117029.

Leightner, Jonathan E and C.A. Lovell. (1998). The impact of financial liberalization on the performance of Thai banks. *Journal of Economics and Business* 50(2): 115–131.

Logan, Andrew. (2000). The early 1990s small bank' crisis: leading indicators. *Bank of England Financial Stability Review* (8): 80–82.

McCulley, Paul. (2007). Teton reflections. *Pimco Global Central Bank Focus*. Online: https://www.pimco.com/insights/economic-and-market-commentary/global-central-bank-focus/teton-reflections.

McGuire, Patrick and Goetz Von Peter. (2009). The US Dollar Shortage in Global Banking. *BIS Quarterly Review*, 47–63.

Milne, Alistair. (2009). *The Fall of the House of Credit*. Cambridge, UK: Cambridge University Press. http://www.cambridge.org/gb/knowledge/isbn/item2428039/?site_locale=en_GB.

Milne, Alistair and Geoffrey E Wood. (2008). Banking crisis solutions old and new. *Federal Reserve Bank of St. Louis Review* 90, Sept/Oct.

Moen, Jon and Ellis W Tallman. 1992. The bank panic of 1907: the role of trust companies. *The Journal of Economic History* 52(03): 611–630.

Pain, Darren. (2003). The provisioning experience of the major UK banks: a small panel investigation. 177. Working Paper.

Pozsar, Zoltan, Tobias Adrian, Adam B. Ashcraft and Haley Boesky. (2010). Shadow Banking. 458. *SSRN Electronic Journal.* Staff Report, doi:10.2139/ssrn.1645337. http://papers.ssrn.com/abstract=1645337.

Pozsar, Zoltan and Manmohan Singh. (2011). The Nonbank-Bank Nexus and the Shadow Banking System. http://papers.ssrn.com/abstract=1971440.

RBS. (2009). Annual Report and Accounts, 2008.

Reid, Margaret. (1982). *The Secondary Banking Crisis, 1973–75: Its Causes and Course.* London and Basingstoke: Macmillan.

Reinhart, Carmen and Rogoff, Kenneth. (2009). *This Time Is Different: Eight Centuries of Financial Folly.* Princeton University Press, Princeton, NJ. http://www.amazon.co.uk/This-Time-Different-Centuries-Financial-ebook/dp/B004EYT932/ref=sr_1_1?ie=UTF8&qid=1404847123&sr=8-1&keywords=this+time+is+different+rogoff.

Singh, Manmohan. (2010). The sizable role of Rehypothecation in the shadow banking system. *SSRN Electronic Journal*, doi:10.2139/ssrn.1670740. http://papers.ssrn.com/abstract=1670740.

Singh, Manmohan and James Aitken. (2009). Deleveraging after Lehman – evidence from reduced Rehypothecation. 09/42. Working Papers. http://papers.ssrn.com/abstract=1366171.

United Dominions Trust Ltd 1966 v. Kirkwood BT – QB., 2 431.

Vander Weyer, Martin. (2000). *Falling Eagle: The Decline of Barclays Bank.* Weidenfeld & Nicolson, London. http://www.amazon.co.uk/Falling-Eagle-Decline-Barclays-Bank/dp/0297644068.

6 Household debt and spending in the United Kingdom

Philip Bunn and May Rostom

6.1 Introduction

A major development in UK household balance sheets over the period between 1992 and 2007 was the build-up of household debt. The stock of debt trebled from around £450 billion in 1992 to £1.5 trillion in 2007 with most of the increase taking place from the late 1990s onwards. In relation to annual disposable income, debt rose by around 60 percentage points over this period to a peak of 160%.

Debt plays no causal role in determining spending in standard economic theory, and the extent to which debt may have implications for aggregate spending is not well understood. In a life-cycle model, households typically borrow to smooth through their consumption, which is determined only by their expected lifetime income and net wealth. But debt could potentially affect consumption, at least temporarily: for example if high debt levels led indebted households to respond to shocks in a different way to other households.

In the context of the UK economy, it is possible that the large build-up of debt over the period leading up to the financial crisis helped to boost household consumption, and that the recession was deeper, and the subsequent recovery slower, as a result of indebted households making larger adjustments to spending than other households. Our work (a simplified version of which was published in the 2014 Q3 Bank of

The views expressed in this chapter are those of the authors, and not necessarily those of the Bank of England or its committees. We are grateful to Orazio Attanasio, Charlie Bean, Jamie Bell, Alan Castle, Tom Crossley, Hamish Low, Paul Mizen, Martin Weale, an anonymous referee and seminar participants at the Bank of England and the 2013 Causes and Consequences of the Long UK Expansion Conference for helpful comments and suggestions. This work contains statistical data from ONS which is Crown Copyright. The use of the ONS statistical data in this work does not imply the endorsement of the ONS in relation to the interpretation or analysis of the statistical data. This work uses research datasets which may not exactly reproduce National Statistics aggregates. This chapter was finalised on 22 September 2014.

England *Quarterly Bulletin* (Bunn and Rostom (2014)) aims to investigate these issues for the UK. Empirical evidence suggests that high debt levels did depress consumer spending in the USA after 2007 (Dynan (2012), Baker (2013) and Mian et al. (2013)).

It is difficult to assess how debt has affected household spending using aggregate data. We use microdata from the Living Costs and Food (LCF) Survey to investigate differences in spending patterns across households with different levels of debt over the period since 1992. This approach can establish whether high-debt households consumed more or less than other households, although it is still difficult to prove whether there is a causal link or not. We therefore use evidence from the Bank of England/NMG Consulting Survey to further investigate the reasons behind households' spending decisions.

Whilst increases in mortgage debt before 2007 were largely matched by an accumulation of financial assets, we find evidence that larger than average increases in spending by indebted households may have provided some modest support to aggregate consumption. But after 2007, households with high levels of debt cut spending by more – relative to income – than households on average. Spending cuts associated with debt are estimated to have reduced the level of aggregate private consumption by around 2% after 2007. Survey evidence suggests that large cuts in spending by indebted households following the financial crisis reflect a combination of tighter credit conditions and increased concerns about ability to make future debt repayments.

The chapter is organised as follows. First we discuss the theory and previous literature around the relationship between debt and consumption. We then provide an overview of developments in household balance sheets in the UK since 1992, before moving on to discuss our research design, the data and our econometric results on the relationship between debt and consumption. Finally, we discuss the interpretation of those results and present some evidence on why households may have cut spending after 2007.

6.2 Theory and literature

In the permanent income/life-cycle model, households borrow or save in order to smooth their consumption over their life cycle. Current consumption depends on expected lifetime income and wealth. Households with debt do not respond differently to those without, whether a household has debt is simply related to how their current income and wealth compares to their average lifetime income and wealth: debt plays no causal role in determining the level of spending.

In the simplest form of the life-cycle model, households can borrow as much as they choose, the cost of borrowing is constant, households are assumed to be able to accurately predict their lifetime income, there is no uncertainty and expectations do not change.

In practice, many of the assumptions that underlie the life-cycle model may not hold. More specifically, households are not certain about their lifetime incomes; they may have unrealistic expectations or may be affected by shocks which change those expectations. They may also not be able to borrow against their future income, or be able to borrow as much as they would like to be able to fully smooth their consumption and their ability to borrow, or the cost of borrowing may change over time. Some theoretical models in the literature do therefore find a direct role for debt in determining spending by allowing changes in income expectations or credit conditions to interact with debt.

The literature on how debt might affect spending dates back to Fisher's (1933) debt deflation theory. Fisher argued that in the US Great Depression, debt helped to amplify the initial shock as it propagated through the economy. King (1994) discusses how Fisher's work might have been relevant in explaining the weakness of UK consumption during the 1990s recession. King puts forward a model in which indebted households, who had borrowed on the expectation of higher future income, suffered adverse shocks to their future income expectations that led them to consume less and repay debt. Even if other households experience offsetting positive shocks, they do not increase consumption by enough to fully offset the effect on aggregate spending.

Since the recent financial crisis, new research on the role of debt has typically tried to incorporate some type of reduction in households' ability to borrow. For example, Eggertsson and Krugman (2012) assume that there is a limit on how much debt individuals can hold, and if that limit is revised down (for example because of a sudden realisation that collateral constraints were too lax), highly indebted households are forced to reduce spending sharply, with no offsetting response from non-debtors. Other models, such those of Guerrieri and Lorenzoni (2011) and Philippon and Midrigan (2011), also try to explain weak consumption by incorporating a tightening in the ability of households to borrow to smooth consumption and by a reduction in the ability of households to withdraw equity from their homes. Changes in ability to borrow can also potentially help to amplify the impact of other shocks through the financial accelerator type mechanism discussed by Bernanke et al. (1999). In a similar vein, Iacoviello (2005) builds a model in which rising debt burdens help to amplify the impact of demand shocks. Increases in demand boost asset prices and increase the borrowing capacity of debtors, allowing them to spend more, whilst consequent increases in prices erode the real value of debt and boost net worth. But high debt levels only amplify the effects of demand shocks in this model – they help to dampen the impact of supply shocks.

There are two main strands of empirical literature that investigate the link between household debt and spending: analysis of how consumer spending varies with debt levels across (i) countries or (ii) households within a given country.

Cross-country evidence typically finds that the recessions preceded by large increases in household debt tend to be more severe and protracted (e.g. IMF (2012), Jorda et al. (2013)). Whilst this relationship is evident during the recent crisis, the evidence is not restricted to recent experience. King (1994) shows that the same was true in the early 1990s, and going back to the 1870s, Jorda et al. (2013) show how excess credit growth is correlated with stronger booms and subsequent deeper recessions and slower recoveries.

There is, however, less evidence that the aggregate level of pre-crisis household debt is a good predictor of the size of the subsequent adjustment in spending. Consistent with that, Cecchetti et al. (2011) find that the level of household debt does not have a statistically significant effect on future growth in a cross-country dataset going back to 1980 (although they do find a significant role for public debt, and in some instances corporate debt). However, Flodén (2014) argues that there is a clearer relationship between the level of debt and changes in consumption after 2007 once the level of consumption is adjusted for prior growth in debt, past consumption and the current account balance.

At the household level, empirical work in the USA has found evidence of a relationship between high pre-crisis debt levels and weak post-crisis consumption. Dynan (2012) uses household-level data to show that households with high loan-to-value ratios experienced larger declines in spending between 2007 and 2009, after controlling for wealth effects and other factors. Mian et al. (2013) show that the decline in US consumption following the crisis was greater in counties with higher leverage prior to the crisis. Baker (2013) finds that spending by highly indebted households has been more sensitive to income fluctuations and that is likely to have increased the depth of the recent recession, although the size of these effects becomes smaller once asset prices and credit conditions are controlled for.

Andersen et al. (2014) find similar evidence of a negative correlation between pre-crisis leverage and consumption during the crisis in Denmark, and they find that this result cannot be fully explained by a contraction in credit supply. They also show that the highly indebted households who made larger adjustments in spending during the crisis had been consuming a greater share of their income before the crisis.

There is no such household-level empirical work for the UK looking at whether high debt levels have weighed on consumption since the financial crisis. Cloyne and Surico (2014) show how between 1978 and 2009 the consumption response of mortgagors to income tax shocks that were not associated with the state of the economy was significantly larger than the response of outright owners, although they do not differentiate between households with different levels of debt. Benito et al. (2007) find little evidence that high- and low-debt households responded differently to changes in their financial positions between 1997 and 2004. But that was over a period of relative stability, and the shocks experienced by households since 2007 are likely to have been much larger. Our work aims to fill this gap in the literature and assess the role of indebted households in explaining movements in UK household spending over the most recent recession, whilst also investigating the extent to which debt may have supported consumption in the period before the crisis.

6.3 An overview of developments in household balance sheets

Over the period from 1992 to 2007, household debt rose from around 100% of annual income to a peak of around 160%, although the debt-to-income ratio only began rising from around 1999 onwards (Figure 6.1). Those increases in debt were also accompanied by an accumulation of financial assets and increases in asset values, such that measures of capital gearing – which measure the stock of debt in relation to the value of assets – were close to their 1992 level in 2007, although gearing fell and then rose during the intervening period (Figure 6.1).

Since 2007, the stock of household debt has stabilised, and the debt-to-income ratio has fallen back from its peak, given continued, albeit modest, growth in nominal incomes. Measures of capital gearing rose during the crisis as asset values fell sharply, but as asset prices recovered, those measures of debt relative to asset values fell back.

This section provides a more detailed discussion of these developments in household balance sheets and then considers how they may have affected household spending.

6.3.1 Trends in household balance sheets

Mortgage debt accounts for around 80% of total household debt, and increases in the aggregate debt-to-income ratio since the late 1990s

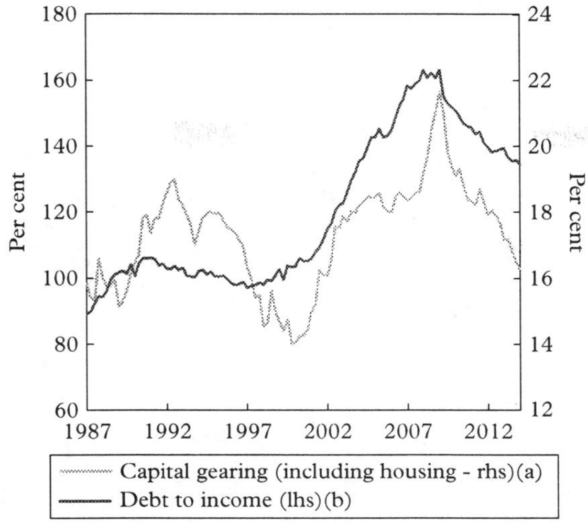

Figure 6.1. Household debt-to-income and capital gearing
(a) Total financial liabilities as a percentage of households' total financial assets and residential building assets.
(b) Total financial liabilities as a percentage of annualised total household resources.
Sources: ONS and authors' calculations.

largely reflect higher levels of secured debt (Figure 6.2). Annual growth in net mortgage lending rose from a trough of around 5% in 1993 to a peak of around 15% in 2004 and remained above 10% until the start of the financial crisis in 2008 (Figure 6.3). Unsecured net lending grew more rapidly than secured lending during most of the 1990s, although it did slow before the financial crisis. Since 2009, there has been little growth in both secured and unsecured net lending.

The increase in household debt relative to income from the late 1990s onwards appears to have been closely related to increases in house prices: there has been a good correlation between the mortgage debt-to-income ratio and the ratio of house prices to income since 1992 (Figure 6.4). Higher house prices mean that new entrants into the housing market have to pay more to buy their house. If sellers were using the proceeds to pay down their debt there would be no overall effect on aggregate debt. But as last-time sellers tend to have either small mortgages or no mortgage, higher house prices tend to lead to higher secured debt.

Although higher house prices have led households to take on more debt since the early 1990s, factors that have increased households' ability

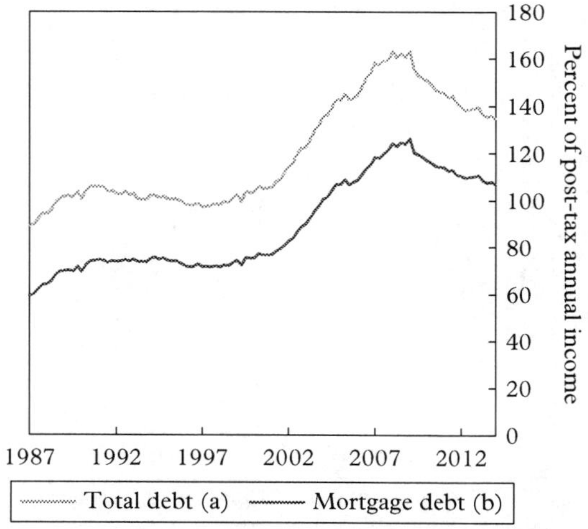

Figure 6.2. Household debt-to-income ratio
(a) Total financial liabilities as a percentage of annualised total household resources.
(b) Loans secured on dwellings as a percentage of annualised total household resources.
Sources: ONS and authors' calculations.

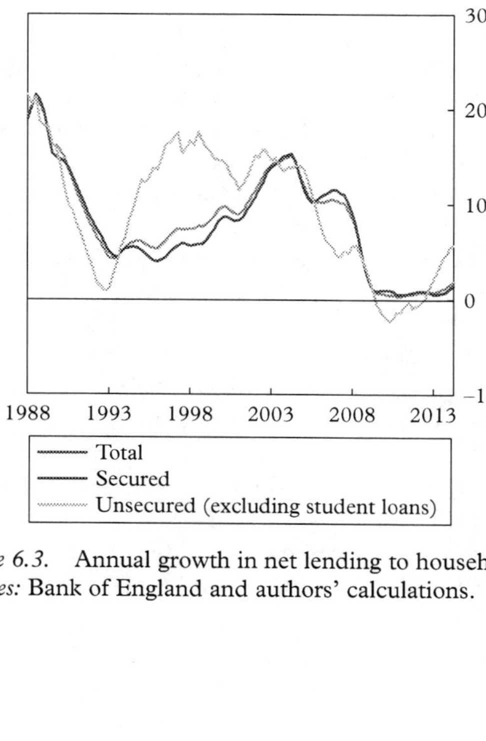

Figure 6.3. Annual growth in net lending to households
Sources: Bank of England and authors' calculations.

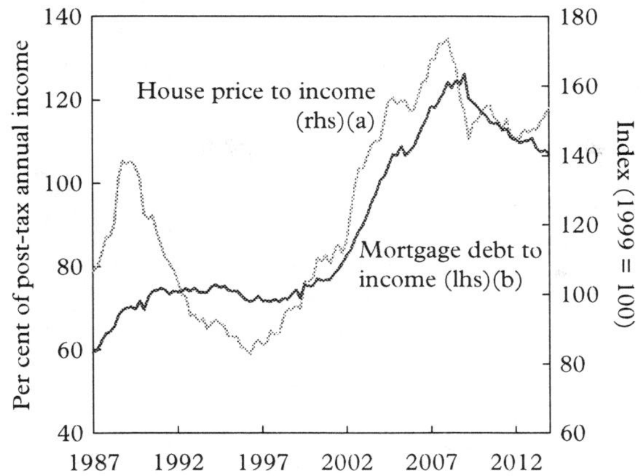

Figure 6.4. House prices-to-income and mortgage debt-to-income
(a) ONS House Price Index divided by annualised total household resources per adult.
(b) Loans secured on dwellings as a percentage of annualised total household resources.
Sources: ONS and authors' calculations.

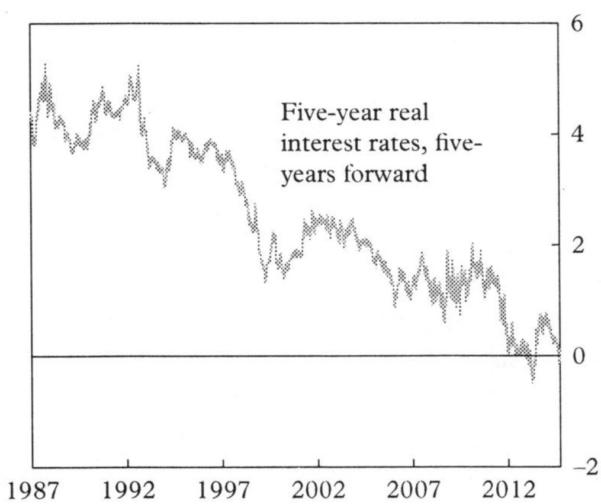

Figure 6.5. Real interest rates
Derived from the Bank's government liability curves.
Source: Bank of England.

to borrow may themselves have contributed to rises in house prices. For example, lower real interest rates will have made it cheaper for households to borrow. There was a substantial and sustained fall in long-run risk-free real interest rates in the late 1990s (Figure 6.5).

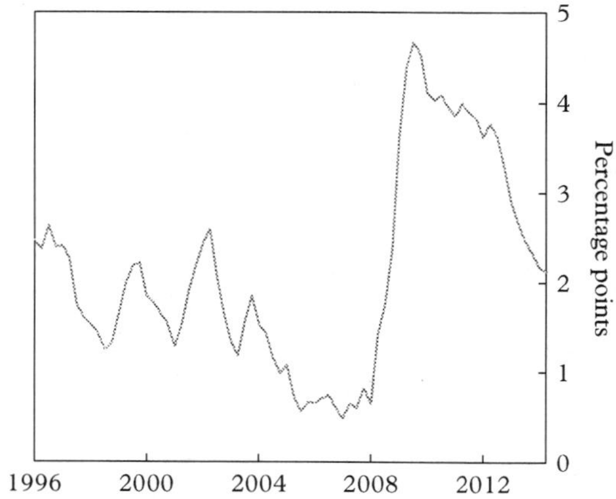

Figure 6.6. Household credit spreads
Weighted average of the spread over Bank Rate of rates on a £10k personal loan (25%), two-year 75% loan-to-value ratio fixed rate mortgage (25%) and a one-year fixed rate bond deposit (50%). Weights are shown in parentheses.
Sources: Bank of England and authors' calculations.

Waldron and Zampolli (2010) argue that the fall in real interest rates is a key factor behind the increases in both house prices and debt from the late 1990s. On top of lower real interest rates, looser credit conditions also made it easier for households to borrow in the period before the financial crisis. For example, banks became more willing to lend to households at high loan-to-income ratios and credit spreads narrowed (Figure 6.6).[1]

Since 2007, lower house prices (relative to income) and a tightening in credit conditions can help to explain why the debt-to-income ratio has fallen back. Evidence from the Bank's Credit Conditions Survey suggests that credit availability fell significantly, particularly at higher loan-to-value ratios, and credit spreads rose sharply (Figure 6.6). The resulting fall in the number of first-time buyers entering the housing market will have weighed on the flow of new lending. Higher deposit requirements and lower house prices will also have reduced the size of

1 The weighted index of the spreads on loan rates and deposits shown in Figure 6.6 is a simpler approximation of the measure of credit spreads described in Butt and Pugh (2014), but has the advantage that it can be extended back further. This simple measure may not fully account for changes in spreads on all types of lending, and in particular on high loan-to-value ratio mortgages.

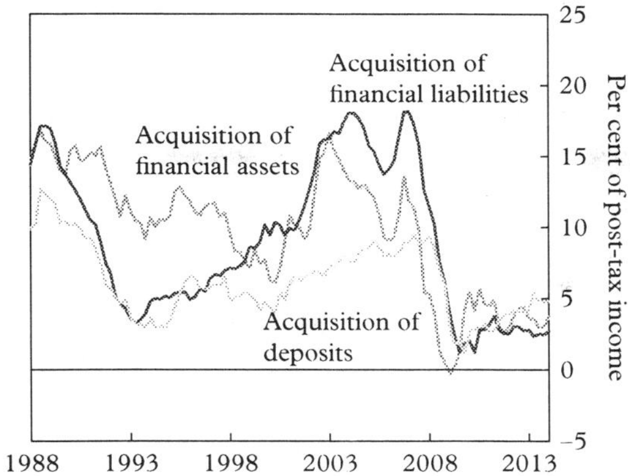

Figure 6.7. Household net acquisition of financial assets and liabilities
Four-quarter moving averages.
Sources: ONS and authors' calculations.

the mortgages taken on by the first-time buyers who were able to enter the market.

In aggregate, the build-up in household debt over the period from 1992 to 2007 was largely matched by a build-up of assets, with a large proportion of these assets being bank deposits. When banks lend money to households they create matching deposits, which are initially held by the borrower. In the case of mortgages, those deposits are then transferred to the home seller when the mortgagor purchases a property and that money subsequently circulates around the economy. It can be retained within the household sector either if households want to hold more deposits in their portfolio, or if it leads to additional housing market transactions. Alternatively, the money may flow to another sector in the economy or to overseas residents if it is used to purchase goods and services or other financial assets.[2] As house prices increased, financial assets were acquired at a broadly similar rate to liabilities, which suggests that the proceeds from the sales of homes at higher prices were largely left on deposit or invested in financial assets (Figure 6.7).

Although higher debt levels may not have been associated with a significant deterioration in the overall state of household balance sheets, they did lead to notable changes in the distribution of balance sheets across households. Large increases in borrowing by one part of the population were largely matched by a big increase in wealth for another

2 See McLeay et al. (2014) for more details on the role of money in a modern economy.

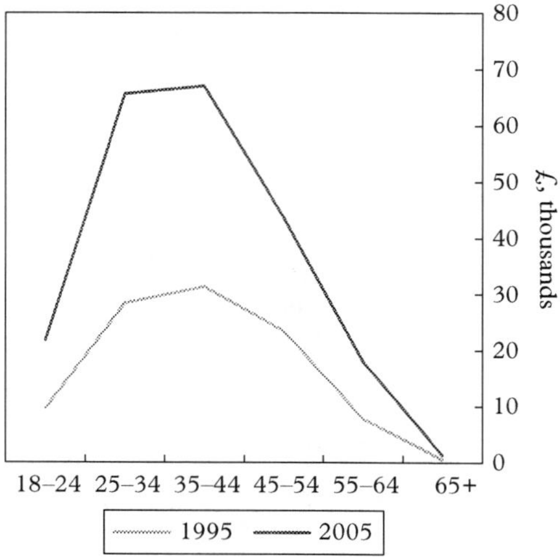

Figure 6.8. Average household debt by age
Sources: British Household Panel Survey (BHPS) and authors' calculations.

part of the population. This is clear from looking at changes in debt and wealth between 1995 and 2005 from the British Household Panel Survey microdata (as previously illustrated by Benito et al. (2007)). Those trading up in the housing market, who tended to be younger households, were made worse off by the increase in house prices because they have had to pay more for their houses and they accumulated more debt (Figure 6.8). At the other end of the spectrum, those who either already owned large houses or who traded down and sold a higher value house, who were more likely to be older households, saw significant increases in their wealth (Figure 6.9).

6.3.2 *How did developments in household balance sheets affect consumption?*

It is difficult to evaluate whether debt has had any impact on UK household spending using aggregate data. Consumption grew at roughly the same rate between 1999 and 2007, when debt was rising rapidly, as it did between 1992 and 1998, when debt did not increase relative to income (Figure 6.10). The household saving rate also fell at a similar pace during these two periods. This, together with the fact that increases in household debt were largely matched by a build-up in

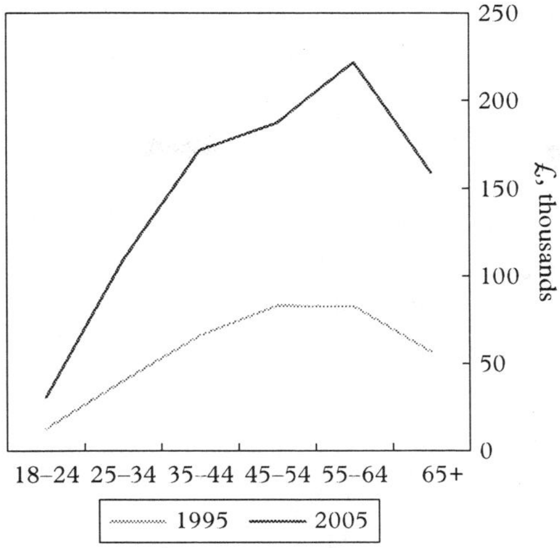

Figure 6.9. Average household gross wealth (including housing assets) by age
Sources: BHPS and authors' calculations.

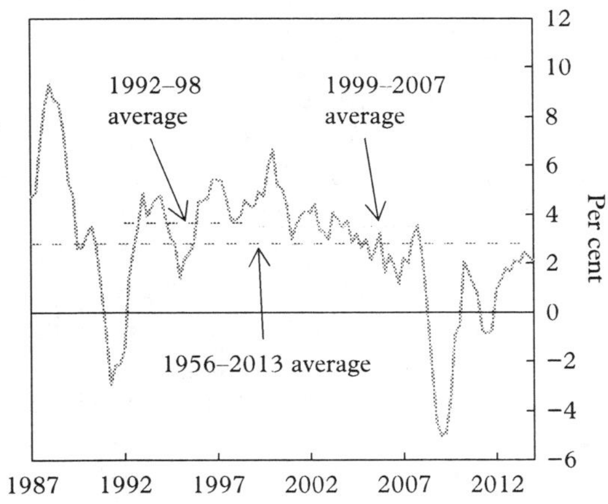

Figure 6.10. Annual consumption growth
Sources: ONS and authors' calculations.

assets, is consistent with the suggestion that increases in debt did not provide significant support to consumption. Bean (2004) and Nickell (2004) expressed similar views at the time when debt was rising rapidly. And post-2008, there are a number of factors other than debt which might explain why spending fell sharply.

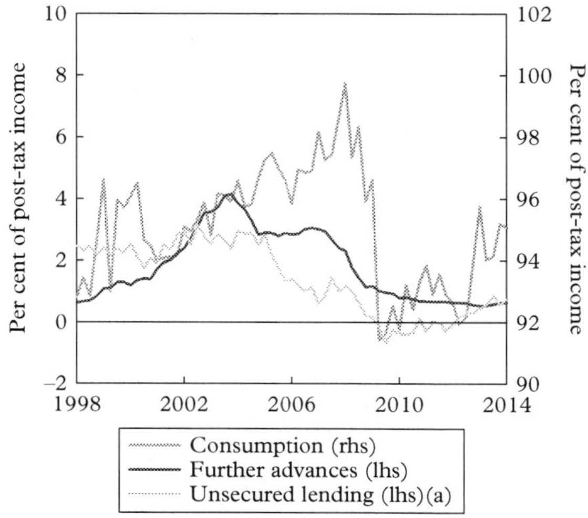

Figure 6.11. Consumption and borrowing available for consumption
(a) Excludes student loans.
Sources: Bank of England, ONS and authors' calculations.

Nevertheless, it is possible to make the case that debt did play some role in supporting spending before 2007. Further advances on mortgages (additional borrowing secured against a house, but not used to buy the property) are an indicator of the secured debt that is available for consumption. There is a correlation between further advances and consumption which might imply that some of this borrowing was used to finance consumption (Figure 6.11). Unsecured borrowing can also be used to finance consumption, and that also picked up when spending was rising relative to income, although the correlation with consumption is weaker than the correlation between spending and further advances.

Changes in the asset side of households' balance sheets may also have implications for household spending. Changes in financial asset prices, primarily equity prices, may lead households to reassess their future wealth and adjust spending in response. Equity prices rose during the 1990s, boosting financial wealth, and that may have supported consumption.

Changes in house prices can potentially affect spending in a number of ways, including by affecting the value of collateral which households can borrow against to fund consumption. There may be a distributional wealth effect from older households, who are the ones most likely to trade down, being made better off by increases in house prices and increasing their consumption in response. But whether there is an

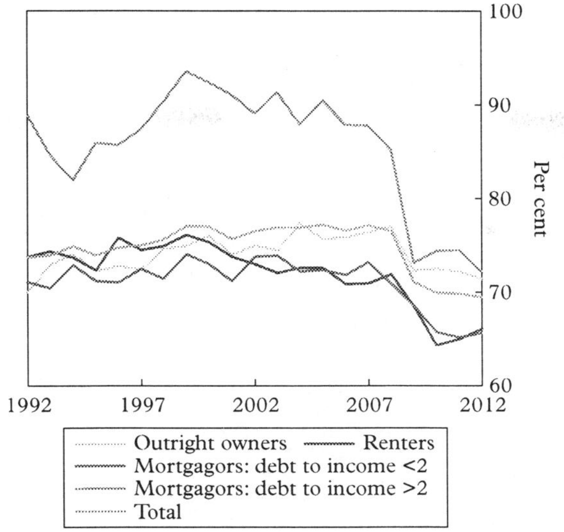

Figure 6.12. Non-housing consumption as a share of income
Non-housing consumption as a share of income net of mortgage interest payments. Data are scaled so that the total matches the National Accounts. Debt-to-income ratio is calculated using secured debt only.
Sources: Living Costs and Food (LCF) Survey, ONS and authors' calculations.

impact on aggregate spending depends on whether those households who want to get into the housing market or trade up reduce their spending by a similar amount when house prices rise. In the data, house prices and consumption are well correlated and increases in house prices could have supported consumption in the period before the crisis. But there is no consensus in the literature on whether that reflects causality (as argued by Campbell and Cocco (2007)) or whether the two simply move together because they are determined by similar factors, such as expectations of future income (Attanasio et al. (2009)).

Given the difficulties in assessing how debt has affected consumption using aggregate data, it is helpful to use microdata to investigate how consumption varies across households with different levels of debt. Figure 6.12 shows the proportion of disposable income (net of mortgage interest payments[3]) spent on non-housing consumption for different groups of households, calculated from the Living Costs and Food (LCF) Survey (see Section 4.2 for further details on this survey).

3 This is consistent with the measurement of income in the National Accounts.

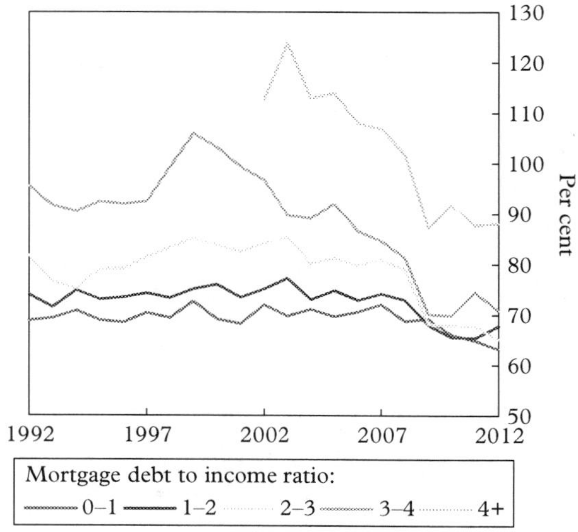

Figure 6.13. Non-housing consumption as a share of income by mortage ratio
Data for 4+ not shown before 2002 as they are erratic and are based on a small sample. Non-housing consumption as a share of income net of mortgage interest payments. Data are scaled so that the total matches the National Accounts. Debt-to-income ratio is calculated using secured debt only.
Sources: LCF Survey, ONS and authors' calculations.

In the second half of the 1990s, households with mortgage debt-to-income ratios greater than two appear to have increased the share of their income spent on non-housing consumption by more than mortgagors with lower debt-to-income ratios (Figure 6.12). But these higher debt mortgagors subsequently made larger than average reductions in spending relative to income after the financial crisis. This analysis focuses on secured debt only, since only limited data on unsecured debt are available in the LCF Survey.

Disaggregating the data for mortgagors further, the largest adjustment in spending relative to income after 2007 came among households with a mortgage debt-to-income ratio above four (Figure 6.13). Cuts in spending were more modest for those with debt-to-income ratios below two.

It is possible that the differences in spending patterns between households with different levels of debt that are evident in the descriptive data reflect factors other than debt. The analysis presented in the rest of the chapter aims to control for other factors and more precisely identify the relationship between household debt and consumer spending in the UK.

6.4 Research design and data

6.4.1 Research design

We investigate the relationship between debt and non-housing consumption by estimating household level consumption equations that incorporate a mortgage debt-to-income variable. Our econometric approach allows us to test whether households with higher levels of debt have different consumption from lower debt households after controlling for all observable characteristics.[4] By allowing the coefficient on the debt-to-income variable to vary over time we are able to investigate whether this relationship was different before and after the financial crisis. It is how the coefficient changes over time that is the focus of our analysis, since debt should only affect aggregate consumption growth if the coefficient does change over time.

Our framework is based on a life-cycle type model that is used in the housing and consumption literature (see Attanasio et al. (2009) as an example), except that we adapt it to also include a debt variable. As discussed above, although debt does not play an important role in the standard life-cycle model there are reasons to think that some of the assumptions underlying that model may not hold, and therefore it is useful to include debt in the model to test whether that is the case.

We estimate the following equation at the household level:

$$c_{it} = \beta_1 dy_{it} + \beta_2' dy^{\star}\ year_{it} + \beta_3' \ year_t + \beta_4' \ cohort_i + \beta_5' \ X_{it} + e_{it}$$

where c_{it} is the log of real non-housing consumption for household i at time t, dy is the ratio of outstanding mortgage debt to households disposable income, *year* is a vector of time dummies to capture time specific shocks and *cohort* is a vector of five-year date-of-birth buckets. X is a vector of controls for age, sex, marital status, highest qualification, economic activity, household composition, tenure, house prices, income and region.

The β_1 coefficient shows how consumption varies by debt level in the reference year (2007) while the vector β_2 captures how that impact changes over time. Our approach allows us to test whether higher debt households consumed more or less than lower debt households at different points in time, but we cannot follow the households who went into the crisis with high levels of debt because our data are only a repeated cross-section. The data being a cross-section means that we

4 By controlling for as many factors as possible, we are aiming to compare the consumption of two households of similar income, age, education etc., but where one household has high debt and the other has low debt.

cannot control for unobserved individual heterogeneity in the way that would be possible if our data were a panel. But we do include cohort dummies (based on five-year birth intervals) which capture a pseudo fixed effect for all the households within a particular cohort.

Identifying whether there is a causal relationship between debt and consumption is difficult. For example, households with more optimistic expectations of future income may be more willing to take on debt and consume more because of those expectations. That would imply high-debt households consumed before the financial crisis, and if those expectations proved unrealistic they may make larger adjustments in spending afterwards, but in there is no causal link: debt is simply correlated with income expectations. US studies such as Mian et al. (2013) and Baker (2013) have tried to address this issue by instrumenting debt using local level housing supply elasticities. But our data does not contain detailed geographic data below government office region level, which makes it difficult to use any instruments based on geographic characteristics. We do not instrument debt in our regressions.

To try to address the issue of why indebted households may have behaved differently from households with less debt over the recent past, we make use of the Bank of England/NMG Consulting Survey. The survey does not contain consumption data, but it does ask households a range of questions about their finances and the influences on their spending decisions. In particular, the survey asks households whether they had cut spending in response to concerns about debt. We use this question and questions on how other factors such as credit conditions have affected spending to try to account for the reasons behind differences in spending patterns between high- and low-debt households.

6.4.2 Data

We use household-level microdata between 1992 and 2012 from the Living Costs & Food (LCF) Survey, previously known as the Family Expenditure Survey. This is an annual, repeated cross-sectional survey, rather than a pure panel, and it contains around 6,000 households per year, although the sample size does decline gradually over time. The survey also switches between calendar and fiscal year collection more than once. For consistency, we convert all data to calendar years. We only include households where the head of the household is aged between 21 and 69 and was born between 1926 and 1989. Our analysis only covers the period from 1992 to 2012, as mortgage debt data is only available from 1992.

We use weekly non-housing expenditure because the methodology for calculating housing consumption in the LCF Survey is not consistent with that used in the National Accounts – for homeowners, the LCF Survey only measures mortgage payments rather than using a measure of imputed rents like the National Accounts.[5] All data are deflated using the National Accounts consumption deflator.

Our measure of debt is the ratio of outstanding mortgage debt to disposable income. The LCF survey does not include data on wealth, so it is not possible to use measures of debt relative to the value of assets. Our decision to scale debt relative to income is therefore a purely practical one. In terms of assessing whether households who entered the financial crisis with high levels of debt made bigger adjustments to their spending, we would ideally use pre-crisis debt-to-income, but given that our data are not a panel those data are not available. We only have data on contemporaneous debt-to-income, although over relatively short periods of the time the two are likely to be well correlated.

The focus of our analysis is largely on secured debt, which again reflects the availability of data.

The LCF Survey does contain information on whether households have unsecured debt, but it does not contain comprehensive data on the amount of unsecured debt currently outstanding and there appears to be a break before 2001. That makes it difficult to distinguish between households with high and low levels of unsecured debt, although we do investigate how the consumption of those with unsecured debt differs from those without in Section 5.3.

We use the Bank of England/NMG Consulting Survey to investigate the reasons for why the spending patterns of indebted households may have differed from other households. This is a cross-sectional survey of households commissioned by the Bank. It has been running since 2004, although we only make use of the 2010 and 2013 surveys, since the most relevant questions were not asked in earlier years. The 2010 survey covered approximately 2,000 households and was carried out face-to-face, while the 2013 survey included around 6,000 households and was conducted online. Nielsen et al. (2010) and Bunn et al. (2013), respectively, contain a detailed discussion of the 2010 and 2013 NMG surveys.

5 Aggregate consumption derived from the LCF Survey under-records spending relative to the National Accounts. In the figures shown we scale up the microdata to match non-housing consumption in the National Accounts, and similarly we also adjust disposable income. We use the unadjusted microdata in our regressions since all the regressions include year dummies, and any scaling factor applied to all households would only be reflected in the coefficients on these year dummies.

6.5 Results

6.5.1 Econometric results for non-housing consumption

The relationship between household spending and debt is estimated to have changed over time.

Figure 6.14 summarises the coefficients on the year/debt-to-income interaction variables.[6] These coefficients show the difference in consumption from having a one unit higher debt-to-income ratio (such as three rather than two) by year, relative to 2007. The gradual increase in the size of these coefficients between 1996 and 2003 suggests that increased spending by higher debt households is likely to have supported consumption over this period, and the change in the coefficients between these two dates is statistically significant. But the fall in the coefficients on the debt/year interactions since 2007, which are significant at the 1% level, implies that bigger reductions in spending by higher debt households have weighed on consumption growth since then. The coefficients imply that a household with a debt-to-income ratio of three cut spending by around 2.5% more after 2007 than a

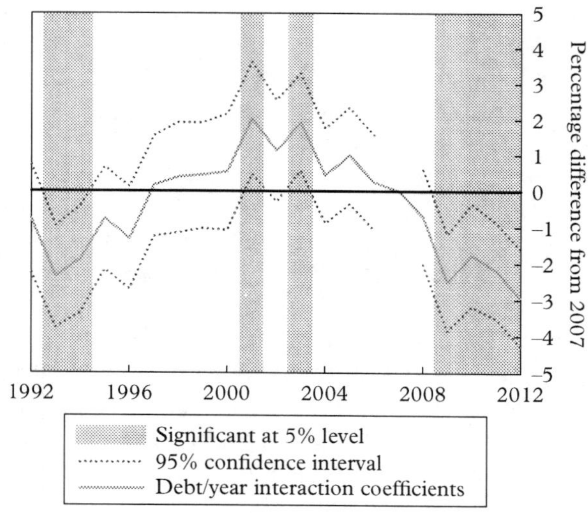

Figure 6.14. Impact of one unit increase in debt-to-income ratio on non-housing consumption, relative to 2007
Sources: LCF Survey and authors' calculations.

6 Precise coefficient estimates can be found in Table A in the Appendix; results shown in Figure 6.14 are from equation [4].

household with all the same other characteristics and a debt-to-income ratio of two.

The relationship between debt and consumption for mortgagors is assumed to be linear. We tested whether there was evidence on a non-linear relationship with higher debt households making disproportionately larger cuts in spending, but there was not clear evidence that was the case (consistent with descriptive analysis shown in Figure 6.13). Our preferred equation (Eq. [4] (i.e. column [4]) in Table A.1 of the Appendix) includes income net of mortgage interest payments, which means that reductions in mortgage rates in 2009 that lowered mortgage interest payments will have helped to cushion the squeeze on incomes for mortgages, and particularly for higher debt mortgagors. This measure captures the amount of income that households have to spend on non-housing items at any point in time. If a definition of income before interest payments is used – which would take no account of how reductions in interest rates in 2009 made mortgagors better off – the change coefficient on the debt-to-income ratio after 2007 is smaller than those before (Eq. [7] (i.e. column [7]) in Table A.1 of the Appendix). The change is only statistically significantly different from 2007 in some years, but taking the 2008–2012 period as a whole, the coefficient on the debt-to-income variables is significantly smaller than it was between 1992 and 2007 (Eq. [6] (i.e. column [6])), with the change in the coefficient after 2007 only being around half as large as if income is measured net of interest payments (shown in Eq. [3] (i.e. column [3])).

An alternative methodology for investigating the differences between the spending patterns of high and low mortgage debt households is simply to look at residuals from a consumption equation that contains no debt variables (this is Eq. [1] (i.e. column [1]) in Table A.1 of the Appendix). Those residuals imply that there was an unexplained fall of around 7% in the non-housing consumption of high-debt mortgagors relative to low-debt mortgagors between 2007 and 2009–12. Our preferred model can explain a fall of a similar magnitude (Figure 6.15) and the differences in the residuals between the high- and low-debt group are then largely eliminated.

In terms of the absolute size of the coefficient, households with high secured debt levels are estimated to have had higher non-housing consumption than those with low debt in all years, once current income is controlled for. Table 6.1 summarises the coefficient on the mortgage debt-to-income ratio variable where it is not allowed to vary over time. Including income (net of interest payments – Eq. [2] (i.e. column [2]) in Table 6.1 and Table A.1 of the Appendix), a household with a

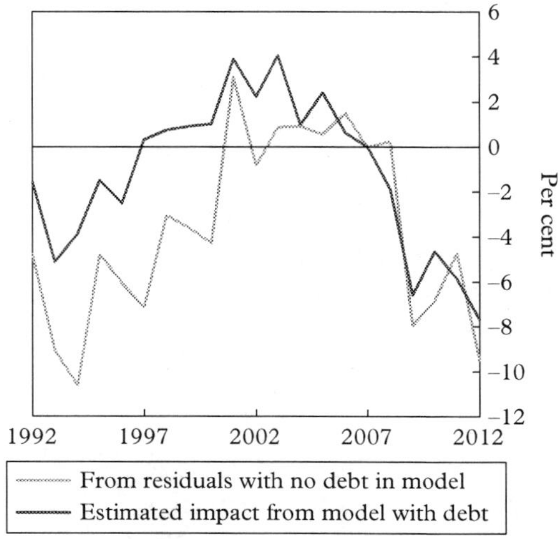

Figure 6.15. Differences between non-housing consumption of high- and low-debt mortgage households, relative to 2007
High-debt mortgagors are defined as having a debt-to-income ratio above two, low-debt mortgagors have a debt-to-income ratio below two.
Sources: LCF Survey and authors' calculations.

mortgage debt-to-income ratio of three rather than two is estimated to have consumed around 4% more, on average, over our sample period, all else being equal. That coefficient is statistically significantly different from zero at the 1% level.

The result that high-debt households consume more is dependent on controlling for current income. If current income is not included in the regression (Eq. [5] (i.e. column [5]) in Table 6.1 and Table A.1 of the Appendix) then the coefficient on the mortgage debt-to-income ratio becomes negative. That suggests that high-debt households do not have higher lifetime income than low-debt households, but taking on debt may enable high-debt households to smooth their consumption and to consume a greater share of current income at the point in their life-cycle when current income is below their average expected lifetime income.

In a pure version of the life-cycle model, spending should be determined by lifetime income and not current income. Once factors such as age, cohort and education are controlled for, current income should not contain additional information about future income and therefore it is not necessary to include it in the regressions. However, current income is highly significant and by incorporating a debt-to-income ratio

Table 6.1. Consumption regression results

	Non-housing consumption	
Dependent variable	**[2]**	**[5]**
Log real income (net of interest payments)	0.493***	–
	(63.75)	
Mortgage debt-to-income ratio	0.042***	−0.030***
	(20.92)	(−17.22)
Mortgage debt-to-income ratio year interactions	No	No
Observations	107,623	107,746
R-squared	0.583	0.478

*** $p < 0.01$, ** $p < 0.05$, * $p < 0.1$. T ratios reported in parentheses. Dependent variable is log of real household consumption. Other variables included, but not reported above, are birth year cohort dummies, age, sex, marital status, highest qualification, economic activity, household composition, tenure, house prices, year and quarter dummies, government office region dummies and a constant. All equations are estimated by OLS with robust standard errors from 1992 to 2012.

in our regressions we are already including some income information, so we retain it in most specifications.[7]

The absolute difference in consumption from having a one unit higher debt-to-income ratio in any particularly year can be calculated by adding the coefficients to the debt/year interactions to the 2007 effect (Figure 6.16). In our preferred specification, taking the two together, a household with a debt-to-income ratio of three rather than two is estimated to have consumed about 5% more in 2007, but only around 2.5% more between 2009 and 2012, after controlling for current income.

6.5.2 *Econometric results for different categories of spending*

In this section we investigate whether households used debt to finance particular types of spending in the period before the crisis and whether subsequent larger than average reductions in spending by more indebted households were concentrated in certain categories of spending.

Most of the strength in spending by high mortgage debt households before the financial crisis and the larger adjustment afterwards was in categories of spending that could be considered as non-essential. While there was still some fluctuation in spending on essential non-durable items, the estimated impact was smaller than for durables

7 Equation [6] in Table A of the Appendix reports full regression results excluding current income.

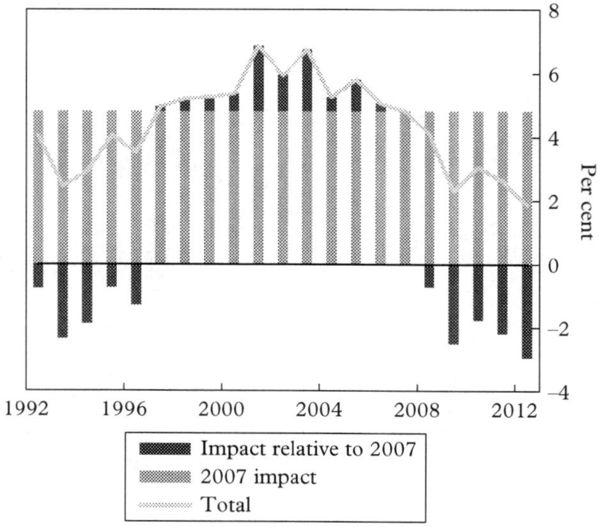

Figure 6.16. Impact of one unit increase in debt-to-income ratio on non-housing consumption
Sources: LCF Survey and authors' calculations.

and non-essential non-durables – consistent with the intuition that households cut back on non-essential spending first when they face financial pressure. Figures 6.17–6.19 show the coefficients on mortgage debt-to-income/year interactions for alternative equations estimated with durable, non-essential non-durable and essential non-durable spending as the respective dependent variables (see Table A.2 in the Appendix for full regression results).[8]

6.5.3 *Unsecured debt econometric results*

The analysis so far has focussed solely on secured debt and its relationship with household spending, but it is also possible that unsecured debt also played a role in determining spending patterns. Although

8 Durables are defined as vehicles, household goods, recreational goods, and clothing and footwear. Non-essential non-durables are recreational services, household services, personal goods and services, alcohol and tobacco. Essential non-durables are defined as food and beverages, transport fares and other transport costs. The definitions of essential and non-essential spending are only based on high-level categories and in practice there will be some elements of essential and non-essential spending within each category. For example, spending on food will include spending on luxury food items, which could be substituted for cheaper alternatives and therefore might be considered as non-essential.

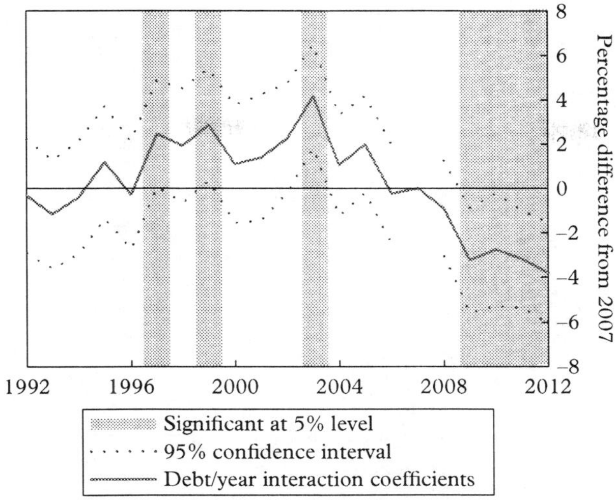

Figure 6.17. Impact of one unit increase in debt-to-income ratio on durable consumption, relative to 2007
Sources: LCF Survey and authors' calculations.

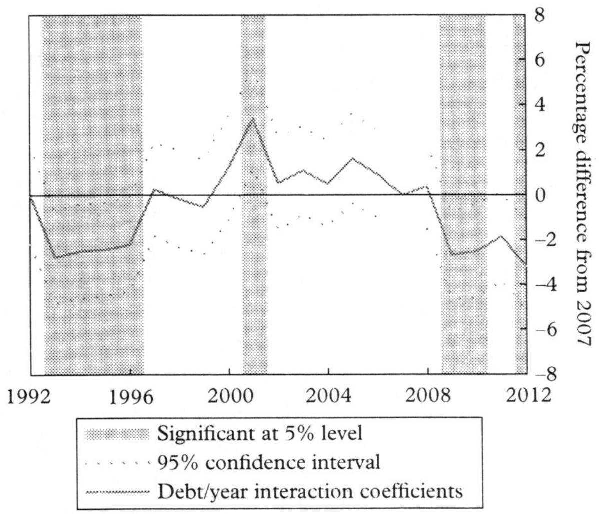

Figure 6.18. Impact of one unit increase in debt-to-income ratio on non-essential non-durable consumption, relative to 2007
Sources: LCF Survey and authors' calculations.

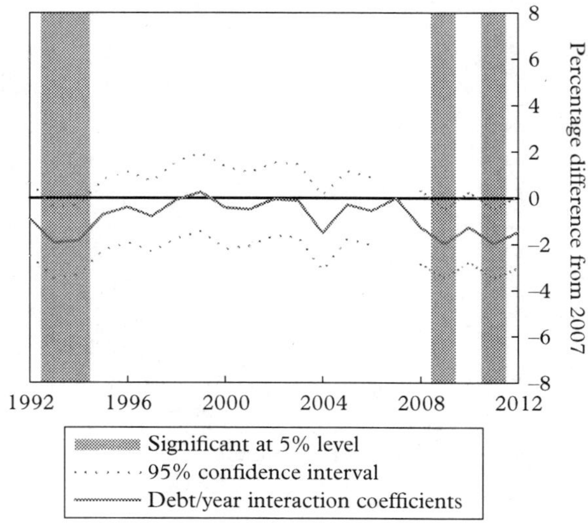

Figure 6.19. Impact of one unit increase in debt-to-income ratio on essential non-durable consumption, relative to 2007
Sources: LCF Survey and authors' calculations.

unsecured loans are typically much smaller than mortgages, they may be more likely to be used to fund consumption than mortgages. But set against that, mortgage debt accounts for 80% of all debt, and as there are fewer consequences of walking away from unsecured debt, households with unsecured debt might be less concerned about having to default and therefore be less willing than mortgagors to reduce spending sharply rather than risk default.

As described in Section 4.2, the LCF data only contain information on whether households have unsecured debt and not on the amount of unsecured debt currently outstanding. We investigate the role of unsecured debt by including a dummy variable for having outstanding unsecured debt in our regressions and we then allow the coefficient on that variable to vary over time by interacting it with year dummies. We only estimate the equations from 2001 because there appears to be a break in the data before that point. The coefficient on the unsecured debt dummy variable is positive, suggesting that unsecured borrowing is likely to be used to fund consumption. On average, households with unsecured debt have around 11% higher consumption than those without (see Table A.3 in the Appendix for full details).

When allowed to vary by year, the coefficients on the dummy variable for having unsecured debt are smaller in the second half of the estimation period, but on a year to year basis standard errors on the unsecured debt/year interactions are large and the differences are not generally statistically significantly different from 2007 (see Eq. [15] (i.e. column [15]) in the Table A.4 of the Appendix for full regression estimates).

The result that the coefficient on our unsecured debt variable does not change significantly over time does not mean that unsecured borrowing played no role in influencing UK household spending patterns. Although we are not able to find statistically significant changes in the spending patterns of those households with and without unsecured debt over time, we are unable to look for differences in spending between those with high and low levels of unsecured debt, which would be a better way of testing the hypothesis.

6.5.4 *Estimating the influence of high-debt households on aggregate consumption*

Our regression results show how spending patterns have varied by mortgage debt levels over time, after controlling for other factors. Our econometric model can also be used to estimate the importance of those differences for aggregate household spending. We do this by taking the fitted values for each household for spending in a given year from our preferred model, and then subtracting what the model predicts they would have spent if debt had had the same estimated influence on spending patterns in each year as it did in 2007, keeping all other characteristics unchanged. Differences are then summed across households. To get a total impact on aggregate private consumption there is assumed to be no impact on either non-housing consumption for those aged under 21 or over 69, aggregate housing consumption or the consumption of non-profit institutions serving households.

Our results suggest that spending cuts associated with mortgage debt reduced aggregate private consumption by around 2% after 2007 (Figure 6.20), out of a total fall of almost 5%. At least until the latest available data in 2012, these effects had not unwound. Mapping the results into aggregate saving ratio space, spending cuts associated with debt are estimated to have added around 2 percentage points to the aggregate households saving ratio since 2007 out of a total increase of around 5 percentage points (Figure 6.21).

These estimates are based on microdata and implicitly assume that most aspects of the economy were not affected by developments in

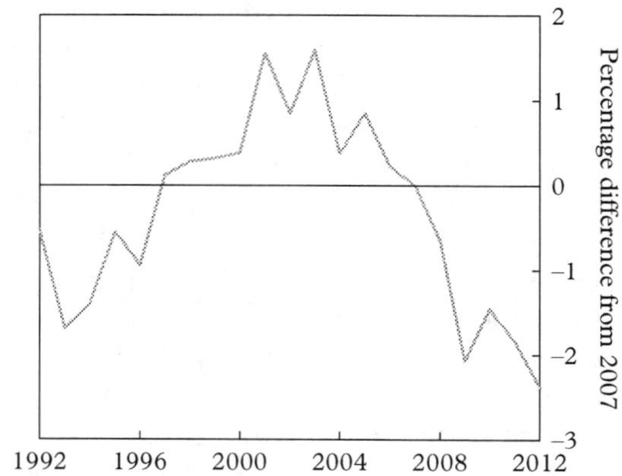

Figure 6.20. Estimated impact of debt on level of aggregate private consumption
The impact on non-housing consumption is constructed by taking predicted spending for each household from Eq. [4] (i.e. column [4]) in Table A.1 of the Appendix, and then subtracting what the model predicts they would have spent if debt had the same estimated influence on spending patterns in each year as it did in 2007, keeping all other characteristics unchanged. Differences are then summed across households. To get to a total impact on aggregate private consumption there is assumed to be no effect on housing consumption or the consumption of non-profit institutions serving households.
Sources: LCF Survey, ONS and authors' calculations.

household debt. Growth in debt could have had macroeconomic effects that may have fed back into consumption, for example through its effects on employment, the public finances and asset prices. Households take on secured debt primarily to finance a house purchase, and to the extent that high borrowing might itself raise house prices, these estimates take no account of how changes in house prices might have affected spending, although as described earlier, there is not a clear consensus in the literature on whether house prices do play an important role in affecting spending decisions. Also, we take no account of any second round general equilibrium effects; for example, lower household spending could feed back into lower household incomes or any impacts on other components of GDP. For some households to hold debt other households have to own assets, and these estimates of the overall impact on aggregate consumption do not take into account any possible responses by the households holding those assets. Evaluating these channels is beyond the scope of our work.

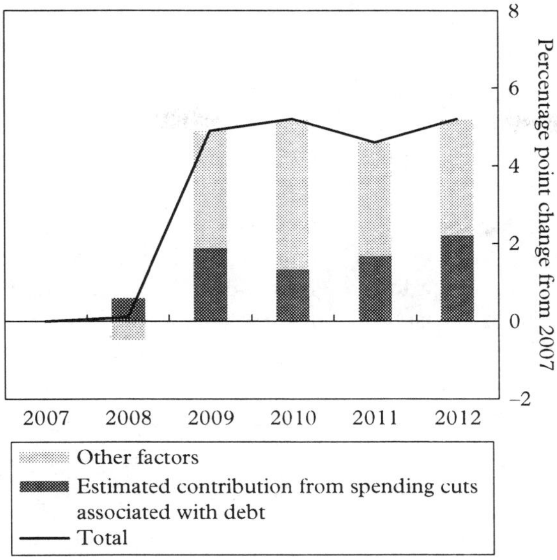

Figure 6.21. Contributions to the change in the National Accounts saving ratio from 2007

Contribution from spending cuts associated with debt is calculated using the estimates from Chart 20, and by assuming no change in aggregate household income.

Sources: LCF Survey, ONS and authors' calculations.

6.6 Explaining differences in consumption by debt level

6.6.1 Hypotheses

The analysis presented so far has focussed on establishing how spending has varied across households with different levels of debt. The remainder of the chapter tries to put forward some explanations for these differences.

Increased spending by more highly indebted households before 2007 could reflect a number of factors. These include:

1. *Lower real interest rates and looser credit conditions.* This may have encouraged some households to take on high levels of debt and bring forward spending from the future.
2. *Household who took on high levels of debt became more optimistic about future income.* An improvement in income expectations may have been what led them to take on debt in the first place, although there may also have been no direct link between their income expectations debt.

We also put forward three possible explanations for why high-debt households made larger adjustments in spending after the crisis:

1. *Highly indebted households were disproportionately affected by tighter credit conditions.* In this case, high existing debt levels caused lower spending by restricting borrowers' ability to renew, or increase, existing debt, and by lowering expectations of future access to credit.
2. *Highly indebted households became more concerned about their ability to make future repayments.* Downward revisions to expected future income and/or uncertainty about future income may have made highly indebted households more concerned about their ability to repay debt in the future. This group may therefore have made larger adjustments to spending than other households, even if high- and low-debt households suffered the same-sized shock to expected future income.
3. *Highly indebted households may have made larger adjustments to future income expectations.* This may be because they were too optimistic before 2007, and overly optimistic income expectations may have been what led these households to take on high debt in the first place. Here, debt has no causal link to the larger adjustment in spending by highly indebted households – households with high debt just happen to have experienced larger shocks to expected future income.

6.6.2 *Evidence on the role of credit using the LCF Survey*

We perform a number of robustness checks within the LCF data to investigate the extent to which developments in credit conditions can explain our results. The first is to include a measure of credit conditions in our regressions, which is a weighted index of credit spreads (shown in Figure 6.7). The coefficient on the credit spreads variable is negative and statistically significant, and if the coefficient is allowed to vary by debt level, credit spreads are estimated to have a significantly larger negative impact on the spending of mortgagors with a debt-to-income ratio above two than is the case for lower debt mortgagors (see Eq. [17] (i.e. column [17]) in Table A.3 of the Appendix for details).[9]

This approach suggests that highly indebted households being disproportionately affected by tighter credit conditions could potentially explain

9 This equation can only be estimated from 1996 as credit spread data are not available before that, but slightly reducing the sample period makes little difference to the results.

at least some of the larger reduction in spending after 2007 by higher debt mortgagors. But even once credit spreads are incorporated into the regressions, the coefficients on the mortgage debt-to-income variable still become significantly smaller after 2007, although the change in those coefficients is more modest than in our preferred specification. Using the model with credit spreads included, spending cuts associated with debt are estimated to have reduced aggregate private consumption by around 1.5% after 2007, compared to 2% in the model without credit spreads.

One way in which looser credit conditions may have supported spending before the crisis is by allowing more households to withdraw more equity from their houses to help finance other forms of spending. And the fact that it became much more difficult to withdraw equity after 2007 could help to explain the fall in spending. However, for equity withdrawal to be able to explain our results, high-debt households should have been more likely to withdraw equity than low-debt households.

The LCF data contains a question asking households whether they have ever remortgaged or topped up their mortgage. This will capture all households who have withdrawn equity, but it will also include households who have simply refinanced, and the date at which the mortgage was refinanced or topped up is not reported. This is therefore an imperfect proxy for withdrawing equity, but nevertheless it does suggest that increases in equity withdrawal were significantly larger for higher debt mortgagors than for low-debt mortgagors between the mid-1990s and mid-2000s (Figure 6.22), which is the period over which spending growth was faster among high-debt households.

The descriptive analysis suggests that increased use of equity withdrawal is a possible explanation for faster spending growth among high-debt mortgagors in the period before the crisis. Including a dummy variable in our regressions for topping up a mortgage shows that households who withdraw equity do have higher consumption after controlling for other factors (Eq. [18] (i.e. column [18]) in Table A.4), but this has little impact on our debt results, even if the coefficient on the topup dummy is allowed to vary by year (Eq. [19] (i.e. column [19]), Table A.4).

Overall, there is some evidence from the LCF data that movements in credit conditions could explain some, but by no means all, of the differences in spending patterns that we observe between high- and low-debt mortgagors, although it is not clear that this relates directly to the ability to withdraw equity.

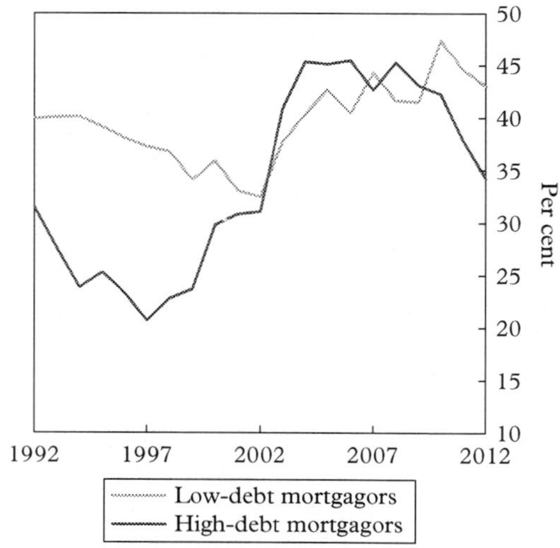

Figure 6.22. Proportion of mortgagors who have topped up their mortgage
High-debt mortgagors are defined as having a mortgage debt-to-income ratio above two, while low-debt mortgagors have a debt-to-income ratio below two. Topping up mortgage is defined as ever having topped up mortgage or remortgaged.
Sources: LCF Survey and authors' calculations.

6.6.3 *Evidence from the Bank of England/NMG survey*

It is difficult to distinguish between the different possible explanations for our results within the LCF data, and therefore we use the Bank of England/NMG Consulting Survey to investigate this further. The NMG Survey asks households about the factors affecting their spending decisions and is therefore potentially useful to discriminate between our competing hypotheses. Given that the most relevant questions in the NMG Survey are only available from 2010 onwards we focus only on trying to explain the larger adjustment in spending by higher debt households after 2007 in this section.

The NMG Survey contains questions that can be used to construct variables that broadly match the three possible explanations for why higher debt households made large adjustments in spending after 2007. Households were asked whether they had cut spending because of concerns about credit availability (hypothesis 1), whether they had cut spending because of concerns about debt (hypothesis 2) and whether they were worse off in 2013 than they had expected in 2006 (hypothesis 3 – being worse off than expected over the past might be correlated with downward revisions to future income expectations).

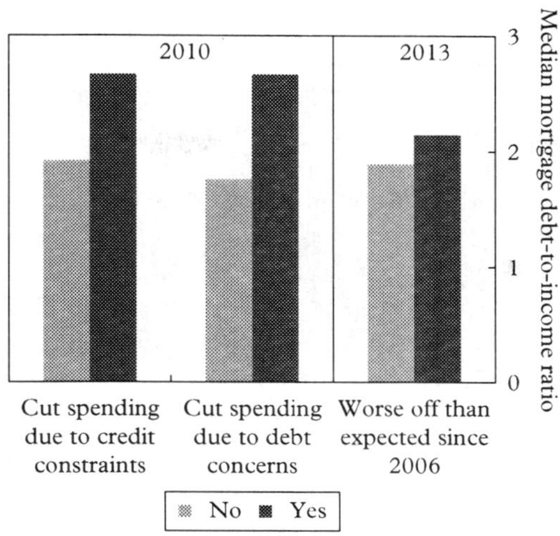

Figure 6.23. Average mortgage debt-to-income ratio by household characteristics
Mortgage debt-to-income ratio is defined as outstanding mortgage debt as a percentage of gross annual income. Questions: 'Have you been put off spending because you are concerned that you will not be able to get further credit when you need it, say because you are close to your credit limit or think your loan application will be turned down?'; 'How concerned are you about your current level of debt?'; 'What actions, if any, are you taking to deal with your concerns about your current level of debt?'; and 'Would you say you are better or worse off than you would have expected at the end of 2006, before the start of the financial crisis?'. Question about whether a household is worse off than expected since 2006 was only asked in 2013. Question about whether a household has cut spending due to debt concerns was first asked in 2010.
Sources: NMG Consulting Survey and authors' calculations.

Mortgagors who reported that they had cut spending due to concerns about credit availability had higher than average mortgage debt-to-income ratios (Figure 6.23). Debt-to-income ratios were also higher for households who had cut spending in relation to concerns about debt. But there is less evidence that households who were worse off than they had previously expected were disproportionately highly indebted, which would imply placing less weight on hypothesis 3.

The descriptive data suggests that credit constraints and concerns about debt are both possible explanations for why highly indebted households spent less after 2007. However, there are substantial overlaps between these two explanations. In 2010, 50% of mortgagors who said they had cut spending in response to debt concerns also reported that they had cut spending due to credit availability. We try to control for these overlaps by estimating a simple regression with mortgage debt-to-income ratio as the dependent variable and cutting spending due to credit constraints and debt concerns as explanatory variables (Eq. [20] (i.e. column [20]) in Table A.5 of the Appendix).

In 2010, households cutting spending due to credit availability are estimated to have had debt-to-income ratios 0.4 units higher than those not reducing spending for this reason, while those who reduced spending in response to debt concerns had debt-to-income ratios 1.1 units higher than those who were not concerned. The coefficient on the concerns about debt variable is significantly different from zero at the 1% level, although the coefficient on credit availability is not quite significant that the 10% level. Outside of our LCF Survey sample period, it is only possible to include the variable for being worse off than expected in 2006 by estimating for 2013. When we do this, households who were worse off than they had expected in 2006 did not have significantly higher debt-to-income ratios (Eq. [21] (i.e. column [21]) in Table A.5). In the 2013 regressions, the extent to which households concerned about debt had higher debt-to-income ratios is only about half as large as in 2010, but the coefficient is still significantly different from zero and the coefficient on the cutting spending due to credit availability variable does become significant (with a similar magnitude, helped by the larger sample size reducing the standard errors).[10]

In summary, the evidence from the NMG Survey suggests that cutting spending due to credit constraints and due to debt concerns have both been positively correlated with mortgage debt-to-income ratios, and therefore these can potentially both explain why we observe larger cuts in spending by more highly indebted households after 2007 in the LCF data. There is less evidence that larger revisions to expected future income were a key explanation because highly indebted households do not appear more likely than average to have become worse off than they expected since 2006.

6.6.4 *Why might concerns about debt have reduced household spending?*

Tighter credit conditions may have restricted the spending of indebted households if existing debts prevented those households from borrowing any further to finance consumption (or lowered expectations of

10 It is also possible that some of these differences are related to the 2013 survey being conducted online rather than face to face, which was the case in 2010. Households appear more likely to disclose sensitive information about the state of their finances in online surveys compared to interviews conducted face to face. See Bunn et al. (2012) for further details.

future access to credit), but the mechanism for why households should cut spending because of concerns about debt is less clear. This section tries to explain why that might be the case. Based on evidence from the NMG Survey, we put forward a possible explanation that outstanding debt may have amplified the impact on spending of the income and uncertainty shocks associated with the financial crisis as increased concerns about ability to make future debt repayments led indebted households to make additional cuts in spending.

Our analysis of why households may have cut spending due to debt concerns has two strands: we directly asked households why they were concerned about debt and we analyse the characteristics of those who reported that they had cut spending because of concerns about debt. In the 2013 NMG Survey, households who reported that they were concerned about debt were asked why that was the case from a list of options (multiple responses were allowed). The most common reasons cited by households were related to concerns about not being able to keep up with repayments in the future if either interest rates were to rise or income were to fall (Table 6.2). The third most cited reason was that current income was already lower than when the loan was taken out. Concerns about ability to make future repayments were much more important than currently having repayment difficulties as reasons

Table 6.2. Reasons for concerns about debt[(a)]

	Percentages of mortgagors who have cut spending due to debt concerns
Concerned about keeping up with repayments if interest rates rise	45
Concerned about keeping up with repayments because income could fall	28
Current income lower than expected when took out loan	23
Currently having repayment difficulties	20
Banks unwilling to lend more because of current level of debt	10
Other	9
House borrowed against worth less than expected	4

(a) Data from 2013 survey. Households were able to choose up to three responses. Questions: 'How concerned are you about your current level of debt?'; 'Why are you concerned about your current level of debt?'.

Sources: NMG Consulting Survey and authors' calculations.

why households reported that they were concerned about debt, which is likely to reflect the low level of interest rates.

Analysis of the characteristics of households cutting spending due to concerns about debt also suggests that lower-than-expected income and uncertainty about future income are important reasons why households were concerned about debt. In 2013, mortgagors cutting spending were much more likely to report that they were worse off than they had expected in 2006 and that they thought their income could fall sharply over the next year (Table 6.3).

We also analyse the influence of income shocks and uncertainty more formally by estimating probit models for the probability of cutting spending due to debt concerns (see Table A.6 in the Appendix). Being much worse off than expected since 2006 increases the probability of being concerned about debt by 0.5% points relative to households who were either better off than, or as well off as, they expected in 2013 (on a scale of 0 to 1), while households who are just worse off than expected have a probability about 0.25% points higher. The marginal effect of a sharp fall in income being quite likely over the next year is smaller at around 0.1% points, but that effect is still statistically significant.

Whilst there is clear evidence that income shocks and uncertainty about future income increase the probability of cutting spending due to concerns about debt, the evidence that this effect is bigger for more highly indebted households is less conclusive. If the mortgage

Table 6.3. Characteristics of mortgagors who have cut spending due to debt concerns[(a)]

	Reduced spending in response to debt concerns (2013 data)	
	Yes	**No**
Median mortgage debt-to-income ratio	2.4	1.7
Proportion who are worse off than they expected in 2006	73%	39%
Proportion who are think that a sharp fall in income is quite likely over the next year	33%	19%

(a) Data from 2013 survey. Mortgage debt-to-income ratio is defined as outstanding mortgage debt as a percentage of gross annual income. Questions: 'Would you say you are better or worse off than you would have expected at the end of 2006, before the start of the financial crisis?' and 'To the best of your knowledge, how likely is it that your household income will fall sharply over the next year or so (for example, because you or someone in your household are made redundant)?'.

Sources: NMG Consulting Survey and authors' calculations.

debt-to-income ratio is not included separately in the model, the marginal impact on the probability of cutting spending due to debt concerns from expecting a fall in income or being worse off since 2006 (but not much worse off) is significantly larger (Eq. [24] (i.e. column [24]) in Table A.6). But once the debt-to-income ratio is included separately as a control variable, the effects are not significantly larger for higher debt households (Eq. [26] (i.e. column [26]) in Table A.6). It is possible that large income shocks make both high- and low-debt households more concerned about their ability to repay debts in the future, but that the spending response among high-debt households is larger. Unfortunately, the NMG Survey does not contain any information on the size of spending responses to allow us to test this.

To summarise, households reported that the main reason that they were concerned about debt was that they were worried about their ability to repay debt in the future. Households who were concerned about debt were also more likely to have suffered negative income and shocks and to be more uncertain about their future income. These results suggest that debt may have amplified the impact of income and uncertainty shocks on spending as increased concerns about ability to make future debt repayments led indebted households to make additional cuts in spending, despite the fact that highly indebted households will have experienced the largest falls in their current debt servicing costs.

6.7 Conclusion

A major development in UK household balance sheets over the decade before the financial crisis was the build-up of household debt. This chapter investigates the extent to which increases in mortgage debt before 2007 helped to finance household spending and whether high debt levels led to a deeper recession in 2008–09.

There is evidence that households with high levels of debt have increased the volatility of household spending in the UK. Debt appears to have provided some support to consumption and GDP during periods of economic growth, but has also contributed to a deeper downturn and more protracted recovery in the wake of the Great Recession. We present microdata evidence showing that highly indebted UK households made larger than average cuts in spending, relative to income, after 2007. But this only represents an unwinding of faster than average spending growth by indebted households before the crisis.

Based on our econometric analysis, spending cuts associated with debt are estimated to have reduced the level of aggregate private consumption by around 2% after 2007. And whilst the increases in mortgage debt before 2007 were predominantly matched by an accumulation of financial assets, larger than average increases in spending by more highly indebted households are estimated to have added around 0.35% points a year to aggregate consumption growth between 1996 and 2003.

It is difficult to prove that more highly indebted households who made large cuts in spending after 2007 did so specifically because of their debts. However, we find evidence that suggests those spending cuts were driven by a combination of tighter credit conditions and increased concerns about ability to make future debt repayments, which is consistent with high indebtedness being the cause of those spending patterns.

Appendix

Table A.1. Consumption regression results

Dependent variable	Non-housing consumption							
	[1]	[2]	[3]	[4]	[5]	[6]	[7]	[8]
Cohort dummies[(a)]								
Born 1926–30	−0.084***	−0.094***	−0.085***	−0.100***	−0.081***	−0.112***	−0.078***	−0.100***
	(−4.42)	(−4.98)	(−4.50)	(−5.21)	(−3.84)	(−5.26)	(−4.12)	(−5.23)
Born 1931–35	−0.063***	−0.070***	−0.063***	−0.067***	−0.061***	−0.077***	−0.059***	−0.067***
	(−4.67)	(−5.18)	(−4.63)	(−4.92)	(−4.07)	(−5.07)	(−4.36)	(−4.93)
Born 1936–40	−0.035***	−0.038***	−0.033***	−0.034***	−0.040***	−0.044***	−0.032***	−0.033***
	(−3.79)	(−4.13)	(−3.59)	(−3.63)	(−3.88)	(−4.24)	(−3.44)	(−3.59)
Born 1946–50	0.002	0.003	0.001	0.002	0.003	0.006	−0.001	0.001
	(0.24)	(0.40)	(0.08)	(0.19)	(0.35)	(0.70)	(−0.11)	(0.11)
Born 1951–55	−0.002	−0.001	−0.004	−0.004	−0.016	−0.012	−0.006	−0.004
	(−0.14)	(−0.05)	(−0.35)	(−0.29)	(−1.18)	(−0.88)	(−0.45)	(−0.30)
Born 1936–60	0.005	0.003	0.000	0.000	−0.010	−0.008	−0.000	0.000
	(0.28)	(0.20)	(0.02)	(0.01)	(−0.51)	(−0.40)	(−0.02)	(0.00)
Born 1961–65	0.016	0.013	0.012	0.009	0.009	0.006	0.012	0.009
	(0.76)	(0.58)	(0.53)	(0.41)	(0.36)	(0.23)	(0.57)	(0.41)
Born 1966–70	0.022	0.014	0.016	0.011	0.025	0.015	0.019	0.011
	(0.82)	(0.54)	(0.61)	(0.40)	(0.85)	(0.50)	(0.71)	(0.40)
Born 1971–75	0.012	0.003	0.009	0.000	0.026	0.009	0.012	0.000
	(0.37)	(0.09)	(0.27)	(0.01)	(0.74)	(0.25)	(0.39)	(0.01)
Born 1976–80	−0.020	−0.031	−0.023	−0.030	−0.001	−0.018	−0.020	−0.032
	(−0.54)	(−0.84)	(−0.61)	(−0.80)	(−0.02)	(−0.45)	(−0.55)	(−0.86)
Born 1981–85	−0.035	−0.045	−0.037	−0.045	−0.008	−0.024	−0.038	−0.049
	(−0.82)	(−1.07)	(−0.87)	(−1.06)	(−0.17)	(−0.50)	(−0.89)	(−1.16)
Born 1986–90	−0.040	−0.043	−0.046	−0.056	−0.009	−0.024	−0.049	−0.061
	(−0.79)	(−0.84)	(−0.90)	(−1.10)	(−0.16)	(−0.43)	(−0.96)	(−1.21)
Head of household characteristics								
	−0.278***	−0.280***	−0.290***	−0.272***	−0.102	−0.073	−0.306***	−0.280***
	(−3.07)	(−3.10)	(−3.20)	(−3.00)	(−1.02)	(−0.73)	(−3.39)	(−3.10)
Age squared	0.014***	0.013***	0.014***	0.013***	0.007	0.006	0.014***	0.013***
	(3.11)	(3.05)	(3.12)	(2.92)	(1.44)	(1.19)	(3.28)	(3.01)

(continued)

Table A.1. (*cont.*)

Dependent variable	Non-housing consumption							
	[1]	[2]	[3]	[4]	[5]	[6]	[7]	[8]
Age cubed	−0.000***	−0.000***	−0.000***	−0.000***	−0.000*	−0.000	−0.000***	−0.000***
	(−3.16)	(−3.04)	(−3.07)	(−2.88)	(−1.73)	(−1.52)	(−3.21)	(−2.96)
Age^4	0.000***	0.000***	0.000***	0.000***	0.000*	0.000*	0.000***	0.000***
	(3.23)	(3.06)	(3.06)	(2.87)	(1.91)	(1.73)	(3.18)	(2.94)
Age^5	−0.000***	−0.000***	−0.000***	−0.000***	−0.000**	−0.000*	−0.000***	−0.000***
	(−3.31)	(−3.11)	(−3.08)	(−2.90)	(−2.01)	(−1.85)	(−3.19)	(−2.97)
Male dummy	−0.018***	−0.020***	−0.021***	−0.021***	0.013***	0.013***	−0.021***	−0.022***
	(−4.51)	(−4.97)	(−5.06)	(−5.15)	(2.99)	(2.85)	(−5.20)	(−5.33)
Married dummy	0.083***	0.085***	0.085***	0.085***	0.131***	0.132***	0.083***	0.084***
	(19.72)	(20.25)	(20.30)	(20.39)	(28.15)	(28.25)	(20.00)	(20.11)
A level dummy[(b)]	0.090***	0.084***	0.084***	0.084***	0.163***	0.164***	0.083***	0.083***
	(23.05)	(21.45)	(21.24)	(21.25)	(38.74)	(38.87)	(20.96)	(21.01)
Degree dummy[(b)]	0.135***	0.125***	0.125***	0.125***	0.308***	0.308***	0.121***	0.121***
	(25.68)	(22.97)	(22.88)	(22.87)	(63.63)	(63.59)	(22.02)	(22.01)
Self-employed dummy[(c)]	0.079***	0.072***	0.071***	0.072***	0.015**	0.016***	0.070***	0.071***
	(14.68)	(13.49)	(13.44)	(13.54)	(2.52)	(2.76)	(13.33)	(13.51)
Unemployed dummy[(c)]	−0.070***	−0.061***	−0.060***	−0.061***	−0.452***	−0.454***	−0.052***	−0.054***
	(−7.00)	(−6.02)	(−5.89)	(−6.02)	(−47.19)	(−47.43)	(−5.15)	(−5.34)
Inactive dummy[(c)]	−0.009	−0.003	−0.003	−0.002	−0.267***	−0.265***	0.003	0.004
	(−1.60)	(−0.59)	(−0.48)	(−0.37)	(−50.28)	(−49.93)	(0.46)	(0.63)
Household characteristics								
Number of children under 5	0.023***	0.018***	0.018***	0.018***	0.024***	0.024***	0.017***	0.017***
	(7.39)	(5.88)	(5.84)	(5.83)	(6.95)	(6.92)	(5.72)	(5.67)
Number of children aged 5–18	0.075***	0.075***	0.075***	0.075***	0.101***	0.100***	0.074***	0.074***
	(42.67)	(42.76)	(42.95)	(42.88)	(50.93)	(50.57)	(42.63)	(42.45)
Number of adults	0.195***	0.195***	0.195***	0.195***	0.358***	0.358***	0.192***	0.192***
	(57.32)	(56.58)	(56.46)	(56.45)	(121.16)	(121.00)	(55.04)	(55.04)
Mortgagor dummy[(d)]	−0.014***	−0.091***	−0.095***	−0.095***	0.024***	0.026***	−0.101***	−0.100***
	(−3.02)	(−16.51)	(−17.09)	(−17.03)	(4.01)	(4.42)	(−18.27)	(−18.13)
Renter dummy[(d)]	−0.265***	−0.245***	−0.243***	−0.244***	−0.393***	−0.397***	−0.240***	−0.242***
	(−47.08)	(−41.48)	(−40.98)	(−40.99)	(−67.13)	(−67.58)	(−40.27)	(−40.51)

House prices								
Log real regional house prices	0.076*** (4.20)	0.070*** (3.88)	0.068*** (3.78)	0.058*** (3.21)	0.122*** (6.08)	0.110*** (5.46)	0.076*** (4.23)	0.063*** (3.47)
Income								
Log real income (net of interest payments)	0.470*** (67.05)	0.493*** (63.75)	0.495*** (63.53)	0.495*** (63.18)	–	–	–	–
Log real income (before interest payments)	–	–	–	–	–	–	0.508*** (63.32)	0.507*** (63.19)
Debt variables								
Mortgage debt-to-income ratio	–	0.042*** (20.92)	0.050*** (22.00)	0.048*** (9.20)	−0.030*** (−17.22)	−0.016*** (−3.11)	0.016*** (8.34)	0.017*** (3.43)
Mortgage debt-to-income ratio year interactions[(e)]:								
2008–12	–	–	−0.022*** (−8.56)	–	–	–	−0.010*** (−4.11)	–
1992	–	–	–	−0.008 (−1.00)	–	−0.043*** (−5.69)	–	−0.026*** (−3.68)
1993	–	–	–	−0.024*** (−3.28)	–	−0.046*** (−6.24)	–	−0.029*** (−4.12)
1994	–	–	–	−0.019** (−2.50)	–	−0.044*** (−5.95)	–	−0.023*** (−3.21)
1995	–	–	–	−0.007 (−1.03)	–	−0.040*** (−5.38)	–	−0.017** (−2.39)
1996	–	–	–	−0.013* (−1.80)	–	−0.046*** (−6.18)	–	−0.019*** (−2.84)
1997	–	–	–	0.002 (0.22)	–	−0.022*** (−2.94)	–	−0.003 (−0.46)
1998	–	–	–	0.004 (0.51)	–	−0.032*** (−4.03)	–	−0.006 (−0.82)
1999	–	–	–	0.005 (0.60)	–	−0.023*** (−3.05)	–	0.001 (0.17)
2000	–	–	–	0.005 (0.67)	–	−0.018** (−2.15)	–	0.002 (0.25)

(continued)

Table A.1. (*cont.*)

Dependent variable	Non-housing consumption							
	[1]	[2]	[3]	[4]	[5]	[6]	[7]	[8]
2001	–	–	–	0.020**	–	−0.000	–	0.018**
		–	–	(2.54)		(−0.03)		(2.42)
2002	–	–	–	0.011	–	−0.008	–	0.012*
				(1.56)		(−0.99)		(1.79)
2003	–	–	–	0.019***	–	0.009	–	0.024***
				(2.77)		(1.21)		(3.50)
2004	–	–	–	0.004	–	0.001	–	0.009
				(0.65)		(0.15)		(1.35)
2005	–	–	–	0.010	–	0.003	–	0.011*
				(1.45)		(0.43)		(1.70)
2006	–	–	–	0.002	–	0.001	–	0.005
				(0.37)		(0.15)		(0.81)
2008	–	–	–	−0.007	–	−0.003	–	−0.007
				(−1.07)		(−0.45)		(−1.05)
2009	–	–	–	−0.025***	–	−0.014*	–	−0.014**
				(−3.71)		(−1.95)		(−2.17)
2010	–	–	–	−0.018**	–	−0.009	–	−0.006
				(−2.44)		(−1.17)		(−0.94)
2011	–	–	–	−0.022***	–	−0.009	–	−0.009
				(−3.25)		(−1.24)		(−1.32)
2012	–	–	–	−0.030***	–	−0.022***	–	−0.015**
				(−4.32)		(−2.96)		(−2.31)
Observations	107,623	107,623	107,623	107,623	107,746	107,746	107,657	107,657
R-squared	0.580	0.583	0.583	0.584	0.478	0.479	0.585	0.586

*** $p < 0.01$, ** $p < 0.05$, * $p < 0.1$. T ratios reported in parentheses. Dependent variable is log of real household non-housing consumption. Other variables included, but not reported above, are year and quarter dummies, government office region dummies and a constant. All equations are estimated by OLS with robust standard errors from 1992 to 2012.

(a) Relative to those born between 1941 and 1945.

(b) Relative those whose highest qualification is GCSEs or lower.

(c) Relative to employees.

(d) Relative to owner occupiers.

(e) Relative to 2007.

Table A.2. Regression results for different components of consumption

Dependent variable	Non-housing consumption	Durable consumption	Non-durable consumption	Essential non-durable consumption	Non-essential non-durable consumption
	[4]	[9]	[10]	[11]	[12]
Debt variables					
Mortgage debt-to-income ratio	0.048***	0.055***	0.049***	0.024***	0.069***
	(9.20)	(6.40)	(8.61)	(4.22)	(9.02)
Mortgage debt-to-income ratio year interactions[(a)]:					
1992	−0.008	−0.003	−0.005	−0.009	0.000
	(−1.00)	(−0.26)	(−0.65)	(−1.11)	(0.03)
1993	−0.024***	−0.012	−0.025***	−0.019**	−0.028***
	(−3.28)	(−0.93)	(−3.29)	(−2.49)	(−2.60)
1994	−0.019**	−0.004	−0.024***	−0.018**	−0.025**
	(−2.50)	(−0.31)	(−3.01)	(−2.36)	(−2.31)
1995	−0.007	0.012	−0.016**	−0.007	−0.024**
	(−1.03)	(0.92)	(−2.03)	(−0.91)	(−2.28)
1996	−0.013*	−0.003	−0.015*	−0.004	−0.022**
	(−1.80)	(−0.24)	(−1.93)	(−0.50)	(−2.05)
1997	0.002	0.025**	−0.001	−0.008	0.003
	(0.22)	(2.01)	(−0.07)	(−1.02)	(0.24)
1998	0.004	0.019	−0.002	−0.001	−0.002
	(0.51)	(1.47)	(−0.23)	(−0.10)	(−0.14)
1999	0.005	0.029**	−0.004	0.003	−0.005
	(0.60)	(2.22)	(−0.46)	(0.31)	(−0.49)
2000	0.005	0.011	0.005	−0.004	0.012
	(0.67)	(0.82)	(0.61)	(−0.45)	(1.02)
2001	0.020**	0.014	0.016*	−0.005	0.034***
	(2.54)	(0.97)	(1.89)	(−0.59)	(3.01)

(continued)

Table A.2. (*cont.*)

	Non-housing consumption	Durable consumption	Non-durable consumption	Essential non-durable consumption	Non-essential non-durable consumption
Dependent variable	**[4]**	**[9]**	**[10]**	**[11]**	**[12]**
2002	0.011	0.023*	0.002	−0.000	0.006
	(1.56)	(1.81)	(0.28)	(−0.04)	(0.51)
2003	0.019***	0.042***	0.006	−0.001	0.011
	(2.77)	(3.47)	(0.83)	(−0.14)	(1.10)
2004	0.004	0.011	−0.001	−0.015*	0.005
	(0.65)	(0.91)	(−0.17)	(−1.80)	(0.53)
2005	0.010	0.020*	0.009	−0.003	0.016
	(1.45)	(1.78)	(1.11)	(−0.38)	(1.62)
2006	0.002	−0.002	0.004	−0.005	0.009
	(0.37)	(−0.21)	(0.50)	(−0.74)	(0.95)
2008	−0.007	−0.009	−0.004	−0.013	0.004
	(−1.07)	(−0.82)	(−0.57)	(−1.55)	(0.39)
2009	−0.025***	−0.032***	−0.025***	−0.020***	−0.027***
	(−3.71)	(−2.69)	(−3.36)	(−2.64)	(−2.70)
2010	−0.018**	−0.028**	−0.018**	−0.013	−0.025**
	(−2.44)	(−2.14)	(−2.25)	(−1.61)	(−2.34)
2011	−0.022***	−0.032***	−0.019**	−0.020***	−0.019*
	(−3.25)	(−2.84)	(−2.51)	(−2.61)	(−1.85)
2012	−0.030***	−0.038***	−0.026***	−0.015*	−0.032***
	(−4.32)	(−3.30)	(−3.25)	(−1.83)	(−3.07)
Observations	107,623	107,250	107,622	107,459	107,592
R-squared	0.584	0.425	0.525	0.473	0.418

*** $p < 0.01$, ** $p < 0.05$, * $p < 0.1$. T ratios reported in parentheses. Dependent variable is log of real household consumption, definition varies across equations. Other variables included, but not reported above, are birth year cohort dummies, age, sex, marital status, highest qualification, economic activity, household composition, tenure, house prices, income (net of mortgage interest payments), year and quarter dummies, government office region dummies and a constant. All equations are estimated by OLS with robust standard errors from 1992 to 2012.
(a) Relative to 2007.

Table A.3. Consumption regression results incorporating unsecured debt variables

	Non-housing consumption		
Dependent variable	**[13]**	**[14]**	**[15]**
Debt variables			
Mortgage debt-to-income ratio	0.048***	0.039***	0.046***
	(8.94)	(16.69)	(8.59)
Mortgage debt-to-income ratio year interactions[(a)]:			
2001	0.016**	–	0.014*
	(1.98)		(1.71)
2002	0.008	–	0.004
	(1.07)		(0.51)
2003	0.016**	–	0.012*
	(2.34)		(1.70)
2004	0.003	–	0.001
	(0.42)		(0.17)
2005	0.009	–	0.008
	(1.36)		(1.19)
2006	0.002	–	0.001
	(0.31)		(0.17)
2008	−0.007	–	−0.007
	(−1.04)		(−1.10)
2009	−0.025***	–	−0.025***
	(−3.64)		(−3.69)
2010	−0.016**	–	−0.016**
	(−2.27)		(−2.14)
2011	−0.021***	–	−0.024***
	(−3.12)		(−3.47)
2012	−0.028***	–	−0.028***
	(−4.13)		(−4.08)
Dummy for unsecured debt	–	0.112***	0.097***
		(26.31)	(6.64)
Dummy for unsecured debt year interactions[(a)]:			
2001	–	–	0.016
			(0.80)
2002	–	–	0.034*
			(1.70)
2003	–	–	0.049**
			(2.52)
2004	–	–	0.029
			(1.45)
2005	–	–	0.021
			(1.06)
2006	–	–	0.012
			(0.59)
2008	–	–	0.000
			(0.02)

(continued)

Table A.3. (*cont.*)

Dependent variable	Non-housing consumption [13]	[14]	[15]
2009	–	–	0.014
			(0.68)
2010	–	–	−0.025
			(−1.19)
2011	–	–	0.017
			(0.82)
2012	–	–	−0.007
			(−0.35)
Observations	59,988	59,988	59,988
R-squared	0.562	0.566	0.567

*** $p < 0.01$, ** $p < 0.05$, * $p < 0.1$. T ratios reported in parentheses. Dependent variable is log of real household non-housing consumption. Other variables included, but not reported above, are birth year cohort dummies, age, sex, marital status, highest qualification, economic activity, household composition, tenure, house prices, income (net of mortgage interest payments), year and quarter dummies, government office region dummies and a constant. All equations are estimated by OLS with robust standard errors from 2001 to 2012.
(a) Relative to 2007.

Table A.4. Consumption regression results incorporating credit condition variables

Dependent variable	Non-housing consumption [4]	[16]	[17]	[18]	[19]
Debt variables					
Mortgage debt-to-income ratio	0.048***	0.049***	0.053***	0.048***	0.048***
	(9.20)	(9.24)	(9.69)	(9.09)	(8.59)
Mortgage debt-to-income ratio year interactions[(a)]:					
1992	−0.008			−0.007	−0.007
	(−1.00)			(−0.87)	(−0.93)
1993	−0.024***			−0.022***	−0.024***
	(−3.28)			(−3.12)	(−3.17)
1994	−0.019**			−0.017**	−0.017**
	(−2.50)			(−2.26)	(−2.10)
1995	−0.007			−0.006	−0.007
	(−1.03)			(−0.78)	(−0.89)
1996	−0.013*	−0.017**	−0.013	−0.011	−0.010
	(−1.80)	(−2.28)	(−1.64)	(−1.55)	(−1.31)

Table A.4. (*cont.*)

Dependent variable	Non-housing consumption				
	[4]	**[16]**	**[17]**	**[18]**	**[19]**
1997	0.002	−0.002	0.001	0.004	0.002
	(0.22)	(−0.24)	(0.20)	(0.55)	(0.30)
1998	0.004	0.001	0.004	0.006	0.005
	(0.51)	(0.13)	(0.46)	(0.78)	(0.59)
1999	0.005	0.002	0.005	0.006	0.005
	(0.60)	(0.31)	(0.67)	(0.86)	(0.68)
2000	0.005	0.003	0.006	0.007	0.007
	(0.67)	(0.38)	(0.73)	(0.82)	(0.76)
2001	0.020**	0.019**	0.022***	0.022***	0.024***
	(2.54)	(2.33)	(2.65)	(2.69)	(2.80)
2002	0.011	0.010	0.013*	0.013*	0.009
	(1.56)	(1.38)	(1.72)	(1.74)	(1.22)
2003	0.019***	0.018***	0.020***	0.019***	0.015**
	(2.77)	(2.62)	(2.90)	(2.77)	(2.00)
2004	0.004	0.004	0.005	0.004	0.004
	(0.65)	(0.54)	(0.75)	(0.60)	(0.59)
2005	0.010	0.010	0.010	0.010	0.009
	(1.45)	(1.42)	(1.48)	(1.45)	(1.20)
2006	0.002	0.002	0.002	0.002	0.003
	(0.37)	(0.36)	(0.36)	(0.32)	(0.36)
2008	−0.007	−0.007	−0.006	−0.007	−0.007
	(−1.07)	(−1.06)	(−0.89)	(−1.10)	(−0.96)
2009	−0.025***	−0.025***	−0.020**	−0.025***	−0.024***
	(−3.71)	(−3.69)	(−2.46)	(−3.72)	(−3.31)
2010	−0.018**	−0.017**	−0.013	−0.018**	−0.018**
	(−2.44)	(−2.37)	(−1.51)	(−2.43)	(−2.33)
2011	−0.022***	−0.022***	−0.017**	−0.021***	−0.022***
	(−3.25)	(−3.19)	(−2.20)	(−3.17)	(−2.98)
2012	−0.030***	−0.029***	−0.025***	−0.029***	−0.029***
	(−4.32)	(−4.23)	(−3.27)	(−4.18)	(−3.95)
Credit variables					
Aggregate credit spreads	–	−0.017***	−0.010	−0.030***	−0.030***
		(−2.62)	(−1.38)	(−3.43)	(−3.44)
Credit spreads * low debt mortgagor	–	–	0.001	–	–
			(0.17)		
Credit spreads * high debt mortgagor	–	–	−0.014**	–	–
			(−2.55)		
Credit spreads * renter	–	–	−0.014***	–	–
			(−3.06)		
Topped up mortgage	–	–		0.043***	0.036**
				(10.95)	(2.05)
Topped up mortgage year interactions[(a)]:					
1992	–	–	–	–	0.009
					(0.40)

(*continued*)

Table A.4. (*cont.*)

Dependent variable	Non-housing consumption				
	[4]	[16]	[17]	[18]	[19]
1993	–	–	–	–	0.021
					(0.91)
1994	–	–	–	–	−0.009
					(−0.40)
1995	–	–	–	–	0.014
					(0.62)
1996	–	–	–	–	−0.021
					(−0.92)
1997	–	–	–	–	0.027
					(1.18)
1998	–	–	–	–	0.019
					(0.79)
1999	–	–	–	–	0.014
					(0.61)
2000	–	–	–	–	0.002
					(0.09)
2001	–	–	–	–	−0.024
					(−1.00)
2002	–	–	–	–	0.041*
					(1.68)
2003	–	–	–	–	0.042*
					(1.75)
2004	–	–	–	–	−0.002
					(−0.07)
2005	–	–	–	–	0.012
					(0.48)
2006	–	–	–	–	−0.005
					(−0.19)
2008	–	–	–	–	−0.005
					(−0.20)
2009	–	–	–	–	−0.012
					(−0.48)
2010	–	–	–	–	0.008
					(0.31)
2011	–	–	–	–	0.002
					(0.08)
2012	–	–	–	–	0.001
					(0.02)
Observations	107,623	86,325	86,325	107,623	107,623
R-squared	0.584	0.576	0.577	0.584	0.584

*** $p < 0.01$, ** $p < 0.05$, * $p < 0.1$. T ratios reported in parentheses. Dependent variable is log of real household non-housing consumption, definition varies across equations. Other variables included, but not reported above, are birth year cohort dummies, age, sex, marital status, highest qualification, economic activity, household composition, tenure, house prices, income (net of mortgage interest payments), year and quarter dummies, government office region dummies and a constant. All equations are estimated by OLS with robust standard errors from 1992 to 2012, except for Eqs. [16] and [17] which are estimated from 1996 to 2012.

(a) Relative to 2007.

Table A.5. Mortgage debt-to-income regressions

	Mortgage debt-to-income ratio		
Dependent variable	**[20]**	**[21]**	**[22]**
Put off spending because of concerns about credit availability	0.431	0.421***	0.424***
	(1.50)	(3.57)	(3.59)
Cut spending because of concerns about debt	1.120***	0.576***	0.515***
	(4.11)	(5.21)	(4.48)
Worse off than expected in 2006			0.151
			(1.47)
Constant	2.125***	2.039***	1.970***
	(14.90)	(32.89)	(26.65)
Year	2010	2013	2013
Observations	368	1,541	1,509
R-squared	0.072	0.041	0.043

***$p < 0.01$, **$p < 0.05$, *$p < 0.1$. T ratios are reported in parentheses. All equations are estimated by OLS. Includes mortgagors only.

Table A.6. Probit models for probability of cutting spending due to debt concerns

	Cut spending due to debt concerns			
Dependent variable	**[23]**	**[24]**	**[25]**	**[26]**
Income shock dummy variables				
Sharp income fall quite likely over next year	0.084**	0.012	0.087***	0.041
	(2.54)	(0.26)	(2.62)	(0.82)
Worse off than expected since 2006	0.248***	0.188***	0.248***	0.242***
	(7.77)	(4.53)	(7.67)	(5.12)
Much worse off than expected since 2006	0.507***	0.499***	0.501***	0.545***
	(12.70)	(8.71)	(12.33)	(8.99)
Interactions with mortgage debt-to-income ratio > 2:				
Sharp income fall quite likely over next year	–	0.134**	–	0.079
		(2.08)		(1.17)
Worse off than expected since 2006	–	0.121**	–	0.012
		(2.36)		(0.20)
Much worse off than expected since 2006	–	0.015	–	−0.082
		(0.21)		(−1.10)
Debt dummy variables				
Mortgage debt-to-income ratio >=1 & <2[(a)]	–	–	0.155***	0.155***
			(3.53)	(3.51)
Mortgage debt-to-income ratio >=2 & <3[(a)]	–	–	0.220***	0.210***
			(4.73)	(3.47)

(*continued*)

Table A.6. (*cont.*)

	Cut spending due to debt concerns			
Dependent variable	**[23]**	**[24]**	**[25]**	**[26]**
Mortgage debt-to-income ratio >=3[(a)]	–	–	0.231***	0.223***
			(5.00)	(3.72)
Has unsecured debt	–	–	0.065***	0.066***
			(3.35)	(3.36)
Observations	1,321	1,321	1,321	1,321

*** $p < 0.01$, ** $p < 0.05$, * $p < 0.1$. Table reports marginal effects on probability of cutting spending due to debt concerns. T ratios are reported in parentheses. Other variables included but not reported are age, income, house value and region. All equations are estimated for 2013 only. Includes mortgagors only.
(a) Relative to those with a mortgage debt-to-income ratio of less than one.

References

Andersen, A.L., Duus, C., and Jensen, T.L. (2014), 'Household debt and consumption during the financial crisis: evidence from Danish micro data', Danmarks National Bank Working Paper No. 89.

Attanasio, O., Blow, L., Hamilton, R., and Leicester, A. (2009), 'Consumption, house prices and expectations', 'Booms and busts: consumption, house prices and expectations', *Economica*, 71, p20–p50.

Baker, S. (2013), '*Debt and the consumption response to household income shocks*', Stanford University, Mimeo.

Bean, C. (2004), 'Some current issues in UK monetary policy', *Bank of England Quarterly Bulletin*, 355–358.

Benito, A., Waldron, M., Young, G., and Zampolli, F. (2007), 'The role of household debt and balance sheets in the monetary transmission mechanism', *Bank of England Quarterly Bulletin*, 47(1), 70–78.

Bernanke, B., Gertler, M., and Gilchrist, S. (1999), 'The financial accelerator in a quantitative business cycle framework' In: Taylor, J and Woodford, M, (eds), Handbook of macroeconomics, vol. 1C.

Bunn, P. and Rostom, M. (2014), 'Household debt and spending', *Bank of England Quarterly Bulletin*, 54(3), 304–315.

Butt, N. and Pugh, A. (2014), 'Credit spreads: capturing credit conditions facing households and firms', *Bank of England Quarterly Bulletin*, 54(2), 137–147.

Bunn, P., Domit, S., Piscitelli, L., Rostom, M., and Worrow, N. (2013), 'The financial position of British households: evidence from the 2013 NMG consulting survey', *Bank of England Quarterly Bulletin*, 53(4), 351–360.

Bunn, P., Johnson, R., Le Roux, J., and McLeay, M. (2012), 'Influences on household spending: evidence from the 2012 NMG consulting survey', *Bank of England Quarterly Bulletin*, 52(4), 332–342.

Campbell, J. and Cocco, J. (2007), 'How do house prices affect consumption? Evidence from microdata', *Journal of Monetary Economics*, 54, 591–621.

Cecchetti, S., Mohanty, M., and Zampolli, F. (2011), 'The real effects of debt', BIS Working Paper No. 352.

Cloyne, J. and Surico, P. (2014), 'Household debt and the dynamic effects of income tax changes', Bank of England Working Paper No. 491.

Dynan, K. (2012), '*Is a household debt overhang holding back consumption?*', Brookings Papers on Economic Activity, Spring.

Eggertsson, G. and Krugman, P. (2012), 'Debt, deleveraging, and the liquidity trap: a Fisher-Minsky-Koo approach', *Quarterly Journal of Economics*, 127(3), 1469–1513.

Fisher, I. (1933), 'The debt-deflation theory of great depressions', *Econometrica*, 1(4), 337–357.

Flodén, M. (2014), 'Did household debt matter in the Great Recession?', available at http://martinfloden.net/files/hhdebt_supplement_2014.pdf.

Guerrieri, V. and Lorenzoni, G. (2011), 'Credit crises, precautionary savings, and the liquidity trap,' NBER Working Paper 17583.

Iacoviello, M. (2005), 'House prices, borrowing constraints and monetary policy in the business cycle', *American Economic Review*, 95(3), 739–764.

International Monetary Fund. (2012), 'Dealing with household debt', World Economic Outlook, April, Chapter 3.

Jorda, O., Schularick, M., and Taylor, A. (2013), 'When credit bites back', *Journal of Money, Credit and Banking*, 45(2), 3–28.

King, M. (1994), 'Debt deflation: theory and evidence', *European Economic Review*, 38(3–4), 419–455.

McLeay, M., Radia, A., and Thomas, R. (2014), 'Money in the modern economy: an introduction', *Bank of England Quarterly Bulletin*, 54(1), 4–13.

Mian, A., Rao, K., and Sufi, A. (2013), 'Household balance sheets, consumption, and the economic slump', *Quarterly Journal of Economics*, 128(1), 687–726.

Nickell, S. (2004), 'Household debt, house prices and consumption growth', *Bank of England Quarterly Bulletin*, 383–389, Autumn.

Nielsen, M., Pezzini Reinhold, K., and William, R. (2010), 'The financial position of British households: evidence from the 2010 NMG Consulting survey', *Bank of England Quarterly Bulletin*, 333–345.

Philippon, T. and Midrigan, V. (2011), 'Household leverage and the recession', NBER Working Paper 16965.

Waldron, M. and Zampolli, F. (2010), 'Household debt, house prices and consumption in the United Kingdom: a quantitative theoretical analysis', Bank of England Working Paper 379.

7 MPC decision-making, the Long Expansion and the crisis: integration with the global economy, heterogeneity and network dynamics

Arnab Bhattacharjee and Sean Holly

7.1 Introduction

There is a substantial literature, for both the United Kingdom and the United States, which uses information from voting records and transcripts of the proceedings – for both the Bank of England's Monetary Policy Committee (MPC) and the Federal Open Markets Committee (FOMC) – to study the monetary policy-making process. This body of work has provided a number of insights into this process and the roles played by individual members, especially the Bank of England Governor or the Federal Reserve Chairman. For representative work for the Bank of England MPC, see, for example, Chadha and Nolan (2001), Cobham (2002, 2003, 2013), Gerlach-Kristen (2004), Besley et al. (2008) and Bhattacharjee and Holly (2015); for the FOMC, see Belden (1989), Edison and Marquez (1998), Chappell and McGregor (2004), Chappell et al. (2005), Bailey and Schonhardt-Bailey (2008) and Meade and Thornton (2012).

Over the Long Expansion period, substantial transformations have taken place in the institutional and operational arrangements of monetary policy around the world. First, monetary policy in most central banks has come to be conducted by MPCs, rather than by an individual central banker. Second, attempting to maintain inflation at a pre-specified target level has emerged as the most important object of monetary policy. In

The editors and a reviewer made numerous constructive comments that helped us revise and improve the chapter substantially. Their contributions are gratefully acknowledged. Besides, the paper has benefited from comments by Richard Barwell, Parantap Basu, Jagjit Chadha, David Cobham, George Evans, Petra Geraats and Charles Nolan, as well as participants at the Conference on 'Causes and Consequences of the Long UK Expansion: 1992 to 2007' (Cambridge, UK, 2013), the Money Macro and Finance Research Group 44th Annual Conference (Dublin, 2012) and Royal Economic Society's 2012 Annual Conference (Cambridge, UK, 2012). The usual disclaimer applies.

1992, the UK, following New Zealand and Sweden, adopted inflation targeting. This was augmented by a much more open system of decision-making, but ultimately decisions on interest rates were still made by the Government. Third, there is growing acknowledgement that credible monetary policy is aided by a central bank that is functionally independent of the fiscal authorities. In 1997 the Bank of England was given full operational independence. To support this new policy regime, very detailed information about interest rate decisions has been provided to the public. Recent literature has used such detailed information, including votes by individual members, to study several aspects of monetary policy-making at the Bank of England's MPC. Finally, many of these far-reaching changes occurred against the backdrop of a major upswing in most countries around the world. This period of sustained economic growth and low inflation (the Great Moderation or the Long Expansion) came to an abrupt end in 2007–08, following an unprecedented worldwide financial crisis.

In this chapter, we consider the monetary policy decision-making process of the Bank of England's MPC since 1997, as the UK economy moved through the phases of expansion, expansion pre-crisis (when many commented unfavourably on developments in global financial and housing markets, but with very few getting the timing or the depth of the crisis right) and finally the crisis. While the above literature has focussed largely on the Long Expansion, we ask whether and how the conduct of monetary policy changed over the period. Our empirical analyses are based on an economic model of MPC decisions, which admits heterogeneity among the members of the committee as well as network interactions within the MPC. Here heterogeneity does not arise so much from differences in preferences about inflation and output, but from differing views about the state of the economy. Based on data on voting records of individual MPC members, we investigate the nature of heterogeneity among members and the network structure between members, and how this has changed over time, over the period 1997–2010.

Our chapter touches on a number of additional issues concerning monetary policy. First, there is a large literature that examines the characterisation of monetary policy in terms of a rule (for further discussion, see Svensson, 1997; Woodford, 1999; Orphanides, 2003). We use the Svensson (1997) inflation forecast targeting model in preference to the Taylor rule (Taylor, 1993), based on the argument that, given the long and variable lags inherent in policy, it might make more sense to target a forecast of inflation rather than its current value. Second, interest rate decisions are made in real time and based on current information, when there is also considerable uncertainty about the current state of the economy; see, among others, Orphanides (1998). In this chapter, we assume that the filtering that is required of current, imperfect measures of economic activity takes place as part of the internal procedures of the Bank of England (Budd, 1998). Indeed, our empirical results indicate that forecasts of inflation and output provide the best explanation for the conduct of UK monetary policy since 1997, which supports the inflation forecast targeting rule. Third, we allow for housing and financial markets to matter, in line with the extensive literature on the role of asset markets in monetary policy decisions; see, for example, Cecchetti et al. (2000), Bernanke and Gertler (2001) and Cobham (2013).

Fourth, information on the actual voting record of each member allows us to investigate heterogeneity among MPC members, as well as network interactions between them. We find substantial evidence in favour of heterogeneity and clear network structures. This raises the question as to why there is heterogeneity across the committee in the first place, given that they all appear to share a common pool of information and that individual members have many opportunities to make their views known before an interest rate decision. It is fair to assume that all MPC members are inflation targeters, so that preference heterogeneity is absent. Instead, we find that heterogeneity reflects differing views of the world, with some members attaching greater importance to particular developments in the economy than others. Some attach greater importance to developments on the supply side, which in the presence of forecast uncertainty translates into different views on the size of the output gap. Similarly, some other members may attach greater importance to asset markets, while others may disagree with the majority view because they believe the transmission mechanism of monetary policy is different. Likewise, some members place more importance on developments in the international economy.

Fifth, we analyse interactions among the members of a committee, once we have conditioned on the factors that influence individual committee members' decisions on interest rates, allowing for the heterogeneous responses of individual members to these factors. The results point to significant interactions between members, both positive and negative. There is also substantial asymmetry in these interactions. In other words, there is considerable asymmetry in the influence that committee members have and how they are influenced in turn by others. The estimated network structures point to interesting dynamics within the committee, and provide some insights into the nature of monetary policy decision-making at the Bank of England's MPC.

Finally, we analyse how the nature of monetary policy-making at the Bank of England's MPC changed over the course of the transition from the expansion to the crisis, through an intermediate period when the crisis was already being anticipated. We chart the three stages of transition – expansion (Regime 1), expansion pre-crisis (Regime 2) and crisis (Regime 3) – in terms of changes in the macroeconomic factors that the MPC would have considered in making their decisions, changes in the nature of heterogeneity across members and changes in the network structure within the committee. Charting these changes over the period is the primary contribution of this chapter.

The plan of the chapter is as follows. In Section 7.2, we present a simple model of inflation forecast targeting in the Bank of England's MPC. We discuss possible sources of heterogeneity and interactions within the MPC. In Section 7.3, we discuss data, the empirical model and the estimation problem. In Section 7.4, we report and discuss our empirical results. Finally, we present our conclusions in Section 7.5.

7.2 Economic model of an MPC

In this section, we discuss briefly a model for monetary policy decision-making by a committee. Our model introduces a role for heterogeneity across policy-makers and considers the signal extraction problem that the MPC and its members face individually. Inter-member interactions arise from deliberation and information sharing, but also like-mindedness and conflicting preferences in private information that cannot be shared between members. Only an outline description is provided here; for further details, see Bhattacharjee and Holly (2015).

7.2.1 Inflation (forecast) targeting

We adopt a very simple model of the monetary policy-making process. This gives us a model that we believe aligns best with how central banks view the monetary transmission process from an initial change in the monetary stance to a target for inflation. This provides a justification for the way in which policy appears to be conducted.

This allows us to emphasise that, when there are delays in the monetary transmission process, so that it takes time for changes in interest rates to affect output, and for output in turn to affect inflation, it is optimal for the MPC to base its interest rate decisions on forecasts of current and future output and inflation rather than on past and present realisations of output and inflation, as with a Taylor rule. We then widen the set of information to which the MPC could also pay attention.

We derive an inflation 'feed forward' rule based on Svensson (1997), where the policy-maker only targets inflation, and the central bank can (in expectation) use the current interest rate to hit the target for inflation, in expectation, two periods hence.

The model is structured as follows:

$$\pi_t = \pi_{t-1} + \alpha y_{t-1} + \varepsilon_t,$$
$$y_t = \beta_1 y_{t-1} + \beta_2 (r_{t-1} - \pi_{t-1}) + \eta_t,$$

where π_t is the inflation rate in period t, y_t is the output gap (the difference between the log of output and the log of potential output), and r_t the nominal interest rate. The supply shock, η_t, and the demand shock, ε_t, are both i.i.d. shocks in period t not observable in period $t-1$. Under the model, current changes in the interest rate affect output in the next period, and this in turn affects inflation in the following period. Setting the inter-temporal loss function for an inflation-targeting central bank as

$$L_t = \frac{1}{2} E_t \sum_{\tau=t}^{\infty} \delta^{\tau-t} (\pi_\tau - \pi^\star)^2$$

where $\pi^\star$ is the inflation target and δ the discount rate, interest rates can be set to hit target inflation, in expectation, in two periods. Controllability allows the inter-temporal problem to be written as a sequence of single-period problems (Svensson, 1997)

$$L_t = \frac{1}{2} (\pi_{t+2|t} - \pi^\star)^2$$

where $\pi_{t+2|t}$ is the forecast of inflation in period $t+2$ based on information available in period t.

Minimising the squared deviation of the current two period ahead inflation forecast $\pi_{t+2|t}$ from the target, the interest rate rule then takes the form:

$$i_t = \pi_{t|t} + \frac{1}{\alpha\beta_2} (\pi_{t+1|t} - \pi^\star) + \frac{\beta_1}{\beta_2} y_{t|t} \tag{7.1}$$

where the subscript $t|t$ reflects the fact that current realisations of the output gap and inflation rate may well be imperfectly observed and may need to be forecasted.

The above inflation forecast targeting decision rule may be contrasted with the Taylor rule (Taylor, 1993), in which the interest rate responds to current or lagged realisations of inflation and output. In Svensson's original formulation, $\pi_{t|t}$ and $y_{t|t}$ are known. However, in practice, current inflation and the current output gap are not observed in real time (Orphanides, 1998). Most importantly, the form of the rule has important implications for the conduct of monetary policy. When a decision is being made to set interest rates, the policy-maker sets the interest rate to achieve (in expectation) the target in two periods' time. The key assumption made in our empirical model is that this policy horizon corresponds to about two years into the future; this bears correspondence to how monetary policy is conducted in the MPC (King, 2002). To quote a former member of the MPC:

> When I was a member of the MPC I thought that I was trying, at each forecast round, to set the level of interest rates so that, without the need for future rate changes, prospective (forecast) inflation would on average equal the target at the policy horizon. This was, I thought, what the exercise was supposed to be. (Goodhart, 2001)

The MPC meets monthly and sets the interest rate in order to achieve the target inflation rate at the policy horizon. A decision to change the interest rate in period t (relative to the decision that was made in period $t-1$) can only be the result of new information becoming available in period t.[1] For example, new information suggesting a build-up in pressures in labour markets may call for a rise in interest rates in order to keep inflation on target in two years' time.

7.2.2 Heterogeneity

There can be substantial heterogeneity, which is reflected in the voting intentions of the members of the MPC. Blinder (2007) has argued that this heterogeneity arises from several different sources: different information sets, different policy preferences (or at least different beliefs as to the impact of interest rates on future inflation and output), different models of the economy, different forecasts of macroeconomic variables and different decision-making heuristics. Sibert (2002) considers the situation where policy-makers have a varying and uncertain aversion to inflation relative to their dislike for output loss – this is a source of heterogeneity. Further, when policy-makers serve on the committee for two periods, she shows how strategic behaviour can lead to different votes in the first and second periods.

Likewise, rational partisan theory (Alesina, 1987; Waller, 1992) can explain how heterogeneity in the effect of forecast uncertainty about the output gap can lead to spatial voting behaviour in a MPC (Bhattacharjee and Holly, 2010). Furthermore, Gerlach-Kristen (2006) argues that if there is uncertainty about potential output then monetary policy should

1 Strictly speaking the introduction of a new member of the MPC (external members serve for a maximum of six years) may also change the decision-making process.

be conducted by a committee rather than a single individual. Imperfect information aggregation is highlighted also as a source of heterogeneity in Claussen et al. (2012), where varying degrees of overconfidence yield disagreement and dissent among decision-makers, which in turn leads to variation in influence across the members. Finally, Riboni and Ruge-Murcia (2010) incorporate heterogeneity through a member-specific discount factor in a utility function aggregating current and future inflation.

In this chapter, we consider an MPC where personalities can be important in the determination of interest rate decisions. In our model, based on Bhattacharjee and Holly (2015), personalities are reflected in heterogeneity in the policy reaction function, as well as in interactions among members. We focus on a strict inflation-targeting regime, so preference heterogeneity between targets for inflation and output does not appear. Instead, heterogeneity arises from three different sources: (a) differing views about the state of the economy, leading to different views about the magnitude of the output gap, (b) varying beliefs about the effect of interest rates on inflation and the output gap ($\alpha\beta_2$ and β_2 respectively) and (c) heterogeneity in the effect of uncertainty on individual members' policy reaction functions. In addition, our model allows for interactions among members, reflecting the extent to which individuals are influenced by other members, and in turn an individual member influences other members. In other words, some members can have more influence on others, and some members are more influenced by other members of the committee.

It is assumed, reasonably, that members come to the committee with different judgements about the state of the economy. As Mervyn King, former Governor of the Bank of England, has pointed out, most of the discussion is focussed on alternative views of the economic environment and a technical economic judgement about what it is necessary to do to hit the inflation target:

> [I]t is precisely the exploration of alternative views about what is happening in the British economy, and the discussion of these views by the Committee in a spirit of investigation not advocacy, that is central to the pooling of knowledge through which committees reach decisions that are superior to those taken by individuals. … Differences of view on our Committee are an honest reflection of the uncertainty about both the data and the structure of the economy. (King, 2002)

It is also assumed that each member has the same public information set, but in addition brings to the committee private information. An individual member may dissent from the consensus forecast or may have a particular expertise in some aspects of the economy so that more weight may be attached to particular kinds of information compared to the average. The summary of discussions in each MPC meeting discussed in Cobham (2003) provides some guidance about how this works. Since the internal dynamics of committee decision-making can result in the sharing of expertise, we assume that the decision of each individual member is ultimately based on commonly shared information as well as on private views that cannot be shared fully with the other members of the MPC, or to which the other members of the Committee attach less importance than an individual member.

Decision-making can be thought of as a two-stage process. In the first stage there is deliberation about the state of the economy. Staff economists (as is the case at any central bank) provide a conjunctural analysis of the current state of the economy, members share information and views, and eventually a central forecast, with agreed error bands in the form of a fan chart, is agreed on. Nevertheless, at this second stage, even though there has been a full sharing of knowledge, many MPC members will choose an interest setting different from the median estimate of a nine-member committee.

A formal way of understanding how a committee comes to a decision is that each member reacts independently to a 'signal' coming from the economy and makes an appropriate decision in the light of this signal and the particular expertise of the member. A voting method then generates a decision that is implemented. Before a decision is made there is a shared discussion of the state of the world as seen by each of the members. Views are exchanged about the interpretation of signals, and an individual member may decide to revise their views depending upon how much weight they place on their own views and those of others.

This process can be cast as a simple signal extraction problem within a highly stylised framework. Once all public information is revealed and sharable private information of all the members has been exchanged, each committee member formulates his or her own initial estimate of the output gap. This estimate is based on $\underline{x}_t^j$, a $(g \times 1)$ vector of variables that the jth MPC member may take notice of (including all publicly available information and shared private information contained in asset and labour market developments, for example), plus private views that cannot be shared with the rest of the committee. This generates a member-specific initial (unbiased) estimate of the output gap (y_t), where members in the committee are indexed $j = 1, \ldots, N$. Then the underlying model for the jth member's private estimate (y_t^j) of the current output gap, y_t, is:

$$y_t^j = \beta_j \underline{x}_t^j + \varpi_t^j, \quad \varpi_t^j \sim N(0, \sigma_{\varpi^j}^2), \quad E(y_t^j) = \beta_j \underline{x}_t^j = y_t, \quad j = 1, \ldots, N.$$

This member-specific estimate of the output gap incorporates heterogeneity in the judgements about the state of the economy through different $\underline{x}_t^j$ and β_j for different members. This is the first important source of cross-member heterogeneity considered here. Since the ϖ_t^j reflect private views not shared by other committee members, we would normally expect that, across members, these estimation errors would be uncorrelated. However, in cases where there is interaction between committee members this may not hold. This will prove to be an important source of our uncovering of network interactions within the committee. However, to discuss such interactions as well as other sources of heterogeneity, we must first consider the decision-making process within the MPC, to which we turn next.

7.2.3 Two-stage committee decision-making process

Following the growing game theoretic literature on committee decision-making involving issues such as strategic voting, the acquisition of information, possible conflicts of interest and how information is communicated in committees (see Gerling et al. (2005) for a survey), we think of the decision-making process by the MPC as a two-stage process. In this first stage there is deliberation about the state of the economy (Gerlach-Kristen, 2003; Meade and Stasavage, 2004): staff economists present conjunctural analyses of recent events, members share information and views, and eventually a central forecast, with agreed error bands in the form of a fan chart, is arrived at. Nevertheless, at the second stage, despite this sharing of knowledge many MPC members will choose an interest setting different from the central estimate.

At the end of discussion and deliberation in the first stage, outlined above, a central estimate, $y_{t|t}$, of the output gap is agreed upon. This common estimate is a weighted average of the initial estimates for the m committee members. Therefore, this central bank estimate is also an unbiased estimate of the true output gap with

$$y_{t|t} = y_t + \varpi_t^b, \quad \varpi_t^b \sim N(0, \sigma_{y_t}^2).$$

This common (pooled) estimate can be thought to correspond to the fan chart of output growth published by the Bank of England. Then, for the jth member, the final estimate of y_t minimises the forecast error variance and combines optimally the central bank estimate ($y_{t|t}$) and the private estimate (y_t^j). In our model this final estimate, denoted y_t^{dj}, is obtained using the Kalman filter; see Bhattacharjee and Holly (2015) for details. This reflects heterogeneity about the effect of (forecast) uncertainty of current estimates of the output gap; seen, for example, in the fan charts of output growth. This is the second source of heterogeneity in our model; for details see Bhattacharjee and Holly (2010).[2]

In addition to heterogeneity in judgements about the state of the economy and the magnitude of the output gap, committee members may also differ in their views of the effect of interest rates on inflation and the output gap – our third important source of heterogeneity. In the context of the interest rate model under inflation forecast targeting presented in the previous subsection, this implies member-specific effects $\alpha_j\beta_{2j}$ and β_{2j} respectively. This form of heterogeneity is, in principle, similar to preference regarding the trade-off between inflation and output loss in the general form of the policy-maker's loss function; see, for example, Sibert (2002).

Accounting for the three sources of heterogeneity discussed above, and using the standard separation of observation from control to plug the optimal estimates of $y_{t|t}$ and $\pi_{t+1|t}$ into the feedback rule in Eq. (7.1), we obtain a member-specific policy rule:

$$i_t = \pi_{t|t} + \varphi_j + \frac{1}{\alpha_j\beta_{2j}}(\pi_{t+1|t} - \pi^\star) + \frac{\beta_1}{\beta_{2j}} y_{t|t} + \beta_j^{(x)} \underline{x}_t^j + + \beta_j^{(\sigma)} \sigma_{y_t} + \vartheta_{jt}, \quad j = 1, \ldots, N. \tag{7.2}$$

We can estimate this decision rule using data on the votes of individual members. This generates several potential sources of heterogeneity, as well as possible interactions between MPC members.

1. The three sources of heterogeneity discussed above are incorporated in the decision rule.
   a. *Heterogeneity of beliefs in the effect of interest rates on output and inflation.* The slope coefficients of inflation and output gap, $1/(\alpha_j\beta_{2j})$ and β_1/β_{2j} respectively, are allowed to vary across committee members.
   b. *Heterogeneity of beliefs about the degree of attention to be given to financial and labour market developments, and the state of the international economy.* Both the macroeconomic variables included in the jth member's initial estimate of the output gap ($\underline{x}_t^j$) and the corresponding coefficient vector ($\beta_j^{(x)}$) vary across MPC members. Attention to other monetary policy issues, such as forward-looking

2 In a discussion of the differing views in the September 2006 meeting of the MPC (Bank of England, 2006), there is explicit acknowledgement that different members place different weights on the same macroeconomic events and implicitly that they may hold differing views on the size of the output gap.

expectations and alternate inflation targeting mechanisms, are also encompassed in our empirical model by including a wide range of macroeconomic variables in the definition of the $\underline{x}_t^j$.

c. *Heterogeneity in the effect of forecast uncertainty*. The coefficient $\beta_j^{(\sigma)}$ on (forecast) uncertainty in current estimates of the output gap captures subjective beliefs about the importance of a member's own estimates relative to the other members and is the third important source of heterogeneity in our model. When there is more uncertainty regarding the future (forecast) output gap and inflation, policy-makers may be more hesitant to change interest rates (Bhattacharjee and Holly, 2010). However, members may differ in their response to this uncertainty. In our empirical work, we use the standard deviation in the one year ahead forecast output growth (from the output growth fan charts published by the Bank of England) as the time-varying measure of uncertainty (σ_{y_t}).
d. *Heterogeneity about where each member is on a 'dove–hawk' scale*. The member-specific fixed effects ϕ_j capture a form of classification on this scale. It measures the extent to which the jth member is a hawk (favouring increases in interest rates) or a dove (favouring decreases in interest rates). However, this classification is after conditioning on all other macro variables rather than an unconditional classification that is used more commonly.

2. Finally, ϑ_{jt} are zero mean errors that are potentially heteroscedastic and correlated across members.
   a. *Heterogeneity in activism*. The magnitude of the variance reflects heterogeneity in the degree of activism for each member (Bhattacharjee and Holly, 2010).
   b. *Network interactions*. For member j, the ϑ_{jt} are uncorrelated across meetings. However, ϑ_{jt} are correlated across members – the degree of correlation reflecting both the nature of deliberation within the committee and the degree of interactions between members. This is the source of cross-member or network interactions in this chapter, which we discuss next.
   c. *Heterogeneity in influence*. This network structure then leads to a final source of heterogeneity in our model – heterogeneity about how influential each MPC member is within the MPC and how much attention individual members pay to the views of others.

7.2.4 Network dynamics

In addition to the above forms of heterogeneity, our model allows for interaction between MPC members through information sharing over the decision-making process, but also by way of strategic interaction among members. First, the process of deliberation within the MPC involves arriving at a common estimate, $y_{t|t}$, of the output gap. This common estimate may be viewed as a weighted average of member-specific initial private estimates, y_t^j. The weights corresponding to different MPC members may be different, with higher weights accorded to MPC members who are more senior or more important within the committee. However, in any case, this averaging process implies that the central bank estimate is correlated with the initial private estimates. Then, in the second stage, the members obtain their final estimates (y_t^{dj}) by combining optimally the central bank estimate ($y_{t|t}$) and the private estimate (y_t^j). Thus, the process of deliberation and information-sharing within the MPC implies that the final estimates, and in particular the estimation errors associated with these final estimates, are expected to be correlated across the members.

Second, covariances between forecast errors in private estimates of the current output gap imply interactions over and above the sharing of individual estimates during deliberations on the output gap. These correlations arise from information that cannot be fully shared within the MPC, and are therefore related to the degree of like-mindedness between any pair. Some share a common background or experiences and may happen to share a common view of the world. In this case there will be positive covariances between the forecast errors of those who share common views.

Likewise, such correlations may also arise from strategic voting behaviour, where a group of members may try to influence the median vote within the MPC. Similarly, there may be conflicts between preferences of other members. The current literature on political economy emphasises several channels through which significant interactions may arise; see Gerling et al. (2005) and Bhattacharjee and Holly (2013) for further discussion.

Finally, recent literature on endogenous network formation also points to important roles for strategic information sharing and links (Goyal, 2007). First, transmission of information may be unidirectional or bidirectional. Granovetter (1973) interprets unidirectional transmission as a weak link and bidirectional as a strong link. Second, the quality of links may vary a lot, and network formation depends endogenously on this quality (Goyal, 2005). Third, certain forms of network architecture often emerge as equilibrium solutions, while others are not stable. For example, a periphery-sponsored star is a Nash equilibrium in Goyal (2005), while under capacity constraints Goyal and Vega-Redondo (2007) find a cycle network more meaningful. In the context of interactions between committee members, this suggests two important points. First, a network where all members try hard to obtain private information from others is often not an equilibrium solution. Second, the architecture of networks which emerges in equilibrium is useful for understanding the nature of information aggregation and constraints. Our framework for inference on cross-member interactions will inform both these aspects.

All of these forms of interaction are incorporated into our model through the network structure of the MPC. In particular, interactions can be asymmetric and even negative. Further, some members are more influenced by others than they in turn influence others, while other members may be more influential but less influenced by others. Estimation of the member-specific decision rules and network structure are discussed later.

7.3 Backdrop, data and empirical model

The backdrop to the empirical work in this chapter is the Long Expansion. For more than 15 years, starting about 1992, inflation in most western countries was consistently between 2 per cent and 3 per cent, while growth rates were consistently positive but moderate. Inflation targeting, either explicitly or implicitly, became the main monetary policy framework and increasingly central banks became more independent. However, in the UK, although an explicit inflation target was adopted in 1992 the Bank of England did not gain operational independence until 1997.

The long period of expansion came to an end in approximately 2008, with the onset of a global financial crisis. Macroeconomic developments over the Long Expansion and the crisis are documented in several papers, for example in a special issue of *Oxford Economic Papers* on 'Monetary Policy Before, During, and After the Crisis'; see, in particular Cobham (2013) and Nelson (2013).

7.3.1 The role of three regimes of the MPC

The subject of our analysis is three sub-groups or regimes of the MPC. The inclusion of members in each regime was guided by the availability of enough voting records for a meaningful empirical study. The first selection (Regime 1) covers the period June 1997 to June 2003. The second (Regime 2) is for the period January 2004 to September 2006; and the final selection (Regime 3) is for October 2006 to October 2011.

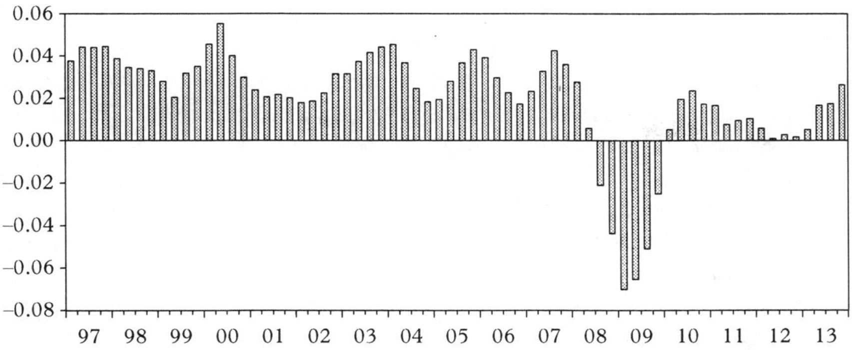

Figure 7.1. Year-on-year quarterly growth in GDP: 1997q1–2013q4

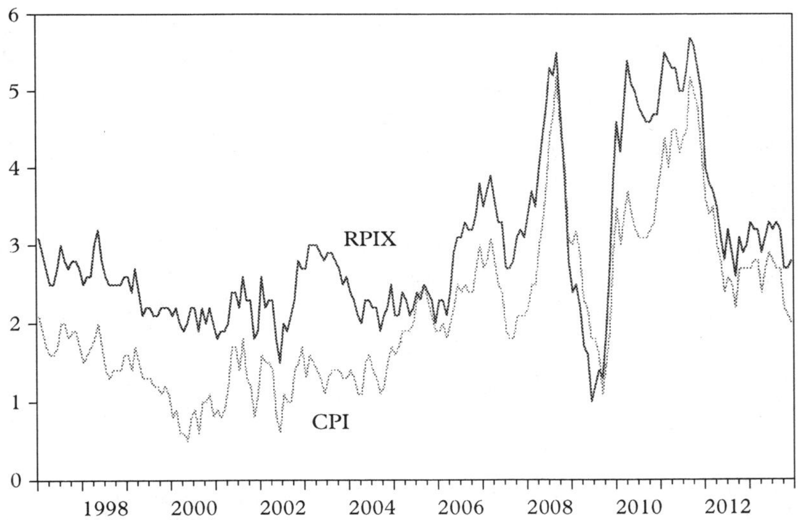

Figure 7.2. Year-on-year inflation: 1997 m1–2013 m12

This classification allows us to examine the possibility of an evolving pattern of cross-member heterogeneity and network structures within the MPC as the membership of the committee changed over time. It also allows us to match differing MPCs to changing economic events.

In Figures 7.1 and 7.2 we plot the quarterly annual percentage change in GDP and the annual monthly percentage change in both RPIX and CPI. The original target set from May 1997 was for a 2.5 per cent ± 1 per cent increase in the RPIX (Retail Price Index (RPI) for the UK, excluding mortgage interest payments). In December 2003 the target was changed to 2 per cent ± 1 per cent for the CPI (Consumer Price Index for the UK, excluding mortgage interest payments and housing costs). This provided the backdrop to the Great Moderation, and our expansion pre-crisis regime (Regime 2) begins in January 2004. The Bank of England successfully guided the RPIX within the target margins up to 2004. It continued to do so with the CPI until March 2007, when for the first time the CPI at 3.1 per cent exceeded the upper margin of 3 per cent. However, while the prospects for inflation and output growth appeared rosy over this period there were a number of developments in UK housing and financial markets that with hindsight suggested that all was not well.

The end of the Great Moderation or Long Expansion period is more ambiguous. It is clear that the volatility of inflation in the UK started to increase in the early part of 2007, but output continued to grow and did not turn down until the end of 2007. The subprime share of the US mortgage market peaked in 2006, and in the latter part of the year the subprime market collapsed. This started the cascade of events that eventually led to the end of the Great Moderation. So our final regime, starting in October 2006, begins before the most likely onset of the financial crisis, but most of its duration lies firmly inside the crisis.

Focussing on transitions between the three regimes, we ask the following question. Did the conduct of monetary policy change over the transition between the three regimes? If so, how?

Specifically, our question focusses on the following three aspects of monetary policy decision-making:

- *The global economy*: What macroeconomic factors did the MPC members consider? We focus on both conventional and somewhat unconventional measures, and in particular, on strong cross-sectional dependence (CD) and integration with the global economy.
- *Heterogeneity*: What role did personalities within the MPC play? In particular, is there evidence of heterogeneity within the MPC and, if so, did the nature of heterogeneity change in the transition between the three regimes?
- *Network dynamics*: Did the network structure of the MPC change over the transitions and, if so, how?

The context in which we seek answers to these questions is one of an inflation (forecast) targeting MPC, where there is potentially heterogeneity between members, reflecting both different personalities and preferences, and therefore incorporating safeguards against an individual conservative central banker (Backus and Driffill, 1985; Waller, 1992; Sibert, 2003). In addition to heterogeneity, our economic model of the

MPC considers an important role for deliberation and exchange of opinions within the committee. This in turn generates network dynamics, reflecting variations in the influence that each member has within the committee and variations in how much each MPC member is influenced by other members of the committee.

7.3.2 Data

The primary objective of the empirical study is to understand changes across the different regimes of the MPC. Our analyses take special account of heterogeneity and interaction in decision-making, within the context of the model of committee decision-making presented in the previous section.

7.3.2.1 Voting records of individual MPC members Our dependent variables are the decisions of the individual members of the MPC. The sources for these data are the minutes of the MPC meetings. Since mid-1997, when data on the votes of individual members started being made publicly available, the MPC has met once a month to decide on the base rate for the next month.[3] Over most of this period, the MPC has had nine members at any given time: the Governor (of the Bank of England), four internal members (senior staff at the Bank of England) and four external members. External members were usually appointed for a period of three years with the possibility of it being extended to a total of six years. Because of changes in the internal and external members, the composition of the MPC has changed reasonably frequently.

For the study of heterogeneity we use the voting records of all members who were ever included in an MPC during each of the three regime periods. However, to facilitate the study of network dynamics within the MPC we focus on five selected members, including the Governor, two internal members and two external members across the three different periods. For the first regime we choose five members who were in the MPC throughout the period: George (the Governor), Clementi and King (the two internal members) and Buiter and Julius (the two external members).[4] However, the votes of all MPC members during this period are used also as instruments when we analyse cross-member heterogeneity and integration with the global economy.

3 The MPC met twice in September 2001. The special meeting was called after the events of 09/11.

4 The sixth member was Ian Plenderleith. However, to retain continuity of structure across different committee compositions under study, we have chosen only five out of the six available members; Plenderleith's votes were very similar to those of Eddie George.

Table 7.1. Voting records of selected MPC members (period: June 1997 to October 2011), reproduced with permission from Bhattacharjee and Holly (2015)

		Votes			Dissent		
Member	**Meetings**	**Lower**	**No change**	**Raise**	**Total**	**Low**	**High**
Barker (Ba)	109	20	78	11	5	4	1
Bean (Be)	134	22	104	8	5	5	0
Buiter (Bu)	36	10	10	16	17	8	9
Clementi (C)	63	14	39	10	4	1	3
George (G)	74	15	51	6	0	0	0
Julius (J)	45	18	25	2	14	14	0
King (K) (all meetings)	174	23	122	29	14	0	14
King (K) (as Governor)	100	10	79	11	2	0	2
Lomax (L)	60	4	49	7	4	3	1
Nickell (N)	73	23	41	9	17	13	4
Sentence (S)	56	8	28	20	17	0	17
Tucker (T)	113	10	90	13	7	1	6

Likewise, we consider two further periods during Mervyn King's Governorship. The first is the 35 month period July 2003 to May 2006,[5] with the five MPC members: Governor King, internal members Bean and Lomax and external members Barker and Nickell. In the last regime – October 2006 to October 2011 – the five members are Governor King, internal members Bean and Tucker and external members Barker and Sentence.[6] So Mervyn King sat on all three committees and Bean for the last two.

The voting patterns[7] of these selected MPC members suggest substantial variation (Table 7.1). For example, of the 45 meetings which Julius attended, 14 votes were against the consensus decision, and all of these were for a lower interest rate. On the other hand, King disagreed with the consensus decision in 14 of the 174 meetings he attended, voting for a higher interest rate each time. By contrast, Buiter dissented in 17 meetings out of 36, voting on eight occasions for a lower interest rate and nine times in favour of a higher one. See also King (2002) and Gerlach-Kristen (2004).

5 Note that this period corresponds only approximately with our periodisation for the expansion pre-crisis regime. Whereas our Regime 2 begins in January 2004, the 35-month period considered here begins in July 2003. We decided not to align the time periods precisely since this would lead to a substantial reduction in sample data.

6 See Bhattacharjee and Holly (2013) for further discussion on the choice of periods and MPC members.

7 It should be noted that Eddie George as Governor was the only member never to dissent. The reason for this is that the Governor deliberately chose to speak last and never went against the view of the committee as a whole.

Furthermore, the votes of MPC members are highly clustered, with a majority of the votes proposing no change in the base rate. The final decisions on interest rate changes are all similarly clustered. For the Bank of England's MPC as a whole over the period June 1997 to October 2011, 75 per cent of the meetings decided to keep the base rate at its current level, 10 per cent recommended a rise of 25 basis points, 9 per cent recommended a reduction of 25 basis points and the remaining 6 per cent a reduction of 50 basis points or more.

This clustering has to be taken into account when studying individual votes and committee decisions of the MPC. We do not observe changes in interest rates on a continuous or unrestricted scale: we have a non-continuous or limited dependent variable. Moreover, changes in interest rates are in multiples of 25 basis points. Therefore we use an interval regression framework; other authors have used other limited dependent variable frameworks, such as the logit/probit or multinomial/ordered logit/probit framework.

7.3.2.2 Macroeconomic indicators In order to explain the votes of MPC members, we collected information on the kinds of data that the MPC would have looked at for each monthly meeting. Not all of this information is made use of in this chapter, but the important issue was to ensure that we conditioned only on what information was actually available at the time of each meeting. Assessing monetary policy decisions in the presence of uncertainty about forecast levels of inflation and the output gap (including uncertainty in both forecast output levels and potential output) requires collection of real-time data available to the policy-makers when interest rate decisions are made, as well as measures of forecast uncertainty. This contrasts with many studies of monetary policy, which are based on realised (and subsequently revised) measures of economic activity (Orphanides, 2003).

We use information on unemployment (where this typically refers to unemployment three months prior to the MPC meeting, as well as data on asset markets (housing prices, share prices and exchange rates). We measure unemployment by the year-on-year change in the International Labour Organization (ILO) rate of unemployment, lagged three months. The ILO rate of unemployment is computed using three-month rolling average estimates of the number of ILO-unemployed persons and size of labour force (ILO definition), both collected from the Office for National Statistics (ONS) Labour Force Survey. Housing prices are measured by the year-on-year growth rates of the Nationwide House Price Index (seasonally adjusted) for the previous month (Source: Nationwide). Share prices and exchange rates are measured by the year-on-year growth rate of the FTSE 100 share index and the effective exchange rate respectively at the end of the previous month (Source: Bank of England). Other information included in the model is the current level of inflation – measured by the year-on-year growth rate of RPIX inflation lagged two months for the Governor George period, and a similar measure based on the CPI for the Governor King period (Source: ONS).[8]

Our model also includes expected rates of future inflation and forecasts of current and future output. One difficulty with using the Bank's forecasts of inflation is that they are not sufficiently informative. For the assumed policy horizon the Bank targets inflation over a two-year horizon, so it always publishes a forecast in which (in expectation) inflation hits the target in two years' time. To do anything else would be internally inconsistent. Instead, as a measure of future inflation, we use the four (or five) year ahead inflation expectations implicit in bond markets at the time of the MPC meeting, data on which can be inferred from the Bank of England's forward yield curve estimates obtained from index-linked bonds.[9]

For current output, we use the annual growth of two-month-lagged monthly GDP published by the National Institute of Economic and Social Research and for one-year-ahead forecast GDP growth, we use the Bank of England's model based mean quarterly forecasts.

Uncertainty about the future macroeconomic environment and private perceptions about the importance of such uncertainty play an important role in the model developed in this chapter. The extent to which there is uncertainty about the forecast of the Bank of England can be inferred from the fan charts published in the Inflation Report. As a measure of uncertainty in the future macroeconomic environment, we use the standard deviation of the one-year-ahead forecast. These measures are obtained from the Bank of England's fan charts of output; details regarding these measures are discussed elsewhere (Britton et al., 1998).

Figure 7.3 shows asset and housing market developments, Figure 7.4 shows output growth and inflation expectations and Figure 7.5 shows forecast uncertainty. It would appear from the plots that our selection of regimes reflects different economic circumstances. The first period is one of economic expansion and stable inflation. The second period begins to show declining growth in housing prices, but a recovery and

8 Since December 2003, the inflation target has been based on CPI inflation rather than RPIX.

9 The two-year-ahead expected inflation figures are not available for the entire sample period. Based on availability, we use the four-year-ahead figures for the first chosen period, and five-year-ahead expectations for the latter two periods. In practice the inflation yield curve tends to be very flat after two years.

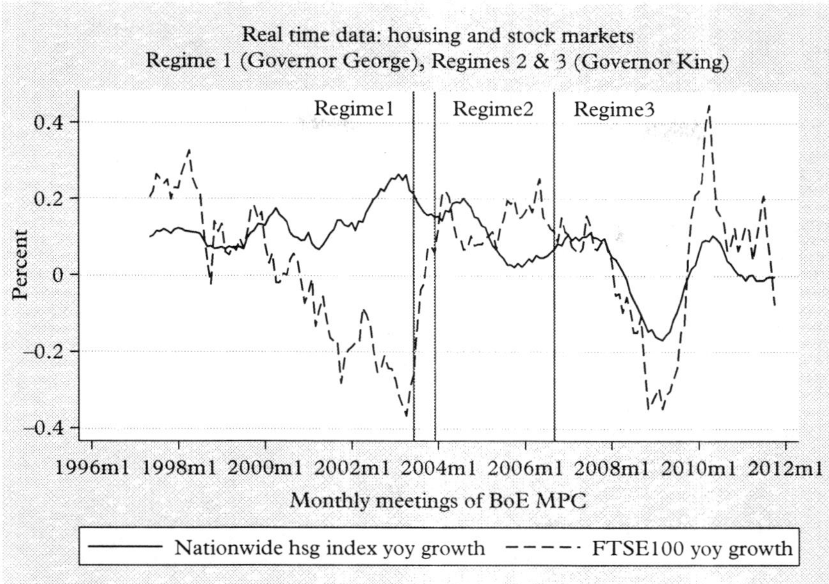

Figure 7.3. Housing and stock markets over time, and over the three regimes

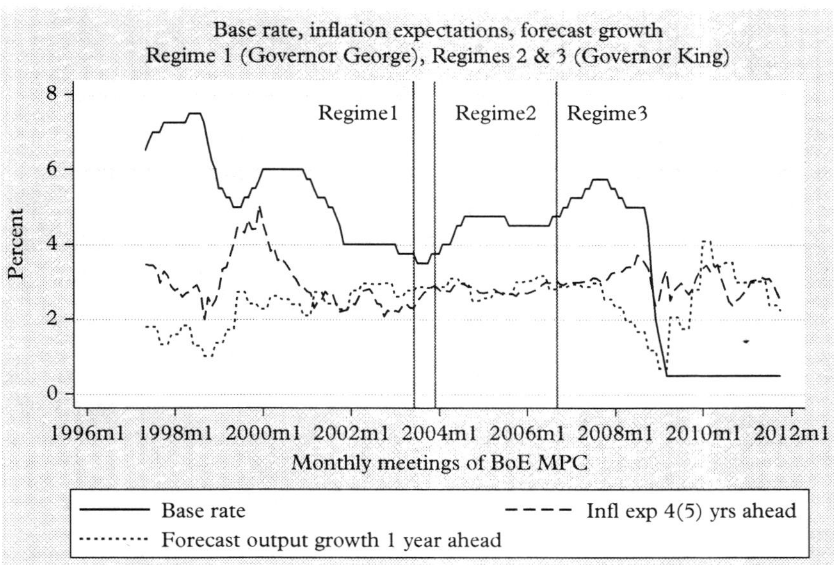

Figure 7.4. (Base) interest rates, inflation expectations and forecast output growth over the regimes

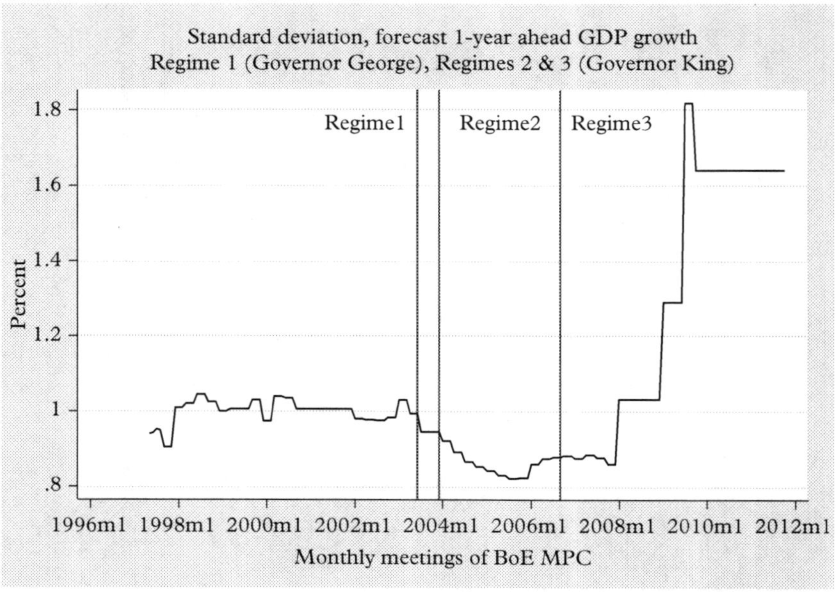

Figure 7.5. Forecast uncertainty (in output growth) over time, and over the three regimes

relative stability in share prices. The final period shows a very sharp increase in forecast uncertainty, a fall in asset and house prices and the end of the Long Expansion.

7.3.2.3 Strong dependence For the last two regimes we increased the conditioning macroeconomic variables because GMM estimates of cross-member interactions suggested a potential violation of the spatial granularity (stationarity) condition (Pesaran and Tosetti, 2011). This suggested the presence of strong dependence, potentially driven by hidden time-specific factors. This led us to re-examine the minutes of MPC meetings and speeches by MPC members to try to identify such latent factors. We found suggestions that, during the Governor King period, monetary policy was increasingly attentive to world developments, and policy itself may also have been coordinated across central banks. Therefore we included as additional explanatory factors several international economic variables: specifically, a measure of global GDP growth (Source: IfW, Kiel Institute for the World Economy) and US interest rates (Source: Federal Reserve).[10]

10 See Bhattacharjee and Holly (2013) for further discussion on spatial strong dependence and our choice of macroeconomic variables to address the issue.

7.3.3 Empirical model

We start with the model of individual voting behaviour within the MPC (Eq. (7.2)) developed in the previous section. The model includes individual specific heterogeneity in the fixed effects and in inflation and the output gap, forecast uncertainty, labour, housing and financial markets, as well as the international economy.

7.3.3.1 Individual decision rules of MPC members We estimate this model where the dependent variable is the *j*th member's preferred change in the (base) interest rate. In other words, our dependent variable, υ_{jt}, represents the deviation of the preferred interest rate for the *j*th member (at the meeting in month *t*) from the current (base) rate of interest r_{t-1}:

$$\upsilon_{jt} = i_{jt} - r_{t-1}.$$

The model is set up in a way that captures the idea that, absent new information sufficiently strong to recommend a change in interest rates, the default vote will be for 'no change'. Therefore we estimate the following empirical model of individual decision rules within the MPC:

$$\begin{aligned} \upsilon_{jt} = \phi_j + \beta_j^{(r)} \Delta r_{t-1} + \beta_j^{(\pi_0)} \pi_t + \beta_j^{(\pi_4)} \pi_{t+4|t} + \beta_j^{(y_0)} y_{t|t} \\ + \beta_j^{(y_1)} y_{t+1|t} + \beta_j^{(\underline{x})} \underline{x}_t + \beta_j^{(\sigma)} \sigma_{y_{t+1|t}} + \vartheta_{jt}, \end{aligned} \quad (7.3)$$

where $\underline{x}_t$ represents current observations on unemployment (Δu_t) and the underlying state of asset markets: housing, equity and the foreign exchange market ($P_{hsg,t}$, $P_{FTSE,t}$ and $P_{exch,t}$ respectively). In addition, for the Governor King regime, we include in $\underline{x}_t$ variables representing the international economic environment: global GDP growth and US interest rates ($y_{World,t|t}$ and $r_{US,t}$ respectively). The standard deviation of the one-year-ahead forecast of output growth is denoted by $\sigma_{y_{t+1|t}}$; this term is included to incorporate the notion that the stance of monetary policy may depend on the uncertainty relating to forecast future levels of output and inflation. Increased uncertainty about the current state of the economy will tend to bias policy towards caution in changing interest rates (Bhattacharjee and Holly, 2010). In particular, the literature suggests that optimal monetary policy may be more cautious (rather than activist) under greater uncertainty in the forecast or real-time estimates of output gap and inflation (Issing, 2002; Aoki, 2003; Orphanides, 2003). Since, as previously discussed, the published inflation forecast is not sufficiently informative, we confined ourselves to uncertainty relating to forecasts of future output growth.

There are two additional features of our data-generating process that render the estimation exercise nonstandard. First, the dependent variable is observed in the form of votes, which are highly clustered interval-censored outcomes based on the underlying decision rules. Second, the regression errors are interrelated across the members.

The observed dependent variable, $v_{jt,obs}$, is the truncated version of the latent policy response variable of the *j*th member, v_{jt}, which we model as

$$v_{jt,obs} = \begin{cases} -0.25 & \text{if} \quad v_{jt} \in [-0.375, -0.20) \\ 0 & \text{if} \quad v_{jt} \in [-0.20, 0.20] \\ 0.25 & \text{if} \quad v_{jt} \in (0.20, 0.375], \text{ and} \end{cases}$$

$$v_{jt} \in (v_{jt,obs} - 0.125, v_{jt,obs} + 0.125) \text{ whenever } |v_{jt,obs}| > 0.325.$$

The wider truncation interval when there is a vote for no change in interest rates (i.e., for $v_{jt,obs} = 0$) may be interpreted as reflecting the conservative stance of monetary policy under uncertainty with a bias in favour of leaving interest rates unchanged; that is, excess zero clustering. The choice of intervals corresponding to different votes is somewhat arbitrary. However, the choices are made using cross-validation and, moreover, our empirical results are robust to alternative interval boundaries.

As discussed in the previous section, the regression errors, ϑ_{jt}, are uncorrelated across different meetings for a given MPC member, but possibly correlated across members. The degree of correlation reflects both the nature of deliberation within the committee before arriving at a common estimate of the output gap, and the degree of like-mindedness or strategic interaction between members. We represent the interrelationship between the ϑ_{jt} as a cross-sectional (spatial) autoregressive process as:

$$\begin{aligned} \vartheta_{jt} &= \sum_{i \neq j} w_{ij} \vartheta_{it} + \psi_{jt}, \quad \text{for } j = 1, \ldots, m, \\ \Rightarrow \underline{\vartheta}_t &= W \underline{\vartheta}_t + \underline{\psi}_t, \end{aligned} \tag{7.4}$$

where $\underline{\vartheta}_t = (\vartheta_{1t}, \vartheta_{2t}, \ldots, \vartheta_{mt})'$, W is a spatial (or cross-sectional) interaction weights matrix with zero diagonal elements such that $(I - W)$ is nonsingular (here, I denotes the identity matrix) and $\underline{\psi}_t = (\psi_{1t}, \psi_{2t}, \ldots, \psi_{mt})'$ is a vector of uncorrelated errors that are possibly heteroscedastic. The square matrix $W_{(m \times m)}$ captures the network structure of the m chosen MPC members; the choice criterion, discussed above, is partly conditioned on data availability and partly based on GMM moment conditions (Bhattacharjee and Holly, 2013).

In combination with the interval regression model (Eq. (7.3)), the residuals (Eq. (7.4)) describe a model known in the spatial econometrics literature as the spatial error model with autoregressive errors (Anselin, 1988, 1999). The elements in the (spatial) weights matrix W describe the strength of interaction between different MPC members. The purely idiosyncratic part in the policy reaction function of each member, ψ_{jt}, are derived from the private and unshared information that each member possesses. These idiosyncratic errors are uncorrelated across the members and are allowed to have different variances for different MPC members; the magnitude of the variance indicates how activist the member is.

7.3.3.2 Estimation The objectives of our empirical exercise are: first, to estimate separate policy reaction functions (Eq. (7.3)) for each MPC member in the three regimes; second, to estimate the corresponding network structure through the spatial weights matrix, W; third, to use estimates of the above model to infer the distribution of heterogeneous coefficients in a random coefficients model (Swamy, 1970) setting; and fourth, to use these estimates to infer changes over the transitions between the three regimes.

Bhattacharjee and Holly (2015) use the differences in the estimates of the policy reaction function across the different MPC members to infer the degree of heterogeneity, and the elements of the estimated spatial weight matrix to study the strength (and direction) of interactions. Furthermore, the interaction weights are used to infer heterogeneity in the influence of each member and the degree to which each member is in turn influenced by other members of the committee. We use these results, but our focus here is in understanding monetary policy decision-making changes over the three periods.

Under the maintained assumptions that (a) the regression errors are uncorrelated and homoscedastic across meetings, but potentially heteroscedastic across members, (b) the errors are Gaussian with zero mean and (c) the response variable is interval-censored, we estimate the policy reaction function for each member (Eq. (7.3)) by interval regression. The interval regression model (Amemiya, 1973) is a generalisation of the tobit model where the truncation in the dependent variable is possibly different for different observation units, and the truncation cutoffs are known.

Based on the random coefficients model (Swamy, 1970), where a random effects assumption is placed on the slope coefficients across MPC members, we simulate data from the joint distribution of the heterogeneous slope coefficient estimates. A kernel density estimator is then used for this cross-sectional distribution (Wand and Jones, 1995) to infer changes over the different regimes, using the cross-sectional distribution of heterogeneous effects across MPC members.

Because the response variable is interval-censored the residuals also exhibit similar limited dependence, and this results in significant challenges in estimating the network structure; see Bhattacharjee and Holly (2013, 2015) for more discussion about the problem and its potential solutions. We estimate the model using interval estimation Amemiya (1973) separately for each member and obtain interval-censored residuals using the initial censoring scheme. We place these interval-censored residuals at their expected values given that they lie in the respective intervals. The cross-sectional interactions weights matrix, W, is then estimated separately for each period under study using the GMM methodology proposed in Bhattacharjee and Holly (2013).

The choice of macroeconomic variables included in the policy reaction function is partly informed by the estimates of the spatial (interaction) matrix W. Specifically, we ensure that adequate explanatory variables are included so that the estimated interaction weights satisfy the spatial granularity condition for 'no strong dependence' (Pesaran and Tosetti, 2011); this condition is verified using the spatial granularity approximate p-value, $G(p)$, proposed by Bhattacharjee and Holly (2013) and the weak CD test (Pesaran, 2015).

7.4 Results and discussion

In this section, we discuss our empirical results, focussing on changes in the nature of monetary policy decisions at the Bank of England's MPC. The transitions between these regimes were marked by some important institutional changes connected with monetary policy at the Bank of England.

7.4.1 Integration with global economy

Interactions between MPC members, by way of deliberation and discussion or like-mindedness and strategic interactions, play a key role in our economic model of MPC decision-making. However, before we can analyse these (hidden) relationships it is important to allow for any factors that influence all members of a committee. Pesaran (2006) has highlighted a key distinction between cross-sectional (or spatial) dependence due to the effect of latent factors (spatial strong dependence) and that arising from the positions of units in space (spatial weak dependence). In essence, strong dependence needs to be explicitly controlled for, and only then can we interpret weak dependence as an indicator of a network structure.

The distinction between strong and weak spatial dependence is therefore crucial. Essentially, all macroeconomic factors that contribute to strong spatial dependence need first to be included in the model before network dynamics (weak dependence) can be studied. Further, Pesaran and Tosetti (2011) relate strong spatial dependence to the spatial granularity (stationarity) condition that the spatial weights matrix has row and column norms less than unity. This ensures weak dependence (structural interactions) rather than strong spatial dependence (factor-based interactions.[11]

Applying these tests to the baseline decision rules[12] during the first regime, we find no evidence that the spatial granularity condition is violated. However, the same is not true for the other two regimes. This led us to examine the minutes of MPC meetings and speeches by MPC members to try to identify such latent factors. We found suggestions that monetary policy was increasingly affected by world developments, and policy itself may also have been coordinated across central banks, especially in response to the events of September 2001. Therefore we included several international economic variables: specifically, a measure of global GDP growth and US interest rates.[13] This eliminated strong spatial dependence for the last two regimes.

It appears that monetary policy at the Bank of England had changed since the first regime. With global integration of economies, and in particular the adverse impact of housing and financial market shocks, the MPC had started to pay much more attention to developments in the global economy.

7.4.2 Heterogeneity between members

Previously we have observed substantial heterogeneity in the estimated reaction functions across different MPC members.[14] Here we ask: has the nature of heterogeneity changed over the three regimes and, if so,

11 See Bhattacharjee and Holly (2011) and Pesaran and Tosetti (2011) for further discussion. The condition can be tested using procedures developed in Bhattacharjee and Holly (2013) and Pesaran (2015).

12 This baseline model includes as explanatory factors: current inflation and output gap; inflation expectations; forecast output growth; housing and financial market conditions; and forecast uncertainty in output growth. Cross-member heterogeneity is allowed for the effect of all these factors.

13 We also experimented with several other variables, including US inflation, euro area inflation and growth rates for the European Union countries, OECD countries and China. The most parsimonious and adequate model was identified as one including the world growth rate and US interest rates; hence only these variables were retained.

14 Bhattacharjee and Holly (2015).

how? For this purpose, we nest our interval regression model within the framework of a random coefficients model (Swamy, 1970). Besley et al. (2008) have modelled heterogeneity across MPC members using a random coefficients model. However, our approach is different. Whereas they assume that the coefficients are independent of regression errors and all included covariates, and that its cross-sectional distribution is Gaussian, we allow for unrestricted heterogeneity. Accordingly, we estimate the model as a heterogeneous (fixed) coefficients model. Then we use the estimated slope coefficients together with their standard errors to infer the cross-sectional features of its distribution.

Specifically, we draw random samples of heterogeneous (across members) coefficients from the cross-sectional distributions implied by our estimates of individual member-specific policy rules. Based on these Monte Carlo draws, we obtain kernel density estimates (Wand and Jones, 1995), using Gaussian kernels, of the implied cross-sectional distribution. These estimated densities are plotted separately for the three regimes and constitute the basis for our analyses.

The kernel density plots in Figure 7.6 represent heterogeneous responses to inflation expectations and growth forecasts. The plots show substantial changes over the three regimes. Comparing the first and third regimes, the MPC are much more concerned with inflation and output in the later period. Although the second regime is more concerned with inflation compared to the first regime, the effect on output expectations is less clear cut.

Similar heterogeneity is evident in the responses to financial and housing market conditions (Figure 7.7). Overall, and somewhat contrary to our *a priori* expectations, MPC members were more mindful of other market factors during the first regime, and paid much less attention to equity and housing markets in the final regime. It would therefore appear that, with a major boom in equity (and house) prices, much more attention was paid to these factors; with the crash, less attention ensued, and the second regime lies somewhere in between. Further, there is distinct evidence of bimodal densities. This may be that MPC members come in two types: those that pay no attention to other markets and those that do. Essentially, what changed during the transition from the first to the third regime is the balance between these two types.

Finally, the changing patterns of heterogeneous responses to forecast uncertainty are also quite illuminating (Figure 7.8). Bhattacharjee and Holly (2010) emphasised an important role for forecast uncertainty in monetary policy decision-making. Supporting evidence is seen from the plots. With the first regime, higher uncertainty leads to passive monetary policy, potentially because the option to wait for stronger signals is

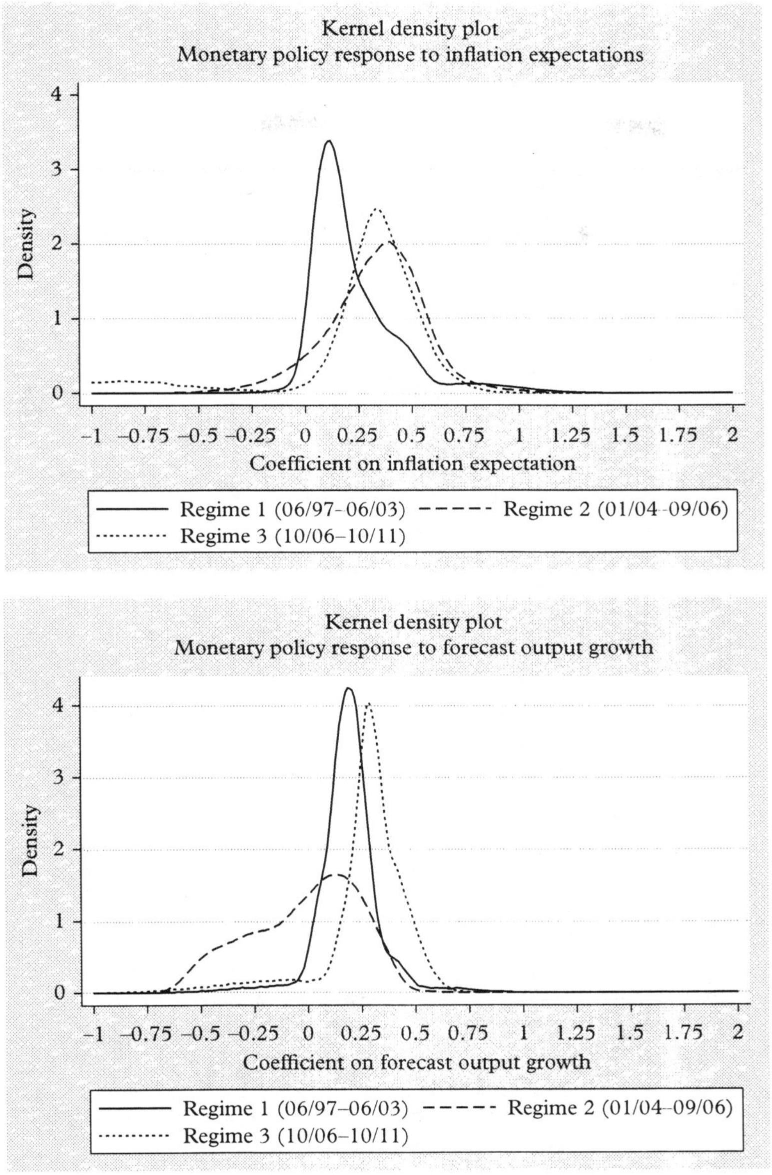

Figure 7.6. Heterogeneity in monetary policy responses to inflation expectations and growth

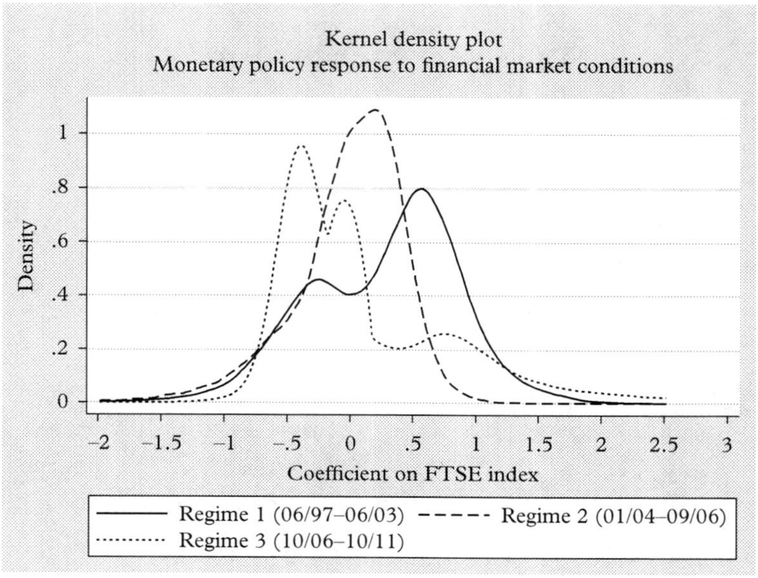

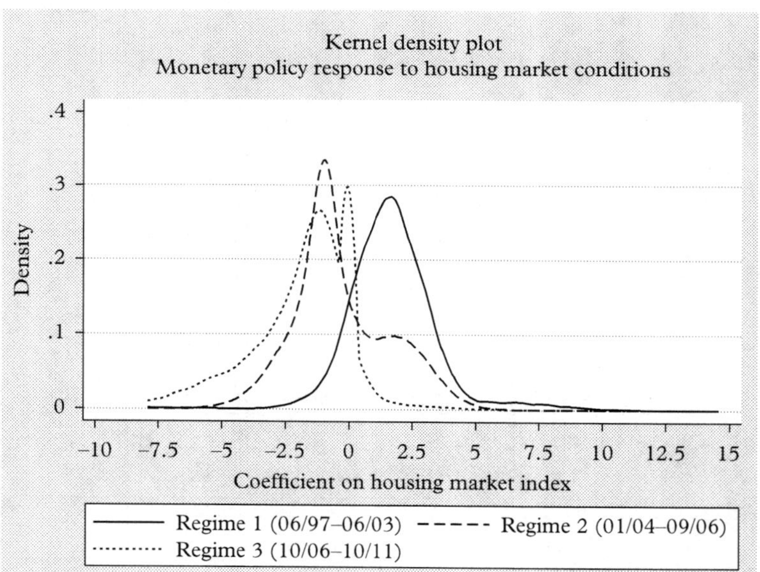

Figure 7.7. Heterogeneity in monetary policy responses to financial and housing markets

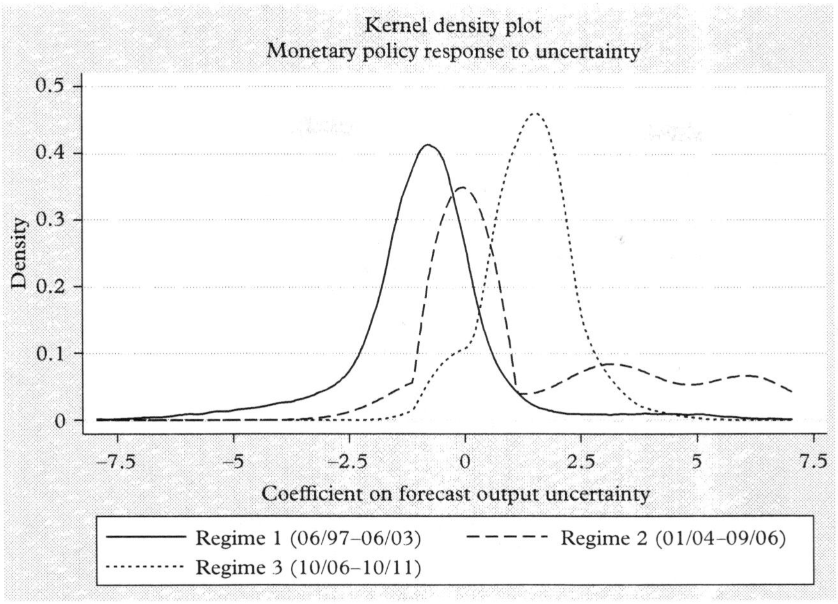

Figure 7.8. Heterogeneity in monetary policy responses to forecast uncertainty

available. However, during the crisis period, higher uncertainty is associated with more aggressive policy.

Overall, our analyses of heterogeneity reflect significant shifts in policy reaction functions of the three regimes. In general, the evidence points towards an enhanced impact of inflation expectations and output growth during the crisis, and a lesser role for financial and housing markets. During the crisis, there is also evidence of more aggressive policy in the face of uncertainty. Importantly, during second regime there was a larger role for heterogeneity and personalities.

7.4.3 Network dynamics

Finally, we estimate the interactions weight matrix, W, for the three regimes. This allows us to draw some implications about network structures. We have discussed the compositions of the three committees in the previous section.

Figure 7.9 plots a graphical representation of each of the three regimes. Each node in the graph is a chosen member from the specific

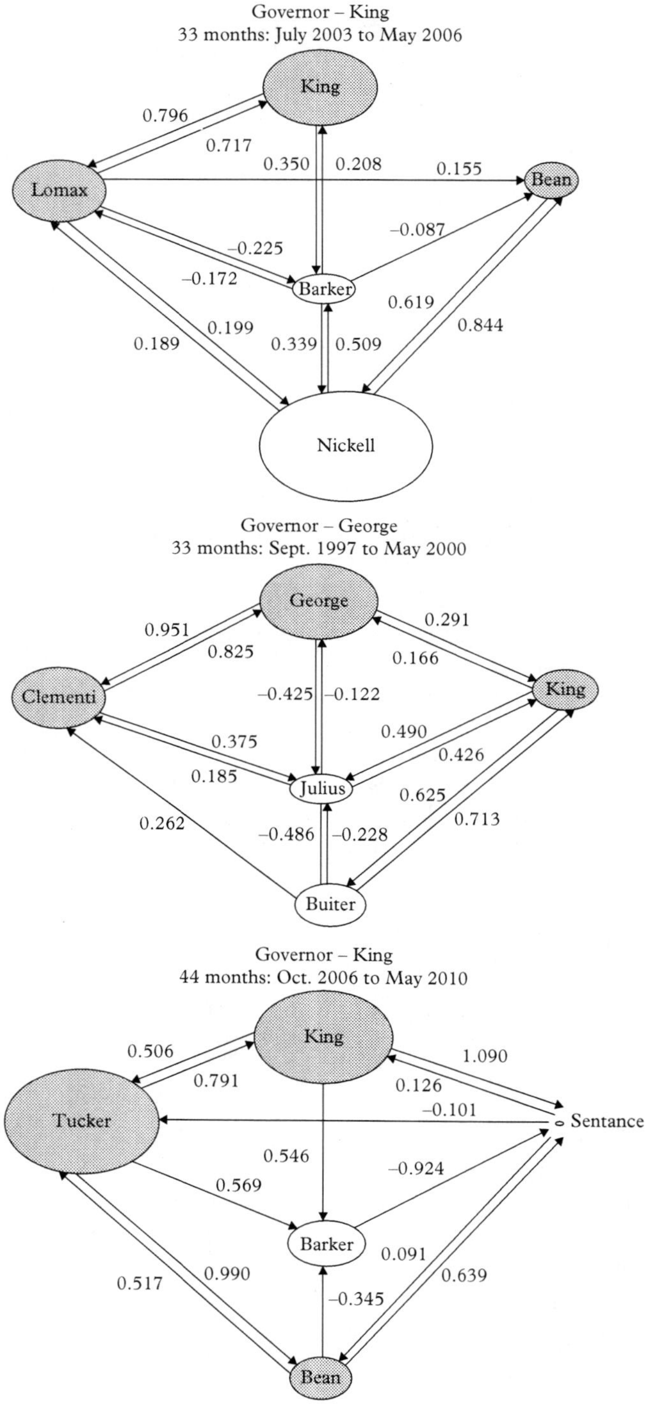

Figure 7.9. MPC network structures over the three regimes
Source: Reproduced with permission from Bhattacharjee and Holly, 2015.

MPC. A pair of nodes (say, node i and node j) are connected by a directed edge $i \rightarrow j$ if, in the estimated interaction weights matrix W, the element w_{ji} is statistically significant at the 5 per cent level.

Some features are common to the network structures during the three regimes. First, the networks are highly asymmetric, which in turn has important theoretical implications. Specifically, they indicate significant constraints within the MPC in communication and information sharing. Second, there are some negative interaction weights, reflecting, perhaps, a lack of like-mindedness or strategic positioning into antagonistic poles. Third, there is large heterogeneity in the degree of influence that each member has within the committee, and the degree to which each member is influenced by other MPC members. In fact, some members listen more to others, but are still very important members within the network. Fourth, internal members (from within the Bank of England) are in general more influential, but the Governor is not always the most influential MPC member.

We measure the strength of the jth member's influence on others by a quantity, influence, obtained as the sum of the squared weights for directed edges originating from node j. We measure the strength of the influence of others on the jth member by 'influenced', the sum of squared weights for directed edges pointing into node j. In other words, influence is the sum of squares of elements in the jth column of W that are significant at the 5 per cent level. Likewise, influenced is computed as the sum of the squared (significant) elements in the jth row of W.

Each node in the network diagram (Figure 7.9) is represented by an ellipse with size proportional to how influential the corresponding MPC member actually was.

Finally, if we look at transitions between the regimes, the MPC network is tighter and well connected in crisis, when it is 'all hands on board' time. By contrast, the network is least closely knit during the second regime, when the personalities are the most important. Furthermore, during the crisis external members were more integrated into the network as well. This reflects how a combination of changing personalities and external economic events shows up in the network dynamics over the three regimes.

7.5 Conclusion

In this chapter we have examined changes in the nature and character of monetary policy decision-making at the Bank of England from the early days of Bank of England independence through to the crisis. We considered three periods in all. Our empirical analysis is based on an economic model that suggests a wide variety of heterogeneity across policy-makers. The model also suggests that voting behaviour across the committee may be interrelated in several ways. While part of the interactions may be due to discussion and deliberation within the committee, it is also possible that there is strategic interaction among committee members; these interactions are partly driven by like-mindedness and conflicting preferences.

Our empirical study of voting behaviour within the Bank of England's MPC over the transition between the three regimes provides a numbers of interesting findings. First, monetary policy in the UK has become increasingly integrated with the global economy. International developments have influenced MPC decision-making much more since the first regime. Second, the nature of heterogeneity has changed over the three regimes. Both inflation expectations and forecast output growth mattered more during the crisis, whereas developments in the financial and housing markets had more impact during the earlier period. Uncertainty led to more aggressive monetary policy during the crisis, but not during the two other regimes pre-crisis. Personalities were more important during the middle regime. Third, network dynamics have also changed substantially, with the network becoming better connected during the crisis, and external members also becoming more integral to the committee network.

These findings contrast sharply with the view, expressed elsewhere in the literature and economic commentaries, that monetary policy in the Bank of England's MPC has been largely passive and has not reacted substantially to the crisis. The instruments of monetary policy have also changed dramatically over the crisis, with Quantitative Easing (QE) playing a major role. Further attention to QE in relation to decision-making within the MPC lies in the domain of future work.

References

Alesina, A., (1987). Macroeconomic policy in a two-party system as a repeated game. Quarterly Journal of Economics 102, 651–678.

Amemiya, T., (1973). Regression analysis when the dependent variable is truncated normal. Econometrica 41, 997–1016.

Anselin, L., (1988). Spatial Econometrics: Methods and Models. Kluwer Academic Publishers, Dordrecht, The Netherlands.

(1999). Spatial econometrics. In: Baltagi, B.H. (Ed.), A Companion to Theoretical Econometrics. Oxford, Basil Blackwell, pp. 310–330.

Aoki, K., (2003). On the optimal monetary policy response to noisy indicators. Journal of Monetary Economics 50(3), 501–523.

Backus, D., Driffill, J., (1985). Inflation and reputation. American Economic Review 75, 530–538.

Bailey, A., Schonhardt-Bailey, C., (2008). Does deliberation matter in FOMC monetary policymaking? The Volcker revolution of 1979. Political Analysis 16, 404–427.

Bank of England, (2006). Minutes of the Monetary Policy Committee meeting held on 6 and 7 September 2006. Available from: http://www.bankofengland.co.uk/publications/minutes/mpc/pdf/2006/index.htm.

Belden, S., (1989). Policy preferences of FOMC members as revealed by dissenting votes. Journal of Money, Credit and Banking 21(4), 432–441.

Bernanke, B.S., Gertler, M., (2001). Should central banks respond to movements in asset prices? American Economic Review 91(2), 253–257.

Besley, T., Meads, N., Surico, P., (2008). Insiders versus outsiders in monetary policymaking. American Economic Review: Papers & Proceedings 98(2), 218–223.

Bhattacharjee, A., Holly, S., (2010). Rational partisan theory, uncertainty and spatial voting: evidence for the Bank of England's MPC. Economics and Politics, 22(2), 151–179.

(2011). Structural interactions in spatial panels. Empirical Economics 40(1), 69–94.

(2013). Understanding interactions in social networks and committees. Spatial Economic Analysis 8(1), 23–53.

Bhattacharjee, A., Holly, S. (2015). Influence, interactions and heterogeneity: taking personalities out of monetary policy decision-making. Manchester School 83(2), 153–182.

Blinder, A.S., (2007). Monetary policy by committee: why and how? European Journal of Political Economy 23, 106–123.

Britton, E., Fisher, P.G., Whitley, J.D., (1998). The inflation report projections: understanding the fan chart. Bank of England Quarterly Bulletin 38, 30–37.

Budd, A., (1998). The role and operations of the bank of England monetary policy committee. Economic Journal 108(451), 1783–1794.

Cecchetti, S.G., Genberg, H., Lipsky, J., Wadhwani, S., (2000). Asset prices and central bank policy. Geneva Reports on the World Economy No. 2, International Center for Monetary and Banking Studies and Centre for Economic Policy Research, Geneva.

Chadha, J., Nolan, C., (2001). Inflation targeting, transparency and interest rate volatility: ditching "monetary mystique" in the UK. Journal of Macroeconomics 23(3), 349–366.

Chappell Jr., H.W., McGregor, R.R., (2004). Did time inconsistency contribute to the great inflation? Evidence from the FOMC transcripts. Economics and Politics 16, 233–251.

Chappell Jr., H.W., McGregor, R.R., Vermilyea, T., (2005). Committee Decisions on Monetary Policy: Evidence from Historical Records of the Federal Open Market Committee. MIT Press.

Claussen, C.A., Matsen, E., Røisland, Ø., Torvik, R., (2012). Overconfidence, monetary policy committees and chairman dominance. Journal of Economic Behavior and Organization 81, 699–711.

Cobham, D., (2002). The exchange rate as a source of disturbances: the UK 1979–2000. National Institute Economic Review 181, 96–112.

(2003). Why does the monetary policy committee smooth interest rates? Oxford Economic Papers 55(3), 467–493.

(2013). Central banks and house prices in the run-up to the crisis. Oxford Economic Papers 65(S1), Special Issue on 'Monetary Policy Before, During and After the Crisis', i42–i65.

Edison, H.J., Marquez, J., (1998). U.S. monetary policy and econometric modeling: tales from the FOMC transcripts 1984–1991. Economic Modelling 15, 411–428.

Gerlach-Kristen, P., (2003). Monetary Policy Committees and the Benefits of Deliberation. Mimeo, University of Basel.

(2004). Is the MPC's voting record informative about future UK monetary policy? Scandinavian Journal of Economics 106, 299–314.

(2006). Monetary policy committees and interest rate setting, European Economic Review 50, 487–507.

Gerling, K., Grüner, H.P., Kiel, A., Schulte, E., (2005). Information acquisition and decision making in committees: a survey. European Journal of Political Economy 21, 563–597.

Goodhart, C.A.E., (2001). Monetary transmission lags and the formulation of the policy decision on interest rates. Federal Reserve Bank of St Louis Review 83(4), 165–181.

Goyal, S., (2005). Strong and weak links. Journal of the European Economic Association 3(2–3), 608–616.

(2007). Connections: An Introduction to the Economics of Networks. Princeton University Press.

Goyal, S., Vega-Redondo, F., (2007). Structural holes in social networks. Journal of Economic Theory 137, 460–492.

Granovetter, M.S., (1973). The strength of weak ties. American Journal of Sociology 78, 1360–1380.

Issing, O., (2002). Monetary policy in a world of uncertainty. Presented at the Economic Policy Forum. Banque de France, Paris, December.

King, M., (2002). The Monetary Policy Committee five years on. Address to the Society of Business Economists, London. Available from: http://www.bankofengland.co.uk/speeches/speaker.htm, May.

Meade, E.E., Stasavage, D., February (2004). Publicity of debate and the incentive to dissent: evidence from the US Federal Reserve. Mimeo, London School of Economics.

Meade, E.E., Thornton, D.L., (2012). The Phillips curve and US monetary policy: what the FOMC transcripts tell us. Oxford Economic Papers 64, 197–216.

Nelson, E., (2013). Key aspects of longer term asset purchase programs in UK and US monetary policy. Oxford Economic Papers 65(S1), Special Issue on 'Monetary Policy Before, During and After the Crisis', i92–i114.

Orphanides, A., (1998). Monetary policy rules based on real-time data. Finance and Economics Discussion Series 1998–03, Board of Governors of the Federal Reserve System.

(2003). Monetary policy evaluation with noisy information. Journal of Monetary Economics 50(3), 605–631.

Pesaran, M.H., (2006). Estimation and inference in large heterogenous panels with multifactor error structure. Econometrica 74, 967–1012.

(2015). Testing weak cross-sectional dependence in large panels. Econometric Reviews 34(6–10), 1089–1117.

Pesaran, M.H., Tosetti, E., (2011). Large panels with common factors and spatial correlation. Journal of Econometrics 161, 182–202.

Riboni, A., Ruge-Murcia, F.J., (2010). Monetary policy by committee: consensus, chairman dominance, or simple majority? Quarterly Journal of Economics 125, 363–416.

Sibert, A., (2002). Monetary policy with uncertain central bank preferences. European Economic Review 46, 1093–1109.

(2003). Monetary policy committees: individual and collective reputations. Review of Economic Studies 70(3), 649–665.

Svensson, L., (1997). Inflation forecast targeting: implementing and monitoring inflation targets. European Economic Review 41(6), 1111–1146.

Swamy, P.A.V.B., (1970). Efficient inference in a random coefficient regression model. Econometrica 38(2), 311–323.

Taylor, J.B., (1993). Discretion versus policy rules in practice. Carnegie-Rochester Conference Series on Public Policy 39, 195–214.

Waller, C.J., (1992). The choice of a conservative central banker in a multisector economy. American Economic Review 82, 1006–1012.

Wand, M.P., Jones, M.C., (1995). Kernel Smoothing. London, Chapman & Hall/CRC.

Woodford, M., (1999). Optimal monetary policy inertia. NBER Working Paper No 7261.

8 Nine votes, one view and the never-ending consensus on the MPC during the great stability

Richard Barwell

8.1 Introduction: 'You've never had it so good'

On 2 May 2007 former Governor of the Bank of England Mervyn King delivered a speech to the Society of Business Economists in which he looked back at the first ten years of the Monetary Policy Committee (MPC). King was able to report a dramatic improvement in UK macroeconomic performance. This was a time when growth and inflation outcomes were improving around the globe, but King could point to an improvement relative to that achieved elsewhere. Having lagged behind the rest of the G7 over the period 1950–96, the UK arguably led the pack between 1997 and 2006 when it came to the average rate of growth and inflation. But the striking feature of this period was not so much the *average* level of inflation, or certainly the average level of growth, but the *stability* of these variables. Indeed, the Bank refers to this period as the Great Stability, although it is better known elsewhere as the Great Moderation.[1] As King noted, the Taylor Curve (Taylor, 1979) – or what he dubbed the 'stability possibility frontier' – had shifted in, such that policy-makers had been able to achieve greater stability of inflation without having to tolerate increased volatility in output.

The question which dominated the policy debate during those twilight years of the Great Stability was whether that increased stability was the result of good policy or mere good luck, and therefore whether the second decade of the Committee's existence – those awkward teenage years – were likely to be as tranquil as the first. Governor King was taking nothing for granted – reminding his audience of the warning given by the then Prime Minister Harold MacMillan the last time the UK

1 See footnote (1) on page 123 of Tucker (2006c) for a discussion of the Bank's views on terminology.

economy had enjoyed such an extended period of prosperity (King, 2007a):

> Indeed, let us be frank about it: most of our people have never had it so good. Go around the country, go to the industrial towns, go to the farms, and you will see a state of prosperity such as we have never had in my lifetime – nor indeed ever in the history of this country. What is beginning to worry some of us is, is it too good to be true? – or perhaps I should say, is too good to last?

Of course, with the benefit of hindsight we know that King was right to be concerned: the Great Stability was already unravelling, with problems already apparent in the market for residential mortgage-backed securities which would soon lead to a major dislocation in financial markets.

This chapter is about monetary policy during the long expansion period, but the objective is not to act as judge and jury of the *decisions* taken by the Monetary Policy Committee during this period – to assess whether the stance of monetary policy was inappropriate *ex post*, and whether the Committee should have known that *ex ante*. Instead, the aim is to highlight a curious and – in the opinion of the author – undesirable feature of that policy debate within the Committee. To all intents and purposes, there was a permanent consensus within the Committee over the current policy stance, even though there was rarely if ever a consensus over the conjuncture. In contrast to the ornithological obsession of financial markets, there were no hawks and there were no doves. Nobody advocated a meaningfully different policy stance from the one favoured by the majority at any point. Everyone agreed, all the time.

We begin by documenting what the Committee believed about the causes and consequences of the long and stable expansion in activity and inflation (in consumer prices) in real time. The aim is not to reveal any new insight about the behaviour of the economy during this period or the precise calibration of the reaction function (for analysis of which see Adam et al., 2005), but instead to complement the analysis elsewhere in this volume by detailing what members of the MPC thought about those key developments as they unfolded. The reader should be left under no illusion that the conduct of monetary policy was 'boring' (to use Governor King's phrase) during the Committee's first ten years. Members of the Committee had to grapple with complex questions of strategy – of how best to respond to events. We shall document the uncertainty within the Committee about the conjuncture and questions of strategy and the differences of view within the Committee.

With that thought in mind we turn to the key contribution of this chapter: *the observation that members of the Committee were more or less in complete agreement with each other throughout this period when it came to the appropriate level of Bank Rate despite the huge uncertainty around the outlook and the optimal policy response to it, and evidence that members of the Committee disagreed with one another on specific issues within the debate.* More generally, we can find little evidence of dissenting members advocating a fundamentally different strategy – that is, a different *path* for Bank Rate to the one implicitly adopted by the majority.

That observation should not sit comfortably with those brought up on the idea of an institutional structure which encourages people to vote their view (Tucker, 2007b):

> … maybe alone amongst central banks, I'm not sure – no one doubts that the MPC does decide Bank Rate by a free vote. That this should be so owes a great deal to the culture of the Committee itself; a culture engendered by its first Chairman and his successor as Governor, but also by the rest of the membership. This is buttressed by the way in which the Bank's Court of nonexecutive directors approaches its statutory responsibility of reviewing the MPC's processes, involving annual bilateral meetings with each MPC member. And, externally, it is similarly underpinned by the Treasury Select Committee holding us individually accountable for our monthly votes, which are published as part of the minutes of our meetings.
>
> This establishes very powerful incentives for each member to reach their own considered view. There is no free-riding in the MPC; and our policy debates are full and free. That lies at the very heart of the MPC's operation, performance and communications

Nor does this observation tally with the ornithological meme of 'hawks' and 'doves': that there is a lively debate and frequent dissent at Threadneedle Street with individual members sticking to their guns and their independence (Besley, 2007a):

> I accepted the invitation to join the MPC last summer on the premise that I would exercise my independent judgement in assessing what the data are telling us about trends in the UK economy. My decisions will be guided by this alone

Nonetheless, despite much attention being lavished on the incidence of dissenting votes on the Committee, we shall argue that there was no *economically meaningful* dissent during this period. At no point in time did a single MPC member advocate a radical change in the stance, let alone the strategy. The exercise of that independent judgement by those nine individuals consistently resulted in consensus.

For completeness, Section 8.2 of this chapter describes the methodology used to document the views of the Committee during this period. Section 8.3 sets the scene, describing the key macroeconomic features of the Great Stability. Sections 8.4 covers the key themes in the policy debate during this period and then Section 8.5 grapples with the thorny question of how to respond to asset prices and financial imbalances. Section 8.6 sets out the basic facts on the voting record of the Committee during this period. Section 8.7 discusses whether there is a contradiction between the observation in this chapter and the literature which suggests that the incidence of dissent during this period contains useful information about the future path of policy. Section 8.8 discusses issues of paradigm and process that guide policy decisions in search of potential explanations for the perma-consensus on the MPC. Section 8.9 concludes by discussing possible changes to the process which might enable a richer discussion of strategy within the Committee.

8.2 Methodology

Clearly, given the purpose of this chapter, no apology will be given for the extensive use of quotations from source material: the intention is to allow Committee members to speak in their own words. The question is simply: what is the best source of information on the views of the Committee?

In theory, our first port of call should be the Minutes of each policy meeting. The Minutes certainly provide a useful record of the broad contours of the policy debate at a particular moment in time. However, they do not go into any great detail on specific subjects and therefore do not offer much in the way of insight into the Committee's perspective on the subtle nuances of the debate.

The text of the *Inflation Report*, published at the end of each quarterly forecast round, should take us a little closer to the substance of the debate. In particular, the material deemed sufficiently important to be discussed in boxes in the first four sections of the *Report* (which together discuss the current state of the economy as the Committee perceives it) and the final section, 'Prospects for inflation', (which discusses the economic outlook), provide valuable information. However, the *Inflation Report* is deliberately written in an inclusive style, with technical detail kept to an absolute minimum, and there is therefore a limit as to what can be gleaned from the text. For example, references to academic research conducted outside the Bank of England are few and far between in *Inflation Report* boxes during this period.

The *Inflation Report* press conferences and the appearances of members of the Committee at the Treasury Select Committee could provide additional source material. However, the discussion in these fora is also rarely of a technical nature. Moreover, in an environment where Committee members cannot prepare answers in advance, one can never be sure if a noteworthy remark in these situations – a heterodox analysis of a particular problem – represents a considered assessment or a slip of the tongue.

It is the speeches that members of the Committee delivered during this period that are most likely to offer a profitable line of enquiry, for two key reasons. First, speeches provide more scope for a policy-maker to provide a considered and comprehensive assessment of the key issues in the policy debate – to elaborate on technical details, to explain complex arguments, to reference key findings in the academic literature. Second, policy-makers choose what material to include in their speeches and what to leave out, and therefore the subject matter of speeches should speak to the issues that troubled particular members and the entire Committee at each moment in time.

Our choice of source material still leaves us with over two hundred speeches to choose from, with many members making similar points on a particular theme, so some criteria are required to guide the selection process: there is not space here to do full justice to a decade of debate within the MPC. Where possible an attempt has been made to cite those MPC members who discussed a particular issue at length, or those who have specific expertise in that area or who arrived at a different conclusion to the majority view. However, the comments of former Governor King loom large in this chapter. King's comments are given added prominence for a number of reasons: he was a member of the Committee throughout this period; he tended to address the key themes in his speeches; and as Governor, his views likely carried great weight within the Committee.

The focus of this chapter is monetary policy. With the benefit of hindsight – and for a select few, not least those at the BIS, before the event too – it is clear that the behaviour of asset prices, credit flows and debt stocks are central to that narrative. However, we will not review what the senior management or the staff of the Bank's Financial Stability (FS) wing had to say in speeches or the *Financial Stability Report* about developments during this period. If the members of the Monetary Policy Committee were persuaded by the arguments of those working in FS, then their comments and votes should reflect them, and if they were not, then whilst that is interesting from a process perspective, those arguments are not relevant to our discussion.

We need to define the beginning and end of the period under investigation. Given our focus on the words and deeds of the MPC, the start point is clear: May 1997. The end of the Great Stability period is ambiguous. In theory, one could stretch this period right up to October 2008 and the demise of Lehman Brothers, which then precipitated chaos in financial markets and in short order the global economy. Indeed, one could view the August 2008 *Inflation Report* as the last instalment of Committee's communication that embodied the long expansion/Great Stability mentality. The projections in the August *Report* reveal that the Committee was still confident that the gathering storm clouds would not capsize the economy.[2] Of course, we now know that external MPC member Danny Blanchflower was right to be gravely concerned that the Long Expansion had already drawn to a close.[3]

In this chapter, we choose a less controversial end point: September 2007. That date precedes the first fall in output, but it was clear by the autumn of 2007 that events had already taken a turn for the worse. The date is not arbitrary. September 2007 saw the Bank of England host an international conference on the sources of macroeconomic stability, and coincidentally on the final day of that conference, the Chancellor of the Exchequer authorised the Bank of England to provide liquidity support to Northern Rock.

For obvious reasons, little use will be made of comments made by members of the Committee in the years that followed the end of the Great Stability. After all, it would be surprising if current and former members of the Committee had not changed their mind on some of the key issues of this period, and in some cases radically so, in light of events in the years that followed the Great Stability.[4]

Given the focus of this chapter, the rounded literature review that one would typically find in an academic enquiry is surplus to requirements: the purpose is to document what the Committee thought, not what academics thought. In any case, one might reasonably assume that the

2 The central projection for activity in the August 2008 *Report* suggested that annual GDP growth would remain in positive territory throughout the forecast horizon, with output broadly flat in the near term, even if interest rates were held constant at 5%.

3 Although strictly speaking outside our period of interest, Blanchflower's comments in spring 2008 are surely worthy of inclusion here: 'We are probably in the grip of world forces that are greater than most people realise. Forecasting is thus very difficult at such times. I believe more action is needed to prevent the UK falling into recession … Monetary policy in my view still remains restrictive currently, and we need to take action to loosen policy sooner rather than later' (Blanchflower, 2008). He was right to be concerned: the latest data suggest that the economy was already contracting at a prodigious pace *before the momentous events of October 2008*. The contraction in activity during 2008Q2 and Q3 is currently estimated to be roughly on a par with the peak to trough fall in output during the early 1990s recession. Finally, in the context of the discussion later in this chapter about the difference between dissent and economically meaningful dissent, it is worth noting that Blanchflower's views about the policy stance were consistently *25 basis points* below the majority view within the Committee during this period.

4 See, for example, former Governor King's advocacy of using interest rates to lean against financial imbalances in the future *even when policy-makers have macroprudential instruments at their disposal* (see King, 2012).

published research of the latter would have percolated into the speeches of the former. Instead, this chapter will only discuss research published by the Bank itself during this period, because that material is likely to be more informative about the internal policy debate. Two different types of useful source material among the 'research' published by the Bank staff spring to mind: first, the pure academic research produced within Threadneedle Street (and eventually published in the form of Bank of England *Working Paper* series, and in some cases academic journals) which is likely to have informed the internal policy debate (at least, the material that staff presented to the MPC); and second, articles in the Bank of England's *Quarterly Bulletin*, which do not include ground-breaking material but are likely to accurately record in considerable detail the Committee's considered assessment of a particular subject.

8.3 Setting the scene

The only place to begin is with a summary of the facts – again from the perspective of Threadneedle Street. It is all too easy to underestimate how surprising macroeconomic performance during the first decade of the MPC was, given what had gone before, as the Bank of England (2007a,b) submission to the Treasury Select Committee (TSC) noted (MPC, 2007):

> inflation has so far not deviated by more than 1 percentage point from the target … That is a much better performance than was expected when the present arrangements were established: calculations at the time suggested that inflation was likely to be more than 1 percentage point away from the target around 40% of the time … And growth is estimated to have been unusually steady, with 58 quarters of unbroken expansion, the longest such run on record. No other G7 country has experienced such a sequence.

Although the focus of that memorandum and this chapter is on the 'MPC years', the turnaround in macroeconomic performance pre-dates the birth of the MPC, to around the time of the introduction of the inflation target (Tucker, 2005). Five years before his speech to the Society of Business Economists, King (2002) gave another speech celebrating a ten-year anniversary – this time, of the inflation target – in which he was able to report much good news:

> Today the UK has low and stable inflation. And that has not come at the expense of either output or employment. Britain has now experienced 41 successive quarters of positive economic growth. And unemployment in this country is lower than in any other G7 country.

Indeed, Governor King would argue on several occasions that the MPC arrived on the scene midway through the best years of the Great Stability. In his first speech as Governor of the Bank, King (2003) coined the phrase *nice* decade to describe the ten-year period since 1992:

> the UK experienced a *n*on-*i*nflationary *c*onsistently *e*xpansionary – or *"nice"* – decade; a decade in which growth was a little above trend, unemployment fell steadily, and supported by the improved terms of trade, real take-home pay rose without adding to employers' cost, thus allowing consumption to grow at above trend rates without putting upward pressure on inflation.

King (2004c) would soon issue a warning that the future may not be quite so nice, but *not so bad* (*n*ot *o*f *t*he *s*ame *o*rder *b*ut *a*lso *d*esirable) either:

> What is clear, however, is that the combination of low and stable inflation and continuously falling unemployment must come to an end at some point, and may already have done so … From time to time shocks will hit our economy, as we have seen with oil prices and world trade, and so there will be fluctuations in growth and unemployment, as well as in inflation. Unemployment can be maintained at lower rates than in the past, even though there will inevitably be times when it will rise because no monetary policy can hope to prevent all fluctuations of demand, output, and hence employment … Moving from a nice to a not-so-bad decade would still represent a significant improvement in our economic fortunes compared with the period of high inflation. We must be conscious of the dangers of hubris.

An influential Bank study published towards the tail-end of the Great Stability documented just how unusual the post-1992 period was. Using data that extended back to 1661 and the Christiano–Fitzgerald band pass filter to extract the business cycle components of macroeconomic series, Benati (2006) documented the unprecedented stability of the inflation targeting era:

> The post-1992 inflation-targeting regime appears to have been characterised, to date, by the most stable macroeconomic environment in recorded UK history, with the volatilities of the business-cycle components of real GDP, national accounts aggregates, and inflation measures having been, post-1992, systematically lower than for any of the pre-1992 monetary regimes/historical periods, often markedly so, as in the case of inflation and real GDP … with the standard deviations of the business-cycle components of real GDP and inflation having fallen by about 50 and 70 per cent, respectively [relative to the period 1972–92].

Benati (2006) noted another key feature of inflation during this period – that 'fluctuations' tended to be short-lived:

> Under inflation targeting, inflation exhibits little or no persistence based on all the price indices we consider … our results provide compelling evidence that high inflation persistence is not an intrinsic, structural feature of the economy.

Instead, the extent of inflation persistence may crucially depend on the monetary regime in place over the sample period.

Not only had inflation become more stable and less persistent, but there was an additional puzzle which went to the very heart of the conduct of monetary policy: inflation appeared to have become less sensitive to shifts in demand. Once again, this was a global phenomenon, but one that appeared to be particularly evident in the UK, as Deputy Governor Charles Bean (2007) noted:

> one of the most striking empirical features of recent history has been the apparent flattening of the Phillips curve as inflation has subsided. This is apparent in many developed economies, but is particularly evident in the United Kingdom.

The Committee was fond of illustrating the apparent flattening of the trade-off with plots of inflation and unemployment outcomes since the 1970s (which cropped up regularly in speeches towards the end of the MPC's first decade). However, those charts might have been an illusion: synchronised movements in the actual and equilibrium rate of unemployment during this period could exaggerate the perceived flattening of the curve. However, Bean (2007) appeared to be in little doubt as to the explanation for this key puzzle:

> One possible explanation runs as follows. The usual inverse short-run trade-off is alive and well, but the natural rate of unemployment has been falling as a result of past and continuing labour market reforms. Policy-makers, seeking to stabilise inflation, have then managed to expand real demand at just the right rate so that actual unemployment has fallen in line with that declining natural rate. The problem is that this assumes an ability to fine-tune that is frankly unbelievable, especially once one recognises the data fog in which policy decisions are taken. If the short-run trade-off were still there, it surely would have revealed itself as control errors pushed inflation either above or below target. The alternative explanation is that the short-run trade-off is indeed flatter now.

Not all members of the Committee were quite so sure. The then Executive Director for the Markets area, Paul Tucker (2006b) sounded a more cautious tone:

> we just do not know enough about the underlying structure and properties of the economy. Quite apart from the change in monetary regime, the extent and variety of the structural change underway in the real economy is profound … In consequence, in the UK for the moment we do not really know whether the short-run trade off between excess (or deficient) demand and inflation has changed; whether the short-run Phillips curve has become flatter.

Indeed, the reforms to the monetary framework – the introduction of inflation targeting and then the granting of operational independence to the Bank – was but one of a number of shocks and structural changes to have occurred during this period which were likely to have had a significant impact on both the state of the economy and system dynamics. It was reasonable to question – as Tucker did – whether there had been a permanent structural shift in the slope of the Phillips Curve, or whether the change in the reduced form trade-off was likely to prove a short-lived phenomenon.

Even with the luxury of reliable data and a mature academic literature on the impact of these new phenomena it would have been difficult to calibrate the optimal stance. However, as Tucker (2006b) would go on to explain, there was an additional complication: members of the Committee were forced to come to a preliminary view on the optimal policy stance with the limited and flawed data at their disposal in real time.

> the data we use give us an unavoidably imperfect read on what is going on. Not infrequently in my experience we debate the various possible explanations for some puzzle in the data, only to find that a year or so later the data have been revised and, as it turned out, there was no puzzle.

This chapter documents the ebb and flow of those debates and puzzles. Before moving on it is important to note that the moniker *Great Stability* is in fact controversial. The first ten years of the MPC was only stable if one took a particular perspective – if one focussed on the traditional arguments of the monetary policy reaction function: output and consumer price inflation. If, instead, one focussed on asset prices, credit flows and balance sheet stocks this period appears anything but stable (for a discussion of these financial imbalances in the UK during this period, see Barwell and Burrows (2013)). In the real economy, there was a rapid build-up of financial assets and liabilities on the household balance sheet as property prices surged ahead of consumer prices. The value of the currency was relatively stable in trade-weighted terms albeit at a level that had been thought unsustainable when sterling first appreciated in the mid-1990s and for most of the decade that followed, but in the stock market there was time enough for boom, bust and recovery, and towards the end of this period balance sheets across the financial system, including those of the banks, ballooned. The Committee's reaction to that *Great Instability* will also feature in the pages that follow. Without further ado we shall now turn to discuss this and other key developments during this period.

8.4 Agreeing to disagree on the heady combination of developments

There are some permanent conjunctural features of the policy debate: the size of the output gap; the momentum in consumer spending; the outlook for global demand; the prospects for commodity prices; the near-term profile for consumer prices given cost pressures in the supply chain; and so on. Given the quality of the real-time data available to policy-makers and the uncertainty about how the economy behaves, there is ample scope for differences of view on these mundane subjects on a scale sufficient to warrant differences of view on the policy stance. For example, consider the Bank's assessment of the uncertainty around the extent of capacity pressures within companies (Ellis and Turnbull, 2007):

> A variety of different methods are presented, each with their own advantages and drawbacks. Ultimately, no measure of capacity pressure is perfect, and the policymaker's judgement is crucial

That emphasis on the importance of judgement crops up again and again in the comments of MPC members. But as we will go on to discuss, the supposedly independent summation of countless judgements by the nine different members of the Committee consistently produced the same answer.

Rather than focus on the ebb and flow of the discussion over these perennial questions of capacity pressures and the like, we shall instead focus on some of the key structural themes during this period. The label *Great Stability* conjures up an impression of a tranquil period, with little economic news for the Committee to process, few shocks to confront. Had that been the case, the debate would have been straightforward and sterile in equal measure, and a perma-consensus on the policy stance would be less surprising. But that impression is misleading.

In a speech aptly titled 'Monetary policy, stability and structural change' (Tucker, 2005), the then Executive Director Paul Tucker summed up the challenge that confronted the Committee:

> Monetary regime change, labour market reform, financial innovation, the technological revolution, globalisation – it is a heady combination, which unavoidably adds to the challenge of discriminating between cyclical and structural influences when forming a view on the macroeconomic outlook. But it is equally unavoidable that policy-makers must try to do just that.

His comments echoed those of former Governor Sir Edward George (George, 2000):

> in part the explanation for this encouraging development may lie in the dampening effect of the strong exchange rate or in the lower and more stable inflationary expectations we are now seeing. But other possible explanations include exceptional competitive pressure in goods markets, structural changes in labour market behaviour or an underlying improvement in productivity growth, or in some combination of all three ... The jury frankly is still very much out on all of this. The difficulty is that most of these possible developments cannot be directly observed in the data, and, even if they could be, we would still not know whether or not, or for how long, they might persist. We certainly have not closed our mind to a continuation of such benign "new economy" effects, indeed we make conscious allowance for them as best we can in our projections. But we cannot bank on them. All we can – and do – do is, continuously and meticulously, to monitor the evolving evidence. We watch it, in fact, like a dove.

We shall now review four of these key debates: the behaviour of inflation expectations; the impact of globalisation on UK costs and prices; the state of the labour market; and a handful of key developments within the UK corporate sector. What follows is not intended as an exhaustive summary of the debate within the Committee on any particular issue.

We could have selected a broader set of structural issues, and explored each in greater depth, but hopefully what follows will be sufficient to demonstrate the point: that members of the Committee were uncertain about the causes and consequences of events as they unfolded and did not always agree in their preliminary assessment. We shall delay discussing the thorny issue of asset prices and financial imbalances until the next section, because that posed a more fundamental challenge to the direction of monetary strategy: no one was under any illusion that a subtle nudge on the interest rate tiller would correct those imbalances.

Two constant themes should strike the reader across the four issues discussed below. First, that there was always considerable uncertainty within the Committee about how events should be interpreted (Tucker, 2006a):

> The introduction of the new monetary regime did not, and of course could not, remove uncertainty about the quarter-to-quarter, or indeed year-to-year, path of the economy and inflation. And so there remains a degree of unavoidable uncertainty about the short-term path of official rates, as the Monetary Policy Committee responds to cyclical developments ... But, like anybody else, we cannot predict with certainty what will happen in the economy. There are always material risks around the central outlook. We have to weigh those risks in our policy decisions.

Second, the Committee were not always in agreement about the outlook – for example, external member Richard Lambert argued that it would difficult for the Bank to give a detailed account of the policy debate immediately after the decision is taken for precisely this reason (Lambert, 2006):

An individualistic committee like ours would find it difficult to agree on a substantive statement in the tight time frame available immediately after each meeting. And it would be very difficult for the Governor to hold an immediate press conference on the decision, since at that short notice he couldn't be expected to reflect the sometimes highly nuanced tone of the policy discussion

8.4.1 Inflation expectations – critical but fragile?

The Committee was not taking all the credit for the improvement in macroeconomic performance during the Great Stability. Where the Committee thought that some credit was due was in the impact of the new institutional arrangements on inflation expectations, and thereby indirectly on the locus of achievable output inflation combinations (King, 2007a).

It seems to me likely that the new framework for monetary policy has been a key, though not the only, driver in moving the frontier inwards. By eliminating uncertainty about the inflation target and ensuring that the objective of low and stable inflation is well understood and credible, the change in the framework in 1997 helped to anchor expectations of inflation in the medium term. By doing so, it has made it possible for the MPC to keep inflation closer to target with smaller changes in monetary policy, and hence fluctuations in output, than would otherwise have been the case. The anchoring of inflation expectations has changed the way businesses respond to unexpected shocks. Faced with changes in their costs stemming from, for example, changes in import or energy prices, businesses can respond in two ways, each consistent with the necessary change in employees' real take-home pay. They can pass those cost changes forwards to prices or backwards to money wages. With inflation expectations well-anchored to the target, companies have restricted the pass-through of changes in costs to prices. The necessary adjustment of real take-home pay has taken place more through fluctuations in money wages than prices.

This is the central message of the Committee's 'ten years on' submission to the Treasury Select Committee:

Inflation expectations are therefore central in determining inflation today. Indeed, the most potent effect of monetary policy is not so much through the consequences of individual monthly interest rate decisions, but rather through the ability of the policy framework to condition those expectations. In a world where inflation expectations are well anchored, an increase in nominal demand relative to supply will lead to a smaller and less persistent increase in inflation than in a world where the increase in nominal demand simultaneously raises expectations of future inflation.

Likewise, Deputy Governor Bean (2007) argued that:

> the expectations channel represents a crucial link in the monetary transmission mechanism. Indeed, Woodford has gone so far as to claim that not only do expectations matter, but that very little else does! One feature of forward-looking behaviour is that expectations of future changes in policy can do a lot of the work, obviating the need for sharp movements in current official interest rates.

The immediate market response to the announcement of operational independence – with a 50 basis point drop in long rates – certainly seemed to corroborate this hypothesis: that the change in the framework shifted beliefs about the loss function that guides the conduct of policy (Chadha et al., 2007). This belief that the new monetary arrangements had anchored inflation expectations, which in turn had engineered a favourable inward shift in the Taylor Curve, led in turn to a good deal of soul searching within the Committee about the fragile nature of that anchor, and what the Committee needed to do in order to preserve the status quo. Indeed, Deputy Governor Rachel Lomax worried that the Committee could become the victim of its own success (Lomax, 2007):

> The less helpful legacy [of the Great Stability] is that even a small movement in inflation away from target – one percentage point – has prompted some highly coloured media coverage, and may have unsettled people's expectations about where inflation is headed in the short run … the MPC can never afford to ignore evidence that medium-term inflation expectations are becoming dislodged: anchoring these expectations is fundamental to the success of the framework. But direct evidence of inflation expectations is very hard to come by; the measures we have are patchy and poor. So there is a difficult dilemma here, which the MPC has been grappling with over the past few months. And it has left me with a nagging worry. My concern is this. If the price of maintaining the public's confidence is that we have to try to keep inflation within a whisker of the target at all times – even in the face very large shocks – the flexibility that is such an important feature of our present arrangements may get significantly eroded.

In short, the Committee didn't seem to think that they could take the Great Stability for granted – in the words of Paul Tucker, the Committee believed that credibility 'has to be achieved, and continually re-achieved' (Tucker, 2005) – and therefore the MPC acted as if it had less latitude than the stable dynamics of this period might have implied.

Quite how much latitude the Committee had – how and when the Committee should respond to Lomax's 'patchy and poor' indicators of inflation expectations, i.e. what needed to be done to constantly re-achieve credibility – was less clear, but was surely a first-order problem of monetary strategy. Indeed, not only was the information set not much to write home about, there was precious little hard theory to guide the Committee on how expectations were formed 'in the real world', and how they would endogenously respond to events to ground an assessment of the risks to inflation expectations (Tucker, 2006b):

> We do not know enough about how households and firms form their expectations – how much forward-looking, how much backward-looking – to be able to model the process rigorously. That is not part of the 'information set' of policymakers in today's world … Crucially, we have to make judgments about whether medium-term inflation expectations are, in fact, securely anchored. We need to resist falling into the trap of thinking that the nominal side is now, and forever, nicely looked after by some miracle of credibility … We absolutely have to attend to indicators of medium-term nominal trends. That is why central bankers like me look at measures of inflation expectations from as many sources as we can: bond markets, surveys etc. And it is why the ECB and others, including at the Bank of England, track the monetary aggregates as a cross check, a potential amber light alerting us to medium-term risks.

Given this unholy trinity of strong conviction that inflation expectations *matter*, patchy data on the current state of expectations and no compelling theory on how expectations are formed one would imagine that reasonable people could arrive at meaningfully different views on the outlook given differences of view on the amplification of shocks through expectations. Indeed, the May 2007 *Inflation Report* noted (Bank of England, 2007a):

> The central projection assumes that inflation expectations return to the target over time. But assessing how rapidly this happens under alternative monetary policy settings is complicated by the fact that little is known about how households and companies form expectations … Though the uncertainties in this area are substantial, the central projection places some weight on this latter possibility.

Indeed, as a footnote to this discussion, it is interesting that Governor King was a co-author of an academic paper which examined the macroeconomic consequences when agents form expectations using simple rules of thumb rather than complex economic models (Brazier et al., 2006), which unsurprisingly yields the result that monetary policy should respond to expectations.

8.4.2 Globalisation – the consequences of cheap imports and expensive energy

Globalisation, defined by Deputy Governor Charles Bean as the integration of China, India and the emerging economies of Eastern Europe into the world economy and the greater ease with which companies can outsource production (Bean, 2003), was more than a buzzword – it was a key development which cut across multiple conversations in the policy debate during the Great Stability era. In this section, we will focus on the *direct* effect of those emerging economies on UK costs and prices which dominated much of the discussion around movements in headline inflation during the Great Stability; but there was also a powerful *indirect* effect via migration on labour supply (see Section 8.4.3) and via global real interest rates on the price of assets including property (see Section 8.5.2).

Given the protracted inflation overshoot in the crisis years it is all too easy to forget that in the early years of the MPC, the inflation problem the Committee confronted was one of too little, not too much. In the early years of the millennium, import prices helped to deliver deflation in consumer goods prices and the rising market share of low-cost producers was a key part of that narrative (King, 2006):

> China, India and the former Soviet Union between them have massively increased the supply of labour available to industry around the world. As labour-intensive goods have become more abundant, they have also become cheaper … As consumers, we have benefited from falling prices of goods made in China and elsewhere in Asia. Between 1995 and 2005, the prices of imported manufactured goods fell by a sixth and, relative to the price of domestically produced output, by no less than a third.

Indeed, as external member Steve Nickell (Nickell, 2005a) noted, small changes in the share of the export basket accounted for by these low-cost producers had the potential to have a marked impact on headline prices:

> between 1999 and 2002, imports to the UK from China and India increased their share by nearly 1.1 percentage points. This does not seem very much, but average prices in these countries are around one quarter of those from developed countries, for example. This apparent small shift in import shares is enough to reduce UK weighted world export price inflation by around 0.5% per annum during the three year period.

Once again, the uncertainty around even the direct effect on UK prices of the rising share of low-cost economies was significant (not least given the data constraints) let alone around the extent of the indirect effects of the low-cost economies on UK prices (for example, on the productivity of domestic producers) or the prospects for this drag to persist – as the Bank's own research suggested (Mac Coille, 2008). In any case, the flip-side of this drag from low-cost economies is that UK households benefited from a surge in the terms of trade, supporting robust consumption growth (King, 2005b)

Industrialisation in China and elsewhere has benefited British consumers. For much of the past decade, the terms on which we were able to trade with the rest of the world moved in our favour. In other words, the average price of our exports rose relative to the price of our imports. And that enabled consumer spending to rise faster than national output. From 1997 until around 2002 consumer spending rose at an average rate of almost 4% a year, whereas GDP rose at an average annual rate of less than 3%.

Indeed, the Committee appears to have concluded that the batting average effect of the rising share of low-cost producers in the basket of goods and services that the UK imports, which likely contributed to a rise in the terms of trade, and hence the purchasing power of UK wages, might have enabled a temporary fall in the equilibrium unemployment rate (MPC, 2007).[5]

In time, the perceived impact of the emerging economies on UK costs and prices would become more nuanced to say the least, with oil prices tripling in the space of two years on the back of rapid growth in the oil-intensive emerging economies. Of course, both phenomena were relative price shocks; the issue was whether a policy response was required to achieve the inflation target (Bean, 2003). Given the behaviour of inflation during the oil shocks of the 1970s one might have expected the Committee to react aggressively to the persistent rise in oil prices, but the combination of the gradual and *surprising*[6] nature of the rise in oil prices, coupled with the relatively muted macroeconomic impact, allowed the Committee to take a more measured response. The Committee concluded that there would be no repeat performance of the 1970s with inflationary second round effects so long as inflation expectations remained anchored, allowing the Committee to focus more on the immediate impact of the cost shock on demand than it otherwise might have done (Walton, 2006).

if the monetary framework is credible, inflation expectations are less likely to be dislodged in the event of a cost shock. Real wage resistance might be reduced if workers realise that the MPC will react to any attempt by workers to be compensated for the unavoidable loss of spending power in the event of an oil shock. Both factors lower the likelihood of second round effects on wages,

5 Note that the Bank's research in this area concluded that the rise in the terms of trade was likely the result of a number of factors, including a shift in global tastes towards the services that the UK exports (Dury, Piscitelli, Sebastia-Barriel and Yates, 2003).

6 Deputy Governor Bean (2006) noted: 'If you had told the MPC in early 2004 that oil prices would triple over the following two years, I think we would have been very worried indeed about the possible inflationary impact'.

reducing the persistence of the inflation shock. There will also be a smaller hit to output if the MPC does not have to raise interest rates to rein in second round effects.

Calibrating the precise policy response to the cost shock was not straightforward, as the then Executive Director Paul Tucker made plain (Tucker, 2007a):

The textbook response to a cost shock is supposedly to allow the price level to rise, with the associated temporary pick up in inflation being just that – temporary. In the jargon of central banking, the 'first round effects should be accommodated' in order to contain output volatility; but any second-round effects on inflation, through wage bargaining and medium-term inflation expectations, should of course be prevented. What of practice? … That the full impact of the rise in costs has not passed through to inflation owes something, I believe, to wariness amongst central bankers of their being able, given uncertainty about the underlying shocks, to calibrate policy with sufficient precision to bring about such a neat but vitally important distinction between first-round and second-round effects; let alone of their being able to communicate such a strategy to the public, the business community and financial markets. Textbook orthodoxy might perhaps have been more compelling if the rise in energy prices had been both sharp and caused purely by interruptions to, or constraints on, the supply of energy. But when, as over the past couple of years, the rise in costs was partly the consequence of increased global demand, and the price rise drawn out, the wariness in fully accommodating the first round effects was, I think, tangible, and reasonable.

Finally, Bean (2003) argued that globalisation could have had a more profound structural impact on price-setting in the UK (which could potentially explain the apparent flattening of the Phillips Curve discussed above) and therefore the conduct of policy – but he acknowledged that the direction (let alone the magnitude) of this channel was ambiguous:

These three factors – increased specialisation; the intensification of product market competition; and the impact of that intensified competition and migration on the behaviour of wages – should all work to flatten the short-run trade-off between inflation and domestic activity. But it is worth mentioning one consequence of globalisation that might work in the opposite direction. An increase in the competitive pressures in product markets will mean that the profits foregone by setting a price at the "wrong" level will be all the greater. That would encourage businesses to revise their prices more frequently, and will tend to steepen, rather than flatten, the trade-off …

By way of providing some evidence on this, we recently asked our regional Agents to conduct a small survey of some of their business contacts in order to see how the frequency of price changes had changed over the past decade … There is a marked tendency towards an increased frequency of price changes in virtually all sectors, including in manufacturing which is probably the sector most exposed to the effects of globalisation.

Again, as in almost every area of the policy debate, there was uncertainty, both about the extent to which globalisation might have depressed UK inflation, and through what channels, and whether that disinflationary 'tailwind' would persist, magnify or abate in the future, and the extent to which a central bank could safely accommodate the first round effects of the shock (Bean, 2003):

Globalisation also offers a special challenge to monetary policy makers. While globalisation is not the ultimate cause of the generally low and stable inflation experienced by most industrialised economies over the past fifteen years, the associated improvement in the industrialised countries' terms of trade has provided a benign backdrop to the widespread pursuit of low inflation through stability-oriented monetary policies. But that beneficial tailwind has waned somewhat in the past couple of years. Moreover, intensified competition in product markets, along with other factors, does seem to have altered the way in which wages and prices are determined, complicating our task. Central bankers are a long way from having a full understanding of what is going on here and further research on these questions is definitely called for. Perhaps when I next give a speech here, some of you will have come up with the answers.

8.4.3 The labour market – new labour, new flexibility

Developments in the labour market played a central role in the Committee's narrative of the Great Stability. We begin with a general discussion of structural change in the labour market and then highlight two specific policy-relevant themes: the impact of migration and the absence of real wage resistance.

The degree of labour market slack – or labour market tightness – is a key diagnostic of inflationary pressure. In a stable economy it is relatively straightforward to infer the sign and scale of slack from the data on the labour market quantities – for example, when one is confident in one's estimate of the equilibrium unemployment rate to one decimal place,[7] there is little uncertainty about the unemployment gap. The UK labour market was anything but stable over this period, complicating the conduct of monetary policy: Committee members had to take a stand on how far employment could increase before they took a stand (King, 1998b):

After all, is not the belief that we could always achieve lower unemployment without an increase in inflation the mark of a kinder, gentler, altogether more civilised approach to economic policy? Or is it simply wishful thinking?

7 See for example Gordon (1997), discussing the US labour market: 'for many years it was reasonable to assume that the NAIRU was 6.0%'.

As Greg Mankiw put it: "Wishful thinking is one reason that monetary policy has historically been excessively inflationary...To my mind, wishful thinking is as worrisome a problem for monetary policy as time inconsistency." Genuine concern for the unemployed means a recognition that sustainable reductions in unemployment require a combination of monetary stability on the demand side and microeconomic reforms such as the New Deal on the supply side. As Alan Blinder has reminded us, we need soft hearts and hard heads, not the other way round. Despite suggestions to the contrary, the MPC does have soft hearts and hard heads.

Those hard heads came to the conclusion that the equilibrium unemployment rate had indeed fallen, as external member and Professor of Labour Economics Steve Nickell observed (Nickell, 2001):

> We have seen a continuing decline in unemployment down to its lowest level for a generation without excessive inflationary pressure. This suggests that equilibrium unemployment has been declining and, in fact, it has been doing so since the mid 1980s. The reasons why this has happened are first, because the balance of power in wage bargaining has shifted away from workers as union coverage has declined significantly over the last twenty years and unions have become far less adversarial. Second, unemployment benefits have also declined over the same period and the whole benefit system has become much more focused on getting the unemployed back into work. These are the most important factors with a small additional contribution from the decline in taxes on employment.

The MPC had to calibrate the macro consequences of a package of labour market reforms – from the National Minimum Wage, to the New Deal, to the Working Time Directive to a whole host of Tax Credits – as well as a whole host of other socio-demographic factors which have the potential to shift equilibrium labour supply. Indeed, alongside the changes in the equilibrium unemployment rate discussed above, the equilibrium participation rate likely rose, with an increase in labour supply among the older members of the population and the mothers of young children, and the equilibrium level of hours worked falling, with a decline in the number of people working very long hours facilitated by the Working Time Directive (Barwell et al., 2007). In every case, there were grounds for reasonable people to take materially different views on the extent to which movements in actual labour input, such as the increase in the participation rate or the decline in average hours worked, were matched by a shift in the equilibrium.

However, the most profound shock to labour supply was the entry of the Accession countries to the European Union, which led to a steep rise in net migrant flows – and one that Governor King argues the Committee spotted earlier than most (FT, 2007).

I think we were among the first to spot the importance and the size of migrant labour, and we did that because we went out and made regional visits ourselves, talked to businesses, and asked our agents around the country what they were seeing. It became very clear to us quite quickly that the scale of the migration was a lot bigger than anyone had really led us to believe … I think it's our equivalent [of Greenspan's observation] that productivity growth has risen.

A migrant-driven increase in the population could in theory boost supply and demand, so its impact on inflationary pressure is ambiguous (Barwell, 2007). However, the Committee was of the view that the boost to supply would likely dominate in the short run, and therefore the inflow of migrants was a beneficial 'tailwind', similar to that offered by globalisation (MPC, 2007). However, the Committee believed that something more profound could be taking place: migration was not only shifting the location of the vertical long-run Phillips Curve (the level of potential employment), but also changing the slope of the short-run curve (King, 2005b):

An increase in spending raises the pressure of demand on supply and leads to upward pressure on wages and prices. But if the increased demand for labour generates its own supply in the form of migrant labour then the link between demand and prices is broken, or at least altered. Indeed, in an economy that can call on unlimited supplies of migrant labour the concept of the output gap is meaningless. The UK is not in that extreme position, but the inflow of migrant labour, especially in the past year or so from Eastern Europe, has probably led to a diminution of inflationary pressure in the labour market relative to previous experience.

It is important not to confuse the Committee's musings on these issues with certainty about the evolving trade-off in the labour market – there was plenty of uncertainty to go around; see, for example the discussion in the November 2004 *Inflation Report* (Bank of England, 2004):

There are a number of risks relating to how a particular path for demand will affect inflation. One risk relates to wages. Wage growth has been unusually subdued, given the low level of unemployment. Part of the explanation probably lies in the impact of government reforms spanning the past twenty-five years that have changed the relationship between wage growth and unemployment. Other factors may have changed the relationship more recently. Additional inward migration or delayed retirement, for example, may have helped to keep wages in check during the past few years. But the MPC remains uncertain about the importance of different factors in explaining the low outturns for earnings growth, and about how long-lasting some of the effects will be.

As we have already seen in the discussion of rising energy prices, the new-found flexibility of the UK labour market would be put to the test in the twilight years of the Great Stability, as cost shocks drove a wedge between the value of domestic output and domestic consumption, which required a fall in real take-home pay. In days gone by an increase in unemployment might have been required to keep wages in check, but in the Great Stability there was precious little evidence of real wage resistance (King, 2007a):

> The acceptance of necessary adjustment in real take-home pay has helped to stabilise employment growth which, over the past decade, has been four times less variable than over the previous five decades. That has shifted the 'stability possibility frontier' faced by the MPC inwards, enabling the MPC to keep inflation more stable than in the past.

With unemployment edging up towards the end of this period, the question was whether wages would continue to 'behave'. The discussion in the August 2007 *Inflation Report* took nothing for granted, and reveals a good deal of uncertainty about the future (Bank of England, 2007b):

> There are marked risks on both sides of this central case, particularly in the labour market. Wage pressures could be weaker than in the central projection if the pickup in unemployment proves to have been primarily cyclical, if any real wage resistance or skills mismatch is short-lived, or if inward migration accelerates. However, if employees seek to claw back past reductions in real earnings growth, or recruitment difficulties prove to be more persistent, wage pressures may be somewhat higher.

Not all of the Committee were in two minds on this issue; external member Danny Blanchflower was in little doubt (Blanchflower, 2007):

> So, in my opinion, at this point in time, it appears that wages are the dog that hasn't barked. My view is that wages are not going to increase much any time soon when insider and outsider pressures are low. By that I mean, firms don't have the ability to pay as their profits have been squeezed (insider power is low) and, as I have said previously, there is a good deal of slack in the labour market resulting from increased unemployment and immigration to the UK (low outsider pressures) (Blanchflower, Oswald and Garrett, 1990 & Blanchflower et al. 2007). I have some sense from my regional visits that the fear of unemployment among workers is elevated, although, there is limited data on the issue (see Blanchflower, 1991 and Campbell et al, 2007). Workers these days seem increasingly aware that they can be replaced by immigrants and/or that their employer can move his or her production facility abroad. This limits workers' bargaining power. These pressures manifest themselves in the recent low settlements figures.

8.4.4 *Corporate sector – a smörgåsbord of structural issues*

Finally, we turn to discuss the uncertainty around developments in the corporate sector. We shall begin with three issues which were important themes in the debate at a particular moment in time during the Great

Stability – the emergence of the internet; the ICT miracle and the productivity puzzle; and structural changes in the distribution sector – before closing this section with a discussion of the puzzling behaviour of business investment, which is of particular interest given the focus of this volume.

Although macroeconomists think of technical change as a smooth process, gradually shifting out the production possibility frontier, it may be more appropriate to think of there being a series of great leaps forward. During the MPC's first decade the Committee had to grapple with one innovation that appeared to be 'the next big thing': the internet.

It is clear that at least a couple of external MPC members believed that the rise of the internet could have meaningful macroeconomic consequences that largely but not exclusively operated through the corporate sector. Wadhwani (2000a) argued that the internet would have 'important disinflationary effects', boosting productivity, compressing margins and lowering the equilibrium unemployment rate. Likewise, Julius (2000) argued that the internet could have a profound impact on prices, through increased competition, by lowering the search costs of consumers and the barriers to entry facing potential new producers, and by stimulating productivity growth.

The essence of the argument at least appears to have been shared by others on the Committee, although perhaps not with the same ardour; for example, Buiter (1999) observed:

> Even if much of the claims made for the New Economy is hype, what remains is substantial enough to matter for the United Kingdom's real economic performance in the medium and long term and for the conduct of monetary policy.

Indeed, discussion of the impact of the internet on headline inflation found its way into the text of the February 2000 *Inflation Report*, although the *Report* made clear that some members thought that the central projection under-cooked the impact of the internet (Bank of England, 2000a):

> The decline in retail goods price inflation could also be indicative of an increase in the degree of price competition in the retail sector more broadly. New technology, such as the Internet, may be enabling new firms with lower unit costs to enter the retail market. That technology may also have lowered the cost to consumers of searching across different retailers to obtain alternative prices. If, as a result, consumer demand has become more price-sensitive, then we might expect to see a decline in retailers' margins. During the period of adjustment to a lower level of unit costs, or margins, retail price inflation may decline temporarily.

The policy debate in the aftermath of the crisis has been dominated by the puzzling behaviour of labour productivity (see, for example, Broadbent, 2012). In the early years of the MPC there were high hopes that the transition to a 'new economy' (NE), with an acceleration in the diffusion of information and communications technology (ICT), could unlock a spurt in labour productivity. Wadhwani (2001) urged caution in reading too much into the hyperbole of the time – 'some of the claims that have been made for the NE are far too extravagant' – but argued that there were grounds for optimism:

> Academic studies are now growingly supportive of the notion that the underlying rate of productivity growth has, in recent years, increased in the US. These studies also suggest that ICT investment has played an important role. Indeed, there is some evidence suggesting that the growth contribution of ICT in the past 25 years outstrips that of electricity and railroads over comparable periods.

Indeed, with puzzlingly low inflation in the mid-noughties, the possibility that there had been an ICT miracle on the supply side could no longer be ignored (Barker, 2005b):

> one possibility is that the UK is now experiencing the kind of improvements in productivity that the US saw around a decade earlier. This was not evident to policymakers in the (official) US productivity data at the time, but became clear through subsequent data revisions. However, on the basis in particular of higher ICT investment, improving profit margins, and anecdotal and survey evidence from business, a number of FOMC members argued that there were signs of a favourable productivity shock, some time ahead of confirmation from the data.

As ever, there was more than enough uncertainty to go around, with the MPC in wait and see mode (Barker, 2005b):

> The evidence is building, but cannot yet support optimism similar to that of the US in the mid-1990s. While the latest data has suggests some productivity improvement, it is too early to reject the alternative explanation that this is simply a cyclical rise. Further, given some signs of relatively poor adoption of best practice management techniques in the UK, a degree of scepticism about productivity gains from ICT seems justified. However, over the coming quarters it will be necessary to look hard at this question, and remain open to the possibility of a structural improvement.

Indeed, measuring and explaining the drivers of productivity, and in particular the impact of the ICT revolution on the contribution of capital goods and the efficiency with which companies were able to combine labour and capital to produce output (TFP), would become key research agendas at the Bank during the Great Stability era, as the

Committee sought to hone its estimate of the supply capacity of the UK economy. Oulton and Srinivasan (2003) developed a more reliable measure of the contribution of capital goods to *current* production, which put a larger weight on assets which were expensive to rent relative to their purchase price (to compensate for the depreciation of the asset) such as ICT goods. That 'capital services' measure suggested that the contribution from capital goods had increased much faster than a traditional wealth measure, which in turn implied that TFP growth had been correspondingly weaker. Indeed, the Bank would eventually reach a somewhat pessimistic conclusion about the productivity miracle – detailed research conducted by Bank staff at the industry level suggested that 'the TFP acceleration appears to have been less widespread across industries in the United Kingdom compared to the United States' (Groth, Nuñez and Srinivasan, 2006).Central bankers tend not to pay too much attention to developments in particular sectors, but exceptions sometimes have to be made when those developments have macroeconomic consequences. Events in the distribution sector during this period – in particular, a compression in profit margins, particularly in the wholesale sector, and an increase in productivity (Nickell, 2005a) – are a case in point. Those developments had direct implications for the relative prices of goods in the consumption basket, and therefore in the short run at least, inflation (Tucker, 2005):

> At a macro level, the effect was, for a period, to open up a gap between producer output price inflation and retail goods price inflation … In other words, for a while some structural changes in the distribution sector reduced the feed-through of demand pressures into retail price inflation. Looking ahead, one downside risk to the MPC's central projection is that we cannot rule out that this process has further to go.

Once again, we find the two perennial themes of these debates. First, the uncertainty, highlighted by Tucker: the Committee was unsure where disinflationary developments unfolding in the distribution sector would persist into the future. Second, the absence of consensus: with, for example, Nickell (2005a) taking a different line on the balance of risks:

> Given the recent stability of distribution sector margins (see Figure 13), there seems no particular reason to expect a repeat of this via a further squeeze on distribution margins.

One might have expected that business investment would have flourished in the twilight years of the Great Stability, in an environment of macroeconomic stability and easy credit, but as Deputy Governor John

Gieve observed, gross fixed capital formation remained puzzlingly weak (Gieve, 2006):

I confess I remain puzzled. The macro environment has never been more stable. Companies have been achieving high rates of return on their investments in the United Kingdom, and finance is readily available. For some years the UK has had a low capital stock per worker relative to most similar economies and – in a truly global market – we might expect that gap to narrow. It is difficult not to think that opportunities are there and in time we will see the long awaited sustained recovery in investment

The Committee was not short of explanations for that puzzling weakness in business investment (MPC, 2007):

This weakness reflects the fact that other factors are likely to be of more importance than the cost of finance in determining the level of investment; certainly empirical studies suggest that the influence of the cost of capital is relatively weak. Expectations of future profitability are key, and heightened uncertainty about prospects can lead to investment being put on hold, which may have been the case in the early stages of the recovery from the 2001–03 slowdown. Balance sheet considerations may also have been important, particularly for smaller companies who have to rely on the banks for finance rather than internally generated funds. And for companies with limited access to outside funds, the need to cover pension deficits may also have been a factor. Finally, the recent investment weakness could in part reflect the unusually high levels of investment in IT ahead of the millennium, which reduced the need for subsequent investment

Of course, the price of ICT goods had fallen significantly relative to the price of capital goods, which in turn had fallen relative to the price of output, and those relative price trends complicated the analysis of the nominal data on business investment. Depending on the elasticity of substitution in the production function – another key unknown structural feature of the economy – one might expect to see a downward trend in the share of investment in demand *in current prices* (Ellis and Groth, 2003). Finally, given the overarching theme of this book, one intriguing explanation for the behaviour of business investment promoted by external member Kate Barker was that the Great Stability was not so stable after all, if one was prepared to look through the microscope at the developments at the company level rather than through a telescope at the developments at the sectoral level (Barker, 2005c):

preliminary work suggests that the 'Great Stability' of the UK economy since the inception of inflation targeting has not been reflected at the level of individual firms – and indeed that in the UK individual firms may have seen increased volatility for sales and for profits. In the US, where a similar contrast is apparent, various explanations for it have been put forward. It is possible that the divergent trends in volatility might be related, to the extent that firms undertake more risky projects in a more stable macro environment. However, an alternative explanation might be that greater firm volatility is due to greater competitive pressures. This latter case would provide some explanation for the fact that business investment in the UK has been weaker than expected given the more stable macroeconomic performance.

Again, one is struck by the diverse range of explanations for the weakness of investment. It is not unreasonable to conclude that this diversity should be reflected in a range of views across the Committee about the prospects for investment, presuming that different members of the Committee attached different weights to these explanations (which have different implications for the future).

8.5 Asset prices and financial imbalance

It sometimes claimed that the MPC were wilfully blind to developments in asset prices and the build-up of financial imbalances during the Great Stability. This is self-evidently false. The Committee clearly believed that the constellation of asset prices influenced the outlook for activity and inflation: from the impact of the price of corporate bonds and equities on investment via the cost of capital and consumption via wealth effects, to the impact of the stock of debt on the transmission mechanism, and so on. These channels (and more) are faithfully recorded in the Committee's description of the transmission mechanism (MPC, 1999) and are described at length in a QB article on this topic written by a senior member of Bank staff (Clews, 2002).

We can also fall back on revealed preference. If the Committee did not feel that information on developments in financial markets was helpful in setting policy it seems unlikely that the Committee would have tolerated sitting through presentations on this material every month during meetings which lasted the best part of a day in the early days of the MPC.

The debate is around whether policy-makers should attach *additional* importance to asset prices and broader developments in financial markets over and above these plain vanilla transmission channels, and in particular, whether central bankers should raise rates to pre-emptively prick bubbles when prices were found to be out of line with fundamentals. Policy-makers faced a trade-off: they had to choose between taking action today and suffering below-target inflation or instead waiting to take action tomorrow – allowing the bubble to expand, which might lead to a more significant inflation undershoot at some unknown point in the future when the bubble eventually burst of its own accord.

Critically, for the purposes of our key observation – that there was no meaningful dissent in the pattern of votes in the first decade of the MPC despite differences of view on aspects of the conjuncture – we shall learn that the Committee did not always see eye to eye on this issue (Lomax, 2007):

> There has been a long running debate among central bankers about how they should respond to asset price booms – and possible busts – with some arguing that there is a case for taking pre-emptive action, over and above what might be warranted to meet the inflation target over the normal two to three year horizon. There have been members of the MPC on both sides of this argument.

We now turn to set out the general parameters of this debate – as the Committee saw it – before turning to discuss a couple of key issues – house prices and household debt, and the currency and the current account – before turning to discuss a related concern: the behaviour of money and credit.

8.5.1 General issues

The Committee was well aware of the warnings issued in Basel that those financial imbalances posed a significant medium-term threat to price stability, and the successful pursuit of price stability in the short run could even aggravate the build-up of financial imbalances (Borio and Lowe, 2002). Indeed, in the early days of the MPC, members of the Committee openly acknowledged that they were consciously encouraging the build-up of those imbalances – boosting domestic demand to compensate for the weak international environment (George, 2001, 2003):

> there is not much that we can do directly, through monetary policy, to affect the various external influences weighing upon our economy. But we can attempt to offset their effects, by encouraging the growth of private sector domestic demand to try to keep overall demand in the economy growing in line with potential supply. And that in effect is what we have done through our recent interest rate cuts. This approach is not, however, without risks. It involves accepting – at least while the dampening external influences persist – a growing imbalance between the internationally-exposed and the domestically-oriented sectors. If we did not accept that, then overall demand and output would be lower, and inflation would tend to fall further below target.
>
> We've had to cope with a painful imbalance within the economy over the past few years as a result of successive storms emanating from overseas. And it has been truly painful for the externally-exposed sectors of our economy. To stay on course while those storms persisted we've had to compensate for the external weakness by accepting – indeed positively encouraging through monetary policy – domestic consumer demand growth at a rate that we knew could not be sustained indefinitely.

The Committee did not contest the idea that there was a potential trade-off between stabilising inflation today and stabilising inflation tomorrow, or that the Committee had the scope to pursue this 'bubble bursting' strategy within the remit (King, 2002):

> The fact that growing imbalances might cause sharp deviations of inflation from target at some point in the future, raises the possibility of a trade off between deviations of inflation from target over the next year or so and deviations of inflation from target further ahead. That, I believe, is the right way to think about the challenge to monetary policy posed by asset price movements. Although there are no simple answers I hope I have shown that inflation targeting is enough, provided that one thinks carefully about the horizon over which policy can hope to affect inflation.

However, at no point during the Great Stability was there a majority within the Committee in favour of exercising that option: of adjusting the policy stance to address the long horizon threat posed by financial imbalances and asset prices.

The house view on the appropriate response to asset prices in the early days of the MPC was presented in a speech by Chief Economist John Vickers:

> This discussion has echoed the findings in the recent paper by Bernanke and Gertler (1999). The main conclusion from their analysis is best quoted verbatim (but with emphasis added): 'Inflation-targeting provides an effective, unified framework for achieving both general macroeconomic stability and financial stability. Given a strong commitment to stabilizing expected inflation, it is neither necessary nor desirable for monetary policy to respond to changes in asset prices, except to the extent that they help to forecast inflationary or deflationary pressures'.

Charles Bean, Vickers' successor as Chief Economist, would go on to discuss this issue at length and the difficulties involved in setting out on a bubble-bursting escapade. His speech to the AEA conference in early 2004 (Bean, 2004) highlighted the three key difficulties in implementing this strategy:

> First, the policymaker must judge whether an asset price increase is warranted by the fundamentals or whether it is instead based on misplaced expectations and furthermore poses a threat to future financial and macroeconomic stability … Given that asset price boom-busts are apt to occur when there has also been an improvement in fundamentals, that is not likely to be a straightforward task, at least in the early stages of the upswing.
>
> Second, once a bubble is large enough to be reliably identified, the presence of lags in the transmission mechanism of monetary policy complicates the calibration of the appropriate policy. Raising official interest rates will be counterproductive if the bubble subsequently bursts, so that the economy is subject

to the twin deflationary impulses of the asset price collapse and the effect of the policy tightening.

Third, a modest increase in interest rates may do little to restrain an asset price boom. But an increase large enough to materially affect the evolution of asset prices is likely to have a significant adverse impact on economic activity. So the policy maker would need to believe that the short-term costs from such a strategy are outweighed by the uncertain longer term gains.

There is a final consideration which will influence the decision whether to proactively intervene and prick a bubble – and that is the degree of confidence policy-makers have in their capacity to manage the fallout if they do not intervene and let the bubble run its course. The experiences of the Greenspan Fed during the dotcom bubble and bust appeared to suggest that it was safe to rely on the reactive 'mop up after' strategy (Blinder and Reis, 2005).[8] That said, not everyone on the Committee was convinced (Tucker, 2006b):

I think I would want to register just a slight qualification to a strong version of the proposition that the central bank should simply – as if it could be simple – 'mop up' after a bubble has burst. Policymakers need to take care that the measures they take to offset the impact on aggregate demand of one type of imbalance unravelling do not themselves create or exacerbate imbalances elsewhere in the economy, including in other asset markets.

The final word on the majority view belongs to Mervyn King, who said the following about the virtues of the leaning against the wind in May 2007 (FT, 2007):

We have always got the option and we've always said that if we felt there was a real risk that there would be a future shock to demand resulting from a collapse in asset prices that would then lead to a sharp fall in inflation that would lead us to below target, we could take that into account and we could then set interest rates in order to smooth a future path of inflation. Both Charlie Bean and I in speeches have made that quite clear over a number of years, but it's actually been extremely hard to identify a point in the past when we felt that was something that was material to our decisions on interest rates. [emphasis added]

8 Blinder and Reis (2005) argued 'The "mop up after" strategy received a severe real world stress test in 2000–02, when the biggest bubble in history imploded, vaporizing some $8 *trillion* in wealth in process. It is noteworthy, but insufficiently noted, that the ensuring recession was tiny and that not a single sizeable bank failed. In fact, and even more amazingly, not a single sizeable stock brokerage or investment bank failed, either. Thus the fears that the "mop up after" strategy might be overwhelmed by the speed and magnitude of the bursting of a giant bubble proved to be unfounded. Regarding Greenspan's legacy, then, we pose a simple rhetorical question. If the mopping up strategy worked this well after the mega-bubble burst in 2000, shouldn't we assume that it will also work well after other, presumably smaller, bubbles burst in the future?'

This view was not universally shared on the MPC. In the early years of the MPC, external member Sushil Wadhwani advocated a more flexible approach to inflation targeting (Wadhwani, 2002):

> an inflation targeting central bank might improve macroeconomic performance by reacting to asset price misalignments over and above the deviation of, say, a two-year ahead inflation forecast from target. One argument for doing so is that 'leaning against the wind', when an asset price moves for 'non-fundamental' reasons, can moderate the impact on the real economy. A second advantage of having a central bank that behaves in such a fashion is that the knowledge of a likely policy response to an inflating bubble should reduce the likelihood of asset price bubbles forming in the first place. I should emphasise that our proposal did not envisage targeting asset prices, as, of course, the central bank would continue to target inflation. Reacting to asset price misalignments would help the central bank fulfil its remit more effectively.

8.5.2 House prices and household debt

If there was one asset price and one financial imbalance that consumed more of the Committee's time than any other during the Great Stability it was the rapid rise in house prices and the build-up in household debt. In this section we will review how the Committee's narrative on the housing market changed through this period; for a more detailed study see Cobham (2013).

The state of the housing market was a constant theme in the policy debate during this period. But in the early days of the Committee, there was an additional reason to fret about house prices: a proxy for house prices (housing depreciation) featured in the basket used to calculate the target measure of inflation (RPIX). Rapid house price inflation was having a meaningful *direct* impact on the headline rate of inflation relative to a measure that excludes housing costs (like the CPI, or HICP as it was then known). The Committee hoped that this state of affairs would not continue, as the Box in the May 2003 *Inflation Report* noted on the differences between RPIX and HICP inflation laid bare (Bank of England, 2003b):

> The contribution of housing costs has been particularly large recently and is the principal reason behind the widening of the difference over the past year … Looking ahead, the gap between RPIX and HICP inflation is likely to diminish as house price inflation subsides. In the Committee's central projection, house prices are broadly stable by the second year of the forecast, so that the contribution from housing depreciation is negligible

Once the transition to the CPI had been made the issues were more straightforward: what did the upward trend in real house prices and the stock of household debt burden imply about the future path of demand, inflation and therefore the appropriate policy stance?

In the early years, the Committee was clearly perturbed about the outlook for house prices, although the debate appeared to be relatively fluid. In the Minutes of the May 2002 meeting the Committee appeared comfortable with the *level* of house prices (Bank of England, 2002a):

> With the ratio of house prices to earnings above its historical average, the question was how soon this house price inflation would begin to slow and the speed with which it would do so. It was by no means obvious that the current level of house prices was unsustainable.

The following month, the Committee were less sanguine about the state of affairs (Bank of England, 2002b):

> The present rate of increase in house prices was unsustainable, and the longer it persisted the greater would be the risk of a subsequent sharp correction.

The Committee was not short on explanations for a sustainable acceleration in real property prices. External member Kate Barker cited four candidate explanations (Barker, 2005a):

> The most obvious is the front-loading effect – the fact that lower nominal interest rates ease the ability to pay at the start of a mortgage … The second support for higher prices over recent years is the fall in long-term real interest rates … The third reason for higher house prices is the slow growth of housing supply relative to demand … A fourth explanation is that effective demand has risen by more than would have been expected, based purely on household growth, because of an increased preference by households for investment in housing, rather than equity or other financial markets

The second factor – the fall in long-term real interest rates – was given particular prominence by several MPC members (Nickell, 2004, Barker, 2005a, King, 2006). Bank research on this subject (Weeken, 2004), which was cited by Nickell and Barker, concluded that:

> a simple 'dividend' discount model of the housing market suggests that lower real interest rates can account for part of the increase in the ratio of house prices to net rentals since 1996. Nevertheless, to account fully for this increase, the housing risk premium would need to have fallen too. Comparing the implied housing risk premium now with that in the late 1980s may suggest that house prices are closer to sustainable levels now than was the case in the late 1980s

In other words, it was not clear that the level of house prices was unsustainable *so long as real interest rates remained very low* (Nickell, 2005b):

> it is impossible to tell whether or not there has been a house price bubble in the light of the fall in UK long-term real interest rates from around 4% in the mid 1990s to around 2% by 2000.

The fate of house prices was thus tied to another probable imbalance – this time in global markets, between savings and investment (King, 2006):

> since we do not know the causes of low long-term rates, can we be sure for how long they will persist. Monetary policy will, therefore, need to be alert to the information contained in a wide range of asset prices, to be forward-looking in its aim of maintaining low and stable inflation, and to be ready to respond to changes in the signposts.

In the meantime, the MPC pushed back against the idea of a strong *mechanical* link between house prices and demand, and specifically a strong net wealth effect for the population as a whole, from the very beginning (King, 1998a):

> The impact of rises in house prices on consumption – which is cause and which is effect – remains hotly contested by economists. A rise in house prices leads not only to an increase in wealth but also to an increase in the cost of housing services. Or, to put it another way, if the price of your home goes up, you will not be able to spend more on other things if you wish to carry on living in your home. So it is not at all clear that changes in house prices will in fact have a significant impact on household spending.

That is not to say that the Committee and the Bank rejected the idea of any link between house prices and aggregate demand (see, for example, Aoki, Proudman and Vlieghe (2001)); simply that the correlation between them was unlikely to prove stable. The house view on house prices and household spending was summarised in a *Quarterly Bulletin* article published towards the end of the Great Stability era (Benito et al., 2006) which examined the likely reasons for the breakdown of that correlation during this period:

> The evidence suggests that causal links have been weaker, and common factors less influential, in the recent past. To what extent is unclear … It seems likely that both common factors and causal links are key to the weaker association between house prices and consumer spending of the past few years.

That said, as in so many areas there was plenty of uncertainty in the view – if not, as we will go on to discuss, in the votes. The MPC was not confident about the likely path of house prices – as Governor King famously remarked 'You'd have to be either mad or a publicity seeker to predict what is going to happen to house prices' – or their impact on the economy (Bean, 2002):

> Our central expectation is that the rate of increase of house prices will slow sharply over the next year, with prices becoming broadly stable in two years' time. And if that happens consumption growth should slow too, although the presence of some unexploited housing collateral may mean that slowdown will only follow with a lag. But this is not a view we hold with great confidence, and there are risks on either side.

As for household debt, that was explained away as one piece of a larger jigsaw: as ownership of the housing stock passed down the generations in an era of rapidly rising house prices, households trading down or out of the market exited the market with an ever larger stock of financial assets, whilst those at the other end of the property ladder were racking up ever larger financial liabilities. In particular, the Committee did not view the build-up of debt as a price that was not worth paying for an unsustainable consumption boom, and therefore did not view this issue as one of first-order importance to the conduct of policy at that moment (Nickell, 2004):

> The fact that household debt accumulation appears not to be closely related to household consumption growth indicates that it will not have a direct impact on monetary policy. However, it may have some small indirect impact if, for example, high levels of debt make the response of the economy to interest rate changes more uncertain.

In passing, the story on unsecured household debt was somewhat different – but the MPC comforted itself that whilst this was a 'significant social issue' it was unlikely to be a macroeconomic concern, because the people concerned accounted for such a small share of consumption (MPC, 2007).

This leads us to the question of what could have been done to restrain house prices. External member Steve Nickell reasserted the mainstream mantra that only a large and sustained increase in Bank Rate would have been required to rein in house prices (Nickell, 2005b):

> Using the Bank of England model and house price equation, we try and answer this question. Of course, any answers we obtain have to be treated with caution since they are bound to be subject to substantial error. However, they should give us the right order of magnitude… what sort of rise in interest rates in 2002 would have been required to eliminate the surge in house price inflation in 2003–4 and generate instead the dotted path ..? It is hard to do this exactly … we need a 300 basis points rise in the interest rate in 2002 Q3 which lasts for 13 quarters. Not surprisingly this interest rate shift has a significant impact on the overall economy, taking more than 1/2 per cent off GDP in 2003 and 1 per cent off inflation in 2004 to have any significant impact on the housing boom, the MPC would have had to raise interest rates by around 300 basis points for three years from late 2002.

Whether the Bank of England model was capable of giving a sensible answer to a serious question about the evolution of financial imbalances is at best debatable (see the discussion in Section 8.3). In any case, it is interesting to contrast this claim with the reaction to the one moment during this period when it appears that the Committee – in the person of the Governor – attempted to talk some sense into the market (King, 2004b):

> After the hectic pace of price rises over the past year it is clear that the chances of falls in house prices are greater than they were. So anyone entering or moving within the housing market should consider carefully the possible future paths of both house prices and interest rates.

The market reaction to this sober assessment appears to have chastened the MPC and discouraged any further attempts at jaw-boning down house price inflation. For example, under the title 'The Great House Price Crash 2005?', the BBC reported one estate agent's recollections of the response to Governor King's speech (Liptrot, 2005):

> We saw visitor numbers to our offices decrease dramatically … Hits to our website fell through the floor, the telephones simply stopped ringing.

There were clear differences of opinion on the Committee over what to do about housing – although not on the scale that Nickell (2005b) indicates was required to make a difference. Concerns about stoking up the housing market bubbled to the surface, but soon submerged. For example, the Minutes of the February 2003 meeting when the Committee cut rates by 25 basis points noted (Bank of England, 2003a):

> any signal of an easier interest rate environment could prompt further, unsustainable, accumulation of debt by households, potentially exacerbating the subsequent adjustment and complicating the operation of monetary policy.

But by July of that year, when rates were once again cut, the Minutes noted (Bank of England, 2003c):

> A repo rate reduction seemed unlikely to cause house prices to accelerate, given the current slowdown in housing activity. There was therefore less risk than earlier in the year of stimulating further increases in household borrowing and so exacerbating the imbalance between domestic demand and net trade.

Clearly, no MPC member advocated a profound shift in strategy to rein in house prices, but it is clear that a couple of MPC members were more concerned than most about the consequences of the inexorable rise in house prices and household debt. In his last speech as an MPC member, Sushil Wadhwani sounded a clear warning about the need for vigilance on house prices (Wadhwani, 2002).

> there is necessarily some uncertainty about whether, at a national level, the housing market is significantly overvalued as yet. However, the current double-digit house price growth cannot go on for very long before the market would start looking overvalued. I believe that a clear signal from monetary policymakers that they would, other things being equal, react to a bubble if one clearly emerged would make the continuance of strong house price growth less likely now.

In the years that followed, Deputy Governor Andrew Large would pick up the cudgels, making the case for slightly higher interest rates to lean against the signature financial imbalance during this period (Large, 2004):

> It is important to remember that we need to consider the fulfilment of our monetary policy remit over time. Not just over the next two years for which our forecast is given, but over the longer term as well. Sudden unexpected shocks of course could threaten monetary stability and might make keeping to the target trickier. We need to ensure that threats of instability from such a shock do not call this into question. With this in mind, each month when we on the MPC make our policy decision I am conscious of the debt situation. In particular the possibility that the potential vulnerabilities stemming from higher debt levels do in fact crystallise at some point and trigger a sharp demand slowdown that could have an adverse impact on monetary stability and make it more difficult to meet the inflation target over time …
>
> I mentioned my tendency to think about the risks, however conscious I am of the central case. And this explains why on several occasions over recent months I have found myself voting for a rise; with a view to discharging our mandate to stabilise inflation at the target level, with stability in the monetary arena.

8.5.3 Sterling

In the early years of the MPC the asset price and imbalance that concerned the MPC most was the currency – and in particular sterling's 'remarkable strength' against the euro (King, 2000) – and the current account deficit. In a speech entitled 'No country is an island' (King, 1999) the then Deputy Governor observed:

> final domestic demand growth, which has averaged 4% a year for four years, has exceeded supply and the trade deficit has risen. Indeed, net trade is now likely to have made a negative contribution to output growth for five consecutive years, the longest such period since the nineteenth century.

The Bank's Chief Economist John Vickers was able to cite a number of factors which might explain the appreciation of the currency, but sterling's strength clearly came as a surprise to the Committee (Vickers, 2000):

> I know of no convincing explanation of the extent of sterling's strength

Vickers argued that while it was likely that sterling would depreciate in the future, there was considerable uncertainty around that view – an observation no doubt informed by the Committee's early track record in this area (see Figure 5 in Wadhwani, 2000b). As an interesting aside, he also acknowledged that there was disagreement within the Committee about the likely path of the exchange rate (Vickers, 2000), which one would imagine might have been reflected in differences of view over the policy stance:

> Some implications of this uncertainty are: that no reasonable person can be confident about where the exchange rate is heading; that people can very reasonably disagree about the chances of different exchange rate paths occurring (and MPC members do).

When it came to the policy response, the house view was that, as per asset prices in general, the Committee should respond to the direct effect of the currency on the outlook, but little could or should be done to address an imbalance (George, 2000):

> Even as a central banker I can understand why many euro-exposed businesses feel hard done by in present circumstances. And I can understand why they in particular might urge the Monetary Policy Committee to signal that UK short-term interest rates have peaked. They make a seductive case. But in fact it's not as straightforward as it sounds. If the intention is that by signalling that our interest rates have peaked we might weaken sterling against the euro, it is not at all obvious that it would in fact have that effect ... it is not at all clear that there is much that we could do – even if we wanted to – to weaken sterling against the euro by marginal changes in short-term interest rates.

External member Sushil Wadhwani was not so sure; he was clear that sterling was 'overvalued' and made the case for an alternative strategy to respond to this asset price misalignment (Wadhwani, 2000b):

> that interest rates be held modestly lower than what is necessary to hit the inflation target 2 years out, because such a policy would, by keeping the pound lower than it would otherwise be, both, reduce the size of the inflation undershoot now, and would plausibly reduce the likely size of the inflation overshoot that might occur if and when the pound falls eventually (because it would fall from a less elevated level).

Governor King (2000) effectively made the opposite case – arguing that the Committee could not persist with its current accommodative strategy indefinitely (i.e. pumping up domestic demand to compensate for weak external demand):

> The message for policy is that it is important not to let domestic demand grow too rapidly for too long. The longer the correction is left, the sharper the required adjustment will be. The higher one end of the see-saw, the greater the subsequent lurch will be. The trade deficit cannot continue to widen indefinitely. Hence, at some point domestic demand will have to grow at below its sustainable trend level rather than significantly above as it has done now for some time – over 4% a year on average over the past four years. By acting pre-emptively, and trying to anticipate developments, the MPC has been able to maintain overall stability in the economy, but the sharp rise in sterling led to a

lurch in the economic see-saw ... Pre-emptive action to slow domestic demand growth to a more sustainable level is the key to avoiding a larger and more painful adjustment at a later date. That is why the MPC has raised interest rates by 100 basis points since September.

However, as time went on, and sterling remained at its elevated level, it appears that concerns over the external imbalance started to fade into the background as just one of a number of risks, with the 'bubble baton' passing from the currency market to the housing market (Nickell, 2005b):

It was the dramatic rise in 1996/7 which led people to refer to unsustainability, misalignment and even bubbles. However, as time passed and sterling remained within the 98/110 band, talk of unsustainability and misalignment died away, so that at the time of writing (Summer 2005), with sterling still within the 98/110 band, misalignment of the trade-weighted UK exchange rate is rarely thought to be a major issue for monetary policy. Indeed, some time in early 2002, house prices took over as the relevant asset price for those who wanted monetary policy to react to misalignments.

Indeed, in a speech about the current account deficit, external member Steve Nickell pivoted from the flow imbalance to the more ambiguous stock position, emphasising the supportive nature of the composition of the UK's foreign assets and liabilities (Nickell, 2006):

So long as average returns on equity type assets continue to exceed average returns on debt type assets, the current position is probably sustainable. Risks include first, a continuing and rapid increase in the trade deficit which might eventually undermine the favourable adjusted net asset position. This would probably take a long time. Second, a significant fall in the long-term returns on equity relative to returns on debt. Third, UK assets held by foreign residents become more weighted towards equity type investments, perhaps by a massive purchase of UK companies by foreign concerns. Finally, a large and permanent real appreciation of sterling which would significantly reduce UK assets relative to UK liabilities. At present, this seems unlikely.

In its summary of its first ten years, the Committee simply concluded that 'at some stage the current account deficit will probably need to close' (MPC, 2007). Within a couple of years, the value of the currency would fall by a quarter in trade-weighted terms.

8.5.4 Money and credit

The other key feature of the financial imbalances story during the Great Stability was the rapid growth in the money supply. In days gone by, central bankers would have interpreted rapid growth in broad money as the precursor of an imminent acceleration in nominal demand and consumer prices – and with good reason, as research done by Bank staff (Benati, 2006) illustrated:

> Only one stylised fact – the high correlation between inflation and the rates of growth of both narrow and broad monetary aggregates at the very low frequencies – has emerged as remarkably invariant to changes in the policy regime and, as such, should be regarded as structural in the sense of Lucas (1976), and should be replicated by any reasonable macroeconomic model.

However, the 'relationship' between broad money and nominal demand and consumer prices appeared to break down in the Great Stability (put another way, the velocity of money turned out to be particularly unstable) – for reasons that largely had to do with an increased demand for money *within financial markets*, summarised in Tucker (2006c):

> Like much of the monetary analysis of the early 1980s, I fear that this is rather inconclusive, other than underlining that one has to get one's hands dirty in analysing the money numbers. It is plausible that a decent chunk of recent UK M4 growth should be seen in the light of structural change in the financial system. Essentially, some types of non-bank financial intermediation have become more significant, and seem to have entailed higher money holdings on the definitions currently employed. If so, recent OFC money growth does not of itself obviously have malign implications for money spending and inflation.

The question was whether this relationship would reassert itself in the future: whether further rapid growth in broad money would pose a clear and present danger to price stability. Indeed, it is noteworthy that Governor King chose to focus on the appropriate role of money in the policy debate in his 'MPC ten years on' speech, in which he challenged the notion that there was no incremental information in money, over and above the signal in inflation expectations, demand or interest rates (King, 2007a):

> I would not want to rely on that for three reasons, which together imply that the growth of money and credit may signal in advance of other indicators that Bank Rate is set at a level inconsistent with bringing inflation back to the target in the medium term. First, we do not have good indicators of the expectations of businesses and employees and, in looking at measures of expectations in financial markets, we must be alert to the possibility that those expectations are formed by people falling into the same trap. Second, the spending of many households and businesses is constrained by the need to use money in transactions and by the availability of credit … Thirdly, official interest rates are not a sufficient statistic for the array of effective interest rates confronting borrowers and lenders … Since many of those rates are unobservable by the MPC, money, credit and asset prices may contain valuable information about the likely outlook for spending.

The majority view on the Committee at this time is probably best summarised by the following comment in the Committee's 2007 submission to the Treasury Select Committee (MPC, 2007):

> The problems of using a monetary target were aptly summed up by Governor Gerry Bouey of the Bank of Canada who reputedly remarked: 'We did not abandon the monetary aggregates; they abandoned us'. Even so, it would be unwise to ignore the money supply entirely. In recent quarters, UK broad money has grown at higher rates, relative to nominal demand, than at any time since 1990.

For many, if not most, members of the Committee there was at least as much to be learned from developments on the other side of banks' balance sheets, and in the analysis of credit conditions as from the monetary aggregates. Paul Tucker's inaugural speech as a member of the MPC provides the clearest insight into how the MPC interrogated the data on money and credit (Tucker, 2003):

> credit conditions as I have discussed them – eg credit spreads to compensate for risk, balance sheet robustness – are real rather than nominal economic variables ... So long as inflation expectations are so anchored, we can afford to focus on the balance of real demand and supply. But that expectations do appear to have been anchored should not seduce us into ignoring monetary (or nominal) barometers. Analysis of credit conditions is a complement to that, not a substitute for it. Credit conditions feed into the assessment of prospective demand pressures, and into gauging how any policy changes will be transmitted in the economy.

This was a period of profound change in financial markets and credit conditions broadly defined. In the early days of the Committee, structural changes in retail credit markets – with the arrival of new entrants and new products – delivered a *de facto* monetary loosening, as a Box in the February 2001 *Inflation Report* outlined (Bank of England, 2001):

> Structural change in retail credit markets has reduced the relative costs and increased the availability of finance in recent years. That may have allowed previously credit-constrained consumers to move closer to their optimal consumption levels, perhaps contributing to recent strong borrowing and consumption growth.

Similar developments were taking place in the corporate sphere, with increased access to asset-based finance for small companies and capital markets for their larger peers (Tucker, 2005). Later, of course, would come the rise of what the then Executive Director Tucker dubbed 'vehicular finance' (Tucker, 2007a).

The MPC did not radically change tack in response to those developments in the tail end of the Great Stability, but one can detect concern if one looks for it. In contrast to the default Great Stability mindset, Paul Tucker gave a decidedly cautious assessment of the outlook for monetary and financial stability given the rapid pace of change in markets (Tucker, 2006c):

> Working with our partners in regulatory organisations and in other central banks, we must seek to understand today's global banking system and capital markets well enough to tell the difference, if and when called upon to do so, between a problem requiring solely a macroeconomic policy response and a more complex financial stability problem. And, most important of all, central banks must strive to maintain the medium-term credibility of monetary policy, as an essential pre-condition for the stability in which both the real and financial economy can thrive. Not pretending that the world is simpler or safer than the reality is one small part of that endeavour.

In the context of our discussion, and in contrast to broader developments in financial markets, it is worth noting that developments in money and credit were influencing the policy stance by the tail end of the Great Stability, leading the Committee to raise rates (Gieve, 2007):

> I voted for a further increase earlier this month partly because I was not convinced that current rates would be sufficient to bring credit growth and nominal demand back to their long term sustainable path.

In passing, and perhaps with the benefit of hindsight, it is interesting to note that the Committee started raising rates in response to one symptom of mounting financial imbalances at this mature stage in the financial cycle given the comments made by Deputy Governor Bean (highlighted earlier) about the risks involved in a 'late in the day' strategy.

8.6 Votes: 'United we stand, united we fall'

President Mario Draghi of the European Central Bank once remarked of his role on the Governing Council (which sets monetary policy in the Eurozone) that 'one of my objectives is that we have as much consensus as possible'. Monetary policy was not supposed to work this way at the Bank of England. The institutional arrangements at Threadneedle Street were designed to encourage individuals to vote their view, and therefore allow dissent to flourish.

Speaking on the first anniversary of the MPC, the then Chief Economist Mervyn King argued that such dissent was desirable – that the motto of the MPC should perhaps be 'divided we stand, united we fall' (King, 1998a):

> there is an additional point which is fundamental to the role of the Monetary Policy Committee ... the evidence suggests that in difficult cases reasonable experts can interpret the evidence in different ways. Rather than take comfort from one self-confident view, which I would find difficult to challenge, I would like to know where the balance of professional opinion lies. That is why in the case of essentially technical judgments it is sensible to rely upon collective wisdom, and there are other areas in which we do precisely that. The Law Lords, for example, reach their decisions by aggregating individual judgments, and the same is true in the United States Supreme Court. The MPC is based on the same principle. For such a system to work it is crucial that the individual members of the MPC give their best judgment and do not try to reach an artificial consensus.

King (2007a) would return to this point in his 'MPC ten years on' speech, making much of the *incidence* of dissent on the Committee:

> Disagreement among the Committee is inevitable; it is also desirable because it represents the individual judgements of members, rather than an attempt to create a false consensus. It is a source of strength. Over the past ten years, there have been 153 dissenting votes, on average more than one per meeting. This institutional encouragement of open debate is in contrast to many other central banks. We don't "do consensus", as one former member put it. Dissent is more frequent than on other central bank committees which publish individual votes ... Not only is the number of dissenting votes greater on the MPC, the frequency of more substantive disagreement – where one quarter or more of the voters dissented – is markedly greater.

It is true that of the 962 votes cast between November 1998 and September 2007 there were 137 dissenting votes – an average of almost exactly one in every seven votes. It is also true that of the 108 meetings during that period there were 18 in which a third or more of the Committee voted against the consensus. However, these data provide a perspective on the nature of dissent within the Committee which is *at best* incomplete.

An alternative approach to measuring dissent within the Committee is to ask *how much* members of the Committee disagreed with each other, not (just) how *often*. Now the picture is radically changed. **Of those 962 votes cast between November 1998 and September 2007 only *one* was more than 25 basis points away from the outcome which eventually won the support of the majority – namely external member Willem Buiter's vote for a 40 basis point cut in March 1999.**[9] The other 136 dissenting votes were all 25 basis points

9 Quantifying the degree of dissent before 1998 is problematic.

away from the majority decision. The question then is whether a dissenting vote of 25 basis points qualifies as *meaningful* dissent – in other words, whether there would be a meaningful economic impact if the Committee followed the alternative monetary strategy 'advocated' by the dissenters. It is the contention of the author that it does not, in which case, contrary to the claim that the MPC didn't 'do consensus', in fact *all the MPC did during this period was consensus.*

If we take the votes of MPC members at face value – as statements about the appropriate level of the overnight rate over the month-long interval before the next policy meeting – then it seems uncontroversial to claim that the dissent observed during the Great Stability was not economically significant. The idea that agents take decisions today on the basis of expectations about the future is a central tenet of modern macroeconomics. It is taken as read that beliefs about the future stance of monetary policy influence asset prices and behaviour today. Few economists would argue that a temporary 25 basis point shock to the policy rate – that is, one which is not expected to persist beyond the next policy meeting – would have a meaningful impact on asset prices and behaviour if those expectations about the future path of policy are not affected.

If instead we interpret dissenting votes as a signal that a member of the Committee believes that policy must remain more/less accommodative than the majority view on the MPC for an extended period (as presumably expressed in the market path for interest rates upon which the forecast is conditioned) and by the amount implied by the vote, then there is more scope for the observed pattern of dissent to be of some economic significance. The question is how much more?

Answering this question is not straightforward. It is dangerous to assume that we can infer the impact of an alternative monetary strategy designed to address specific concerns from the results of the literature on 'monetary policy shocks' – that is simulations in which the policymaker is assumed to deviate from the 'optimal' rule for no good reason – especially if that alternative strategy is to be pursued for an extended period. If the model on which the simulation is run does not include the concern which guides the alternative strategy – for example, the threat posed by financial imbalances – then it is not obvious what can be learned. Moreover, any Lucas Critique compliant counterfactual simulation should allow for the fact that agents revise their priors about the reaction function and adjust their expectations and behaviour accordingly; if the simulation does not capture this shift in behaviour it is unlikely to prove a reliable guide to the impact of a meaningful and persistent departure from the observed strategy.

Nonetheless, the literature on monetary policy shocks provides the most accessible evidence on this question. Of course, even within the confines of that literature, what we would like to know is what the typical MPC member thought the impact of a standard monetary policy shock was. Fortunately, we do have some information about that – we can look to the simulations run on the macroeconomic model used to produce the *Inflation Report* projections, since it is reasonable to assume that the model will have been calibrated to deliver ready reckoners which accord with the Committee's collective priors.

The Bank has published results of the same simulation on the two models that have been used to inform the internal debate over this period: an unanticipated shock to the policy rate of one percentage point which lasts one year, after which time policy follows a standard reaction function. The impact of the shock on the vintage of the Bank's main macroeconomic model presented in the September 2000 update of the *Economic models at the Bank of England* publication is described as follows Bank of England, (2000b):[10]

> The maximum effect of the temporary interest rate increase on real activity occurs after about one year, and the maximum effect on inflation occurs after about two years. For the benchmark simulation, where the Taylor rule with a weight of 0.5 on the deviation of inflation from target is adopted, the level of GDP falls by about 0.3% at the end of the first year, recovering to base after three years. Inflation remains broadly unchanged during the first year, reflecting the degree of nominal inertia in the economy, but by the beginning of the third year has fallen by just over 0.3 percentage points. Thereafter, it returns slowly to base.

In other words, even with shocks which are four times larger than the extent of the dissent expressed in the votes (100 basis points versus 25 basis points) and that are expected to persist for an entire year the results are hardly staggering – a peak impact of about 30 basis points on the level of activity and the rate of inflation. Judged relative to the *perceived* uncertainty about the future path of the economy and even about the current state – as described by the width of the *Inflation Report* fan charts around activity and inflation – these numbers are not large.

Given what the Committee appeared to believe about the size of the interest rate multiplier and the fact that dissent is almost always limited to 25 basis points we can infer by revealed preference that the disagreement within the Committee about the economic outlook must also be

10 Harrison et al. (2005) report that running the same simulation on BEQM yields 'broadly similar' results to those described above.

on a very modest scale – presuming, that is, that members of the Committee agreed on the broad strategy (that is, how they should respond to a given economic outlook). If members of the Committee disagreed about the likely level of output and inflation two years hence by say 30 basis points (again a relatively small amount given the perceived uncertainty expressed in the fan charts) then the Committee ought to be disagreeing about the appropriate level of interest rates by around a percentage point. They did not.

Of course, we cannot take it for granted that the Committee agreed on strategy. For example, members of the Committee may not have agreed on the exact specification of the loss function which guides monetary policy decisions – the relative weights attached to stabilising output and inflation – which is why Lars Svensson (2003) encouraged the MPC to be explicit on this point.[11] Small differences of opinion over the relative merits of stabilising output and inflation should be reflected in differences of opinion over the appropriate policy stance even when Committee members share the same assessment of the outlook. Alternatively, members of the Committee may disagree on the merits of gradual or abrupt approach to adjusting interest rates, or on the merits of dealing with uncertain long horizon threats to stability (such as those posed by bubbles) which might both imply meaningful differences of opinion over the appropriate level of interest rates *today*.[12]

In short, dissent on the scale evident in the pattern of votes throughout this period suggests that if the votes reflected the best judgement of individuals and not an artificial consensus – as King argued that they would – then at no point was there a meaningful difference of opinion within the Committee about either the economic outlook or the appropriate policy response to a given outlook. Put another way, the motto of the Committee has to all intents and purposes been 'united we stand, united we fall'. In passing, we suspect that those economists who do not follow the monetary policy debate closely will be surprised by that explanation: Fuchs, Krueger and Poterba (1998) report considerable disagreement among economists about policy proposals in other spheres.

11 The Bank of England has recently conceded the point: that there is some uncertainty about the loss function which guides policy decisions by arguing that a key virtue of the forward guidance regime is that it 'provides greater clarity regarding the MPC's view of the appropriate trade-off between the speed with which inflation is returned to the target and the support given to the recovery'.

12 Governor King acknowledged this point when in 2012 he discussed an alternative strategy that might have been pursued during the Great Stability period of 'setting interest rates at a much higher level'.

8.7 But what about the evidence that there is useful information in dissenting votes?

The magnitude of dissent expressed in the votes may not be meaningful from an economic perspective, but it does not appear to be random in nature. Gerlach-Kristen (2004) demonstrated that the votes are informative about the future path of policy, and that the market processes news on the pattern of votes into market prices which embody expectations of the future policy stance. What then should we make of the fact that 'epsilon dissent' during the Great Stability is informative about future policy decisions? The answer depends on whether there was an 'artificial consensus', to use King's (1998a) phrase, or whether there was a genuine consensus during this period.

8.7.1 False consensus

It is possible that there were genuine (i.e. economically meaningful) differences of opinion about the appropriate policy stance on the Committee, but those opinions were not *fully* expressed in the votes. In other words, there was latent dissent on the Committee.

Dissenting members of the Committee may choose to vote the direction but not the distance of their dissent – i.e. they signal only that interest rates need to be higher or lower than the majority believes, but not by how much, and it turns out that those signals turn out to be informative about the future path of policy. This still leaves us with the question: why do dissenting members only register the *direction* of their dissent, even if the expression of their dissent is capable of steering expectations?

Similar forces may be at work to those which deliver a typically gradual pace of change in the policy stance and infrequent reversals (changes of direction). External MPC member Richard Lambert (2005a) gave a number of reasons why the Committee preferred a gradual approach:

> There are several reasons why the MPC likes to take small steps in the same direction, as opposed to making a leap. One is to do with uncertainty. Despite all the staff work, members are aware that their knowledge of the economy is far from perfect. The data are often subject to revision, and new information is coming in all the time. There is also room for doubt about how much a particular interest rate change will impact on the economy going forward. Members tend to feel that by moving in small steps they have a better chance of assessing their action, and perhaps refining their views about how much further rates might have to move in the future. On top of this, there is a quite a strong feeling on the Committee that sharp movements which will surprise the public are to be avoided unless they are essential. Better to signal and to explain the need for change than to spring it on to a startled world.

Similar logic could be applied to dissenting votes: the member in question may prefer not to express his or her view in terms of one great leap, but rather as the first of a series of small steps. Of course, this argument only works to the extent that Committee members believe that *markets get the message*: that the observed pattern of dissent, and the explanations provided for it, can deliver the desired change in monetary conditions (Tucker, 2007b):

> Each member wants their individual decisions to matter – to the current Bank Rate, and to the expected path of policy and so the monetary conditions embodied in the money market yield curve. One votes in a minority when one disagrees with the immediate decision and the strategy it might convey. Occasionally, doing so, with the reasons disclosed in the minutes, can be an effective way of influencing monetary conditions.

One factor that could prove particularly powerful in the case of dissenting votes is the impact of those votes on the reputation of both the institution and the individual.

Members of the Committee may feel that evidence of *significant* differences of opinion expressed in the votes may damage confidence in the entire process, leading the market to question the competence of the MPC and the Bank (*'if you can't agree amongst yourselves …'*). Those members advocating a significantly different policy setting to the one agreed by the majority would surely come under pressure to explain why they thought that the actual policy stance was inappropriate (or why their peers had 'got it wrong'). Evidence of major disagreements within the Committee might sap confidence in the narrative supplied by either camp. Moreover, the Committee may find it more difficult to steer expectations of the future path of policy in a world in which there is a large spread in views about the current stance – there would be more scope for a large change in policy in the near future – and that might reduce the capacity of the Bank to stabilise the economy. As a consequence, the MPC may agree to present a *broadly* united front. This brings us neatly to a speech by external member Kate Barker, in which she explains why reversals are relatively few and far between (Barker (2007)):

> One definition of waiting is caution about making a change in interest rates which reverses the direction of the previous change. An early move back towards tightening after a period of loosening, or vice versa, tends to create the impression that the previous set of changes had moved too far, and therefore could be damaging to credibility. Equally, this suggests that clear evidence in support of any change of direction is needed, as the risks attached to a second reversal (concerns about provoking sharp money market movements and public appearance of policy confusion) may increase the cost of a mistake.

In the case of dissent which implies a change of direction, issues of personal reputation may come to the fore: the central-bank-watching community may criticise those policy-makers who appear to 'flip flop' – i.e. constantly changing their minds about the appropriate policy stance.[13] Special opprobrium may be reserved for those policy-makers who stray from the majority position only to rapidly return to the fold. This brings us neatly to a comment by external member Charles Goodhart (1998), who, in response to claims by one central bank watcher that he would not change his mind (and vote) for 'reasons of credibility', said the following:

> Yet let me reprise once again. If policy is roughly on course to deliver the desired objective, then policy should be finely balanced and should react to incoming unanticipated news in an approximately random walk fashion. A committee, or an individual within that, who consistently votes the same way for month after month either has got the balance of policy seriously wrong, or individually must think that that balance is seriously wrong.

An alternative explanation for latent dissent within the Committee lies in the politics of persuasion. The only way to change policy is to convince four other people on the Committee of the merits of your arguments for a change in stance. Dissenting Committee members may have perceived that they stood more chance of shifting the policy stance in the right direction by repeatedly making the case for an epsilon change meeting after meeting, forecast round after forecast round. Dissenting members may have perceived that making the case for a more radical discrete shift in the stance would have proved counter-productive.

8.7.2 Genuine consensus

The other explanation for the observed pattern of votes is that the Committee was of one mind: the votes of so-called dissenting members of the Committee do indeed reflect their views on the optimal policy setting. The literature on the predictive power of dissenting votes may suggest that there is still useful information in these votes of epsilon dissent, but it is harder to make the case that dissenting members end up 'winning the argument' because there is no argument to be had. In this case, there is no meaningful difference in the views or the votes of the

13 See for example the criticism cited by Goodhart (1998): 'Where the committee lost credibility last week is in its inconsistency … What is the outside world meant to make of members who can change their view so readily? It suggests a fickle committee, influenced by the latest anecdotal or statistical evidence, swaying its opinions one way or the other and back again'.

MPC. If Committee members do vote their views then it is fair to say that the Committee was in near complete agreement on both the outlook and the appropriate policy response throughout this period – a permanent genuine consensus in the policy debate which appears to be *prima facie* evidence of *Groupthink*.

Consider the huge number of judgements that need to be made in order to arrive at a considered view of the outlook – about the current state of the economy (for example, the size of the output gap), the nature of the steady state to which the economy is headed (for example, the level of the stock–output ratio which companies wish to maintain in the long run), how the economy responds to shocks (for example, how sensitive consumption is to real interest rates) or the appropriate path of the exogenous variables on which the forecast is conditioned (for example, the rate at which world trade is assumed to expand). Governor King alluded to this point in the August 2007 press conference (King, 2007b):

> Well there are differences of judgement about almost everything I think. The key one would be that there are bound to be nuance differences in judgements about the amount of spare capacity in the economy that we start with. There are likely to be nuance differences in the speed at which demand is likely to slow over the coming year or so. There are going to be nuance differences about the extent to which prices are likely to rise given the surveys of pricing intentions, or indeed about the path of inflation expectations. These are judgements that I would expect there to be differences of view on. I think if any two of you from this room were to go out and have a coffee after the meeting wouldn't you be amazed if you had exactly the same view on every single detail that went into a judgement about the future for the economy? Of course there are going to be differences of nuance. But these are not particularly large.

Indeed, this author would be amazed if the differences of opinion over each of those details always amounted only to a matter of nuance, and therefore summing across all those differences one consistently ended up with trivial differences in the overall assessment *if the people concerned arrived at their views independently of one another*. But of course that is not the way that the process works.

8.8 Framework: One paradigm, one process and one model to rule them all?

The discussion thus far has not touched on the institutional setup of the Bank of England. In this section we shall briefly review what members of the Committee thought about the policy process from a conceptual and practical point of view before ending with the elephant in the room: the forecast model.

8.8.1 *Paradigm issues*

If one reads the speeches of the dominant figure on the Committee throughout this period, Sir Mervyn King, one can hear a constant refrain of the dangers of relying on one model, one view of the world. In a speech entitled 'Monetary Policy: Practice ahead of theory' (King (2005a) argued:

> No economist can point to a particular model, and in honesty say 'that is how the world works'. A crucial difference between economic and, say, meteorological analysis is that in economics there are no natural constants, not even for the natural rate of unemployment. Our understanding of the economy is incomplete and constantly evolving, sometimes in small steps, sometimes in big leaps. The stock of knowledge is not static … monetary policy in practice is characterised by a continuous process of learning embedded, in the case of the Bank of England, in the rounds of meetings and forecasts that are the daily life of the Monetary Policy Committee.

King argued that this was a key lesson he had learned from Alan Greenspan (King, 2005c):

> Above all, it is vital never to confuse the world with a model. The whole point of a model is to abstract from a wide range of factors in order to think clearly about one particular issue. Let me describe an example of what I shall call 'the Greenspan approach to economics'. It concerns the 'Lucas critique'. Robert Lucas' 1976 paper encouraged economists to construct models which incorporated explicit optimising behaviour by households and firms. Unfortunately, some of them urged policy-makers to apply the lessons from their models as literally as the enthusiasts of the engineering approach to macroeconomic policy had done so in the 1950s and 1960s. The Greenspan approach to economics would advise great caution. The insight of the Lucas critique is that we need to think about the responses of rational households and firms when analysing the consequences of alternative policies. But the likelihood that any particular model captures how the real economy would respond to a given change in policy is vanishingly small. Lucas did not pretend that there existed a single 'true' model from which could be drawn unequivocal predictions about the impact of policy changes.

This was a consistent theme of King's communication throughout the period – constantly rejecting the premise that there was one paradigm which should guide policy. King (2004a) argued that alongside sophisticated structural models, central bankers:

> should also use their judgement; compare current experiences with previous, similar episodes; and continually test and update a range of reduced-form models, which should help give some insight into how the economy is evolving. This is the approach taken at the Bank of England.

Equally, Governor King was not one for putting his faith in 'mindless regressions' (FT, 2007):

> That in a nutshell I think is my philosophy of how you should do policy. Don't rely on regressions from the past. They could be spurious, they can be meaningless, at the very best, they are no more than average correlations of variables in the past, try to think through the economics of the shocks that are hitting the economy.

Although King's comments extolling the virtues of judgement over slavish devotion to models or regressions are likely an excellent guide to the Bank's *modus operandi* it is clear from reading through the speeches of MPC members during this period that different individuals approached the problem of how to 'do policy' in slightly different ways, as Deputy Governor Lomax (2005) observed:

> Judgement always plays a large role – although different people frame their judgements in more or less model-based ways.

At one end of the spectrum we have external member Danny Blanchflower advocating a data driven approach (Blanchflower, 2007):

> I hope this has shown you the importance of 'sniffing the air', and putting the data before the theory where this seems warranted. This is of particular relevance in my role as a member of the MPC, where rate setting decisions must be made on the basis of a wide variety of data, both quantitative and qualitative.

On the other hand, external member Tim Besley advocated a 'from first principles' theory-driven approach (Besley, 2007b).

> In thinking about any economic issue, I am a firm believer in beginning from economic first principles. My relatively brief experience on the MPC has only served to reinforce this. The MPC is updated daily on a myriad of surveys and data sources. But the trick is to find ways of joining up the facts revealed this way and to find a coherent and consistent view of what is going on behind the data. Basic principles of economics are the glue that we need for this exercise to hold together.

Of course, setting policy is more than just a choice of which model to use to process the news. It is also about an assessment of the current state of the economy (i.e. the inputs to those models). In a world without measurement error and publication lags this would be a matter of no importance: in practice, the MPC spends a good deal of its time trying to penetrate the 'statistical fog' to get a clearer picture of the true state of the economy (Lomax, 2004):

> few subjects consume more of our time and energy than another, more insidious, source of uncertainty: one with which the MPC does daily battle – the data … as Lord Peston, Chairman of the House of Lords Select Committee on

Economic Affairs, recently observed, referring to our foot high data pack: 'Statistics seem to be [the MPC's] life blood'.

A key element of that counter data uncertainty strategy was the feedback that the Committee received direct from companies via the Bank's network of Agents (see Ellis and Pike, 2005). Committee members regularly emphasised the importance they attached to that intelligence in supplementing the more traditional information set that central bankers rely on (Julius, 1999, Sentance, 2007):

> If model-based forecasts are highly uncertain and potentially misleading, then it is especially important to seek out complementary sources of information and interpretations of economic developments from those actually in the thick of the action. The Bank's regional agents hold detailed discussions with business people around the country to provide us with such feedback.
>
> One of the strengths of the way the Monetary Policy Committee operates is that this direct contact and feedback from business is built into our processes. First of all, we benefit at our monthly meetings from the reports compiled by the Bank's Agents, who maintain a network of around 8,000 business contacts across the country … In addition, Monetary Policy Committee members each undertake a regular programme of visits to business contacts throughout the country, including company visits, lunch and dinner meetings with groups of business contacts and larger business briefings.

This is not simply a signal extraction problem, of drawing upon a wide range of survey and official data to arrive at the best possible estimate of the current state; it is also about dealing with the more fundamental revisions to the historical data, which can change your view of the behaviour of the economy (Bell, 2004):

> Revisions to data stemming either from more information or methodological improvements will inevitably lead us to reassess our view of the underlying truth. As the prisoners in Plato's cave found when the Guardian tried to enlighten them, this is not always comfortable. But it is an inevitable part of the policy maker's job, and that of other users of statistics, to make sense of revisions

Reading the above only makes it harder to explain how the Committee was in a state of permanent consensus during this period. If Committee members only had access to a small information set of data (that were not subject to revision) and one model then it would not be such a surprise if they arrived at a similar assessment of the outlook and the appropriate response. Surely, the larger the information set which can be used to inform the current state of the economy, the more noisy the data and the more diverse the set of models which can be used to process news and model the dynamics of the economy, the greater the scope for disagreement – as Deputy Governor Rachel Lomax (2005) observed:

> It may be more remarkable that nine economists, labouring under the burden of individual accountability, have so far succeeded in signing off 31 editions of the Inflation Report, and found ways of dealing with the inevitable range of views.

That, in a nutshell, is the insight of this chapter: it is remarkable, and not obviously desirable.

8.8.2 *Practical issues*

It is hard not to reach the conclusion that it is the process itself – discussing the outlook and the response as a Committee – which breeds consensus, although whether taking decisions in this way is likely to lead to the 'right' outcome is a different question.[14] Indeed, one could argue that the whole point of the Committee structure was to foster agreement: policy-makers would learn from one another through discussion and debate (Lambert, 2005b):[15]

> Studies in both the US and the UK suggest that groups of people who are prepared to debate with and learn from each other are capable of producing better results than their smartest individual member, and my experience of the past two years has convinced me of why this is the case.

Indeed, one might view the forecast round, in which the Committee updates the projections published in the *Inflation Report* in light of the news on the quarter and any changes in economic judgements, as the perfect forum in which to hammer out a consensus. Committee members certainly seem to view the crescendo of the forecast round as the moment when the big judgements are taken (Lambert, 2005a):

> the period leading up to publication is when the Committee discusses most intensively how the various pieces of the economic jigsaw all fit together. It builds these discussions around forecasts for growth and inflation which it updates every three months, and which provide the framework for its forward-looking policy decisions. The quarterly round is thus an opportunity to stand back from the daily news agenda and think about longer-term trends. It is for this reason that interest rate changes in the past have often come in the month when the *Inflation Report* has been published: members of the Committee have spent many hours thinking together about the outlook for inflation, during the course of which they may have decided to modify their views.

14 See the discussion in Section 2.5, Part 7 in Barwell (2013).

15 An experiment conducted by Bank staff into the benefits of setting policy by committee did not identify an improvement in performance when individuals were allowed to discuss the outlook, although people did gain from observing the votes of their peers (Lombardelli, Talbot and Proudman, 2002).

The point about the forecast round, with its tight timetable of a small number of set-piece meetings and a looming publication deadline, is that it can focus the mind on reaching a consensus. Without this discipline device, it is easier to imagine the onset of 'paralysis by analysis': with the Committee endlessly commissioning new analysis and never reaching a conclusion King (1999).

> It would be strange if the uncertainties facing the Committee were not reflected in small differences of opinion. And views of the appropriate level of rates have never differed by more than 0.5 percentage points. Nor have these technical disagreements led to "paralysis by analysis".

An (unintended) illustration of the way in which the policy process breeds consensus can be found in a comment by Deputy Governor Lomax concerning the way in which the fan charts are constructed. Lomax argues that differences of opinion *do* emerge in the construction of the *Inflation Report* fan charts, but then goes on to make a surprising claim: that members of the Committee manage to agree on the shape of that distribution, but not necessarily for the same reason (Lomax, 2005):

> The MPC's approach to constructing fan charts can help the members come to an agreement on the substantive issues, while retaining their individual views. This is because the risks are often where the major differences of opinion amongst members lie. And while the members may be able to agree on a collective view of the overall outlook including the degree of uncertainty and balance of risks, it might be for slightly different reasons.

One of two things is happening here: either by sheer fluke Committee members can still agree about the 'big picture' (the overall balance of the risks) without managing to reach agreement about the individual brushstrokes (the nature of the individual risks to the outlook), or members reach a consensus about the shape of the fan chart first and then allow each other the freedom to explain that consensus in different ways. To the author at least, the latter seems a much more plausible explanation.

Of course, one could arrive at a more disturbing conclusion. The central objective of the quarterly forecast round is to process the news: to update the central projection in light of the news on the quarter. There has always been a concern that the Committee would fall victim to one of two potential pitfalls in this process. First, the focus on the central projection encourages policy-makers to devote too much attention to the single most likely outcome, and relative small deviations around it, at the expense of the entire distribution, or a summary statistic of it (like the mean). Second, the focus on processing the news encourages policy-makers to think in terms of changes, not levels – that is, whether a change in the policy stance is warranted, rather than whether the absolute level is inappropriate. It seems likely that a debate framed in terms of the change in the modal projection and the implications for the change in the policy stance is more conducive to the kind of *perma-consensus* we have documented here than a debate framed in terms of the absolute mean outlook and the implications for the absolute policy stance. The evidence presented above is therefore broadly consistent with, but does not decisively prove, that the Committee may indeed have fallen victim to one or both of these pitfalls at certain moments during the Long Expansion.

8.8.3 Forecast models

It is not possible to discuss the impact of the internal policy process in general and the forecast round in particular on the outcome without a word or two about the design of forecast model and its impact on the policy debate – the perfect intersection between questions of paradigm and questions of process.

During our period of interest, the Bank chose to change the design of the model used to drive the analysis in the quarterly round, moving from a tractable macroeconometric model (the Medium-Term Macro Model, or MTMM) towards a much sophisticated and complex alternative (the Bank of England Quarterly Model, or BEQM[16]). The reason for the change in model was set out in the introduction to the BEQM book (Harrison et al., 2005):

> the decision to develop a new model reflected the view that recent advances in both economic understanding and, importantly, in computational power meant that it was possible to improve upon the articulation of the economic structure within the MTMM. As Pagan (2003) noted in his report on modelling and forecasting at the Bank of England, the MTMM was no longer 'state of the art'. In particular, Pagan concluded that 'It seems highly likely that [a new model] could achieve the same empirical coherence [as the MTMM] with a stronger theoretical perspective'. In doing so, this would provide the Committee with a more flexible and coherent framework to aid its economic deliberations. That, in short, is what the new model tries to achieve through a clearer articulation of the underlying structure of the economy and a more explicit identification of the role expectations play.

The importance of the forecast model can be overplayed: the idea that MPC members were slaves to the main model is fanciful. As the quotes above make clear, the forecast process is a judgement-driven not

16 Pronounced Beckham, as in the name of the England football captain of that era.

model-driven process. Equally, it is unreasonable to claim that the design of the model has *no* impact on the process, on the basis of revealed preference. The Bank would not have invested a huge amount of resource into building a new model on a couple of occasions if the design of the model was irrelevant. The particular way in which BEQM achieved a 'clearer articulation of the underlying structure of the economy' mattered: the design of the model will influence the forecast process – the default treatment of news. Arguably, the design also gives us an insight into the mindset of the Committee: how MPC members thought the world worked.

Unsurprisingly, the core economic structure of the BEQM mirrored the current convention in the academic literature – in Cochrane's phrase 'playing by Kydland and Prescott rules but adding some frictions'. Unfortunately, playing by Kydland and Prescott rules meant that the model was poorly equipped to handle significant departures from optimising behaviour and rational expectations in general and the causes and consequences of financial imbalances in particular. Just because the model had a blind spot where the threat posed by financial imbalances was concerned it does not necessarily follow that the Committee was oblivious to what was going on – but it is hard not to reach the conclusion that the design of the model was more hindrance than help when it came to the conduct of monetary policy in the final years of the Great Stability.

In theory the switch from the MTMM to BEQM created an opportunity for a dissenting member of the Committee to challenge the fundamental economic story that underpinned the forecast by examining the sensitivity of the forecast to a different view on the deep structural parameters of the model, as Deputy Governor Lomax (2005) notes:

> There is a high degree of simultaneity in the way the model is solved. It no longer makes sense, nor is it at all easy, to consider the model equation by equation. This provides a greater degree of discipline on Committee members and staff, who are now forced to confront the full implications of their judgements more explicitly. If someone wants to change one of the economic relationships, they need to say.

However, significant changes to a key parameter of a large, complex dynamic general equilibrium (DGE) model are likely to have major implications for the behaviour of the model and fundamental changes to the structure of the model certainly will. But changes to the calibration and structure of the model will typically be constrained such that they approximately preserve certain whole model properties (such as the interest rate multiplier) and therefore any major change will typically require a model recalibration exercise to preserve those properties.

For example, you cannot keep adding fresh sources of real and nominal rigidity to a model without revisiting the calibration of the mechanisms that you had originally included – which with a model as large and complex as BEQM is a time-consuming process not obviously suited to a tight forecast round. Likewise, it is difficult to evaluate the impact of alternative policy paths within a forecast model which has a simple policy reaction function hard-wired into expectations in the model, since all deviations from that simple rule are treated as inexplicable shocks.

In practice it was possible to manipulate the model in the usual fashion given the hybrid structure of BEQM by making changes in the 'non-core' of the model – the atheoretic mapping equations which connected the output of the DGE model in the 'core' to the data. However, it is difficult to put an economic interpretation on adjustments made via coefficients and residuals in the non-core of BEQM or the equations of the MTMM , or to be confident that the 'non-core' can act as an effective sticking plaster for economic mechanisms that are not articulated in the core of BEQM or at all in the case of the MTMM.

In short, it is not clear that the design of the new model (BEQM) was any better suited than the old model (the MTMM) to handle fundamental challenges to the forecast, such as evaluating the relative merits of proactive and reactive strategies for dealing with mounting financial imbalances. Nor for that matter, was it any worse. The key mechanisms involved were absent from both models, and there was no obvious way to integrate analysis from other models into the main forecast model.[17]

8.9 Conclusions and recommendations

This chapter is not intended as an indictment of monetary policy and monetary policy-makers during the Great Stability. No attempt has been made to articulate an alternative monetary strategy which might have confronted the build-up of financial imbalances during this period, let alone demonstrate that this alternative strategy was superior. In passing, the key lesson learned is surely that the increasingly fragile state of the UK economy was crying out for tighter micro- and macroprudential regulation, rather than higher Bank Rate (Barwell, 2013). It is far from

17 In passing, it is not obvious that the Bank's new forecast model (COMPASS) addresses this problem either. The new framework may allow Bank staff to embed the impulse response of a 'credit shock' into the forecast (see Burgess et al., 2013), but if the mechanisms which give rise to that response are not present in the model itself then COMPASS will not process news accurately – the amplification through these financial channels will be lost. The first best solution is full model recalibration when a new feature is included, but that is a resource-intensive process.

clear that monetary policy alone could have averted the disaster: for example, an increase in Bank Rate does little to ameliorate the threat posed to UK monetary and financial stability posed by the structured credit exposures that were accumulating on the balance sheets of the UK banks. Nonetheless, MPC members had to play with the hand that fate dealt them and given that no microprudential response was forthcoming (and there was no macroprudential authority) the Committee had to choose whether to act or not, and it is not obvious that a different monetary policy strategy in the boom could not have made an extremely bad situation in the bust a little better. Clearly, the mop up after strategy proved wholly insufficient, but we leave a more comprehensive discussion of alternative strategies during the Long Expansion to another time and another place.

The concern highlighted by this chapter is that the alternative strategy was never seriously *discussed*, let alone advocated by a dissenting member. A handful of MPC members talked about the merits of a bubble-bursting strategy, but that discussion rarely got as far as seriously calibrating and promoting a radically different policy stance. Indeed, one might be concerned that the Bank did not get as far as seriously calibrating the risks posed by the financial cycle, let alone thinking through the cost–benefit of an alternative strategy.

Arguably the clearest explanation of the *modus operandi* of the Committee – how the Committee thought about low-probability, high-impact tail risk – can be found in the speeches of Executive Director Paul Tucker (Tucker, 2006b,c):

> In my experience, it is not sensible to respond to all possible risks, even some that would have a big impact if they crystallised. Take, for example, global imbalances. If they were to unravel abruptly, with a big fall in the dollar against the euro, aggregate demand in the euro area might fall for a while. Depending on what had happened to sterling's bilateral exchange rates, the UK would not be immune from spillovers, as the euro area is by far our largest trading partner. For some time, therefore, global imbalances have been a real source of risk to the UK as well as to the global economy. Should I have been voting to cut interest rates to head off those risks? I don't think so. It would not have made sense to try to anticipate the effects of a shock that had not yet occurred and over which we had effectively no influence. A number of external 'tail risks' are rather like that.
>
> Yet policymakers also stress a wide range of uncertainties, threatening at least interruptions to the benign conditions of the past decade or so. This is not just an occupational disposition of central bankers. To varying degrees, these uncertainties do feature in real-world policy debates. I have argued previously that some risks — such as those posed by global current account imbalances — could not sensibly be factored in to policy settings ahead of their crystallising.

In truth, this debate is not just about the low-probability, high-impact risks. The extent of the consensus within the MPC during this period was such that it is hard to find any evidence within the votes of differences of view on the high-probability, low-impact risks, or even the appropriate response to the central projection *despite the fact that it is easy to find evidence of differences in view expressed in the speeches.* To repeat: on only one occasion during the first decade of the Committee did a member of the Committee make a case for an interest rate setting more than 25 basis points away from the position agreed by the majority of the MPC.

A similar point can be made about the fan charts. There was a moment in time when certain MPC members felt sufficiently uncomfortable with the view expressed in the fan chart that they insisted upon an alternative view being expressed in the *Inflation Report.* As the Kohn Report noted (Kohn, 2000):

> The MPC needs to continue examining what it means by 'best collective judgment' to refine its understanding and possibly to consider alternative approaches. Originally, apparently, the forecast was a consensus of Committee members, forged through compromise and trade-offs. But as views became more diverse, compromise to achieve a single forecast was no longer possible, and members created Table 6B, which contains alternative assumptions and outcomes for the inflation forecast eight quarters out. Although the Outlook section indicates generally how far from the central tendency some members' forecasts might be, that indication is not explicitly related to the information in Table 6B. The public does not know the number of members at odds with the central projection, and except for that general statement, the distribution of forecasts around the center. Table 6B also has complicated the construction of skews, since members who would have argued for skews to allow them to join the consensus now see themselves on Table 6B.

However, that innovation proved relatively short-lived, so that by the end of the Great Stability all Committee members were happy to sign up to the exact same illustration of the outlook, *despite clear differences of view on the building blocks of those fan charts*.

In short, the behaviour of the Committee during this period is best summarised as 'nine votes, one view'. If the votes or the fan charts are your metrics then there was only token dissent on the Committee, despite the fact that members of the Committee clearly disagreed with each other on the details. Occam's razor suggests that the institutional design contributes towards this strong convergence towards consensus: it seems hard to believe that members of the Committee would continue to agree on the policy setting if they voted in isolation of one another, and the anchor of the lagged dependent variable in the reaction function (i.e. the collective decision the previous month) was removed. The author suspects that the policy settings would soon drift apart, even if one allowed the Committee members to observe the impact of their preferred policy stance on the economy.

The reader will no doubt reach her own conclusion about whether this is a satisfactory state of affairs. One can make the argument that the market would punish those policy institutions where there is evidence of profound disagreement over the stance: market prices which embed an expectation of the future path of policy may price in greater uncertainty about the policy stance and may prove less susceptible to central bank communication or data outturns.

However, the author is not convinced that this argument is sufficiently compelling to justify the 'nine votes, one view' model. It is very hard to disagree with the proposition that the Committee should discuss the risks as well as the central projection in detail and alternative strategy responses behind closed doors. We cannot be sure (it has yet to be proved) that this process would have led to an alternative strategy during the long expansion and superior outcomes in the crash that followed; but there seem clear risks from placing too much emphasis on the mode in the internal policy debate. Moreover, I believe that there is a strong case for individual members communicating to the outside world the differences of view on the policy stance which are implied by their comments on the conjuncture, but which are not apparent in their votes.

We will now briefly discuss possible reforms to the process which might lean against the tendency to artificial or genuine consensus. The solution to this problem of MPC members herding on a common strategy despite clear differences of view on the conjuncture is likely to be found in encouraging members of the Committee to speak more (and therefore think more) about *their own personal views* on why the current policy stance is optimal (or not) relative to an alternative strategy, rather than confining their views largely to the conjuncture – i.e. talk and think more about the outputs of the reaction function rather than just the inputs. Requiring members of the Committee to publish those views sounds like the most effective way to encourage MPC members to think about these issues in the first place.

The Committee was (is) clearly not in favour of such an 'individualistic' approach. Paul Tucker explained at length why he was opposed to including paragraphs in the Minutes which described the views of named MPC members (Tucker, 2007b):

> My reluctance to go down that route stems from a concern that we would slip towards a degree of individualism where members were no longer listening to each other. It would not be possible for members to polish their statements after

the meeting, as they would then be able to tweak their text, ever so slightly of course, in the light of the market reaction to our decision and so on. So highly polished statements would be brought to the meeting, with perhaps even a degree of competition in the depth of the analysis or the beauty of the prose. But the very point of a committee is that we should listen to each other, and then make up our own minds. That includes trying to persuade one's colleagues. Over the years, I have definitely seen occasions where individual members have altered their position during the course of a meeting.

Tucker's argument makes perfect sense – but if one buys the argument in this chapter that potentially dissenting Committee members are too open to persuasion, are too willing to shift their position on policy too much, then a mechanism which throws sand in the herding process and encourages members to 'stick to their guns' is to be welcomed.

However, this issue goes deeper than just the immediate policy decision. The current level of Bank Rate is not a sufficient statistic for the policy stance (the impact of monetary policy on the outlook). The decisions which the markets and agents in the real economy expect the Committee to make in the future will influence behaviour today. Those expectations are in turn based on the past and present behaviour of the Committee – which reveals information about the reaction function – as well as beliefs about the outlook. Members of the Committee should care about those beliefs, and they should have a view about whether those expectations are consistent with their own assessment of the outlook and optimal strategy.

Independent of the arguments advanced in this chapter, there is a strong case for the Bank of England to enhance its communication strategy with markets by signalling what the Committee believes to be an optimal path for policy which respects the uncertainty: in short, publish a fan chart for Bank Rate and the stock of purchased assets (Barwell and Chadha, 2013a,b, 2014). One criticism of this suggestion is that the Committee would be unable to agree upon the optimal path. This does not seem an insurmountable barrier – but it would require individual members to come to their own view about the outlook and the optimal response, so that the Committee could then calibrate fan charts which reflect their collective view, and the differences of opinion between them.

Those individual views could – and in the view of the author should – be published. To repeat, it is not unreasonable to believe that the process of producing a personal view on the outlook and the policy response should make it a lot more likely that the Committee will at least discuss alternative strategies and increase the chance that individual members will make the case for different strategies which reflect the views they express on the outlook.

Of course, there is nothing to guarantee that MPC members will not end up publishing near identical paths for the policy rate – in just the same way that they vote on near identical levels of Bank Rate – but at the very least that would bring the state of near-perfect consensus within the Committee out into the open. Even in a state of near-perfect consensus it seems likely that the process would force the Committee to confront alternative strategies. The Committee would be obliged to explain the narrative behind 'off central case' policy paths implicit within those fan charts in its communication with markets (Barwell and Chadha, 2013a), and in order to conduct that conversation with the outside world the Committee would surely want to explore the merits of a wide set of alternative outcomes and strategies (rather than just those proposed by members of the Committee) within the internal policy debate.

The final constraint here is the resources required to produce alternative forecasts or assessments of alternative strategies. There is no doubt that a more detailed discussion about the risks to the consensus view within the Committee and the costs and benefits of alternative strategy responses would consume additional resources – the precious time of staff to produce additional analysis and of the Committee to digest and discuss it. But that seems a price worth paying; in the words of David Stockton (Stockton, 2012):

> The current focus on best collective judgment may round off differences of view that, if brought into sharper focus, could help the MPC better understand the vulnerabilities in its outlook for the economy and its policies. Surfacing those differences more visibly and systematically could also provide valuable perspective to the public about key areas of dispute in the policy debate.

As discussed in Section 8.3, it is not easy to interrogate the consequences of different interpretations of the way the economy functions or alternative reaction functions within a forecast model. The Committee would need to have access to a large suite of models and considerable analytical support to have a fruitful discussion of these issues. For a discussion of a set of proposals which might enrich the policy debate and enhance the staff's capacity to fulfil this role see Barwell (2014).

To be clear, these proposals are in no way original. The excellent Stockton Review includes the following options for reform (Stockton, 2012):

> 10. Analysis of monetary policy options and strategies could be included routinely in the background materials and briefings prepared by the staff for every forecast round.

11. Consider creating a forecast with an extended horizon beyond the current three-year period – a horizon of sufficient length to allow consideration of the development and likely unwinding of major economic and financial imbalances.

12. Consider publishing some alternative scenarios.

...

15. Consider publishing a summary of the individual forecasts of the MPC members as a supplement to the fan charts in the Inflation Report.

16. Consider increasing communication about the outlook for policy as part of the forecast process.

17. Consider publishing a vote by MPC members on the forecast in addition to a vote on the policy decision.

The Bank has already made good progress in implementing some of the reforms outlined by David Stockton, but if the Bank wants a clear break with the 'nine votes, one view' model of the past, then it is likely that more needs to be done.

Select Bibliography

Adam, C., Cobham, D. and Girardin, E. (2005), 'Monetary frameworks and institutional constraints', *Oxford Bulletin of Economics and Statistics*, 67(4), 497–516.

Aoki, K., Proudman, J. and Vlieghe, G. (Winter 2001), 'Why house prices matter', *Bank of England Quarterly Bulletin*, 460–468.

Bank of England (1998), *Minutes of the June 1998 Meeting.*

(2000a), *Economic models at the Bank of England: September 2000 update.*

(2000b), *February 2000 Inflation Report.*

(2001), *February 2001 Inflation Report.*

(2002a), *Minutes of the May 2002 Meeting.*

(2002b), *Minutes of the June 2002 Meeting.*

(2003a), *Minutes of the February 2003 Meeting.*

(2003b), *May 2003 Inflation Report.*

(2003c), *Minutes of the July 2003 Meeting.*

(2004), *November 2004 Inflation Report.*

(2007a), *May 2007 Inflation Report.*

(2007b), *August 2007 Inflation Report.*

Barker, K. (2005a), 'The housing market and the wider economy?', *Speech*, 24 January.

(2005b), 'Monetary policy in the UK – The framework and current issues', *Speech*, 21 March.

(2005c), 'Economic stability and the business climate', *Speech*, 24 November.

(2007), 'Interest rate changes – too many or too few?', *Speech*, 20 March.

Barwell, R. (2007), 'The macroeconomic impact of international migration', *Bank of England Quarterly Bulletin*, Q1, 48–59.

Barwell, R., Bell, V., Bunn, P. and Gutiérrez-Domènech, M. (2007), 'Potential employment', *Bank of England Quarterly Bulletin*, Q1, 60–69.

Barwell, R. (2013), *Macroprudential policy*, Palgrave Macmillan, London.

Barwell, R. and Burrows, O. (2013), 'Growing fragilities? Balance sheets in The Great Moderation', in Winkler, B, van Riet, A and Bull, P (eds.), *Flow-of Funds Perspective on the Financial Crisis, Volume II: Macroeconomic Imbalances and Risks to Financial Stability*.

Barwell, R. and Chadha, J. (2013a), 'Turning forward guidance into 20:20 vision', *Central Banking Journal*, 24(2).

(2013b), 'Complete forward guidance', in den Haan, W (ed.), *Forward Guidance*.

(2014), 'Forward guidance publish or be damned – or why central banks need to say more about the path of their policy rates', *Vox, 31 August*.

Barwell, R. (2014), 'A new vision for the Old Lady', *Central Banking Journal*, 24(3).

Bean, C. (2002), 'The MPC and UK economy: should we fear the D-words?', *Paper*, 25 November.

(2003), 'Asset prices, financial imbalances and monetary policy: are inflation targets enough?', *Paper*, 19 August.

(2004), 'Asset prices, monetary policy and financial stability: a central banker's view', *Speech*, 3 January.

(2006), Globalisation and inflation, *Speech*, 24 October.

(2007), 'Is there a new consensus in monetary policy?', in Arestis, P (ed.), *Is there a new consensus in macroeconomics?*.

Bell, M. (2004), 'Monetary policy, data uncertainty and the supply side', *Speech*, 15 September.

Benati, L. (2006), 'UK monetary regimes and macroeconomic stylised facts', *Bank of England Working Paper* 290.

Benito, A., Thompson, J., Waldron, M. and Wood, R. (Summer 2006), 'House prices and consumer spending' *Bank of England Quarterly Bulletin*, 142–154.

Besley, T. (2007a), 'Inflation and the service sector', *Speech*, 18 January.

(2007b), 'Consumption and interest rates', *Speech*, 19 July.

Blanchflower, D. (2007), 'Recent developments in the UK economy: the economics of walking about', *Speech*, 30 May.

(2008), 'Inflation, expectations and monetary policy', *Speech*, 29 April.

Blinder, A. and Reis, R. (2005), 'Understanding the Greenspan Standard', *CEPS Working Paper 114*.

Borio, P. and Lowe, P. (2002), 'Asset prices, financial and monetary stability: exploring the nexus', BIS Working Paper 114.

Brazier, A., King, M., Harrison, R. and Yates, A. (2006), 'The danger of inflating expectations of macroeconomic stability', *Bank of England working paper 303*.

Broadbent, B. (2012), 'Productivity and the allocation of resources', *Speech*, 12 September.

Buiter, W. (1999), 'The new economy and the old monetary economics', Speech, 27 October.

Burgess, S., Fernandez-Corugedo, E., Groth, C., Harrison, R., Monti, F., Theodoridis, K. and Waldron, M. (2013), 'The Bank of England's forecasting platform: COMPASS, MAPS, EASE and the suite of models', *Bank of England working paper 471*.

Chadha, J., Macmillan, P. and Nolan, C. (2007), 'Independence day for the 'Old Lady': a natural experiment on the implications of central bank independence', *Manchester School*, 3(6), 311–327.

Christiano, L. and Fitzgerald, T. (2003), 'The band-pass filter', *International Economic Review*, 44 (2), 435–465.

Clews, R. (Summer 2002), 'Asset prices and inflation', *Bank of England Quarterly Bulletin*, 178–185.

Cobham, D. (2013), 'Central banks and house prices in the run-up to the crisis', *Oxford Economic Papers*, 65, 42–65.

Dury, K., Piscitelli, L., Sebastia-Barriel, M. and Yates, T. (Summer 2003), 'What caused the rise in the UK terms of trade', *Bank of England Quarterly Bulletin*, 164–176.

Ellis, C. and Groth, C. (2003), 'Long-run equilibrium ratios of business investment to output in the United Kingdom, *Bank of England Quarterly Bulletin*, 177–187.

Ellis, C. and Pike, T. (2005), 'Introducing the agents' scores', *Bank of England Quarterly Bulletin*, 424–430.

Ellis, C. and Turnbull, K. (2007), 'Gauging capacity pressures within businesses', *Bank of England Quarterly Bulletin*, Q1, 79–85.

Financial Times (2007), *Transcript of interview with Mervyn King conducted on 1 May.*

Fuchs, V., Krueger, A. and Poterba, J. (1998), 'Economists views about parameters, values, and policy: survey results in labor and public finance', *Journal of Economic Literature*, 36(3), 1387–1425.

George, E. (2000), 'New economy – same old problems', *Speech*, 7 November.

(2001), 'Mansion House Speech', *Speech*, 20 June.

(2003), 'Mansion House Speech', *Speech*, 18 June

Gerlach-Kristen, P. (2004), 'Is the MPC's voting record informative about future UK monetary policy?', *Scandinavian Journal of Economics*, 106(2), 299–313.

Gieve, J. (2006), 'The puzzle of UK business investment', Speech, 26 September.

(2007), 'London, money and the UK economy', Speech, 26 June.

Goodhart, C. (1998), 'Central bankers and uncertainty', *Speech*, 29 October.

Gordon, R. (1997), 'The time-varying NAIRU and its implications for economic policy', *Journal of Economic Perspectives*, 11(1), 11–32.

Groth, C., Nuñez, S. and Srinivasan, S. (2006), 'Productivity growth, adjustment costs and variable factor utilisation: the UK case', *Bank of England Working Paper 295.*

Harrison, R., Nikolov, K., Quinn, M., Ramsay, G., Scott, A. and Thomas, R. (2005), *The Bank of England Quarterly Model*, Bank of England, London.

Julius, D.-A. (1999), 'Back to the future of low global inflation', *Speech*, 20 October.

(2000), 'New trends in a new economy', *Speech*, 15 March.

King, M. (1998a), 'The UK economy and monetary policy – looking ahead', *Speech*, 27 May.

(1998b), 'Monetary Policy and the labour market', *Speech*, 1 December.

(1999), 'The Monetary Policy Committee two years on', *Speech*, 17 May.
(2000), 'Balancing the economic see-saw', *Speech*, 14 April.
(2002), 'The inflation target ten years on', *Speech*, 19 November.
(2003), 'Speech to the East Midlands Development Agency', *Speech*, 14 October.
(2004a), 'Comments on 'Risk and uncertainty in monetary policy', 3 January.
(2004b), 'Speech to the CBI Scotland Dinner', 14 June.
(2004c), 'Speech at the Bank of England's Court Dinner at the Eden Project', *Speech*, 12 October.
(2005a), 'Monetary policy: practice ahead of theory', *Speech*, 17 May.
(2005b), 'Speech at Salt Mills', *Speech*, 13 June.
(2005c), 'Remarks at Jackson Hole', 27 August.
(2006), 'Speech at a dinner for Kent Business contacts', *Speech*, 16 January.
(2007a), 'The MPC ten years on', *Speech*, 2 May.
(2007b), 'Comments in August Inflation Report press conference', 8 *August*.
(2012), 'Twenty years of inflation targeting', *Speech*, 9 October.
Kohn, D. (2000), *Report to the Non-Executive Directors of the Court of the Bank of England o monetary policy processes and the work of monetary analysis.*
Lambert, R. (2005a), 'Inside the MPC', *Bank of England Quarterly Bulletin*, 56–65.
Lambert, R. (2005b), 'Monetary policy-making: fact and fiction', *Speech*, 24 May.
(2006), 'Central bank communications: best practices in advanced economies', *Speech*, 23 January.
Large, A. (2004), 'Puzzles in today's economy – the build-up of household debt', *Speech*, 23 March.
Liptrot, H. (2005), 'The Great House Price Crash 2005?', *BBC website*.
Lomax, R. (2004), 'Stability and statistics', *Speech*, 23 November.
(2005), 'Inflation targeting in practice: models, forecasts and hunches', *Speech*, 12 March.
(2007), 'The MPC comes of age', *Speech*, 28 February.
Lombardelli, C., Talbot, J. and Proudman, J. (Autumn 2002), 'Committees versus individuals', *Bank of England Quarterly Bulletin*, 262–273.
Mac Coille, C. (2008), 'The impact of low-cost economies on UK import prices', *Bank of England Quarterly Bulletin*, Q1, 58–65.
Monetary Policy Committee (1999), *The transmission mechanism of monetary policy.*
(2007), 'The Monetary Policy Committee of the Bank of England: ten years on', *Bank of England Quarterly Bulletin*, Q1, 24–38.
Nickell, S. and Quintini, G. (2001), 'The recent performance of the UK labour market', *Speech*, 4 September.
Nickell (2004), 'Household debt, house prices and consumption', *Speech*, 14 September.
(2005a), 'Why has inflation been so low since 1999?', *Speech*, 13 January.
(2005b), 'Practical issues in UK monetary policy?', *Speech*, 20 September.
(2006), 'The UK current account deficit and all that', *Speech*, 25 April.

Oulton, N. and Srinivasan, S. (2003), 'Capital stocks, capital services and depreciation', *Bank of England Working Paper 192.*

Sentance, A. (2007), 'UK monetary policy: good for business?', *Speech*, 10 July.

Stockton, D. (2012), 'Review of the Monetary Policy Committee's forecasting capability', *Report presented to the Court of the Bank of England.*

Svensson, L. (2003), 'The inflation forecast and the loss function', in Mizen, P. (ed.), *Central Banking, Monetary Theory and Practice: Essays in Honour of Charles Goodhart*, Edward Elgar, Chichester.

Taylor, J. (1979), 'Estimation and control of a macroeconomic model with rational expectations', *Econometrica*, 47(5), 1267–1286.

Tucker, P. (2003), 'Credit conditions and monetary policy', *Speech*, 28 August.

(2005), 'Monetary policy, stability and structural change', *Speech*, 1 March.

(2006a), 'Uncertainty, the implementation of monetary policy and the management of risk', *Speech*, 19 May.

(2006b), 'Reflections on operating inflation targeting', *Speech*, 25 May.

(2006c), 'Macro, asset price, and financial system uncertainties', *Speech*, 11 December.

(2007a), 'A perspective on recent monetary and financial system developments', *Speech*, 26 April.

(2007b), 'Central banking and political economy', *Speech*, 15 June.

Vickers, J. (1999), 'Monetary policy and asset prices', *Speech*, 22 September.

(2000), 'Monetary policy and the exchange rate', *Speech*, 18 April.

Wadhwani, S. (2000a), 'The impact of the internet on UK inflation', *Speech*, 23 February.

(2000b), 'The exchange rate and the MPC: what can we do?', *Speech*, 31 May.

(2001), 'The new economy: myths and realities', *Speech*, 20 March.

(2002a), 'Household indebtedness, the exchange rate and risks to the UK economy', *Speech*, 25 March.

(2002b), 'The MPC: some further challenges', *Speech*, 16 May.

Walton, D. (2006), 'Has oil lost the capacity to shock?', *Speech*, 23 February.

Weeken, O. (Spring 2004), 'Asset pricing and the housing market', *Bank of England Quarterly Bulletin*, 32–41.

9 Emerging markets and import prices during the Long Expansion

John Lewis and Jumana Saleheen

9.1 Introduction

The Long Expansion occurred at about the same time as a period of prolonged growth in emerging market economies (EMEs). This process of globalisation had several dimensions, including greater trade integration between advanced and emerging economies, a lengthening in global supply chains and an increase in the share of global output accounted for by EMEs. At the same time, this process has sparked considerable discussion about how the rise of EMEs has affected inflation in the developed world. The goal of this chapter to examine how the rise of EMEs has affected inflationary pressure via the import price channel during the Great Stability.

On the one hand, the rise of EMEs is often associated with a reduction in the price of imported goods, as low-cost EME producers either displaced traditional producers or forced them to lower their prices to stay competitive. Several policy-makers have pointed to the resultant terms of trade gain as a help to achieving price stability during the Long Expansion period (Dudley, 2011). Cheaper imports, so the argument runs, reduce inflationary pressure and allow the policy-maker to run the domestic economy at a higher rate of domestically generated inflation and/or a faster rate of growth than would otherwise be possible (Bean, 2006).

More recently, however, some have argued that EMEs may have contributed to upward inflation pressure. Consumer and producer price inflation rates in EMEs have typically been higher than in advanced economies, and if this feeds through into export prices, greater exposure to EMEs may result in stronger inflationary pressure. In addition, the growth in manufacturing seen in EMEs has increased demand for commodities, which may have pushed up their price.

The views expressed are those of the authors and not necessarily those of the Bank of England. The authors are grateful to Kate Stratford and Joanna Konings for useful discussions on the role of EMEs and commodity prices.

EMEs may also have exerted downward pressure on domestic producer prices via competition effects. Several papers have found evidence of a competition effect from EME import penetration (e.g. Auer et al., 2013). Also, the rise of EMEs may have increased demand for commodities and may have boosted inflationary pressure via the commodity price channel.

Since the focus here is on import and producer prices, we do not directly address the issue of how import price inflation feeds through to CPI inflation. Ball and Mankiw (1995) has argued that any shock to the terms of trade is a relative price shock, which therefore should have no effect on the general price level. On the other hand, others (e.g. Mishkin, 2009) have argued the contrary, with Auer and Fischer (2010) finding that because the distribution of relative price shocks has a strong negative skew, this may interact with menu costs to produce downward pressure.

The remainder of the chapter is organised as follows. Section 9.2 sets out some stylised facts – about how much the UK imports form EMEs, and about the relative price differentials. Section 9.3 presents the results of panel regressions on import prices. Section 9.4 puts these into the broader context of the literature on other potential channels. Section 9.5 concludes.

9.2 Some stylised facts

In what follows, we split up EME producers into three groups: China (by far the largest single EME exporter to the UK), the New EU Members from Central and Eastern Europe (NMS);[1] and Other Low Wage Countries (LWC);[2] – which includes Brazil, India and several others.

Figure 9.1 shows how the market share of each group has evolved since 1999, and reveals an important distinction between the manufacturing and non-manufacturing sectors.

In the manufacturing industries EME import penetration has risen, with all three groups seeing a rise market share. China has seen the strongest growth with a rise of around 10 percentage points (pp). The share of NMS has risen consistently too, with a strong rate of growth after the 2004 EU Accession, but LWCs have seen a much slower growth in market share. By contrast, in the non-manufacturing sectors,

1 Bulgaria, the Czech Republic, Estonia, Hungary, Latvia, Lithuania, Poland, Slovakia, Slovenia and Romania.

2 Brazil, India, Indonesia, Mexico, Pakistan, Philippines, Russia, Thailand, Turkey, Vietnam.

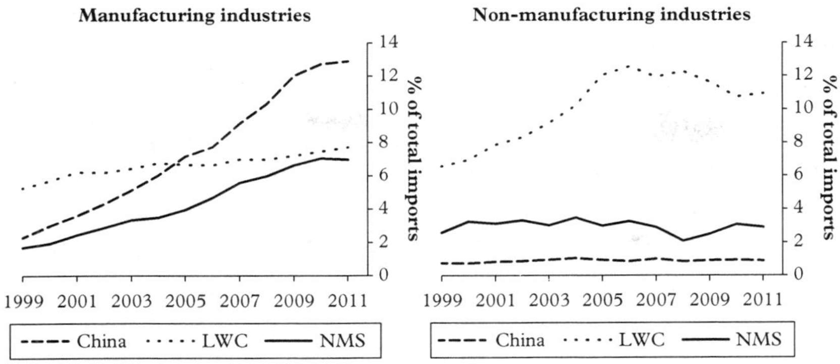

Figure 9.1. Import market share of EMEs, 1999–2011
Source: HMRC, own calculations.

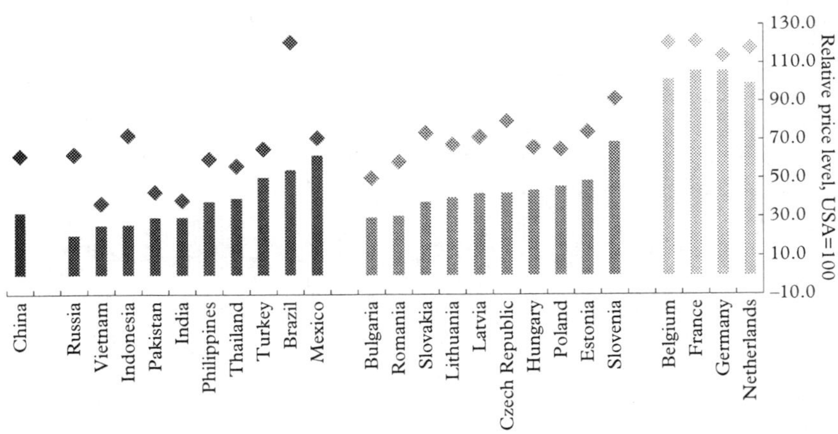

Figure 9.2. Relative price of GDP
Note: Bars denote relative prices in 1999, diamonds denote relative prices in 2011.
Source: Penn World Tables, own calculations.

the market share of China and NMS has been flat, with LWCs gaining market share initially before a partial falling back later on.

Data on the relative prices of exported goods in levels are difficult to come by, but the Penn World Tables do report figures on the relative price levels for all goods and services in the domestic economy, which provide a proxy for the cost advantage of EMEs. These are shown in Figure 9.2.

The bars depict the starting values (i.e. in 1999), and the diamonds show values at the end of the sample in 2011. To the extent that these price differentials translate into lower production costs – for example through lower wages – they suggest EMEs may have enjoyed a sizeable cost advantage relative to advanced economies. But at the same time, it is evident that many EMEs have seen quite sharp rises in their relative price level over the same period. If those fed through as higher sterling export prices, then this may have been a source of upward pressure on import prices.

9.3 A panel regression approach

Our primary data source is the *Tradeinfo* database, produced by HMRC which records the value and volume of imports by exporter for over 3,000 product types. From this data we can compute a unit value measure which we use as a proxy for price. The data are classified using the five-digit SITC system. The first digit of each industry's SITC code is the broadest classification, subsequent digits give a finer classification.

We aggregate this data across countries to yield a measure of the rate of change of unit values π_{it}, where i denotes industry type and t denotes the year. We then estimate regressions of the form:

$$\pi_{it} = \alpha + \beta_1 S_{it-1}^{CHINA} + \beta_2 \Delta S_{it}^{CHINA} + \gamma_1 S_{it-1}^{NMS} + \gamma_2 \Delta S_{it}^{NMS} + \varphi_1 S_{it-1}^{LWC} + \varphi_2 \Delta S_{it}^{LWC} + \theta exch_{it} + \mu_i + \lambda_t + \psi' X_{it} + \varepsilon_{it}$$

The effects of emerging markets are captured by the S terms. S^X refers to the share in imports of each NMS group, in industry i at time t. A reduction in prices attributable to the rise in 'cheap imports' from EMEs will show up via the *change* in market share. Suppose China begins to export cheaper shoes, which gain market share at the expense of Italy. The marginal effect of this gain in market share ($\Delta S^{CHINA} > 0$) leads to a fall in prices ($\pi < 0$). The regression coefficient will capture the sum of both the direct switching effect (the Chinese shoes are cheaper than the Italian ones they have replaced) and the indirect competition effect (the strengthening in Chinese market share leads to the remaining Italian producers cutting their margins). Now suppose that after some period of time, China's market share levels off, and settles at permanently higher level. With no additional market share growth there is no switching, and the competition from Chinese producers is no longer increasing over time, so neither effect is in operation – hence the *change* rather than the *level* is the appropriate variable to capture this.

An increase in prices attributable to higher inflation in EMEs will show up via the lagged *level* of market share. Suppose that China experiences a cost shock which increases the (sterling) price of its exports. The marginal impact on import price inflation will be equal to the extra inflation times the lag of China's market share. In a regression context, that means – *ceteris paribus* – industries with a higher exposure to China (i.e. a higher S^{CHINA}) will experience higher inflation, and so will show up via the coefficient on the lagged level.

We also include several control variables – an industry-specific exchange rate index *exch*, (defined in the European way so that a rise denotes an appreciation of the currency) as well as time and industry fixed effects. Finally, we control for the existence of common correlated effects using the approach of Kapetanios et al. (2011) by including within period averages of each of the regressors and the dependent variables at the four-digit level. This is represented by the final term $\psi' X$.

We begin by running pooled regressions, split into manufacturing vs. non-manufacturing industries. These results are shown in Table 9.1.

In the non-manufacturing sector there is little evidence of an EME effect on import prices over the period. The coefficient on the change in NMS share is just significant at the 10% level, but since the overall market share of NMS has remained essentially flat over the sample period, this implies a negligible aggregate effect. By contrast, in manufacturing there is a highly significant coefficient on the change in Chinese market share – which implies that for every percentage point of market share China gains, import price inflation is reduced by 0.5 pp. There is also a significant coefficient in the change in share of LWCs, though the size is around half. The lagged market share coefficients are

Table 9.1. Pooled regressions, manufacturing vs. non-manufacturing industries

Sample (one-digit industries)	Non-manufacturing	Manufacturing
Lagged China share	−0.015 (0.120)	−0.002 *(0.066)*
Change in China share	0.003 *(0.117)*	−0.550*** *(0.093)*
Lagged NMS share	−0.151 *(0.161)*	0.019 *(0.075)*
Change in NMS share	−0.349* *(0.209)*	−0.173 *(0.117)*
Lagged Other LWC share	0.114 *(0.084)*	−0.072 *(0.060)*
Change in Other LWC share	−0.039 *(0.137)*	−0.264*** *(0.080)*
Exchange rate	−0.121 *(0.138)*	−0.472*** *(0.165)*
N (no. of obs)	7,983	21,902
I (no. of industries)	724	1,947
R2 (overall)	0.343	0.273

Notes: Standard errors in brackets; *, **, *** denote significance at 10, 5 and 1% levels respectively; all standard errors are in italics.

not significant, suggesting that the countervailing channel – greater exposure to emerging markets leading to greater 'imported inflation' has not been present. Given the above results, we restrict our attention to the manufacturing sector, in keeping with the bulk of the literature.

There are good theoretical reasons to assume that the price level effects of EMEs may vary across industries. For example, differences in labour input required, transport costs and tariff barriers may all generate differences in the price advantage that EMEs enjoy in different product groups. Formal testing for poolability rejects the null hypothesis that coefficients are equal across all industries, or within each of the one-digit industries. We therefore run a separate regression for each two-digit industry, which are not reported here for space reasons.

Since the goal of the analysis is to understand the total size of the EME pricing effect, we combine the estimated coefficients for each industry with the observed values and sum across all groups. For example, the total effect of China gaining market share is:

$$E_t^P = \sum_{i=1}^{I} w_{it} \cdot \beta_{2i} \cdot \Delta S_{it}^{CHINA}$$

Figure 9.3 shows the total size of the effect attributable to changes in EME market share.

Looking at the sum across all EMEs (the diamonds), there did appear to be sizeable downward pressure on import prices as a result of EMEs

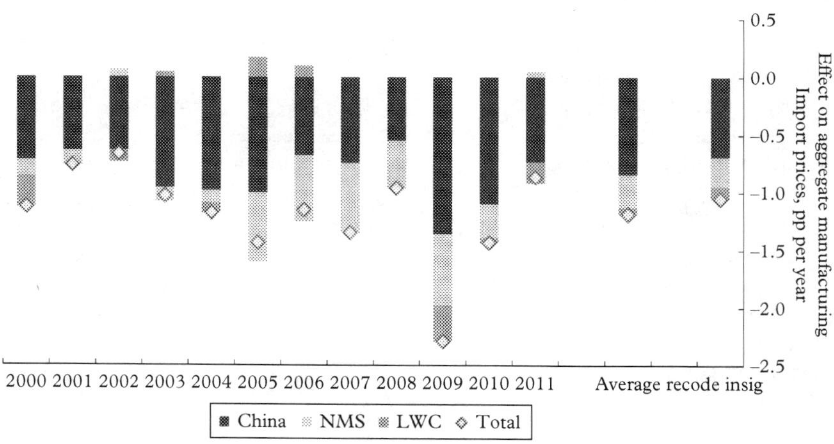

Figure 9.3. Effect of EMEs gaining market share
Note: 'Recode insig' reports the results for computation where insignificant coefficients are recoded to zero.

gaining market share, worth around 1 pp off import price inflation per year. The bulk of this took place courtesy of China gaining export market share. Averaging over the whole sample period, China accounts for around 0.85 pp, NMS for around 0.3 pp and LWCs for a negligible 0.05 pp. Looking at the time profile of the diamonds suggests no clear waning in this effect over time.

Formal significance testing is not straightforward here, since these estimates rely on combining coefficients from 27 individual regressions. To gauge whether these results are driven by statistically significant relationships, we repeated the exercise recoding to zero any coefficients that were insignificant at the 10% level. These results are shown on the far right of Figure 9.3, and demonstrate very similar estimates are obtained when insignificant coefficients are dropped. The estimate size of the effects shrinks only marginally, suggesting that the result is driven by statistically significant coefficients.

As a further check, we computed a 95% confidence interval using Monte Carlo methods. Specifically, given the parameter distribution from the regressions, we take one draw of each parameter, and given these construct an estimate of the total EME effect. We then discard the top and bottom 2.5% of these to yield a 95% confidence interval. These confidence intervals are shown in Table 9.2.

The second channel under investigation is that greater exposure to EMEs may have raised inflationary pressure if higher domestic inflation also shows up in higher import prices. To gauge the size of this effect, we apply a similar formula to the estimated coefficients on the lag of each EME's market share. Using China as an example, this formula is

$$E_t^P = \sum_{i=1}^{I} w_{it} \cdot \beta_{1i} \cdot S_{it-1}^{CHINA}$$

The point estimates, together with the 95% confidence interval are shown in Table 9.3.

These estimated confidence intervals include zero, so we therefore conclude that there has been no statistically significant effect in aggregate.

Table 9.2. Effects of EMEs gaining market share

	Mean	Upper bound	Lower bound
China	−0.8	−0.4	−1.2
NMS	−0.3	0	−0.6
LWC	−0.1	+0.2	−0.3

Table 9.3. Effects of greater EME market share

	Mean	Upper bound	Lower bound
China	−1.2	0.3	−2.6
NMS	0.4	1.5	−0.8
LWC	−1.6	0.0	−3.2

9.4 Putting these estimates in a broader context

These results suggest that only China has exerted a significant downward effect on import prices. This may partly reflect the fact that whilst NMS enjoyed a similar price level to China, their rate of market share acquisition has been around half that of China. And the lack of effect is broadly consistent with Auer et al. (2013), who found no evidence that increased NMS market shares put downward pressure on domestic producers' prices. Nevertheless, our finding is at odds with the results of an ECB (2006) exercise which found that NMS had lowered import price inflation in the Euro Area by around 1 pp over the period 1995–2005.

The lack of a significant LWC effect is perhaps not surprising given the relatively slow rate of market share acquisition over the period (2.5 pp over 12 years, compared to 10.5 pp for China). In an international context, it is worth noting that the rise in import penetration from this group of countries has been much smaller for the UK than for, say, the USA. For the latter, Auer and Fischer (2010) document that China accounts for only about a third of EME import penetration, and Mexico and China collectively for just over a half, with emerging Asia and Brazil accounting for the remainder.

To put our estimates of the overall China effect in the context of the rest of the literature, Table 9.4 shows our result alongside estimates from other studies.

To derive an equivalent in terms of the import price inflation measure that many other studies do, we multiply our estimate by the share of manufactured goods in total goods imports. Pain et al. and Wheeler assume that relative price shifts do translate into movements in the general price level. To aid comparison, we report what our estimates would imply if that assumption held. Since the share of imports in the UK CPI is estimated to be around one-third, we multiply our overall import price number by a third to get a figure of around 0.2.

This comparison suggests that in terms of the effect on either measure of import price inflation, our estimates are at or near the top of the range found in the literature. For overall HICP inflation, our results are of similar magnitude, but towards the lower end of the range.

Table 9.4. External estimates of the effect of EMEs

Country	Author(s)	Sample period	Estimated effect, per annum, pp: Import price inflation	Manuf. import price inflation	HICP inflation
USA	Kamin et al. (2006)	1993–2001	−0.53		
USA	Pain et al. (2008)	2001–05	−0.12		
OECD	Kamin et al. (2006)	1993–2001	−0.13		
€A	ECB (2006)	1995–2005		−1	
€A	Pain et al. (2006)	2001–05			−0.19
UK	Kamin et al. (2006)	1993–2001	0		
UK	McCoille (2008)	1999–2006		−0.5	
UK	Nickell (2005)	1999–2005	−0.55		
UK	Wheeler (2008)	1990–2004	−0.5		−0.35
UK	Pain et al. (2006) (non-OECD Asia)	2000–05			−0.2 to −0.3
UK	Lewis/Saleheen	1999–2011	−0.60	−0.87	≈−0.20

But aside from the channels considered so far, other mechanisms could also have been at play. Pushing up on import prices is the potential effect of rising EME demand on commodity prices. Going the other way – in domestic inflation terms – is the effect of EME competition lowering the price domestic producers are able to charge.

Looking at the commodity price channel, Figure 9.4 shows that in simple accounting terms EMEs account for virtually all of the rise in demand for commodities since 2000.

Estimates of how this rising demand from China and other EMEs affected commodity prices are relatively scarce.[3] A key issue here is that if commodity prices are forward-looking, then the effects of stronger EME growth (if anticipated) will already be priced in, so only the effect to shocks to growth rates can be estimated. Killian and Hicks (2013) estimate the effect of growth surprises, and find that stronger than expected growth in China and India explains around half of the rise in

3 There is a broader literature looking at the effect of global industrial production on oil prices, as opposed to a shock to output which is specifically Chinese in origin. But as Roach (2012) argues, since Chinese output is more commodity-intensive than the global average, a Chinese output shock may have a larger effect on prices than an equivalent sized shock to global output originating elsewhere.

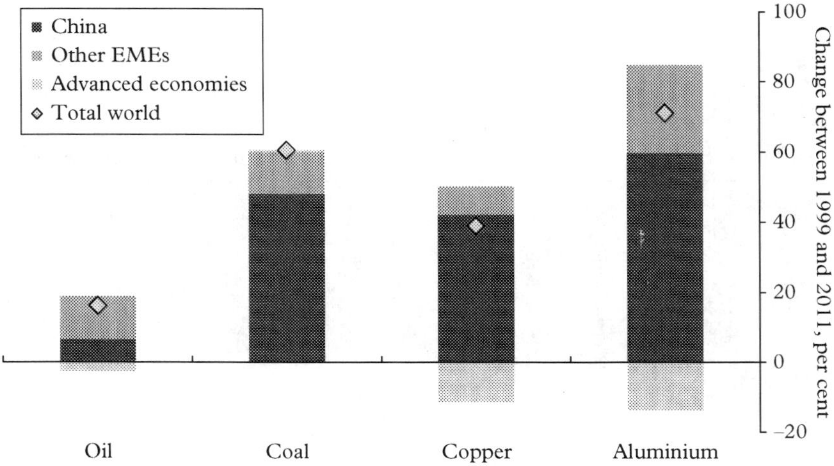

Figure 9.4. Contributions to commodity demand growth

oil prices from their 2000 level over our sample period. So assuming that EMEs 'caused' £50 of the £100 rise in sterling oil prices from 1999 to 2011, and taking the OBR's (2010) estimate that a £10 rise in sterling oil prices adds 0.25 pp to the CPI, that would imply an EME effect of 1.25 pp over 12 years on CPI, or 0.1 pp per annum. Abstracting from the issue of relative price offsets, this impact is both small and about half the estimated downward pressure from switching to cheaper imports.

Elsewhere, Pain et al. (2006, 2008) have estimated that the impact of rising EME demand for commodities added around $35 to the price of a barrel of oil, and that the overall commodity price effect added 0.1 pp per annum on UK CPI inflation over the period 1995–2005.

There are, to our knowledge, no direct estimates of the effect of EME import competition on domestic producers' prices for the UK. Auer and Fischer (2012) find strong effects on US producer prices from EME import competition over the period 1993–2001. In a companion paper (Auer et al., 2013) performing a similar analysis for the UK, significant coefficient estimates on Chinese import penetration are found, but the overall effect on producer prices is not computed.

9.5 Conclusions

The rise of EMEs during the Great Stability led to a major reshaping of UK trade patterns, with EMEs trebling their share of UK imports over the period. We find evidence that the growth in 'cheap imports' that displaced and competed with producers from advanced economies is associated with a reduction in import price. We estimate that this switching process reduced manufactured import price inflation by 0.87 pp per annum on average, and overall import price inflation by around 0.6 pp per annum. On the other hand, we find no evidence that higher inflation in EMEs has spilled over into import prices. Finally, on the commodity price channel, other studies have found that rising growth in EMEs has increased the demand for and price of commodities such as oil, but the estimated impact of this in CPI terms is still relatively modest.

In sum, it is likely that EMEs have exerted downward rather than upward pressure on UK import prices during the Great Stability period. This has been a helpful tailwind for policy-makers, but can explain at best only a fraction of the reduction in goods price inflation seen over the period. There does not appear to have been a pronounced slackening off of this tailwind over our sample period, but given its initial size, as and when the effect wanes it is unlikely to lead to a large change in inflationary pressure via the import price channel.

References

Auer, R., Dregen, K., and Fischer, A. (2013) "Low-wage import competition, inflationary pressure, and industry dynamics in Europe", *European Economic Review*, 59, 141–166.

Auer, R. and Fischer, A. (2010) "The effect of low-wage import competition on U.S. inflationary pressure", *Journal of Monetary Economics*, 57, 491–503.

Ball, L. and Mankiw, N.G. (1995) "Relative price changes as aggregate supply shocks", *Quarterly Journal of Economics*, 110(1), 163–193.

Bean, C. (2006) "Globalisation and inflation", *Bank of England Quarterly Bulletin* Q4, 468–475.

Dudley, W. (2011) "*US Economic Policy in a Global Context*", Remarks at the Foreign Policy Association Corporate Dinner, New York. http://www.newyorkfed.org/newsevents/speeches/2011/dud110607.html

European Central Bank (2006) "Effects of the rising trade integration of low-cost countries on euro area import prices", Box 6, *Monthly Bulletin*, August.

Kamin, S., Marazzi, M., and Schindler, J. (2006) "The impact of Chinese exports on global import prices", *Review of International Economics*, 14(2), 179–201.

Kapetanios, G., Pesaran, H., and Yamagata, T. (2011) Panels with non-stationary multifactor error structures, *Journal of Econometrics*, 160, 326–348.

Killian, L. and Hicks, B. (2013) "Did unexpectedly strong economic growth cause the oil price shock of 2003–2008", *Journal of Forecasting*, 32, 385–394.

McCoille, C. (2008) "The impact of low-cost economies on UK import prices", *Bank of England Quarterly Bulletin* Q1, 58–63.

Nickell, S. (2005) "Why has inflation been so low since 1999?", *Bank of England Quarterly Bulletin* Q2, 92–107.

Mishkin, F. (2009) "Globalization, macroeconomic performance and monetary policy", *Journal of Money, Credit and Banking*, 41(S1), 187–196.

Office for Budgetary Responsibility (2010) "Assessment of the Effect of Oil Price Fluctuations on Public Finances", http://budgetresponsibility.org.uk/wordpress/docs/assessment_oilprice_publicfinances.pdf.

Pain, N., Koske, I., and Sollie, M. (2006) "Globalisation and Inflation in the OECD Economies", OECD Working Paper No 524.

(2008) "Globalisation and OECD Consumer Price Inflation", OECD Economic Studies 44 2008/1.

Roach, S. (2012) "China's Impact on World Commodity Markets", IMF Working Paper 12/115, International Monetary Fund.

Wheeler, T. (2008) "Has Trade with China Affected UK Inflation?", External MPC Unit Discussion Paper 22, Bank of England.

10 UK fiscal policy before the crisis

Paul Johnson

10.1 Introduction and summary

We are currently in the middle of the most substantial fiscal consolidation since the end of the last war. Government borrowing hit a post-war record of more than 11% of GDP, public sector net debt is set to exceed 80% of GDP and, as of the start of 2014, the government is planning a consolidation of 10% of GDP.

Much has been written about the scale of the problem and the policies put in place to deal with it. What we focus on here, however, is fiscal policy in the two decades or so before the great recession hit. We look at what happened to borrowing and national debt over that period and how levels of spending and taxation changed.

The UK did enter the crisis with one of the larger structural budget deficits in the industrial world and a bigger public debt than most OECD countries. Nevertheless, the primary idea is not to ask whether our current problems were *created* by fiscal policy over that period. There is no good reason for believing that the economic crisis was created by excessively loose fiscal policy in the UK. And while the scale of the current required consolidation would have been different had somewhat different policies been pursued, it seems most unlikely that a large fiscal problem could have been avoided. While it is easy to argue with hindsight that the period up to 2008 involved an unsustainable economic boom, that was apparent to almost nobody at the time. Certainly spending could, and perhaps should, have been more tightly controlled, but it is hard to see circumstances in which the scale of the deficit which appeared post-crisis could have been reduced by more than, at most, 20% or so by tighter fiscal policy pre-crisis. That would have required a chancellor with both remarkable economic foresight and powers of political persuasion who had been able both to predict the scale of the looming recession and to persuade his colleagues and the electorate of the

This chapter was completed in 2014 and the data and analysis was correct as of that date.

case for significantly lower public spending or higher taxes. In those circumstances one has to wonder what would have been the reaction through monetary policy of an independent MPC to a significantly tighter fiscal policy. That said, the government, in the run-up to 2008, had lost a degree of credibility in seeming to test both the letter and the spirit of its own fiscal rules to, and perhaps beyond, breaking point. This won't have helped confidence that it was serious about a medium-term strategy to deal with the impact of the crisis on the public finances.

The purpose of this chapter is to consider the conduct of fiscal policy over the pre-recession period and ask what lessons one might draw from it. It starts by looking at how the fiscal aggregates developed over the decade or two before the crisis, with a particular focus on how they stood on the eve of the crisis. It then reflects on the fiscal objectives that the government claimed to be aiming for in the period from 1997, before looking in a little more detail at how and why public spending rose over this period and also at the evolution of tax receipts.

One can draw a number of tentative conclusions about the conduct of fiscal policy, and possible lessons for future governments.

10.1.1 Public finances

The last Labour government in many ways replicated the fiscal experience of its predecessor Conservative government. Its first three years in office involved a substantial fiscal consolidation resulting in a structural surplus. There followed a period of loosening based, as it turned out, on an overly optimistic reading of the strength of the economy. This was driven in particular by increased public service spending (and increases in some benefits and tax credits) under the Labour government, and by tax cuts under the Conservatives. When recession hit (in 1990 and in 2008) the fiscal situation deteriorated very rapidly and a substantial hole opened up in the public finances.

The biggest problem with managing the public finances in the 1980s and the 2000s turned out to flow from overly optimistic assessments of the performance of the economy. In each case, economic performance which the Chancellors of the day – Nigel Lawson and Gordon Brown – thought was sustainable proved in fact not to be so. Fiscal policy was therefore also shown not to be sustainable and a sharp correction was required and implemented.

10.1.2 Fiscal rules

Whilst they had some sensible underpinnings, and were an improvement on the *ad hoc* approach of previous governments, the fiscal rules pursued by the last government were inadequate in practice. They were not appropriately binding, were not well designed and arguably were gamed by the government that introduced them. A much better fiscal framework is required.

The main 'golden rule' was backward looking and, arguably, open to the possibility of manipulation. Justifying large deficits in the latter half of the 2000s on the basis that there were surpluses in the earlier part of the decade because the period was all part of the same economic cycle made little sense. The debt rule – that national debt should not exceed 40% of national income – was barely being honoured even before the crisis became apparent. Central pre-crisis forecasts suggested that debt would come very close to 40% of national income, with very little room for error. There is some evidence that decisions were made to structure activities to keep certain debts 'off balance sheet' in order to avoid breaching the rule.

10.1.3 Public spending

The government of the 2000s used the apparent growth dividend to fund substantial increases in public service spending. Indeed, total public spending rose somewhat more quickly than national income over the period from 1999–2000 to 2007–08. Despite substantial discretionary increases in some elements, spending on social security actually fell as a proportion of all spending. By contrast, spending on public services, notably health, rose.

Over long periods the pattern of changes in public spending looks unlikely to be compatible with sensible long-term decision-making. After a long period of very tight spending settlements the loosening of the purse strings after 2000 was dramatic. We are now going through a period of considerable retrenchment. Whatever the appropriate level and distribution of public spending, such (pro-cyclical) periods of cuts, increases and cuts again are unlikely to be efficient.

While the current fiscal consolidation will take the size of the state back to roughly its level in the early 2000s, the shape of the state will be very different indeed. It is unclear to what extent this is an unintended consequence of unstable fiscal policy. It would certainly seem to be the case that spending decisions are taken with little heed to long-term commitments.

10.1.4 Taxation

Tax revenues also increased more quickly than national income in the period between 1997–98 and 2007–08, following a period of decline over the previous two decades – declines which occurred despite the fact that discretionary tax increases were responsible for roughly half the fiscal consolidation between 1991–92 and 1996–97.

There is some evidence that elements of tax revenues in both the late 1980s and the 2000s were not sustainable. Most obviously, revenues from North Sea oil reached a peak of 3.5% of national income in the mid-1980s, falling precipitously to less than 0.5% in the early 1990s. During the 2000s corporation tax revenues were particularly buoyant, supported in part by the financial sector. One clear difference between the period prior to 2008 and that prior to 1990 was the substantial discretionary reductions in the earlier period, which were not repeated later on.

10.2 Fiscal outturns to 2007–08

While its scale was bigger, the crisis of 2008 was not the first significant recession in recent times, nor was it the first to cause a major fiscal problem. The recession of 1990 also led to a substantial deficit which required a prolonged period of fiscal tightening to fill. This is well illustrated in Figure 10.1, which shows how a budget surplus in 1989–90 turned into a deficit of more than 7% of GDP just three years later. This was driven not just by a fall in output, but by the fact that growth was much slower than the assumed 3% trend rate of growth which had underpinned Chancellor Lawson's substantial tax cuts in the late 1980s.

The figure also shows the most recent OBR view of cyclically adjusted net borrowing, a measure which looks rather less positive in the late 1980s.

Not surprisingly, then, the 1990s were a decade of substantial fiscal tightening. After the 1992 election, the then Chancellor Norman Lamont announced significant tax-raising measures. Kenneth Clarke, who became Chancellor in May 1993, continued this process and also cut public spending as a share of national income. Borrowing fell swiftly. Mr Clarke forecast in his November 1996 Budget that revenues would continue to rise and spending would continue to fall as shares of national income. The Treasury expected this to get the budget back into surplus by 2000–01. In fact, surpluses were achieved in each year from 1998–99 to 2000–01, with the total budget surplus reaching 1.9% of national income in 2000–01, comprising an estimated structural surplus of 1.1% of national income and a cyclical surplus of 0.8%, as the new Labour government largely adhered to the very tight spending

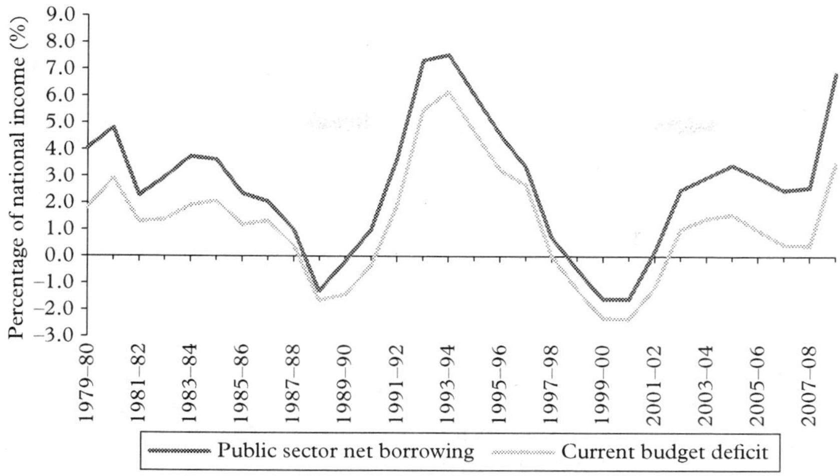

Figure 10.1. Current budget deficit and public sector net borrowing as a proportion of national income

Note: All excluding the temporary effects of the financial interventions, and adjusting for the one-off effects of the £23.5 billion sale of the 3G spectrum in 2000–01 and the £28 billion transfer of the Royal Mail pension fund in 2012–13.

Source: OBR databank, August 2013 (http://budgetresponsibility.independent.gov.uk/data/).

plans set out by its predecessor and indeed increased taxes relative to the November 1996 plans.

Over the period from the start of the 1980s to the early 2000s public sector net debt followed the equivalent path as is readily seen in Figure 10.2. It fell from about 45% of national income to a low of 25% by 1990 rising again to above 40% in 1995, before dropping just under 30% by 2001–02.

So by 2001 the public finances appeared to be in their best shape for a generation. The budget was in surplus and net debt stood at less than 30% of national income. In part this was because the first-term Labour government reduced total public spending (TME) by 3.1% of national income, with falls in both current spending and investment spending. (Notwithstanding Chancellor Brown's complaints about Conservative underinvestment, public sector net investment was lower on average in Labour's first term – at 0.6% of national income – than in any other four-year period since the Second World War.) The same government also saw tax revenues increase by more than 2% of national income, in part driven by fiscal drag in the face of strong economic growth. Note

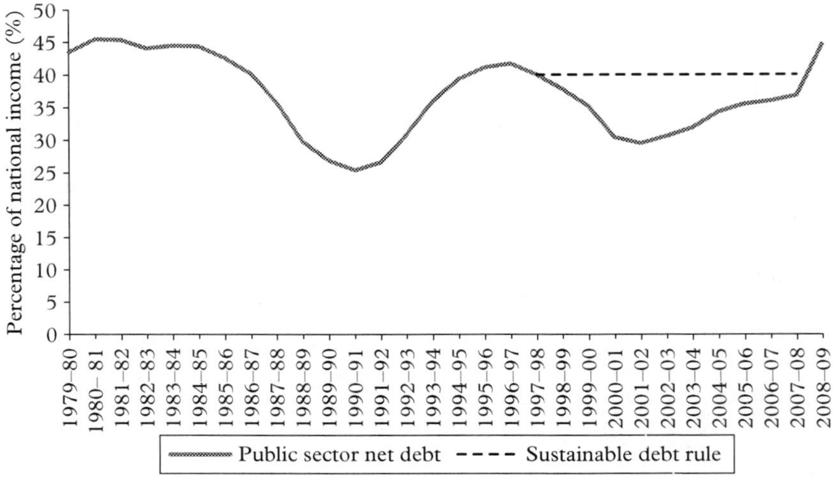

Figure 10.2. Net debt as a proportion of GDP
Source: OBR databank, August 2013 (http://budgetresponsibility.independent.gov.uk/data/).

though that the effect of fiscal drag on strengthening the public finances over the period from 1996–2001 was no more than was expected at the time of the November 1996 Budget.[1]

The period from 2001 was rather different. Mr Brown had described his determination to reduce borrowing in Labour's early years in office as 'prudence for a purpose'.[2] The purpose became clear as the government reversed its earlier cuts in public spending, with health, education and lower-income pensioners and families with children the main beneficiaries. However, as spending rose by 3.9% of national income over Labour's second term, tax revenues weakened unexpectedly when the stock market fell in 2000 and 2001, reducing tax payments by financial sector firms and their employees. The tax-raising Budget of April 2002 helped begin to reverse the decline, but government revenues still ended Labour's second term 1.2% of national income lower than they began it, despite the fact that the net effect of new policy measures during the second term had been to raise revenue.

1 Note that part of the extra revenue relative to the November 1996 Budget is 'unexplained' – i.e. not due to specific measures nor due to the standard impact of growth on the public finances.

2 Mr Brown's 1998 Budget Speech: 'I said that this would be a Budget based on prudence for a purpose and that guides us also in our approach to public spending' (http://www.hm-treasury.gov.uk/bud_budget98_speech.htm).

The combination of higher spending and weaker tax revenues unwound the improvement in the public finances. The current budget balance moved from a surplus of 2.4% of national income at the end of the first term to a deficit of 1.6% of national income by 2004–05. The swing in the overall budget balance was even larger, reflecting the fact that public sector net investment had at last begun to increase. The return to sizeable overall budget deficits began to push public sector net debt up again, reaching 34.1% of national income in 2004–05.

The 2004 Spending Review began to slow the increase in public service spending, but the real growth rate still averaged 3.2% between 2005–06 and 2007–08 and total spending was at 41.1% of national income in 2007–08, up from 40.7% in 2004–05. Net tax increases followed the 2005 election, despite assurances to the contrary[3] (a not uncommon feature of post-election periods), and revenues rose by 1% point to 38.5% of national income in 2007–08. This resulted in the modest narrowing of the budget deficit which can be seen in Figure 10.1 in 2006–07, with the current budget deficit at less than 0.5% of GDP. But with borrowing remaining high relative to the growth rate of the economy, and high relative to the stock of debt, public sector net debt continued to rise – from 34.1% of national income in 2004–05 to 36.4% of national income in 2007–08.

Before moving on to look in more detail at the state of the public finances immediately pre-crisis it is worth reflecting on how the pattern of borrowing over the whole period from 1979–80 is clearly driven by the economic cycle. The deficit in the early 1980s was more than eliminated in the boom at the end of the decade. A big deficit reappeared as a result of the recession of 1990. A decade of retrenchment followed, with a surplus achieved by the early 2000s. A period of modest but growing deficits followed, taking off once the 2008 recession hit. This is also the story of two governments which rode waves of economic growth to cut taxes on the one hand and increase spending on the other, only to find that the economic performance was not as sustained and sustainable as had been hoped.

This is related in part to how estimates of the *structural* deficit are arrived at. We mention that briefly below. But it also raises questions about the accuracy of more straightforward fiscal forecasts. Figure 10.3 shows how forecasts for borrowing related to outturns in the four key

3 'People say we won't meet our fiscal rules. Once again, with the public finances strong, we will prove them wrong', Gordon Brown, quoted in http://www.guardian.co.uk/money/2005/apr/22/pubcfinances.politics.

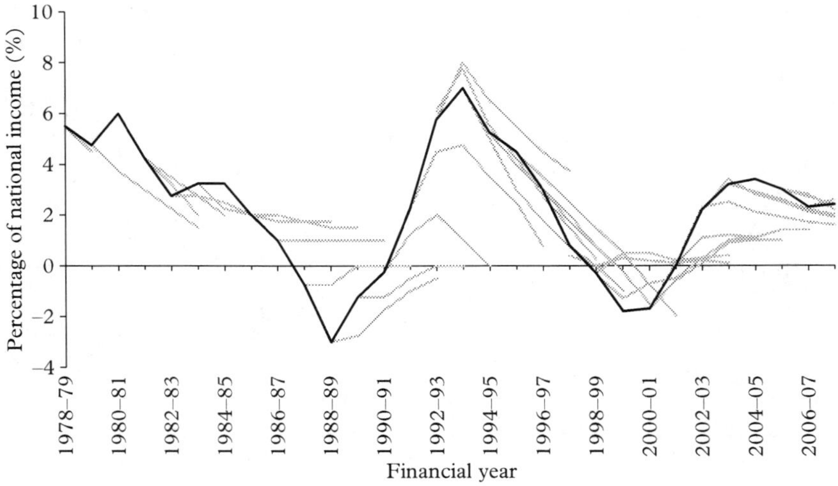

Figure 10.3. Revisions to borrowing forecasts
Notes: The black line shows estimated out-turn a year after the fiscal year in question had ended. More recent out-turns differ, but often due to definitional changes, which are less of a fair reflection of the aggregate that was being forecast at the time. The grey lines show forecasts from all previous Budget statements.
Sources: Office for Budget Responsibility, using data from various HM Treasury forecasts.

periods we have been considering – the period before the 1990 recession when borrowing was generally falling, the period of swiftly rising borrowing around that recession, the falls up to 2001 or so and the rises thereafter. The black line shows actual borrowing. The grey lines show forecasts at each Budget. It is nearly always the case that the grey lines are above the black line when it is sloping down and below it when it is sloping up. In other words, forecasts have tended to be too optimistic when borrowing has been increasing and too pessimistic when it falls. The Treasury was generally taken by surprise by the rate of change – the deficit fell faster than expected in the 1980s, grew faster than expected during the recession, fell more than expected through the 1990s and then grew faster than forecast in the 2000s.

10.2.1 The state of the public finances pre-crisis

The overall pattern of the public finances in the three decades before the crisis hit is fairly clear. One question that remains a topic of some contention is whether there was anything in the stewardship of the public finances by the last government which left the UK worse placed to cope than it should have been with the huge increase in public sector borrowing that would follow.

- In his PBR statement of November 2008, the then Chancellor Alistair Darling said:[4] 'Mr Speaker, the economic crisis, and the action by governments across the world, will inevitably mean sharp increases in national debt relative to GDP. Again the UK will be no exception. But because we started from a stronger position, our debt will remain below that of most other major countries'.
- George Osborne, the then Conservative Shadow Chancellor, responded:[5] 'He ran a huge budget deficit on the unstable premise that he could milk the City every year, and never considered what would happen to public finances when the money ran dry. He did not fix the roof when the sun was shining'.

At a high level the facts are clear though. A significant budget deficit was being run before the crisis hit – indeed it was the third highest of any OECD country. On the other hand, the large majority of the deficit which the current government is dealing with became apparent only after the crisis hit.

It is worth stressing that the deficit in 2007–08 was smaller than in 1996–97, as Labour had allowed the tax burden to rise by more than it had increased spending as a share of GDP. In addition more of the deficit in 2007–08 was explained by investment spending than in 1996–97. Less than wholly cautious it may have been, but we should not use the benefit of hindsight to suggest that overall fiscal policy over the period was somehow completely unconstrained.

In assessing the state of the public finances in the run up to the crisis one has to take a view on the level not just of the actual deficit, but of the structural deficit. In 2007–08, total PSNB stood at 2.4% of national income (a current budget deficit of 0.4% of national income). Since, at the time, the Treasury thought that the UK economy was operating slightly above its productive potential, underlying structural borrowing

4 http://webarchive.nationalarchives.gov.uk/20130129110402/http://www.hm-treasury.gov.uk/prebud_pbr08_speech.htm

5 http://www.publications.parliament.uk/pa/cm200708/cmhansrd/cm081124/debtext/81124-0006.htm

was estimated to be a slightly higher 2.6% of national income. The most recent OBR figures suggest that the output gap was in fact larger than that and hence structural borrowing in 2007–08 in fact stood at around 3.7% of national income.[6]

So, with the benefit of hindsight, the OBR now thinks that the public finances were structurally weaker back in 2007–08 than the government believed (or at least admitted to) at the time. Had the government of the time based their policy on the OBR's latest estimate of the output gap in 2007, they would have needed to have tightened fiscal policy (i.e. increased taxes or cut spending) by around £12 billion in order to have forecast the fall in borrowing that they were projecting at the time. While a fiscal tightening of this size is considerable in normal times, it is only a small fraction of the 8.6% of national income (or £133 billion in today's terms) additional hole we estimate is implied by the March 2013 official forecast compared with the March 2008 one.[7]

What about the UK's position by comparison with that of other countries on the eve of the recession though? Were we in a better or worse position than our competitors – and were any differences big enough to matter?

Table 10.1 provides some international comparisons drawn from the OECD's most recent estimates (as of August 2013). International comparisons suggest that most other OECD countries were doing more to strengthen their finances in the decade running up to the crisis. On the OECD measure, the UK had a structural budget deficit of 4.5% of national income in 2007. This was the largest structural budget deficit among the G7 economies and the third highest of the 26 industrial countries for which the OECD has data (behind only Hungary and Greece). Over the period it moved decisively down the OECD league tables in terms of borrowing levels and debt levels. Most OECD countries did more to reduce their indebtedness and – in particular – their structural deficits than the UK in the decade before the crisis.

10.3 Fiscal rules and objectives

We have seen, then, broadly how the public finances developed in the years up to 2007–08. But what guided the governments of the time as to the appropriate levels of debt and borrowing?

6 OBR databank August 2013. See also T. Pybus, 'Estimating the UK's historical output gap', Office for Budget Responsibility, Working Paper 1, 2011

7 Emmerson, Keynes and Tetlow (2013) http://www.ifs.org.uk/budgets/gb2013/GB2013_Ch5.pdf

Table 10.1. Key fiscal indicators on the eve of the crisis

% of national income unless otherwise stated rankings: OECD member countries	Pre-crisis position (2007)	Change, 1997–2007 (% points)
Spending		
General government spending	43.7%	+3.3
Place in OECD league table	12th/30 highest spending	2nd/30 largest increase
Revenues		
Tax and other revenues	41.0%	+2.8
Place in OECD league table	18th/30 highest revenues	6th/30 largest increase
Borrowing		
General government net borrowing	2.7%	+0.5
Place in OECD league table	6th/30 highest borrowing	4th/30 largest increase
General government net borrowing: structural	4.5%	+2.3
Place in OECD league table	3rd/26 highest borrowing	6th/26 largest increase
Net worth, debt and debt interest		
Public sector net debt	28.3%	–2.1
Place in OECD league table	11th/23 highest debt	9th/23 largest increase
Public sector net debt interest	1.8%	–1.3
Place in OECD league table	10th/30 highest debt interest	17th/30 largest reduction

Note: OECD figures for UK fiscal aggregates differ to those of HM Treasury as they constructed are on an internationally comparable basis.
Source: OECD, *Economic Outlook No. 93*, September 2013 (http://www.oecd.org/oecdEconomicOutlook).

The Conservative government of the early to mid-1990s did not have a clear set of fiscal rules – though it was certainly aiming at (and achieving) significant reductions in borrowing. For example, the 1995 FSBR simply said that the objective was to 'bring the PSBR back towards balance over the medium term', with the definition of the medium term left vague. The 1996 Budget was a little more explicit, but inconsistent with this statement, committing 'to ensure that when the economy is next on trend, the public sector borrows no more than is required to finance its net capital spending'. (This has considerable similarities to the current government's 'fiscal mandate', which is that the structural current budget must be forecast to be in balance or in surplus by the end of the rolling, five-year forecast horizon.)

From 1997 the Labour government had a more explicit fiscal framework and set of rules designed to provide it with some credibility and to tie its own hands. The key elements were:

- the *Code for Fiscal Stability*, which set out the broad principles of fiscal policy as well as requiring the Treasury to be transparent about its goals and record; and
- publicly stated *fiscal rules*, which turned broad principles of 'sound' fiscal policy into specific operational targets against which success or failure could be judged.

The fiscal rules which made Labour's four broad objectives for fiscal policy more concrete were:

- The *golden rule* required the public sector to borrow only to pay for capital investment, and to finance its remaining 'current' spending from tax and other revenues. In other words, the government had to keep the current budget (revenues minus current spending) in balance or in surplus. To avoid exacerbating swings in the economy, the rule had to be met on average over the cycle rather than every year.
- The *sustainable investment rule* required the government to keep the public sector's debt (net of its short-term financial assets) at a 'stable and prudent' level. The Treasury defined this as less than 40% of national income (GDP) at the end of each financial year of the economic cycle.

The government claimed to have complied with these rules over the economic cycle that it eventually chose to define as running from 1997–98 to 2006–07 (though both start and end dates were revised during that period). The golden rule, however, suffered from a number of problems as a rule for guiding fiscal decisions, not least that it required that the start and end of an economic cycle be dated and that borrowing be adjusted to any shocks over that period. The start and end dates of an economic cycle are not easily verifiable in real time (if ever). This inevitably raised suspicions when, just after the 2005 general election and when the public finances appeared to be on course to breach rather than meet the golden rule, Mr Brown decided to push back the start of the then current economic cycle from 1999 to 1997, making it easier to meet the rule.[8] It is hard to believe that the correct fiscal policy this year and next should depend on fine judgements in the dating of the

8 For a discussion, see C. Emmerson, 'Bending the rules?', *Public Finance Magazine*, August 2005 (http://www.publicfinance.co.uk/features/2005/bending-the-rules-by-carl-emmerson/).

cycle or indeed on exactly what the scale of surpluses or deficits were earlier in the cycle. As well as being based on an event or period that is hard to date, the rule is also backward-looking. As a guide to policy it looks (and was) inadequate.

The sustainable investment rule was intended to place a cap on government debt. Inevitably the precise level of the cap is somewhat arbitrary, though some 'anchor' for total debt is no doubt needed. Doubts about the efficacy of the particular rule are threefold. First is the question of the seriousness with which the rule was applied. The 2008 Budget, published at a time when the Treasury's central prediction was that the economy would suffer no more than a very slight slowdown (with the central expectation being for growth of 2% in 2008 and more than that thereafter), projected that debt would rise to 39.8% of GDP in 2010–11. The number 39.8 is less than 40, but as a central projection at a time of considerable uncertainty it does not suggest that a 40% debt ceiling was taken terribly seriously. Second, a range of public–private finance deals and structures were put in place which, deliberately or otherwise, kept debt off the public balance sheet. Following the demise of Railtrack, for example, Network Rail was carefully constructed as an entity in a way that, by coincidence or otherwise, kept multiple billions of pounds of debt (£18 billion as of September 2007) outside of officially measured public debt.[9] A rule which results in the reality or perception of gaming like this can have negative economic consequences. Third, it was clear at the time, and has become all too obvious since, that it was in no sense robust to any economic downturn. On other hand, what keeping debt at or below 40% of national income did ensure was that there was headroom for a very large increase in national debt in the face of the downturn.

In addition to the specific problems with these two rules as expressed and operated, the pre-recession fiscal framework suffered from the fact that all the judgements over fiscal rules were made within the Treasury and not in any way at arm's length from government. The Chancellor was effectively judge and jury on his own rules. The judgement on whether they were being met, and therefore whether tax increases or spending cuts were required, depended on Treasury macroeconomic forecasts, Treasury judgements over the dating of the cycle and Treasury forecasts of the public finances. As IFS researchers argued at the time, this arrangement had the potential to reduce the credibility of

9 In fact, in December 2013 the Office for National Statistics announced that Networks Rail's debt should after all be counted as public debt, adding £30 billion to official debt figures.

the commitments and hence there was a strong case for some independent body to act as arbiter on the fiscal rules. The Office for Budget Responsibility now plays that role.

The fact of the OBR, though, does not make some of the judgements required to operationalise fiscal rules any easier to come to. The current fiscal mandate states that the structural current budget must be forecast to be in balance or surplus by the end of the rolling five-year forecast horizon. The structure of this rule has much to commend it. The difficulty lies in the degree of judgement required to determine not just what the actual budget deficit will be five years hence, but what the *structural* deficit will be. That in turn requires a judgement about what the output gap will be. The uncertainties inherent in this judgement have already been alluded to in relation to the adjustments made to estimates of the output gap and hence the structural deficit in the run-up to the recession. Looking further back, the OBR's estimates of the output gap and structural deficit in the 1980s are now quite dramatically different from those used by the Treasury. For example, the most recent Treasury estimate of the output gap for 1981–82 was 6.4% of GDP. The OBR now puts the output gap in that year at 2.8% of GDP.[10] So what looked like a structural surplus in that year now looks like a deficit.

10.4 Taxes and spending

We have so far looked at overall fiscal outcomes. But the amount that is borrowed in any year is of course the difference between two very big numbers – the amount spent by the government and the amount raised in taxes. If each, or either, could be costlessly adjusted year by year then much of the fiscal problem would disappear. But of course that is not possible. That is in part because of the potential effects of changes on the macroeconomy. But pressures on spending are long term, both in the sense that any increase can be difficult to unwind and in the sense that exogenous factors such as population ageing and increasing costs in, for example, provision of health care can drive totals. The structure of the tax system also matters for the sustainability of the fiscal stance. Reliance on taxes that are especially volatile or sensitive to the point in the economic cycle can create fiscal instability. And of course frequent and substantial changes to levels and structures can be destabilising.

10 See T. Pybus *op cit.*

In this section, then, we look at long-term changes in the levels and composition of spending and taxes since 1980, focussing on both choices and external forces which have driven change.

10.4.1 Spending

As illustrated in Figure 10.4, total government spending as a share of national income shows a clear cyclical pattern over the past three decades, falling as GDP rose in the 1980s, rising during the recession and falling in the 1990s, before gradually rising again as a result of policy choices in the 2000s with a very sharp rise after the 2008 recession.

The pattern, though, is by no means driven entirely by the cycle – policy decisions matter too. This is well illustrated in Figures 10.5 and 10.6, the first of which shows annual changes in spending on public services, with the second showing changes in social security spending.

The most striking element of the public services picture is the year-to-year volatility of spending over the 1980s and 1990s – a pattern which was in fact evident for most of the period since the late 1940s – followed by the consistent and substantial increases in spending from 2000 on. This contrasts with the pattern of spending on social security

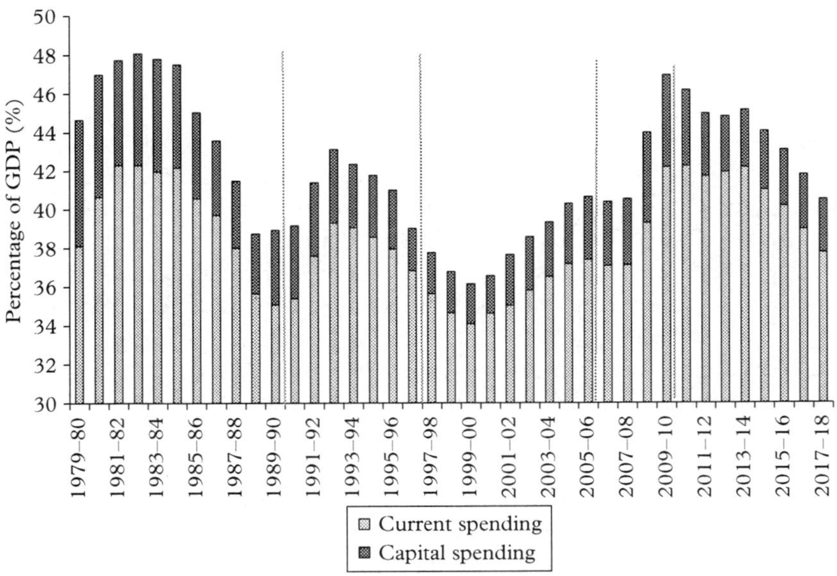

Figure 10.4. Current and total spending as a proportion of national income
Source: OBR databank, http://budgetresponsibility.independent.gov.uk/data/.

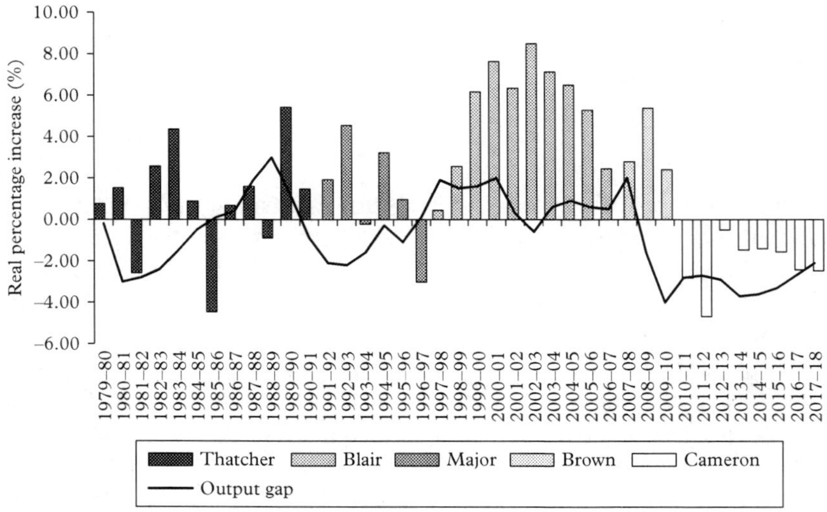

Figure 10.5. Annual increases in spending on public services since 1979–80

Notes: Projections consistent with March 2013 OBR forecasts. Excludes £28 billion of negative spending associated with the transfer of Royal Mail assets to the public sector.

Sources: ONS series JW2Q, JW2Z, JW2S and JW2P, forecasts from OBR *Economic and Fiscal Outlook*, March 2013.

benefits shown in Figure 10.6. Spending on these was highly countercyclical during the 1980s and 1990s, though with total spending rising substantially over the period. Spending continued to increase during the 2000s, despite low and falling unemployment.

These spending increases have not proved sustainable in the face of lost economic output. Plans set out in the 2013 Autumn Statement imply cuts in public service spending of around 20% in real (price-adjusted) terms between 2010–11 and 2018–19. A series of reforms is due to cut spending on working age social security benefits by more than £20 billion by 2015–16 by comparison with a no policy change counterfactual, and the Chancellor has mooted an additional £12 billion of cuts over the next parliament.

Is this evidence that spending was 'too high' pre-recession? Returning to our previous discussion of the fiscal aggregates, it seems hard to argue that the then government should have been spending a great deal less (or taxing more) for reasons of short- to medium-term fiscal sustainability given what was known at the time. Two important

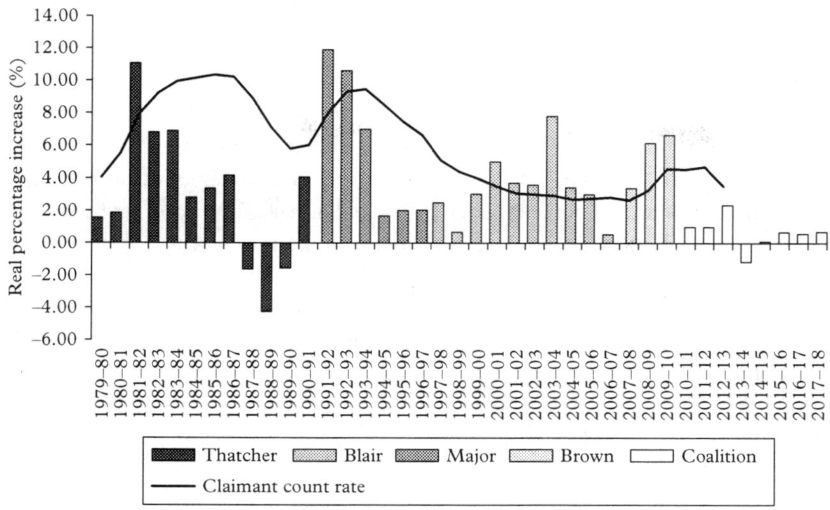

Figure 10.6. Annual increases in social security spending since 1979–80

Notes: GB benefits and tax credits.

Sources: DWP benefit expenditure statistics, https://www.gov.uk/government/publications/benefit-expenditure-and-caseload-tables-2013.

considerations related to long-term sustainability, though, might argue against quite such a generous assessment.

First, given the experience of the 1980s as well, there might be a case for building significant additional caution into spending decisions,[11] such that they are robust to a possible, if not expected, economic slowdown. Several years of historically large increases in public spending looked sustainable on the presumption that economic growth would continue at least at a modest rate. Chancellor Brown repeated on numerous occasions that growth had continued unabated for longer than any period in Britain's economic history[12] and that there would be 'no return to boom and bust'. It is not a statement of deep economic insight to wonder whether a degree of hubris underpinned some of the decisions over total spending levels. It is probably never wise to proceed on the assumption that economic cycles have been consigned to history.

11 We refer to spending decisions here but of course the point is essentially about fiscal decisions and should encompass tax decisions also.

12 See for example the 2006 pre-Budget report "I can report not only the longer period of sustained growth in our history"

That of course rather begs the question about the degree of caution that should be exercised. That might depend on the view one takes over whether we have just experienced a once in 20 years, 50 years or 100 years event. Keeping fiscal policy robust to one in 100 years events is likely over-cautious. Building in some robustness to one in 20 years events may make more sense. Certainly if you truly believe, for example, that debt should never exceed 40% of national income, then building in some robustness (as opposed to none) to poor economic news is surely important.

A second and related reason for wondering whether pre-2008 spending plans were set appropriately relates to the process by which spending decisions are made. Little if any attention is in practice given to the likely medium-term consequences of policy decisions. In the period from 1997, spending decisions were made at spending reviews covering the subsequent three years. Whilst an improvement on previous practice which often involved decisions on a year-by-year basis, this still involved Treasury working to the fiction that spending decisions really were for three years only – no decision committed to spending in the period after the spending review period. But spending is sticky, decisions are hard to reverse and decisions, for example, to increase the number of health service workers, to extend the reach of the welfare state into childcare provision or to implement substantial rises in some welfare benefits can be painful and/or costly to unwind and effectively commit the government to higher spending for a long period.

Given the cost and difficulty associated with unwinding spending decisions, the case both for ensuring that decisions are made which are robust to relatively pessimistic scenarios and which take full account of the 'stickiness' of decisions seems strong. The pattern, for example, of public sector employment is illustrated in Figure 10.7 – a pattern that looks, to say the least, unlikely to be efficient.

10.4.2 Demography and longer-term change

Figures 10.5 and 10.6 showed how public service spending and spending on social security each grew over time. It is natural to ask about the extent to which these were driven by underlying demographic and other changes. We don't go into that in detail here, but to understand these patterns further consider the figures in Table 10.2, which show average annual increases in spending on public services as a whole, on health specifically, on working age social security and on pensioner benefits, for the periods 1978/79–1988/89, 1988/89–1999/2000 and

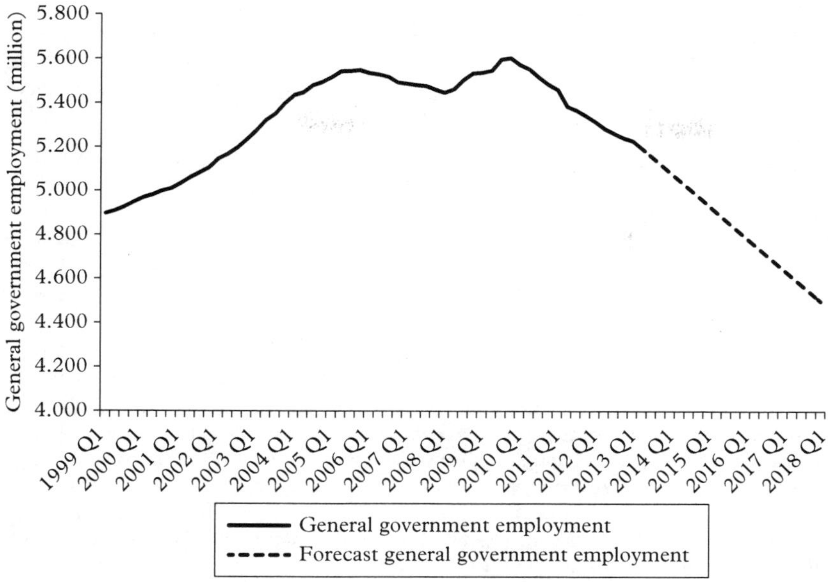

Figure 10.7. General government employment
Notes: General government employment excludes FE colleges and Sixth Form College Corporations prior to 2012Q1, up until then they were considered part of general government. Forecast general government employment is a linear projection from the latest data in 2013Q2 to the OBR forecast in 2018Q1 (the methodology employed by the OBR).
Source: Outturn data from Office for National Statistics, Public Employment Statistics, forecast for 2018Q1 from Office for Budget Responsibility, Economic and Fiscal Outlook March 2013.

1999/2000–2007/08. The table also includes figures for the change in unemployment and the number of pensioners over each period.

A lot of emphasis is put on the fiscal challenges that will in the future be caused by an ageing population. Less effort tends to be put into understanding how ageing has already caused significant changes to the fiscal landscape. The increased scale of spending on health and pensioner benefits in the decades running up to the crisis clearly, in a purely mechanistic way, put additional pressure on the public finances (despite the fact that the main pensioner benefit, the basic state pension, rose only in line with prices – and thus considerably more slowly than GDP and total spending – over the period). In fact it is spending on health, rather than benefits for pensioners, which rose most

Table 10.2. Changes in spending on selected areas over time

	1978–79 to 1988–89	1988–89 to 1999–2000	1999–2000 to 2007–08
Av. annual real increase:			
Public service spending	0.4%	2.3%	5.8%
– Health spending	3.0%	4.3%	7.0%
– Non-health spending	–0.1%	1.8%	5.4%
GB benefit and tax credit spending	3.2%	3.9%	3.8%
– On pensioners	2.3%	3.8%	3.8%
– On working age	4.3%	4.0%	3.8%
Average annual change:			
Claimant count	+6.6%	–5.0%	–4.1%
Number of pensioners	+1.3%	+1.0%	+1.2%

Notes: Pensioner-specific benefit and tax credit spending includes state pensions, pension credit (from 2003–04, and income support spending on pensioners in prior years), winter fuel payments, over-65s/70s payments and over-75s TV licences.
Sources: Office for National Statistics, Office for Budget Responsibility, Department for Work and Pensions, DWP benefit expenditure statistics, https://www.gov.uk/government/publications/benefit-expenditure-and-caseload-tables-2013.

consistently relative to other spending over the period.[13] Indeed, in the first two periods spending on working age benefits rose more quickly than spending on pensioner benefits, and rose at the same rate as pensioner benefit spending in the last period. The lack of a relationship between the rise in the claimant count and the rise in working age benefit spending is striking.

Post recession, it is spending on health and pensioner benefits which have been protected, and increases in spending elsewhere which have not been sustained. The resultant change in the composition of public spending is illustrated in Table 10.3. Health spending is forecast to reach nearly 18% of total public spending by 2017–18, up from 10% in 1980, while the share of pensioner-specific benefits in total spending over the period is due to have risen from 10% to 14%. It is spending on other public services which is falling the most by comparison. One cannot understand what was happening to spending as a whole before the recession without understanding these trends. Equally one cannot think about the appropriate way to manage the spending and public finances

13 See Emmerson, Frayne and Goodman (2000) for a discussion of the role of population ageing in health costs (http://www.ifs.org.uk/comms/nhsspending.pdf).

Table 10.3. Spending on selected functions over time

	1980–81	2000–01	2007–08	2017–18
% national income				
Health	5.0%	5.4%	7.0%	7.2%
Other public services	26.2%	15.2%	20.5%	16.3%
Pensioner-specific benefits	4.7%	4.5%	4.7%	5.7%
Other GB benefits and tax credits	4.3%	5.5%	5.8%	6.2%
% total public spending				
Health	10.6%	14.8%	17.2%	17.8%
Other public services	55.8%	41.7%	50.5%	40.2%
Pensioner-specific benefits	10.0%	12.3%	11.5%	14.0%
Other GB benefits and tax credits	9.2%	15.1%	14.3%	15.2%

Notes: Pensioner-specific benefit and tax credit spending includes state pensions, pension credit (from 2003–04, and income support spending on pensioners in prior years), winter fuel payments, over-65s/70s payments and over-75s TV licences.
Forecast for health spending assumes a real freeze in health spending from 2012–13 onwards. Forecasts for benefit spending from DWP.

going forward without a clear appreciation of the challenges posed by the likely continuation of the same trends.

10.4.3 Taxation

Figure 10.8 shows tax revenues over time as a proportion of national income, while Figure 10.9 shows how real revenues changed year by year. Note that the effect of both policy changes and of automatic responses to economic growth is included in these figures.[14]

Figure 10.9 illustrates the expected pro-cyclicality of receipts. The scale of discretionary decisions is illustrated in Figure 10.10, drawn from the 2013 IFS Green Budget.

The Budgets of 1987 and 1988 cut taxes by £28 billion (in 2013 prices). There was only a very modest tax increase in 1990 and 1991 when the fiscal effects of the recession were becoming clear, followed by a pre-election tax giveaway in 1992, a giveaway comprehensively reversed many times over in the two Budgets of 1993. As Norman Lamont so memorably put it the 1992 Budget was ‘not a very good budget. But it did help us to win the 1992 election’ while the 1993

14 Net taxes and National Insurance Contributions are defined as taxes collected by HMRC and its predecessors, VED, Council Tax, Business Rates and other taxes and royalties. Current receipts also include interest and dividends, gross operating surplus, rent and other receipts and adjustments.

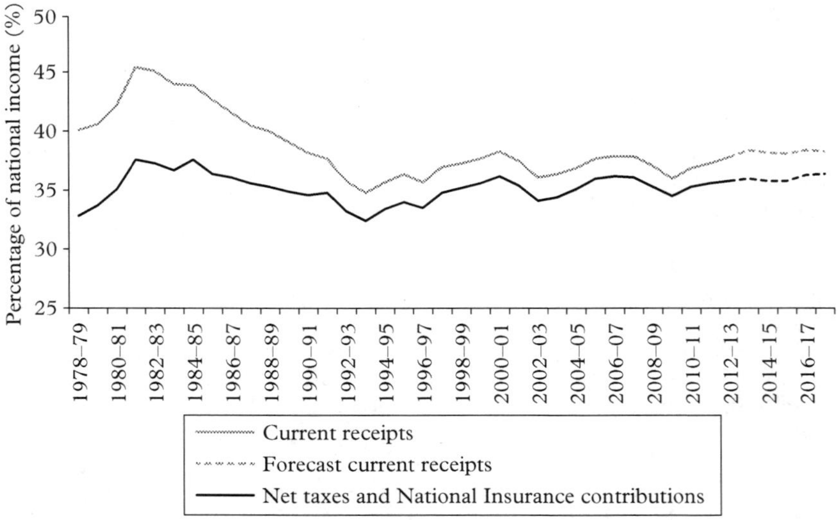

Figure 10.8. Government revenues since 1978–79
Note: Projections are from the OBR's March 2013 *Economic and Fiscal Outlook*.
Sources: OBR databank, Net taxes and National Insurance contributions, from HM Treasury, *Public Finances Databank*, April 2013.

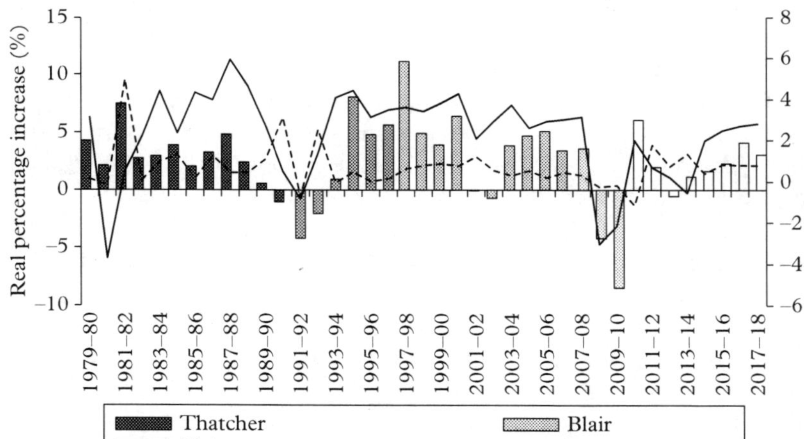

Figure 10.9. Annual real increases in net taxes and NI contributions, since 1979–80

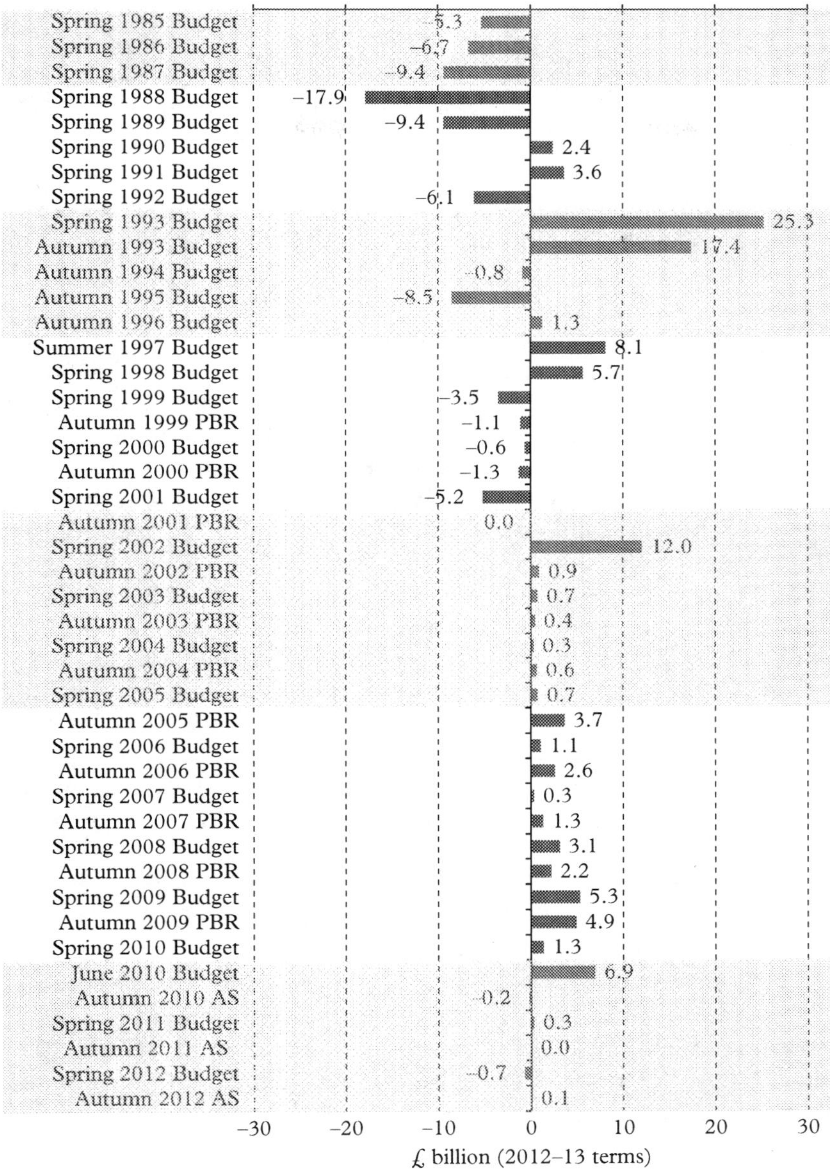

Figure 10.10. Discretionary tax increases by Budget – long-term effects

Budget 'helped to lose the 1997 election for the Conservatives, but it was definitely my best budget'.[15] One can draw parallels here with the more recent period on the spending side, where we saw in Figure 10.4 how the large increases in public service spending in the 2000s are being followed by large reductions in the 2010s. In much the same way, in the late 1980s there were large discretionary tax cuts which, in total, were more than fully reversed just a few years later as the lack of sustainability of the public finances became evident following the recession (although the specific cuts were not reversed).

Two other important patterns emerge from Figure 10.9. First, the Labour government in the six years prior to the 2008 crisis did introduce around £24 billion worth of discretionary tax increases, half of them in the Spring 2002 Budget. Second, the big tax increases in 1993 and 2002 on which we have just commented are part of a broader pattern of increases in taxes in the budgets immediately following elections. With the exception of the 1988 Budget, which saw the abolition of income tax rates above 40%, every post-election Budget over these three decades was a tax increasing Budget. Over the 28 years since 1985, there has been an average net discretionary tax increase announced each year of £1.3 billion (in 2012–13 terms). But, in the 12 months before elections, governments have tended to announce tax giveaways – amounting on average to £2.2 billion a year in 2012–13 terms. And in immediate post-election Budgets announced tax increases have averaged £7.5 billion.[16] It is hard to think of a clearer demonstration of the role played by the electoral cycle in the development of fiscal policy in recent decades.

Like the composition of spending, the composition of tax revenues has changed over time, though perhaps less dramatically. Broadly speaking, governments have come to rely more on revenue from National Insurance Contributions and VAT and, since the late 1980s at least, on income tax. The importance of a range of smaller taxes, notably excise duties, has diminished over time. As Crawford et al (2014) show, one important feature of the changing composition of revenues has been the increasing dependence on a small number of the very rich for a large share of total revenues and especially of revenues from income tax. This fact may become important for managing the public finances going forward. Certainly the cyclicality of revenues illustrated

15 Quoted in *The Chancellors' Tales: Managing the British Economy* edited by Howard Davies.

16 Figures from Emmerson et al. (2014).

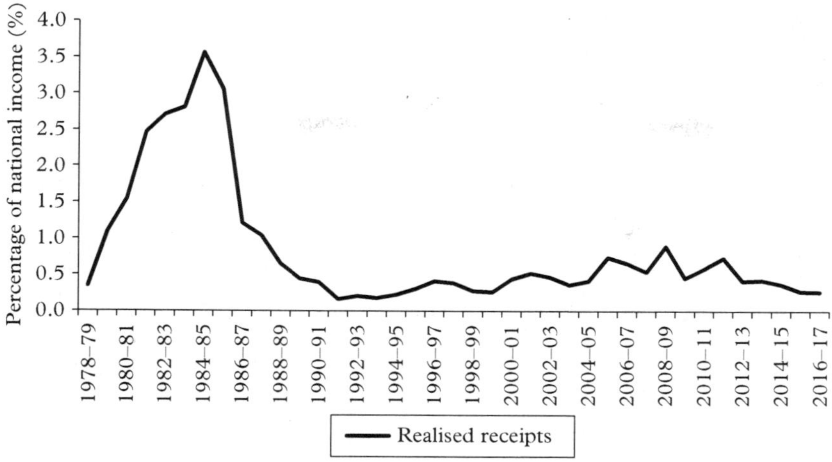

Figure 10.11. North Sea oil revenues as percentage of national income

in Figure 10.7 matters a great deal. Revenues were robust through the late 1980s, despite tax cuts, before collapsing with the economy in the recession. The crash following the 2008 recession is even more dramatic.

Two specific features of those two periods are worth mentioning – revenues from oil and from corporate taxes. The mid-1980s saw a boom in tax revenues from the North Sea, which very rapidly collapsed towards the end of the decade and reached historic lows in 1991–92 just as other revenues were also at a minimum. These revenues were large enough in the earlier period to make a substantial difference to the fiscal arithmetic. The government at no point treated these revenues differently from other revenues in judging the fiscal position or in considering appropriate levels of borrowing. No oil fund was set up and no effort made to spread the benefits of the revenue over more than the immediate generation (Figure 10.11).

A phenomenon from the 1980s and 1990s more relevant to the recent past is the cyclical nature of receipts from corporation tax. Cash receipts from onshore corporation tax fell by over a fifth between 2007–08 and 2009–10.[17] With an increased reliance on the financial sector a substantial reduction in receipts after 2008 is no surprise. And

17 The sensitivity of corporate tax receipts to economic growth is discussed in Devereux et al. (2004).

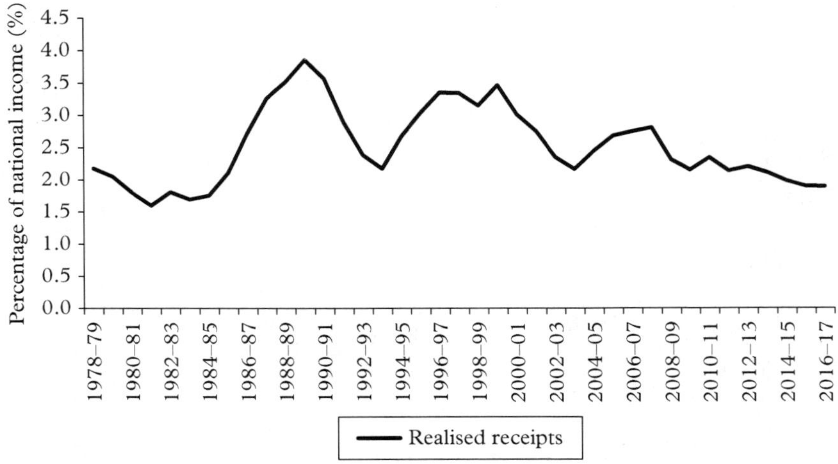

Figure 10.12. Onshore corporation tax receipts as a proportion of national income

the proportionate loss in corporate tax receipts was greater than that for any other major tax, though, as Figure 10.12 illustrates, less dramatic than had been the case in previous downturns.

10.5 Conclusions

The UK public finances suffered two major busts within a period of less than 20 years, first after 1990 and then after 2008. Both were associated with recessions. In each case fiscal policy before the recession had been predicated on a presumption that economic growth would continue at a robust rate. In the late 1980s this presumption was used to justify significant tax cuts; in the early 2000s big increases in public spending. The 1990s then saw a long period of fiscal repair with some substantial tax increases. An even bigger and longer repair job is being carried out during the 2010s involving the most substantial public spending cuts on record. Could these fiscal busts, and in particular the most recent one, have been avoided through better managed fiscal policy in the run-up to recession?

With the benefit of hindsight the answer looks obvious. The UK was running a deficit of nearly 3% of national income in 2007 at a time when the economy had, as the then Chancellor never tired of reminding us, been growing for the longest continuous period in centuries. The UK entered the recession with one of the biggest structural deficits in the OECD. And the scale of fiscal consolidation now being carried out is one of the very biggest in the OECD. The fiscal rules being followed pre-recession were inadequate, and were described as such by many commentators. Even then they were barely followed and the government's behaviour was enough to suggest that they weren't taken terribly seriously. That, in a nutshell, is the case for the prosecution.

The case for the defence is that nobody saw the crisis coming. On the basis of the best information then available, forecasts suggested that the public finances were sustainable into the medium term. Spending increases had largely been matched by tax increases. And even if the fiscal rules were sub-optimal and barely honoured in the breach, they did exert a real constraint on behaviour and ensured that neither debt nor borrowing looked unsustainable at the time.

The truth, of course, is not as black and white as either of these summaries would suggest. What is clear is that, just as happened in the late 1980s, a degree of hubris allowed the government to convince itself that it had achieved what no government has previously achieved – in Nigel Lawson's case that the trend growth of the economy had risen to much higher levels and in Gordon Brown's case that he had abolished the economic cycle, or 'boom and bust' as he put it. Lessons need to be learnt. It was a mistake to assume that the economy was so strong. It was a mistake to rely so heavily on pro-cyclical revenue streams. It was a mistake to think that public spending could continue growing so fast. It was a mistake to run substantial deficits on the basis that an ill-conceived backward looking fiscal rule 'allowed' it. And there were many other mistakes associated with letting definitions of what counted as on- and off-balance sheet to drive policy decisions, with acting as though spending decisions were easily reversible, and with not appearing to take adequate account of the long-term drivers of increased public spending.

In part those mistakes are understandable, some even excusable. It would have taken a strong Chancellor indeed to have resisted blandishments for spending increases or tax cuts in the face of apparently strong public finances and something of a consensus that growth was entrenched. But the need for better fiscal rules, more caution, less games-playing, more focus on the future and a lot less hubris should surely provide lessons for future Chancellors in running fiscal policy.

References

Brown, G. (1998), *Budget Speech* (available here: http://webarchive.nationalarchives.gov.uk/20100407010852/http:/www.hm-treasury.gov.uk/bud_budget98_speech.htm).

(2006), *Pre Budget Report Statement Speech.*

Crawford, R., C. Emmerson and S. Keynes (2014), "Public finances: risks on tax, bigger risks on spending?" in Emmerson, C., P. Johnson and H. Miller (eds) *The IFS Green Budget.*

Darling, A. (2008), *Pre-Budget Report Statement* (available here: http://webarchive.nationalarchives.gov.uk/20100407010852/http://www.hm-treasury.gov.uk/prebud_pbr08_speech.htm).

Davies, H. (2006), *The Chancellors' Tales: Managing the British Economy*, Wiley, London.

Department for Work and Pensions (2013), *Benefit Expenditure Statistics* (available here: https://www.gov.uk/government/publications/benefit-expenditure-and-caseload-tables-2013).

Devereux, M., R. Griffith and A. Klemm (2004), 'Why has the UK corporation tax raised so much revenue?' *Fiscal Studies*, November.

Emmerson, C. (2005) 'Bending the rules?' *Public Finance Magazine.*

Emmerson, C., C. Frayne and A. Goodman (2000), *Pressures in UK Healthcare: Challenges for the NHS*, IFS, London.

Emmerson, C., S. Keynes and G. Tetlow (2013), August "Public finances: outlook and risks" in Emmerson, C., P. Johnson and H. Miller (eds) *IFS Green Budget 2013*, IFS: London.

Osborne, G. (2008), *Response to Pre-Budget Statement* (available here: http://www.publications.parliament.uk/pa/cm200708/cmhansrd/cm081124/debtext/81124–0006.htm).

Office for Budget Responsibility (2013), *Economic and Fiscal Outlook 2013*, OBR, London.

Pybus, T. (2011), *Estimating the UK's historical output gap*, Office for Budget Responsibility, Working Paper 1.

OECD (2013), *Economic Outlook No. 93.*

Index

Note: Page numbers in **bold** refer to figures and tables.

Printed in the United States
By Bookmasters